Second Workshop on Speech and Language Technologies for Dravidian Languages (DravidianLangTech 2022)

Dublin, Ireland
26 May 2022

ISBN: 978-1-7138-6735-7

Printed from e-media with permission by:

Curran Associates, Inc.
57 Morehouse Lane
Red Hook, NY 12571

Some format issues inherent in the e-media version may also appear in this print version.

Printed with permission by Curran Associates, Inc. (2023)

For permission requests, please contact the Association for Computational Linguistics at the address below.

Association for Computational Linguistics
209 N. Eighth Street
Stroudsburg, Pennsylvania 18360

Phone: 1-570-476-8006
Fax: 1-570-476-0860

acl@aclweb.org

Additional copies of this publication are available from:

Curran Associates, Inc.
57 Morehouse Lane
Red Hook, NY 12571 USA
Phone: 845-758-0400
Fax: 845-758-2633
Email: curran@proceedings.com
Web: www.proceedings.com

DravidianLangTech 2022

The Second Workshop on Speech and Language Technologies for Dravidian Languages

Proceedings of the Workshop

May 26, 2022

The DravidianLangTech organizers gratefully acknowledge the support from the following sponsors.

In cooperation with

Introduction

We are excited to welcome you to DravidianLangTech 2022, the 60th Annual Meeting of the Association for Computational Linguistics. This year the workshop is being held hybrid (online and at Dublin), on May 26, 2022 with ACL 2022 that will take place also hybrid May 22-27, 2022.

The development of technology increases our internet use, and most of the global languages have adapted themselves to the digital era. However, many regional, under-resourced languages face challenges as they still lack developments in language technology. One such language family is the Dravidian (Tamil) family of languages. Dravidian is the name for the Tamil languages or Tamil people in Sanskrit, and all the current Dravidian languages were called a branch of Tamil in old Jain, Bhraminic, and Buddhist literature (Caldwell, 1875). Tamil languages are primarily spoken in south India, Sri Lanka, and Singapore. Pockets of speakers are found in Nepal, Pakistan, Malaysia, other parts of India, and elsewhere globally. The Tamil languages, which are 4,500 years old and spoken by millions of speakers, are under-resourced in speech and natural language processing. The Dravidian languages were first documented in Tamili script on pottery and cave walls in the Keezhadi (Keeladi), Madurai and Tirunelveli regions of Tamil Nadu, India, from the 6th century BCE. The Tamil languages are divided into four groups: South, South-Central, Central, and North groups. Tamil morphology is agglutinating and exclusively suffixal. Syntactically, Tamil languages are head- final and left-branching. They are free-constituent order languages. To improve access to and production of information for monolingual speakers of Dravidian (Tamil) languages, it is necessary to have speech and languages technologies. These workshops aim to save the Dravidian languages from extinction in technology.

This is the first workshop on speech and language technologies for Dravidian languages. The broader objective of DravidianLangTech-2021 was

To investigate challenges related to speech and language resource creation for Dravidian languages.

To promote a research in speech and language technology in Dravidian languages.

To adopt appropriate language technology models which suit Dravidian languages.

To provide opportunities for researchers from the Dravidian language community from around the world to collaborate with other researchers

Bharathi Raja Chakravarthi, Ruba Priyadharshini, Anand Kumar Madasamy, Parameswari Krishnamurty, Elizabeth Sherly, Sinnathamby Mahesan, General Chair

Organizing Committee

General Chair

Bharathi Raja Chakravarthi, National University of Ireland Galway
Ruba Priyadharshini, Gandhigram Rural University, Tamil Nadu, India
Anand Kumar Madasamy, National Institute of Technology Karnataka, India
Parameswari Krishnamurthy, University of Hyderabad, Telangana, India
Elizabeth Sherly, Indian Institue of Information Technology and Management-Kerala, India
Sinnathamby Mahesan, University of Jaffna, Sri Lanka

Program Committee

Program Committee

Aanisha Bhattacharyya, Institute of Engineering and Management, India
Adeep Hande, Indian Institute of Information Technology Tiruchirappalli
Aditya Yadavalli, International Institute of Information Technology, Hyderabad
Akhter Al, Rochester Institute of Technology
Akshat Gupta, Carnegie Mellon University
Amandalynne Paullada, University of Washington
Anil Vuppala, IIIT Hyderabad
Asha Hegde, Mangalore University
Barathi Ganesh, Amrita Vishwa Vidyapeetham (Deemed University)
Bharathi B, Sri Sivasubramaniya Nadar College Of Engineering, Tamil Nadu
Bhargav Dave, Dharamsinh Desai University, India
Bhavish Pahwa, BITS Pilani, Birla Institute of Technology and Science
C S, Amrita Vishwa Vidyapeetham (Deemed University)
Christine Basta, Universidad Politécnica de Cataluna
Firoj Alam, Qatar Computing Research Institute
Gaurang Prasad, wikiHow Inc.
Gokul Karthik, Mohamed bin Zayed University of Artificial Intelligence
Hariharan RamakrishnaIyer, National Institute of Technology Karnataka
Iris Hendrickx, Radboud University Nijmegen, the Netherlands
Josephine Varsha, Sri Sivasubramaniya Nadar College Of Engineering
José Antonio, Universidad de Murcia
Judith Jeyafreeda, University of Manchester
Karthik Nandakumar, Mohamed Bin Zayed University of Artificial Intelligence
Kinjal Bhargavkumar, Uka Tarsadia University
Krishnakumari K, A.V.C.College of Engineering
Laurie Burchell, University of Edinburgh
Liji S, University of Pennsylvania
Maithili Lohakare, Pandit Deendayal Petroleum University
Manikandan Ravikiran, Georgia Institute of Technology
Mithun Das, Indian Institute of Technology Kharagpur
Musica Supriya, Manipal University
NIRMALADEVI JAGANATHAN, Anna University
Nandu Chandran, University of Trento
Piyushi Goyal, Manipal University
Pradeep Kumar, NIT Patna
Prajit Dhar, University of Groningen
Prasanna Kumar, Indian Institute Of Information Technology and Management-Kerala, India.
Premjith B, Amrita Vishwa Vidyapeetham (Deemed University)
Priya Rani, National University of Ireland, Galway
Pulkit Madaan, Wadhwani Institute for Artificial Intelligence
Rabindra Nath, BJIT Limited, Dhaka
Rafael Valencia-García, Universidad de Murcia
Rahul Ponnusamy, Indian Institute of Information Technology and Management - Kerala, Dhirubhai Ambani Institute Of Information and Communication Technology
Rahul Tangsali, Pune Institute of Computer Technology
Rajasekar M, Hindustan Institute of Technology and Science

Ramaneswaran S, Vellore Institute of Technology
Richard Saldanha, National Institute of Technology Karnataka
Rudali Huidrom, Dublin City University
Sainik Kumar, institute of engineering and management
Sarika Esackimuthu, Sri Sivasubramaniya Nadar College Of Engineering
Sean Benhur, PSG College of Arts and Science
Shankar Biradar, Indian Institute of Information Technology Dharwad
Shaswat P, Netaji Subhas University of Technology
Siddhanth U, Bangalore University
Sripriya N, sri sivasubramaniya nadar college of engineering
Suman Dowlagar, International Institute of Information Technology Hyderabad
Sunil Gundapu, International Institute of Information Technology Hyderabad, Dhirubhai Ambani Institute Of Information and Communication Technology
Surangika Ranathunga, University of Moratuwa, Sri Lanka
Thenmozhi Durairaj, Sri Sivasubramaniya Nadar College Of Engineering
Theodorus Fransen, National University of Ireland, Galway
Vasanth Palanikumar, Chennai Institute of Technology, Tamil Nadu
Viktor Hangya, The Center for Information and Language Processing, University of Munich
Yuta Koreeda, Hitachi America, Ltd.
Yves Lepage, Waseda University

Keynote Talk: Development of e-resources for Tulu – An Under-resourced Language

Shashirekha HL
Mangalore University

Abstract: Tulu is one of the Dravidian languages predominantly spoken in Southern part of India, mainly by the people of Dakshina Kannada, Udupi and some places of Kasaragod. More than 2.5 million people speak Tulu and they consider it as their mother tongue. Tulu speaking community with its distinct sociocultural traits, religious practices, artistic traditions and theatrical forms has made significant contribution to the cultural heritage of Karnataka and through it to the totality of Indian culture and civilization. Even though Tulu has its own script called 'Tigalari', most people predominantly use Kannada script to write Tulu articles. Tulu is a free word order language with a high level of agglutination and rich morphological structure and follow similar strategy for its phonology like other Dravidian languages. A word is formed by adding suffixes or prefixes to the root word in a series similar to other Dravidian languages and the word complexity increases with the number of prefixes and/or suffixes where suffixes indicate the number, tense, case and gender related information. Verbs have both affirmative and negative voice and with verb-final inflectional patterns, Tulu is an inflectional language like Kannada.
In spite of several literary works in Tulu, digital presence of Tulu is almost zero making it an under-resourced language. The size of Tulu Wikipedia text and Tulu text corpus are of very less size making it difficult to construct datasets for any applications. BPEmb - pre-trained subword embeddings with a vocabulary of size 10,000 and fasttext - pre-trained word vectors, are the only digital resources available for Tulu natural language processing. Due to lack of resources, computational tools such as Morphological Generator and Analyser, POS tagger, NER and so on and applications such as Sentiment analysis, Offensive language identification, Fake news and are not available for Tulu. This talk addresses the needs and the possible solutions for the development of resources, tools and applications for Tulu language.

Bio: Professor, Department of Computer Science, Mangalore University, Mangalore

Table of Contents

Program

Thursday, May 26, 2022

09:15 - 09:30 *Opening Remarks*

09:30 - 10:00 *Keynote*

10:00 - 11:00 *Multitask and Multimodal Learning in Dravidian Languages*

Findings of the Shared Task on Multi-task Learning in Dravidian Languages
Bharathi Raja Chakravarthi, Ruba Priyadharshini, Subalalitha CN, Sangeetha S, Malliga Subramanian, Kogilavani Shanmugavadivel, Parameswari Krishnamurthy, Adeep Hande, Siddhanth U Hegde, Roshan Nayak and Swetha Valli

MuCoT: Multilingual Contrastive Training for Question-Answering in Low-resource Languages
Gokul Karthik Kumar, Abhishek Singh Gehlot, Sahal Shaji Mullappilly and Karthik Nandakumar

Findings of the Shared Task on Multimodal Sentiment Analysis and Troll Meme Classification in Dravidian Languages
Premjith B, Bharathi Raja Chakravarthi, Malliga Subramanian, Bharathi B, Soman KP, Dhanalakshmi V, Sreelakshmi K, Arunaggiri Pandian and Prasanna Kumar Kumaresan

A Dataset for Detecting Humor in Telugu Social Media Text
Sriphani Vardhan Bellamkonda, Maithili Lohakare and Shaswat P Patel

11:00 - 11:30 *Break*

11:00 - 13:00 *Identifying Emotions, Troll, Abuse and Offensive Contents in Dravidian Languages*

Findings of the Shared Task on Offensive Span Identification fromCode-Mixed Tamil-English Comments
Manikandan Ravikiran, Bharathi Raja Chakravarthi, Anand Kumar Madasamy, Sangeetha S, Ratnavel Rajalakshmi, Sajeetha Thavareesan, Rahul Ponnusamy and Shankar Mahadevan

Overview of the Shared Task on Machine Translation in Dravidian Languages
Anand Kumar Madasamy, Asha Hegde, Shubhanker Banerjee, Bharathi Raja Chakravarthi, Ruba Priyadharshini, Hosahalli Lakshmaiah Shashirekha and John Philip McCrae

BERT-Based Sequence Labelling Approach for Dependency Parsing in Tamil
C S Ayush Kumar, Advaith Das Maharana, Srinath Murali, Premjith B and Soman KP

Zero-shot Code-Mixed Offensive Span Identification through Rationale Extraction
Manikandan Ravikiran and Bharathi Raja Chakravarthi

Overview of Abusive Comment Detection in Tamil-ACL 2022
Ruba Priyadharshini, Bharathi Raja Chakravarthi, Subalalitha CN, Thenmozhi Durairaj, Malliga Subramanian, Kogilavani Shanmugavadivel, Siddhanth U Hegde and Prasanna Kumar Kumaresan

TamilATIS: Dataset for Task-Oriented Dialog in Tamil
Ramaneswaran S, Sanchit Vijay and Kathiravan Srinivasan

Findings of the Shared Task on Emotion Analysis in Tamil
Anbukkarasi Sampath, Thenmozhi Durairaj, Bharathi Raja Chakravarthi, Ruba Priyadharshini, Subalalitha CN, Kogilavani Shanmugavadivel, Sajeetha Thavareesan, Sathiyaraj Thangasamy, Parameswari Krishnamurthy, Adeep Hande, Sean Benhur, Kishore Kumar Ponnusamy and Santhiya Pandiyan

Sentiment Analysis on Code-Switched Dravidian Languages with Kernel Based Extreme Learning Machines
Mithun Kumar S R, Lov Kumar and Aruna Malapati

13:00 - 14:00 *Break*

14:00 - 17:00 *Poster Session: Shared Task Papers*

hate-alert@DravidianLangTech-ACL2022: Ensembling Multi-Modalities for Tamil TrollMeme Classification
Mithun Das, Somnath Banerjee and Animesh Mukherjee

TeamX@DravidianLangTech-ACL2022: A Comparative Analysis for Troll-Based Meme Classification
Rabindra Nath Nandi, Firoj Alam and Preslav Nakov

Translation Techies @DravidianLangTech-ACL2022-Machine Translation in Dravidian Languages
Piyushi Goyal, Musica Supriya, Dinesh Acharya U and Ashalatha Nayak

SSN_MLRG1@DravidianLangTech-ACL2022: Troll Meme Classification in Tamil using Transformer Models
Shruthi Hariprasad, Sarika Esackimuthu, Saritha Madhavan, Rajalakshmi Sivanaiah and Angel Deborah S

BPHC@DravidianLangTech-ACL2022-A comparative analysis of classical and pre-trained models for troll meme classification in Tamil
Achyuta Krishna V, Mithun Kumar S R, Aruna Malapati and Lov Kumar

CUET-NLP@DravidianLangTech-ACL2022: Investigating Deep Learning Techniques to Detect Multimodal Troll Memes
Md Maruf Hasan, Nusratul Jannat, Eftekhar Hossain, Omar Sharif and Mohammed Moshiul Hoque

PICT@DravidianLangTech-ACL2022: Neural Machine Translation On Dravidian Languages
Aditya Vyawahare, Rahul Tangsali, Aditya Mandke, Onkar Rupesh Litake and Dipali Kadam

CUET-NLP@DravidianLangTech-ACL2022: Exploiting Textual Features to Classify Sentiment of Multimodal Movie Reviews
Nasehatul Mustakim, Nusratul Jannat, Md Maruf Hasan, Eftekhar Hossain, Omar Sharif and Mohammed Moshiul Hoque

Thursday, May 26, 2022 (continued)

17:00 - 17:15 *Meeting, Awards, Closing (TBD)*

BERT-Based Sequence Labelling Approach for Dependency Parsing in Tamil

C S Ayush Kumar, Advaith Das Maharana, Srinath Murali Krishnan, Premjith B, and Soman K P
Center for Computational Engineering and Networking (CEN)
Amrita School of Engineering, Coimbatore
Amrita Vishwa Vidyapeetham, India
b_premjith@cb.amrita.edu

Abstract

Dependency parsing is a method for doing surface-level syntactic analysis on natural language texts. The scarcity of any viable tools for doing these tasks in Dravidian Languages has introduced a new line of research into these topics. This paper focuses on a novel approach that uses word-to-word dependency tagging using BERT models to improve the malt parser performance. We used Tamil, a morphologically rich and free word order language. The individual words are tokenized using BERT models and the dependency relations are recognized using Machine Learning Algorithms. Oversampling algorithms such as SMOTE (Chawla et al., 2002) and ADASYN (He et al., 2008) are used to tackle data imbalance and consequently improve parsing results. The results obtained after oversampling (label accuracy of 69.94% IndicBERT-SVM) are used in the malt parser and this can be accustomed to further highlight that feature-based approaches can be used for such tasks.

1 Introduction

Grammatical structures are directly involved in social interactions in the use of languages and this is central for language variation and change. A dependency parser examines a sentence's grammatical structure, finding linkages between head words and modifier words. Dependency parsing is a method for doing surface-level syntactic analysis on natural language texts. The dependency parser creates a parse tree by scanning the words of a sentence in linear time. It keeps a partial parse, a stack of words presently being processed, and a buffer of words yet to be processed at each step.

In contrast to its corresponding constituency structure, the dependency tree structure is considered a cutting-edge approach for parsing free word order languages such as Dravidian languages. A typical challenge for developing parsers in such low resource languages is non-projectivity, which emerges because of languages with free word order or long-distance dependencies, leading to a significant proportion of sentences in many languages requiring a non-projective dependency analysis.

Tamil is a Dravidian language spoken mostly in Malaysia, Sri Lanka, Singapore and southern India (Chakravarthi et al., 2021). Tamil is agglutinative and contains many morphological suffixes. Tamil has two core word classes: nouns and verbs, with hundreds of distinct word forms possible through concatenative and derivational morphology (Premjith and Soman, 2021). With the exception of head-final, Tamil has a rich morphology that allows it to have any word order. This is a critical challenge in Dravidian languages since the subtask of proper label prediction in dependency parsing is extremely imprecise. Enhancing the prediction of these proper dependency relations betters the dependency parsing scores considerably on parsing tasks in transition-based parsing algorithms.

Only a few works on dependency parsing for Indic languages have been mentioned in the literature, let alone focusing on improving the prediction of dependency relation labels because there are a limited number of tools available. The lack of organized data makes this process extremely challenging, as unstructured text is difficult to parse on its own. The necessity of developing and improving a parser for Tamil is known to find applications in tasks like semantic parsing, machine translation, relation extraction, and many others. A key advantage of dependency parser is its ability to gain important semantic information for languages that are flexible with the placement of their part of speech (Butt et al., 2020).

In this paper, we tried to bring about machine learning approaches built upon a novel way of generating word embeddings through various pretrained multilingual BERT models (Barua et al., 2020) for improving the dependency relation prediction. These models are fine-tuned to improve

Proceedings of the Second Workshop on Speech and Language Technologies for Dravidian Languages, pages 1 - 8
May 26, 2022 ©2022 Association for Computational Linguistics

and study the variational changes within the models and improving the performance of dependency parsing for Tamil Language. The currently available parsers deal with word and sentence level embeddings, but for a free word language, the word's dependency tags information is held at elementary character level which is fed onto machine learning algorithms like Regression, Decision Tree, Random Forrest Classification, and Support Vector Machine (Devlin et al., 2019).

The models chosen are specific to understanding the relationship of embeddings of words at character level, where learning through regression and SVM infers the dimensional separability and feature space projections, while Decision Tree and Random Forest are well known relevant feature extractors. The four different models for dependency parsing compared directly and analyzed. To train the models we have tokenized sentences of Tamil TTB into individual words and extracted its respective dependency tags, further this data is embedded and then used to train our models.

Initial results suggest bias towards the majority dependency class tags, appearing due to the imbalances in dependency tag distribution. Where models like SVM become difficult to use as the class wise accuracy is strikingly low for minority class labels. One method of tackling the issue of data imbalance is through Oversampling Algorithms, yielding a higher-class wise accuracy while slightly compromising the overall accuracy which are discussed over the experiment section. The CoNLL-U formatted data is processed and then BERT case models are used for the token embedding which is used to train the machine learning models. The dependency of each word is label encoded which is then further used in training the models. Our best observed values were for the support vector machines fed with embedding generated by IndicBERT (Kakwani et al., 2020) with label accuracy of 67%, which was further passed onto a transition-based parser giving 52% labeled and 89% unlabeled attachment score. Due to the high imbalance in the dataset, on oversampling of the data, the observed labeled accuracy was around 56% with improvement in the overall class wise accuracy for some of the minority classes.

2 Dataset Description

Universal Dependencies (UD) (McDonald et al., 2013) is a project that aims to create cross-linguistically consistent treebank annotation for a variety of languages. The purpose is to facilitate multilingual parser creation, cross-lingual learning, and parsing research from the standpoint of language typology. The Universal Dependency formalism is now widely used to construct Universal Dependency Treebanks (UDTs) with annotations (Nivre et al., 2016), where in UDv2.7, Indian languages like Tamil have fewer than 12K tokens.

This paper is worked on over Tamil Tree Bank (Ramasamy and Žabokrtský, 2012), which has longer sentences over Multi-Word Tamil Tree Bank (MWTT). Cored with complex concepts such as elision, relative clauses, conjunct propagation, raising and control structures, and expanded case marking based on the Enhanced Universal Dependency annotation, it forms around 536 sentences (Sarveswaran and Dias, 2020). There are 400 training sentences and 120 testing sentences in the Tamil UDT (Universal Dependency Treebanks), with around 30 unique observed dependency tags in the dataset.

3 Related Works

Dependency parsing and the building of annotated treebanks are currently being researched for Hindi and Telugu (Bharati et al., 2009; Nivre, 2009; Zeman, 2009). In 2009, as part of the ICON 2009 conference, there was an NLP tools contest focused on parsing Indian languages (Hindi, Bangla, and Telugu). As the data were feasible, the building of a large-scale treebank dependency (Begum et al., 2008) for Telugu (with a goal of 1 million words) that has about 1500 annotated sentences were one such notable attempt for building a dependency parser in Dravidian languages.

Previous works that used Tamil dependency treebanks have been published, a paper (Dhanalakshmi et al., 2010) that used a machine learning approach to Tamil dependency parsing. This paper described grammar teaching tools in the sentence and word analyzing level for Tamil language. As part of the parser development, Selvam et al. (2009) created small dependency corpora with 5000 words. Other works such as Janarthanam et al. (2007) focused on parsing the spoken language utterances using dependency framework. Those works did not make use of treebank to the parser development, rather they were based on linguistic rules. The work (Janarthanam et al., 2007) used relative position of words to identify semantic relations. Along with the previously mentioned work there was one more work (Liyanage et al., 2014) that discussed Tamil syntactic parsing. Liyanage et al. (2014) used morphological analyzer and heuristic rules to identify phrase structures.

Paper Title	UAS Score
Goutam (2012)	94.5
Kolachina and Agarwal (2010)	91.82
Husain (2009)	85.76

Table 1: UAS Scores of Parsing Indian Languages.

Paper Title	LAS Score
Sarveswaran and Dias (2020)	62.39
Goutam (2012)	88.60
Kolachina and Agarwal (2010)	70.12
Husain (2009)	65.01

Table 2: LAS Scores of Parsing Indian Languages.

The literature on Tamil dependency parsing is sparse, though there are some recent works on developing a Tamil Dependency parser which has been studied in many contexts, a neural based parser (Sarveswaran and Dias, 2020) and a rule-based parsing (Ramasamy and Zabokrtsky, 2011). To our idea, these are the initial attempts to create a Tamil dependency treebank.

4 Methodology

The dependency parser's internal structure is made up entirely of directed relationships between lexical components in the sentence. Vital information that is typically buried in the more sophisticated phrase-structure parses is explicitly encoded by these head-dependent interactions. Another reason to employ a dependency-based method is that head-dependent connections approximate the semantic link between predicates and their arguments, making them valuable in a variety of applications including question answering, information extraction, and co-reference resolution. Hence the correct dependent prediction is crucial in the task of Dependency Parsing. Learning contextual information is essential over generating contextual-independent word embeddings for effectively encoding sentence-level features even inside single-word embeddings, yielding results that are equivalent or even superior to those achieved with sentence representations (Miaschi and Dell'Orletta, 2020).

The data extracted with morphological and part of speech information is fed on to various pre-trained multilingual Bidirectional Encoder Representation like mBERT, XLM-RoBERTA, IndicBERT and DistilBERT for generating the embedding at character level. The generated embedding is of different dimensions based on the morphology, unified by taking linear combinations of all vectors generated for each word in a sentence. These embeddings are passed on to various machine learning models to analyze performance of which the best model jointly works with transition-based dependency parsing.

We follow the Transition-based dependency parser (Nivre, 2008) which, includes two important systems; a transition mechanism that transforms a phrase into a dependency tree, and a machine learning classifier that can predict the next transition for each system structure that passes a statement. Dependency parsing can be accomplished as a deterministic search over the transition system, led by the classifier, given these two components. A stack of partially processed tokens, an input buffer containing the remaining tokens, and a collection of arcs representing the partially created dependency tree make up a parser configuration in this system. There are four transitions possible in this system that can only capture projective dependency trees:

- Left-Arc(r): From next to the top, add an arc labelled r; pop the stack.
- Right-Arc(r): Add an arc from top to next, labelled r, and put next onto the stack.
- Reduce: Pop the stack.
- Shift: Push next onto the stack.

Reduce operations, such as Left-Arc and Right-Arc, are named after shift-reduce parsing metaphor in which reducing involves merging components on the stack. When it comes to using operators, there are few prerequisites. When ROOT is the second member on the stack, the Left-Arc operator cannot be used (since by definition the ROOT node cannot have any incoming arcs). Both the Left-Arc and Right-Arc operators must have two components on the stack before they may be used.

A transition-based parser can also be defined by expressing the current state of the parse as a configuration, which includes the stack, an input buffer of words or tokens and a collection of relations that create a dependency tree. We begin with an initial configuration in which the ROOT node is on the stack, the tokens in the sentence are in the buffer and the parsing is represented by an empty set of relations. The stack and word list should be empty in the end target state and the set of relations will represent the final parse.

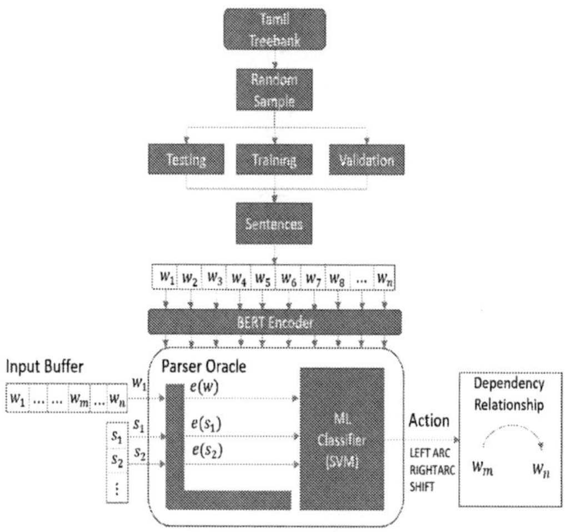

Figure 1: Schematic block for proposed methodology

The approach is similar to neural based parser oracle of Wang et al. (2020), which is replaced with machine learning algorithms for arc prediction (see Figure 1), where a sentence with 'n' words $w = [w1, w2, w3, \ldots, wn]$ is fed to the Encoder for obtaining the concatenation of several token embeddings is $E = [e1, e2, e3, \ldots, en]$ from BERT models pretrained with Indian Languages. The best model architecture was observed based on the test set. We used MaltParser, an open-source implementation of transition-based dependency parsing with a range of transition systems and customized classifiers, receives the embeddings equipped with a machine learning classifier. To overcome the problem of highly imbalanced label distribution oversampling algorithms such as SMOTE and ADASYN algorithms to up sample the Tamil training set which improved the results from initial experiments.

5 Experiments & Results

UD Treebanks in CoNLL-U format annotations are marked with the morphological, POS and dependency label information required for construction of the parse tree. Tamil UDT provides dataset segregations for training, validation, and testing. To induce the randomness, the data is combined and random sampled same ratio, following the approach of Loganathan et al. (Green et al., 2012). As part of exploratory data analysis, we analyzed the distribution of dependency relations in the Train-Test dataset combined (see Figure 2).

As observed, the classification task was highly biased towards the majority classes on account of the high imbalance in the dataset. To extract the character level significance of Tamil language, the sentences are broken down on to tokens as specified in the CoNLL-U formatting. In the encoder module, we have used different types of BERT models for this task, namely mBERT, XLM-RoBERTa, IndicBERT and DistilBERT with a range of different results. These tokens are embedded using these models which are trained with Tamil and other Indic languages to retain the contextual information of the token.

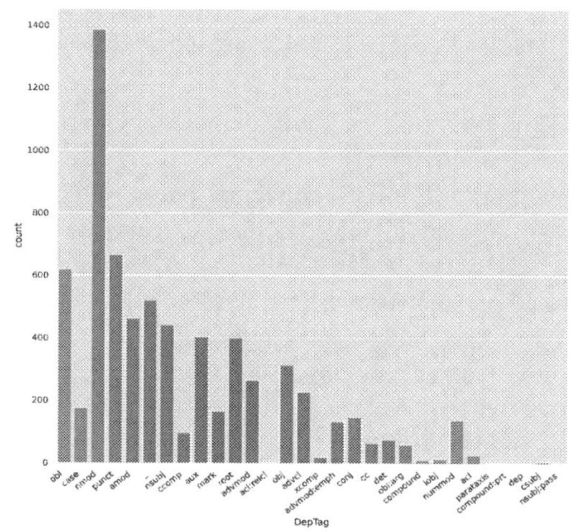

Figure 2: Class Distribution of Dependency Relation Label

We have used BERT embedding for the tokenization of the input sentences solely because the individual word tokens are exclusively dependent on the sentence itself rather than having just a corresponding index for the word itself like Word2Vec. Each individual sentence requires its own input id's which are a sequence of integers which map every input token with its respective token index in the BERT tokenizer vocabulary. The large BERT model that is used here has around 24 transformer encoders and each output per token from one of the layers can be used as a work embedding. Further as mentioned these embedded tokens can be fed to the Parser Oracle of the Malt parser.

Malt parser works based on a transition system

and two stacks. At each step, a transition is predicted using machine learning models, altered from liblinear and libsvm provided by the open-sourced parser. The input to these models is composed of the encoding of tokens in stacks and the current state of the machine. The embeddings passed on to the oracle are experimented with learning algorithms like linear regression to understand the separability of the data in its dimension in an attempt to establish linear relationship with the words. Decision Tree and Random Forrest classifiers are well performing important feature extractors, which is implemented to better the parsing task and study the head-dependent tag relation based from the generated BERT embeddings.

The algorithm closely follows a rule-based approach for parsing tasks. The sentences are tokenized and fed on to classifier trees, which improved the results over the regression models. A Support Vector Machine classifier is employed to solve the parsing task, which is a multi-class classification problem. The multi-class problem is divided into a series of binary-class problems since SVMs are binary classifiers, that classify the embeddings generated by projecting it into higher dimension to achieve separability.

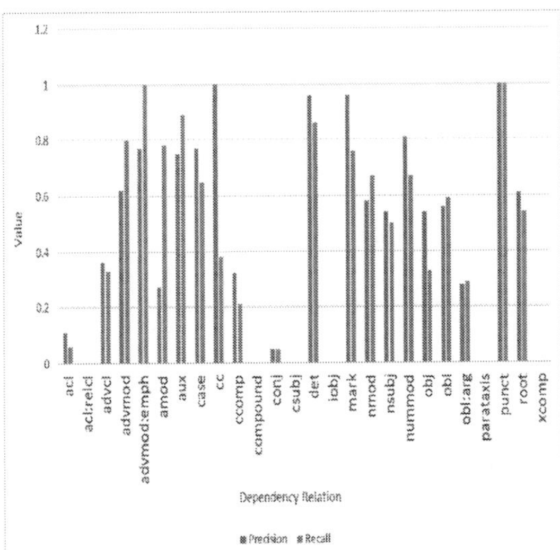

Figure 3: Precision & Recall Before Oversampling (IndicBERT-SVM)

The graph above (see Figure 3) , we can clearly observe that there is a large amount of misclassification in quite a few classes. This is mainly because of the high amount of imbalance in our dataset. To counter this issue, we have over-sampled the data using algorithms like ADASYN and SMOTE. The main goal of using these techniques was to improve class-wise accuracy.

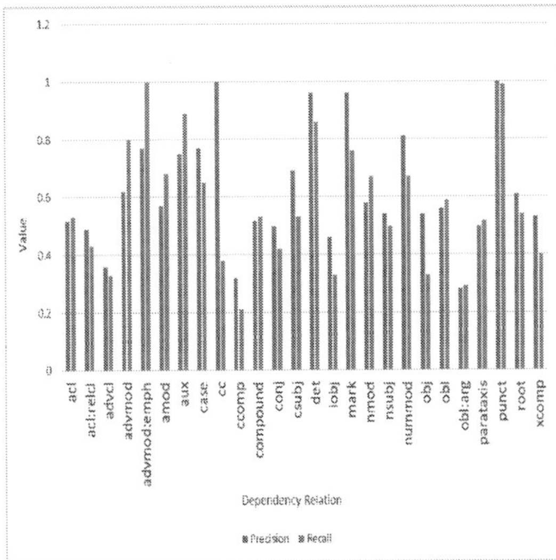

Figure 4: Precision & Recall After Oversampling (IndicBERT-SVM)

As observed (see Figure 4), there was a significant improvement in the class-wise accuracy while the overall accuracy remained constant. Both ADASYN and SMOTE functions are based on the K-Nearest Neighbours (KNN), difference being that ADASYN uses density distribution to determine the number of synthetic samples generated respectively for every minority class. This is done by changing the weights of the various minority samples adaptively which compensates for the skewed distributions. SMOTE creates an equivalent number of synthetic samples for each original minority sample. With respect to our experiment, we have seen that ADASYN yields better results as compared to SMOTE.

The difference being that ADASYN uses density distribution to determine the number of synthetic samples generated respectively for every minority class. This is done by changing the weights of the various minority samples adaptively which compensates for the skewed distributions. SMOTE creates an equivalent number of synthetic samples for each original minority sample.

We experimented with four different BERT models for this task and have achieved varying results based on the model used. IndicBERT being a multilingual ALBERT pre-trained model trained upon 11 Indian languages, outperformed every other BERT

Encoder/Model	Regression	Decision Tree	Random Forest	SVM
mBERT	53.33	52.26	55.35	58.21
XLM-RoBERTa	50.47	55.19	57.98	59.64
IndicBERT	54.21	56.93	60.71	62.33
DistilBERT	48.76	51.52	55.44	58.31

Table 3: Label Accuracy Before Oversampling

Encoder/Model	Regression	Decision Tree	Random Forest	SVM
mBERT	50.75	53.64	57.47	65.94
XLM-RoBERTa	52.82	59.66	61.31	66.35
IndicBERT	56.40	59.91	63.38	67.94
DistilBERT	49.36	52.36	56.23	63.57

Table 4: Label Accuracy After Oversampling

model. XLM-Roberta and mBERT had comparable results but often XLM-RoBERTA gave better results as it uses sentence wise tokenization compared to the word wise tokenization observed in mBERT. While DistilBERT is more compact and shows equivalent results to the other models it was observed to be the least performing model out of the four used. We included DistilBERT in our experiments to demonstrate the effectiveness of Transformer-based language models in a production context. The results suggests (see Table 3) IndicBERT-SVM as the better performing model, when parsed through Malt Parser we observed **Label Attachment Score of 52**. Which is lower compared to the approaches followed by Bharati et al. (2009), Kolachina and Agarwal (2010) & Sarveswaran and Dias (2020) (see Table 1), trained by mixing tree banks of various languages to calculate the respective LAS score, leading to higher scores, focused on 3 languages-Tamil, Telugu and Hindi.

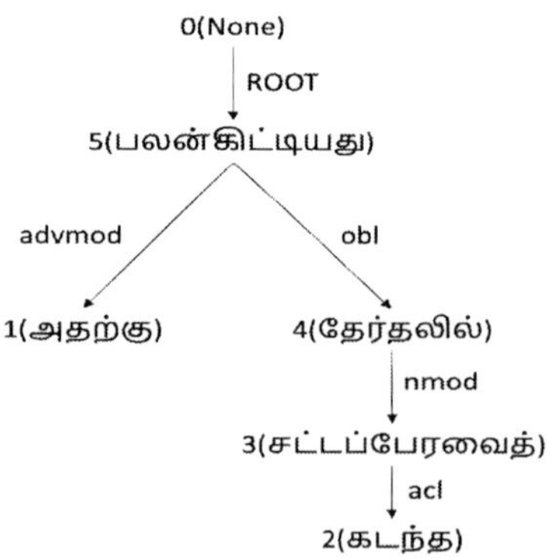

Figure 5: Ground Truth - Parsed Sentence

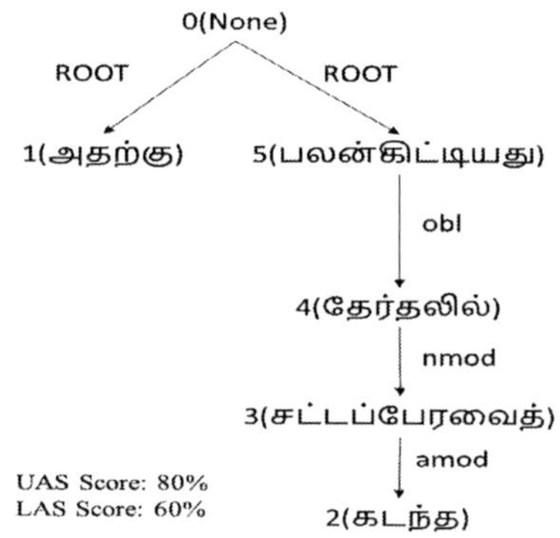

Figure 6: Parsed Sentence Before Over Sampling

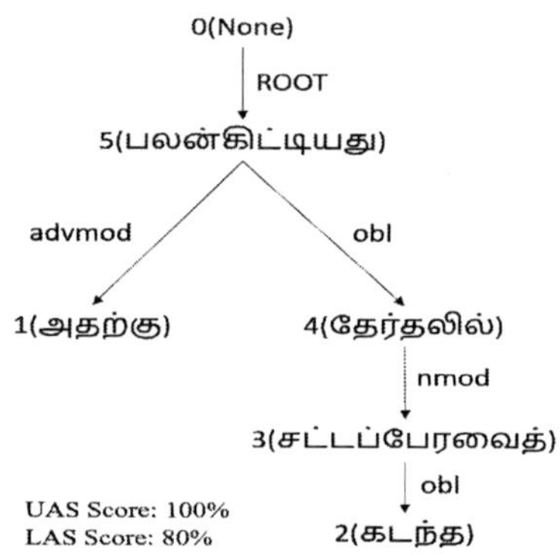

Figure 7: Parsed Sentence After Over Sampling

To overcome such low scores, we move ahead with the method of oversampling, which yielded better results due to the fact that for distinct minority class instances. ADASYN uses a weighted distribution based on how difficult it is to learn, with more synthetic data generated and trained for challenging minority class cases lesser in samples. Alongside increasing the number of data samples. As perceived (see Table 4), LS Scores have drastically improved upon training with synthetically generated data to improve the parser performance. Our best performing model IndicBERT-SVM's scores are closer to method of Nivre (2009) for Telugu Language and Sarveswaran and Dias (2020) (see Table 1) without mixed language training giving **Label Attachment Score of 56**. Considering a sample sentence from our test set (see Figure 5) marked with it's ground truth dependency relation and syntactic heads. The LAS and UAS scores was significantly improved by assigning the right dependency tags before (see Figure 6) and after the oversampling algorithm (see Figure 7).

6 Conclusion & Future Works

This paper explores the use of a malt parser for transition-based dependency parsing of Tamil language and how an improvement in LS scores can directly improve the overall parser performance. We show that for a morphologically rich, agglutinative language like Tamil, with appropriate vector representations from BERT trained by Indic languages yields enhanced parsing. Various Bert models were used to improve the dependency relation prediction accuracy and the best performing model's scores are comparable to other methods without mixed language training. The synthetic data generated by oversampling algorithms eliminates the need for more data to an extent, but we suggest training the model using a variety of datasets for the low-resource language to efficiently build a parser with strong contextual embeddings for Dravidian Languages.

We plan to use these techniques to improve our results in the near future on building effective parser for Dravidian Languages. In the future, we'd like to explore how the outcomes of our data split evolve when additional data is added, this may be an excellent tool for self-training. Because the amount of the tuning data for the SVM (Soman et al., 2009), (Premjith et al., 2019) appears to be the most relevant, the UAS may be improved by including self-training data in our tuning sets. The approach of contextual embedding and oversampling algorithms can be extended to other parsing algorithms like graph based parsing techniques, which open up wide variety of possibilities of improving the task of Dependency Parsing for Dravidian Languages.

References

Aindriya Barua, S Thara, B Premjith, and KP Soman. 2020. Analysis of contextual and non-contextual word embedding models for hindi ner with web application for data collection. In *International Advanced Computing Conference*, pages 183–202. Springer.

Rafiya Begum, Samar Husain, Arun Dhwaj, Dipti Misra Sharma, Lakshmi Bai, and Rajeev Sangal. 2008. Dependency annotation scheme for Indian languages. In *Proceedings of the Third International Joint Conference on Natural Language Processing: Volume-II*.

Akshar Bharati, Mridul Gupta, Vineet Yadav, Karthik Gali, and Dipti Misra Sharma. 2009. Simple parser for Indian languages in a dependency framework. In *Proceedings of the Third Linguistic Annotation Workshop (LAW III)*, pages 162–165, Suntec, Singapore. Association for Computational Linguistics.

Miriam Butt, Rajamathangi S., and Sarveswaran Kengatharaiyer. 2020. Mixed categories in tamil via complex categories.

Bharathi Raja Chakravarthi, KP Soman, Rahul Ponnusamy, Prasanna Kumar Kumaresan, Kingston Pal Thamburaj, John P McCrae, et al. 2021. Dravidian-multimodality: A dataset for multi-modal sentiment analysis in tamil and malayalam. *arXiv preprint arXiv:2106.04853*.

Nitesh V Chawla, Kevin W Bowyer, Lawrence O Hall, and W Philip Kegelmeyer. 2002. Smote: synthetic minority over-sampling technique. *Journal of artificial intelligence research*, 16:321–357.

Jacob Devlin, Ming-Wei Chang, Kenton Lee, and Kristina Toutanova. 2019. BERT: Pre-training of deep bidirectional transformers for language understanding. In *Proceedings of the 2019 Conference of the North American Chapter of the Association for Computational Linguistics: Human Language Technologies, Volume 1 (Long and Short Papers)*, pages 4171–4186, Minneapolis, Minnesota. Association for Computational Linguistics.

Velliangiri Dhanalakshmi, M Anand Kumar, R U Rekha, K P Soman, and S Rajendran. 2010. Grammar teaching tools for tamil language. In *2010 International Conference on Technology for Education*, pages 85–88.

Rahul Goutam. 2012. Exploring self-training and co-training for hindi dependency parsing using partial parses. In *2012 International Conference on Asian Language Processing*, pages 37–40.

Nathan Green, Loganathan Ramasamy, and Zdeněk Žabokrtský. 2012. Using an SVM ensemble system for improved Tamil dependency parsing. In *Proceedings of the ACL 2012 Joint Workshop on Statistical Parsing and Semantic Processing of Morphologically Rich Languages*, pages 72–77, Jeju, Republic of Korea. Association for Computational Linguistics.

Haibo He, Yang Bai, Edwardo A Garcia, and Shutao Li. 2008. Adasyn: Adaptive synthetic sampling approach for imbalanced learning. In *2008 IEEE international joint conference on neural networks (IEEE world congress on computational intelligence)*, pages 1322–1328. IEEE.

Samar Husain. 2009. Dependency parsers for indian languages.

Srinivasan Janarthanam, Udhaykumar Nallasamy, Loganathan Ramasamy, and C Santhoshkumar. 2007. Robust dependency parser for natural language dialog systems in tamil. In *Proceedings of the 5th Workshop on Knowledge and Reasoning in Practical Dialogue Systems, IJCAI KRPDS*, pages 1–6.

Divyanshu Kakwani, Anoop Kunchukuttan, Satish Golla, NC Gokul, Avik Bhattacharyya, Mitesh M Khapra, and Pratyush Kumar. 2020. Indicnlpsuite: Monolingual corpora, evaluation benchmarks and pre-trained multilingual language models for indian languages. In *Findings of the Association for Computational Linguistics: EMNLP 2020*, pages 4948–4961.

Sudheer Kolachina and Manish Agarwal. 2010. Experiments with maltparser for parsing indian languages.

Chamila Liyanage, Ifancy Ariaratnam, and Ruvan Weerasinghe. 2014. A shallow parser for tamil.

Ryan McDonald, Joakim Nivre, Yvonne Quirmbach-Brundage, Yoav Goldberg, Dipanjan Das, Kuzman Ganchev, Keith Hall, Slav Petrov, Hao Zhang, Oscar Täckström, et al. 2013. Universal dependency annotation for multilingual parsing. In *Proceedings of the 51st Annual Meeting of the Association for Computational Linguistics (Volume 2: Short Papers)*, pages 92–97.

Alessio Miaschi and Felice Dell'Orletta. 2020. Contextual and non-contextual word embeddings: an in-depth linguistic investigation. In *Proceedings of the 5th Workshop on Representation Learning for NLP*, pages 110–119, Online. Association for Computational Linguistics.

Joakim Nivre. 2008. Algorithms for deterministic incremental dependency parsing. *Comput. Linguist.*, 34(4):513–553.

Joakim Nivre. 2009. Parsing indian languages with maltparser.

Joakim Nivre, Marie-Catherine de Marneffe, Filip Ginter, Yoav Goldberg, Jan Hajič, Christopher D. Manning, Ryan McDonald, Slav Petrov, Sampo Pyysalo, Natalia Silveira, Reut Tsarfaty, and Daniel Zeman. 2016. Universal Dependencies v1: A multilingual treebank collection. In *Proceedings of the Tenth International Conference on Language Resources and Evaluation (LREC'16)*, pages 1659–1666, Portorož, Slovenia. European Language Resources Association (ELRA).

B Premjith and KP Soman. 2021. Deep learning approach for the morphological synthesis in malayalam and tamil at the character level. *Transactions on Asian and Low-Resource Language Information Processing*, 20(6):1–17.

B Premjith, KP Soman, M Anand Kumar, and D Jyothi Ratnam. 2019. Embedding linguistic features in word embedding for preposition sense disambiguation in english—malayalam machine translation context. In *Recent Advances in Computational Intelligence*, pages 341–370. Springer.

Loganathan Ramasamy and Zdeněk Žabokrtský. 2012. Prague dependency style treebank for Tamil. In *Proceedings of Eighth International Conference on Language Resources and Evaluation (LREC 2012)*, pages 1888–1894, İstanbul, Turkey.

Loganathan Ramasamy and Zdenek Zabokrtsky. 2011. Tamil dependency parsing: Results using rule based and corpus based approaches. volume 6608, pages 82–95.

Kengatharaiyer Sarveswaran and Gihan Dias. 2020. Thamizhiudp: A dependency parser for tamil.

Manu Selvam, A. Natarajan, and R. Thangarajan. 2009. Structural parsing of natural language text in tamil language using dependency model. *Int. J. Comput. Proc. Oriental Lang.*, 22:237–256.

KP Soman, R Loganathan, and V Ajay. 2009. *Machine learning with SVM and other kernel methods*. PHI Learning Pvt. Ltd.

Xinyu Wang, Yong Jiang, and Kewei Tu. 2020. Enhanced Universal Dependency parsing with second-order inference and mixture of training data. In *Proceedings of the 16th International Conference on Parsing Technologies and the IWPT 2020 Shared Task on Parsing into Enhanced Universal Dependencies*, pages 215–220, Online. Association for Computational Linguistics.

Daniel Zeman. 2009. Maximum spanning malt: Hiring world's leading dependency parsers to plant indian trees.

A Dataset for Detecting Humor in Telugu Social Media Text

Sriphani Vardhan Bellamkonda
National Institute of Technology Warangal
Telangana, India
sriphani345v@gmail.com

Maithili Lohakare
Pandit Deendayal Energy University
Gandhinagar, Gujarat, India
maithililohakare@gmail.com

Shaswat P Patel
Netaji Subhas University of Technology
New Delhi, India
shaswat178@gmail.com

Abstract

Increased use of online social media sites has given rise to tremendous amounts of user generated data. Social media sites have become a platform where users express and voice their opinions in a real-time environment. Social media sites such as Twitter limit the number of characters used to express a thought in a tweet, leading to increased use of creative, humorous and confusing language in order to convey the message. Due to this, automatic humor detection has become a difficult task, especially for low-resource languages such as the Dravidian languages. Humor detection has been a well studied area for resource rich languages due to the availability of rich and accurate data. In this paper, we have attempted to solve this issue by working on low-resource languages, such as, Telugu, a Dravidian language, by collecting and annotating Telugu tweets and performing automatic humor detection on the collected data. We experimented on the corpus using various transformer models such as Multilingual BERT, Multilingual DistillBERT and XLM-RoBERTa to establish a baseline classification system. We concluded that XLM-RoBERTa was the best-performing model and it achieved an F1-score of 0.82 with 81.5% accuracy.

1 Introduction

The use of social media sites has increased exponentially over the decade giving rise to vast amount of user generated content. Social media sites offer the ability to reach large number of users in real time which enable users to share their experiences easily. The content usually consists of creative and figurative use of languages such as humor, insults, sarcasm and irony. In the past couple of years, research in these linguistic elements has increased tremendously due to requirements in academia as well as in organizations.

Natural language processing(NLP) has evolved significantly leading to improvements in most of the fundamental tasks like Named-Entity recognition, sentiment analysis, etc (Singh etal., 2021). While the advancement is not only attributed to improvements in architecture of models but also due to the increased availability of data. Plethora of work exists for resource rich languages such as English (VanHee etal., 2018; A. and Sonawane, 2016; Patel etal., 2022). However, the same cannot be said for low-resource languages originating from the Indian subcontinent such as the Dravidian languages. Telugu is one of the four major Dravidian languages that stem from India, it is spoken by more than 75 million people (top, 2005). Hence, it is vital to establish a baseline system for automatic humor detection in Telugu language.

In this paper, we explore the task of humor detection, one of the critical elements of a natural language (Kruger, 1996). Humor is subtle and yet plays a significant part in our linguistic and social lives (Martin, 2007). The primary challenge in working with humor detection is the subjective nature of humor and capturing it in higher order is a challenge in NLP (deOliveira and Rodrigo, 2015). Yet, a large amount of research work has been carried out on English tweets and has achieved significant results.

One of the major challenges in building any social media analysis model in low-resource languages is the unavailability of high quality annotated data for conducting various experiments. In this paper, we address this issue by collecting Telugu tweets data by scraping Twitter and performing annotations on it. Furthermore, the dataset we collected is publicly available [1]. Below is an example of humorous tweet in Telugu:

[1] https://github.com/shaswa123/telugu_humour_dataset

Proceedings of the Second Workshop on Speech and Language Technologies for Dravidian Languages, pages 9 - 14
May 26, 2022

నవ్వు రాకపోయినా నవ్వేవాలని ఏమంటారో కానీ ?
What do you call those people who laugh even when laughter is not induced.

Context: This tweet intends to mock the judges of a Telugu comedy show who laugh a lot.

Additionally, we trained three multilingual transformer-based models, namely: Multilingual BERT, Multilingual DistilBERT, and XLM-RoBERTa and compared their performances to establish baseline classification system for humor detection in Telugu.

The rest of the paper is organized into related works (Section 2), detailed description of the dataset (Section 3), brief description of the methodology used(Section 4), analysis of results (Section 5), and finally conclusion (Section 6).

2 Related works

Plenty of work exists on social media text analysis including humor detection. Various works related to humor detection exist in English language, such as statistical and N-gram analysis (Rayz and Mazlack, 2004), Regression Trees (Purandare and Litman, 2006), Word2Vec combined with K-NN Human Centric Features (Yang etal., 2015), Convolutional Neural Networks (Chen and Soo, 2018) and transformer models (Weller and Seppi, 2019).

Previous work related to humor detection in Hindi-English mixed language dataset consists of scraping Hindi-English tweets and building N-grams, Bag-of-words, LSTM, Bi-directional LSTM, and Attention Based Bi-directional LSTM (Khandelwal etal., 2018; Agarwal etal., 2021; Sane etal., 2019).

Related works for humor detection in Telugu language is scarce. Vaishnavi et. al (Pamulapati and Mamidi, 2021) proposed conversational data in Telugu language for humor detection and experimented with TextGCN, FastText, Multilingual BERT, MuRIL, Indic-BERT, and Multilingual DistilBERT models. Automatic humor detection in Telugu for Twitter data is an under-explored area. According to our knowledge, this paper is the first attempt at building a novel telugu dataset and then proceeding with experimenting on various classifiers for humor detection task.

Category	Tweets	Words
Humorous	458	5477
Non-Humorous	1918	18098
Other	273	4213

Table1: Telugu Twitter humor corpus statistics

3 Dataset

3.1 Corpus Creation

For the creation of our dataset, we have scraped tweets from Twitter by filtering specific tags. For collecting humorous tweets, we searched using the tags such as humour, humor, funny, telugu-jokes. Additionally, we also searched using telugu hashtags such a s తమాషా and నవ్వు. In total we collected 1649 tweets using the above-mentioned tags. For non-humorous tweets we searched using tags such as news, sports, cooking, cinema etc. in order to include tweets from various domains in our dataset. Additional 1000 tweets were collected with these tags. The statistics of the resulting dataset is shown in Table 1. All these tweets were then annotated via two human annotators.

3.2 Humor annotation

The annotation of our tweets was done by two native multilingual Telugu speakers. Around 50 human hours was spent in tagging tweets into 3 categories: 0 for non-humorous, 1 for humorous, and n for tweets which do not have enough context to be considered informative or whose body was repeated. A tweet was considered humorous if it consisted sarcasm, irony, comedy, mockery, comment, or insult. Tweets which were just stating facts, general speech, quotes, or did not have any sort of amusement were considered non-humorous. These humor specifications were taken from (Khandelwal etal., 2018). The 2649 tweets were fairly split between the 2 annotators. Below are few examples of tweets from our corpus:

1. అరటి ఆకులో 66 కూరలు ఉన్నా ఆవకాయ లేదా అని అదిగెవాడే మన తెలుగు వాడు
   Even though there are 66 curries in a banana leaf, the one asking for mongo pickle is the true telugu person.
   Explanation: This tweet is classified as humorous as it wittily describes the telugu people's liking for mango pickle. Obviously, not all have this preference, but it is considered as a popular liked dish in the region.

2. మన సినిమా ల కి ఆడియన్సే రారు ..ఇక ' ఆస్కార్ ' రాటానికి అస్కారం ఎక్కడుంటుంది .
   Our movies aren't even watched by our own audience, so for getting oscars we have no scope.
   Explanation: This tweet is classified as humorous as it is satirical in nature and the user makes a clever word play between oscar, prestigious award given to movies, and "askaram", a telugu word which means having scope for.

3. సమతామూర్తి విగ్రహాన్ని దర్శించుకున్న కేంద్ర మంత్రి రాజ్‌నాథ్ సింగ్
   Union Minister Rajnath Singh visited the Samathamurthy statue
   Explanation: This tweet is classified as non humorous as it just states a fact and doesn't contain any comedy, satire, or amusement.

4. ఎయిర్‌టెల్ ఇంటర్నెట్ డౌన్... ఫన్నీ మీమ్‌లతో పిచ్చెక్కిచ్చిన నెటిజన్లు!
   Airtel internet down ... insane netizens with funny memes!
   Explanation: This tweet is marked as other and will be discarded as it isn't inherently humorous but refers to some memes which might be.

3.3 Inter Annotator Agreement

We used the Cohens Kappa coefficient for calculating the Inter Annotator Agreement as only 2 annotators were involved. The annotators are Telugu-native speakers whose second language is English. We extracted a set of 100 tweets and provided it to the annotators to measure their agreement score. The first 50 were sampled from the 1649 tweets intended to be humorous and the next 50 were sampled from the 1000 tweets intended to be non-humorous. We obtained a Kappa score of 0.84, implying that the annotation is of high quality.

4 Methodology

4.1 Preprocessing

In order to convert the humorous and non-humorous data to a favorable format for performing humor detection task, several changes were made to the collected tweets. Preprocessing steps such as removal of emojis, hashtags and URL links were implemented. In the tweets, URL links do not add any information to the data and were hence, removed. Additionally, hashtags were removed so that the models would classify effectively without any bias towards the tags used for filtering the tweets while scraping.

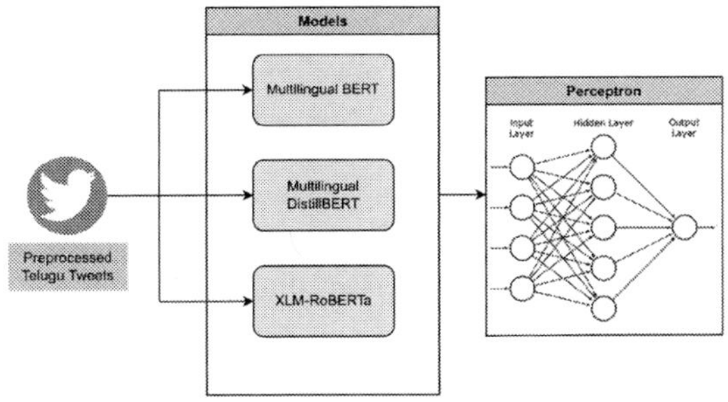

Figure1: Outline of Methodology

4.2 Outline of Methodology

The preprocessed data was then used by the transformer-based models in order to learn distinguishable features to classify tweets into humorous and non-humorous. The input text was intitally tokenzied using Subword or Sentencepiece tokenzation method (Devlin etal., 2019; Liu etal., 2019). The tokenized tweet in addition with segment ID and attention mask is fed to the transformer models to generate meaningful vectors summarizing the context of the tweet. The fix size vector is then classified using a single layered perceptron as shown Figure 1.

5 Modelling

We have trained three transformer models on our corpus for humor detection task. Transformer models with their improved architecture have achieved state-of-the-art results in numerous benchmark datasets including text classification tasks (Young etal., 2018; Alam etal., 2021). Hence, we decided to train these models to establish a suitable baseline for future work.

5.1 Transformers

We have used BERT and its variations such as Multilingual BERT, Multilingual Distill BERT and XML-RoBERTa, which are all transformer-based models, as our primary models for performing the humor detection task. Transformers are a set of deep learning models which use attention-based mechanism and are used for transforming one sequence into another using encoders and decoders. The architecture of a Transformer model consists of the input being passed through an encoder which has two parts: a multi-headed self attention layer and a feed-forward network. This information from the encoder is then presented as output into the decoder which includes the same above-mentioned parts but with an additional masked attention step. Lastly, it is transformed through a softmax layer into the output. The Transformer's self-attention layers are greatly attributed for its success. And hence, we chose to use the Transformer based models for their efficiency at recognizing and attending to the relevant words in sentences and paragraphs which would help classify the tweets with more accuracy and precision.

5.2 Multilingual BERT

Bidirectional Encoder Representations from Transformers or BERT is a transformer-based architecture (Devlin etal., 2019) that has greatly outperformed previous models like RNN-based models in various benchmark datasets. This is due to the ability of the model to capture latent information from text successfully into a fixed sized vector. This is mainly attributed to the following two tasks on which the BERT model was trained on:

1. Masked Language Model(MLM): From the given input sequence, 15% of tokens are randomly chosen and replaced with [MASK] tokens. The objective of this task is to correctly predict the masked tokens.

2. Next sentence prediction(NSP): From the given input segments, the task is to predict whether the input segments follow each other in the original text.

Multilingual BERT is trained on Wikipedia data consisting of 104 different languages (Pires etal., 2019). It has shown better accuracy as compared to BERT for NLP tasks involving machine translation and tasks dealing with multiple languages. Moreover, out of 104 languages, Telugu was one of the languages the multilingual BERT was pre-trained on. Hence, it became crucial to test our corpus by training this model on it.

5.3 Multilingual DistilBERT

Multilingual DistilBERT is the distilled version of Multilingual BERT (Sanh etal., 2019). It is also trained on text belonging to 104 different languages including Telugu and on the same Wikipedia dataset as Multilingual BERT. It consists of 134 million parameters making it on average twice as faster as multilingual BERT, hence, making it cheaper to train and convenient to test on our corpus.

5.4 XLM-RoBERTa

XLM-RoBERTa is a multilingual version of RoBERTa (Conneau etal., 2020). RoBERTa is a transformer based model which also happens to be an improved version of BERT. The following modifications were implemented on training of BERT to improve it's performance:

1. Model was trained on bigger batches and for more epochs.

2. Removing next sentence prediction task from the training objective.

3. Longer sequences were considered for training the model.

4. Changing the masking pattern dynamically for the training data.

The XLM-RoBERTa was pre-trained on 100 different languages using over 2.5TB of filtered CommonCrawl data (Conneau etal., 2020). Moreover, the vocabulary size was also significantly larger in comparison to multilingual BERT. These modifications to BERT have made the XLM-RoBERTa a more robust model and made it outperform multilingual BERT significantly in most of the multilingual NLP tasks. Therefore, XLM-RoBERTa was the best choice for our task.

6 Results

The corpus was split into 80% train and 20% test. We have downsampled the non-humorous tweets to match the number of humorous tweets. At the end, we have 732 training examples and 184 test examples. We have considered macro F1-score as our metric to select the best model out of the three models trained on our corpus. XLM-BERT has outperformed other models with a F1-score of 0.82 and an accuracy of 81.5% as shown in Table 2. XLM-RoBERTa has shown a significant improvement over multilingual BERT in various multilingual tasks (Conneau etal., 2020). This is mainly due to the increase in vocabulary size and in the amount of training data over multilingual BERT.

Model	Accuracy	F1-score
Multilingual BERT	81.5	0.81
Multilingual DistilBERT	73.4	0.73
XLM-RoBERTa	81.5	0.82

Table2: Results of various models trained and tested on our corpus.

7 Conclusion and Future work

In this paper, we introduced the Telugu Twitter Humor Dataset and have addressed the need to annotate low-resource languages and create datasets in languages such as Telugu. We have also described our data collection and annotation process. Additionally, we have trained multiple transformer-based models, namely, Multilingual BERT, Multilingual DistillBERT, and XML-RoBERTa, to perform automatic humor detection on our collected dataset. The performance of these models is compared and a baseline for classification of humorous and non-humorous Telugu tweets is established in this paper. Out of the above-mentioned models used for training our data, XLM-RoBERTa performed the best with a F1-score of 0.82 and an accuracy of 81.5%. We would like to expand this work in the future by incorporating the information detected from emojis into the classifiers and by making a multi-modal humor detection classifier as a large number of tweets which were discarded had images present in them too.

Acknowledgements

We thank our anonymous reviewers for providing their valuable feedbacks. All the opinions, conclusions and findings presented in this material are those of the authors only and do not reflect the views of their graduate schools or employing organizations. We would also like to thank our annotators, Mrs. Bellamkonda Aruna and Mr. Bellamkonda Kiran Kumar for their effort in annotating the data and review.

References

2005. Top 30 languages by number of native speakers.

Vishal A. and S.S. Sonawane. 2016. Sentiment analysis of twitter data: A survey of techniques. *International Journal of Computer Applications*, 139(11):515.

Kaustubh Agarwal, , and RhythmNarula and. 2021. Humor generation and detection in code-mixed hindi-english. In *Proceedings of the Student Research Workshop Associated with RANLP 2021*. INCOMA Ltd. Shoumen, BULGARIA.

Firoj Alam, Arid Hasan, Tanvirul Alam, Akib Khan, Janntatul Tajrin, Naira Khan, and ShammurAbsar Chowdhury. 2021. A review of bangla natural language processing tasks and the utility of transformer models.

Peng-Yu Chen and Von-Wun Soo. 2018. Humor recognition using deep learning. In *Proceedings of the 2018 Conference of the North American Chapter of the Association for Computational Linguistics: Human Language Technologies, Volume 2 (Short Papers)*, pages 113–117, New Orleans, Louisiana. Association for Computational Linguistics.

Alexis Conneau, Kartikay Khandelwal, Naman Goyal, Vishrav Chaudhary, Guillaume Wenzek, Francisco Guzmán, Edouard Grave, Myle Ott, Luke Zettlemoyer, and Veselin Stoyanov. 2020. Unsupervised cross-lingual representation learning at scale.

Luke deOliveira and AlfredoLáinez Rodrigo. 2015. Humor detection in yelp reviews.

Jacob Devlin, Ming-Wei Chang, Kenton Lee, and Kristina Toutanova. 2019. Bert: Pre-training of deep bidirectional transformers for language understanding.

Ankush Khandelwal, Sahil Swami, SyedS. Akhtar, and Manish Shrivastava. 2018. Humor detection in english-hindi code-mixed social media content : Corpus and baseline system.

Arnold Kruger. 1996. The nature of humor in human nature: Cross-cultural commonalities. *Counselling Psychology Quarterly*, 9(3):235–241.

Yinhan Liu, Myle Ott, Naman Goyal, Jingfei Du, Mandar Joshi, Danqi Chen, Omer Levy, Mike Lewis, Luke Zettlemoyer, and Veselin Stoyanov. 2019. Roberta: A robustly optimized bert pretraining approach.

RodA. Martin. 2007. *The Psychology of Humor*. Elsevier.

Vaishnavi Pamulapati and Radhika Mamidi. 2021. Developing conversational data and detection of conversational humor in Telugu. In *Proceedings of the 2nd Workshop on Computational Approaches to Discourse*, pages 12–19, Punta Cana, Dominican Republic and Online. Association for Computational Linguistics.

Shaswat Patel, Binil Shah, and Preeti Kaur. 2022. Leveraging user comments in tweets for rumor detection. In *International Conference on Innovative Computing and Communications*, pages 87–99, Singapore. Springer Singapore.

Telmo Pires, Eva Schlinger, and Dan Garrette. 2019. How multilingual is multilingual BERT? In *Proceedings of the 57th Annual Meeting of the Association for Computational Linguistics*, pages 4996–5001, Florence, Italy. Association for Computational Linguistics.

Amruta Purandare and Diane Litman. 2006. Humor: Prosody analysis and automatic recognition for F*R*I*E*N*D*S*. In *Proceedings of the 2006 Conference on Empirical Methods in Natural Language Processing*, pages 208–215, Sydney, Australia. Association for Computational Linguistics.

JuliaTaylor Rayz and LawrenceJ. Mazlack. 2004. Computationally recognizing wordplay in jokes.

SushmithaReddy Sane, Suraj Tripathi, KoushikReddy Sane, and Radhika Mamidi. 2019. Deep learning techniques for humor detection in Hindi-English code-mixed tweets. In *Proceedings of the Tenth Workshop on Computational Approaches to Subjectivity, Sentiment and Social Media Analysis*, pages 57–61, Minneapolis, USA. Association for Computational Linguistics.

Victor Sanh, Lysandre Debut, Julien Chaumond, and Thomas Wolf. 2019. Distilbert, a distilled version of bert: smaller, faster, cheaper and lighter. *ArXiv*, abs/1910.01108.

Shaanya Singh, Maithili Lohakare, Keval Sayar, and Shivi Sharma. 2021. Recnn: A deep neural network based recommendation system. In *2021 International Conference on Artificial Intelligence and Machine Vision (AIMV)*, pages 1–5.

Cynthia VanHee, Els Lefever, and Véronique Hoste. 2018. SemEval-2018 task 3: Irony detection in English tweets. In *Proceedings of The 12th International Workshop on Semantic Evaluation*, pages 39–50, New Orleans, Louisiana. Association for Computational Linguistics.

Orion Weller and Kevin Seppi. 2019. Humor detection: A transformer gets the last laugh.

Diyi Yang, Alon Lavie, Chris Dyer, and Eduard Hovy. 2015. Humor recognition and humor anchor extraction. In *Proceedings of the 2015 Conference on Empirical Methods in Natural Language Processing*, pages 2367–2376, Lisbon, Portugal. Association for Computational Linguistics.

Tom Young, Devamanyu Hazarika, Soujanya Poria, and Erik Cambria. 2018. Recent trends in deep learning based natural language processing.

MuCoT: Multilingual Contrastive Training for Question-Answering in Low-resource Languages

Gokul Karthik Kumar **Abhishek Singh Gehlot**
Sahal Shaji Mullappilly **Karthik Nandakumar**
Mohamed Bin Zayed University of Artificial Intelligence (MBZUAI)
Abu Dhabi, UAE
{gokul.kumar, abhishek.gehlot}@mbzuai.ac.ae
{sahal.mullappilly, karthik.nandakumar}@mbzuai.ac.ae

Abstract

Accuracy of English-language Question Answering (QA) systems has improved significantly in recent years with the advent of Transformer-based models (e.g., BERT). These models are pre-trained in a self-supervised fashion with a large English text corpus and further fine-tuned with a massive English QA dataset (e.g., SQuAD). However, QA datasets on such a scale are not available for most of the other languages. Multi-lingual BERT-based models (mBERT) are often used to transfer knowledge from high-resource languages to low-resource languages. Since these models are pre-trained with huge text corpora containing multiple languages, they typically learn language-agnostic embeddings for tokens from different languages. However, directly training an mBERT-based QA system for low-resource languages is challenging due to the paucity of training data. In this work, we augment the QA samples of the target language using translation and transliteration into other languages and use the augmented data to fine-tune an mBERT-based QA model, which is already pre-trained in English. Experiments on the Google ChAII dataset show that fine-tuning the mBERT model with translations from the same language family boosts the question-answering performance, whereas the performance degrades in the case of cross-language families. We further show that introducing a contrastive loss between the translated question-context feature pairs during the fine-tuning process, prevents such degradation with cross-lingual family translations and leads to marginal improvement. The code for this work is available at `https://github.com/gokulkarthik/mucot`.

1 Introduction

India has a population of 1.4 billion people speaking 447 languages and over 10,000 dialects, making it the country with the fourth-highest number of languages (Chakravarthi, 2020). However, Indian languages are highly under-represented on the Internet and Natural Language Processing (NLP) systems for Indian languages are in their nascency (Bharathi et al., 2022; Priyadharshini et al., 2021).Tamil is a member of the southern branch of the Dravidian languages, a group of about 26 languages indigenous to the Indian subcontinent. It is also classed as a member of the Tamil language family, which contains the languages of around 35 ethnolinguistic groups, including the Irula and Yerukula languages (Sakuntharaj and Mahesan, 2021, 2017, 2016; Thavareesan and Mahesan, 2019, 2020a,b, 2021). Malayalam is Tamil's closest significant cousin; the two began splitting during the 9th century AD. Although several variations between Tamil and Malayalam indicate a pre-historic break of the western dialect, the process of separating into a different language, Malayalam, did not occur until the 13th or 14th century (Anita and Subalalitha, 2019b,a; Subalalitha and Poovammal, 2018; Subalalitha, 2019). Even state-of-the-art multilingual NLP systems perform sub-optimally on Dravidian languages (Google, 2021). This can be explained by the fact that multilingual language models are often jointly trained on 100+ languages and Indian languages constitute only a small fraction of their vocabulary and training data (as shown in Figure 2).

Machine learning models and tools have been proposed for many Natural Language Understanding tasks. In this work, we focus on Extractive Question-Answering (QA), where the goal is to localize the answer to a question within a large context (see Figure 1). Specifically, we aim to develop a common multilingual question answering model for multiple Indian languages. A multilingual model has several advantages: (1) learning of cues across different languages, (2) a single model for many languages, and (3) avoiding dependency on English translation during inference. In this work, we start with a pre-trained multilingual Bidi-

Proceedings of the Second Workshop on Speech and Language Technologies for Dravidian Languages, pages 15 - 24
May 26, 2022 ©2022 Association for Computational Linguistics

Context	Question	Answer	Start Position	Language
ஒரு சாதாரண வளர்ந்த மனிதனுடைய எலும்புக்கூடு பின்வரும் 206 (மார்பெலும்பு மூன்று பகுதிகளாகக் கருதப்பட்டால் 208) எண்ணிக்கையான எலும்புகளைக் கொண்டிருக்கும் ...	மனித உடலில் எத்தனை எலும்புகள் உள்ளன?	206	53	Tamil
Translation				
A normal adult human skeleton consists of the following 206 (208 if the breast is thought to be three parts) ...	How many bones do you have in your body?	206	56	English
एक सामान्य वयस्क मानव कंकाल में निम्नलिखित 206 होते हैं (यदि स्तन को तीन भाग माना जाता है) ...	आपके शरीर में कितनी हड्डियां हैं?	206	43	Hindi
Transliteration				
Woru sadharan valarnt manidhani elumbukkoodu finwarum 206 (marbelumbu moondau bakudikalagak karudapattal 208) annikkaiyana elumbugalack kontrukkum...	Manit udalil atans elumbues ulsana?	206	54	English

Figure 1: Example of a QA record from the ChAII QA dataset along with the translation and transliteration done on that record.

rectional Encoder Representations from Transformers (mBERT) model and further pre-train it with SQuAD (Rajpurkar et al., 2016), a large-scale question answering dataset in English. The resulting English-language mBERT-QA model is fine-tuned and evaluated for Indian languages Tamil and Hindi using the ChAII dataset (Google, 2021).

Fine-tuning the mBERT-QA model using only the training instances in the ChAII dataset is less effective because of the small number of training samples (1114 records with approximately two-thirds in Hindi and the rest in Tamil). To overcome this problem, we use translation and transliteration to other languages as a data augmentation strategy. The translation is the process of transforming the source content from one language to another, while the transliteration just involves modifying each word from the source content into another script. Both these operations are executed on the training dataset for the contexts, questions, and answers separately; then new locations of transformed answers in the transformed contexts are computed as shown in Figure 1. Using translation and transliteration increases the size of the ChAII dataset manifold.

The choice of languages used for translation and transliteration is critical. Kudugunta et al. (2019) showed that languages under the same family have similar representations in multilingual models. Hence, we put together translations and transliterations from related languages within the same language family to achieve better performance. This will also help with better use of the vocabulary corpora from the low-resource languages. We also study the impact of translation and transliteration on languages outside the family of the target language. Since the cross-family language transfer degraded the QA performance, we introduce a contrastive loss (Radford et al., 2021) between the translated pairs to help retain or improve the original performance by encouraging the embeddings from all languages to be similar regardless of the family group. Thus, the contributions of the paper are three-fold:

- We propose a three-stage training pipeline for question-answering in low-resource languages.
- We evaluate mBERT for question-answering in Tamil and Hindi with translations and transliterations as data augmentation techniques and show that same language family translations improve the performance. In contrast, we show that transliterations do not improve the QA performance on the ChAII dataset, regardless of the language family combinations.
- We propose a contrastive loss between the features of translated pairs to align the cross-family language representations.

2 Related Work

Bidirectional Encoder Representations from Transformers (BERT) (Devlin et al., 2018) is a deep learning model for general-purpose language representations. BERT is often used as the backbone model for several NLP tasks like semantic analysis, question answering, and named entity recognition. The bidirectional transformer used in BERT has a deeper sense of language context and generates intricate semantic feature representations. These representations are learned through a pre-training step using Next Sentence Prediction (NSP) and Masked Language Modelling (MLM) as pretext tasks and transferred to the downstream NLP tasks. The goal of the Next Sentence Prediction task is to identify whether the two input sentences are consecutive or not. In Masked Language Modelling, BERT is trained to predict randomly masked words in a sentence. The Transformer network receives a sequence of tokens as input and utilizes the attention mechanism to learn the contextual relationships between words in a text. These relationships can then be used to extract high-quality

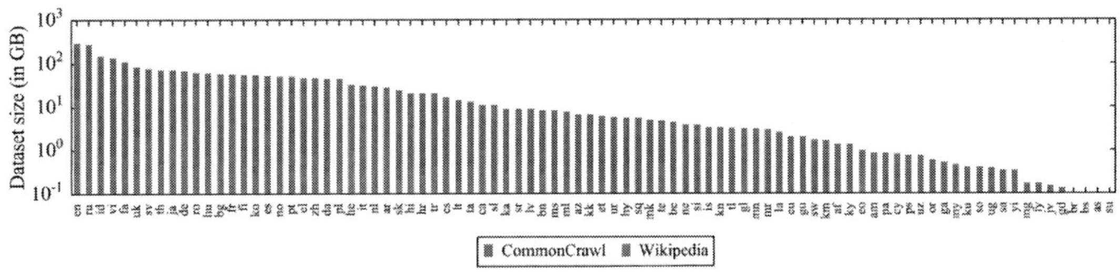

Figure 2: Amount of data in GB (log-scale) for the 88 languages that appear in both the Wiki-100 (Merity et al., 2016) corpus used for mBERT and XLM-100 (Conneau et al., 2020). None of the Indian languages feature among top-25 languages with the largest amount of data.

language features, which can be fine-tuned for applications like semantic analysis and question answering. Multi-lingual-BERT (mBERT) is a BERT model pre-trained using the Wikipedia text corpus (Merity et al., 2016) in more than 100 languages around the world. XLM-RoBERTa (Conneau et al., 2020) scaled this idea with more than 2 terabytes of common crawl data.

Deep models such as Transformers rely heavily on the availability of a large amount of annotated data, which is available only for prominent languages like English, Russian, German or Spanish (Ponti et al., 2019; Joshi et al., 2020). For a majority of other languages with a minimal number of annotations, cross-lingual transfer learning (Prettenhofer and Stein, 2011; Wan et al., 2011; Ruder et al., 2019) has been proposed as a possible solution. This approach can transfer knowledge from the annotation-rich source language to low-resource or zero-resource target languages. Furthermore, multilingual models (Lewis et al., 2019; Clark et al., 2020) can be used to mitigate the data scarcity problem. For example, LASER (Artetxe and Schwenk, 2019) used a bidirectional LSTM (Hochreiter and Schmidhuber, 1997) encoder with a byte pair encoding vocabulary shared between languages. This work showed that joint training of multiple languages helped to improve the model performance for low-resource languages. LaBSE (Feng et al., 2020) used the mBERT (Devlin et al., 2018) encoder pre-trained with masked language modelling and translation language modelling (Lample and Conneau, 2019) tasks. It attempted to optimize the dual encoder translation ranking (Guo et al., 2018) loss during pre-training to achieve similar embedding for the same text in different languages.

The work of Bornea et al. (2020) showed that large pre-trained multilingual models are not enough for question-answering in under-represented languages and presented several novel strategies to improve the performance of mBERT with translations. This work achieved language-independent embeddings, which improved the cross-lingual transfer performance with additional pre-training on adversarial tasks. It also introduced a Language Arbitration Framework (LAF), which consolidated the embedding representations across languages using properties of translation. Cross-lingual manifold mixup (X-Mixup) (Yang et al., 2021) achieved better cross-lingual transfer by calibrating the representation discrepancy, which resulted in a compromised representation for target languages. It was shown that the multilingual pre-training process can be improved by implementing X-Mixup on parallel data. Contrastive Language-Image pre-training (CLIP) (Radford et al., 2021) introduced an efficient way to learn scalable image representations with natural language supervision. Drawing inspiration from ConVIRT (Zhang et al., 2020), CLIP used a contrastive objective that maximizes the cosine similarity of the correct pairs of images and text, while minimizing the same for incorrect pairs.

Building upon the work of (Bornea et al., 2020), we show that translations of a small-scale dataset into cross-family languages could degrade the QA performance. To overcome this problem, we propose multilingual contrastive training to encourage cross-lingual invariance. Our approach is relatively simpler compared to adversarial training and LAF used in Bornea et al. (2020). Though the proposed contrastive loss has a similar objective to the pre-training loss in (Guo et al., 2018), there are subtle differences because we use it in multi-task learning setup along with the original task loss for fine-tuning.

3 Methodology

3.1 Data Representation and Baseline Model

We adopt the standard data representations that are commonly used in Transformer-based question-answering models. We use the same word-piece Tokenizer of mBERT to tokenize the concatenated input of question-context pairs. For the question answering task, the context is usually very long. In some NLP applications, truncating the input text is a viable choice because it leads to only loss of information. But in the extractive question answering task, removing part of the context may result in loss of answer as well. To overcome this challenge, we follow the popular approach of splitting the long context into parts that fit into the model and regulate this splitting using an additional hyper-parameter called 'max length'. Moreover, to cover for cases where the answer might be distributed over multiple splits of the context, an overlap factor is introduced, which in turn is controlled by another hyper-parameter 'doc stride'.

Our baseline is the mBERT model (Devlin et al., 2018), which is pre-trained using pretext tasks like Masked Language Modelling and Next Sentence Prediction on a multilingual text corpus that includes our target languages, Hindi and Tamil. The default output head of mBERT is replaced with the head for the question-answering task. This is done by adding separate output heads for classifying the start and end positions as shown in Devlin et al. (2018).

3.2 Proposed Framework for Effective Cross-lingual Transfer

We propose a three-stage pipeline called Multilingual Constrative Training (MuCoT) to effectively train the mBERT model for question-answering in low-resource languages. An illustration of this pipeline for two low-resource languages, namely Tamil and Hindi, is shown in Figure 3. The first stage is pre-training the baseline multilingual model (mBERT). The second stage involves pre-training the QA head using the large-scale dataset(s) in high resource language(s). In Figure 3, English is considered the high-resource language and SQuAD (Rajpurkar et al., 2016) dataset is used to pre-train the QA head and obtain the mBERT-QA model. The final stage involves fine-tuning the mBERT-QA model using both original and augmented samples from the target low-resource languages. In this work, ChAII (Google, 2021) dataset is used for obtaining training samples in Tamil and Hindi.

Since SQuAD (Rajpurkar et al., 2016) and ChAII (Google, 2021) datasets have similar Wikipedia[1] style contexts, it is possible to train a multilingual QA model jointly using both datasets. However, to take advantage of the engineering and training efforts of publicly available models, we sequentially use both these datasets. After obtaining the mBERT-QA model pre-trained for the English language QA task, we fine-tune it on the ChAII dataset using the following loss function.

$$L_{total} = L_{task} + w_{contrastive} * L_{contrastive}, \quad (1)$$

where L_{task} and $L_{contrastive}$ are the QA task loss and multilingual contrastive loss, respectively, L_{total} is the total loss, and $w_{contrastive}$ is the relative weight assigned to the contrastive loss. Note that fine-tuning using only the QA task loss is often not sufficient to achieve good performance, especially if the dataset used for fine-tuning is small. To mitigate this problem, we translate the training samples into other languages and use both original and translated samples for fine-tuning. While this approach works well for translations into other languages within the same language family, it leads to sub-optimal performance in the case of cross-family language translations, due to divergence in the representations across language families. To solve this issue, we introduce the multi-lingual contrastive loss $L_{contrastive}$.

3.3 Multilingual Contrastive Loss

During fine-tuning, for each data point in the original batch (B_o) of size n, we pick one of its corresponding translations uniformly at random and form a translated batch (B_p) of the same size n. It is important to note that B_o itself is taken from the combined dataset of source instances and translated instances. The two batches that form a pair are denoted as original batch and pair batch, respectively, in Figure 4. We use the same mBERT network up to a specific layer as our encoder (enc) to transform B_o and B_p to get the embeddings, $E_o, E_p \in \mathbb{R}^{n*t*d}$, respectively. Then, we apply a global average pooling (gap) operation to aggregate the vector representations of t tokens into a single vector representation of dimension d for each instance in each batch. This will result in the

[1] `https://www.wikipedia.org/`

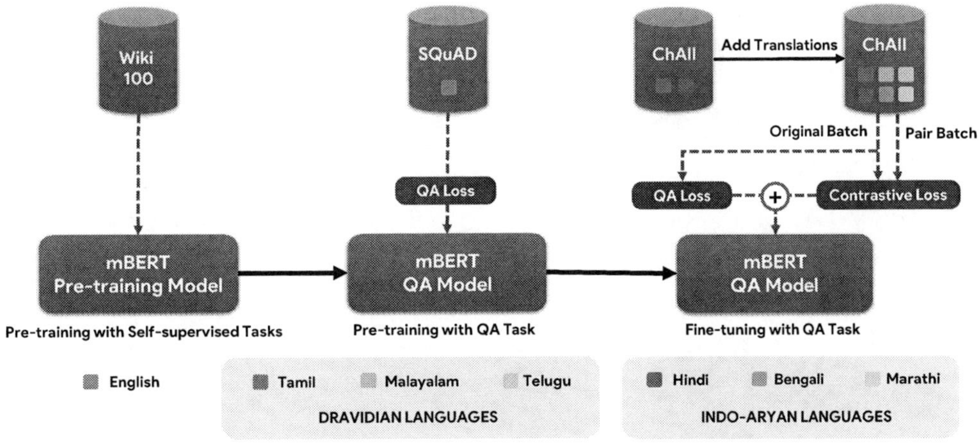

Figure 3: Proposed training pipeline of MuCoT for question answering in low resource languages Tamil and Hindi.

aggregated embeddings $O, P \in \mathbb{R}^{n*d}$ for B_o and B_p, respectively. With these n feature vectors in the original and the translated batch, we follow the CLIP (Radford et al., 2021) approach and compute the contrastive loss using the cross-entropy loss (L_{ce}). Specifically, we multiply the matrices O and P^T to get the logits matrix $Q \in \mathbb{R}^{n*n}$. Then, we apply the cross-entropy loss L_{ce} row-wise and column-wise to the logits matrix Q, with its diagonal locations as original classes for each row and column, respectively.

$$O = gap(enc(B_o)), \tag{2}$$

$$P = gap(enc(B_p)), \tag{3}$$

$$Q = OP^T, \tag{4}$$

$$L_{contrastive} = \frac{L_{ce}^{row}(Q) + L_{ce}^{column}(Q)}{2}. \tag{5}$$

4 Experimental Results

4.1 Datasets

In our experiments, we use ChAII (Google, 2021) question-answering dataset for fine-tuning and evaluation. This dataset was recently released by Google Research India and has 1,114 records of context, question, answer, and its corresponding start position in the context for Tamil and Hindi languages. Hindi is represented predominantly in the dataset with nearly two-thirds of the records. As the ChAII dataset has been published as part of an ongoing Kaggle competition (Google, 2021), the complete test dataset has not been disclosed to the public. Hence, we have used Scikit-learn's train_test_split method with a test size of 100, stratified on language and with a random seed of 0, to get the *test* split from the training data. Similarly, we applied the same method over the filtered *train* split to get the *validation* split of 100 samples. We also use the translations and transliterations of this training split as augmented samples for fine-tuning the QA model.

Stanford Question Answering Dataset (SQuAD) (Rajpurkar et al., 2016) is the most popular question-answering dataset in English. This dataset had been crowdsourced to form 100K records of answerable question-answer pairs along with the context. This dataset is used to pre-train the QA head added to the pre-trained mBERT model, which is subsequently fine-tuned using the ChAII dataset.

4.2 Translation and Transliteration Details

We use AI4Bharat's IndicTrans[2] (Ramesh et al., 2021) for translation, which is a Transformer-4X model trained on *Samanantar* dataset (Ramesh et al., 2021). In IndicTrans, translation can be done from Indian languages to English and vice versa. Available Indian languages include Assamese, Bengali, Gujarati, Hindi, Kannada, Malayalam, Marathi, Oriya, Punjabi, Tamil, and Telugu. At first, we translate the ChAII dataset from Hindi and Tamil to English and then to Bengali, Marathi, Malayalam, and Telugu. In the FLORES devset benchmark (Goyal et al., 2021), the BLEU scores of IndicTrans for translating Hindi and Tamil to English are 37.9 and 28.6, respectively. The scores

[2] https://indicnlp.ai4bharat.org/indic-trans/

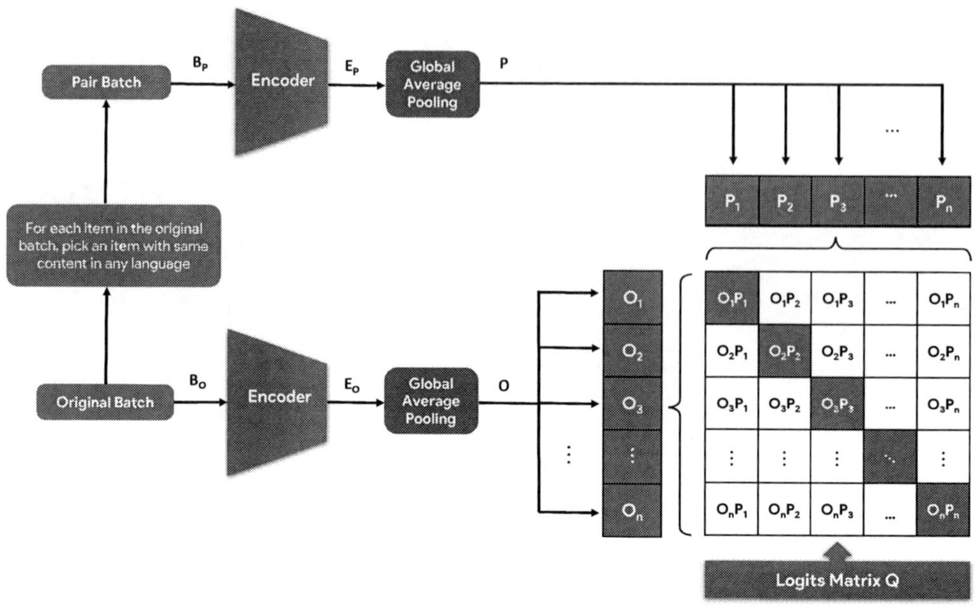

Figure 4: Logits matrix computation for the input to contrastive loss, similar to CLIP (Radford et al., 2021)

for translating English to Bengali, Marathi, Malayalam, and Telugu are 20.3, 16.1, 16.3, and 22.0, respectively. We were not able to translate nearly 500 of the ChAII instances to English as the automatic search for the translated answers in the translated contexts failed. This happened because the same word got translated differently in the context and the answer. For the same reason, we lost nearly another 200 instances when translating from English to other Indian languages.

For transliteration, we use the open-source Indic-trans transliteration module[3] (Bhat et al., 2015), which is available for many Indian language scripts including English and Urdu. Here, we directly transliterate from Hindi and Tamil to Bengali, Marathi, Malayalam, and Telugu.

4.3 Model Training Details

We used mBERT[4] as our baseline model. It is modified for the question-answering task by replacing the output head using HuggingFace's auto model. At first, we evaluated this model after directly fine-tuning on the train split of the ChAII dataset. Then, we introduced intermediate SQuAD pre-training and fine-tuned on the train split of the ChAII dataset with and without translations or transliterations.

[3]https://indic-trans.readthedocs.io/en/latest/index.html

[4]https://huggingface.co/bert-base-multilingual-cased

The hyperparameter settings listed in Table 1 are used for all the experiments. We have experimented with different levels of mBERT layers to compute the contrastive loss. Layer 3 performed consistently well compared to the initial layer 1 and the deeper layers such as 5. Initially, we used contrastive training for all the steps. However, forcing the model to learn exact representations across languages could make the model forget the task-specific patterns learned with intermediate pre-training on a large-scale dataset. Hence, we applied the contrastive loss only for training steps that are a multiple of 500 and picked the best one. Other hyperparameters are tuned based on a standard search over multiple choices.

Hyperparameter	Value
Maximum feature length	128
Document stride	384
Batch size	16
Maximum optimization steps	5000
Learning rate	0.00003
Weight decay	0.01
Contrastive loss layer	3
Contrastive loss weight	0.05
Maximum contrastive steps	1000

Table 1: Hyperparameter configuration of all the models for fine-tuning on ChAII dataset

SQuAD pre-training	No	Yes	Yes		Yes		Yes	
Translations	No	No	Dravidian (ml, te)		Indo-Aryan (bn, mr)		All languages	
Contrastive Training	*No*	*No*	*No*	*Yes*	*No*	*Yes*	*No*	*Yes*
Overall	0.44	0.5	0.49	**0.53**	0.51	0.52	0.49	0.52
Hindi	0.47	0.57	0.52	0.57	**0.59**	0.58	0.54	0.57
Tamil	0.39	0.37	0.44	**0.45**	0.35	0.4	0.39	0.41

Table 2: Jaccard scores with translation used as augmentation in different training settings. ml, te, bn, and mr denote Malayalam, Telugu, Bengali, and Marathi, respectively.

SQuAD pre-training	No	Yes	Yes		Yes		Yes	
Transliterations	No	No	Dravidian (ml, te)		Indo-Aryan (bn, mr)		All languages	
Contrastive Training	*No*	*No*	*No*	*Yes*	*No*	*Yes*	*No*	*Yes*
Overall	0.44	0.5	0.5	0.49	**0.53**	0.47	0.49	0.46
Hindi	0.47	0.57	0.52	0.55	**0.56**	0.53	0.52	0.53
Tamil	0.39	0.37	**0.45**	0.36	0.44	0.36	0.44	0.32

Table 3: Jaccard scores with transliteration used as augmentation in different training settings. ml, te, bn, and mr denote Malayalam, Telugu, Bengali, and Marathi, respectively.

4.4 Evaluation Metric

Given the noisy nature of the ChAII dataset, we employed the Jaccard score as the evaluation metric. Jaccard similarity coefficient is widely used for determining similarity between sets/intervals and is defined as $J(A, B) = \frac{|A \cap B|}{|A \cup B|}$. Here, A and B are sets/intervals, and $\cap$ and $\cup$ represent intersection and union, respectively. We compute the evaluation metric for the overall test split as well as for individual language test sets in intervals of 500 optimization steps. For each experiment, we pick the model at a specific optimization step that gives the best overall Jaccard score and reports its performance.

4.5 Performance

As shown in Tables 2 and 3, translation and transliteration affect the performance in different ways. While some data is lost during the translation process due to failed automatic search of translated text in the translated context. transliteration does not cause any such loss. However, to ensure a fair comparison, records lost during translation are dropped from transliterated testing as well. Note that we use the same hyper-parameters from Table 1 for evaluating the models and later stages with additional augmentation and contrastive training.

First, we observe from Table 2 that just having intermediate SQuAD pre-training in English, improves the overall Jaccard score significantly from 0.44 to 0.5. Furthermore, we fine-tune by dividing translated and transliterated data into Indo-Aryan and Dravidian language families to study how translated and transliterated pairs serve as supervised cross-lingual signals when languages share semantics and structure (Mikolov et al., 2013). Although transliteration improves the Jaccard scores in certain cases compared to the baseline, the trend is not consistent. Moreover, contrastive training does not help in the case of transliteration as shown in Table 3. This could be because the QA model is pre-trained only with regular text and not with transliteration style text.

From Table 2, we observe that grouped translated data in the same language family helps in improving performance. The translated Indo-Aryan data (Bengali and Marathi) increases the Jaccard score of Hindi answers to 0.59 from 0.57. Similarly, Dravidian language data (Telugu and Malayalam) significantly increase the Jaccard similarity of Tamil answers from 0.37 to 0.44. At the same time, the overall Jaccard score did not change much because of the degradation in cross-family language performance. Interestingly, we could observe in Table 2 that the contrastive training helps in preventing such degradation and improves the overall score by encouraging similar representations between languages from across families.

5 Conclusion and Future Work

With Internet usage expanding every day, there is an increasing need to develop better NLP models for a variety of downstream tasks in vernacular languages. As most of these languages do not have labeled resources that are sufficient to train standalone modern deep learning models, we need to rely on multilingual models and enhance them. Our work is a step in this direction and is an attempt to understand and evaluate the impact of cross-lingual knowledge transfer through pre-training and fine-tuning. We utilize modern open-source deep learning models to translate the ChAII dataset into different languages from two language families namely, Dravidian, and Indo-Aryan, and use them to improve the question-answering performance. Our analysis shows an effective way to pick languages for translation, which can be used for fine-tuning. We also showed that introducing a contrastive loss with the original task training loss increases the performance even for cross-family languages.

Despite the inclusion of translations and contrastive loss, we observed that there is only a marginal improvement in the QA performance. This can be attributed to the smaller size of the ChAII dataset with 1114 instances (Tamil and Hindi combined; Train, Validation, and Test combined), which is clearly insufficient to fine-tune a 177M parameter model. Hence, the proposed techniques have to be evaluated on other larger datasets as well as using other multilingual models like XLM-RoBERTa (Conneau et al., 2020), DistillmBERT (Sanh et al., 2019), MURIL (Khanuja et al., 2021) and Indic-BERT (Kakwani et al., 2020). We hope that the proposed techniques will motivate further research in this field, including exploration of the same phenomenon of cross-lingual transfer in other language families and multilingual tasks.

References

R Anita and CN Subalalitha. 2019a. An approach to cluster Tamil literatures using discourse connectives. In *2019 IEEE 1st International Conference on Energy, Systems and Information Processing (ICESIP)*, pages 1–4. IEEE.

R Anita and CN Subalalitha. 2019b. Building discourse parser for Thirukkural. In *Proceedings of the 16th International Conference on Natural Language Processing*, pages 18–25.

Mikel Artetxe and Holger Schwenk. 2019. Massively multilingual sentence embeddings for zero-shot cross-lingual transfer and beyond. *Transactions of the Association for Computational Linguistics*, 7:597–610.

B Bharathi, Bharathi Raja Chakravarthi, Subalalitha Chinnaudayar Navaneethakrishnan, N Sripriya, Arunaggiri Pandian, and Swetha Valli. 2022. Findings of the shared task on Speech Recognition for Vulnerable Individuals in Tamil. In *Proceedings of the Second Workshop on Language Technology for Equality, Diversity and Inclusion*. Association for Computational Linguistics.

Irshad Ahmad Bhat, Vandan Mujadia, Aniruddha Tammewar, Riyaz Ahmad Bhat, and Manish Shrivastava. 2015. Iiit-h system submission for fire2014 shared task on transliterated search. In *Proceedings of the Forum for Information Retrieval Evaluation*, FIRE '14, pages 48–53, New York, NY, USA. ACM.

Mihaela Bornea, Lin Pan, Sara Rosenthal, Radu Florian, and Avirup Sil. 2020. Multilingual transfer learning for qa using translation as data augmentation. *arXiv preprint arXiv:2012.05958*.

Bharathi Raja Chakravarthi. 2020. HopeEDI: A multilingual hope speech detection dataset for equality, diversity, and inclusion. In *Proceedings of the Third Workshop on Computational Modeling of People's Opinions, Personality, and Emotion's in Social Media*, pages 41–53, Barcelona, Spain (Online). Association for Computational Linguistics.

Jonathan H Clark, Eunsol Choi, Michael Collins, Dan Garrette, Tom Kwiatkowski, Vitaly Nikolaev, and Jennimaria Palomaki. 2020. Tydi qa: A benchmark for information-seeking question answering in typologically diverse languages. *Transactions of the Association for Computational Linguistics*, 8:454–470.

Alexis Conneau, Kartikay Khandelwal, Naman Goyal, Vishrav Chaudhary, Guillaume Wenzek, Francisco Guzmán, Edouard Grave, Myle Ott, Luke Zettlemoyer, and Veselin Stoyanov. 2020. Unsupervised cross-lingual representation learning at scale. In *Proceedings of the 58th Annual Meeting of the Association for Computational Linguistics*, pages 8440–8451.

Jacob Devlin, Ming-Wei Chang, Kenton Lee, and Kristina N. Toutanova. 2018. Bert: Pre-training of deep bidirectional transformers for language understanding. In *Proceedings of the 2019 Conference of the North American Chapter of the Association for Computational Linguistics: Human Language Technologies, Volume 1 (Long and Short Papers)*, pages 4171–4186.

Fangxiaoyu Feng, Yinfei Yang, Daniel Cer, Naveen Arivazhagan, and Wei Wang. 2020. Language-agnostic bert sentence embedding. *arXiv preprint arXiv:2007.01852*.

Google. 2021. ChAII - Hindi and Tamil question answering. `https://www.kaggle.com/c/chaii-hindi-and-tamil-question-answering` [Accessed: 01-Oct-2021].

Naman Goyal, Cynthia Gao, Vishrav Chaudhary, Peng-Jen Chen, Guillaume Wenzek, Da Ju, Sanjana Krishnan, Marc'Aurelio Ranzato, Francisco Guzman, and Angela Fan. 2021. The flores-101 evaluation benchmark for low-resource and multilingual machine translation. *arXiv preprint arXiv:2106.03193*.

Mandy Guo, Qinlan Shen, Yinfei Yang, Heming Ge, Daniel Cer, Gustavo Hernandez Abrego, Keith Stevens, Noah Constant, Yun-Hsuan Sung, Brian Strope, and Ray Kurzweil. 2018. Effective parallel corpus mining using bilingual sentence embeddings. In *Proceedings of the Third Conference on Machine Translation: Research Papers*, pages 165–176, Brussels, Belgium. Association for Computational Linguistics.

Sepp Hochreiter and Jürgen Schmidhuber. 1997. Long Short-Term Memory. *Neural Computation*, 9(8):1735–1780.

Pratik Joshi, Sebastin Santy, Amar Budhiraja, Kalika Bali, and Monojit Choudhury. 2020. The state and fate of linguistic diversity and inclusion in the nlp world. *arXiv preprint arXiv:2004.09095*.

Divyanshu Kakwani, Anoop Kunchukuttan, Satish Golla, N C Gokul, Avik Bhattacharyya, Mitesh M. Khapra, and Pratyush Kumar. 2020. Indicnlpsuite: Monolingual corpora, evaluation benchmarks and pre-trained multilingual language models for indian languages. In *Findings of the Association for Computational Linguistics: EMNLP 2020*, pages 4948–4961.

Simran Khanuja, Diksha Bansal, Sarvesh Mehtani, Savya Khosla, Atreyee Dey, Balaji Gopalan, Dilip Kumar Margam, Pooja Aggarwal, Rajiv Teja Nagipogu, Shachi Dave, Shruti Gupta, Subhash Chandra Bose Gali, Vish Subramanian, and Partha P. Talukdar. 2021. Muril: Multilingual representations for indian languages. *arXiv preprint arXiv:2103.10730*.

Sneha Reddy Kudugunta, Ankur Bapna, Isaac Caswell, Naveen Arivazhagan, and Orhan Firat. 2019. Investigating multilingual nmt representations at scale. *arXiv preprint arXiv:1909.02197*.

Guillaume Lample and Alexis Conneau. 2019. Cross-lingual language model pretraining. *arXiv preprint arXiv:1901.07291*.

Patrick Lewis, Barlas Oğuz, Ruty Rinott, Sebastian Riedel, and Holger Schwenk. 2019. Mlqa: Evaluating cross-lingual extractive question answering. *arXiv preprint arXiv:1910.07475*.

Stephen Merity, Caiming Xiong, James Bradbury, and Richard Socher. 2016. Pointer sentinel mixture models. *arXiv preprint arXiv:1609.07843*.

Tomas Mikolov, Quoc V Le, and Ilya Sutskever. 2013. Exploiting similarities among languages for machine translation. *arXiv preprint arXiv:1309.4168*.

Edoardo Maria Ponti, Helen O'horan, Yevgeni Berzak, Ivan Vulić, Roi Reichart, Thierry Poibeau, Ekaterina Shutova, and Anna Korhonen. 2019. Modeling language variation and universals: A survey on typological linguistics for natural language processing. *Computational Linguistics*, 45(3):559–601.

Peter Prettenhofer and Benno Stein. 2011. Cross-lingual adaptation using structural correspondence learning. *ACM Transactions on Intelligent Systems and Technology (TIST)*, 3(1):1–22.

Ruba Priyadharshini, Bharathi Raja Chakravarthi, Sajeetha Thavareesan, Dhivya Chinnappa, Durairaj Thenmozhi, and Rahul Ponnusamy. 2021. Overview of the DravidianCodeMix 2021 shared task on sentiment detection in Tamil, Malayalam, and Kannada. In *Forum for Information Retrieval Evaluation*, pages 4–6.

Alec Radford, Jong Wook Kim, Chris Hallacy, Aditya Ramesh, Gabriel Goh, Sandhini Agarwal, Girish Sastry, Amanda Askell, Pamela Mishkin, Jack Clark, et al. 2021. Learning transferable visual models from natural language supervision. In *International Conference on Machine Learning*, pages 8748–8763. PMLR.

Pranav Rajpurkar, Jian Zhang, Konstantin Lopyrev, and Percy Liang. 2016. Squad: 100,000+ questions for machine comprehension of text. In *Proceedings of the 2016 Conference on Empirical Methods in Natural Language Processing*, pages 2383–2392.

Gowtham Ramesh, Sumanth Doddapaneni, Aravinth Bheemaraj, Mayank Jobanputra, Raghavan AK, Ajitesh Sharma, Sujit Sahoo, Harshita Diddee, Divyanshu Kakwani, Navneet Kumar, et al. 2021. Samanantar: The largest publicly available parallel corpora collection for 11 indic languages. *arXiv preprint arXiv:2104.05596*.

Sebastian Ruder, Ivan Vulić, and Anders Søgaard. 2019. A survey of cross-lingual word embedding models. *Journal of Artificial Intelligence Research*, 65:569–631.

Ratnasingam Sakuntharaj and Sinnathamby Mahesan. 2016. A novel hybrid approach to detect and correct spelling in Tamil text. In *2016 IEEE International Conference on Information and Automation for Sustainability (ICIAfS)*, pages 1–6.

Ratnasingam Sakuntharaj and Sinnathamby Mahesan. 2017. Use of a novel hash-table for speeding-up suggestions for misspelt tamil words. In *2017 IEEE International Conference on Industrial and Information Systems (ICIIS)*, pages 1–5.

Ratnasingam Sakuntharaj and Sinnathamby Mahesan. 2021. Missing word detection and correction based on context of Tamil sentences using n-grams. In *2021 10th International Conference on Information and Automation for Sustainability (ICIAfS)*, pages 42–47.

Victor Sanh, Lysandre Debut, Julien Chaumond, and Thomas Wolf. 2019. Distilbert, a distilled version of bert: smaller, faster, cheaper and lighter. *arXiv preprint arXiv:1910.01108*.

C. N. Subalalitha. 2019. Information extraction framework for Kurunthogai. *Sādhanā*, 44(7):156.

CN Subalalitha and E Poovammal. 2018. Automatic bilingual dictionary construction for Tirukural. *Applied Artificial Intelligence*, 32(6):558–567.

Sajeetha Thavareesan and Sinnathamby Mahesan. 2019. Sentiment analysis in Tamil texts: A study on machine learning techniques and feature representation. In *2019 14th Conference on Industrial and Information Systems (ICIIS)*, pages 320–325.

Sajeetha Thavareesan and Sinnathamby Mahesan. 2020a. Sentiment lexicon expansion using Word2vec and fastText for sentiment prediction in Tamil texts. In *2020 Moratuwa Engineering Research Conference (MERCon)*, pages 272–276.

Sajeetha Thavareesan and Sinnathamby Mahesan. 2020b. Word embedding-based part of speech tagging in Tamil texts. In *2020 IEEE 15th International Conference on Industrial and Information Systems (ICIIS)*, pages 478–482.

Sajeetha Thavareesan and Sinnathamby Mahesan. 2021. Sentiment analysis in Tamil texts using k-means and k-nearest neighbour. In *2021 10th International Conference on Information and Automation for Sustainability (ICIAfS)*, pages 48–53.

Chang Wan, Rong Pan, and Jiefei Li. 2011. Biweighting domain adaptation for cross-language text classification. In *Twenty-Second International Joint Conference on Artificial Intelligence*.

Huiyun Yang, Huadong Chen, Hao Zhou, and Lei Li. 2021. Enhancing cross-lingual transfer by manifold mixup. In *International Conference on Learning Representations*.

Yuhao Zhang, Hang Jiang, Yasuhide Miura, Christopher D Manning, and Curtis P Langlotz. 2020. Contrastive learning of medical visual representations from paired images and text. *arXiv preprint arXiv:2010.00747*.

TamilATIS: Dataset for Task-Oriented Dialog in Tamil

Ramaneswaran S and **Sanchit Vijay** and **Kathiravan Srinivasan**
Vellore Institute Of Technology, Vellore
kathiravan.srinivasan@vit.ac.in
{s.ramaneswaran2018, sanchit.vijay2018}@vitstudent.ac.in

Abstract

Task-Oriented Dialogue (TOD) systems allow users to accomplish tasks by giving directions to the system using natural language utterances. With the widespread adoption of conversational agents and chat platforms, TOD has become mainstream in NLP research today. However, developing TOD systems require massive amounts of data, and there has been limited work done for TOD in low-resource languages like Tamil. Towards this objective, we introduce TamilATIS - a TOD dataset for Tamil which contains 4874 utterances. We present a detailed account of the entire data collection and data annotation process. We train state-of-the-art NLU models and report their performances. The Joint BERT model with XLM-Roberta as utterance encoder achieved the highest score with an intent accuracy of 96.26% and slot F1 of 94.01%.

1 Introduction

Task-oriented dialog (TOD) systems enable a user to use natural language directions to complete specific tasks. Recently, such systems have been successfully deployed in smart applications such as Amazon's Echo and Spotify's Car Thing.

There are several components that are critical to the performance of a TOD system. These components are Natural Language Understanding, Dialogue State Tracking (DST), and Response Selection. In this work, we focus on the NLU component. NLU aims to semantically parse an input utterance and typically has two tasks: intent classification and slot filling (refer Table 1 for example).

Intent classification deals with identifying the underlying motivation or the goal of the user query. It is modelled as a sequence classification task. The simplicity and conciseness of the utterances, paired with the necessity to scale to multiple domains, pose bottlenecks to intent detection. Slot filling deals with identifying entities present in an utterance that corresponds to certain slots in the user query. This is typically cast as a token classification or span identification task. Slot filling is a challenging task in NLU. The model needs to adapt to unseen domains and identify entities that it has not encountered in training before.

Find	morning	flights	to	Chennai
O	B-period	O	O	B-fromcity
Intent: find-flight				

Table 1: Example of user utterance with their corresponding BIO annotation and intent.

Intent classification and slot filling have been widely researched for the English language. The approaches presented in these works achieve excellent performance due to the availability of large amounts of high-quality and human-annotated datasets. However, such performance has not been achieved for several low-resource languages due to a lack of data. Developing TOD datasets for low-resource languages is essential to the proliferation of NLP technologies in these communities and contributes towards inclusivity and diversity of language resources.

To facilitate this, we present a dataset named TamilATIS, which contains 4874 utterances in Tamil and their corresponding slots and intent annotations. The following are some of the main contributions of this work:

- We present a TOD dataset for Tamil - TamilATIS with 4874 utterances.
- We perform initial experiments with state-of-the art slot filling and intent detection models to establish the baselines.

The full dataset and the source code of the baseline models are available at `https://github.com/ramaneswaran/tamil_atis`

Proceedings of the Second Workshop on Speech and Language Technologies for Dravidian Languages, pages 25 - 32
May 26, 2022 ©2022 Association for Computational Linguistics

	Utterance	Intent
Ex. 1	(Morning flights from Vadodara to Vijayawada on April 20) ஏப்ரல் 20 அன்று வதோதராவில் இருந்து விஜயவாடாவிற்கு காலை விமானங்கள்	atis_flight
Slots	B.MN B.DN O B.FCN O B.TCN B.POD	
Ex. 2	(What is the fare for a taxi to Agartala?) அகர்தலாவிற்கு ஒரு டாக்ஸிக்கு என்ன கட்டணம்	atis_ground_fare
Slots	B.CN O B.TPT O O	
Ex. 3	(What is the seat capacity of the 733?) 733 இன் இருக்கை திறன் என்ன?	atis_capacity
Slots	B.AC O O O O	
Ex. 4	(I would like to take a flight from Kochi to Tiruchirappalli on Saturday morning in Vistara) விஸ்தாராவில் சனிக்கிழமை காலை கொச்சியிலிருந்து திருச்சிராப்பள்ளிக்கு விமானம் செல்ல விரும்புகிறேன்	atis_flight
Slots	B.AN B.DDN B.DPD B.FCN B.TCN O O O	

Figure 1: Examples of utterances and their annotations from the Tamil ATIS dataset. The words in blue are the slot values

2 Related Work

Intent classification and slot filling are two key challenges modelled separately or jointly for Natural Language Understanding (NLU). Joint modelling approaches have attained state-of-the-art performance, and have demonstrated that there exists a significant correlation between the two tasks. Prior works have implemented CNN-CRF (Xu and Sarikaya, 2013), RecNN (Guo et al., 2014), joint RNN-LSTM (Hakkani-Tür et al., 2016), attention-based BiRNN (Liu and Lane, 2016), and slot-gated attention-based model (Goo et al., 2018) and more recently have used BERT (Chen et al., 2019a) and BiLSTM based (Haihong et al., 2019) approaches.

Intent classification and slot filling functions are core modules for NLU in Task-Oriented Dialogue (TOD) systems (Chen et al., 2016; Takanobu et al., 2019; Kummerfeld et al., 2019; Liang et al., 2019; Campagna et al., 2020; Hosseini-Asl et al., 2020; Ham et al., 2020). Since these tasks are characterized as sequence classification and token tagging tasks, sentence encoder models have been utilized to solve them. The two extensively utilized large scale datasets in English (high resource language) for this purpose in NLU are: ATIS (Price, 1990), which features audio recordings of individuals booking flight reservations, and SNIPS (Coucke et al., 2018), which is gathered from Snips' personal voice assistant. Dao et al. (2021) introduced a low-resource language dataset in Vietnamese. Apart from these monolingual English corpora, Schuster et al. (2019) presented a new dataset of 57k annotated utterances in English (43k), including low-resource Spanish (8.6k), and Thai (5k), spanning the topics of weather, alarm, and reminder.

In Indian languages, there have been works to synthesize training data by using Google Translate and proposed CNN+LSTM based architecture (Gupta et al., 2020). Malviya et al. (2021) released a Hindi Dialogue Restaurant Search (HDRS) corpus consisting of 1.4k human-to-human typed dialogues collected using the Wizard-of-Oz paradigm and compared various state-of-the-art DST models. Small sized datasets were constructed manually and used with Indic and Code-Switched TOD systems (Jayarao and Srivastava, 2018). (Kanakagiri and Radhakrishnan, 2021) used mBERT based semantic tracking to associate the slot tokens to the respective tokens in the utterance and employed Google Translate API, morphological characteristics and semantics based heuristic slot aligner to publish a dataset for dravidian languages like Kannada and Tamil.

3 Tamil ATIS

The earliest Old Tamil documents are small inscriptions in Adichanallur dating from 905 BC to 696

Name	Language	Intent	Slot	Description
HDRS 2021	hi	No	Yes	H2H dialogue corpus for restaurant domain in Hindi
TaskMaster-1 2018	hi,mr,bn,gj	Yes	No	Google's Taskmaster-1 dataset for intent classification automatically translated to 4 indian languages
CoMTIC 2021	hi-en	Yes	No	Hindi-english code-mixed dataset for intent classification
Codemix-DSTC2 2018	hi,bn,gj,ta	Yes	Yes	DSTC2 dataset manually converted to codemix and slot labels manually annotated
Codemix-SNIPS 2020	hi-en	Yes	No	SNIPs dataset manually converted to hindi-english code-mixed form.
TOD-Dravidian 2021	kn, ta	Yes	Yes	MTOD dataset automatically translated and slots automatically annotated
Ours	ta	Yes	Yes	ATIS dataset automatically translated to Tamil and slot labels manually annotated

Table 2: Comparison of various datasets for TOD in Indian languages.

Vistara from delhi to mumbai
டெல்லியிலிருந்து மும்பை வரை விஸ்தாரா
விஸ்தாரா-தில்லி முதல் மும்பை வரை
Air asia flights to delhi
டெல்லிக்கு ஏர் ஏசியா விமானங்கள்
தில்லிக்கு விமானங்கள்

Figure 2: Translation results from Google Translate API (in blue) and IndicTrans (in red).

BC. Tamil has the oldest ancient non-Sanskritic Indian literature of any Indian language. Tamil uses agglutinative grammar, which uses suffixes to indicate noun class, number, case, verb tense, and other grammatical categories. Tamil's standard metalinguistic terminology and scholarly vocabulary is itself Tamil, as opposed to the Sanskrit that is standard for most Aryan languages. Tamil has many forms, in addition to dialects: a classical literary style based on the ancient language (cankattami), a modern literary and formal style (centami), and a current colloquial form (kotuntami) (Sakuntharaj and Mahesan, 2021, 2017, 2016; Thavareesan and Mahesan, 2019, 2020a,b, 2021). These styles blend into one another, creating a stylistic continuity. It is conceivable, for example, to write centami using cankattami vocabulary, or to utilize forms connected with one of the other varieties while speaking kotuntami (Subalalitha, 2019; Srinivasan and Subalalitha, 2019; Narasimhan et al., 2018). Tamil words are made up of a lexical root and one or more affixes. The majority of Tamil affixes are suffixes. Tamil suffixes are either derivational suffixes, which modify the part of speech or meaning of the word, or inflectional suffixes, which designate categories like as person, number, mood, tense, and so on. There is no ultimate limit to the length and scope of agglutination, which might result in large words with several suffixes, requiring many words or a sentence in English (Anita and Subalalitha, 2019b,a; Subalalitha and Poovammal, 2018).

The TamilATIS corpus is collected to promote research and development in the field of task-oriented dialogue systems for the Tamil language. It contains 4874 utterances related to airline-related enquiries.

Table 2 gives an overview of various TOD datasets available for Indian languages. We observe that only two of them, TOD-Dravidian and Codemix-DSTC2 contain Tamil utterances. Our dataset is different from these two. While TOD-Dravidian is annotated using automatic methods, TamilATIS is curated by hand. Codemix-DSTC2 contains Tamil-english code-mixed utterances, unlike ours which does not focus on code-mixing and rather contains utterances in pure Tamil.

Below, we describe the data collection and data annotation processes and give detailed statistics about the TamilATIS dataset.

3.1 Data Collection

We derive the Tamil ATIS dataset by automatically translating a modified version of the ATIS dataset (Hemphill et al., 1990) to Tamil and then manually annotating the slot labels. The ATIS dataset is a standard benchmark dataset for intent classification and slot filling. It consists of audio recordings and manual transcripts of humans enquiring about

Annotator Identity	Educational Background	Native Proficiency
1	Bachelors	✓
2	Bachelors	✓
3	Masters	✓

Table 3: Annotators and their details

Annotators	κ
α_1 α_2	0.94
α_1 α_3	0.95
α_2 α_3	0.97

Table 4: Cohen's κ agreement obtained during the annotation dry run. α_1 α_2 α_3 are the three annotators

flight-related information on an automated airline travel inquiry system.

We experiment with two methods for translation: IndicTrans (Ramesh et al., 2021) and Google Translate API. We randomly sampled 50 utterances from the ATIS dataset and translated them using IndicTrans and the Google Translate API and manually inspected the translation quality. We noticed that translated utterances obtained from Google Translate were of much higher quality. Figure 2 shows some examples where IndicTrans did not give correct translations. For eg. in the first example, IndicTrans is not able to identify Vistara as an airline and combines it with Delhi, and in the second example, airline information is lost in translation. However, in both these cases, Google translate was able to provide proper translations.

3.2 Annotation Setup

For annotation, we follow earlier work on TOD (Malviya et al., 2021) where each utterance is annotated by one annotator. Since we derive utterances from ATIS, we already have a list of slot labels expected in each utterance and the annotator has to correctly map the slot label to the correct value in the utterance.

To aid with the annotation, we designed an interface that provides the annotators with an easy-to-use platform for annotation. Each annotator was assigned random batches of utterances and they worked independently in their own schedule.

3.3 Annotators

For the annotation process, we had 3 annotators. Two of the annotators are bachelor's student and one of them is a master's student. All three of the annotators have native language proficiency in Tamil. The details of the annotators are summarized in Table 3.

3.4 Annotation Process

Before the start of the annotation process, we briefed the annotators about TOD and trained them

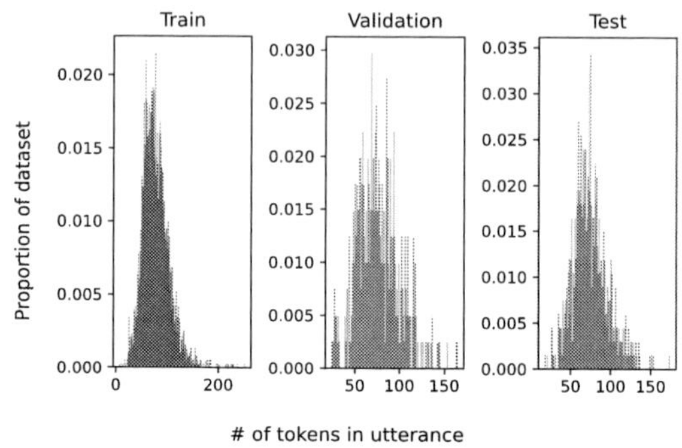

Figure 3: Distribution of number of tokens in each utterance

to identify intent and slots in an utterance from the TamilATIS dataset using examples covering all the different intent and slot labels. We conducted the annotation in two phases the dry run and a final annotation.

Dry run. We conducted a dry run on a subset of 200 utterances. We ensure that we uniformly sample the utterances from the dataset to ensure we have all the intents and slot labels in this subset. We then asked each of the three annotators to independently annotate each utterance. After this annotation, we computed the Cohen's κ for each pair of annotators. Table 4 shows the κ scores obtained. The high κ scores indicate that the annotators got a good grasp of the annotation process.

Final annotation. After the dry run, we started the final annotation process. In this stage, we also asked the annotators to reject an utterance if the translation was not correct. A total of 78 utterances were rejected in this phase.

3.5 Corpus Statistics

The corpus statistics for the TamilATIS dataset are given in Table 5. The minimum and maximum utterance lengths are 7 and 252 respectively, while the minimum and the maximum number of tokens in the utterance are 2 and 29. However, these are edge cases and the average utterance length and number of tokens are 76 and 8 respectively. We

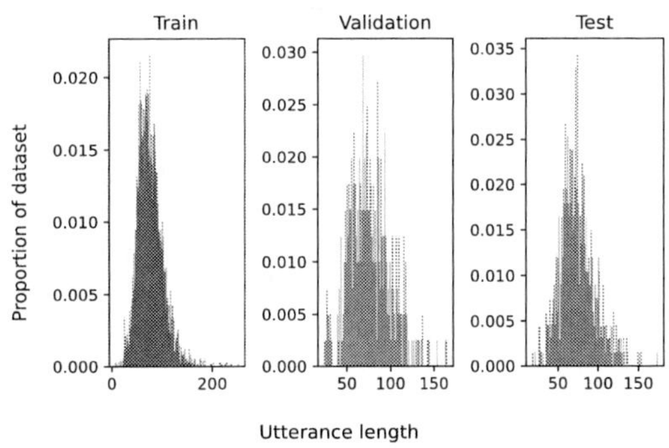

Figure 4: Distribution of utterance length

Vocabulary Size	1819
Total utterances	4874
# of intents	23
# of slot labels	45
# of unique slot values	885
Average length of utterances	76
Average # of tokens in utterance	8
Min & Max # tokens	2, 29
Min & Max utterance length	7, 252

Table 5: Statistics of the TamilATIS dataset

can observe in Figure 4 and 3 that the length and number of tokens in the utterances are consistent across the train, validation and test split.

4 Experimental Settings

We benchmark the TamilATIS dataset on eight state-of-the-art NLU models. In this section, we describe the models used and present the baseline results obtained. The problem of intent detection and slot filling can be cast as a generation task or a classification task, and in our baseline models, we include both of these types of architectures.

- **Seq2seq**:(Liu and Lane, 2016) propose an attention-based encoder-decoder model for joint intent detection and slot filling. Due to the explicit alignment requirement in the slot-filling task, the authors use an attention mechanism to incorporate alignment information into the encoder-decoder framework.

- **Slot-Gated:**(Goo et al., 2018) propose a slot-gated joint model that explicitly models the relationship between the slot and the intent attention vectors.

- **Capsule NLU:**(Zhang et al., 2019) propose hierarchical capsule nets to model the semantic hierarchy present among words, slots, and the intent of the utterance. They use context-aware word representations and dynamic routing to perform intent detection and slot-filling.

- **SF-ID:**(E et al., 2019) propose a bi-directional interrelated model for joint intent detection and slot filling. An SF-ID network is used to establish connections between the two tasks to help them promote each other mutually.

- **Stack-Propagation:**(Qin et al., 2019) propose a stack-propagation framework to incorporate the intent information during slot tagging. This allows the model to capture the intent of semantic knowledge. Moreover, to avoid error propagation in the model, token-level intent detection is performed.

- **SlotRefine:**(Wu et al., 2020) cast the task of joint intent detection and slot filling as a tag generation task and propose a non-autoregressive model for it. They use a two-pass mechanism to explicitly predict the slot boundary.

- **GL-GIN:**(Qin et al., 2021) propose a non-autoregressive model for joint intent detection and slot filling. It employs graph interaction networks to model slot dependency to model the interaction between intents and all the slots in the utterance.

- **JointBERT:**(Chen et al., 2019b) propose a joint model for intent detection and slot filling using the BERT model. The intent detection task is modelled as sequence classification while the slot filling task is modelled as token classification and the losses from the two models are jointly optimized.

5 Result and Analysis

In this section, we report the results obtained by the baseline models. We evaluate the NLU performance for slot filling using the F1(Micro) score and intent prediction using accuracy. The score obtained by each of the baselines is shown in Table 6.

Since the focus of these experiments is to just establish baselines and provide a starting point for further exploration, we restrict ourselves from in-depth error analysis.

Model	Intent (Acc)	Slot (F1)
Seq2seq ♣	83.11	56.99
Slot-Gated	93.87	91.31
Capsule NLU	89.33	88.48
SF-ID	91.92	92.47
Stack-Propagation ♣	93.27	91.84
SlotRefine ♣	94.30	92.10
GL-GIN ♣	91.33	91.94
JointBERT	96.26	94.01

Table 6: Performance of various baselines on the TamilATIS dataset. ♣ indicates that the model uses a generative approach and the rest of the models use a classification approach.

Encoder	Intent (Acc)	Slot (F1)
mBERT	95.21	93.64
indicBERT	93.57	89.28
Muril	87.44	81.74
XLM-Roberta	96.26	94.01

Table 7: Performance obtained from the JointBERT architecture by using different multilingual models as utterance encoders.

The baselines can be broadly classified into two approaches, generative approaches and classification-based approaches. The lowest scoring model is Seq2seq, which uses a simple encoder-decoder architecture to generate intent and slot details. This approach scores a decent accuracy of 83.11 for intent detection but a low F1 score of 56.99 for slot filling. Other generative approaches like Stack-Propagation, SlotRefine and GL-GIN achieve much better performances. These approaches have components in their architecture (like Stack-propagation framework, graph interaction layers etc) that help them explicitly model the relationship between the slots and intent leading to superior performance.

Classification based approaches like SF-ID, Capsule NLU and Slot-Gated achieve performance similar to the three generative architectures mentioned before. All of these approaches we discussed use sophisticated techniques to better model the interaction between intent and slot information and yield noticeable improvements over a simple architecture like Seq2Seq.

However, the best score is obtained by JointBERT. It obtains an intent accuracy of 96.26% and slot F1 score of 94.01%. This is an absolute improvement of 1.96% and 1.91% in intent accuracy and slot F1 over the second-best performing model (SlotRefine). JointBERT shows the effectiveness of transformer architectures pre-trained on large datasets when applied to downstream tasks like intent detection and slot filling.

We further investigate the JointBERT architecture by using different multilingual models as utterance encoders. Table 7 gives an overview of the score obtained by using different utterance encoders. XLM-Roberta and mBERT perform similarly, with XLM-Roberta getting slightly scores. IndicBERT and Muril, two transformer models pretrained on Indian languages however fail to produce scores as good as mBERT and XLM-Roberta. The superior performance of these two encoders could be attributed to the robust architecture and training strategy of XLM-Roberta and the large amount of data used to pretrain XLM-Roberta and mBERT.

6 Conclusion

In this paper, we presented TamilATIS, a TOD dataset in Tamil with 4874 utterances. We benchmarked the dataset with eight state-of-the-art NLU models and reported their intent accuracy and slot F1. Both generative and classification-based approaches perform similarly and achieve high intent accuracy and slot F1 score. We also highlighted the importance of modelling the relation between intent detection and slot labelling to yield performance improvement. The Joint BERT model with XLM-Roberta as utterance encoder achieved the highest score with an intent accuracy of 96.26% and slot F1 of 94.01%.

In future work, we plan to extend this dataset to other low-resource Dravidian languages like Malayalam, Kannada and Telugu. This would contribute towards the proliferation of TOD technology in the communities that speak these languages and also promote the development of multi-lingual TOD models for Dravidian languages. Having multi-domain utterances is another important research direction.

References

R Anita and CN Subalalitha. 2019a. An approach to cluster Tamil literatures using discourse connectives. In *2019 IEEE 1st International Conference on Energy, Systems and Information Processing (ICESIP)*, pages 1–4. IEEE.

R Anita and CN Subalalitha. 2019b. Building discourse parser for Thirukkural. In *Proceedings of the 16th*

International Conference on Natural Language Processing, pages 18–25.

Suman Banerjee, Nikita Moghe, Siddharth Arora, and Mitesh M. Khapra. 2018. A dataset for building code-mixed goal oriented conversation systems. In *COLING*.

Giovanni Campagna, Agata Foryciarz, Mehrad Moradshahi, and Monica Lam. 2020. Zero-shot transfer learning with synthesized data for multi-domain dialogue state tracking. pages 122–132.

Qian Chen, Zhu Zhuo, and Wen Wang. 2019a. Bert for joint intent classification and slot filling.

Qian Chen, Zhu Zhuo, and Wen Wang. 2019b. Bert for joint intent classification and slot filling.

Yun-Nung (Vivian) Chen, Dilek Z. Hakkani-Tür, Gökhan Tür, Jianfeng Gao, and Li Deng. 2016. End-to-end memory networks with knowledge carryover for multi-turn spoken language understanding. In *INTERSPEECH*.

Alice Coucke, Alaa Saade, Adrien Ball, Théodore Bluche, Alexandre Caulier, David Leroy, Clément Doumouro, Thibault Gisselbrecht, Francesco Caltagirone, Thibaut Lavril, Maël Primet, and Joseph Dureau. 2018. Snips voice platform: an embedded spoken language understanding system for private-by-design voice interfaces. *ArXiv*, abs/1805.10190.

Mai Hoang Dao, Thinh Hung Truong, and Dat Quoc Nguyen. 2021. Intent detection and slot filling for vietnamese.

Haihong E, Peiqing Niu, Zhongfu Chen, and Meina Song. 2019. A novel bi-directional interrelated model for joint intent detection and slot filling.

Chih-Wen Goo, Guang Gao, Yun-Kai Hsu, Chih-Li Huo, Tsung-Chieh Chen, Keng-Wei Hsu, and Yun-Nung Chen. 2018. Slot-gated modeling for joint slot filling and intent prediction. In *Proceedings of the 2018 Conference of the North American Chapter of the Association for Computational Linguistics: Human Language Technologies, Volume 2 (Short Papers)*, pages 753–757, New Orleans, Louisiana. Association for Computational Linguistics.

Daniel Guo, Gokhan Tur, Wen-tau Yih, and Geoffrey Zweig. 2014. Joint semantic utterance classification and slot filling with recursive neural networks. In *2014 IEEE Spoken Language Technology Workshop (SLT)*, pages 554–559.

Akshat Gupta, Xinjian Li, Sai Rallabandi, and Alan Black. 2020. Acoustics based intent recognition using discovered phonetic units for low resource languages.

E. Haihong, Peiqing Niu, Zhongfu Chen, and Meina Song. 2019. A novel bi-directional interrelated model for joint intent detection and slot filling. In *ACL*.

Dilek Hakkani-Tür, Gokhan Tur, Asli Celikyilmaz, Yun-Nung Vivian Chen, Jianfeng Gao, Li Deng, and Ye-Yi Wang. 2016. Multi-domain joint semantic frame parsing using bi-directional rnn-lstm. In *Proceedings of The 17th Annual Meeting of the International Speech Communication Association (INTERSPEECH 2016)*. ISCA.

Donghoon Ham, Jeong-Gwan Lee, Youngsoo Jang, and Kee-Eung Kim. 2020. End-to-end neural pipeline for goal-oriented dialogue systems using GPT-2. In *Proceedings of the 58th Annual Meeting of the Association for Computational Linguistics*, pages 583–592, Online. Association for Computational Linguistics.

Charles T. Hemphill, John J. Godfrey, and George R. Doddington. 1990. The atis spoken language systems pilot corpus. HLT '90, page 96–101, USA. Association for Computational Linguistics.

Ehsan Hosseini-Asl, Bryan McCann, Chien-Sheng Wu, Semih Yavuz, and Richard Socher. 2020. A simple language model for task-oriented dialogue. In *Advances in Neural Information Processing Systems*, volume 33, pages 20179–20191. Curran Associates, Inc.

Pratik Jayarao and Aman Srivastava. 2018. Intent detection for code-mix utterances in task oriented dialogue systems. *2018 International Conference on Electrical, Electronics, Communication, Computer, and Optimization Techniques (ICEECCOT)*, pages 583–587.

Tushar Kanakagiri and Karthik Radhakrishnan. 2021. Task-oriented dialog systems for Dravidian languages. In *Proceedings of the First Workshop on Speech and Language Technologies for Dravidian Languages*, pages 85–93, Kyiv. Association for Computational Linguistics.

Jonathan K. Kummerfeld, Sai R. Gouravajhala, Joseph J. Peper, Vignesh Athreya, Chulaka Gunasekara, Jatin Ganhotra, Siva Sankalp Patel, Lazaros C Polymenakos, and Walter Lasecki. 2019. A large-scale corpus for conversation disentanglement. In *Proceedings of the 57th Annual Meeting of the Association for Computational Linguistics*, pages 3846–3856, Florence, Italy. Association for Computational Linguistics.

Weixin Liang, Youzhi Tian, Chengcai Chen, and Zhou Yu. 2019. Moss: End-to-end dialog system framework with modular supervision.

Bing Liu and Ian Lane. 2016. Attention-based recurrent neural network models for joint intent detection and slot filling.

Shrikant Malviya, Rohit Mishra, Santosh Barnwal, and Uma Shanker Tiwary. 2021. Hdrs: Hindi dialogue restaurant search corpus for dialogue state tracking in task-oriented environment. *IEEE/ACM Transactions on Audio, Speech, and Language Processing*, PP:1–1.

Siddhartha Mukherjee, Anish Nediyanchath, Abhishek Singh, Vinuthkumar Prasan, Divya Verma Gogoi, and Surya Pratap Singh Parmar. 2021. Intent classification from code mixed input for virtual assistants. In *2021 IEEE 15th International Conference on Semantic Computing (ICSC)*, pages 108–111.

Anitha Narasimhan, Aarthy Anandan, Madhan Karky, and CN Subalalitha. 2018. Porul: Option generation and selection and scoring algorithms for a tamil flash card game. *International Journal of Cognitive and Language Sciences*, 12(2):225–228.

P. J. Price. 1990. Evaluation of spoken language systems: the ATIS domain. In *Speech and Natural Language: Proceedings of a Workshop Held at Hidden Valley, Pennsylvania, June 24-27,1990.*

Libo Qin, Wanxiang Che, Yangming Li, Haoyang Wen, and Ting Liu. 2019. A stack-propagation framework with token-level intent detection for spoken language understanding.

Libo Qin, Fuxuan Wei, Tianbao Xie, Xiao Xu, Wanxiang Che, and Ting Liu. 2021. Gl-gin: Fast and accurate non-autoregressive model for joint multiple intent detection and slot filling.

Gowtham Ramesh, Sumanth Doddapaneni, Aravinth Bheemaraj, Mayank Jobanputra, Raghavan AK, Ajitesh Sharma, Sujit Sahoo, Harshita Diddee, Mahalakshmi J, Divyanshu Kakwani, Navneet Kumar, Aswin Pradeep, Kumar Deepak, Vivek Raghavan, Anoop Kunchukuttan, Pratyush Kumar, and Mitesh Shantadevi Khapra. 2021. Samanantar: The largest publicly available parallel corpora collection for 11 indic languages.

Ratnasingam Sakuntharaj and Sinnathamby Mahesan. 2016. A novel hybrid approach to detect and correct spelling in Tamil text. In *2016 IEEE International Conference on Information and Automation for Sustainability (ICIAfS)*, pages 1–6.

Ratnasingam Sakuntharaj and Sinnathamby Mahesan. 2017. Use of a novel hash-table for speeding-up suggestions for misspelt Tamil words. In *2017 IEEE International Conference on Industrial and Information Systems (ICIIS)*, pages 1–5.

Ratnasingam Sakuntharaj and Sinnathamby Mahesan. 2021. Missing word detection and correction based on context of Tamil sentences using n-grams. In *2021 10th International Conference on Information and Automation for Sustainability (ICIAfS)*, pages 42–47.

Sebastian Schuster, S. Gupta, Rushin Shah, and Mike Lewis. 2019. Cross-lingual transfer learning for multilingual task oriented dialog. In *NAACL*.

R Srinivasan and CN Subalalitha. 2019. Automated named entity recognition from tamil documents. In *2019 IEEE 1st International Conference on Energy, Systems and Information Processing (ICESIP)*, pages 1–5. IEEE.

C. N. Subalalitha. 2019. Information extraction framework for Kurunthogai. *Sādhanā*, 44(7):156.

CN Subalalitha and E Poovammal. 2018. Automatic bilingual dictionary construction for Tirukural. *Applied Artificial Intelligence*, 32(6):558–567.

Ryuichi Takanobu, Hanlin Zhu, and Minlie Huang. 2019. Guided dialog policy learning: Reward estimation for multi-domain task-oriented dialog. In *Proceedings of the 2019 Conference on Empirical Methods in Natural Language Processing and the 9th International Joint Conference on Natural Language Processing (EMNLP-IJCNLP)*, pages 100–110, Hong Kong, China. Association for Computational Linguistics.

Sajeetha Thavareesan and Sinnathamby Mahesan. 2019. Sentiment analysis in Tamil texts: A study on machine learning techniques and feature representation. In *2019 14th Conference on Industrial and Information Systems (ICIIS)*, pages 320–325.

Sajeetha Thavareesan and Sinnathamby Mahesan. 2020a. Sentiment lexicon expansion using Word2vec and fastText for sentiment prediction in Tamil texts. In *2020 Moratuwa Engineering Research Conference (MERCon)*, pages 272–276.

Sajeetha Thavareesan and Sinnathamby Mahesan. 2020b. Word embedding-based part of speech tagging in Tamil texts. In *2020 IEEE 15th International Conference on Industrial and Information Systems (ICIIS)*, pages 478–482.

Sajeetha Thavareesan and Sinnathamby Mahesan. 2021. Sentiment analysis in Tamil texts using k-means and k-nearest neighbour. In *2021 10th International Conference on Information and Automation for Sustainability (ICIAfS)*, pages 48–53.

Di Wu, Liang Ding, Fan Lu, and Jian Xie. 2020. Slotrefine: A fast non-autoregressive model for joint intent detection and slot filling.

Puyang Xu and Ruhi Sarikaya. 2013. Convolutional neural network based triangular crf for joint intent detection and slot filling. IEEE - Institute of Electrical and Electronics Engineers. Best Paper Award.

Chenwei Zhang, Yaliang Li, Nan Du, Wei Fan, and Philip S. Yu. 2019. Joint slot filling and intent detection via capsule neural networks.

DE-ABUSE@TamilNLP-ACL 2022: Transliteration as Data Augmentation for Abuse Detection in Tamil

Vasanth Palanikumar[1], **Sean Benhur**[2], **Adeep Hande** [3]
Bharathi Raja Chakravarthi[4]
[1]Chennai Institute of Technology [2]PSG College of Arts and Science
[3] Indian Institute of Information Technology Tiruchirappalli
[4]National University of Ireland Galway
vasanthpcse2019@citchennai.net, seanbenhur@gmail.com
adeeph18c@iiitt.ac.in, bharathi.raja@insight-centre.org

Abstract

With the rise of social media and internet, there is a necessity to provide an inclusive space and prevent the abusive topics against any gender, race or community. This paper describes the system submitted to the ACL-2022 shared task on fine-grained abuse detection in Tamil. In our approach we transliterated code-mixed dataset as an augmentation technique to increase the size of the data. Using this method we were able to rank 3rd on the task with a 0.290 macro average F1 score and a 0.590 weighted F1 score.

1 Introduction

Internet is a global computer network that provides a variety of information and facilitates communication between users from any part of the world. The world population is 7.9 billion as of January 2022 of which around 5.2 billion are live internet users[1]. In recent times, people have become more communicative and inclusive. People want to share their views on a common platform, where social media comes into the picture (Chakravarthi, 2020; Chakravarthi and Muralidaran, 2021; Puranik et al., 2021; Ghanghor et al., 2021). People can post their opinions which are productive and efficient for their society but at times people also post their opinions which could be abusive to others. There are many social media platforms like YouTube, Facebook, Instagram, Twitter and many more (Priyadharshini et al., 2021; Kumaresan et al., 2021) where the users are given the liberty to put forward their opinion. On an average as per statistics around 250 M tweets are posted, 2 million blogs are written on various websites and 80 B mails are sent per day. Social media platforms could be both a boon and bane.

Comments that humiliates or denigrates an individual or a group based on various characteristics such as colour, ethnicity, sexual orientation, nationality, race and religion are called abusive comments(Saumya et al., 2021). Abuse caused via social media can cause many negative impacts in users' lives. This will affect the mental state of the specific individual terribly causing depression and sleeplessness (Chakravarthi et al., 2021c; Sampath et al., 2022; Chakravarthi et al., 2022). Some of these comments also can create a controversy over the social media on a specific individual or a group of people. This shows the need for restricting these kind of abusive comments from being posted in the social media. Once abusive comments have been posted onto the social media it should be flagged and immediately removed.

This world is a diverse one which comprises of different kinds of people from different origin. But when it comes to the comments of people the language plays a very important role ("Bharathi et al., 2022). Though most of the people use English as their language to show their opinion some of them also use other languages instead of English. For example in a diverse nation like India where people are not restricted to communicate in English, people comment in different languages like Tamil, Telugu, Kannada, Malayalam, Hindi, Marathi and many others.

Tamil is one of the oldest and longest surviving language in this world(Chakravarthi et al., 2020). It is an old Dravidian language mostly spoken by people of South Indian origin with a history of over 3000 years[2] that has lot of dialects. Therefore it is very tough to classify posts which have abusive comments in Tamil language.

Lately, after the advent of machine learning, researches are carried over onto this area for classifying the abusive comments.

In our work we have used Transformer (Vaswani et al., 2017) models for the given task of classifying the abusive comments. The rest of the paper is

[1]https://www.internetlivestats.com/

[2]https://www.cal.org/heritage/pdfs/Heritage-Voice-Language-Tamil.pdf

Proceedings of the Second Workshop on Speech and Language Technologies for Dravidian Languages, pages 33 - 38
May 26, 2022 ©2022 Association for Computational Linguistics

structured as follows section 2 describes the related works which are carried over in this field. The section 3 describes the methodology used in the system. The 2nd section describes the results we obtained in our research experiments.We discuss our results on Section 4. Finally in the 5th section we conclude this research paper followed by the references section.

2 Related Work

2.1 NLP on Tamil

NLP in Tamil have been recently carried out extensively through various shared tasks(Chakravarthi et al., 2021b,a) focusing on tasks such as offensive language detection, machine translation and sentiment analysis. Participants have used different methods including intelligent feature extraction (Dave et al., 2021) and ensembles of deep learning methods (Saha et al., 2021). Tamil is an agglutinative language, due to the ease of typing many users use Tamil in roman script in the social media and internet, this is known as code-switching (Jose et al., 2020), since it is also a morphologically rich language, developing NLP systems in Tamil is hard.

2.2 Abuse detection

Tasks such as abuse detection, offensive language detection and hate speech detection have been a focus of research for the past decade due to a surge in the internet and social media platform users. With the emergence of deep learning and transformers, current approaches for abusive language detection heavily relies on deep learning methods due to the rise of transformers and pretrained language models, since pretrained language models require less data.

3 Methodology

In this section, we describe the methodology based on which our system is designed, including the data preparation phase, modelling phase and model evaluation phase.

3.1 Data Preprocessing

In the shared task, two datasets (Priyadharshini et al., 2022) were provided where one comprises of Tamil sentences while the other comprising of code-mixed Tamil-English sentences. The Tamil dataset comprises of 2,240 sentences for training and 560 sentences for validation. In the code-mixed dataset there are 5,948 training sentences and 1,488 validation sentences.Table 1 shows the distribution of data among different classes before and after combining Tamil and Transliterated dataset.

We first removed punctuations present in both the dataset. The datasets comprises of some categories like Transphobic there were only very few sentences corresponding to it. To overcome this data shortage issue we performed transliteration on the code-mixed dataset and we converted the sentences in that dataset also to its corresponding Tamil sentences (Hande et al., 2021) by using ai4bharat-transliteration [3] Python package. Before combining the dataset, we removed all those sentences which fell under the category of not-Tamil and then combined the Tamil dataset with the transliterated dataset ending up with 8,186 sentences which is approximately 4 times the size of the previous dataset. By this the imbalance in the dataset was reduced and we overcame the data-shortage as well.

Figure 1 depicts the data preparation phase graphically.

3.1.1 Transliteration

Transliteration refers to the process of converting a word from one script to another wherein the semantic meaning of the sentence is not changed and the syntactical structure of the target language is strictly followed (Hande et al., 2021). By this we have increased our data size considerably. For this Transliteration we have used ai4bharat-transliteration Python package.

3.2 Modelling

In our experimentation, MURIL model outperformed all the other models which we experimented on. For evaluation we considered macro and weighted F1-score.

3.2.1 ML Models with N-gram TF-IDF Vectorization

For experimenting with ML models, we created a pipeline where first the text is vectorized by using CountVectorizer and is transformed by TfIdf-Transformer. Once the transformation of the data is completed, it is trained on the following Machine Learning models: LightGBM, Catboost, RandomForest, Support Vector Machines classifer and Multinomial Naive Naive Bayes. Of the all models

[3] https://github.com/AI4Bharat/IndianNLP-Transliteration

Classes	Tamil Dataset	Transliterated dataset	Combined dataset
Counter-speech	149	348	497
Homophobia	35	172	207
Hope-Speech	86	213	299
Misandry	446	830	1276
Misogyny	125	211	336
None-of-the-above	1296	3715	5011
Transphobic	6	157	163
Xenophobia	95	297	392

Table 1: Distribution of Dataset

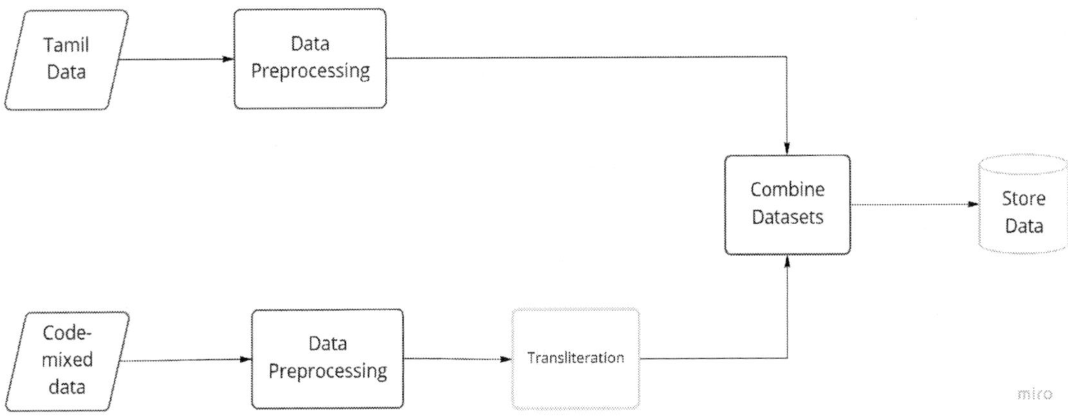

Figure 1: Data Preparation phase

experimented LightGBM (Ke et al., 2017) outperformed all the other algorithms by having 0.32 macro average f1-score and 0.65 weighted average f1-score followed by Catboost. Therfore we performed hyperparameter tuning on Optuna on LightGBM where we ended up having 0.36 macro average f1-score and 0.63 weighted average f1-score which was the highest metric of our experiments on traditional ML models.

3.2.2 MURIL

MURIL (Khanuja et al., 2021) is a pretrained bert model created by Google for tasks on Indian languages trained on 17 Indian languages. It was parallely trained on Translated Data and Transliterated Data. Based on the XTREME (Hu et al., 2020) benchmark, MURIL outperformed mBERT for all the languages in all standard downstream tasks. Hence, this model handles translated and transliterated data very well. We fine-tuned the MURIL model with the parameters listed in the Table 3. The metric we obtained from MURIL showed us that it outperformed all other ML models.

4 Results

MURIL and other Machine Learning models were trained on the training set and was validated on the dev set. For this competition, submission, macro f1-score was considered as the metric of evaluation by the organisers. By this MURIL trained on both Tamil and Transliterated dataset combined together had a very high macro f1-score of 0.49 and weighted f1-score of 0.76 on the validation dataset and a macro f1-score of 0.290 on test dataset and weighted f1-score of 0.590. With this result we secured the 3rd rank in the task. The Table 2 shows the results of all the experimentations carried on during the modelling phase.

5 Conclusion

In this paper, we conclude that with a relatively smaller-size dataset, we can use Transliteration as an efficient data augmentation technique to increase the volume of data available which played a very important role for getting a better F1-score is evident from the results Table 2 shows that Transliteration of dataset works very well. We also con-

Model	Dataset	MP	MR	MF	WP	WR	WF
MURIL	Tamil	0.37	0.34	0.33	0.67	0.70	0.68
MURIL	Combined	0.52	0.44	0.46	0.72	0.72	0.71
LightGBM	Tamil	0.30	0.42	0.33	0.76	0.65	0.69
LightGBM	Combined	0.28	0.46	0.31	0.78	0.66	0.71
CatBoost	Tamil	0.28	0.52	0.33	0.82	0.66	0.72
CatBoost	Combined	0.26	0.43	0.29	0.82	0.66	0.72
Random Forest	Tamil	0.23	0.55	0.25	0.81	0.63	0.70
Random Forest	Combined	0.23	0.39	0.24	0.85	0.65	0.73
Support Vector Machine	Tamil	0.24	0.53	0.26	0.87	0.65	0.73
Support Vector Machine	Combined	0.26	0.45	0.28	0.88	0.66	0.75
Multinomial Naive Bayes	Tamil	0.16	0.16	0.14	0.94	0.64	0.74
Multinomial Naive Bayes	Combined	0.18	0.29	0.18	0.93	0.65	0.75

Table 2: Experimental Results on various models **MF** - macro F1-score; **WF** - weighted F1-score; **MP** - macro Precision; **WP** - weighted Precision; **MR** - macro Recall; **WR** - weighted Recall

Hyperparameters	Values
Learning Rate	2e-5
Batch Size	16
Epochs	3
Weight Decay	0.001
Dropout	0.3

Table 3: Hyperparameters used across experiments

clude that Transformer models outperform traditional Machine Learning and Deep Learning models for this task.

References

B "Bharathi, Bharathi Raja Chakravarthi, Subalalitha Chinnaudayar Navaneethakrishnan, N Sripriya, Arunaggiri Pandian, and Swetha" Valli. 2022. Findings of the shared task on Speech Recognition for Vulnerable Individuals in Tamil. In *Proceedings of the Second Workshop on Language Technology for Equality, Diversity and Inclusion*. Association for Computational Linguistics.

Bharathi Raja Chakravarthi. 2020. HopeEDI: A multilingual hope speech detection dataset for equality, diversity, and inclusion. In *Proceedings of the Third Workshop on Computational Modeling of People's Opinions, Personality, and Emotion's in Social Media*, pages 41–53, Barcelona, Spain (Online). Association for Computational Linguistics.

Bharathi Raja Chakravarthi, Dhivya Chinnappa, Ruba Priyadharshini, Anand Kumar Madasamy, Sangeetha Sivanesan, Subalalitha Chinnaudayar Navaneethakrishnan, Sajeetha Thavareesan, Dhanalakshmi Vadivel, Rahul Ponnusamy, and Prasanna Kumar Kumaresan. 2021a. Developing successful shared tasks on offensive language identification for dravidian languages.

Bharathi Raja Chakravarthi and Vigneshwaran Muralidaran. 2021. Findings of the shared task on hope speech detection for equality, diversity, and inclusion. In *Proceedings of the First Workshop on Language Technology for Equality, Diversity and Inclusion*, pages 61–72, Kyiv. Association for Computational Linguistics.

Bharathi Raja Chakravarthi, Vigneshwaran Muralidaran, Ruba Priyadharshini, and John Philip McCrae. 2020. Corpus creation for sentiment analysis in code-mixed Tamil-English text. In *Proceedings of the 1st Joint Workshop on Spoken Language Technologies for Under-resourced languages (SLTU) and Collaboration and Computing for Under-Resourced Languages (CCURL)*, pages 202–210, Marseille, France. European Language Resources association.

Bharathi Raja Chakravarthi, Ruba Priyadharshini, Thenmozhi Durairaj, John Phillip McCrae, Paul Buitaleer, Prasanna Kumar Kumaresan, and Rahul Ponnusamy. 2022. Findings of the shared task on Homophobia Transphobia Detection in Social Media Comments. In *Proceedings of the Second Workshop on Language Technology for Equality, Diversity and Inclusion*. Association for Computational Linguistics.

Bharathi Raja Chakravarthi, Ruba Priyadharshini, Navya Jose, Anand Kumar M, Thomas Mandl, Prasanna Kumar Kumaresan, Rahul Ponnusamy, Hariharan R L, John P. McCrae, and Elizabeth Sherly. 2021b. Findings of the shared task on offensive language identification in Tamil, Malayalam, and

Kannada. In *Proceedings of the First Workshop on Speech and Language Technologies for Dravidian Languages*, pages 133–145, Kyiv. Association for Computational Linguistics.

Bharathi Raja Chakravarthi, Ruba Priyadharshini, Rahul Ponnusamy, Prasanna Kumar Kumaresan, Kayalvizhi Sampath, Durairaj Thenmozhi, Sathiyaraj Thangasamy, Rajendran Nallathambi, and John Phillip McCrae. 2021c. Dataset for identification of homophobia and transophobia in multilingual youtube comments. *arXiv preprint arXiv:2109.00227*.

Bhargav Dave, Shripad Bhat, and Prasenjit Majumder. 2021. IRNLP_DAIICT@DravidianLangTech-EACL2021:offensive language identification in Dravidian languages using TF-IDF char n-grams and MuRIL. In *Proceedings of the First Workshop on Speech and Language Technologies for Dravidian Languages*, pages 266–269, Kyiv. Association for Computational Linguistics.

Nikhil Ghanghor, Rahul Ponnusamy, Prasanna Kumar Kumaresan, Ruba Priyadharshini, Sajeetha Thavareesan, and Bharathi Raja Chakravarthi. 2021. IIITK@LT-EDI-EACL2021: Hope speech detection for equality, diversity, and inclusion in Tamil , Malayalam and English. In *Proceedings of the First Workshop on Language Technology for Equality, Diversity and Inclusion*, pages 197–203, Kyiv. Association for Computational Linguistics.

Adeep Hande, Karthik Puranik, Konthala Yasaswini, Ruba Priyadharshini, Sajeetha Thavareesan, Anbukkarasi Sampath, Kogilavani Shanmugavadivel, Durairaj Thenmozhi, and Bharathi Raja Chakravarthi. 2021. Offensive language identification in low-resourced code-mixed dravidian languages using pseudo-labeling. *CoRR*, abs/2108.12177.

Junjie Hu, Sebastian Ruder, Aditya Siddhant, Graham Neubig, Orhan Firat, and Melvin Johnson. 2020. XTREME: A massively multilingual multi-task benchmark for evaluating cross-lingual generalization. *CoRR*, abs/2003.11080.

Navya Jose, Bharathi Raja Chakravarthi, Shardul Suryawanshi, Elizabeth Sherly, and John P. McCrae. 2020. A survey of current datasets for code-switching research. In *2020 6th International Conference on Advanced Computing and Communication Systems (ICACCS)*, pages 136–141.

Guolin Ke, Qi Meng, Thomas Finley, Taifeng Wang, Wei Chen, Weidong Ma, Qiwei Ye, and Tie-Yan Liu. 2017. Lightgbm: A highly efficient gradient boosting decision tree. In *NIPS*.

Simran Khanuja, Diksha Bansal, Sarvesh Mehtani, Savya Khosla, Atreyee Dey, Balaji Gopalan, Dilip Kumar Margam, Pooja Aggarwal, Rajiv Teja Nagipogu, Shachi Dave, Shruti Gupta, Subhash Chandra Bose Gali, Vish Subramanian, and Partha P. Talukdar. 2021. Muril: Multilingual representations for indian languages. *CoRR*, abs/2103.10730.

Prasanna Kumar Kumaresan, Ratnasingam Sakuntharaj, Sajeetha Thavareesan, Subalalitha Navaneethakrishnan, Anand Kumar Madasamy, Bharathi Raja Chakravarthi, and John P McCrae. 2021. Findings of shared task on offensive language identification in tamil and malayalam. In *Forum for Information Retrieval Evaluation*, pages 16–18.

Ruba Priyadharshini, Bharathi Raja Chakravarthi, Subalalitha Chinnaudayar Navaneethakrishnan, Thenmozhi Durairaj, Malliga Subramanian, Kogilavani Shanmugavadivel, Siddhanth U Hegde, and Prasanna Kumar Kumaresan. 2022. Findings of the shared task on Abusive Comment Detection in Tamil. In *Proceedings of the Second Workshop on Speech and Language Technologies for Dravidian Languages*. Association for Computational Linguistics.

Ruba Priyadharshini, Bharathi Raja Chakravarthi, Sajeetha Thavareesan, Dhivya Chinnappa, Durairaj Thenmozhi, and Rahul Ponnusamy. 2021. Overview of the dravidiancodemix 2021 shared task on sentiment detection in tamil, malayalam, and kannada. In *Forum for Information Retrieval Evaluation*, pages 4–6.

Karthik Puranik, Adeep Hande, Ruba Priyadharshini, Sajeetha Thavareesan, and Bharathi Raja Chakravarthi. 2021. IIITT@LT-EDI-EACL2021-hope speech detection: There is always hope in transformers. In *Proceedings of the First Workshop on Language Technology for Equality, Diversity and Inclusion*, pages 98–106, Kyiv. Association for Computational Linguistics.

Debjoy Saha, Naman Paharia, Debajit Chakraborty, Punyajoy Saha, and Animesh Mukherjee. 2021. Hate-alert@DravidianLangTech-EACL2021: Ensembling strategies for transformer-based offensive language detection. In *Proceedings of the First Workshop on Speech and Language Technologies for Dravidian Languages*, pages 270–276, Kyiv. Association for Computational Linguistics.

Anbukkarasi Sampath, Thenmozhi Durairaj, Bharathi Raja Chakravarthi, Ruba Priyadharshini, Subalalitha Chinnaudayar Navaneethakrishnan, Kogilavani Shanmugavadivel, Sajeetha Thavareesan, Sathiyaraj Thangasamy, Parameswari Krishnamurthy, Adeep Hande, Sean Benhur, and Santhiya Ponnusamy, Kishor Kumar Pandiyan. 2022. Findings of the shared task on Emotion Analysis in Tamil. In *Proceedings of the Second Workshop on Speech and Language Technologies for Dravidian Languages*. Association for Computational Linguistics.

Sunil Saumya, Abhinav Kumar, and Jyoti Prakash Singh. 2021. Offensive language identification in Dravidian code mixed social media text. In *Proceedings of the First Workshop on Speech and Language Technologies for Dravidian Languages*, pages 36–45, Kyiv. Association for Computational Linguistics.

Ashish Vaswani, Noam Shazeer, Niki Parmar, Jakob Uszkoreit, Llion Jones, Aidan N. Gomez, Lukasz Kaiser, and Illia Polosukhin. 2017. Attention is all you need. *CoRR*, abs/1706.03762.

UMUTeam@TamilNLP-ACL2022: Emotional Analysis in Tamil

José Antonio García-Díaz and **Rafael Valencia-García***
Facultad de Informática, Universidad de Murcia, Campus de Espinardo, 30100, Spain
{joseantonio.garcia8,valencia}@um.es

Miguel Ángel Rodríguez-García
Departamento de Ciencias de la Computación, Universidad Rey Juan Carlos,
28933 Madrid, Spain
miguel.rodriguez@urjc.es

Abstract

This working notes summarises the participation of the UMUTeam on the TamilNLP (ACL 2022) shared task concerning emotion analysis in Tamil. We participated in the two multi-classification challenges proposed with a neural network that combines linguistic features with different feature sets based on contextual and non-contextual sentence embeddings. Our proposal achieved the 1st result for the second subtask, with an f1-score of 15.1% discerning among 30 different emotions. However, our results for the first subtask were not recorded in the official leader board. Accordingly, we report our results for this subtask with the validation split, reaching a macro f1-score of 32.360%.

1 Introduction

In this work, we detail the participation of the UMUTeam in the shared-task Tamil NLP (ACL 2022), concerning Emotion Analysis (EA) in Tamil (Sampath et al., 2022). Emotion detection is a recent field of research included in the broader research area of sentiment analysis. Here, the target of emotion detection aims at detecting types of feelings in natural language like anger, fear, disgust, happiness, surprise and sadness (Iqbal et al., 2022). In literature, strategies can be found addressing emotion detection in quite different domains. For instance, Shelke et al., (Shelke et al., 2022) propose an architecture based on Leaky Relu activated Deep Neural Network (LRA-DNN) to address emotion analysis on social media. The architecture is comprised of four steps: (1) preprocessing to clean the data and change it representation in a more understandable format; (2) feature extraction step to extract the most relevant characteristics; (3) ranking step where extracted features are assigned to ranks that they are optimised by using a nature-inspired meta-heuristic optimisation algorithm; and (4) classification where the LRA-DNN is employed. Yong et al., (Yong et al., 2022) describe a BCBLAC model designed to tackle emotion analysis in a food review. Its name is due to its layer architecture: Bert Layer, CNN layer, BLSTM layer, Attention layer and CRF layer. Each layer represents a step that the input must go through to carry out the emotion classification process.

In this shared task, the organisers challenged the participants to extract one emotion per document from a collection of social media comments written in Tamil. The organisers provided the participants with three sets: development, training and test. It is worth mentioning that we use these splits as expected, that is, we train with the training set and validate with the development set. This shared task was divided into two minor subtasks. The first subtask distinguishes among 11 emotions whereas the second subtask with 30 emotions. The name of the emotions, and the number of instances per training and validation are depicted in Figure 1.

Our research group has experience dealing with EA tasks. For example, we participated in the EmoEvalEs shared task, proposed in IberLef 2021 (Plaza-del Arco et al., 2021) concerning EA in Spanish. This task consisted into a multi classification task with the Ekman basic emotions. We achieved the 6th position with an accuracy of 68.5990% (4.1667% below the best result) (García-Díaz et al., 2021c). In this shared-task we participated with similar methods to the ones described in (García-Díaz et al., 2021c). However, here we conduct a more advance hyperparameter tuning stage. Besides, we use this task to validate a subset of language-independent linguistic features extracted with a custom tool that is part of the doctoral thesis of one the members of the team. In fact, we had participated in different automatic document classification tasks in Spanish to validate these linguistic features. We have observed that these linguistic features contribute to improve state-of-the-art models

*Corresponding author

Proceedings of the Second Workshop on Speech and Language Technologies for Dravidian Languages, pages 39 - 44
May 26, 2022 ©2022 Association for Computational Linguistics

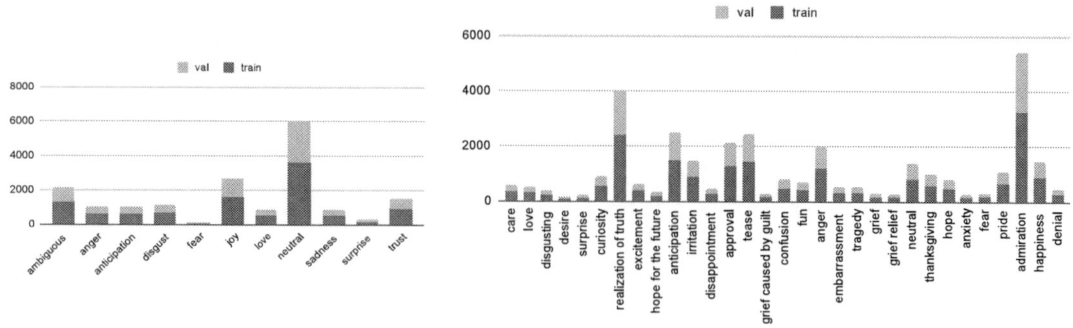

Figure 1: Label distribution for the first (left) and second (right) subtasks

based on Transformers. One of the secondary objectives of our participation is therefore to observe whether the subset of these linguistic features that are language-independent still improve the performance of automatic document classification in non-Latin languages. This subset of linguistic features are based on stylometry, which different metrics concerning word and sentence length as well as punctuation symbols. There are, in addition, features that capture emojis, hyperlinks, and social network jargon.

2 Methodology

In a nutshell, our participation consists in the development of a classifier based on neural network that uses four feature sets combined using a knowledge integration strategy. During the development stage, other methods for combining these features, such as ensemble learning, are evaluated.

Next, we describe the four feature sets in detail. The first feature set is **LF**, a subset of language-independent linguistic features extracted using the UMUTextStats tool (García-Díaz et al., 2021b; García-Díaz and Valencia-García, 2022). These features are stylometric features, PoS features based on the Tamil model of Stanza (Qi et al., 2020), and social media features that includes the detection of emojis. The second feature set is **SE**, that are non-contextual sentence embeddings from the Tamil pretrained model from fastText (Grave et al., 2018). The third and forth feature sets are **BF** and **RF**. These features are, respectively, sentence embeddings from multilingual BERT (Devlin et al., 2018) and multilingual RoBERTa (Conneau et al., 2019).

To obtain the sentence embeddings from BERT and RoBERTa, we fine-tuned them separately for each task with RayTune (Liaw et al., 2018). During this stage, 10 models with Tree of Parzen Estimators (TPE) (Bergstra et al., 2013) were trained to obtain the optimum values for the (1) weight decay, (2) batch size, (3) warm-up speed, (4) number of epochs, and (5) learning rate. TPE strategy selects the next hyperparameters using Bayesian reasoning and the expected improvement. Next, we extract the `[CLS]` token from the best models in a similar way as described in (Reimers and Gurevych, 2019).

Next, we train a neural network per feature set separately. We use these neural networks to build two classifiers based on ensemble learning. For this, we use Keras (TensorFlow) and RayTune for the hyperparameter stage. Besides, we train another neural network that combines all the feature sets at once using a knowledge integration strategy. For this, we fed each feature set in a separate hidden layer and then combine their outputs in the hidden layers.

The details of the hyperparameter optimisation stages are the following. As all feature sets are of a fixed size, we evaluate only MultiLayer Perceptrons (MLP) as the network architecture. These MLPs are divided into shallow and deep neural networks. This category is based on the number of hidden layers and the number of neurons per layer. Specifically, for the shallow neural networks we only try one or two hidden layers maximum. The number of neurons is the same in all layers. In deep neural networks, however, we try a larger number of hidden layers (between 3 and 8). Besides, the number of neurons per layer are arranged in different shapes (brick, triangle, diamond, rhombus, and short and long funnel). We also try several activation functions to connect the hidden layers as well as several learning rates and ratios of a dropout mechanism. We also handle class imbalance evaluating larger batch sizes and class weights.

The best configuration for the knowledge integration strategy for subtask 1 is a deep neural network composed of 3 hidden layers, with 128 neurons stacked in a triangle shape. The batch size is 64, the dropout of .2, the learning rate is 0.001, and the activation function that connects the layers is a sigmoid. On the other hand, the best configuration for subtask 2 is a batch size of 32, no dropout, 4 hidden layers with 57 neurons stacked with a rhombus shape (the value of 57 is the max value of neurons per hidden layer), a learning rate of 0.001, and *selu* as activation function.

3 Results and discussion

Table 1 reports the results with the validation split for subtask 1 and 2. These results include each feature set separately, the knowledge integration strategy and two ensembles, one based on the mode of the predictions and another based on averaging the probabilities.

	Subtask 1		
	precision	recall	f1-score
LF	17.84	15.35	13.70
SE	26.74	33.50	26.71
BF	29.25	29.26	28.84
RF	33.69	**35.29**	**33.74**
K.I.	**33.90**	32.85	32.36
mode	32.56	34.53	32.27
average	33.16	34.09	32.99
	Subtask 2		
	precision	recall	f1-score
LF	8.56	6.73	5.40
SE	14.39	**16.30**	13.00
BF	13.67	14.12	13.38
RF	13.54	14.64	12.92
K.I.	13.97	14.29	13.33
mode	**15.10**	15.59	12.98
average	15.01	17.13	**15.12**

Table 1: Macro precision, recall and f1-score for the first and second subtask: LF stands for the Linguistic Features, SE stands for Sentence embeddings from fastText, BF and RF stands for Sentence embeddings from BERT and RoBERTa transformers, respectively. K.I. stands for knowledge integration strategy, and mode and average for the two ensemble strategies evaluated

As it can be observed from the first subtask (see Table 1 -top-), the best result for the models trained with only one feature set is achieved with the RF (XML RoBERTa). This result outperforms SE and BF. Besides, the performance of LF is more limited than the rest of the features based on embeddings. This is expected as the linguistic features (LF) is a small subset of features. The knowledge integration strategy (K.I.) achieves a macro average f1-score of 32.36. This f1-score is lower than the result achieved with RF used in isolation, which suggests that the combination of RF with other features within the same neural network downplays RF. We also check what is the macro f1-score of using other strategies for combining the features. We test two ensemble learning strategies, one based on the mode of the predictions, and another one based on averaging the probabilities of each class. The macro f1-score achieved is 32.274 for the mode, and 32.992 for averaging the predictions. These results are also lower than the ones achieved by RF in isolation.

As it can be observed from the first subtask (see Table 1 -bottom-), no larger difference between RF and BF is observed. In fact, RF achieves a lower score than BF and SE. The knowledge integration strategy reported a macro f1-score of 13.33%, which is better than the ensemble based on the mode but limited compared with the average of the predictions.

In view of these results, and as we only have one chance to submit our proposal, we decided to send the results with the knowledge integration strategy because, in our experience, it tends to produce better results with unseen test splits.

The classification report of the knowledge integration strategy for the first subtask is depicted in Table 2. Concerning the sentiments explored individually, we observed that *joy* and *ambiguous* are the emotions with higher score, with a f1-score of 57.63% and 57.38% respectively whereas *surprise* was the label with lower score, with a f1-score of 8.16%. These scores are related to the distribution of the labels, as documents labelled as *surprise* are underrepresented. However, documents labelled as *neutral*, which is the majority class, only achieves a f1-score of 47.73%. We calculate the confusion matrix (see Figure 2) to analyse this behaviour. Neutral documents are mismatched with the rest of the emotions. For instance, a 10% of the neutral documents are labelled as *joy*, and another 10% as *disgust*. This behaviour is not observed in the rest of the emotions. For example, documents labelled as *love* are sometimes incorrectly labelled as *joy* (34%) or *trust* (13%). Moreover, the majority of wrong classifications with the emotions are related to the *neutral* class. In fact, a 42% of documents labelled as *surprise* are predicted as *neutral*.

	precision	recall	f1-score
ambiguous	58.65	56.17	57.38
anger	36.44	10.54	16.35
anticipation	27.39	29.50	28.41
disguist	22.37	34.60	27.17
fear	33.33	22.00	26.51
joy	56.69	58.59	57.63
love	18.10	24.28	20.74
neutral	49.49	46.08	47.73
sadness	34.44	43.94	38.61
surprise	6.94	9.92	8.16
trust	29.07	25.70	27.28
macro avg	33.90	32.85	32.36
weighted avg	43.05	41.74	41.81

Table 2: Classification report for the first subtask, with the validation split

Besides, in order to observe the correlation of the linguistic features with the class, we calculate the Information Gain. We observed that the most relevant linguistic features are related to positive emotions by the usage of certain emojis (0.03413). Regarding stylometric features, the most relevant ones are based on the average word length (0.03226) and concerning PoS features we found a important correlation between words that does not have defined grammatical gender.

The classification report for the second subtask is depicted in Table 3. The name of labels were translated using Google Translate. The macro f1-score is 13.329%. According to the individual emotions, the best result was achieved for *thanksgiving* (f1-score of 51.665%) and *admiration* (f1-score of 47.074%). The *neutral* documents achieved low performance (f1-score of 7.484%).

The results are also lower than the best of the feature sets in isolation: BF (macro f1-score of 13.38). In this case, the macro f1-score of combining the features using ensembles are 12.98% for the mode, and 15.12% for averaging the predictions of each model. As it can be observed, the result with the ensemble learning outperforms both the results achieved with BF and the combination of features into the same neural network. However, we decided to send the results using the same strat-

	precision	recall	f1-score
care	3.49	5.26	4.20
love	12.58	19.71	15.36
disgusting	12.73	17.83	14.85
desire	1.35	1.52	1.43
surprise	2.05	8.70	3.31
curiosity	15.89	16.99	16.42
realization of truth	26.77	22.33	24.35
excitement	7.17	8.95	7.96
hope for the future	6.18	11.59	8.06
anticipation	33.50	27.47	30.19
irritation	12.19	11.77	11.98
disappointment	4.32	10.99	6.20
approval	17.50	9.10	11.98
tease	28.05	26.26	27.13
grief caused by guilt	3.74	3.70	3.72
confusion	8.22	5.56	6.63
fun	5.57	10.00	7.15
anger	26.36	30.41	28.24
embarrassment	1.69	0.45	0.72
tragedy	23.40	5.14	8.43
grief	1.72	0.85	1.14
grief relief	0.78	0.92	0.84
neutral	13.24	5.22	7.48
thanksgiving	47.67	56.39	51.66
hope	10.08	8.13	9.00
anxiety	1.30	0.87	1.04
fear	2.44	13.64	4.13
pride	26.76	36.20	30.77
admiration	54.16	41.63	47.07
happiness	15.69	10.85	12.83
denial	6.48	14.43	8.95
macro avg	13.97	14.29	13.33
weighted avg	24.79	21.80	22.66

Table 3: Classification report for the second subtask

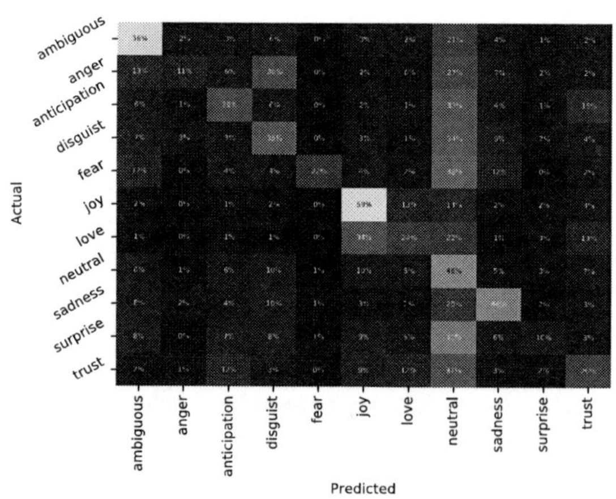

Figure 2: Confusion matrix for the first subtask

egy for both subtasks (as commented above, we could not receive any type of feedback using the CodaLab platform, which made the competition more challenging).

Next, we report the results for the official leader board. However, our participation was not considered for the first subtask. We suspect that the problem is related to a wrong format of the submission. It is worth mentioning that the results were not sending using the Codalab platform and we did not received feedback until the end of the evaluation phase.

Table 4 depicts the results for the second task, in which we achieve the first position, with a macro f1-score of 15.1% and improving the second best result (12.5%) in 0.026. Our system achieved the best precision and recall, being the most relevant the recall. This result is superior to the one achieved with the validation split. We assume, therefore, that the documents and their distribution in the validation and test sets are similar and that the performance of each label is similar.

team	precision	recall	f1-score
UMUTeam	15.0	17.1	15.1
GJG	14.2	14.4	12.5
Optimize_Prime	13.2	14.0	12.5
IIITSurat	15.6	9.9	9.0
Judith Jeyafreeda	9.4	6.8	5.7
GA	3.3	3.1	2.8
VCNVegetable	0.5	3.2	0.9

Table 4: Official results for the second task, sorted by rank. We include the macro averaged metrics of precision, recall and F1-score

4 Conclusions and further research lines

In this working notes we have described the participation of the UMUTeam in a shared task regarding emotion analysis in Tamil. We achieved the 1st position in a fine-grained emotion analysis classification in which 30 emotions can be defined. However, our results for the first multi-classification task were not reported due to an unknown error. We report our results for this task using the validation split. Our proposal to solve this problem was grounded on knowledge integration to combine linguistic features and different kind of sentence embeddings. As commented in the Introduction Section, we wanted to evaluate a subset of language-independent linguistic features in a non-Latin language. However, multilingual RoBERTa separately outperformed slightly the results of combining different feature sets with ensemble learning or knowledge integration.

As future work, we would like to extend the presented architecture by incorporating new feature extraction techniques to analyse their impact in precision. Furthermore, we will focus on interpretability techniques. Besides, regarding the application of emotions, we will evaluate the correlation of some linguistic features regarding anger and sadness with hate-speech in Spanish with the datasets published at (García-Díaz et al., 2022) and (García-Díaz et al., 2021a).

Acknowledgements

This work is part of the research project LaTe4PSP (PID2019-107652RB-I00) funded by MCIN/AEI/10.13039/501100011033. This work is also part of the research project PDC2021-121112-I00 funded by MCIN/AEI/10.13039/501100011033 and by the European Union NextGenerationEU/PRTR. In addition, José Antonio García-Díaz is supported by Banco Santander and the University of Murcia through the Doctorado Industrial programme.

References

James Bergstra, Daniel Yamins, and David Cox. 2013. Making a science of model search: Hyperparameter optimization in hundreds of dimensions for vision architectures. In *International conference on machine learning*, pages 115–123. PMLR.

Alexis Conneau, Kartikay Khandelwal, Naman Goyal, Vishrav Chaudhary, Guillaume Wenzek, Francisco Guzmán, Edouard Grave, Myle Ott, Luke Zettlemoyer, and Veselin Stoyanov. 2019. Unsupervised cross-lingual representation learning at scale. *CoRR*, abs/1911.02116.

Jacob Devlin, Ming-Wei Chang, Kenton Lee, and Kristina Toutanova. 2018. BERT: pre-training of deep bidirectional transformers for language understanding. *CoRR*, abs/1810.04805.

José Antonio García-Díaz, Mar Cánovas-García, Ricardo Colomo-Palacios, and Rafael Valencia-García. 2021a. Detecting misogyny in spanish tweets. an approach based on linguistics features and word embeddings. *Future Generation Computer Systems*, 114:506–518.

José Antonio García-Díaz, Ricardo Colomo-Palacios, and Rafael Valencia-García. 2021b. Psychographic traits identification based on political ideology: An author analysis study on spanish politicians' tweets posted in 2020. *Future Generation Computer Systems*.

José Antonio García-Díaz, Ricardo Colomo-Palacios, and Rafael Valencia-Garcia. 2021c. Umuteam at emoevales 2021: Emosjon analysis for spanish based on explainable linguistic features and transformers.

José Antonio García-Díaz, Salud María Jiménez-Zafra, Miguel Angel García-Cumbreras, and Rafael Valencia-García. 2022. Evaluating feature combination strategies for hate-speech detection in spanish using linguistic features and transformers. *Complex & Intelligent Systems*, pages 1–22.

José Antonio García-Díaz and Rafael Valencia-García. 2022. Compilation and evaluation of the spanish saticorpus 2021 for satire identification using linguistic features and transformers. *Complex & Intelligent Systems*, pages 1–14.

Edouard Grave, Piotr Bojanowski, Prakhar Gupta, Armand Joulin, and Tomas Mikolov. 2018. Learning word vectors for 157 languages. In *Proceedings of the International Conference on Language Resources and Evaluation (LREC 2018)*.

MD Iqbal, Avishek Das, Omar Sharif, Mohammed Moshiul Hoque, and Iqbal H Sarker. 2022. Bemoc: A corpus for identifying emotion in bengali texts. *SN Computer Science*, 3(2):1–17.

Richard Liaw, Eric Liang, Robert Nishihara, Philipp Moritz, Joseph E Gonzalez, and Ion Stoica. 2018. Tune: A research platform for distributed model selection and training. *arXiv preprint arXiv:1807.05118*.

Flor Miriam Plaza-del Arco, Salud M Jiménez Zafra, Arturo Montejo Ráez, M Dolores Molina González, Luis Alfonso Ureña López, and María Teresa Martín Valdivia. 2021. Overview of the emoevales task on emotion detection for spanish at iberlef 2021.

Peng Qi, Yuhao Zhang, Yuhui Zhang, Jason Bolton, and Christopher D Manning. 2020. Stanza: A python natural language processing toolkit for many human languages. *arXiv preprint arXiv:2003.07082*.

Nils Reimers and Iryna Gurevych. 2019. Sentence-bert: Sentence embeddings using siamese bert-networks. In *Proceedings of the 2019 Conference on Empirical Methods in Natural Language Processing*. Association for Computational Linguistics.

Anbukkarasi Sampath, Thenmozhi Durairaj, Bharathi Raja Chakravarthi, Ruba Priyadharshini, Subalalitha Chinnaudayar Navaneethakrishnan, Kogilavani Shanmugavadivel, Sajeetha Thavareesan, Sathiyaraj Thangasamy, Parameswari Krishnamurthy, Adeep Hande, Sean Benhur, and Santhiya Ponnusamy, Kishor Kumar Pandiyan. 2022. Findings of the shared task on Emotion Analysis in Tamil. In *Proceedings of the Second Workshop on Speech and Language Technologies for Dravidian Languages*. Association for Computational Linguistics.

Nilesh Shelke, Sushovan Chaudhury, Sudakshina Chakrabarti, Sunil L Bangare, G Yogapriya, and Pratibha Pandey. 2022. An efficient way of text-based emotion analysis from social media using lra-dnn. *Neuroscience Informatics*, page 100048.

Li Yong, Yang Xiaojun, Liu Yi, Liu Ruijun, and Jin Qingyu. 2022. A new emotion analysis fusion and complementary model based on online food reviews. *Computers & Electrical Engineering*, 98:107679.

UMUTeam@TamilNLP-ACL2022: Abusive Detection in Tamil using Linguistic Features and Transformers

José Antonio García-Díaz and **Manuel Valencia-García** and **Rafael Valencia-García***
Facultad de Informática, Universidad de Murcia, Campus de Espinardo, 30100, Spain
{joseantonio.garcia8,manuelv,valencia}@um.es

Abstract

Social media has become a dangerous place as bullies take advantage of the anonymity the Internet provides to target and intimidate vulnerable individuals and groups. In the past few years, the research community has focused on developing automatic classification tools for detecting hate-speech, its variants, and other types of abusive behaviour. However, these methods are still at an early stage in low-resource languages. With the aim of reducing this barrier, the TamilNLP shared task has proposed a multi-classification challenge for Tamil written in Tamil script and code-mixed to detect abusive comments and hope-speech. Our participation consists of a knowledge integration strategy that combines sentence embeddings from BERT, RoBERTa, FastText and a subset of language-independent linguistic features. We achieved our best result in code-mixed, reaching 3rd position with a macro-average f1-score of 35%.

1 Introduction

Some users make use of social networks to attack others. Bullies target vulnerable individuals groups with the goal of putting them down. This harassment is done on basis of traits such as sexual orientation, religious affiliation, gender, or ethnicity. This speech is known as hate-speech and its automatic detection has recently been explored because the number of daily posts on social networks make it impossible to review all of them manually. The biggest challenges of automatic hate classification are the use of figurative language and that it is not enough just to use offensive language to consider a document as hate speech. Besides, although the performance of hate-speech detectors is not bad (at least in controlled environments), they are language and cultural dependent. This makes it difficult to automatically detect hope and hate speech in low-resource languages like Tamil, where some of the state-of-the-art techniques have yet to be explored.

In these working-notes, the participation of the UMUTeam in the TamilNLP shared task (Priyadharshini et al., 2022) (ACL-2022) is described. In this shared task, the organisers want the participants to detect abusive comments in comments posted in YouTube (Chakravarthi, 2020; Chakravarthi and Muralidaran, 2021; Hande et al., 2021). This is a multi-classification task. The labels are *misandry*, *counter-speech*, *misogyny*, *xenophobia*, *hope-speech*, *homophobia*, *transphobia*, and *none-of-the-above*. The overall performance of each submission is measured using the macro average precision, recall and f1-score.

Two datasets are published. One in Tamil script and another in Tamil using Latin characters (code-mixed). The comments from YouTube are mostly composed by only one sentence. The dataset annotators rate each comment individually (that is, the annotators did not know if the comment is response to another comment or which is the context of the video). The task organisers published the datasets divided into training and development. Table 1 depicts the number of labels per dataset. It can be seen that, on the one hand, there is a strong imbalance between the labels and, on the other, that the code-mixed dataset is much larger.

Label	Tamil-script	Code-mixed
none-of-the-above	1642	4639
misandry	550	1048
counter-speech	185	443
misogyny	149	367
xenophobia	124	266
hope-speech	97	261
homophobia	43	215
transphobic	8	197

Table 1: Dataset statistics per label

*Corresponding author

Proceedings of the Second Workshop on Speech and Language Technologies for Dravidian Languages, pages 45 - 50
May 26, 2022

2 Related work

Automatic abusive comment detection has gained academic relevance. In fact, it is a trending topic in international workshops on Natural Language Processing. For instance, the MEX-A3T shared-task (IberLEF-2019), Germ-Eval 2018 (Wiegand et al., 2018), or EvalIta 2018 (Bosco et al., 2018) among others.

The common approaches for the development of automatic abusive comment detectors are based on automatic document classification. Therefore, the most common way to do it is by building an automatic classifier based on supervised learning. To do this, some approaches rely on extracting statistical features, such as Bag-of-words, TF–IDF, word or sentence embeddings, and use them to train an automatic classifier based on traditional machine-learning models or neural networks with a convolutional, recurrent or based on transformers architecture.

Modern approaches for detecting abusive comments are based on ensemble learning. For instance, the authors of (Molina-González et al., 2019), which participated in the MEX-A3T, proposed an ensemble learning model based on a soft-voting strategy. To the best of our knowledge, nevertheless, little research has evaluated knowledge integration strategies for abusive comment detection. In (Ahuja et al., 2021), the authors combined four traditional machine-learning models based Bag-of-Words features, and two deep-learning architectures (a convolutional and a recurrent neural network) based on pretrained word embeddings from FastText and GloVe. In (García-Díaz et al., 2022), the authors compared ensemble learning strategies with knowledge integration with four datasets of hate-speech datasets in Spanish. Their evaluation suggest that knowledge integration outperforms ensemble learning slightly.

There is also some work focused on specific types of hate-speech. Our research group, for example, compiled the Spanish MisoCorpus 2020 (García-Díaz et al., 2021a), concerning different types of misogynistic behaviour in Spanish.

3 Methodology

Our methodology is depicted in Figure 1. In a nutshell, it can be described as follows. For both datasets, we extract four feature sets: LF, SE, BF, and RF. The details of each feature set are described in more detail in these working notes. Next, we train a neural network model for each feature set. We use these neural networks to build a new model based on ensemble learning. This new model combines the predictions of each model. Besides, we also evaluate a knowledge integration strategy. With the knowledge integration strategy, a new neural network is trained with all the feature sets at once. For this, we connect each feature set to a input layer and combine their weights in a new hidden layer. Finally, we select the best strategy and obtain the predictions of the official test split.

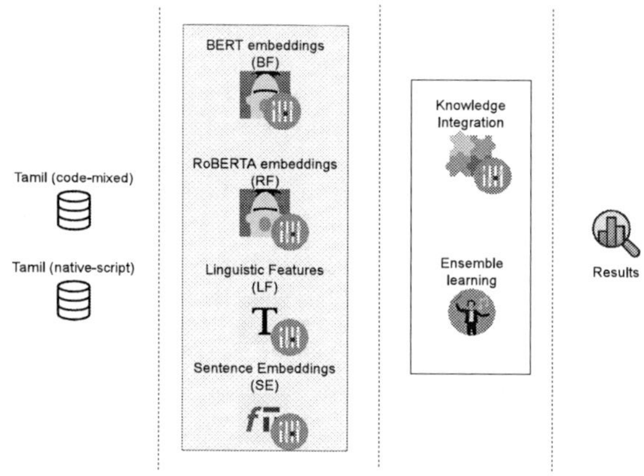

Figure 1: System architecture

Next, the feature sets are explained in detail. The first feature set (LF) is a subset of language-independent linguistic features from the UMU-TextStats tool[1] (García-Díaz et al., 2021b; García-Díaz and Valencia-García, 2022). These features include stylometric features (for instance, word and sentence average and Type-Token Ratio), emojis, and Part-of-Speech features. The second feature set (SE) are non-contextual sentence embeddings from FastText (Mikolov et al., 2018). It is worth noting that FastText has a model for Tamil (Grave et al., 2018). FastText provides a tool to extract sentence embeddings. These embeddings are made up of the average of all the words in each document. The embeddings obtained from FastText are non contextual (they ignore word order). The third and forth feature sets are sentence embeddings from BERT (BF) (Devlin et al., 2018) and RoBERTa (RF) (Liu et al., 2019). In case of Tamil, we use multilingual BERT (Devlin et al., 2018) and XLM RoBERTa (Conneau et al., 2019).

To extract the sentence embeddings from BERT and RoBERTa we conduct a hyperparameter se-

[1] https://umuteam.inf.um.es/umutextstats

lection stage that consisted in the evaluation of 10 models with Tree of Parzen Estimators (TPE) (Bergstra et al., 2013). We evaluate a weight decay between 0 and .3, 2 batch sizes (8 and 16[2]), four warm-up speeds (between 0 and 1000 with steps of 250), from 1 to 5 epochs, and a learning rate between 1e–5 and 5e–5. Once we obtained the best configuration for BERT and for RoBERTa, we extract their sentence embeddings extracting the `[CLS]` token (Reimers and Gurevych, 2019).

The next step in our pipeline is the training of the neural network models. For this, we conduct several hyperparameter optimisation stages with Tensorflow and RayTune (Liaw et al., 2018). This stage is used for each feature set (LF, SE, BF, RF) and for the knowledge integration strategy (LF + SE + BF + RF). Each hyperparameter optimisation stage evaluated 20 shallow neural networks and 5 deep neural networks. The shallow neural networks contains one or two hidden layers max with the same number of neurons per layer. For these, we evaluate `linear`, `ReLU`, `sigmoid`, and `tanh` as activation functions. The deep-learning networks can be from 3 to 8 layers. Besides, each hidden layer can have different number of neurons. These hidden layers and their neurons are arranged in shapes, namely brick, triangle, diamond, rhombus, and funnel. For the deep neural networks we evaluated `sigmoid`, `tanh`, `SELU` and `ELU` as activation functions. In these experiments, we test two learning rates: `10e-03` and `10e-04`. We also evaluate large batch sizes (128, 256, 512) due to class imbalance. Our objective is that every batch has sufficient number of instances of all classes. Besides, we also include a regularisation mechanism based on dropout, testing different ratios between .1 and .3.

Due to page length restrictions, we only report the results achieved with the knowledge integration strategy, as it is the neural network that we use for our official participation. The results achieved with the validation split are depicted in Table 2. We report a macro f1-score of 49.834% for Code-mixed and 46.167% for Tamil-script. Concerning the individual labels, the best results are obtained with the *none-of-the-above* label (the majority class). We observed that documents labelled as *transphobic* label in Tamil-script (66.667%) achieved promising results whereas its counter-part in Code-mixed achieved limited results (24.561%). This behaviour is explained due to the limited number of examples of this label in Code-mixed. In fact, the results are usually better for Tamil except with documents labelled as *xenophobia*, in which our model achieved very good precision in Code-mixed (80.357%) but limited in Tamil (48.936%).

Besides, we include the confusion matrix for Code-mixed (top) and Tamil-script (bottom) in Figure 2. With the confusion matrix, we can observe what are the wrong classifications made by each model. As expected, the *none-of-the-above-label* (that is, the neutral label) is the label that has the larger number of wrong classifications. In case of Tamil-script, we can observe that documents labelled as *hope-speech* are commonly misclassified.

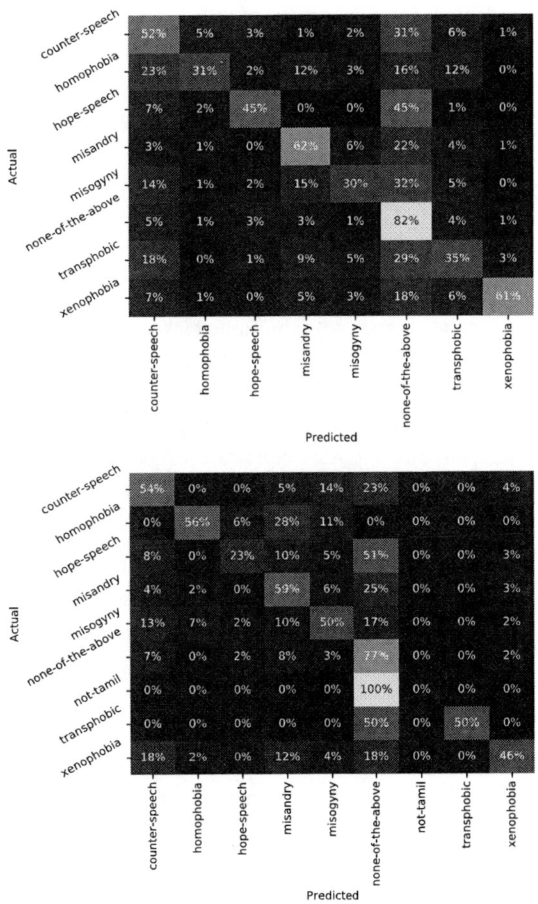

Figure 2: Confusion matrix for report for Code-mixed (top) and Tamil-script (bottom) with the validation split in the neural network that combines all feature sets

[2]In case of Tamil, our GPU does not support batch size of 16, so we only evaluate 8

	precision	recall	f1-score	precision	recall	f1-score
	Code-mixed			Tamil-script		
none-of-the-above	83.93	82.44	83.17	81.64	77.17	79.34
misandry	71.98	62.38	66.84	62.20	59.09	60.61
counter-speech	34.85	51.69	41.63	35.09	54.05	42.55
xenophobia	80.36	61.22	69.50	48.94	46.00	47.42
hope-speech	41.74	44.86	43.24	33.33	23.08	27.27
misogyny	34.78	30.48	32.49	37.50	50.00	42.86
homophobia	45.76	31.40	37.24	43.48	55.56	48.78
transphobic	18.79	35.44	24.56	100.00	50.00	66.67
macro avg	51.52	49.99	49.83	49.13	46.11	46.17
weighted avg	73.05	70.82	71.61	68.65	66.87	67.46

Table 2: Precision, recall, and f1-score for Code-mixed (left) and Tamil-script (right). These results are obtained with the knowledge integration strategy that combined LF, SE, BF, and BF

4 Results and discussion

One of the biggest challenges in this shared task is that the CodaLab leader board is disabled. Therefore, we could not review that the output file is correct.

Table 3 depicts the official leader board for Code-mixed and Table 4 for Tamil-script. Note that these results were provided by the organisers and we can not report more precision. It can be seen that we achieved the 3rd position in the official leader board for code-mixed, with the same f1-score that the second participant (with fewer accuracy and precision but a higher recall). We achieved very limited results in Tamil-script, reaching 9th position in the official ranking. As it can be observed, we obtained very limited precision and recall. In view of these results, it is possible that our neural network model has not learn to classify correctly the labels and it is always predicting the same result.

Team	Acc	m-P	m-R	m-F1
abusive-checker	65	46	38	41
GJG_TamilEnglish	60	37	34	35
UMUTeam	59	35	37	35
Optimize_Prime	45	31	38	32
MUCIC	54	40	28	29
CEN-Tamil	56	30	23	25
DLRG	60	18	15	14
BpHigh	15	14	16	10

Table 3: Official results for the code-mixed, showing the accuracy and the macro precision, recall, and F1-score

Team	Acc	m-P	m-R	m-F1
CEN-Tamil	63	38	29	32
COMBATANT	53	29	33	30
DE-ABUSE	61	33	29	29
DLRG	60	34	26	27
TROOPER	61	40	23	25
abusive-checker	45	14	14	14
Optimize_Prime	44	13	13	13
GJG_Tamil	43	13	14	13
UMUTeam	39	13	13	13
MUCIC	46	12	13	12
BpHigh_tamil	7	18	12	6

Table 4: Official results for Tamil-script, showing the accuracy and the macro precision, recall, and F1-score

5 Conclusions and promising research lines

This working notes describe the participation of the UMUTeam in the TamilNLP-ACL2022 shared task, concerning abusive detection in Tamil written in Tamil-script and code-mixed. In this work, we have combined four feature sets from linguistic features to three types of sentences embeddings. We have combined these features in a knowledge integration strategy. We reached the 3rd position in Code-mixed and 9th position in Tamil-script.

As future work, we will focus on the development of language-independent linguistic features. For example, we have adapted UMUTextStats to use different PoS models from Stanza (Qi et al., 2020), which has allowed to extend the subset of the linguistic features for Tamil. Besides, we will compile idioms and extending the dictionaries to improve the figurative language identification (del

Pilar Salas-Zárate et al., 2020), thus improving the performance of automatic document classification.

Acknowledgements

This work is part of the research project LaTe4PSP (PID2019-107652RB-I00) funded by MCIN/AEI/10.13039/501100011033. This work is also part of the research project PDC2021-121112-I00 funded by MCIN/AEI/10.13039/501100011033 and by the European Union NextGenerationEU/PRTR. In addition, José Antonio García-Díaz is supported by Banco Santander and the University of Murcia through the Doctorado Industrial programme.

References

Ravinder Ahuja, Alisha Banga, and SC Sharma. 2021. Detecting abusive comments using ensemble deep learning algorithms. In *Malware Analysis Using Artificial Intelligence and Deep Learning*, pages 515–534. Springer.

James Bergstra, Daniel Yamins, and David Cox. 2013. Making a science of model search: Hyperparameter optimization in hundreds of dimensions for vision architectures. In *International conference on machine learning*, pages 115–123. PMLR.

Cristina Bosco, Dell'Orletta Felice, Fabio Poletto, Manuela Sanguinetti, and Tesconi Maurizio. 2018. Overview of the evalita 2018 hate speech detection task. In *EVALITA 2018-Sixth Evaluation Campaign of Natural Language Processing and Speech Tools for Italian*, volume 2263, pages 1–9. CEUR.

Bharathi Raja Chakravarthi. 2020. HopeEDI: A multilingual hope speech detection dataset for equality, diversity, and inclusion. In *Proceedings of the Third Workshop on Computational Modeling of People's Opinions, Personality, and Emotion's in Social Media*, pages 41–53, Barcelona, Spain (Online). Association for Computational Linguistics.

Bharathi Raja Chakravarthi and Vigneshwaran Muralidaran. 2021. Findings of the shared task on hope speech detection for equality, diversity, and inclusion. In *Proceedings of the First Workshop on Language Technology for Equality, Diversity and Inclusion*, pages 61–72, Kyiv. Association for Computational Linguistics.

Alexis Conneau, Kartikay Khandelwal, Naman Goyal, Vishrav Chaudhary, Guillaume Wenzek, Francisco Guzmán, Edouard Grave, Myle Ott, Luke Zettlemoyer, and Veselin Stoyanov. 2019. Unsupervised cross-lingual representation learning at scale. *CoRR*, abs/1911.02116.

María del Pilar Salas-Zárate, Giner Alor-Hernández, José Luis Sánchez-Cervantes, Mario Andrés Paredes-Valverde, Jorge Luis García-Alcaraz, and Rafael Valencia-García. 2020. Review of english literature on figurative language applied to social networks. *Knowledge and Information Systems*, 62(6):2105–2137.

Jacob Devlin, Ming-Wei Chang, Kenton Lee, and Kristina Toutanova. 2018. BERT: pre-training of deep bidirectional transformers for language understanding. *CoRR*, abs/1810.04805.

José Antonio García-Díaz, Mar Cánovas-García, Ricardo Colomo-Palacios, and Rafael Valencia-García. 2021a. Detecting misogyny in spanish tweets. an approach based on linguistics features and word embeddings. *Future Generation Computer Systems*, 114:506–518.

José Antonio García-Díaz, Ricardo Colomo-Palacios, and Rafael Valencia-García. 2021b. Psychographic traits identification based on political ideology: An author analysis study on spanish politicians' tweets posted in 2020. *Future Generation Computer Systems*.

José Antonio García-Díaz, Salud María Jiménez-Zafra, Miguel Angel García-Cumbreras, and Rafael Valencia-García. 2022. Evaluating feature combination strategies for hate-speech detection in spanish using linguistic features and transformers. *Complex & Intelligent Systems*, pages 1–22.

José Antonio García-Díaz and Rafael Valencia-García. 2022. Compilation and evaluation of the spanish saticorpus 2021 for satire identification using linguistic features and transformers. *Complex & Intelligent Systems*, pages 1–14.

Edouard Grave, Piotr Bojanowski, Prakhar Gupta, Armand Joulin, and Tomas Mikolov. 2018. Learning word vectors for 157 languages. In *Proceedings of the International Conference on Language Resources and Evaluation (LREC 2018)*.

Adeep Hande, Ruba Priyadharshini, Anbukkarasi Sampath, Kingston Pal Thamburaj, Prabakaran Chandran, and Bharathi Raja Chakravarthi. 2021. Hope speech detection in under-resourced kannada language.

Richard Liaw, Eric Liang, Robert Nishihara, Philipp Moritz, Joseph E Gonzalez, and Ion Stoica. 2018. Tune: A research platform for distributed model selection and training. *arXiv preprint arXiv:1807.05118*.

Yinhan Liu, Myle Ott, Naman Goyal, Jingfei Du, Mandar Joshi, Danqi Chen, Omer Levy, Mike Lewis, Luke Zettlemoyer, and Veselin Stoyanov. 2019. Roberta: A robustly optimized BERT pretraining approach. *CoRR*, abs/1907.11692.

Tomas Mikolov, Edouard Grave, Piotr Bojanowski, Christian Puhrsch, and Armand Joulin. 2018. Advances in pre-training distributed word representations. In *Proceedings of the International Conference on Language Resources and Evaluation (LREC 2018)*.

María Dolores Molina-González, Flor Miriam Plaza del Arco, María Teresa Martín-Valdivia, and Luis Alfonso Ureña López. 2019. Ensemble learning to detect aggressiveness in mexican spanish tweets. In *IberLEF@ SEPLN*, pages 495–501.

Ruba Priyadharshini, Bharathi Raja Chakravarthi, Subalalitha Chinnaudayar Navaneethakrishnan, Thenmozhi Durairaj, Malliga Subramanian, Kogilavani Shanmugavadivel, Siddhanth U Hegde, and Prasanna Kumar Kumaresan. 2022. Findings of the shared task on Abusive Comment Detection in Tamil. In *Proceedings of the Second Workshop on Speech and Language Technologies for Dravidian Languages*. Association for Computational Linguistics.

Peng Qi, Yuhao Zhang, Yuhui Zhang, Jason Bolton, and Christopher D Manning. 2020. Stanza: A python natural language processing toolkit for many human languages. *arXiv preprint arXiv:2003.07082*.

Nils Reimers and Iryna Gurevych. 2019. Sentence-bert: Sentence embeddings using siamese bert-networks. In *Proceedings of the 2019 Conference on Empirical Methods in Natural Language Processing*. Association for Computational Linguistics.

Michael Wiegand, Melanie Siegel, and Josef Ruppenhofer. 2018. Overview of the germeval 2018 shared task on the identification of offensive language.

hate-alert@DravidianLangTech-ACL2022: Ensembling Multi-Modalities for Tamil TrollMeme Classification

Mithun Das, Somnath Banerjee, Animesh Mukherjee
Indian Institute of Technology, Kharagpur, India
mithundas@iitkgp.ac.in, som.iitkgpcse@kgpian.iitkgp.ac.in, animeshm@cse.iitkgp.ac.in

Abstract

Social media platforms often act as breeding grounds for various forms of trolling or malicious content targeting users or communities. One way of trolling users is by creating memes, which in most cases unites an image with a short piece of text embedded on top of it. The situation is more complex for multilingual(e.g., Tamil) memes due to the lack of benchmark datasets and models. We explore several models to detect Troll memes in Tamil based on the shared task, "Troll Meme Classification in DravidianLangTech2022" at ACL-2022. We observe while the text-based model MURIL performs better for Non-troll meme classification, the image-based model VGG16 performs better for Troll-meme classification. Further fusing these two modalities help us achieve stable outcomes in both classes. Our fusion model achieved a 0.561 weighted average F1 score and ranked **second** in this task.

1 Introduction

Over the past few years, social media platforms have been expanding rapidly. Users of the platform interact by sharing content to enrich their knowledge and social connections. Although most of the content on social media platforms that existed so far was textual, recently, a unique message was born: the *meme* (Chakravarthi, 2020; Chakravarthi and Muralidaran, 2021). A meme is usually created by an image and a short piece of text on top of it, entrenched as part of the image. Memes are generally meant to be harmless and conceived to look humorous, but sometimes, bad actors use memes for threatening and abusing individuals or specific target communities (Ghanghor et al., 2021a,b; Yasaswini et al., 2021). Such memes are collectively known as Offensive/Troll memes in social media.

Trolling is the exercise of publicizing a message via social media that is planned to be abusive, inciting, or threatening to distract, which often has rambling or off-topic content to provoke the audience(Bishop, 2014; Suryawanshi et al., 2020a). In addition, such memes can be treacherous as they can easily harm the reputation of individuals, famous celebs, political entities, businesses, or social groups, e.g., minorities. Although various studies have been conducted to detect offensive posts using different natural language techniques, Troll meme classification has not yet been explored.

The situation for countries like India is more complicated due to the immense lanuage diverisy[1]. The meme in the Indian context, can be composed in English, local language (native or foreign script) or in combination of both language and script (Sampath et al., 2022; Ravikiran et al., 2022; Chakravarthi et al., 2022; Bharathi et al., 2022; Priyadharshini et al., 2022). This adds another challenge for the troll meme classification. Tamil is one of the world's longest-surviving classical languages (Anita and Subalalitha, 2019b,a; Subalalitha and Poovammal, 2018). Tamil is a member of the southern branch of the Dravidian languages, a group of about 26 languages indigenous to the Indian subcontinent (Subalalitha, 2019; Srinivasan and Subalalitha, 2019; Narasimhan et al., 2018). It is also classed as a member of the Tamil language family, which contains the languages of around 35 ethnolinguistic groups, including the Irula and Yerukula languages (Sakuntharaj and Mahesan, 2021, 2017, 2016; Thavareesan and Mahesan, 2019, 2020a,b, 2021).

Recently, there has been a lot of effort to investigate the malicious side of memes, e.g., focusing on hate(Gomez et al., 2020), offensive(Suryawanshi et al., 2020a), and harmful(Pramanick et al., 2021) memes. However, the majority of the studies are centralized around the English language. Further several shared tasks like HASOC 2021(Modha et al., 2021), DravidianLangTech

[1] https://en.wikipedia.org/wiki/Languages_of_India

Proceedings of the Second Workshop on Speech and Language Technologies for Dravidian Languages, pages 51 - 57
May 26, 2022

(a) An example of a Troll meme

(b) An example of a Non-troll meme

Figure 1: Examples of troll and not-troll meme

Split	Troll	Non-troll	Total
Train	1,282	1,018	2,300
Test	395	272	667
Total	1,677	1,290	2,967

Table 1: Dataset statistics

2021(Chakravarthi et al., 2021), have been organized on multiple languages for hostile content detection in the Indian context, but it is limited to textual classification. Extending those tasks further, the organizer of this shared task has organized a classification task to identify troll memes in Tamil by providing 2,967 memes. This paper illustrates the methodologies we used to identify Tamil troll memes, which helped us achieve **second** place in the final leader-board standings of shared tasks.

2 Related Work

This section discusses some of the text-based abusive content detection methods and briefly explains the multi-modal techniques used so far to detect malicious memes.

2.1 Text-based abusive content detection

Recently, a lot of work has been carried out to identify abusive speech using text from social media posts (Das et al., 2020). In 2017, Davidson et al. (2017) made public a Twitter dataset in which thousands of tweets were labeled offensive, hate, and neither. The earlier efforts to create such classifiers used easy methods such as linguistic features, word n-grams, bag-of-words, etc (Davidson et al., 2017). With the availability of larger datasets, researchers have started utilizing complex models such as deep learning and graph embedding(Das et al., 2021b) strategies to improve the classifier performance of hate speech detection in social media posts. In 2018, Pitsilis et al. (2018) used deep learning-based models, such as the recurrent neural networks (RNNs), to detect the abusive tweets in the English language and witnessed that it was pretty effective in this task. In contrast, RNNs have been established to perform well with several language models. In addition, other neural network models, such as LSTM and CNN, have succeeded in detecting abusive speech (Goldberg, 2015; la Peña Sarracén et al., 2018). Recently, Transformer-based (Vaswani et al., 2017) language models such as BERT, (Devlin et al., 2019) are becoming quite prevalent in several downstream tasks, such as spam detection, classification(Das et al., 2021a; Banerjee et al., 2021), etc. Having observed the exceptional performance of these Transformer based models, we also utilize a Transformer based model, MURIL, which is pre-trained explicitly in Indian Languages.

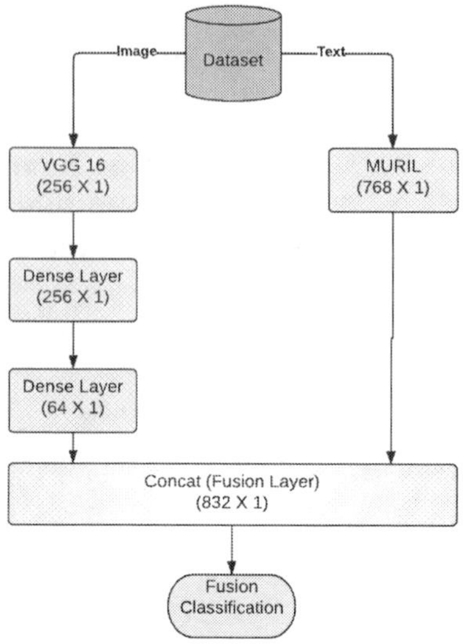

Figure 2: Our fusion model architecture with VGG16 and MURIL

Model	Accuracy	F1 Score(T)	F1 Score(w)	Precision(w)	Recall(w)
MURIL	0.556	0.637	0.552	0.549	0.556
VGG16	**0.587**	**0.736**	0.458	0.522	**0.587**
Fusion	0.566	0.649	**0.561**	**0.558**	0.567

Table 2: Performance Comparisons of Each Model. T: Troll Class. w: Weighted-Average. The best performance in each column is marked in **bold** and second best is underlined

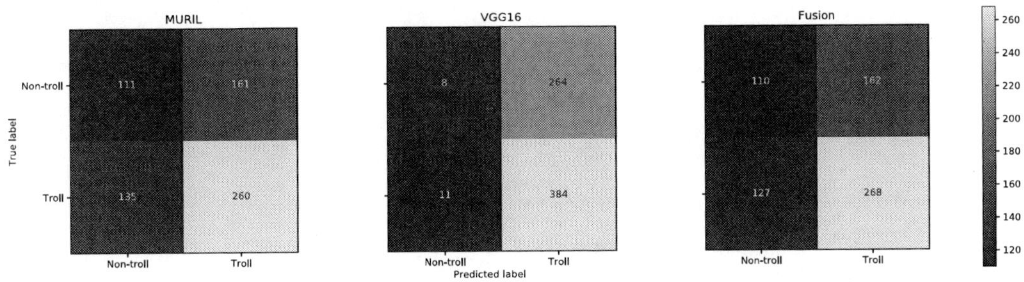

Figure 3: Confusion Matrix on Test Data for Each Model

2.2 Multi-modal abusive content detection

Lately, several datasets have been made public to the research community for abusive meme detection. Sabat et al.(2019) created a dataset of 5,020 memes for hate speech detection. The MMHS150K hate meme dataset developed by Gomez et al.(2020) is one of the enormous datasets collected from Twitter, consisting of 150K posts. Similarly, Facebook AI (Kiela et al., 2020) introduced another Hateful Meme dataset of 10K+ posts labeled hateful and non-hateful. As part of the hateful meme detection, an array of techniques with diverse architecture ranging from the text-based model, image-based model, and multi-modal models have been employed, including Glove embedding, FastText embedding, ResNet-152, VGG16, VisualBERT, UNITER, ViLBERT CC, V-BERT COCO(Pramanick et al., 2021; Chandra et al., 2021).

In this work, we use the VGG16 model, which is extensively used for several classification problems, to extract the features of all the memes and finally use it with the textual features to design our final model.

3 Dataset Description

The shared task on Troll Meme Classification in DravidianLangTech2022 (Suryawanshi et al., 2022) at ACL-2022 is based on a classification problem with the aim of moderating and minimizing the offensive/harmful content in social media. The objective of the shared task is to devise methodologies and vision-language models for troll meme detection in Tamil. We show the class distribution of the dataset(Suryawanshi et al., 2020b; Suryawanshi and Chakravarthi, 2021) in Table 1. The training set consisting of 2,300 memes (out of which 1,282 memes were labeled as troll meme) and the test set consisting of 667 memes. In addition, the latin transcribed texts were shared for all memes. We show example of both Troll and Non-troll memes in Figure 1.

4 Methodology

In this section, we discuss the different parts of the pipeline that we pursued for the detection of troll meme using the dataset.

4.1 Uni-modal Models

As part of our initial experiments, we created the following two uni-model models, one utilizing text features and the other using image-based features.
MURIL: MURIL(Khanuja et al., 2021) is a transformer encoder having 12 layers with 12 attention heads and 768 dimensions. We used the pre-trained model which has been trained on 17 Indian languages and their transliterated counterparts using the MLM (masked language model) and the next sentence prediction (NSP) loss functions. The dataset used for pre-training is obtained by using the publicly available corpora from Wikipedia and Common Crawl. We pass all the texts associated with the meme via pre-trained MURIL [2] to get the

[2] https://huggingface.co/google/

768-dimensional feature vectors for each meme and then finally fed it to a output node for the final prediction.

VGG16: VGG16 (Simonyan and Zisserman, 2014) is a Convolutional Neural Network architecture, a variant of the VGG model which consists of 16 layers and is very appealing because of its very uniform architecture. We pass all the images(meme) via VGG16 and get the 256-dimensional feature vectors, then we pass it to the two dense layer of size 256 (with dropout of 0.5), 64 and finally fed it two the output node for the final prediction.

4.2 Fusion Model

The uni-modal models we used so far do not use the relation between the text and image present in the meme. To have better understanding between the text and image, we design a new MURIL+VGG16 fusion classifier, where we first concatenate the embedding from the both MURIL and VGG16 models discussed above, then we pass the concatenated embedding to a classification node for the final prediction. The detail of the pipeline is presented in Figure 2.

All the models are trained with binary cross-entropy loss functions and Adam optimizer for 20 epochs.

5 Results

Table 2 demonstrates the performance of each model. We observe among the uni-modal models, VGG16 has the highest Accuracy(MURIL: 0.556, VGG16: 0.587) and F1 score (MURIL: 0.637, VGG16: 0.736) for troll class. Though in terms of weighted F1 score(MURIL: 0.552, VGG16: 0.458), the text-based model MURIL performs better. When we fuse these two models, the fusion model achieves the highest weighted F1 score(0.561) among all the models. To further understand the model's weakness, we show the confusion matrix of each model in Figure 3. We observe that while the MURIL performs better on the Non-troll meme datapoints, VGG16 performs better on the troll meme datapoints. Whereas on the non-troll meme data points, VGG16 shows inferior performance. The fusion model brings the positive characteristics of both MURIL and VGG16 and performs the best by understanding better connections between the text and image of the memes.

muril-base-cased

6 Conclusion

In this shared task, we deal with a novel problem of detecting Tamil troll memes. We evaluated different uni-modal models and introduced a fusion model. We found that text-based model MURIL performs better on the Non-troll class, whereas VGG16 performs better on the Troll class. Ensembling these two models help us in gaining stable outcomes in both classes. We plan to explore further other vision-based models to improve classification performance as an immediate next step.

References

R Anita and CN Subalalitha. 2019a. An approach to cluster Tamil literatures using discourse connectives. In *2019 IEEE 1st International Conference on Energy, Systems and Information Processing (ICESIP)*, pages 1–4. IEEE.

R Anita and CN Subalalitha. 2019b. Building discourse parser for Thirukkural. In *Proceedings of the 16th International Conference on Natural Language Processing*, pages 18–25.

Somnath Banerjee, Maulindu Sarkar, Nancy Agrawal, Punyajoy Saha, and Mithun Das. 2021. Exploring transformer based models to identify hate speech and offensive content in english and indo-aryan languages. *arXiv preprint arXiv:2111.13974*.

B Bharathi, Bharathi Raja Chakravarthi, Subalalitha Chinnaudayar Navaneethakrishnan, N Sripriya, Arunaggiri Pandian, and Swetha Valli. 2022. Findings of the shared task on Speech Recognition for Vulnerable Individuals in Tamil. In *Proceedings of the Second Workshop on Language Technology for Equality, Diversity and Inclusion*. Association for Computational Linguistics.

Jonathan Bishop. 2014. Dealing with internet trolling in political online communities: Towards the this is why we can't have nice things scale. *International Journal of E-Politics (IJEP)*, 5(4):1–20.

Bharathi Raja Chakravarthi. 2020. HopeEDI: A multilingual hope speech detection dataset for equality, diversity, and inclusion. In *Proceedings of the Third Workshop on Computational Modeling of People's Opinions, Personality, and Emotion's in Social Media*, pages 41–53, Barcelona, Spain (Online). Association for Computational Linguistics.

Bharathi Raja Chakravarthi and Vigneshwaran Muralidaran. 2021. Findings of the shared task on hope speech detection for equality, diversity, and inclusion. In *Proceedings of the First Workshop on Language Technology for Equality, Diversity and Inclusion*, pages 61–72, Kyiv. Association for Computational Linguistics.

Bharathi Raja Chakravarthi, Ruba Priyadharshini, Thenmozhi Durairaj, John Phillip McCrae, Paul Buitaleer, Prasanna Kumar Kumaresan, and Rahul Ponnusamy. 2022. Findings of the shared task on Homophobia Transphobia Detection in Social Media Comments. In *Proceedings of the Second Workshop on Language Technology for Equality, Diversity and Inclusion*. Association for Computational Linguistics.

Bharathi Raja Chakravarthi, Ruba Priyadharshini, Navya Jose, Thomas Mandl, Prasanna Kumar Kumaresan, Rahul Ponnusamy, RL Hariharan, John Philip McCrae, Elizabeth Sherly, et al. 2021. Findings of the shared task on offensive language identification in tamil, malayalam, and kannada. In *Proceedings of the first workshop on speech and language technologies for Dravidian languages*, pages 133–145.

Mohit Chandra, Dheeraj Pailla, Himanshu Bhatia, Aadilmehdi Sanchawala, Manish Gupta, Manish Shrivastava, and Ponnurangam Kumaraguru. 2021. "subverting the jewtocracy": Online antisemitism detection using multimodal deep learning. In *13th ACM Web Science Conference 2021*, pages 148–157.

Mithun Das, Somnath Banerjee, and Punyajoy Saha. 2021a. Abusive and threatening language detection in urdu using boosting based and bert based models: A comparative approach. *arXiv preprint arXiv:2111.14830*.

Mithun Das, Binny Mathew, Punyajoy Saha, Pawan Goyal, and Animesh Mukherjee. 2020. Hate speech in online social media. *ACM SIGWEB Newsletter*, (Autumn):1–8.

Mithun Das, Punyajoy Saha, Ritam Dutt, Pawan Goyal, Animesh Mukherjee, and Binny Mathew. 2021b. You too brutus! trapping hateful users in social media: Challenges, solutions & insights. In *Proceedings of the 32nd ACM Conference on Hypertext and Social Media*, pages 79–89.

Thomas Davidson, Dana Warmsley, M. Macy, and Ingmar Weber. 2017. Automated hate speech detection and the problem of offensive language. In *ICWSM*.

J. Devlin, Ming-Wei Chang, Kenton Lee, and Kristina Toutanova. 2019. Bert: Pre-training of deep bidirectional transformers for language understanding. In *NAACL*.

Nikhil Ghanghor, Parameswari Krishnamurthy, Sajeetha Thavareesan, Ruba Priyadharshini, and Bharathi Raja Chakravarthi. 2021a. IIITK@DravidianLangTech-EACL2021: Offensive language identification and meme classification in Tamil, Malayalam and Kannada. In *Proceedings of the First Workshop on Speech and Language Technologies for Dravidian Languages*, pages 222–229, Kyiv. Association for Computational Linguistics.

Nikhil Ghanghor, Rahul Ponnusamy, Prasanna Kumar Kumaresan, Ruba Priyadharshini, Sajeetha Thavareesan, and Bharathi Raja Chakravarthi. 2021b. IIITK@LT-EDI-EACL2021: Hope speech detection for equality, diversity, and inclusion in Tamil , Malayalam and English. In *Proceedings of the First Workshop on Language Technology for Equality, Diversity and Inclusion*, pages 197–203, Kyiv. Association for Computational Linguistics.

Yoav Goldberg. 2015. A primer on neural network models for natural language processing. *Journal of Artificial Intelligence Research*, 57.

Raul Gomez, Jaume Gibert, Lluis Gomez, and Dimosthenis Karatzas. 2020. Exploring hate speech detection in multimodal publications. In *Proceedings of the IEEE/CVF winter conference on applications of computer vision*, pages 1470–1478.

Simran Khanuja, Diksha Bansal, Sarvesh Mehtani, Savya Khosla, Atreyee Dey, Balaji Gopalan, Dilip Kumar Margam, Pooja Aggarwal, Rajiv Teja Nagipogu, Shachi Dave, et al. 2021. Muril: Multilingual representations for indian languages. *arXiv preprint arXiv:2103.10730*.

Douwe Kiela, Hamed Firooz, Aravind Mohan, Vedanuj Goswami, Amanpreet Singh, Pratik Ringshia, and Davide Testuggine. 2020. The hateful memes challenge: Detecting hate speech in multimodal memes. *Advances in Neural Information Processing Systems*, 33:2611–2624.

Gretel Liz De la Peña Sarracén, Reynaldo Gil Pons, C. E. Muñiz-Cuza, and P. Rosso. 2018. Hate speech detection using attention-based lstm. In *EVALITA@CLiC-it*.

Sandip Modha, Thomas Mandl, Gautam Kishore Shahi, Hiren Madhu, Shrey Satapara, Tharindu Ranasinghe, and Marcos Zampieri. 2021. Overview of the hasoc subtrack at fire 2021: Hate speech and offensive content identification in english and indo-aryan languages and conversational hate speech. In *Forum for Information Retrieval Evaluation*, pages 1–3.

Anitha Narasimhan, Aarthy Anandan, Madhan Karky, and CN Subalalitha. 2018. Porul: Option generation and selection and scoring algorithms for a tamil flash card game. *International Journal of Cognitive and Language Sciences*, 12(2):225–228.

Georgios K. Pitsilis, H. Ramampiaro, and H. Langseth. 2018. Detecting offensive language in tweets using deep learning. *ArXiv*, abs/1801.04433.

Shraman Pramanick, Shivam Sharma, Dimitar Dimitrov, Md Shad Akhtar, Preslav Nakov, and Tanmoy Chakraborty. 2021. Momenta: A multimodal framework for detecting harmful memes and their targets. In *Findings of the Association for Computational Linguistics: EMNLP 2021*, pages 4439–4455.

Ruba Priyadharshini, Bharathi Raja Chakravarthi, Subalalitha Chinnaudayar Navaneethakrishnan, Thenmozhi Durairaj, Malliga Subramanian, Kogilavani Shanmugavadivel, Siddhanth U Hegde, and Prasanna Kumar Kumaresan. 2022. Findings of the shared task on Abusive Comment Detection in Tamil. In *Proceedings of the Second Workshop on Speech and Language Technologies for Dravidian Languages*. Association for Computational Linguistics.

Manikandan Ravikiran, Bharathi Raja Chakravarthi, Anand Kumar Madasamy, Sangeetha Sivanesan, Ratnavel Rajalakshmi, Sajeetha Thavareesan, Rahul Ponnusamy, and Shankar Mahadevan. 2022. Findings of the shared task on Offensive Span Identification in code-mixed Tamil-English comments. In *Proceedings of the Second Workshop on Speech and Language Technologies for Dravidian Languages*. Association for Computational Linguistics.

Benet Oriol Sabat, Cristian Canton Ferrer, and Xavier Giro-i Nieto. 2019. Hate speech in pixels: Detection of offensive memes towards automatic moderation. *arXiv preprint arXiv:1910.02334*.

Ratnasingam Sakuntharaj and Sinnathamby Mahesan. 2016. A novel hybrid approach to detect and correct spelling in Tamil text. In *2016 IEEE International Conference on Information and Automation for Sustainability (ICIAfS)*, pages 1–6.

Ratnasingam Sakuntharaj and Sinnathamby Mahesan. 2017. Use of a novel hash-table for speeding-up suggestions for misspelt Tamil words. In *2017 IEEE International Conference on Industrial and Information Systems (ICIIS)*, pages 1–5.

Ratnasingam Sakuntharaj and Sinnathamby Mahesan. 2021. Missing word detection and correction based on context of Tamil sentences using n-grams. In *2021 10th International Conference on Information and Automation for Sustainability (ICIAfS)*, pages 42–47.

Anbukkarasi Sampath, Thenmozhi Durairaj, Bharathi Raja Chakravarthi, Ruba Priyadharshini, Subalalitha Chinnaudayar Navaneethakrishnan, Kogilavani Shanmugavadivel, Sajeetha Thavareesan, Sathiyaraj Thangasamy, Parameswari Krishnamurthy, Adeep Hande, Sean Benhur, Kishor Kumar Ponnusamy, and Santhiya Pandiyan. 2022. Findings of the shared task on Emotion Analysis in Tamil. In *Proceedings of the Second Workshop on Speech and Language Technologies for Dravidian Languages*. Association for Computational Linguistics.

Karen Simonyan and Andrew Zisserman. 2014. Very deep convolutional networks for large-scale image recognition. *arXiv preprint arXiv:1409.1556*.

R Srinivasan and CN Subalalitha. 2019. Automated named entity recognition from tamil documents. In *2019 IEEE 1st International Conference on Energy, Systems and Information Processing (ICESIP)*, pages 1–5. IEEE.

C. N. Subalalitha. 2019. Information extraction framework for Kurunthogai. *Sādhanā*, 44(7):156.

CN Subalalitha and E Poovammal. 2018. Automatic bilingual dictionary construction for Tirukural. *Applied Artificial Intelligence*, 32(6):558–567.

Shardul Suryawanshi and Bharathi Raja Chakravarthi. 2021. Findings of the shared task on Troll Meme Classification in Tamil. In *Proceedings of the First Workshop on Speech and Language Technologies for Dravidian Languages*. Association for Computational Linguistics.

Shardul Suryawanshi, Bharathi Raja Chakravarthi, Mihael Arcan, and Paul Buitelaar. 2020a. Multimodal meme dataset (multioff) for identifying offensive content in image and text. In *Proceedings of the second workshop on trolling, aggression and cyberbullying*, pages 32–41.

Shardul Suryawanshi, Bharathi Raja Chakravarthi, Mihael Arcan, Susan Levy, Paul Buitaleer, Prasanna Kumar Kumaresan, Rahul Ponnusamy, and Adeep Hande. 2022. Findings of the second shared task on Troll Meme Classification in Tamil. In *Proceedings of the Second Workshop on Speech and Language Technologies for Dravidian Languages*. Association for Computational Linguistics.

Shardul Suryawanshi, Bharathi Raja Chakravarthi, Pranav Verma, Mihael Arcan, John Philip McCrae, and Paul Buitelaar. 2020b. A dataset for troll classification of TamilMemes. In *Proceedings of the WILDRE5– 5th Workshop on Indian Language Data: Resources and Evaluation*, pages 7–13, Marseille, France. European Language Resources Association (ELRA).

Sajeetha Thavareesan and Sinnathamby Mahesan. 2019. Sentiment analysis in Tamil texts: A study on machine learning techniques and feature representation. In *2019 14th Conference on Industrial and Information Systems (ICIIS)*, pages 320–325.

Sajeetha Thavareesan and Sinnathamby Mahesan. 2020a. Sentiment lexicon expansion using Word2vec and fastText for sentiment prediction in Tamil texts. In *2020 Moratuwa Engineering Research Conference (MERCon)*, pages 272–276.

Sajeetha Thavareesan and Sinnathamby Mahesan. 2020b. Word embedding-based part of speech tagging in Tamil texts. In *2020 IEEE 15th International Conference on Industrial and Information Systems (ICIIS)*, pages 478–482.

Sajeetha Thavareesan and Sinnathamby Mahesan. 2021. Sentiment analysis in Tamil texts using k-means and k-nearest neighbour. In *2021 10th International Conference on Information and Automation for Sustainability (ICIAfS)*, pages 48–53.

Ashish Vaswani, Noam M. Shazeer, Niki Parmar, Jakob Uszkoreit, Llion Jones, Aidan N. Gomez, Lukasz Kaiser, and Illia Polosukhin. 2017. Attention is all you need. *ArXiv*, abs/1706.03762.

Konthala Yasaswini, Karthik Puranik, Adeep Hande, Ruba Priyadharshini, Sajeetha Thavareesan, and Bharathi Raja Chakravarthi. 2021. IIITT@DravidianLangTech-EACL2021: Transfer learning for offensive language detection in Dravidian languages. In *Proceedings of the First Workshop on Speech and Language Technologies for Dravidian Languages*, pages 187–194, Kyiv. Association for Computational Linguistics.

JudithJeyafreedaAndrew@TamilNLP-ACL2022:CNN for Emotion Analysis in Tamil

Judith Jeyafreeda Andrew
The University of Manchester, Oxford road, Manchester, United Kingdom
judithjeyafreeda@gmail.com

Abstract

Using technology for analysis of human emotion is a relatively nascent research area. There are several types of data where emotion recognition can be employed, such as - text, images, audio and video. In this paper, the focus is on emotion recognition in text data. Emotion recognition in text can be performed from both written comments and from conversations. In this paper, the dataset used for emotion recognition is a list of comments. While extensive research is being performed in this area, the language of the text plays a very important role. In this work, the focus is on the Dravidian language of Tamil. The language and its script demands an extensive pre-processing. The paper contributes to this by adapting various pre-processing methods to the Dravidian Language of Tamil. A CNN method has been adopted for the task at hand. The proposed method has achieved a comparable result.

1 Introduction

Emotion Analysis is a task of classification of emotions in text. There are several application for this task such as reviews analysis in e-commerce, public opinion analysis, extensive search, personalized recommendation, healthcare, and online teaching (Sampath et al., 2022a; Ravikiran et al., 2022; Chakravarthi et al., 2022; Bharathi et al., 2022; Priyadharshini et al., 2022). A lot of research has been done on classifying comments, opinions, movie/product reviews, ratings, recommendations and other forms of online expression into positive or negative sentiments (Priyadharshini et al., 2021; Kumaresan et al., 2021; Chakravarthi, 2020; Chakravarthi and Muralidaran, 2021; Chakravarthi et al., 2020b).

Though there have been several research works around emotion recognition in English language, there are not many in Dravidian languages (Chakravarthi et al., 2021a,b, 2020a; Priyadharshini et al., 2020). The four major Dravidian languages are Tamil, Telugu, Malayalam and Kannada. This paper explores the idea of using deep neural networks specifically CNN for the purpose of Emotion Recognition in text from the Dravidian Language of Tamil (Ghanghor et al., 2021a,b; Yasaswini et al., 2021).

Tamil is one of the world's longest-surviving classical languages (Anita and Subalalitha, 2019b,a; Subalalitha and Poovammal, 2018; Subalalitha, 2019). According to A. K. Ramanujan, it is "the only language of modern India that is recognizably continuous with a classical history." Because of the range and quality of ancient Tamil literature, it has been referred to as "one of the world's major classical traditions and literatures." For about 2600 years, there has been a recorded Tamil literature (Sakuntharaj and Mahesan, 2021, 2017,?, 2016). The earliest period of Tamil literature, known as Sangam literature, is said to have lasted from from 600 BC to AD 300. Among Dravidian languages, it possesses the oldest existing literature. The earliest epigraphic documents discovered on rock edicts and "hero stones" date from the 6th century BC (Thavareesan and Mahesan, 2019, 2020a,b, 2021).

The task in (Sampath et al., 2022b) is categorized in two subtasks, both of which dealing with a corpus in the Dravidian language of Tamil. The first one aims at classifying social media comments in 8-10 classes where the classes are in English. The second subtask involves classifying text into one of the 30 classes, where the classes are also in tamil. The classification systems performance has been measured in terms of macro averaged Precision, macro averaged Recall and macro averaged F-Score across all the classes.

2 Related Work

With the increase in social media content in the recent past, a lot of focus has been given to Emotion Analysis. Several Machine Learning and Deep

Proceedings of the Second Workshop on Speech and Language Technologies for Dravidian Languages, pages 58 - 63
May 26, 2022

Learning approaches have been developed for this cause. (Wiebe et al., 2005) proposed a manual corpus annotation for emotions and sentiments in news articles. (Strapparava and Mihalcea, 2008) describes an experiment for automatic identification of six different emotions in text including Anger, Disgust, Fear, Joy, Sadness and Surprise. The authors propose both knowledge based and corpus based methods for this purpose. (Liu, 2017) uses emotion detection to predict the future stock returns by applying a emotion classifier to tweets from the 2016 presidential election and financial tweets. (Gaind et al., 2019) uses a supervised model.The model developed is a hybrid one consisting of two completely different approaches. The first approach uses Emotion-Words Set and several textual features to classify and score text according to the emotions. The second approach uses standard classifiers like SMO and J48 to classify tweets. Finally, these approaches are combined to detect emotions in text more effectively. (Stojanovski et al., 2015) uses convolutional neural network architecture for emotion identification in Twitter messages. The model has been applied on Twitter messages for emotion identification related to public local services. This is an unsupervised method. (Savigny and Purwarianti, 2017) compared many methods for using word embedding in a classification task, namely average word vector, average word vector with TF-IDF, paragraph vector, and by using Convolutional Neural Network (CNN) algorithm. The authors showed that the accuracy of the classification increases while word embeddings are used in combination with CNN. (Zhang et al., 2018) addresses the problem where a sentence can evoke more than one emotion. For this purpose, the authors introduce an emotion distribution learning and propose a multi-task convolutional neural network for text emotion analysis.

(Andrew, 2020) proposes several machine learning techniques to classify sentiments from YouTube comments in the Dravidian languages of Tamil and Malayalam. The corpus in (Andrew, 2020) is YouTube comments in code mixed Dravidian languages of Tamil and Malayalam. It is noted that a Naïve Bayes method performs the best for sentiment analysis if YouTube comments on code mixed Dravidian language of Tamil. (Andrew, 2021) performs offensive language detection on YouTube comments in Dravidian languages of Tamil, Malayalam and Kannada. The authors perform a preprocessing step that allows the substitution of Dravidian language script to Latin script, replacement of emojis with words and the standard method of removing stop words. This is then followed by the use of several machine language techniques.

3 Data

The datset for the two subtasks are from (Sampath et al., 2022b).

3.1 Subtask A

The goal of subtask A is to classify emotions in Tamil text into 8-10 classes. The classes are in English. The classes are: Ambiguous, Anger, Anticipation, Disgust, Joy, Love, Neutral, Sadness and Trust. The train set consists of 14208 sentences, the development sets consists of 3552 sentences and the test set consists of 4440 sentences.

3.2 Subtask B

The goal of subtask B is to classify emotions in Tamil text into 30 classes. However, unlike subtask A, the classes are in Tamil as well. The train set consists of 30179 sentences, the development sets consists of 4269 sentences and the test set consists of 4268 sentences.

4 Pre-Processing

The Tamil text needs some pre-processing before training a deep learning algorithm. The preprocessing techniques are similar to ones in (Andrew, 2021).

- The words in the script of the Dravidian language of Tamil are replaced by latin text. For subtask B, both the text and the classes are replaced by latin text (IPA). This is performed using the anyascii package in Python.

- The emojis found in the text are replaced by the words that the emoji represents like happy, sad etc.

- Remove stop words and punctuations. For this purpose, python packages for language specific stop words. The advertools and stopwordsiso are used for language specific stopwords.

5 Deep Learning Methods for emotion classification

5.1 Pre-Processing

In this paper, a first preprocessing is done in order to change the script of Tamil to IPA, as described in the previous section. However, in order to be able to trained for a deep learning model, pre-processing methods like tokenization and stemming is performed on the transformed text. For this purpose, the inbuilt 'keras' python package is used.

5.2 Embedding

There have been several word embeddings proposed for the Dravidian language of Tamil. (Thavareesan and Mahesan, 2020c) proposes a word embedding-based Part of Speech (POS) tagger for Tamil, with experiments conducted on BoW, TF-IDF, Word2vec, fastText and GloVe. (Kumar et al., 2020) presents word-embedding for 14 different Indian languages including Tamil. A total of 422 embeddings have been released. In this paper, the embeddings from (Kumar et al., 2020) is used.

5.3 Deep Learning Models

In this paper, a Convolutional Neural Network (CNN) is used for emotion classification. The 'Keras' python CNN package is used for this purpose.

5.3.1 CNN

The central idea behind a CNN is the convolving or sliding pre-determined window of data. The data is first represented using word vectors. A weight matrix, called a filter consisting of an activation function, is then slid horizontally across the sentences by one step. Backpropagation will ensure that the weights of these filters are learned from the data. The next step is to calculate the convoluted feature. This layer is calculated by summing over the element-wise multiplication as each filter slides over the window of data one stride at a time and is multiplied by its corresponding weight in the filter. In cases where the filter doesnt exactly fit the matrix with a given number of slides, a **padding** is necessary. This can be done in two ways: (i) Pad the outer edges with zero vectors (zero-padding) (ii) ignore the part of the matrix that does not fit the filter (valid padding). In order to help the algorithm learn higher-order representations of the data while reducing the number of parameters, **pooling** can be performed. There are three types of pooling - Sum pooling, Max pooling and average pooling.

Finally, the fully connected layer receives the input from the previous pooling and convolutional layers. It then performs a classification task (cnn). This process is shown in Figure 1

Task	Precision	Recall	F1-score
A	0.150	0.122	0.094
B	0.094	0.068	0.057

Table 1: Results.

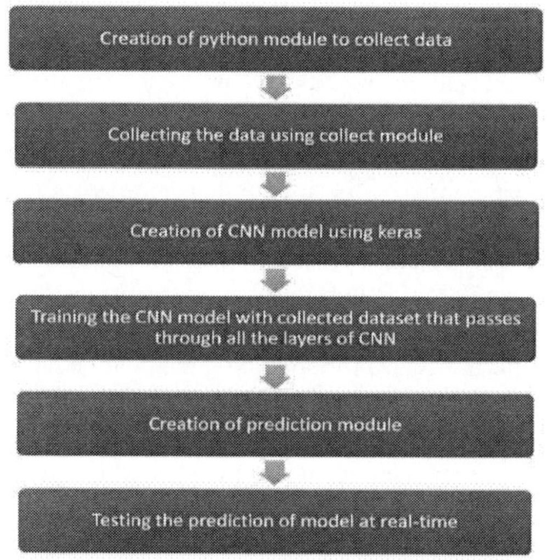

Figure 1: General Process Flow for a Convolution Neural Network (Pathak and Khan, 2021)

6 Results

The performance of the classification system has been evaluated in terms of macro averaged Precision, macro averaged Recall and macro averaged F-Score across all the classes. The evaluation has been performed with the sklearn package on python (Pedregosa et al., 2011).

The results for both tasks A and B are shown in Table 1.

A precision of 0.150, a recall of 0.122 and a F1-score of 0.094 is achieved for Task A. The highest scores of metrics achieved for Task A are precision is 0.220, recall is 0.250 and F1 score is 0.210.

A precision of 0.094, a recall of 0.068 and a F1-score of 0.054 is achieved for Task B. The highest scores of metrics achieved for Task B are precision is 0.15, recall is 0.171 and F1 score is 0.151.

In general this is quite low. It has to be kept in mind that task 2 had both the text and labels in the Dravidian language of Tamil.

It can be noted that when the language of the labels/category is in English, the results are better than when both the labels/category is in Tamil. (Andrew, 2021) shows that pre-processing Dravidian texts help improve the results when used with Machine Learning models, however, this does not seem to be the case with deep learning techniques. This is because deep learning techniques requires huge amount of training data. For a language like Tamil, such models are not easily available due to the lack if data. Using language models such as BERT trained for the Dravidian language of Tamil over a large corpus could help in more accurate classification of emotions.

There is clearly a huge amount of efforts that needs to go in encoding and decoding of Dravidian language scripts. Translating Dravidian Language scripts to Latin alphabets might not be the best approach for emotion classification. This is a critical point of pre-processing that needs to be considered in future works. Any new model built should be able to process the text with the script of the Dravidian language itself.

References

Nlp with cnns. `https://towardsdatascience.com/nlp-with-cnns-a6aa743bdc1e`.

Judith Jeyafreeda Andrew. 2020. Judithjeyafreeda@dravidian-codemix-fire2020: Sentiment analysis of youtube comments for dravidian languages. In *FIRE (Working Notes)*, pages 522–527.

Judith Jeyafreeda Andrew. 2021. Judithjeyafreedaandrew@ dravidianlangtech-eacl2021: offensive language detection for dravidian code-mixed youtube comments. In *Proceedings of the First Workshop on Speech and Language Technologies for Dravidian Languages*, pages 169–174.

R Anita and CN Subalalitha. 2019a. An approach to cluster Tamil literatures using discourse connectives. In *2019 IEEE 1st International Conference on Energy, Systems and Information Processing (ICESIP)*, pages 1–4. IEEE.

R Anita and CN Subalalitha. 2019b. Building discourse parser for Thirukkural. In *Proceedings of the 16th International Conference on Natural Language Processing*, pages 18–25.

B Bharathi, Bharathi Raja Chakravarthi, Subalalitha Chinnaudayar Navaneethakrishnan, N Sripriya, Arunaggiri Pandian, and Swetha Valli. 2022. Findings of the shared task on Speech Recognition for Vulnerable Individuals in Tamil. In *Proceedings of the Second Workshop on Language Technology for Equality, Diversity and Inclusion*. Association for Computational Linguistics.

Bharathi Raja Chakravarthi. 2020. HopeEDI: A multilingual hope speech detection dataset for equality, diversity, and inclusion. In *Proceedings of the Third Workshop on Computational Modeling of People's Opinions, Personality, and Emotion's in Social Media*, pages 41–53, Barcelona, Spain (Online). Association for Computational Linguistics.

Bharathi Raja Chakravarthi and Vigneshwaran Muralidaran. 2021. Findings of the shared task on hope speech detection for equality, diversity, and inclusion. In *Proceedings of the First Workshop on Language Technology for Equality, Diversity and Inclusion*, pages 61–72, Kyiv. Association for Computational Linguistics.

Bharathi Raja Chakravarthi, Vigneshwaran Muralidaran, Ruba Priyadharshini, and John Philip McCrae. 2020a. Corpus creation for sentiment analysis in code-mixed Tamil-English text. In *Proceedings of the 1st Joint Workshop on Spoken Language Technologies for Under-resourced languages (SLTU) and Collaboration and Computing for Under-Resourced Languages (CCURL)*, pages 202–210, Marseille, France. European Language Resources association.

Bharathi Raja Chakravarthi, Ruba Priyadharshini, Thenmozhi Durairaj, John Phillip McCrae, Paul Buitaleer, Prasanna Kumar Kumaresan, and Rahul Ponnusamy. 2022. Findings of the shared task on Homophobia Transphobia Detection in Social Media Comments. In *Proceedings of the Second Workshop on Language Technology for Equality, Diversity and Inclusion*. Association for Computational Linguistics.

Bharathi Raja Chakravarthi, Ruba Priyadharshini, Vigneshwaran Muralidaran, Shardul Suryawanshi, Navya Jose, Elizabeth Sherly, and John P McCrae. 2020b. Overview of the track on sentiment analysis for Dravidian languages in code-mixed text. In *Forum for Information Retrieval Evaluation*, pages 21–24.

Bharathi Raja Chakravarthi, Ruba Priyadharshini, Rahul Ponnusamy, Prasanna Kumar Kumaresan, Kayalvizhi Sampath, Durairaj Thenmozhi, Sathiyaraj Thangasamy, Rajendran Nallathambi, and John Phillip McCrae. 2021a. Dataset for identification of homophobia and transophobia in multilingual YouTube comments. *arXiv preprint arXiv:2109.00227*.

Bharathi Raja Chakravarthi, Priya Rani, Mihael Arcan, and John P McCrae. 2021b. A survey of orthographic information in machine translation. *SN Computer Science*, 2(4):1–19.

Bharat Gaind, Varun Syal, and Sneha Padgalwar. 2019. Emotion detection and analysis on social media. *arXiv preprint arXiv:1901.08458*.

Nikhil Ghanghor, Parameswari Krishnamurthy, Sajeetha Thavareesan, Ruba Priyadharshini, and Bharathi Raja Chakravarthi. 2021a. IIITK@DravidianLangTech-EACL2021: Offensive language identification and meme classification in Tamil, Malayalam and Kannada. In *Proceedings of the First Workshop on Speech and Language Technologies for Dravidian Languages*, pages 222–229, Kyiv. Association for Computational Linguistics.

Nikhil Ghanghor, Rahul Ponnusamy, Prasanna Kumar Kumaresan, Ruba Priyadharshini, Sajeetha Thavareesan, and Bharathi Raja Chakravarthi. 2021b. IIITK@LT-EDI-EACL2021: Hope speech detection for equality, diversity, and inclusion in Tamil , Malayalam and English. In *Proceedings of the First Workshop on Language Technology for Equality, Diversity and Inclusion*, pages 197–203, Kyiv. Association for Computational Linguistics.

Saurav Kumar, Saunack Kumar, Diptesh Kanojia, and Pushpak Bhattacharyya. 2020. "a passage to India": Pre-trained word embeddings for Indian languages. In *Proceedings of the 1st Joint Workshop on Spoken Language Technologies for Under-resourced languages (SLTU) and Collaboration and Computing for Under-Resourced Languages (CCURL)*, pages 352–357, Marseille, France. European Language Resources association.

Prasanna Kumar Kumaresan, Ratnasingam Sakuntharaj, Sajeetha Thavareesan, Subalalitha Navaneethakrishnan, Anand Kumar Madasamy, Bharathi Raja Chakravarthi, and John P McCrae. 2021. Findings of shared task on offensive language identification in Tamil and Malayalam. In *Forum for Information Retrieval Evaluation*, pages 16–18.

Clare H Liu. 2017. *Applications of twitter emotion detection for stock market prediction*. Ph.D. thesis, Massachusetts Institute of Technology.

Adarsh Pathak and Faraz Khan. 2021. Comparison of cnn and contour algorithm for number identification using hand gesture recognition.

F. Pedregosa, G. Varoquaux, A. Gramfort, V. Michel, B. Thirion, O. Grisel, M. Blondel, P. Prettenhofer, R. Weiss, V. Dubourg, J. Vanderplas, A. Passos, D. Cournapeau, M. Brucher, M. Perrot, and E. Duchesnay. 2011. Scikit-learn: Machine learning in Python. *Journal of Machine Learning Research*, 12:2825–2830.

Ruba Priyadharshini, Bharathi Raja Chakravarthi, Subalalitha Chinnaudayar Navaneethakrishnan, Thenmozhi Durairaj, Malliga Subramanian, Kogilavani Shanmugavadivel, Siddhanth U Hegde, and Prasanna Kumar Kumaresan. 2022. Findings of the shared task on Abusive Comment Detection in Tamil. In *Proceedings of the Second Workshop on Speech and Language Technologies for Dravidian Languages*. Association for Computational Linguistics.

Ruba Priyadharshini, Bharathi Raja Chakravarthi, Sajeetha Thavareesan, Dhivya Chinnappa, Durairaj Thenmozhi, and Rahul Ponnusamy. 2021. Overview of the DravidianCodeMix 2021 shared task on sentiment detection in Tamil, Malayalam, and Kannada. In *Forum for Information Retrieval Evaluation*, pages 4–6.

Ruba Priyadharshini, Bharathi Raja Chakravarthi, Mani Vegupatti, and John P McCrae. 2020. Named entity recognition for code-mixed Indian corpus using meta embedding. In *2020 6th international conference on advanced computing and communication systems (ICACCS)*, pages 68–72. IEEE.

Manikandan Ravikiran, Bharathi Raja Chakravarthi, Anand Kumar Madasamy, Sangeetha Sivanesan, Ratnavel Rajalakshmi, Sajeetha Thavareesan, Rahul Ponnusamy, and Shankar Mahadevan. 2022. Findings of the shared task on Offensive Span Identification in code-mixed Tamil-English comments. In *Proceedings of the Second Workshop on Speech and Language Technologies for Dravidian Languages*. Association for Computational Linguistics.

Ratnasingam Sakuntharaj and Sinnathamby Mahesan. 2016. A novel hybrid approach to detect and correct spelling in Tamil text. In *2016 IEEE International Conference on Information and Automation for Sustainability (ICIAfS)*, pages 1–6.

Ratnasingam Sakuntharaj and Sinnathamby Mahesan. 2017. Use of a novel hash-table for speeding-up suggestions for misspelt tamil words. In *2017 IEEE International Conference on Industrial and Information Systems (ICIIS)*, pages 1–5.

Ratnasingam Sakuntharaj and Sinnathamby Mahesan. 2021. Missing word detection and correction based on context of Tamil sentences using n-grams. In *2021 10th International Conference on Information and Automation for Sustainability (ICIAfS)*, pages 42–47.

Anbukkarasi Sampath, Thenmozhi Durairaj, Bharathi Raja Chakravarthi, Ruba Priyadharshini, Subalalitha Chinnaudayar Navaneethakrishnan, Kogilavani Shanmugavadivel, Sajeetha Thavareesan, Sathiyaraj Thangasamy, Parameswari Krishnamurthy, Adeep Hande, Sean Benhur, and Santhiya Ponnusamy, Kishor Kumar Pandiyan. 2022a. Findings of the shared task on Emotion Analysis in Tamil. In *Proceedings of the Second Workshop on Speech and Language Technologies for Dravidian Languages*. Association for Computational Linguistics.

Anbukkarasi Sampath, Thenmozhi Durairaj, Bharathi Raja Chakravarthi, Ruba Priyadharshini, Subalalitha Chinnaudayar Navaneethakrishnan, Kogilavani Shanmugavadivel, Sajeetha Thavareesan, Sathiyaraj Thangasamy, Parameswari Krishnamurthy,

Adeep Hande, Sean Benhur, and Santhiya Ponnusamy, Kishor Kumar Pandiyan. 2022b. Findings of the shared task on Emotion Analysis in Tamil.

Julio Savigny and Ayu Purwarianti. 2017. Emotion classification on youtube comments using word embedding. In *2017 international conference on advanced informatics, concepts, theory, and applications (ICAICTA)*, pages 1–5. IEEE.

Dario Stojanovski, Gjorgji Strezoski, Gjorgji Madjarov, and Ivica Dimitrovski. 2015. Emotion identification in fifa world cup tweets using convolutional neural network. In *2015 11th International Conference on Innovations in Information Technology (IIT)*, pages 52–57. IEEE.

Carlo Strapparava and Rada Mihalcea. 2008. Learning to identify emotions in text. In *Proceedings of the 2008 ACM Symposium on Applied Computing*, SAC '08, page 15561560, New York, NY, USA. Association for Computing Machinery.

C. N. Subalalitha. 2019. Information extraction framework for Kurunthogai. *Sādhanā*, 44(7):156.

CN Subalalitha and E Poovammal. 2018. Automatic bilingual dictionary construction for Tirukural. *Applied Artificial Intelligence*, 32(6):558–567.

Sajeetha Thavareesan and Sinnathamby Mahesan. 2019. Sentiment analysis in Tamil texts: A study on machine learning techniques and feature representation. In *2019 14th Conference on Industrial and Information Systems (ICIIS)*, pages 320–325.

Sajeetha Thavareesan and Sinnathamby Mahesan. 2020a. Sentiment lexicon expansion using Word2vec and fastText for sentiment prediction in Tamil texts. In *2020 Moratuwa Engineering Research Conference (MERCon)*, pages 272–276.

Sajeetha Thavareesan and Sinnathamby Mahesan. 2020b. Word embedding-based part of speech tagging in Tamil texts. In *2020 IEEE 15th International Conference on Industrial and Information Systems (ICIIS)*, pages 478–482.

Sajeetha Thavareesan and Sinnathamby Mahesan. 2020c. Word embedding-based part of speech tagging in tamil texts. In *2020 IEEE 15th International Conference on Industrial and Information Systems (ICIIS)*, pages 478–482.

Sajeetha Thavareesan and Sinnathamby Mahesan. 2021. Sentiment analysis in Tamil texts using k-means and k-nearest neighbour. In *2021 10th International Conference on Information and Automation for Sustainability (ICIAfS)*, pages 48–53.

Janyce Wiebe, Theresa Wilson, and Claire Cardie. 2005. Annotating expressions of opinions and emotions in language. *Language resources and evaluation*, 39(2):165–210.

Konthala Yasaswini, Karthik Puranik, Adeep Hande, Ruba Priyadharshini, Sajeetha Thavareesan, and Bharathi Raja Chakravarthi. 2021. IIITT@DravidianLangTech-EACL2021: Transfer learning for offensive language detection in Dravidian languages. In *Proceedings of the First Workshop on Speech and Language Technologies for Dravidian Languages*, pages 187–194, Kyiv. Association for Computational Linguistics.

Yuxiang Zhang, Jiamei Fu, Dongyu She, Ying Zhang, Senzhang Wang, and Jufeng Yang. 2018. Text emotion distribution learning via multi-task convolutional neural network. In *IJCAI*, pages 4595–4601.

MUCIC@TamilNLP-ACL2022: Abusive Comment Detection in Tamil Language using 1D Conv-LSTM

F. Balouchzahi [1, a], **M. D. Anusha** [2, b], **H. L. Shashirekha** [2, c], **G. Sidorov** [1, d]
[1]Instituto Politécnico Nacional, Centro de Investigación en Computación, CDMX, Mexico
[2]Department of Computer Science, Mangalore University, Mangalore, India
{[b]anugowda251, [c]hlsrekha}@gmail.com,
{[a]fbalouchzahi2021, [d]sidorov}@cic.ipn.mx

Abstract

Abusive language content such as hate speech, profanity, and cyberbullying etc., which is common in online platforms is creating lot of problems to the users as well as policy makers. Hence, detection of such abusive language in user-generated online content has become increasingly important over the past few years. Online platforms strive hard to moderate the abusive content to reduce societal harm, comply with laws, and create a more inclusive environment for their users. In spite of various methods to automatically detect abusive languages in online platforms, the problem still persists. To address the automatic detection of abusive languages in online platforms, this paper describes the models submitted by our team - MUCIC to the shared task on "Abusive Comment Detection in Tamil-ACL 2022". This shared task addresses the abusive comment detection in native Tamil script texts and code-mixed Tamil texts. To address this challenge, two models: i) n-gram-Multilayer Perceptron (n-gram-MLP) model utilizing MLP classifier fed with char-n gram features and ii) 1D Convolutional Long Short-Term Memory (1D Conv-LSTM) model, were submitted. The n-gram-MLP model fared well among these two models with weighted F1-scores of 0.560 and 0.430 for code-mixed Tamil and native Tamil script texts, respectively. This work may be reproduced using the code available in Gthub[1].

1 Introduction

Abusive language refers to the usage of words for any type of insult, vulgarity, profanity, sexism, or misogyny (Butt et al., 2021) that debases the target, as well as anything that causes aggravation (Spertus, 1997). The term abusive language is often reframed as offensive language (Razavi et al., 2010) and hate speech (Djuric et al., 2015; Chakravarthi et al., 2021b). In recent years, an increasing number of users have witnessed the offensive behavior on social media (Duggan, 2017) targeting individuals, group or community. In spite of many social media companies using a variety of tools such as human reviewers, user reporting procedures, etc., to censor the offensive language, the problem is growing day by day mainly because the offensive/abusive language detection algorithms fail to capture the subject and context-dependent characteristics of the text (Chatzakou et al., 2017; Priyadharshini et al., 2021; Kumaresan et al., 2021). For example, an individual message may appear harmless, but when viewed in the context of previous threads, it may appear abusive, and vice versa. It is challenging even for human beings to detect such abusive language.

Social media texts are usually written mixing regional languages such as Tamil, Kannada, Malayalam, etc., with English at sub-word, word or sentence level (Sampath et al., 2022; Ravikiran et al., 2022; Chakravarthi et al., 2022; Bharathi et al., 2022; Priyadharshini et al., 2022). Further, the usage of internet slangs, words in short forms, words of other languages, emojis etc., adds to the problem of tackling abusive language (Balouchzahi and Shashirekha, 2021; Anusha and Shashirekha, 2020). The focus of abusive comment detection algorithms on low-resources like Tamil is rarely explored due to scarcity and unavailability of annotated dataset Amjad et al. (2021b).

"Abusive Comment Detection in Tamil-ACL 2022"[2] shared task (Priyadharshini et al., 2022) encourages researchers to develop models for detecting comments in native Tamil script texts as well as code-mixed Tamil texts. The objective of the shared task is to identify the abusive content in Tamil and categorize it into predefined abusive language categories. To address the challenges of the shared task, we - team MUCIC, submitted two models: i) n-gram-MLP model utilizing MLP classifier fed with char-n gram features and ii) 1D

[1]https://github.com/anushamdgowda/abusive-detection

[2]https://competitions.codalab.org/competitions/36403

Proceedings of the Second Workshop on Speech and Language Technologies for Dravidian Languages, pages 64 - 69
May 26, 2022 ©2022 Association for Computational Linguistics

Conv-LSTM model, to detect abusive comments in Tamil. This paper describes the methodology of the proposed models and the results obtained.

The rest of the paper is arranged as follows: A review of related work is included in Section 2, and the methodology is discussed in Section 3. Experiments, and results are described in Section 4 followed by concluding the paper with future work in Section 5.

2 Related Work

Most of the abusive comment detection works focus on high-resource languages like English, leaving the low-resource languages such as Dravidian languages, Arabic, Persian, Urdu, etc., unexplored for the task (Amjad et al., 2021a).

A brief description of some of the recent abusive language detection works are given below:

The main problem with low-resource languages are the annotated datasets for abusive language detection. Even human annotators find it difficult to annotate some of the comments as abusive because of which building a large and reliable dataset becomes challenging. Chatzakou et al. (2017) found that datasets openly available for abusive language detection on Twitter ranged from 10K to 35K in size and are insufficient to train Deep Learning (DL) models.

Ashraf et al. (2021) explored abusive comment detection in YouTube comments using several Machine Learning (ML) and DL models as baselines and used n-grams features and pre-trained Glove embeddings to train ML and DL models respectively. Ada-boost (ML model) and 1-Dimensional Convolutional Neural Network (1D-CNN) (DL model) models obtained 87.29 and 89.24 F1-scores on comments without replies. Adding replies as conversational context enhanced the results to 91.96 and 91.68 F1-scores for Ada-boost and 1D-CNN respectively.

Lee et al. (2018) compared various learning models using Hate and Abusive Speech Twitter dataset (Founta et al., 2018). In addition to traditional ML approaches (NB, LR, SVM, and RF), they also investigated Neural Network (NN) models (CNN, Recurrent Neural Networks (RNN) and Bidirectional Gated Recurrent Unit (BiGRU)). Term Frequency-Inverse Document Frequency (TF-IDF) of word vectors and pre-trained GloVe vectors were used to train ML and NN models. Further, Latent Topic Clustering (LTC) which extracts latent topic information from the hidden states of RNN is used as additional information in classifying the text data. BiGRU model based on word features and LTC out performed the other models with an F1-score of 0.805.

Eshan and Hasan (2017) experimented TF-IDF of unigram, bigram, and trigram features to train ML algorithms (RF, Multinomial NB, SVM with Linear, Radial Basis Function, Polynomial, and Sigmoid kernels) and evaluated Facebook dataset of Bengali abusive text. SVM with Linear kernel and trigram feature achieved the best accuracy of 76% accuracy among all the models.

ML (Linear Support Vector Classifier (LinearSVC), LR, MNB, RF) and DL (RNN with Long Short Term Memory (LSTM)) algorithms, were used to detect multi-type abusive Bengali text by Emon et al. (2019). LinearSVC, LR, and MNB models were trained with filtered non-Bengali data transformed to vectors using a CountVectorizer[3]. and RF classifier was trained with the TF-IDF vectors obtained after filtering punctuation, numerals, and emotions. For DL model, the raw dataset is stemmed and word embedding is utilized to encode the text. RNN with LSTM outperforms other algorithms with the highest accuracy of 82.20%.

Several code-mixed Tamil datasets are used in various shared tasks, such as Sentiment Analysis in Tamil (Chakravarthi et al., 2020), Hate Speech Detection in Dravidian Languages (Mandl et al., 2020), Hope Speech Detection (Chakravarthi, 2020), Offensive Language Identification (OLI) in Dravidian Languages, (Chakravarthi et al., 2021a), etc. Since code-mixed texts do not follow any grammar, Balouchzahi et al. (2021a) proposed a learning model using sub-words generated by char sequences to deal with code-mixed texts for the task of OLI in Dravidian languages (Chakravarthi et al., 2021a). They used word n-grams with sub-words and a majority voting classifier with eXtreme Gradient Boosting (XGB), LR, and MLP estimators and obtained a weighted average F1-score of 0.75.

In another experiment on code-mixed Tamil texts, Balouchzahi et al. (2021b) combined char sequences with syntactic bi-grams and tri-grams for Hope Speech Detection task (Chakravarthi, 2020) and fed a voting classifier with three ML estimators, namely: LR, XGB and MLP. The authors created a code-mixed BERT language model from

[3]https://scikit-learn.org/stable/modules/generated/sklearn.feature_extraction.text.CountVectorizer.html

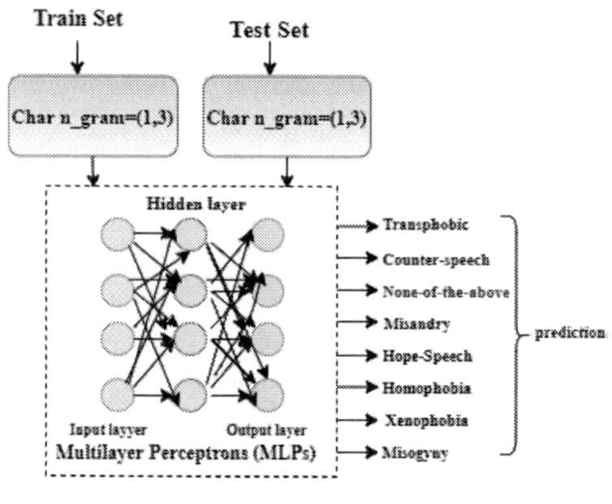

Figure 1: Framework of n-gram-MLP model

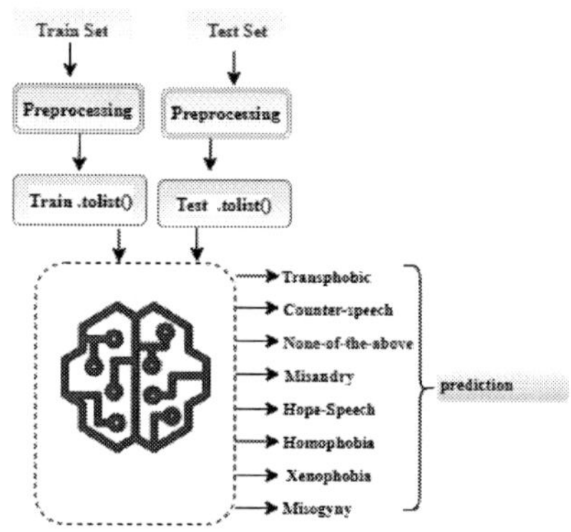

Figure 2: Framework of 1D Conv-LSTM model

scratch and obtained an average weighted F1-score of 0.54. However, in this study, the best performance was that of hard voting classifier with an average weighted F1-score of 0.59 that secured third rank in the competition.

3 Methodology

The first step in processing text data is to clean the text by removing the punctuation symbols, numerical data, frequently occurring words, and stopwords, as these features do not help in identifying the abusive content. Clean data is expected to improve the performance of the learning models. Two models: i) n-gram-MLP trained with char n-grams and ii) 1D Conv-LSTM model, were proposed to identify the abusive comment from native Tamil script and code-mixed Tamil texts. The framework of the proposed models are shown in Figure 1 and 2 and explanation of the models follows:

3.1 n-gram-MLP model

Many text processing projects utilize n-grams features since they are easy to implement and are scalable. A model with a larger 'n' value can store more contexts with a well-understood space-time tradeoff (Balouchzahi and Shashirekha, 2020) allowing many text processing experiments to scale up efficiently.

char n-grams in the range (1, 3) are extracted from the texts and vectorized using TfidfVectorizer[4]. These vectors are used to train MLP classifier by setting hidden layer sizes to (150, 100, 50), maximum iterations to 300, Random state to 1, activation to Relu and solver to Adam.

3.2 1D Conv-LSTM model

Keras Tokenizer[5] tokenizes the text and transforms it into a vector where the coefficient for each token could be binary, based on word count or TF-IDF. Further, the vocabulary size and maximum length of sequences are set to 60,000 and 50 respectively. "Pad_sequences" was utilized to keep all sequences at same length. The three parameters: "input dim", "output dim" and "input length" are set to 60,000 (vocabulary size), 1,000 (vector length of word) and 500 (maximum length of a sequence) respectively. Eventually, a 1D convolutional layer with 64 filtres, two pooling layers, and a relu activation function, followed by 100 fully connected LSTM layers and a soft-max output layer are used in this model to classify the given input.

4 Experiments and Results

The datasets provided by the shared task organizers contains native Tamil script (Tamil) and code-mixed Tamil (Ta-En) texts and the task is to classify the input text into different categories as shown in Table 1. Further, the table also gives the breakup of Train and Test sets for both Tamil and Ta-En datasets. The observation of data distribution reveals that both native and code-mixed Tamil datasets are imbalanced and that makes the classification task more problematic. Fox example, there are only 35, 6, and 2 samples in Homophobia, Transphobic, and not-Tamil classes respectively against 446, 149 and 95 samples in Misandry, Counter-speech and Xenophobia respectively, in the Train set of Tamil dataset. Few samples of the native script and code-mixed texts in the datasets are shown in Table 2.

[4]https://scikit-learn.org/stable/modules/generated/sklearn.feature_extraction.text.TfidfVectorizer.html

[5]https://www.tensorflow.org/api_docs/python/tf/keras/preprocessing/text/Tokenizer

Label\Set	Train		Test	
	Tamil	**Ta-En**	**Tamil**	**Ta-En**
None-of-the-above	1296	3720	346	919
Misandry	446	830	104	218
Counter-speech	149	348	36	95
Xenophobia	95	297	29	70
Hope-Speech	86	213	11	53
Misogyny	125	211	24	50
Homophobia	35	172	8	43
Transphobic	6	157	2	40
Not-Tamil	2	-	-	-
Total	2240	5791	560	1488

Table 1: Distribution of labels in the given datasets

Language	Text	label
Tamil	தாசி மகன் சைமன் என்ற சீமான் என்ற பைத்தியகார பன்னி	Misandry
	செக்ஸ்சாஸ்திரி ஸ்கூல் ஆகா என்ன அருமையான பெயர். இனிமேல்	Homophobia
	சீமான் ஒரு தமிழர் அல்ல	Xenophobia
Ta-En	Guru murthi dhevudiyalukku porantha dhevudiya pullaiya	Misogyny
	Ama manigandan unmaitham.evaroda comments thappa peasra unga ellorukum samarpanam	Counter-speech
	Sappa nose ah udaikum alavukku	Xenophobia

Table 2: Samples of texts in the given dataset

The unlabeled Test sets shared by the organizers were used to evaluate the proposed models and the predictions were submitted to the organizers for final evaluation and ranking. As per the results in the final leaderboard of the shared task, the proposed n-gram-MLP model obtained average weighted F1-scores of 0.560 and 0.430 for Tamil and Ta-En texts respectively. Results of the proposed models on Development set and Test set are shown in Table 3 and 4 respectively. The comparison of average weighted F1-scores among the participating teams in the shared task shown in Figure 3 illustrates that the performance of the n-gram-MLP model is considerate.

5 Conclusion

This paper describes the participation of our team MUCIC in "Abusive Comment Detection in Tamil-ACL 2022" shared task. The objective of this shared task is to identify the different categories of abusive comments in native Tamil script and code-mixed Tamil texts. Among the two models, n-gram-MLP trained with n-grams and 1D Conv-LSTM model submitted for this shared task, n-gram-MLP classifier outperformed on both code-mixed Tamil and native Tamil script texts with average weighted F1-scores of 0.560 and 0.430, respectively.

Model	Language	w_F1-score	m_F1-score
MLP	Ta-En	0.64	0.28
	Tamil	0.56	0.33
1D Conv-LSTM	Ta-En	0.54	0.29
	Tamil	0.60	0.27

Table 3: Macro F1-score(m_F1-score) and Weighted F1-score(w_F1-score) F1-score on Development set

Language /Metric	w_F1-score	m_F1-score	Rank
Ta-En	0.560	0.290	6
Tamil	0.430	0.120	10

Table 4: Macro F1-score(m_F1-score) and Weighted F1-score(w_F1-score) F1-score on Test set

References

Maaz Amjad, Noman Ashraf, Alisa Zhila, Grigori Sidorov, Arkaitz Zubiaga, and Alexander Gelbukh. 2021a. Threatening Language Detection and Target Identification in Urdu Tweets. *IEEE Access*, 9:128302–128313.

Maaz Amjad, Alisa Zhila, Grigori Sidorov, Andrey Labunets, Sabur Butt, Hamza Imam Amjad, Oxana Vitman, and Alexander Gelbukh. 2021b. UrduThreat@ FIRE2021: Shared Track on Abusive Threat Identification in Urdu. In *Forum for Information Retrieval Evaluation*, pages 9–11.

MD Anusha and HL Shashirekha. 2020. An Ensemble Model for Hate Speech and Offensive Content Identification in Indo-European Languages. In *FIRE (Working Notes)*, pages 253–259.

Noman Ashraf, Arkaitz Zubiaga, and Alexander Gelbukh. 2021. Abusive Language Detection in YouTube Comments Leveraging Replies as Conversational Context. *PeerJ. Computer science*, 7:e742.

Fazlourrahman Balouchzahi, Aparna B K, and H L Shashirekha. 2021a. MUCS@DravidianLangTech-EACL2021: COOLI-Code-Mixing Offensive Language Identification. In *Proceedings of the First Workshop on Speech and Language Technologies for Dravidian Languages*, pages 323–329, Kyiv. Association for Computational Linguistics.

Fazlourrahman Balouchzahi, Aparna B K, and H L Shashirekha. 2021b. MUCS@LT-EDI-EACL2021:

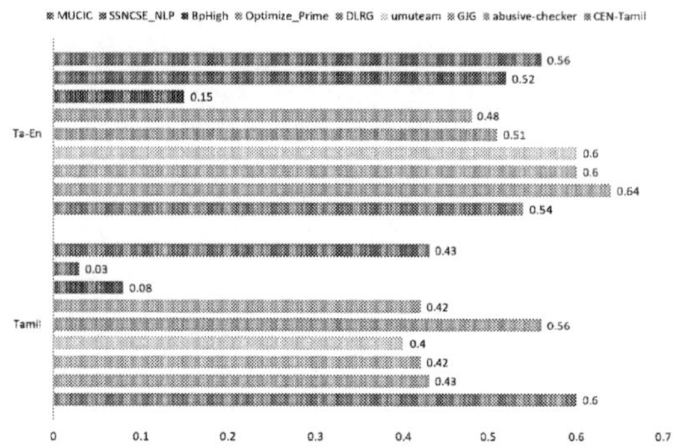

Figure 3: Comparison of average weighted F1-scores of the participating teams

CoHope-Hope Speech Detection for Equality, Diversity, and Inclusion in Code-Mixed Texts. In *Proceedings of the First Workshop on Language Technology for Equality, Diversity and Inclusion*, pages 180–187, Kyiv. Association for Computational Linguistics.

Fazlourrahman Balouchzahi and H L Shashirekha. 2021. LA-SACo: A Study of Learning Approaches for Sentiments Analysis in Code-Mixing Texts. In *Proceedings of the First Workshop on Speech and Language Technologies for Dravidian Languages*, pages 109–118, Kyiv. Association for Computational Linguistics.

Fazlourrahman Balouchzahi and HL Shashirekha. 2020. Puner-Parsi ULMFiT for Named-Entity Recognition in Persian Texts. In *Congress on Intelligent Systems*, pages 75–88. Springer.

B Bharathi, Bharathi Raja Chakravarthi, Subalalitha Chinnaudayar Navaneethakrishnan, N Sripriya, Arunaggiri Pandian, and Swetha Valli. 2022. Findings of the shared task on Speech Recognition for Vulnerable Individuals in Tamil. In *Proceedings of the Second Workshop on Language Technology for Equality, Diversity and Inclusion*. Association for Computational Linguistics.

Sabur Butt, Noman Ashraf, Grigori Sidorov, and Alexander Gelbukh. 2021. Sexism Identification using BERT and Data Augmentation-EXIST2021. In *International Conference of the Spanish Society for Natural Language Processing SEPLN 2021, IberLEF 2021*.

Bharathi Raja Chakravarthi. 2020. HopeEDI: A Multilingual Hope Speech Detection Dataset for Equality, Diversity, and Inclusion. In *Proceedings of the Third Workshop on Computational Modeling of People's Opinions, Personality, and Emotion's in Social Media*, pages 41–53, Barcelona, Spain (Online). Association for Computational Linguistics.

Bharathi Raja Chakravarthi, Vigneshwaran Muralidaran, Ruba Priyadharshini, and John Philip McCrae. 2020. Corpus Creation for Sentiment Analysis in Code-Mixed Tamil-English Text. In *Proceedings of the 1st Joint Workshop on Spoken Language Technologies for Under-resourced languages (SLTU) and Collaboration and Computing for Under-Resourced Languages (CCURL)*, pages 202–210.

Bharathi Raja Chakravarthi, Ruba Priyadharshini, Thenmozhi Durairaj, John Phillip McCrae, Paul Buitaleer, Prasanna Kumar Kumaresan, and Rahul Ponnusamy. 2022. Findings of the shared task on Homophobia Transphobia Detection in Social Media Comments. In *Proceedings of the Second Workshop on Language Technology for Equality, Diversity and Inclusion*. Association for Computational Linguistics.

Bharathi Raja Chakravarthi, Ruba Priyadharshini, Navya Jose, Anand Kumar M, Thomas Mandl, Prasanna Kumar Kumaresan, Rahul Ponnusamy, Hariharan R L, John P. McCrae, and Elizabeth Sherly. 2021a. Findings of the Shared Task on Offensive Language Identification in Tamil, Malayalam, and Kannada. In *Proceedings of the First Workshop on Speech and Language Technologies for Dravidian Languages*, pages 133–145, Kyiv. Association for Computational Linguistics.

Bharathi Raja Chakravarthi, Ruba Priyadharshini, Rahul Ponnusamy, Prasanna Kumar Kumaresan, Kayalvizhi Sampath, Durairaj Thenmozhi, Sathiyaraj Thangasamy, Rajendran Nallathambi, and John Phillip McCrae. 2021b. Dataset for identification of homophobia and transophobia in multilingual YouTube comments. *arXiv preprint arXiv:2109.00227*.

Despoina Chatzakou, Nicolas Kourtellis, Jeremy Blackburn, Emiliano De Cristofaro, Gianluca Stringhini, and Athena Vakali. 2017. Mean Birds: Detecting Aggression and Bullying on Twitter. In *Proceedings of the 2017 ACM on web science conference*, pages 13–22.

Nemanja Djuric, Jing Zhou, Robin Morris, Mihajlo Grbovic, Vladan Radosavljevic, and Narayan Bhamidipati. 2015. Hate Speech Detection with Comment Embeddings. In *Proceedings of the 24th international conference on world wide web*, pages 29–30.

Maeve Duggan. 2017. Online Harassment 2017.

Estiak Ahmed Emon, Shihab Rahman, Joti Banarjee, Amit Kumar Das, and Tanni Mittra. 2019. A Deep Learning Approach to Detect Abusive Bengali Text. In *2019 7th International Conference on Smart Computing & Communications (ICSCC)*, pages 1–5. IEEE.

Shahnoor C Eshan and Mohammad S Hasan. 2017. An Application of Machine Learning to Detect Abusive Bengali Text. In *2017 20th International Conference of Computer and Information Technology (ICCIT)*, pages 1–6. IEEE.

Antigoni Maria Founta, Constantinos Djouvas, Despoina Chatzakou, Ilias Leontiadis, Jeremy Blackburn, Gianluca Stringhini, Athena Vakali, Michael

Sirivianos, and Nicolas Kourtellis. 2018. Large Scale Crowdsourcing and Characterization of Twitter Abusive Behavior. In *Twelfth International AAAI Conference on Web and Social Media*.

Prasanna Kumar Kumaresan, Ratnasingam Sakuntharaj, Sajeetha Thavareesan, Subalalitha Navaneethakrishnan, Anand Kumar Madasamy, Bharathi Raja Chakravarthi, and John P McCrae. 2021. Findings of shared task on offensive language identification in Tamil and Malayalam. In *Forum for Information Retrieval Evaluation*, pages 16–18.

Younghun Lee, Seunghyun Yoon, and Kyomin Jung. 2018. Comparative Studies of Detecting Abusive Language on Twitter. *arXiv preprint arXiv:1808.10245*.

Thomas Mandl, Sandip Modha, Anand Kumar M, and Bharathi Raja Chakravarthi. 2020. Overview of the Hasoc Track at FIRE 2020: Hate Speech and Offensive Language Identification in Tamil, Malayalam, Hindi, English and German. In *Forum for Information Retrieval Evaluation*, pages 29–32.

Ruba Priyadharshini, Bharathi Raja Chakravarthi, Subalalitha Chinnaudayar Navaneethakrishnan, Thenmozhi Durairaj, Malliga Subramanian, Kogilavani Shanmugavadivel, Siddhanth U Hegde, and Prasanna Kumar Kumaresan. 2022. Findings of the shared task on Abusive Comment Detection in Tamil. In *Proceedings of the Second Workshop on Speech and Language Technologies for Dravidian Languages*. Association for Computational Linguistics.

Ruba Priyadharshini, Bharathi Raja Chakravarthi, Sajeetha Thavareesan, Dhivya Chinnappa, Durairaj Thenmozhi, and Rahul Ponnusamy. 2021. Overview of the DravidianCodeMix 2021 shared task on sentiment detection in Tamil, Malayalam, and Kannada. In *Forum for Information Retrieval Evaluation*, pages 4–6.

Manikandan Ravikiran, Bharathi Raja Chakravarthi, Anand Kumar Madasamy, Sangeetha Sivanesan, Ratnavel Rajalakshmi, Sajeetha Thavareesan, Rahul Ponnusamy, and Shankar Mahadevan. 2022. Findings of the shared task on Offensive Span Identification in code-mixed Tamil-English comments. In *Proceedings of the Second Workshop on Speech and Language Technologies for Dravidian Languages*. Association for Computational Linguistics.

Amir H Razavi, Diana Inkpen, Sasha Uritsky, and Stan Matwin. 2010. Offensive Language Detection using Multi-level Classification. In *Canadian Conference on Artificial Intelligence*, pages 16–27. Springer.

Anbukkarasi Sampath, Thenmozhi Durairaj, Bharathi Raja Chakravarthi, Ruba Priyadharshini, Subalalitha Chinnaudayar Navaneethakrishnan, Kogilavani Shanmugavadivel, Sajeetha Thavareesan, Sathiyaraj Thangasamy, Parameswari Krishnamurthy, Adeep Hande, Sean Benhur, Kishor Kumar Ponnusamy, and Santhiya Pandiyan. 2022. Findings of the shared task on Emotion Analysis in Tamil. In *Proceedings of the Second Workshop on Speech and Language Technologies for Dravidian Languages*. Association for Computational Linguistics.

Ellen Spertus. 1997. Smokey: Automatic Recognition of Hostile Messages. In *Aaai/iaai*, pages 1058–1065.

CEN-Tamil@DravidianLangTech-ACL2022: Abusive Comment detection in Tamil using TF-IDF and Random Kitchen Sink Algorithm

Prasanth S N, R Aswin Raj, Adhithan P, Premjith B, Soman K P
Centre for Computation Engineering and Networking (CEN)
Amrita School of Engineering, Coimbatore
Amrita Vishwa Vidyapeetham, India
b_premjith@cb.amrita.edu

Abstract

This paper describes the approach of team CENTamil used for abusive comment detection in Tamil. This task aims to identify whether a given comment contains abusive comments. We used TF-IDF with char-wb analyzers with Random Kitchen Sink (RKS) algorithm to create feature vectors and the Support Vector Machine (SVM) classifier with polynomial kernel for classification. We used this method for both Tamil and Tamil-English datasets and secured first place with an f1-score of 0.32 and seventh place with an f1-score of 0.25, respectively. The code for our approach is shared in the GitHub repository.[1]

1 Introduction

Abusive speech refers to any form of communication done with the intention to humiliate, or spread hatred against a vulnerable individual or a vulnerable group on the basis of gender, race, religion, ethnicity, skin color or disability using abusive or vulgar words. It causes psychological effects on the targeted individual and leading them towards unrightful act.

In recent years, there has been significant growth in the volume of digital content exchanged by people through social media. Online social networks have grown in importance, becoming a source for acquiring news, information, and entertainment. Despite the apparent advantages of using online social networks, there is an ever-increasing number of malevolent actors who use social media to harm others.

The goal of the shared task is to identify abusive comments in Tamil and code-mixed Tamil-English data developed by collecting YouTube comments. The code-mix Tamil-English dataset consists of eight different classes namely, 'Counter-speech', 'Homophobia', 'Hope-Speech', 'Misandry','Misogyny', 'None-of-the-above', 'Transphobic', 'Xenophobia'. In addition to the aforementioned eight classes, the Tamil dataset consists of one more class, 'Not-Tamil'.

We used Random Kitchen Sink (RKS) (Sathyan et al., 2018) algorithms with character word-bound based Term Frequency-Inverse Document Frequency (TF-IDF) (Barathi Ganesh et al., 2016) for text representation and classification was performed using Support Vector Machines (SVM) classifier (Soman et al., 2009), (Premjith et al., 2019). The rest of the paper is organised as follows: Section 2 describes about the related works, Section 3 describes about the Datasets, Section 4 describes about the preprocessing and different methods used, Section 5 describes about the result and analysis and Section 6 concludes the paper.

2 Related Works

Analysis of Online Social Networks' content is an active research area with tasks like Offensive Language Identification and Hope Speech Detection. Recent work in Hope Speech Detection in Dravidan languages includes the shared task on hope speech detection in LT-EDI in EACL (Chakravarthi, 2020; Chakravarthi and Muralidaran, 2021). Abusive language detection for other languages has been done in literature (Jahan et al.; Akhter et al.; Sundar et al.) but as far as we know, this is the first shared task on abusive detection in Tamil at this fine-grained level.

We used TF-IDF because it helps in understanding the importance of a word in the corpus(Sammut and Webb, 2010) and we used Random Kitchen Sink (RKS) on top of it because RKS helps in mapping the data from the feature space to a higher dimensional space(S et al.). We used SVM because of its ability to perform well in the higher dimensional data(Cortes and Vapnik, 1995).

[1]https://github.com/Prasanth-s-n/CEN-Tamil_Abusive_Comment_Detection

Proceedings of the Second Workshop on Speech and Language Technologies for Dravidian Languages, pages 70 - 74
May 26, 2022

3 Dataset

The organisers of the Abusive Comment Detection shared task provided two datasets, where one contains Tamil comments and the another one contains code-mixed Tamil-English comments(Chakravarthi, 2020).

Table 1 shows the classwise distribution of data for Tamil dataset and Table 2 shows the classwise distribution of data for Tamil-English dataset. Table 3 shows the statistics of the datasets given for this task.

4 Methods

We started with preprocessing the YouTube comments in the datasets, and the preprocessed texts were converted into vectors. The classification of the YouTube comments was carried out by supplying the text vectors to a classifier, SVM. Figure 1 shows the pipeline of the methodology we followed for this task.

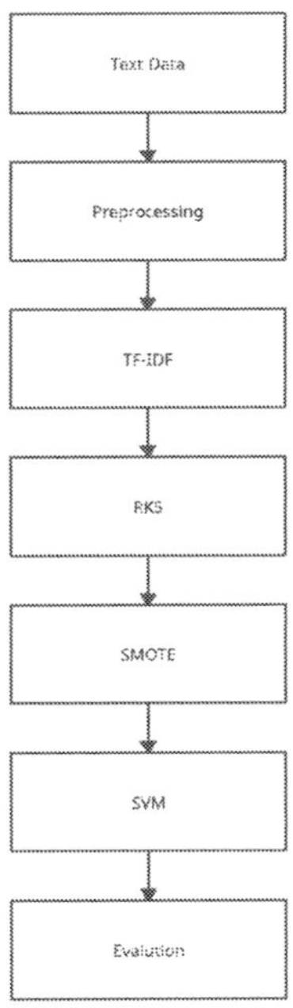

Figure 1: Steps involved in training our submitted Model

4.1 Preprocessing

The datasets used for this shared task contains comment with words in Tamil and English. The social media text contains noise such as URLs, Hashtags and other unwanted characters such as punctuation. The preprocessing step includes the removal of noise to make the data clean. In this step, we removed emojis, hashtags, URLs and non-alphabetical characters.

4.2 Text Representation and Classifier

Text Representation is one of the fundamental task in Natural Language Processing where the text is represented with array of numbers. We used TF-IDF with RKS for text representation. TF-IDF (Term Frequency - Inverse Document Frequency) is vector semantics text representation technique which uses the frequency of a word in a given document and the number of documents in which the particular word is present(Sammut and Webb, 2010). We used character character word bound n-grams based TF-IDF with RKS for increasing the dimension of the data. We used different max features for TF-IDF and different dimension size for RKS.

From Table 2 and Table 3 it is evident that the datasets are highly imbalanced. In order to solve this class imbalance problem, we used a oversampling technique called SMOTE (Synthetic Minority Over-sampling Technique) with k neighbors being 1. It uses the k-nearest neighbor algorithm by creating a plane based on the k neighbors and generates new samples from the plane(Chawla et al.). In our work, we used SMOTE by utilizing imblearn API.

RKS (Random Kitchen Sink) is an effective method for mapping features from their feature space to a higher dimensional space without explicit kernel mapping by using Fourier coefficients. The methodology is able to emulate the characteristics of the shift invariant kernel functions satisfactorily (S et al.).

SVM Classifier is used for classification due to its ability to perform well in case of higher dimensional data (Cortes and Vapnik, 1995). We used Polynomial Kernel with the regularization parameter set to 1. We used Scikit-learn API to do the classification task.

4.3 Hyperparameters

Hyperparameter tuning is an important step in building a model. The model performance is heavily dependent on hyperparameters. We selected the hyperparameters from a set of values and reported the models with hyperparameters that gave better result while valdating the model (trained and validated on Tamil Dataset) in terms of F1-score. Table

Class Name	Train Data	Val Data	Test Data
Counter-speech	149	36	47
Homophobia	35	8	8
Hope-Speech	86	11	26
Misandry	446	104	127
Misogyny	125	24	48
None-of-the-above	1296	346	416
Not-Tamil	2	0	0
Transphobic	6	2	2
Xenophobia	95	29	25

Table 1: Classwise distribuiton of Tamil dataset

Class Name	Train Data	Val Data	Test Data
Counter-speech	348	95	88
Homophobia	172	43	56
Hope-Speech	213	53	70
Misandry	830	218	292
Misogyny	211	50	57
None-of-the-above	3720	919	1143
Transphobic	157	40	58
Xenophobia	297	70	95

Table 2: Classwise distribuiton of Tamil-English dataset

Language	Train	Valid	Test
Tamil	2240	560	699
Tamil-English	5948	1488	1859

Table 3: Shared Task Dataset Statistics

Hyperparameter	Value
TFIDF ngram range	(1,5)
TFIDF Max-Features	2000
RKS Dimension	10*Max-Features
SVM Kernel	Poly
SVM C Parameter	100

Table 4: Hyperparameter used for building the models

4 shows the optimal hyperparameter used for building the models and we used the same parameters for both the datasets.

5 Result and Analysis

We experimented with four different machine learning classification models. All the four models initially uses TF-IDF with char-wb analyzer and max features being 2000 and SVM classifier with polynomial kernel and regularization parameter being 100. Model-1 uses only SVM and TF-IDF. Model-2 additionally uses SMOTE oversampling technique. Model-3 additionally uses RKS for increasing the size of text representation. Model-4 additionally uses RKS and SMOTE. The classification models' performance are measured in terms of macro average Precision, marco average Recall and marco average F1-Score across all the classes. Table 5 and Table 6 shows the performance of the models on validation dataset, Tamil and Tamil-English respectively. We used Model-4 in both cases due to its higher macro F1-score and secured rank 1 for Tamil and rank 7 for Tamil-English in the shared task (Priyadharshini et al., 2022). Table 7 contains the result obtained for Tamil and Tamil-English test datasets using model 4.

By comparing our predictions from the model-4 for Tamil dataset against the ground truth of Tamil test data, we found that None-of-the-above class has the highest individual f1-score of 0.83 and Transphobic class has the lowest individual f1-score of 0 since it has only two data points in the test data. In Tamil-English dataset, None-of-the-above class has the highest individual f1-score of 0.85 and Misogyny class has the lowest individual f1-score of 0.18. Table 8 contains the class-wise f1-score for both the datasets.

Model	Precision	Recall	F1-Score
Model-1	**0.51**	0.28	0.31
Model-2	0.41	0.31	0.33
Model-3	0.50	0.29	0.32
Model-4	0.43	**0.32**	**0.34**

Table 5: Results For Tamil Validation dataset

Model	Precision	Recall	F1-Score
Model-1	0.68	0.40	0.47
Model-2	0.64	0.45	0.51
Model-3	**0.70**	0.42	0.48
Model-4	0.67	**0.46**	**0.52**

Table 6: Results For Tamil-English Validation dataset

Dataset	Precision	Recall	F1-Score
Tamil	0.38	0.29	0.32
Tamil-English	0.30	0.23	0.25

Table 7: Results For Test datasets

Class Name	Tamil	Tamil-English
Counter-speech	0.35	0.38
Homophobia	0.67	0.37
Hope-Speech	0.26	0.23
Misandry	0.71	0.68
Misogyny	0.54	0.18
None-of-the-above	0.83	0.85
Transphobic	0.00	0.32
Xenophobia	0.18	0.65

Table 8: Classwise F1-Score Obtained Using Model-4

6 Conclusion and Future work

This paper briefs the submission of team CEN-Tamil to the shared task at ACL 2022 on Abusive Comments Detection in Tamil. We experimented character word bound n-grams based TF-IDF with and without RKS. The max features for the TF-IDF is taken to be 2000. The highly class imbalance problem was solved using SMOTE. We also reported the results obtained without using SMOTE. The SVM classifier with polynomial kernel and 100 as regularization with TF-IDF, RKS and SMOTE gave high macro F1-Score of 0.32 for Tamil and 0.25 for Tamil-English which secured first and seventh place in the shared task respectively.

We have not explored Transformers based approaches for abusive comment detection. As future works we like to experiment with different transformers like BERT and LaBSE along with deep learning architecture like LSTM and CNN to improve the results.

References

Muhammad Pervez Akhter, Zheng Jiangbin, Irfan Raza Naqvi, Mohammed AbdelMajeed, and Tehseen Zia. Abusive language detection from social media comments using conventional machine learning and deep learning approaches.

HB Barathi Ganesh, M Anand Kumar, and KP Soman. 2016. From vector space models to vector space models of semantics. In *Forum for Information Retrieval Evaluation*, pages 50–60. Springer.

Bharathi Raja Chakravarthi. 2020. HopeEDI: A multilingual hope speech detection dataset for equality, diversity, and inclusion. In *Proceedings of the Third Workshop on Computational Modeling of People's Opinions, Personality, and Emotion's in Social Media*, pages 41–53, Barcelona, Spain (Online). Association for Computational Linguistics.

Bharathi Raja Chakravarthi and Vigneshwaran Muralidaran. 2021. Findings of the shared task on hope speech detection for equality, diversity, and inclusion. In *Proceedings of the First Workshop on Language Technology for Equality, Diversity and Inclusion*, pages 61–72, Kyiv. Association for Computational Linguistics.

Nitesh V. Chawla, Kevin W. Boyer, Lawrence O. Hall, and W. Philip Kegelmeyer. Smote: Synthetic minority over-sampling technique.

Corinna Cortes and Vladimir Vapnik. 1995. Support-vector networks. *Machine learning*, 20(3):273–297.

Maliha Jahan, Istiak Ahamed, Md. Rayanuzzaman Bishwas, and Swakkhar Shatabda. Abusive comments detection in bangla-english code-mixed and transliterated text.

B Premjith, KP Soman, M Anand Kumar, and D Jyothi Ratnam. 2019. Embedding linguistic features in word embedding for preposition sense disambiguation in english—malayalam machine translation context. In *Recent Advances in Computational Intelligence*, pages 341–370. Springer.

Ruba Priyadharshini, Bharathi Raja Chakravarthi, Subalalitha Chinnaudayar Navaneethakrishnan, Thenmozhi Durairaj, Malliga Subramanian, Kogilavani Shanmugavadivel, Siddhanth U Hegde, and Prasanna Kumar Kumaresan. 2022. Findings of the shared task on Abusive Comment Detection in Tamil. In *Proceedings of the Second Workshop on Speech and Language Technologies for Dravidian Languages*. Association for Computational Linguistics.

Athira S, Harikumar K, Sowmya V, and Soman K P. Parameter analysis of random kitchen sink algorithm.

Claude Sammut and Geoffrey I. Webb, editors. 2010. *TF-IDF*, pages 986–987. Springer US, Boston, MA.

Dhanya Sathyan, Kalpathy Balakrishnan Anand, Aravind Jaya Prakash, and Bhavukam Premjith. 2018. Modeling the fresh and hardened stage properties of self-compacting concrete using random kitchen sink algorithm. *International journal of concrete structures and materials*, 12(1):1–10.

KP Soman, R Loganathan, and V Ajay. 2009. *Machine learning with SVM and other kernel methods*. PHI Learning Pvt. Ltd.

Arunima Sundar, Akshay Ramakrishnan, Avantika Balaji, and Thenmozhi Durairaj. Hope speech detection for dravidian languages using cross-lingual embeddings with stacked encoder architecture.

NITK-IT_NLP@TamilNLP-ACL2022: Transformer based model for Offensive Span Identification in Tamil

Hariharan RamakrishnaIyer LekshmiAmmal[1], Manikandan Ravikiran[2], Anand Kumar Madasamy[1]

[1]Department of Information Technology,
National Institute of Technology Karnataka, Surathkal
[2]Georgia Institute of technology, Atlanta, Georgia
hariharanrl.197it003@nitk.edu.in, mravikiran3@gatech.edu
m_anandkumar@nitk.edu.in

Abstract

Offensive Span identification in Tamil is a shared task that focuses on identifying harmful content, contributing to offensiveness. In this work, we have built a model that can efficiently identify the span of text contributing to offensive content. We have used various transformer-based models to develop the system, out of which the fine-tuned MuRIL model was able to achieve the best overall character F1-score of 0.4489.

1 Introduction

As far as social media and entities involved in content moderation are concerned, identifying offensive content is critical. However, most of these companies employ content moderators for determining and mitigating offensive content, but they are frequently swamped by their volume (Arsht and Etcovitch, 2018). Small firms cannot utilize human moderators because of the cost, and hence they turn off their comment sections fully.

Code-mixing is the mixing of various linguistic units from two or more languages in a conversation or even in a single utterance. When the Indian perspective is considered, English is primarily influenced by all Indian languages, including Dravidian languages like Tamil, Malayalam, and Kannada (Chakravarthi et al., 2020). Hence this has become a part of different conversations in social media. Many recent works address the whole comment classification as offensive or not but do not consider the span of text that makes it offensive. Identifying this span of text will further help moderators who deal with these contents.

Offensive Span identification is a shared task organised as a part of DravidianLangTech @ACL-2022[1]. They had two subtasks, Supervised Offensive Span Identification and Semi-Supervised Offensive Span Identification, where we were given annotated as well as non-annotated data. The task was to identify the offensive span of text content.

In this paper, we have used multilingual transformer-based models and Local Interpretable Model Agnostic Explanations (LIME) (Ribeiro et al., 2016) to identify the span of text. The paper is presented as follows; Section 2 explains the Dataset, Section 3 is about the Methodology used, Section 4 explains the Experiments and Results, which follows the Conclusions and Future Scope.

2 Related Works

Offensive language identification is one of the widely explored problems. Most of the work on offensive language identification tasks is of classification type rather than identifying the span of texts. Recent works (Kedia and Nandy, 2021; Sharif et al., 2021; Jayanthi and Gupta, 2021) have explored various transformer-based models and some (Saha et al., 2021; Zhao and Tao, 2021) have made an ensemble of different ones which are focused on classification task. Offensive Span identification is in its developing stage, (Pavlopoulos et al., 2021) was the first to introduced a shared task and Offensive Span dataset.

3 Dataset Description

Two subtasks were given on the codalab competition website[2] for Offensive Span identification in Tamil, namely Supervised Offensive Span Identification and Semi-Supervised Offensive Span Identification. The Dataset (Ravikiran and Annamalai, 2021; Ravikiran et al., 2022) had training and testing sets for both tasks, which are retrieved from YouTube, whose details are given in Table 1, which contained Code-mixed Tamil comments. The supervised task had annotated data for spans (some entire comments are annotated for full spans);

[1]https://dravidianlangtech.github.io/2022/

[2]https://competitions.codalab.org/competitions/36395

Proceedings of the Second Workshop on Speech and Language Technologies for Dravidian Languages, pages 75 - 78
May 26, 2022

along with that, we had partial annotated data. The test data had 876 comments for prediction. We have used the HASOC-2021 (Chakravarthi et al., 2021) shared task dataset for training, which had 4000 comments with an equal number of offensive and not-offensive labels.

Task	Comments
Supervised	4816

Table 1: Dataset Details

4 Methodology

We had two subtasks as a part of this shared task on Offensive Span Identification. The first task was to use a supervised method to identify offensive span of text in the data, and the second task was to use a semi-supervised method to do the same. We used the supervised method, which uses the transformer-based model to train the data for classifying offensive content. This trained model is used to predict whether the given comment is offensive or not. On top of this, we further examine the results on each class individually using input perturbation-based explanation method involving Local Interpretable Model Agnostic Explanations (LIME) (Ribeiro et al., 2016).

Here we are training the model for offensive content identification from comment text. We have used data from the HASOC-2021 shared task[3] (Chakravarthi et al., 2021), which contains comments extracted from YouTube annotated with labels 'offensive' and 'not-offensive.' The comments are Preprocessed, Tokenized, and fed to the pre-trained model and further fine-tuned to make predictions.

Hyperparameter	Model		
	M-BERT	ELECTRA	MuRIL
Learning rate	3e-5	3e-5	3e-5
Batch_size	32	32	32
Optimizer	ADAM	ADAM	ADAM
Epochs	10	10	10
Sequence length	160	160	160

Table 2: Hyperparameter Values

4.1 Text Preprocessing and Tokenization

We have used code-mixed data from HASOC-2021 for training our model. The data given was retrieved from YouTube comments which we cleaned using cleantext[4] library from python for removing unknown characters and ASCII conversions.

We use the tokenization[5] method, which corresponds to the pre-trained models[6] and expects tokens to be in some explicit format.

4.2 Model Description

We have used three pre-trained models named Multilingual BERT (M-BERT) (Kenton et al., 2018), MuRIL (Khanuja et al., 2021) and Electra (Clark et al., 2020) from Google. Among these, the M-BERT and MuRIL were trained on multilingual data. MuRIL was specially trained for the Indian context, with multilingual representations for Indian languages, and they have explicitly augmented monolingual text with translated and transliterated document pairs for training. As shown in Table 2 we used the recommended hyperparameters for all the models.

5 Experiments and Result

We have fine-tuned the pre-trained models for the HASOC 2021 data using the hyperparameters mentioned in Table 2, we have used Adam (Kingma and Ba, 2014) as the optimizer. The experiments were performed on Tesla P100 16GB GPU provided by Kaggle.

Model	Overall F1-Score	F1@30[a]	F1@50[b]	F1@100[c]
MuRIL	0.4489[1]	0.3726	0.2844	0.2968
DLRG-Run1	0.1727	0.3890	0.2522	0.1628

[a]This is character level F1 score calculated for sentences with less than 30 characters

[b]This is character level F1 score calculated for sentences with less than 50 characters but greater than 30 characters

[c]This is character level F1 score calculated for sentences with less than 50 characters but greater than 100 characters

Table 3: Final Results

We initially trained our model with M-BERT for the code-mixed offensive data. This model is used to predict the test data given for identifying offensive/harmful content. The final prediction is interpreted using LIME, which will give a score for each of the words contributing to the offensive and non-offensive contents. Those words contributing to the offensive texts are extracted and predicted for

[3]https://competitions.codalab.org/competitions/31146

[4]https://pypi.org/project/clean-text/

[5]https://huggingface.co/docs/tokenizers/python/latest

[6]http://huggingface.co/models

the given task and its span in the whole comment. We employed a similar procedure for the Electra and MuRIL model; because of the better representation for the Indian context, MuRIL was able to give a more reasonable prediction and we got first position for the same which is given in Table 3. Hence, it got the best score among the others. The Table 3 gives the final score of our MuRIL model and the next best score from participants, and we have not included the scores from M-BERT and Electra as they were not released. The figure 1,2 shows examples of LIME interpretations for given comment text along with contributing words for offensive and not-offensive.

Example Comment text [offensive] :

@USER Ungotha ku rate ellam illa ,free eh othukittu irukan da ungotha thevidiya mundaiyae.

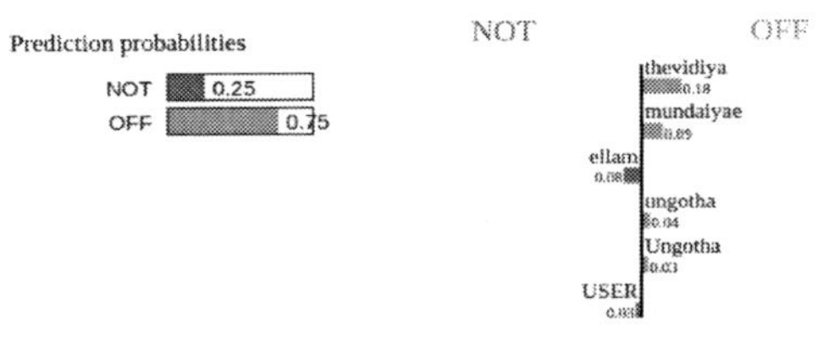

Figure 1: Example of LIME Interpretation for Offensive Class

Example Comment text [Not-offensive]:

*Ellarum Saptacha ..??? *** : Yen Sapadu Vangi kuduka Poriya ?? Unaku RT dhana Venum .... Straight ah Kelu !! Ama..!! Tag #TAG.*

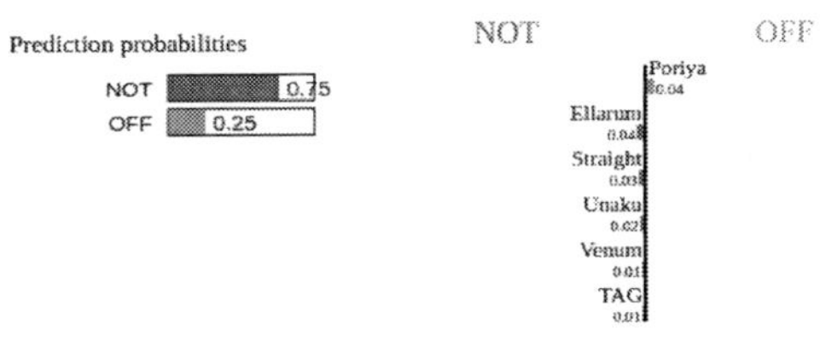

Figure 2: Example of LIME Interpretation for Not-Offensive Class

6 Conclusions and Future Scope

Social media is the primary source from which people use to get information. Hence, the companies that handle these need to moderate content so that the offensive and harmful content are not propagated. In this paper, we have explored the transformer-based model along with LIME interpretations to identify the span of harmful content in comments. Google's MuRIL achieved the best result from different models, which came first in the leaderboard for the shared task. In the future, we would like to explore more on the Code-mixed data and develop improved solutions to this problem.

References

Andrew Arsht and Daniel Etcovitch. 2018. The human cost of online content moderation.

Bharathi Raja Chakravarthi, Prasanna Kumar Kumaresan, Ratnasingam Sakuntharaj, Anand Kumar Madasamy, Sajeetha Thavareesan, Premjith B, Subalalitha Chinnaudayar Navaneethakrishnan, John P. McCrae, and Thomas Mandl. 2021. Overview of the HASOC-DravidianCodeMix Shared Task on Offensive Language Detection in Tamil and Malayalam. In *Working Notes of FIRE 2021 - Forum for Information Retrieval Evaluation*. CEUR.

Bharathi Raja Chakravarthi, Vigneshwaran Muralidaran, Ruba Priyadharshini, and John Philip McCrae. 2020. Corpus creation for sentiment analysis in code-mixed Tamil-English text. In *Proceedings of the 1st Joint Workshop on Spoken Language Technologies for Under-resourced languages (SLTU) and Collaboration and Computing for Under-Resourced Languages (CCURL)*, pages 202–210, Marseille, France. European Language Resources association.

Kevin Clark, Minh-Thang Luong, Quoc V. Le, and Christopher D Manning. 2020. ELECTRA: Pre-training Text Encoders as Discriminators Rather Than Generators.

Sai Muralidhar Jayanthi and Akshat Gupta. 2021. SJ_AJ@DravidianLangTech-EACL2021: Task-adaptive pre-training of multilingual BERT models for offensive language identification. In *Proceedings of the First Workshop on Speech and Language Technologies for Dravidian Languages*, pages 307–312, Kyiv. Association for Computational Linguistics.

Kushal Kedia and Abhilash Nandy. 2021. indicnlp@kgp at DravidianLangTech-EACL2021: Offensive language identification in Dravidian languages. In *Proceedings of the First Workshop on Speech and Language Technologies for Dravidian Languages*, pages 330–335, Kyiv. Association for Computational Linguistics.

Ming-wei Chang Kenton, Lee Kristina, and Jacob Devlin. 2018. BERT: Pre-training of Deep Bidirectional Transformers for Language Understanding. (Mlm).

Simran Khanuja, Diksha Bansal, Sarvesh Mehtani, Savya Khosla, Atreyee Dey, Balaji Gopalan, Dilip Kumar Margam, Pooja Aggarwal, Rajiv Teja Nagipogu, Shachi Dave, Shruti Gupta, Subhash Chandra Bose Gali, Vish Subramanian, and Partha Talukdar. 2021. MuRIL: Multilingual Representations for Indian Languages.

Diederik P Kingma and Jimmy Ba. 2014. Adam: A method for stochastic optimization. *arXiv preprint arXiv:1412.6980.*

John Pavlopoulos, Jeffrey Sorensen, Léo Laugier, and Ion Androutsopoulos. 2021. SemEval-2021 task 5: Toxic spans detection. In *Proceedings of the 15th International Workshop on Semantic Evaluation (SemEval-2021)*, pages 59–69, Online. Association for Computational Linguistics.

Manikandan Ravikiran and Subbiah Annamalai. 2021. DOSA: Dravidian code-mixed offensive span identification dataset. In *Proceedings of the First Workshop on Speech and Language Technologies for Dravidian Languages*, pages 10–17, Kyiv. Association for Computational Linguistics.

Manikandan Ravikiran, Bharathi Raja Chakravarthi, Anand Kumar Madasamy, Sangeetha Sivanesan, Ratnavel Rajalakshmi, Sajeetha Thavareesan, Rahul Ponnusamy, and Shankar Mahadevan. 2022. Findings of the shared task on Toxic Span Identification in Tamil. In *Proceedings of the Second Workshop on Speech and Language Technologies for Dravidian Languages*. Association for Computational Linguistics.

Marco Tulio Ribeiro, Sameer Singh, and Carlos Guestrin. 2016. "why should I trust you?": Explaining the predictions of any classifier. In *Proceedings of the 22nd ACM SIGKDD International Conference on Knowledge Discovery and Data Mining, San Francisco, CA, USA, August 13-17, 2016*, pages 1135–1144.

Debjoy Saha, Naman Paharia, Debajit Chakraborty, Punyajoy Saha, and Animesh Mukherjee. 2021. Hate-alert@DravidianLangTech-EACL2021: Ensembling strategies for transformer-based offensive language detection. In *Proceedings of the First Workshop on Speech and Language Technologies for Dravidian Languages*, pages 270–276, Kyiv. Association for Computational Linguistics.

Omar Sharif, Eftekhar Hossain, and Mohammed Moshiul Hoque. 2021. NLP-CUET@DravidianLangTech-EACL2021: Offensive language detection from multilingual code-mixed text using transformers. In *Proceedings of the First Workshop on Speech and Language Technologies for Dravidian Languages*, pages 255–261, Kyiv. Association for Computational Linguistics.

Yingjia Zhao and Xin Tao. 2021. ZYJ123@DravidianLangTech-EACL2021: Offensive language identification based on XLM-RoBERTa with DPCNN. In *Proceedings of the First Workshop on Speech and Language Technologies for Dravidian Languages*, pages 216–221, Kyiv. Association for Computational Linguistics.

TeamX@DravidianLangTech-ACL2022: A Comparative Analysis for Troll-Based Meme Classification

Rabindra Nath Nandi[1], **Firoj Alam**[2], **Preslav Nakov**[2]
[1]BJIT Limited, Dhaka, Bangladesh
[2]Qatar Computing Research Institute, HBKU, Doha, Qatar
rabindra.nath@bjitgroup.com, {falam,pnakov}@hbku.edu.qa

Abstract

The spread of fake news, propaganda, misinformation, disinformation, and harmful content online raised concerns among social media platforms, government agencies, policymakers, and society as a whole. This is because such harmful or abusive content leads to several consequences to people such as physical, emotional, relational, and financial. Among different harmful content *trolling-based* online content is one of them, where the idea is to post a message that is provocative, offensive, or menacing with an intent to mislead the audience. The content can be textual, visual, a combination of both, or a meme. In this study, we provide a comparative analysis of troll-based memes classification using the textual, visual, and multimodal content. We report several interesting findings in terms of code-mixed text, multimodal setting, and combining an additional dataset, which shows improvements over the majority baseline.

1 Introduction

Social media have become one of the main communication channels for the propagation of information through textual, visual, or audio-visual content. While the content shared on social media creates a positive impact, however, there are also content that spread harm and hostility (Brooke, 2019), including abusive language (Mubarak et al., 2017), propaganda (Da San Martino et al., 2020, 2019) cyberbullying (Van Hee et al., 2015), cyber-aggression (Kumar et al., 2018), and other kinds of harmful content (Pramanick et al., 2021). The propagation of such content most often is done by an automated tool, troll, or coordinated groups, which target specific users, communities (e.g., minority groups), individuals, and companies. To detect such content there has been effort to develop automatic tools (see most recent surveys on disinformation (Alam et al., 2021c), rumours (Bondielli and Marcelloni, 2019), propaganda (Da San Martino et al., 2020), and multimodal memes (Afridi et al., 2021), hate speech (Fortuna and Nunes, 2018), cyberbullying (Haidar et al., 2016), and offensive content (Husain and Uzuner, 2021). In addition, shared tasks has also been organized in the past years addressing factuality, fake news and harmful content (Nakov et al., 2021; Kiela et al., 2020).

Among other social media content, recently, the uses of *internet memes* became popular and they are often shared for the purpose of humor or fun with no bad intentions. However, memes are also created and shared with harmful intentions. This include attack on people based on the characteristics such as ethnicity, race, sex, gender identity, disability, disease, nationality, and immigration status (Kiela et al., 2020). There has been research effort to develop computational method to detect such memes, such as detecting hateful memes (Kiela et al., 2020), propaganda (Dimitrov et al., 2021a,b), offensive (Suryawanshi et al., 2020a), sexist meme (Fersini et al., 2019) and troll based meme (Suryawanshi and Chakravarthi, 2021).

In this study, we focus on troll-based meme classification based on the dataset released in the shared task discussed in (Suryawanshi et al., 2022). While meme contains both textual and visual elements, hence, we investigate textual, visual content and their combination using different pretraind transformer models. In addition, we explored combining an external dataset, and use of code-mixed text (i.e., Tamil and English) extracted using OCR. Note that the text provided with the dataset is transcribed in Latin. While prior work focuses on the text provided with the dataset, here, we also follow a different strategy, directly using the text from the OCR without any cleaning.

Our contributions include:

- we investigate classical algorithm (e.g., SVM), pretraind transformer and deep CNN models for both text and images, respectively;

Proceedings of the Second Workshop on Speech and Language Technologies for Dravidian Languages, pages 79 - 85

- we combine an additional dataset and use code-mixed text, extracted using OCR and compare the performance;
- we also experiment with different pretrained multimodal models.

2 Related Work

Prior work on detecting harmful aspects of memes include categorizing hateful memes (Kiela et al., 2020), antisemitism (Chandra et al., 2021) and propaganda detection techniques in memes (Dimitrov et al., 2021a), harmful memes and their target (Pramanick et al., 2021), identifying protected category such as race, sex that has been attacked (Zia et al., 2021), and identifying offensive content (Suryawanshi et al., 2020a). Among the studies most notable effort that streamlined the research work include shared tasks such as "Hateful Memes Challenge" (Kiela et al., 2020), detection of persuasion techniques (Dimitrov et al., 2021b) and troll meme classification (Suryawanshi and Chakravarthi, 2021).

The work by Chandra et al. (2021) investigates antisemitism along with its types by addressing the tasks as binary and multi-class classification using pretrained transformers and CNN as modality-specific encoders along with various multimodal fusion strategies. Dimitrov et al. (2021a) developed a dataset with 22 propaganda techniques and investigates the different state-of-the-art pretrained models and demonstrate that joint vision-language models perform best. Pramanick et al. (2021) address two tasks such as detecting harmful memes and identifying the social entities they target and propose a multimodal model, which utilizes local and global information. Zia et al. (2021) goes one step further than a binary classification of hateful memes – more fine-grained categorization based on protected category (i.e., race, disability, religion, nationality, sex) and their attack types (i.e., contempt, mocking, inferiority, slurs, exclusion, dehumanizing, inciting violence) using the dataset released in the WOAH 2020 Shared Task.[1] Fersini et al. (2019) studied sexist meme detection and investigate textual cues with a late-fusion strategy, which suggest that fusion approach performs better. The same authors also developed a dataset of 800 misogynistic memes covering different manifestations of hatred against women (e.g., body shaming, stereotyping, objectification and violence), which are collected from different social media (Gasparini et al., 2021).

In the "Hateful Memes Challenge", the participants addressed the hateful meme classification task by fine-tuning the state-of-art multi-modal transformer models (Kiela et al., 2021) and best system in the competition used different unimodal and multimodal pre-training models such as VisualBERT (Li et al., 2019) VL-BERT (Su et al., 2019), UNITER (Chen et al., 2019), VILLA (Gan et al., 2020) and ensembles (Kiela et al., 2021). The SemEval-2021 propaganda detection shared task (Dimitrov et al., 2021b) was organized with a focus on fine-grained propaganda techniques in text and the entire meme, and from the participants' systems, they conclude that multimodal cues are important for automated propaganda detection. In the troll meme classification shared task (Suryawanshi and Chakravarthi, 2021), the best system used ResNet152, BERT with multimodal attention, and the majority of the system used pretrained transformer models for text, CNN models for images, and early fusion approaches.

3 Experiments

3.1 Data

We use the dataset provided in the troll-based Tamil meme classification shared task discussed in (Suryawanshi et al., 2020b, 2022). The dataset is comprised of meme and transcribed text in Latin, which are annotated and transcribed by native Tamil speakers. There is a total of 2,300, 667 memes for training and testing, respectively. For our experiments, we split the training set into training and development set with 80 and 20%, respectively. The development set is used for fine-tuning the models.

In Table 1, we report the distribution of the dataset that we used for the experiments.

Class	Train	Dev	Test
Troll	1013	269	395
Non-Troll	827	191	272

Table 1: Distribution of the Troll-based Tamil Meme dataset. We split original training set into training and development set.

[1] github.com/facebookresearch/fine_grained_hateful_memes

3.2 Settings

For the classification, we run different unimodal experiments: *(i)* only text, *(ii)* only meme, and *(iii)* text and meme together. For each setting, we also run several baseline experiments. One such baseline is the *majority class* baseline, which predicts the label based on the most frequent label in the training set. This has been most commonly used in shared tasks (Nakov et al., 2021). Furthermore, we run a few advanced experiments using an additional dataset and code-mixed text from OCR. To measure the performance of each model we used a weighted F_1 score to maintain shared task guideline.

3.2.1 Text Modality

For the baseline using text modality, we used bag-of-n-gram vectors weighted with logarithmic term frequencies (tf) multiplied with inverse document frequencies (idf) and train the model using Support Vector Machines (SVM) (Platt, 1998). Note that we extracted unigram, bigram, and tri-gram features. We used grid search to optimize the SVM hyper-parameters.

We then experiment using multilingual BERT (mBERT) model (Devlin et al., 2019). We performed ten reruns for each experiment using different random seeds, then we picked the model that performed best on the development set. We used a batch size of 8, a learning rate of 2e-5, maximum sequence length 128, three epochs, and used the 'categorical cross-entropy' as the loss function.

3.2.2 Image Modality

Similar to the text modality, for the baseline experiment with image modality, we extract features from a pre-trained model, then train the model using SVM. We extracted features from the penultimate layer of the EfficientNet (b1) model (Tan and Le, 2019), which was trained using ImageNet. For training the model using SVM we used the default parameters setting.

For the later experiments we used the transfer learning approach, fine-tuning the pre-trained deep CNN models (e.g., VGG16), which has been shown success for visual recognition tasks. We used the weights of the model pre-trained on ImageNet to initialize our model. We adapt the last layer (i.e., softmax layer) of the network for the binary classification task. We trained models using three popular neural network architectures such as VGG16 (Simonyan and Zisserman, 2015), ResNet101 (He et al., 2016) and EfficientNet (Tan and Le, 2019), which showed state-of-art performance in similar tasks (Ofli et al., 2020; Alam et al., 2021a,b). For training, we used the Adam optimizer (Kingma and Ba, 2015) with an initial learning rate of 10^{-5}, which is decreased by a factor of 10 when accuracy on the dev set stops improving for 10 epochs. From our experiment, we observe that the model converse within 50-60 epochs. As the dataset size is small, fine-tuning the entire network did not yield better results, therefore, we freeze the network and fine-tune the penultimate layer.

3.2.3 Multimodal: Text and Image

For the multimodel experiments, we used Vision Transformer (ViT) (Kolesnikov et al., 2021) for image feature encoding and multilingual BERT (mBERT) for the textual representation. We used BLOCK fusion (Ben-younes et al., 2019) to merge the features from two different modalities. BLOCK fusion is a multimodal fusion based on block-superdiagonal tensor decomposition. Previously, Kolesnikov et al. (2021) showed a better performance using BLOCK fusion over several bilinear fusion techniques for Visual Question Answering (VQA) and Visual Relationship Detection (VRD) tasks. We conduct two major experiments by varying the textual data, *(i)* using the provided text, and *(ii)* using the code-mixed text.

3.2.4 Additional Experiments

Code-mixed Tamil and English text: The dataset comes with extracted text in a transcribed form in Latin. Given that current multilingual transformer models have not trained using such a latin form of text, therefore, to further understand the problem we extract text from memes using *tesseract* (Smith, 2007).[2] We then train the same mBERT model using the extracted code-mixed Tamil and English text. Note that the extracted text contains noise that comes from the output of the OCR.

Additional data: While we visually inspected the dataset we realized that textual and visual elements of memes have similarities with memes in hateful meme dataset (Kiela et al., 2020). We then mapped the labels from hateful memes dataset to troll labels, *(i) hateful* to *troll*, and *(ii) not-hateful* to *non-troll*. We combined all training and test set memes from the hateful memes dataset with the training set of the troll meme dataset. The dev set

[2] `https://pypi.org/project/pytesseract/`

Exp	Acc	P	R	F1
Maj.	59.2	35.1	59.2	44.1
Text modality				
Tf-Idf + SVM	46.2	47.9	46.2	**46.6**
mBERT	52.6	51.0	52.6	**51.4**
Add. data + mBERT	56.5	52.8	56.5	**51.8**
Code-mixed text + mBERT	57.3	55.2	57.3	**55.2**
Image modality				
EffNet feat +SVM	59.1	55.6	59.1	**50.1**
VGG16	55.8	50.2	55.8	**49.2**
ResNet101	60.4	58.6	60.4	**53.8**
EffNet (b1)	61.5	61.5	61.5	**53.6**
Multimodality				
ViT + mBERT	57.9	55.1	57.9	**54.2**
ViT + mBERT (code-mixed text)	55.3	57.0	55.3	**55.7**
Image modality + Additional data				
VGG16	54.4	52.0	54.4	**52.3**
ResNet101	60.7	58.9	60.7	**56.2**
EffNet (b1)	60.7	58.9	60.7	**<u>56.6</u>**

Table 2: Evaluation results on the test set. The results that improve over the majority class baseline are in **bold**, and the best one is underlined. Maj.: Majority baseline, Add. data: Additional data.

of the hateful meme dataset is combined with the dev set of the troll dataset. After combining the datasets we experiment with both text and image modalities using the same models.

4 Results and Discussion

In Table 2, we present the results for different modalities and settings. Overall, all results are better than majority baseline. In the unimodal experiments, the image-only models perform better than the text-only models. Our experiments on text-only models suggest that code-mixed data help in improving the performance using the same multiligual mBERT model compared to the transcribed latin text, which suggest that multilingual model is not able to capture the information in latin Tamil text. The additional data, which is in English only, slightly improved the performance for text-only experiment.

For the image-only experiments, we obtain a comparative performance with ResNet101 and EfficientNet (EffNet (b1)).

Our experiments on multimodel experiments provide better results compared to text and image modalities as shown in the Table 2. For the two multimodel experiments, we obtained weighted-F1 scores of 54.2 and 55.7 for text and for code-mixed text, respectively, which are better than the best weighted-F1 score from text modality (51.4) and from image modality (53.8). Note that, the performance of our multimodel experiments is better than Hegde et al. (2021), where a weighted F1 score of 0.47 has been reported for a similar task. That implies BLOCK fusion has advantages over late fusion for troll meme classification tasks.

With additional data, results improved significantly for all image-only models. It confirms our observation that visual elements in memes share information across different datasets, and possibly different cultures too.

Our future plan is to apply the data augmentation technique for multimodality experiments and also we have a plan to explore the performance of popular multimodel algorithms.

During the shared task participation, we submitted one run, using only image modality, where our system was not showing promising performance. However, our subsequent experiments and analysis show several promising directions in terms of original code-mixed data and additional data from the other task.

5 Conclusion and Future Work

We present a comparative analysis of different modalities for the troll-based meme classification task. We show that the multilingual model capture more information for code-mixed text than its Latin counterpart. We present higher performance with multimodality compared to unimodal models. Our experiments also suggest that additional data from the other task helps in capturing visual information. In the future, we plan to further develop multimodal models that can capture information in code-mixed noisy conditions.

References

Tariq Habib Afridi, Aftab Alam, Muhammad Numan Khan, Jawad Khan, and Young Koo Lee. 2021. A multimodal memes classification: A survey and open research issues. In *5th International Conference on Smart City Applications, SCA 2020*, pages 1451–1466. Springer Science and Business Media Deutschland GmbH.

Firoj Alam, Tanvirul Alam, Md Hasan, Abul Hasnat, Muhammad Imran, Ferda Ofli, et al. 2021a. MEDIC: a multi-task learning dataset for disaster image classification. *arXiv:2108.12828*.

Firoj Alam, Tanvirul Alam, Muhammad Imran, and Ferda Ofli. 2021b. Robust training of social media image classification models for rapid disaster response. *arXiv:2104.04184*.

Firoj Alam, Stefano Cresci, Tanmoy Chakraborty, Fabrizio Silvestri, Dimiter Dimitrov, Giovanni Da San Martino, Shaden Shaar, Hamed Firooz, and Preslav Nakov. 2021c. A survey on multimodal disinformation detection. *arXiv:2103.12541*.

Hedi Ben-younes, Remi Cadene, Nicolas Thome, and Matthieu Cord. 2019. Block:bilinear superdiagonal fusion for visual question answeringand visual relationship detection. In *Proceedings of the 33st Conference on Artificial Intelligence (AAAI)*, volume 15.

Alessandro Bondielli and Francesco Marcelloni. 2019. A survey on fake news and rumour detection techniques. *Information Sciences*, 497:38–55.

Sian Brooke. 2019. "Condescending, Rude, Assholes": Framing gender and hostility on Stack Overflow. In *Proceedings of the Third Workshop on Abusive Language Online*, pages 172–180, Florence, Italy. Association for Computational Linguistics.

Mohit Chandra, Dheeraj Pailla, Himanshu Bhatia, Aadilmehdi Sanchawala, Manish Gupta, Manish Shrivastava, and Ponnurangam Kumaraguru. 2021. "Subverting the Jewtocracy": Online antisemitism detection using multimodal deep learning. *arXiv:2104.05947*.

Yen-Chun Chen, Linjie Li, Licheng Yu, Ahmed El Kholy, Faisal Ahmed, Zhe Gan, Yu Cheng, and Jingjing Liu. 2019. UNITER: Learning universal image-text representations.

Giovanni Da San Martino, Stefano Cresci, Alberto Barrón-Cedeño, Seunghak Yu, Roberto Di Pietro, and Preslav Nakov. 2020. A survey on computational propaganda detection. In *Proceedings of the Twenty-Ninth International Joint Conference on Artificial Intelligence, IJCAI 2020*, pages 4826–4832. ijcai.org.

Giovanni Da San Martino, Seunghak Yu, Alberto Barrón-Cedeño, Rostislav Petrov, and Preslav Nakov. 2019. Fine-grained analysis of propaganda in news article. In *Proceedings of the 2019 Conference on Empirical Methods in Natural Language Processing and the 9th International Joint Conference on Natural Language Processing (EMNLP-IJCNLP)*, pages 5636–5646, Hong Kong, China. Association for Computational Linguistics.

Jacob Devlin, Ming-Wei Chang, Kenton Lee, and Kristina Toutanova. 2019. BERT: Pre-training of deep bidirectional transformers for language understanding. In *Proceedings of the 2019 Conference of the North American Chapter of the Association for Computational Linguistics: Human Language Technologies, Volume 1 (Long and Short Papers)*, pages 4171–4186, Minneapolis, Minnesota. Association for Computational Linguistics.

Dimitar Dimitrov, Bishr Bin Ali, Shaden Shaar, Firoj Alam, Fabrizio Silvestri, Hamed Firooz, Preslav Nakov, and Giovanni Da San Martino. 2021a. Detecting propaganda techniques in memes. In *Proceedings of the 59th Annual Meeting of the Association for Computational Linguistics and the 11th International Joint Conference on Natural Language Processing*, ACL-IJCNLP '21, pages 6603–6617, Online. Association for Computational Linguistics.

Dimitar Dimitrov, Bishr Bin Ali, Shaden Shaar, Firoj Alam, Fabrizio Silvestri, Hamed Firooz, Preslav Nakov, and Giovanni Da San Martino. 2021b. Task 6 at SemEval-2021: Detection of persuasion techniques in texts and images. In *Proceedings of the 15th International Workshop on Semantic Evaluation*, SemEval '21, Bangkok, Thailand. Association for Computational Linguistics.

Elisabetta Fersini, Francesca Gasparini, and Silvia Corchs. 2019. Detecting sexist meme on the web: A study on textual and visual cues. In *2019 8th International Conference on Affective Computing and Intelligent Interaction Workshops and Demos (ACIIW)*, pages 226–231. IEEE.

Paula Fortuna and Sérgio Nunes. 2018. A survey on automatic detection of hate speech in text. *ACM Computing Surveys (CSUR)*, 51(4):1–30.

Zhe Gan, Yen-Chun Chen, Linjie Li, Chen Zhu, Yu Cheng, and Jingjing Liu. 2020. Large-scale adversarial training for vision-and-language representation learning. *Advances in Neural Information Processing Systems*, 33:6616–6628.

Francesca Gasparini, Giulia Rizzi, Aurora Saibene, and Elisabetta Fersini. 2021. Benchmark dataset of memes with text transcriptions for automatic detection of multi-modal misogynistic content. *CoRR*, abs/2106.08409.

Batoul Haidar, Maroun Chamoun, and Fadi Yamout. 2016. Cyberbullying detection: A survey on multilingual techniques. In *2016 European Modelling Symposium (EMS)*, pages 165–171.

Kaiming He, Xiangyu Zhang, Shaoqing Ren, and Jian Sun. 2016. Deep residual learning for image recognition. In *Proceedings of the IEEE conference on computer vision and pattern recognition*, pages 770–778.

Siddhanth U Hegde, Adeep Hande, Ruba Priyadharshini, Sajeetha Thavareesan, and Bharathi Raja Chakravarthi. 2021. Uvce-iiitt@ dravidianlangtech-eacl2021: Tamil troll meme classification: You need to pay more attention. In *Proceedings of the First Workshop on Speech and Language Technologies for Dravidian Languages*, pages 180–186.

Fatemah Husain and Ozlem Uzuner. 2021. A survey of offensive language detection for the arabic language. *ACM Transactions on Asian and Low-Resource Language Information Processing (TALLIP)*, 20(1):1–44.

Douwe Kiela, Hamed Firooz, Aravind Mohan, Vedanuj Goswami, Amanpreet Singh, Casey A Fitzpatrick, Peter Bull, Greg Lipstein, Tony Nelli, Ron Zhu, et al. 2021. The hateful memes challenge: competition report. In *NeurIPS 2020 Competition and Demonstration Track*, pages 344–360. PMLR.

Douwe Kiela, Hamed Firooz, Aravind Mohan, Vedanuj Goswami, Amanpreet Singh, Pratik Ringshia, and Davide Testuggine. 2020. The hateful memes challenge: Detecting hate speech in multimodal memes. In *Advances in Neural Information Processing Systems*, Online.

Diederik P. Kingma and Jimmy Ba. 2015. Adam: A method for stochastic optimization. In *International Conference on Learning Representations*.

Alexander Kolesnikov, Alexey Dosovitskiy, Dirk Weissenborn, Georg Heigold, Jakob Uszkoreit, Lucas Beyer, Matthias Minderer, Mostafa Dehghani, Neil Houlsby, Sylvain Gelly, Thomas Unterthiner, and Xiaohua Zhai. 2021. An image is worth 16x16 words: Transformers for image recognition at scale. In *International Conference on Learning Representations*.

Ritesh Kumar, Atul Kr Ojha, Shervin Malmasi, and Marcos Zampieri. 2018. Benchmarking aggression identification in social media. In *Proceedings of the First Workshop on Trolling, Aggression and Cyberbullying*, pages 1–11.

Liunian Harold Li, Mark Yatskar, Da Yin, Cho-Jui Hsieh, and Kai-Wei Chang. 2019. VisualBERT: A simple and performant baseline for vision and language. *arXiv:1908.03557*.

Hamdy Mubarak, Kareem Darwish, and Walid Magdy. 2017. Abusive language detection on arabic social media. In *Proceedings of the first workshop on abusive language online*, pages 52–56.

Preslav Nakov, Da San Martino Giovanni, Tamer Elsayed, Alberto Barrón-Cedeño, Rubén Míguez, Shaden Shaar, Firoj Alam, Fatima Haouari, Maram Hasanain, Watheq Mansour, Bayan Hamdan, Zien Sheikh Ali, Nikolay Babulkov, Alex Nikolov, Gautam Kishore Shahi, Julia Maria Struß, Thomas Mandl, Mucahid Kutlu, and Yavuz Selim Kartal. 2021. Overview of the CLEF-2021 CheckThat! lab on detecting check-worthy claims, previously fact-checked claims, and fake news. LNCS (12880). Springer.

Ferda Ofli, Firoj Alam, and Muhammad Imran. 2020. Analysis of social media data using multimodal deep learning for disaster response. In *Proceedings of the Information Systems for Crisis Response and Management*.

John Platt. 1998. Sequential minimal optimization: A fast algorithm for training support vector machines.

Shraman Pramanick, Shivam Sharma, Dimitar Dimitrov, Md. Shad Akhtar, Preslav Nakov, and Tanmoy Chakraborty. 2021. MOMENTA: A multimodal framework for detecting harmful memes and their targets. In *Findings of the Association for Computational Linguistics: EMNLP 2021*, pages 4439–4455, Punta Cana, Dominican Republic. Association for Computational Linguistics.

Karen Simonyan and Andrew Zisserman. 2015. Very deep convolutional networks for large-scale image recognition. In *3rd International Conference on Learning Representations*, an Diego, CA, USA.

Ray Smith. 2007. An overview of the tesseract ocr engine. In *Ninth international conference on document analysis and recognition*, volume 2, pages 629–633.

Weijie Su, Xizhou Zhu, Yue Cao, Bin Li, Lewei Lu, Furu Wei, and Jifeng Dai. 2019. VL-BERT: Pre-training of generic visual-linguistic representations. *arXiv:1908.08530*.

Shardul Suryawanshi and Bharathi Raja Chakravarthi. 2021. Findings of the shared task on Troll Meme Classification in Tamil. In *Proceedings of the First Workshop on Speech and Language Technologies for Dravidian Languages*. Association for Computational Linguistics.

Shardul Suryawanshi, Bharathi Raja Chakravarthi, Mihael Arcan, and Paul Buitelaar. 2020a. Multimodal meme dataset (MultiOFF) for identifying offensive content in image and text. In *Proceedings of the Second Workshop on Trolling, Aggression and Cyberbullying*, pages 32–41, Marseille, France. European Language Resources Association (ELRA).

Shardul Suryawanshi, Bharathi Raja Chakravarthi, Mihael Arcan, Susan Levy, Paul Buitaleer, Prasanna Kumar Kumaresan, Rahul Ponnusamy, and Adeep Hande. 2022. Findings of the second shared task on Troll Meme Classification in Tamil. In *Proceedings of the Second Workshop on Speech and Language Technologies for Dravidian Languages*. Association for Computational Linguistics.

Shardul Suryawanshi, Bharathi Raja Chakravarthi, Pranav Verma, Mihael Arcan, John Philip McCrae, and Paul Buitelaar. 2020b. A dataset for troll classification of TamilMemes. In *Proceedings of the WILDRE5– 5th Workshop on Indian Language Data: Resources and Evaluation*, pages 7–13, Marseille, France. European Language Resources Association (ELRA).

Mingxing Tan and Quoc V Le. 2019. EfficientNet: rethinking model scaling for convolutional neural networks. *arXiv:1905.11946*.

Cynthia Van Hee, Els Lefever, Ben Verhoeven, Julie Mennes, Bart Desmet, Guy De Pauw, Walter Daelemans, and Veronique Hoste. 2015. Detection and fine-grained classification of cyberbullying events. In *Proceedings of the International Conference Recent Advances in Natural Language Processing*, pages 672–680, Hissar, Bulgaria. INCOMA Ltd. Shoumen, BULGARIA.

Haris Bin Zia, Ignacio Castro, and Gareth Tyson. 2021. Racist or sexist meme? classifying memes beyond hateful. In *Proceedings of the 5th Workshop on Online Abuse and Harms (WOAH 2021)*, pages 215–219, Online. Association for Computational Linguistics.

GJG@TamilNLP-ACL2022: Emotion Analysis and Classification in Tamil using Transformers

Janvi Prasad*
Vellore Institute of Technology
Vellore, India
janvi.prasad@gmail.com

Gaurang Prasad*
wikiHow Inc.
Palo Alto, CA, USA
gaurang@wikihow.com

Gunavathi Chellamuthu
Vellore Institute of Technology
Vellore, India
gunavathi.cm@vit.ac.in

Abstract

This paper describes the systems built by our team for the "Emotion Analysis in Tamil" shared task at the Second Workshop on Speech and Language Technologies for Dravidian Languages at ACL 2022. There were two multi-class classification sub-tasks as a part of this shared task. The dataset for sub-task A contained 11 types of emotions while sub-task B was more fine-grained with 31 emotions. We fine-tuned an XLM-RoBERTa and DeBERTA base model for each sub-task. For sub-task A, the XLM-RoBERTa model achieved an accuracy of 0.46 and the DeBERTa model achieved an accuracy of 0.45. We had the best classification performance out of 11 teams for sub-task A. For sub-task B, the XLM-RoBERTa model's accuracy was 0.33 and the DeBERTa model had an accuracy of 0.26. We ranked 2nd out of 7 teams for sub-task B.

1 Introduction

Emotions are a fundamental component of any language that are used to express how people feel about different things. Emotion detection and classification has becomes an important task in the field of Natural Language Processing (NLP) (Chakravarthi et al., 2021). Emotion analysis enables the improved understanding of user-generated text and has applications in understanding public opinions, healthcare, development of voice and language-based assistants, recommendation engines, etc (Chakravarthi, 2020; Chakravarthi and Muralidaran, 2021a).

Over the past two decades, the internet has become the central avenue for communication. With the advent of web-based services and digital publication platforms, the volume of text-based content across all languages have sky rocketed (B and A, 2021b,a). This not only includes articles, blog posts, and scientific publications, but also user-generated opinions and comments in social networks (Priyadharshini et al., 2021; Kumaresan et al., 2021). People who feel apprehensive about in-person conversations and physical interactions also rely on social media to express their thoughts (Sampath et al., 2022; Ravikiran et al., 2022; Chakravarthi et al., 2022; Bharathi et al., 2022; Priyadharshini et al., 2022). Due to this, social media has become a modern channel of public expression for the people irrespective of the socio-economic boundaries (Priyadharshini et al., 2020). These mediums are not only used to express constructive and positive emotions but also a lot of negativity and hatred (Ghanghor et al., 2021a,b; Yasaswini et al., 2021). A lot of communities express these emotions in their native language. Identifying all these different kinds of emotions is extremely important for the development and improvement of software systems, NLP models, and Human-Computer Interaction.

India is a vast, multi-cultural, and multi-lingual country. A substantial amount of research work has been done for text classification tasks in global languages like English, Spanish, and Mandarin. There has also been NLP-research for Indian languages like Hindi and Urdu (Anita and Subalalitha, 2019b,a; Subalalitha and Poovammal, 2018). However, very little work has been done for Dravidian languages. Dravidian languages are a big part of the Indian culture. Even outside India, they are used in multiple regions for digital and in-person communication and publication (Sakuntharaj and Mahesan, 2021, 2017, 2016; Thavareesan and Mahesan, 2019, 2020a,b, 2021).

The lack of research in Dravidian Language NLP tasks is largely due to the lack of annotated

*These authors contributed equally to this work

Proceedings of the Second Workshop on Speech and Language Technologies for Dravidian Languages, pages 86 - 92
May 26, 2022

datasets. This task provides two datasets for researchers to work with - one coarse-grained and one fine-grained. The availability and publication of such datasets and shared tasks invites multiple approaches to solve downsteam NLP tasks for a Dravidian language like Tamil (Subalalitha, 2019; Srinivasan and Subalalitha, 2019; Narasimhan et al., 2018). In this shared task, we participated in both the sub-tasks: the coarse-grained classification sub-task A with 11 classes, and the fine-grained sub-task B with 31 output classes. The goal of our work is to demonstrate the performance of fine-tuning large pre-trained transformer-based models for a text-classification task in Tamil. We train an XLM-RoBERTa and DeBERTa model, both of which are pre-trained models, for each sub-task on the given train splits, optimize parameters, and evaluate their performance on the respective test splits (Conneau et al., 2019; He et al., 2021).

The rest of our paper is organized as follows: we discuss related work in Tamil emotion recognition, describe the datasets, our methodology, and conclude with the results and performance metrics.

We provide a link to our models and evaluations to provide reproducability, and empower future research in this space[1]. We hope to build on the learnings from this shared task to architect and build models specifically for downstream Tamil NLP tasks.

2 Related Work

There has been a lot of work in emotion analysis and classification for high-resource languages. Even for a low-resource language like Tamil, there have been multiple published works. Renjith and Manju (2017) used Cepstral Coefficients (LPCC) along with Neural Networks to detect emotions. They demonstrated higher accuracy with Hurst parameters as compared to LPCC, when considering individual features for a language like Tamil. Ram and Ponnusamy (2014) used Support Vector Machine (SVM) for emotion recognition in Tamil. They used Cepstral Coefficients for training their model. Sowmya and Rajeswari (2019) extracted features from Tamil audio signals and trained an SVM classifier. They demonstrated a classification accuracy of 85.4%. Saste and Jagdale (2017) also trained an SVM classifier using a feature vector formed by fusion of MFCCs and DWT. Poorna et al. (2018) demonstrated a weight-based emotion recognition system using audio signals for three South Indian languages. They used K-Nearest Neighbor, SVM, and a Neural Network as their classification models. Srikanth et al. (2017) proposed a Deep Belief Network (DBN) over Gaussian Mixture model (GMM) for Tamil emotion recognition. Fernandes and Mannepalli (2021) trained four LSTM-based models for emotion recognition in Tamil speech. They found that Deep Hierarchical LSTM and BiLSTM (DHLB) achieves the highest precision of about 84%. All of the aforementioned research has been focused on emotion detection and recognition using speech signals or features extracted from Tamil speech signals.

There has also been some work in emotion and sentiment analysis based on Tamil text. Raveendirarasa and Amalraj (2020) used sub-word level LSTM to build a behavioural profile for Facebook users, to be able to detect sentiment from Facebook comments. Priyadharshini et al. (2021) presented the findings of the shared task on sentiment analysis in Tamil, Malayalam, and Kannada. Chakravarthi and Muralidaran (2021b) presented the findings of a shared task on hope speech detection. These also focus on text classification tasks in Tamil, but emphasize other emotional and sentimental classes.

There have also been multiple published work that fine-tunes XLM-RoBERTa for text classification tasks. Zhao and Tao (2021) proposed a system using XLM-RoBERTa and DPCNN for detecting offensive text in Dravidian languages. Qu et al. (2021) used TextCNN and XLM-RoBERTa from emotion classification in Spanish. Ou and Li (2020) also demonstrated using XLM-RoBERTa for a hate speech identification classification task.

The number of published works using DeBERTa is fewer than that of XLM-RoBERTa. There have been some studies that use DeBERTa for entity extraction and text-classification tasks. (Martin and Pedersen, 2021; Khan et al., 2022)

3 Data

The annotated training and development datasets, for both the sub-tasks, were provided by the workshop organizers. The testing dataset, without labels, was released a few days prior to the run submission deadline for the teams to run their models on. Once the results were announced, the organizers released the labeled test dataset for

[1]https://tinyurl.com/GJGEmotionAnalysis

Label	Count	Label	Count
Neutral	4841	Anticipation	828
Joy	2134	Sadness	695
Ambiguous	1689	Love	675
Trust	1254	Surprise	248
Disgust	910	Fear	100
Anger	834		

Table 1: Classification labels for sub-task A and the number of rows under each label in the training set.

validation and verification purposes.

The datasets for both the sub-tasks consisted of Tamil sentences obtained from social media comments. A post/ row within the corpus may contain one or more sentences. However, the organizers ensured that the average sentence length of the corpora was 1. The annotations in the corpus were made at a comment / post level (Sampath et al., 2022). The posts could also contain extended words, emojis, and other special characters. The grammatical and lexical accuracy of the sentences were unchanged, in order to be representative of user-generated social media comments.

3.1 Sub-Task A

Sub-task A, the coarse-grained classification task, had a total of 11 output classes/ labels. The training dataset had a total of 14,208 rows while the development dataset had 3,552 rows. The test dataset had 4,440 rows. The classification labels along with the total count in the train set are represented in Table 1. The entire dataset was annotated with English labels, as compared to the sentences - which were in Tamil.

3.2 Sub-Task B

Sub-task B was significantly more fine-grained as compared to the sub-task A and contained a total of 31 output classes/ labels. Unlike sub-task A, the class labels for this sub-task were in Tamil and not English. The training dataset had a total of 30,179 rows, making it much larger than the training split for the coarse-grained classification task. The development dataset had 4,269 rows and the test dataset had 4,269 rows. Table 2 represents all the class labels in the train split (translated to English) along with the total number of rows in each label.

Label	Count	Label	Count
Admiration	4760	Caring	497
Realization	3499	Embarrass	484
Anticipation	2191	Sadness	470
Teasing	2128	Love	453
Approval	1853	Disappoint	422
Anger	1738	Disapproval	421
Annoyance	1277	Disgust	343
Joy	1276	Optimism	292
Neutral	1232	Fear	288
Pride	963	Grief	259
Gratitude	880	Nervous	255
Curiosity	782	Relief	238
Trust	713	Remorse	235
Confusion	709	Surprise	201
Amusement	625	Desire	147
Excitement	548		

Table 2: Translated classification labels for sub-task B and the number of rows under each in the training set.

4 Methodology

For each classification sub-task, we fine-tune an XLM-RoBERTa and DeBERTa base model on sentences from the training splits to create a classification model. We do not remove any stop words, special characters, or emojis from the test splits, in order to preserve the context of the comment. Extended train of special characters (examples: !!!, ..., etc.) and emojis provide useful context, especially for an emotion analysis task.

XLM-RoBERTa is a multilingual version of RoBERTa, which in itself was an improvement over BERT to achieve state-of-the-art results in multiple NLP tasks. XLM-RoBERTa is pre-trained on 2.5TB of filtered CommonCrawl data containing 100 languages (Conneau et al., 2019). DeBERTa uses disentangled attention and enhanced mask decoder to enhance RoBERTa and outperform it in a majority of NLP tasks (He et al., 2021).

Table 3 represents the parameters used to fine-tune the XLM-RoBERTa and DeBERTa base models for both the sub-tasks.

5 Results

We use accuracy and the weighted averages of precision, recall, and F1-score as performance metrics to evaluate our classification models. While the shared task results were based on the macro average F1-score, we calculate all four evaluation metrics to get a better sense of the performance.

	Parameter Value			
	Sub-Task A		**Sub-Task B**	
	XLM-RoBERTa	DeBERTa	XLM-RoBERTa	DeBERTa
Batch Size	20	8	32	8
Max. Sequence Length	256	256	256	256
Number of Epochs	6	10	6	6
Learning Rate	1e-5	1e-5	1e-5	1e-5
Weight Decay	0	0	0	0
Use Class Weights	False	False	False	False

Table 3: Fine-tuning parameters of XLM-RoBERTa and DeBERTA models for both sub-tasks

Task	Model	Accuracy	F1-score	Precision	Recall
Sub-Task A	XLM-RoBERTa	0.46	0.44	0.44	0.46
	DeBERTa	0.45	0.38	0.38	0.45
Sub-Task B	XLM-RoBERTa	0.33	0.26	0.25	0.33
	DeBERTa	0.26	0.2	0.18	0.26

Table 4: Performance metrics for both sub-tasks.

For sub-task A, we find that the XLM-RoBERTa outperforms the DeBERTa in all evaluation metrics. There is a difference of 0.06 in the weighted F1-score and Precision between the two models. Despite the DeBERTa model using a smaller batch size and being trained for a higher number of epochs, the better performance of the XLM-RoBERTa is evident from the metrics.

The overall classification performance for sub-task 2 was lower than that for sub-task A. The fine-grained nature of the task made it a significantly more complex challenge. However, we still find that XLM-RoBERTa model easily outperforms the DeBERTa model (Table 4).

6 Conclusion

This paper presents the fine-tuning of a pre-trained XLM-RoBERTa and DeBERTa models for two multi-class text classification tasks in Tamil. The objective of the shared task was to classify a Tamil text into an emotion class. There were two sub-tasks: the coarse-grained sub-task A with 11 output classes and the fine-grained sub-task B with 31 classes. The dataset, including the training and validation splits, for both the sub-tasks were released by the organizers. The dataset consisted of Tamil text extracted from social media comments. The training split for sub-task A had a total of 14,208 rows and used English classification labels. The training split for sub-task B had 30,179 rows with Tamil classification labels.

We propose the fine-tuning of pre-trained transformer-based models for classifying Tamil text into emotion classes. We trained an XLM-RoBERTa and DeBERTa model for each sub-task while using the training split as-is. For sub-task A, the XLM-RoBERTa achieved a classification accuracy of 46% with a weighted F-1 of 0.44, precision of 0.44, and a recall value of 0.46. The DeBERTa model achieved an accuracy of 45% with weighted F-1 of 0.38, precision of 0.38, and 0.45 recall. For sub-task B, the XLM-RoBERTa achieved a classification accuracy of 33% with a weighted F-1 of 0.26, precision of 0.25, and a recall value of 0.33. The DeBERTa model achieved an accuracy of 26% with weighted F-1 of 0.2, precision of 0.18, and 0.26 recall.

We show that the XLM-RoBERTa model outperforms DeBERTa for both the sub-tasks. By using the training split as-is, we retain the information provided by special characters like emojis and extended punctuations. The XLM-RoBERTa model had the best classification performance out of 11 teams for the first sub-task and was the second-best in sub-task B out of 7 teams. We have open-sourced the code used in this study in a public GitHub repository.

References

R Anita and CN Subalalitha. 2019a. An approach to cluster Tamil literatures using discourse connectives. In *2019 IEEE 1st International Conference on*

Energy, Systems and Information Processing (ICESIP), pages 1–4. IEEE.

R Anita and CN Subalalitha. 2019b. Building discourse parser for Thirukkural. In *Proceedings of the 16th International Conference on Natural Language Processing*, pages 18–25.

Bharathi B and Agnusimmaculate Silvia A. 2021a. SSNCSE_NLP@DravidianLangTech-EACL2021: Meme classification for Tamil using machine learning approach. In *Proceedings of the First Workshop on Speech and Language Technologies for Dravidian Languages*, pages 336–339, Kyiv. Association for Computational Linguistics.

Bharathi B and Agnusimmaculate Silvia A. 2021b. SSNCSE_NLP@DravidianLangTech-EACL2021: Offensive language identification on multilingual code mixing text. In *Proceedings of the First Workshop on Speech and Language Technologies for Dravidian Languages*, pages 313–318, Kyiv. Association for Computational Linguistics.

B Bharathi, Bharathi Raja Chakravarthi, Subalalitha Chinnaudayar Navaneethakrishnan, N Sripriya, Arunaggiri Pandian, and Swetha Valli. 2022. Findings of the shared task on Speech Recognition for Vulnerable Individuals in Tamil. In *Proceedings of the Second Workshop on Language Technology for Equality, Diversity and Inclusion*. Association for Computational Linguistics.

Bharathi Raja Chakravarthi. 2020. HopeEDI: A multilingual hope speech detection dataset for equality, diversity, and inclusion. In *Proceedings of the Third Workshop on Computational Modeling of People's Opinions, Personality, and Emotion's in Social Media*, pages 41–53, Barcelona, Spain (Online). Association for Computational Linguistics.

Bharathi Raja Chakravarthi and Vigneshwaran Muralidaran. 2021a. Findings of the shared task on hope speech detection for equality, diversity, and inclusion. In *Proceedings of the First Workshop on Language Technology for Equality, Diversity and Inclusion*, pages 61–72, Kyiv. Association for Computational Linguistics.

Bharathi Raja Chakravarthi and Vigneshwaran Muralidaran. 2021b. Findings of the shared task on hope speech detection for equality, diversity, and inclusion. In *Proceedings of the First Workshop on Language Technology for Equality, Diversity and Inclusion*, pages 61–72.

Bharathi Raja Chakravarthi, Ruba Priyadharshini, Thenmozhi Durairaj, John Phillip McCrae, Paul Buitaleer, Prasanna Kumar Kumaresan, and Rahul Ponnusamy. 2022. Findings of the shared task on Homophobia Transphobia Detection in Social Media Comments. In *Proceedings of the Second Workshop on Language Technology for Equality, Diversity and Inclusion*. Association for Computational Linguistics.

Bharathi Raja Chakravarthi, Ruba Priyadharshini, Rahul Ponnusamy, Prasanna Kumar Kumaresan, Kayalvizhi Sampath, Durairaj Thenmozhi, Sathiyaraj Thangasamy, Rajendran Nallathambi, and John Phillip McCrae. 2021. Dataset for identification of homophobia and transophobia in multilingual YouTube comments. *arXiv preprint arXiv:2109.00227*.

Alexis Conneau, Kartikay Khandelwal, Naman Goyal, Vishrav Chaudhary, Guillaume Wenzek, Francisco Guzmán, Edouard Grave, Myle Ott, Luke Zettlemoyer, and Veselin Stoyanov. 2019. Unsupervised cross-lingual representation learning at scale. *CoRR*, abs/1911.02116.

Bennilo Fernandes and Kasiprasad Mannepalli. 2021. Speech emotion recognition using deep learning lstm for tamil language. *Pertanika Journal of Science & Technology*, 29(3).

Nikhil Ghanghor, Parameswari Krishnamurthy, Sajeetha Thavareesan, Ruba Priyadharshini, and Bharathi Raja Chakravarthi. 2021a. IIITK@DravidianLangTech-EACL2021: Offensive language identification and meme classification in Tamil, Malayalam and Kannada. In *Proceedings of the First Workshop on Speech and Language Technologies for Dravidian Languages*, pages 222–229, Kyiv. Association for Computational Linguistics.

Nikhil Ghanghor, Rahul Ponnusamy, Prasanna Kumar Kumaresan, Ruba Priyadharshini, Sajeetha Thavareesan, and Bharathi Raja Chakravarthi. 2021b. IIITK@LT-EDI-EACL2021: Hope speech detection for equality, diversity, and inclusion in Tamil , Malayalam and English. In *Proceedings of the First Workshop on Language Technology for Equality, Diversity and Inclusion*, pages 197–203, Kyiv. Association for Computational Linguistics.

Pengcheng He, Xiaodong Liu, Jianfeng Gao, and Weizhu Chen. 2021. Deberta: Decoding-enhanced bert with disentangled attention. In *International Conference on Learning Representations*.

Pervaiz Iqbal Khan, Imran Razzak, Andreas Dengel, and Sheraz Ahmed. 2022. Performance comparison of transformer-based models on twitter health mention classification. *IEEE Transactions on Computational Social Systems*.

Prasanna Kumar Kumaresan, Ratnasingam Sakuntharaj, Sajeetha Thavareesan, Subalalitha Navaneethakrishnan, Anand Kumar Madasamy, Bharathi Raja Chakravarthi, and John P McCrae. 2021. Findings of shared task on offensive language identification in Tamil and Malayalam. In *Forum for Information Retrieval Evaluation*, pages 16–18.

Anna Martin and Ted Pedersen. 2021. Duluth at semeval-2021 task 11: Applying deberta to contributing sentence selection and dependency parsing for entity extraction. In *Proceedings of the 15th International Workshop on Semantic Evaluation (SemEval-2021)*, pages 490–501.

Anitha Narasimhan, Aarthy Anandan, Madhan Karky, and CN Subalalitha. 2018. Porul: Option generation and selection and scoring algorithms for a tamil flash card game. *International Journal of Cognitive and Language Sciences*, 12(2):225–228.

Xiaozhi Ou and Hongling Li. 2020. Ynu_oxz@ haspeede 2 and ami: Xlm-roberta with ordered neurons lstm for classification task at evalita 2020. *EVALITA Evaluation of NLP and Speech Tools for Italian*, 2765:102–109.

SS Poorna, K Anuraj, and GJ Nair. 2018. A weight based approach for emotion recognition from speech: an analysis using south indian languages. In *International Conference on Soft Computing Systems*, pages 14–24. Springer.

Ruba Priyadharshini, Bharathi Raja Chakravarthi, Subalalitha Chinnaudayar Navaneethakrishnan, Thenmozhi Durairaj, Malliga Subramanian, Kogilavani Shanmugavadivel, Siddhanth U Hegde, and Prasanna Kumar Kumaresan. 2022. Findings of the shared task on Abusive Comment Detection in Tamil. In *Proceedings of the Second Workshop on Speech and Language Technologies for Dravidian Languages*. Association for Computational Linguistics.

Ruba Priyadharshini, Bharathi Raja Chakravarthi, Sajeetha Thavareesan, Dhivya Chinnappa, Durairaj Thenmozhi, and Rahul Ponnusamy. 2021. Overview of the dravidiancodemix 2021 shared task on sentiment detection in tamil, malayalam, and kannada. In *Forum for Information Retrieval Evaluation*, pages 4–6.

Ruba Priyadharshini, Bharathi Raja Chakravarthi, Mani Vegupatti, and John P McCrae. 2020. Named entity recognition for code-mixed Indian corpus using meta embedding. In *2020 6th international conference on advanced computing and communication systems (ICACCS)*, pages 68–72. IEEE.

S Qu, Y Yang, and Q Que. 2021. Emotion classification for spanish with xlm-roberta and textcnn. In *Proceedings of the Iberian Languages Evaluation Forum (IberLEF 2021). CEUR Workshop Proceedings, CEUR-WS, Málaga, Spain.*

C Sunitha Ram and R Ponnusamy. 2014. An effective automatic speech emotion recognition for tamil language using support vector machine. In *2014 International Conference on Issues and Challenges in Intelligent Computing Techniques (ICICT)*, pages 19–23. IEEE.

Vidyapiratha Raveendirarasa and CRJ Amalraj. 2020. Sentiment analysis of tamil-english code-switched text on social media using sub-word level lstm. In *2020 5th International Conference on Information Technology Research (ICITR)*, pages 1–5. IEEE.

Manikandan Ravikiran, Bharathi Raja Chakravarthi, Anand Kumar Madasamy, Sangeetha Sivanesan, Ratnavel Rajalakshmi, Sajeetha Thavareesan, Rahul Ponnusamy, and Shankar Mahadevan. 2022. Findings of the shared task on Offensive Span Identification in code-mixed Tamil-English comments. In *Proceedings of the Second Workshop on Speech and Language Technologies for Dravidian Languages*. Association for Computational Linguistics.

S Renjith and KG Manju. 2017. Speech based emotion recognition in tamil and telugu using lpcc and hurst parameters—a comparitive study using knn and ann classifiers. In *2017 International conference on circuit, power and computing technologies (ICCPCT)*, pages 1–6. IEEE.

Ratnasingam Sakuntharaj and Sinnathamby Mahesan. 2016. A novel hybrid approach to detect and correct spelling in Tamil text. In *2016 IEEE International Conference on Information and Automation for Sustainability (ICIAfS)*, pages 1–6.

Ratnasingam Sakuntharaj and Sinnathamby Mahesan. 2017. Use of a novel hash-table for speeding-up suggestions for misspelt Tamil words. In *2017 IEEE International Conference on Industrial and Information Systems (ICIIS)*, pages 1–5.

Ratnasingam Sakuntharaj and Sinnathamby Mahesan. 2021. Missing word detection and correction based on context of Tamil sentences using n-grams. In *2021 10th International Conference on Information and Automation for Sustainability (ICIAfS)*, pages 42–47.

Anbukkarasi Sampath, Thenmozhi Durairaj, Bharathi Raja Chakravarthi, Ruba Priyadharshini, Subalalitha Chinnaudayar Navaneethakrishnan, Kogilavani Shanmugavadivel, Sajeetha Thavareesan, Sathiyaraj Thangasamy, Parameswari Krishnamurthy, Adeep Hande, Sean Benhur, and Santhiya Ponnusamy, Kishor Kumar Pandiyan. 2022. Findings of the shared task on Emotion Analysis in Tamil. In *Proceedings of the Second Workshop on Speech and Language Technologies for Dravidian Languages*. Association for Computational Linguistics.

Sonali T Saste and SM Jagdale. 2017. Emotion recognition from speech using mfcc and dwt for security system. In *2017 international conference of electronics, communication and aerospace technology*, volume 1, pages 701–704. IEEE.

V Sowmya and A Rajeswari. 2019. Speech emotion recognition for tamil language speakers. In *International Conference on Machine Intelligence and Signal Processing*, pages 125–136. Springer.

M Srikanth, D Pravena, and D Govind. 2017. Tamil speech emotion recognition using deep belief network (dbn). In *International Symposium on Signal Processing and Intelligent Recognition Systems*, pages 328–336. Springer.

R Srinivasan and CN Subalalitha. 2019. Automated named entity recognition from tamil documents. In *2019 IEEE 1st International Conference on Energy, Systems and Information Processing (ICESIP)*, pages 1–5. IEEE.

C. N. Subalalitha. 2019. Information extraction framework for Kurunthogai. *Sādhanā*, 44(7):156.

CN Subalalitha and E Poovammal. 2018. Automatic bilingual dictionary construction for Tirukural. *Applied Artificial Intelligence*, 32(6):558–567.

Sajeetha Thavareesan and Sinnathamby Mahesan. 2019. Sentiment analysis in Tamil texts: A study on machine learning techniques and feature representation. In *2019 14th Conference on Industrial and Information Systems (ICIIS)*, pages 320–325.

Sajeetha Thavareesan and Sinnathamby Mahesan. 2020a. Sentiment lexicon expansion using Word2vec and fastText for sentiment prediction in Tamil texts. In *2020 Moratuwa Engineering Research Conference (MERCon)*, pages 272–276.

Sajeetha Thavareesan and Sinnathamby Mahesan. 2020b. Word embedding-based part of speech tagging in Tamil texts. In *2020 IEEE 15th International Conference on Industrial and Information Systems (ICIIS)*, pages 478–482.

Sajeetha Thavareesan and Sinnathamby Mahesan. 2021. Sentiment analysis in Tamil texts using k-means and k-nearest neighbour. In *2021 10th International Conference on Information and Automation for Sustainability (ICIAfS)*, pages 48–53.

Konthala Yasaswini, Karthik Puranik, Adeep Hande, Ruba Priyadharshini, Sajeetha Thavareesan, and Bharathi Raja Chakravarthi. 2021. IIITT@DravidianLangTech-EACL2021: Transfer learning for offensive language detection in Dravidian languages. In *Proceedings of the First Workshop on Speech and Language Technologies for Dravidian Languages*, pages 187–194, Kyiv. Association for Computational Linguistics.

Yingjia Zhao and Xin Tao. 2021. Zyj123@ dravidianlangtech-eacl2021: Offensive language identification based on xlm-roberta with dpcnn. In *Proceedings of the First Workshop on Speech and Language Technologies for Dravidian Languages*, pages 216–221.

GJG@TamilNLP-ACL2022: Using Transformers for Abusive Comment Classification in Tamil

Gaurang Prasad*
wikiHow Inc.
Palo Alto, CA, USA
gaurang@wikihow.com

Janvi Prasad*
Vellore Institute of Technology
Vellore, India
janvi.prasad@gmail.com

Gunavathi Chellamuthu
Vellore Institute of Technology
Vellore, India
gunavathi.cm@vit.ac.in

Abstract

This paper presents transformer-based models for the "Abusive Comment Detection" shared task at the Second Workshop on Speech and Language Technologies for Dravidian Languages at ACL 2022. Our team participated in both the multi-class classification sub-tasks as a part of this shared task. The dataset for sub-task A was in Tamil text; while B was code-mixed Tamil-English text. Both the datasets contained 8 classes of abusive comments. We trained an XLM-RoBERTa and DeBERTA base model on the training splits for each sub-task. For sub-task A, the XLM-RoBERTa model achieved an accuracy of 0.66 and the DeBERTa model achieved an accuracy of 0.62. For sub-task B, both the models achieved a classification accuracy of 0.72; however, the DeBERTa model performed better in other classification metrics. Our team ranked 2nd in the code-mixed classification sub-task and 8th in Tamil-text sub-task.

1 Introduction

The advent of social media and social networks have completely revolutionized the way people communicate with one another (Priyadharshini et al., 2021; Kumaresan et al., 2021). There are many positive aspects of social media - improved connectivity, real-time conversation across multiple locations, a new type of social construct, etc. However, this surge of internet-based communication has also brought about an increase in the volume of negative comments (Sampath et al., 2022; Ravikiran et al., 2022; Chakravarthi et al., 2022; Bharathi et al., 2022; Priyadharshini et al., 2022). Being able to detect and classify such negative and abusive comments is a fundamental and challenging problem to solve. It is fundamental because better hate & abusive comment detection leads to the improvement of spam detection systems, improves web-inclusivity, and ultimately makes the internet a better place for everybody (Ghanghor et al., 2021a,b; Yasaswini et al., 2021).

Abusive Comment detection and classification falls under the broader spectrum of text classification tasks in Natural Language Processing (NLP). Improvements in abusive comment classifiers can directly enhance content filtering systems, digital well-being software, spam detection, etc (Chakravarthi et al., 2021b, 2020). It also leads to a better physical and mental experience for the end-user, as these classifiers can be used to reduce the various types of abusive comments in the digital world.

Just as with any other NLP task, building good abusive comment classifiers requires annotated datasets. There are plenty of such datasets available for high-resource languages like English, which has lead to a lot of published research in this space. However, for low-resource languages like Tamil, there are very few publicly available datasets for downstream NLP tasks (Anita and Subalalitha, 2019b,a; Subalalitha and Poovammal, 2018). Tamil is a Dravidian classical language used by the Tamil people of South Asia. Tamil is an official language of Tamil Nadu, Sri Lanka, Singapore, and the Union Territory of Puducherry in India (Subalalitha, 2019; Srinivasan and Subalalitha, 2019; Narasimhan et al., 2018). Significant minority speak Tamil in the four other South Indian states of Kerala, Karnataka, Andhra Pradesh, and Telangana, as well as the Union Territory of the Andaman and Nicobar Islands. It is also spoken by the Tamil diaspora, which may be found in Malaysia, Myanmar, South Africa, the United Kingdom, the United States, Canada, Australia,

*These authors contributed equally to this work

Proceedings of the Second Workshop on Speech and Language Technologies for Dravidian Languages, pages 93 - 99
May 26, 2022

and Mauritius (Sakuntharaj and Mahesan, 2021, 2017, 2016; Thavareesan and Mahesan, 2019, 2020a,b, 2021). Tamil is also the native language of Sri Lankan Moors. Tamil, one of the 22 scheduled languages in the Indian Constitution, was the first to be designated as a classical language of India (B and A, 2021b,a).

This shared task is an attempt to promote research in abusive comment detection and classification in Tamil. This novel dataset, generated from YouTube comments, consists of 8 types of abusive comments. The publication of the Tamil-text as well as the code-mixed Tamil-English datasets also provides an opportunity to learn about the performance of models on different character sets. In this shared task, we participated in both the sub-tasks: the Tamil-text classification sub-task A, and the code-mixed sub-task B. The goal of this paper is to demonstrate the performance of fine-tuning pre-trained transformer-based models for such a text-classification task in Tamil. We train an XLM-RoBERTa and DeBERTa model for each sub-task on the given train splits, optimize parameters, and evaluate the performance on the test split.

The rest of our paper is organized as follows: we discuss related work in Tamil emotion recognition, describe the datasets, our methodology, and conclude with the results and performance metrics.

We provide a link to our models and evaluations to provide reproducability, and empower future research in this domain[1].

2 Related Work

As mentioned above, a lot of published work exists in the domain of offensive language detection for high-resource languages. Kwok and Wang (2013) trained a binary classifer to detect racist tweets in English. Xu et al. (2012) presented off-the-shelf NLP approaches to identify bullying in social media, in English. Kumar et al. (2018) present their findings from a shared task for aggression identification in social media. Nobata et al. (2016) demonstrated a Machine Learning approach to detect abusive language in English online content.

The volume of published research in abusive comment detection for low-resource languages is much lower than that of English and other high-resource languages. Wiegand et al. (2018) provided an overview of a shared abusive comment detection task in German. Kannan and Mitrović (2021), Kamal et al. (2021), and Jha et al. (2020) have presented their work in detecting abusive comments in Hindi. Eshan and Hasan (2017), Emon et al. (2019), and Romim et al. (2021) have demonstrated popular approaches for Bengali.

Chakravarthi (2020), Chakravarthi and Muralidaran (2021), and Hande et al. (2021) have published their findings from other text classification-related shared tasks in Dravidian Languages (hope speech detection).

Mandl et al. (2020) organized a workshop track for hate speech detection in Tamil, Malayalam, Hindi, English and German. We believe this was the first big focus on developing abusive content identification and classification techniques for Dravidian languages. This was followed up by Chakravarthi et al. (2021a), who organized a shared task for offensive language identification in Tamil, Malayalam, and Kannada.

There have also been multiple previous works that use XLM-RoBERTa for text classification tasks. Zhao and Tao (2021) proposed a system using XLM-RoBERTa and DPCNN for detecting offensive text in Dravidian languages. Qu et al. (2021) used TextCNN and XLM-RoBERTa from emotion classification in Spanish. Ou and Li (2020) also demonstrated using XLM-RoBERTa for a hate speech identification classification task.

The number of published works using DeBERTa is fewer than that of XLM-RoBERTa. There have been some studies that use DeBERTa for entity extraction and text-classification tasks. (Martin and Pedersen, 2021; Khan et al., 2022)

3 Data

The organizers of the shared task released the annotated training and development splits for both the sub-tasks. The testing dataset, without labels, was released a few days prior to the run submission deadline. Once the results were announced, the organizers released the labeled test dataset for verification purposes.

For sub-task A, the dataset consisted of Tamil sentences annotated to one of eight English abusive categories: Misandry, Counter Speech (Sp.), Misogyny, Xenophobia, Hope Sp., Homophobia, Transphobia, or None of the Above (N.O.T.A). The dataset for sub-task B was code-mixed Tamil-English with the same eight English abusive comment classes as sub-task A. The average length of a sentence in the corpora was 1 (Priyadharshini

[1]https://tinyurl.com/GJGAbusiveComments

Label	Count	Label	Count
N.O.T.A	1296	Hope Sp.	86
Misandry	446	Homophob.	35
Counter Sp.	149	Transphob.	6
Misogyny	125	Not Tamil	2
Xenophobia	95		

Table 1: Classification labels for sub-task A and the number of rows under each label in the train split.

Label	Count	Label	Count
N.O.T.A	3720	Hope Sp.	213
Misandry	830	Misogyny	211
Counter Sp.	348	Homophob.	172
Xenophobia	297	Transphob.	157

Table 2: Classification labels for sub-task B and the number of rows under each label in the training split.

et al., 2022). The sentences in both the datasets contained extended words, special characters, emojis, grammatical, and lexical inconsistencies.

3.1 Sub-Task A

The training split for classification sub-task A had a total of 2,240 rows. 2,238 of these rows were classified under one of the eight categories of abusive comments. 2 rows were not in Tamil. Including the "Not Tamil" category, there were a total of 9 category labels in the test split. The development dataset contained 560 rows. The test split had 698 rows. The classification labels along with the total count for each label in the train split are represented in Table 1.

3.2 Sub-Task B

Sub-task B used the code-mixed Tamil-English dataset with the same 8 abusive category labels. The training split did not include any rows of the "Not Tamil" category, which was seen in sub-task A. The dataset splits were larger than that of sub-task A: the training split had a total of 5,948 rows. The development dataset had 1,488 rows and the test split had 1,856 rows. Table 2 represents all the class labels in the train split along with the total number of rows under each label.

4 Methodology

For each classification sub-task, we fine-tune an XLM-RoBERTa and DeBERTa base model on sentences from the training splits to create a classification model. We do not remove any stop words, special characters, or emojis from the test splits, in order to preserve the context of the comment. Special characters and emojis provide useful context, especially for a text classification task. For sub-task A, we also did not remove the 2 instances of "Not Tamil" from the training set.

XLM-RoBERTa is a multilingual version of RoBERTa, which in itself was an improvement over BERT to achieve state-of-the-art results in multiple NLP tasks. XLM-RoBERTa is pre-trained on 2.5TB of filtered CommonCrawl data containing 100 languages (Conneau et al., 2019). DeBERTa uses disentangled attention and enhanced mask decoder to enhance RoBERTa and outperform it in a majority of NLP tasks (He et al., 2021).

Table 3 represents the parameters used to fine-tune the XLM-RoBERTa and DeBERTa base models for both the sub-tasks.

5 Results

We use accuracy and the weighted averages of precision, recall, and F1-score as performance metrics to evaluate our classification models. We calculate all four evaluation metrics to get a better sense of the classification performance.

For sub-task A, we find that the XLM-RoBERTa outperforms the DeBERTa in all evaluation metrics. Both models used the same training splits and parameters. The multi-lingual nature of XLM-RoBERTa is evident from its better performance.

The overall classification performance for sub-task 2 was higher than that for sub-task A. We believe this is because of the English charater set used by the code-mixed dataset. Both the transformer-models are pre-trained on large English datasets. DeBERTa outperforms XLM-RoBERTa in all metrics, which justifies DeBERTa's improvement over XLM-RoBERTa for English-character-NLP tasks (Table 4).

6 Conclusion and Future Work

We present XLM-RoBERTa and DeBERTa models for two multi-class text classification tasks in Tamil. The objective of the shared task was to identify abusive content in Tamil text. There were two sub-tasks: sub-task A in Tamil text, and sub-task B which used Tamil-English code-mixed text. The classes of abusive comments were the same for both the sub-tasks. The Tamil dataset, for sub-task A, consisted of 2,240 rows in the training split. The

	Parameter Value			
	Sub-Task A		**Sub-Task B**	
	XLM-RoBERTa	DeBERTa	XLM-RoBERTa	DeBERTa
Batch Size	9	9	10	10
Max. Sequence Length	256	256	256	256
Number of Epochs	10	10	10	10
Learning Rate	1e-5	1e-5	1e-5	1e-5
Weight Decay	0	0	0	0
Use Class Weights	False	False	False	False

Table 3: Fine-tuning parameters of XLM-RoBERTa and DeBERTA models for both sub-tasks

Task	Model	Accuracy	F1-score	Precision	Recall
Sub-Task A	XLM-RoBERTa	0.66	0.65	0.65	0.66
	DeBERTa	0.62	0.57	0.62	0.56
Sub-Task B	XLM-RoBERTa	0.72	0.70	0.70	0.72
	DeBERTa	0.72	0.72	0.72	0.72

Table 4: Classification metrics for both sub-tasks.

code-mixed training split, for sub-task B, was much bigger with 5,948 rows.

We propose the fine-tuning of pre-trained XLM-RoBERTa and DeBERTa, which are transformer-based models, for classifying Tamil text into abusive comment classes. We trained all the models using the respective training splits as-is. For sub-task A, the XLM-RoBERTa achieved a classification accuracy of 66% with a weighted F-1 of 0.65, precision of 0.65, and a recall value of 0.66. The DeBERTa model achieved an accuracy of 62% with weighted F-1 of 0.57, precision of 0.62, and 0.56 recall. For sub-task B, the XLM-RoBERTa achieved a classification accuracy of 72% with a weighted F-1 of 0.70, precision of 0.70, and a recall value of 0.72. The DeBERTa model achieved an accuracy of 72% with weighted F-1 of 0.72, precision of 0.72, and 0.72 recall.

We show that the XLM-RoBERTa model outperforms DeBERTa for sub-task A, which used Tamil text. For the code-mixed Tamil-English text (sub-task B), the DeBERTa model outperforms the XLM-RoBERTa. This validates the strength of the DeBERTa model on English character tasks, and the superiority of the XLM-RoBERTa for non-English languages. By using the training split as-is, we retain the information provided by special characters like emojis and extended punctuation symbols. The XLM-RoBERTa model had the eight best classification performance in the shared task for sub-task A, and the DeBERTa model ranked second best. We have open-sourced the code used in this study in a public GitHub repository.

For future-work, removing the "Not Tamil" rows from the training split for sub-task A would eliminate an extremely under-sampled class, which may lead to performance improvements. Extracting emojis separately from the text and incorporating emoji-information in identifying abusive comments is also an area for potential study. Using pre-trained models is a good starting point in this domain, however, we feel that custom model architectures and systems have to be studied for such classification tasks in Tamil.

References

R Anita and CN Subalalitha. 2019a. An approach to cluster Tamil literatures using discourse connectives. In *2019 IEEE 1st International Conference on Energy, Systems and Information Processing (ICESIP)*, pages 1–4. IEEE.

R Anita and CN Subalalitha. 2019b. Building discourse parser for Thirukkural. In *Proceedings of the 16th International Conference on Natural Language Processing*, pages 18–25.

Bharathi B and Agnusimmaculate Silvia A. 2021a. SSNCSE_NLP@DravidianLangTech-EACL2021: Meme classification for Tamil using machine learning approach. In *Proceedings of the First Workshop on Speech and Language Technologies for Dravidian Languages*, pages 336–339, Kyiv. Association for Computational Linguistics.

Bharathi B and Agnusimmaculate Silvia A. 2021b.

SSNCSE_NLP@DravidianLangTech-EACL2021: Offensive language identification on multilingual code mixing text. In *Proceedings of the First Workshop on Speech and Language Technologies for Dravidian Languages*, pages 313–318, Kyiv. Association for Computational Linguistics.

B Bharathi, Bharathi Raja Chakravarthi, Subalalitha Chinnaudayar Navaneethakrishnan, N Sripriya, Arunaggiri Pandian, and Swetha Valli. 2022. Findings of the shared task on Speech Recognition for Vulnerable Individuals in Tamil. In *Proceedings of the Second Workshop on Language Technology for Equality, Diversity and Inclusion*. Association for Computational Linguistics.

Bharathi Raja Chakravarthi. 2020. HopeEDI: A multilingual hope speech detection dataset for equality, diversity, and inclusion. In *Proceedings of the Third Workshop on Computational Modeling of People's Opinions, Personality, and Emotion's in Social Media*, pages 41–53, Barcelona, Spain (Online). Association for Computational Linguistics.

Bharathi Raja Chakravarthi and Vigneshwaran Muralidaran. 2021. Findings of the shared task on hope speech detection for equality, diversity, and inclusion. In *Proceedings of the First Workshop on Language Technology for Equality, Diversity and Inclusion*, pages 61–72, Kyiv. Association for Computational Linguistics.

Bharathi Raja Chakravarthi, Vigneshwaran Muralidaran, Ruba Priyadharshini, and John Philip McCrae. 2020. Corpus creation for sentiment analysis in code-mixed Tamil-English text. In *Proceedings of the 1st Joint Workshop on Spoken Language Technologies for Under-resourced languages (SLTU) and Collaboration and Computing for Under-Resourced Languages (CCURL)*, pages 202–210, Marseille, France. European Language Resources association.

Bharathi Raja Chakravarthi, Ruba Priyadharshini, Thenmozhi Durairaj, John Phillip McCrae, Paul Buitaleer, Prasanna Kumar Kumaresan, and Rahul Ponnusamy. 2022. Findings of the shared task on Homophobia Transphobia Detection in Social Media Comments. In *Proceedings of the Second Workshop on Language Technology for Equality, Diversity and Inclusion*. Association for Computational Linguistics.

Bharathi Raja Chakravarthi, Ruba Priyadharshini, Navya Jose, Thomas Mandl, Prasanna Kumar Kumaresan, Rahul Ponnusamy, RL Hariharan, John Philip McCrae, Elizabeth Sherly, et al. 2021a. Findings of the shared task on offensive language identification in tamil, malayalam, and kannada. In *Proceedings of the first workshop on speech and language technologies for Dravidian languages*, pages 133–145.

Bharathi Raja Chakravarthi, Ruba Priyadharshini, Rahul Ponnusamy, Prasanna Kumar Kumaresan, Kayalvizhi Sampath, Durairaj Thenmozhi, Sathiyaraj Thangasamy, Rajendran Nallathambi, and John Phillip McCrae. 2021b. Dataset for identification of homophobia and transophobia in multilingual YouTube comments. *arXiv preprint arXiv:2109.00227*.

Alexis Conneau, Kartikay Khandelwal, Naman Goyal, Vishrav Chaudhary, Guillaume Wenzek, Francisco Guzmán, Edouard Grave, Myle Ott, Luke Zettlemoyer, and Veselin Stoyanov. 2019. Unsupervised cross-lingual representation learning at scale. *CoRR*, abs/1911.02116.

Estiak Ahmed Emon, Shihab Rahman, Joti Banarjee, Amit Kumar Das, and Tanni Mittra. 2019. A deep learning approach to detect abusive bengali text. In *2019 7th International Conference on Smart Computing & Communications (ICSCC)*, pages 1–5. IEEE.

Shahnoor C Eshan and Mohammad S Hasan. 2017. An application of machine learning to detect abusive bengali text. In *2017 20th International Conference of Computer and Information Technology (ICCIT)*, pages 1–6. IEEE.

Nikhil Ghanghor, Parameswari Krishnamurthy, Sajeetha Thavareesan, Ruba Priyadharshini, and Bharathi Raja Chakravarthi. 2021a. IIITK@DravidianLangTech-EACL2021: Offensive language identification and meme classification in Tamil, Malayalam and Kannada. In *Proceedings of the First Workshop on Speech and Language Technologies for Dravidian Languages*, pages 222–229, Kyiv. Association for Computational Linguistics.

Nikhil Ghanghor, Rahul Ponnusamy, Prasanna Kumar Kumaresan, Ruba Priyadharshini, Sajeetha Thavareesan, and Bharathi Raja Chakravarthi. 2021b. IIITK@LT-EDI-EACL2021: Hope speech detection for equality, diversity, and inclusion in Tamil , Malayalam and English. In *Proceedings of the First Workshop on Language Technology for Equality, Diversity and Inclusion*, pages 197–203, Kyiv. Association for Computational Linguistics.

Adeep Hande, Ruba Priyadharshini, Anbukkarasi Sampath, Kingston Pal Thamburaj, Prabakaran Chandran, and Bharathi Raja Chakravarthi. 2021. Hope speech detection in under-resourced kannada language.

Pengcheng He, Xiaodong Liu, Jianfeng Gao, and Weizhu Chen. 2021. Deberta: Decoding-enhanced bert with disentangled attention. In *International Conference on Learning Representations*.

Vikas Kumar Jha, Pa Hrudya, PN Vinu, Vishnu Vijayan, and Pa Prabaharan. 2020. Dhot-repository and classification of offensive tweets in the hindi language. *Procedia Computer Science*, 171:2324–2333.

Ojasv Kamal, Adarsh Kumar, and Tejas Vaidhya. 2021. Hostility detection in hindi leveraging pre-trained language models. In *International Workshop on Combating On line Ho st ile Posts in Regional Languages dur ing Emerge ncy Si tuation*, pages 213–223. Springer.

Sudharsana Kannan and Jelena Mitrović. 2021. Hatespeech and offensive content detection in hindi language using c-bigru. In *Forum for Information Retrieval Evaluation (Working Notes)(FIRE), CEUR-WS. org*.

Pervaiz Iqbal Khan, Imran Razzak, Andreas Dengel, and Sheraz Ahmed. 2022. Performance comparison of transformer-based models on twitter health mention classification. *IEEE Transactions on Computational Social Systems*.

Ritesh Kumar, Atul Kr Ojha, Shervin Malmasi, and Marcos Zampieri. 2018. Benchmarking aggression identification in social media. In *Proceedings of the first workshop on trolling, aggression and cyberbullying (TRAC-2018)*, pages 1–11.

Prasanna Kumar Kumaresan, Ratnasingam Sakuntharaj, Sajeetha Thavareesan, Subalalitha Navaneethakrishnan, Anand Kumar Madasamy, Bharathi Raja Chakravarthi, and John P McCrae. 2021. Findings of shared task on offensive language identification in Tamil and Malayalam. In *Forum for Information Retrieval Evaluation*, pages 16–18.

Irene Kwok and Yuzhou Wang. 2013. Locate the hate: Detecting tweets against blacks. In *Twenty-seventh AAAI conference on artificial intelligence*.

Thomas Mandl, Sandip Modha, Anand Kumar M, and Bharathi Raja Chakravarthi. 2020. Overview of the hasoc track at fire 2020: Hate speech and offensive language identification in tamil, malayalam, hindi, english and german. In *Forum for Information Retrieval Evaluation*, pages 29–32.

Anna Martin and Ted Pedersen. 2021. Duluth at semeval-2021 task 11: Applying deberta to contributing sentence selection and dependency parsing for entity extraction. In *Proceedings of the 15th International Workshop on Semantic Evaluation (SemEval-2021)*, pages 490–501.

Anitha Narasimhan, Aarthy Anandan, Madhan Karky, and CN Subalalitha. 2018. Porul: Option generation and selection and scoring algorithms for a tamil flash card game. *International Journal of Cognitive and Language Sciences*, 12(2):225–228.

Chikashi Nobata, Joel Tetreault, Achint Thomas, Yashar Mehdad, and Yi Chang. 2016. Abusive language detection in online user content. In *Proceedings of the 25th international conference on world wide web*, pages 145–153.

Xiaozhi Ou and Hongling Li. 2020. Ynu_oxz@ haspeede 2 and ami: Xlm-roberta with ordered neurons lstm for classification task at evalita 2020. *EVALITA Evaluation of NLP and Speech Tools for Italian*, 2765:102–109.

Ruba Priyadharshini, Bharathi Raja Chakravarthi, Subalalitha Chinnaudayar Navaneethakrishnan, Thenmozhi Durairaj, Malliga Subramanian, Kogilavani Shanmugavadivel, Siddhanth U Hegde, and Prasanna Kumar Kumaresan. 2022. Findings of the shared task on Abusive Comment Detection in Tamil. In *Proceedings of the Second Workshop on Speech and Language Technologies for Dravidian Languages*. Association for Computational Linguistics.

Ruba Priyadharshini, Bharathi Raja Chakravarthi, Sajeetha Thavareesan, Dhivya Chinnappa, Durairaj Thenmozhi, and Rahul Ponnusamy. 2021. Overview of the DravidianCodeMix 2021 shared task on sentiment detection in Tamil, Malayalam, and Kannada. In *Forum for Information Retrieval Evaluation*, pages 4–6.

S Qu, Y Yang, and Q Que. 2021. Emotion classification for spanish with xlm-roberta and textcnn. In *Proceedings of the Iberian Languages Evaluation Forum (IberLEF 2021). CEUR Workshop Proceedings, CEUR-WS, Málaga, Spain*.

Manikandan Ravikiran, Bharathi Raja Chakravarthi, Anand Kumar Madasamy, Sangeetha Sivanesan, Ratnavel Rajalakshmi, Sajeetha Thavareesan, Rahul Ponnusamy, and Shankar Mahadevan. 2022. Findings of the shared task on Offensive Span Identification in code-mixed Tamil-English comments. In *Proceedings of the Second Workshop on Speech and Language Technologies for Dravidian Languages*. Association for Computational Linguistics.

Nauros Romim, Mosahed Ahmed, Hriteshwar Talukder, Saiful Islam, et al. 2021. Hate speech detection in the bengali language: A dataset and its baseline evaluation. In *Proceedings of International Joint Conference on Advances in Computational Intelligence*, pages 457–468. Springer.

Ratnasingam Sakuntharaj and Sinnathamby Mahesan. 2016. A novel hybrid approach to detect and correct spelling in Tamil text. In *2016 IEEE International Conference on Information and Automation for Sustainability (ICIAfS)*, pages 1–6.

Ratnasingam Sakuntharaj and Sinnathamby Mahesan. 2017. Use of a novel hash-table for speeding-up suggestions for misspelt Tamil words. In *2017 IEEE International Conference on Industrial and Information Systems (ICIIS)*, pages 1–5.

Ratnasingam Sakuntharaj and Sinnathamby Mahesan. 2021. Missing word detection and correction based on context of Tamil sentences using n-grams. In *2021 10th International Conference on Information and Automation for Sustainability (ICIAfS)*, pages 42–47.

Anbukkarasi Sampath, Thenmozhi Durairaj, Bharathi Raja Chakravarthi, Ruba Priyadharshini, Subalalitha Chinnaudayar Navaneethakrishnan, Kogilavani Shanmugavadivel, Sajeetha Thavareesan, Sathiyaraj Thangasamy, Parameswari Krishnamurthy, Adeep Hande, Sean Benhur, and Santhiya Ponnusamy, Kishor Kumar Pandiyan. 2022. Findings of the shared task on Emotion Analysis in Tamil. In *Proceedings of the Second Workshop on Speech and Language Technologies for Dravidian Languages*. Association for Computational Linguistics.

R Srinivasan and CN Subalalitha. 2019. Automated named entity recognition from tamil documents. In *2019 IEEE 1st International Conference on Energy, Systems and Information Processing (ICESIP)*, pages 1–5. IEEE.

C. N. Subalalitha. 2019. Information extraction framework for Kurunthogai. *Sādhanā*, 44(7):156.

CN Subalalitha and E Poovammal. 2018. Automatic bilingual dictionary construction for Tirukural. *Applied Artificial Intelligence*, 32(6):558–567.

Sajeetha Thavareesan and Sinnathamby Mahesan. 2019. Sentiment analysis in Tamil texts: A study on machine learning techniques and feature representation. In *2019 14th Conference on Industrial and Information Systems (ICIIS)*, pages 320–325.

Sajeetha Thavareesan and Sinnathamby Mahesan. 2020a. Sentiment lexicon expansion using Word2vec and fastText for sentiment prediction in Tamil texts. In *2020 Moratuwa Engineering Research Conference (MERCon)*, pages 272–276.

Sajeetha Thavareesan and Sinnathamby Mahesan. 2020b. Word embedding-based part of speech tagging in Tamil texts. In *2020 IEEE 15th International Conference on Industrial and Information Systems (ICIIS)*, pages 478–482.

Sajeetha Thavareesan and Sinnathamby Mahesan. 2021. Sentiment analysis in Tamil texts using k-means and k-nearest neighbour. In *2021 10th International Conference on Information and Automation for Sustainability (ICIAfS)*, pages 48–53.

Michael Wiegand, Melanie Siegel, and Josef Ruppenhofer. 2018. Overview of the germeval 2018 shared task on the identification of offensive language.

Jun-Ming Xu, Kwang-Sung Jun, Xiaojin Zhu, and Amy Bellmore. 2012. Learning from bullying traces in social media. In *Proceedings of the 2012 conference of the North American chapter of the association for computational linguistics: Human language technologies*, pages 656–666.

Konthala Yasaswini, Karthik Puranik, Adeep Hande, Ruba Priyadharshini, Sajeetha Thavareesan, and Bharathi Raja Chakravarthi. 2021. IIITT@DravidianLangTech-EACL2021: Transfer learning for offensive language detection in Dravidian languages. In *Proceedings of the First Workshop on Speech and Language Technologies for Dravidian Languages*, pages 187–194, Kyiv. Association for Computational Linguistics.

Yingjia Zhao and Xin Tao. 2021. Zyj123@ dravidianlangtech-eacl2021: Offensive language identification based on xlm-roberta with dpcnn. In *Proceedings of the First Workshop on Speech and Language Technologies for Dravidian Languages*, pages 216–221.

IIITDWD@TamilNLP-ACL2022: Transformer-based approach to classify abusive content in Dravidian Code-mixed text

Shankar Biradar and **Sunil Saumya**
Department of Computer Science and Engineering
Indian Institute of Information Technology
Dharwad, Karnatka, India
(shankar,sunil.saumya)@iiitdwd.ac.in

Abstract

Identifying abusive content or hate speech in social media text has raised the research community's interest in recent times. The major driving force behind this is the widespread use of social media websites. Further, it also leads to identifying abusive content in low-resource regional languages, which is an important research problem in computational linguistics. As part of ACL-2022, organizers of DravidianLangTech@ACL 2022 have released a shared task on abusive category identification in Tamil and Tamil-English code-mixed text to encourage further research on offensive content identification in low-resource Indic languages. This paper presents the working notes for the model submitted by IIITDWD at DravidianLangTech@ACL 2022. Our team competed in Sub-Task B and finished in 9th place among the participating teams. In our proposed approach, we used a pre-trained transformer model such as Indic-bert for feature extraction, and on top of that, SVM classifier is used for stance detection. Further, our model achieved 62 % accuracy on code-mixed Tamil-English text.

1 Introduction

Many people from various demographics and linguistic backgrounds have been using social media sites to exchange information and interact with others. Further, these speakers tend to combine their mother tongue with a second language during the conversation. This leads to code-mixed text; code-mixing refers to two or more languages appearing one after another during a conversation (Poplack and Walker, 2003). Monitoring code-mixed content from social media sites has caught the research community's interest in natural language processing. Currently, many social media networks use a manual content screening method to deal with abusive content posted by the users. Here a human reviewer will go through the user posts and determine whether they violate the norms or not (Mandl et al., 2020; Biradar et al., 2022). However, as the number of social media users grows, massive amounts of data are generated, making it virtually difficult to monitor every data point personally. As a result, the manual technique of dealing with abusive content has become unsuccessful. Further, it increased the demand for automated abusive language identification models in a social media text, which is largely code-mixed.

The existing models have been trained on high-resource monolingual languages such as English and Hindi. Further, due to the complexity induced by code-mixing at different language levels, models trained with monolingual text failed to identify objectionable features in the code-mixed text. As a result, identifying abusive content in Indic languages poses a significantly greater problem for the NLP community. Hence identifying abusive content in low-resource Dravidian languages such as Tamil, Kannada, and Malayalam is made more difficult due to a lack of pre-trained models and a scarcity of training data to further train models.

To bridge this gap, DravidianLangTech@ACL 2022(Priyadharshini et al., 2022) organizers have provided a gold standard data set for abusive content identification in Dravidian languages such as Tamil and Tanglish Code-mixed text. The task's objective is to identify abusive categories from YouTube comments at the sentence/comment level. The original task is divided into two sub-Tasks: Sub-Task A involves sentence level abusive category detection from monolingual Tamil script, and Sub-Task B involves comment level abusive category identification from code-mixed Tamil-English text. Our team has participated in Sub-Task B and secured 9th rank among the participating teams, and this paper presents working notes of our presented model.

The remainder of the paper is organized as follows: Section 2 provides a review of existing work,

Proceedings of the Second Workshop on Speech and Language Technologies for Dravidian Languages, pages 100 - 104
May 26, 2022

Section 3 provides insight into the suggested model, and Section 4 concludes by offering information about outcomes.

2 Litrature review

The subject of automatic detection of hostile and harmful information from social media has attracted the interest of many researchers and practitioners from industry and academia. However, most of the past research has focused on high-resource languages. Previous attempts have been made to develop hate speech detection models in English, German (Mandl et al., 2019), and Italian (Corazza et al., 2020). But on the other hand, low-resource Indic languages are rarely explored. The first such attempt was made by (Bohra et al., 2018), they have created annotated corpus in Hindi-English code mixed text. They used traditional machine learning models to classify features extracted from the data set, such as character n-grams, word n-grams, punctuation, negation words, and hate lexicons. (Mathur et al., 2018) used a CNN-based transfer learning approach to detect abusive tweets in Hindi-English code-mixed text. They also introduced the HEOT data set and the Profanity Lexicon Set.

Abusive content identification in Indic languages is also the topic of a few shared tasks. Chakravarthi et al. created a shared task in low resource code-mixed Dravidian languages like Tamil-English, Malayalam-English, and Kannada-English (Chakravarthi et al., 2021). The objective of the task is to identify abusive content in a social media text. The shared task presents a new gold standard corpus for abusive language identification of code-mixed text in three Dravidian languages: Tamil-English (Chakravarthi et al., 2020b), Malayalam-English (Chakravarthi et al., 2020a), and Kannada-English (Hande et al., 2020). (Dowlagar and Mamidi, 2021) built a transformer-based transliteration and class balancing loss model to identify abusive content from code-mixed Dravidian languages. TIF-DNN, a transformer-based interpretation and feature extraction model to identify abusive content in Hindi-English code-mixed text, is built by (Biradar et al., 2021)

3 Data and methods

3.1 Task and data set information

We have taken the data set from Dravidian-LangTech@ACL 2022. As part of the competition, organizers have provided two sub-Tasks. Sub-Task A: comment/post-level abusive categories identification in monolingual Tamil text. Sub-Task B: Given a code-mixed text in Tamil-English, the user must identify abusive categories at the post/comment level. Our team took part in Sub-Task B, which involves the identification of abusive categories in Tamil-English code-mixed text. According to the task coordinators, Tamil-English data is gathered from YouTube comments (Priyadharshini et al., 2022). The organizers have provided train, validation, and test data sets. The train data set contained 5948 comments and labels, the validation data set contained 1488 comments, and the test data set contained 1857 comments. Details of the data set are provided in table 1.

3.2 Model description

The model architecture is divided into three steps in our proposed approach, as indicated in Fig 1. The model is comprised of an initial data pre-treatment stage, a transformer-based feature extraction layer, and an outer classification layer. The succeeding subsections will provide a complete details of each these stages.

3.3 Data pre-processing

The data collected from the organizers contains a lot of extraneous information. A few data preparation processes were performed on the text and label fields to make the data appropriate for model building. We removed digits, special characters, hyperlinks, and Twitter user handles from the data set because they are not useful for abusive content detection. Furthermore, the data provided by the user is taken from social media sites, and social media data does not follow grammatical rules. Lemmatization is carried out to convert the data to its usable basic form. Converting upper case text to lower case is also done to avoid redundant words. We used the NLTK toolbox from the python library (Bird et al., 2009) to perform these pre-processing steps.

Next, tokens are created by passing pre-processed text through a tokenizer. For this purpose, we employed the IndicBERT tokenizer[1] in our proposed approach. Additional padding and masking are applied on tokenized data to manage varying length sentences. At the end of the pre-treatment stage, we generate tokenized padded data,

[1]https://indicnlp.ai4bharat.org/indic-bert/

	None	Misandry	Xenop -hobia	Counter-speech	Hope-speech	Trans phobic	misog -yny	homop -hobia	Total
Train	3720	830	297	348	213	157	211	172	5948
Validation	919	218	70	95	53	40	50	43	1488
Test	1142	292	95	88	70	58	57	56	1857
Total	5781	1340	462	531	336	255	318	271	9293

Table 1: Data set distribution

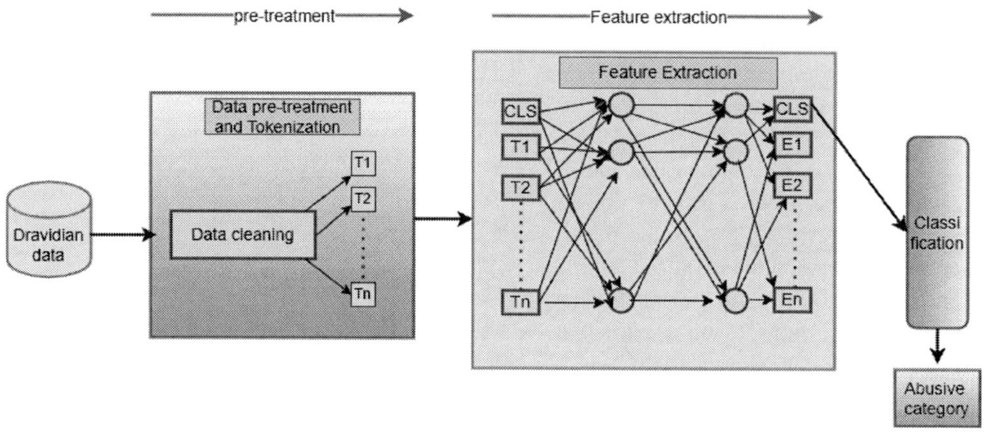

Figure 1: Overall Architecture of proposed system

which will be used as input for the feature extraction stage.

3.4 Feature extraction

Our proposed approach used the transformer-based IndicBERT (Kakwani et al., 2020) model for feature extraction. IndicBERT is a multilingual ALBERT model covering 12 main Indian languages: Assamese, Bengali, English, Gujarati, Hindi, Kannada, Malayalam, Marathi, Oriya, Punjabi, Tamil, and Telugu. It was trained on large-scale corpora. IndicBERT has fewer parameters than other public models like mBERT and XLM-R, yet it performs very well on various tasks. The architecture of IndicBERT is similar to that of the original BERT (Devlin et al., 2018). BERT is a non-regression model consisting of a transformer layer. Here transformer part of the model acts as an attention mechanism through which the model can learn contextual information from the data. We have used embedding from the CLS token in our proposed model, which gives full-sentence embedding. Embeddings are then passed through the outer classification layer for Stance detection.

3.5 Classification Layer

A conventional support vector machine (SVM) classifier is used for stance detection in the classification layer. SVM is built for binary classification problems and does not natively support multi-class classification problems. However, data provided by the organizers consist of linearly separable data with eight different classes. As a result, we utilized the One-vs-rest method from the Scikit-learn Python package[2] to transform a multi-class problem into a binary classification problem. Our experiment built a linear SVM classifier with ten-fold cross-validation using the sklearn SVM.LinearSVC model type and the OnevsRestClassifer wrapper. Experiment findings show that the penalty parameter value "1" and kernel type "linear" generate the best outcomes for the proposed model. Experimental trials determine these hyper-parameter values. The model uses embedding from IndicBERT as input and outputs one of the eight abusive categories. Implementation details of the proposed model are provided in GitHub repository[3].

[2]https://scikit-learn.org/stable/

[3]https://github.com/shankarb14/dravidian-codemix/blob/main/IndicBERT

	Precision	Recall	F1-score
Counter speech	0.55	0.32	0.40
Homo phobia	0.34	0.51	0.41
Hope speech	0.19	0.36	0.25
Misandry	0.63	0.69	0.66
Misogyny	0.05	0.27	0.09
None	0.89	0.81	0.85
Transphobic	0.21	0.40	0.27
Xenophobic	0.59	0.73	0.63
Accuracy	-	-	0.73

Table 2: Classification report for proposed model

4 Results

In the competition, teams were ranked based upon macro averaged Precision, macro averaged Recall and macro averaged F1-Score across all the classes. Our suggested model came in 9th place for abusive category recognition on a code-mixed Tamil-English data set among the participating teams. Table 3 shows the top-five rated teams and the performance of our proposed model. From the table, the performance of our model is indicated in bold letters. According to the table, our model ranks second among the top-performing models with an accuracy of 62%. However, our model underperformed in identifying some of the abusive categories, and as a result of this unevenness, the overall model macro F1 score has decreased to 18.7. In addition, our model scored lower in the macro F1 score since it did not capture some abusive traits such as Trans-phobic, Hope-speech, and misogyny, as illustrated in table 2. The absence of sufficient training data in the categories mentioned contributed to our model's poor performance; nevertheless, our model's performance can be improved further by balancing the overall data set across all categories.

5 Conclusion and future enhancement

Our work presented a model proposed by team IIITDWD for detecting abusive categories in Tamil-English code mixed text as part of the shared task DravidianLangTech@ACL 2022. Our proposed model came in 9th place among the participating teams, with a significant accuracy value of 62%. In the proposed model, we employed the transformer-based IndicBERT, trained on Indic languages, to

Team name	Acc	m_F1
abusive-checker	0.65	0.41
GJG_TamilEnglish _deBERTa	0.60	0.35
umuteam	0.59	0.35
pandas	0.52	0.34
Optimize_Prime_Tamil _English_Run2	0.45	0.29
IITDWD	**0.626**	**0.187**

Table 3: Top performing models

extract features for classification with improved results. We can further improve the model performance by fine-tuning the model on Dravidian languages and including domain-specific embeddings.

References

Shankar Biradar, Sunil Saumya, and Arun Chauhan. 2021. Hate or non-hate: Translation based hate speech identification in code-mixed hinglish data set. In *2021 IEEE International Conference on Big Data (Big Data)*, pages 2470–2475. IEEE.

Shankar Biradar, Sunil Saumya, and Arun Chauhan. 2022. Combating the infodemic: Covid-19 induced fake news recognition in social media networks. *Complex & Intelligent Systems*, pages 1–13.

Steven Bird, Ewan Klein, and Edward Loper. 2009. *Natural language processing with Python: analyzing text with the natural language toolkit.* " O'Reilly Media, Inc.".

Aditya Bohra, Deepanshu Vijay, Vinay Singh, Syed Sarfaraz Akhtar, and Manish Shrivastava. 2018. A dataset of hindi-english code-mixed social media text for hate speech detection. In *Proceedings of the second workshop on computational modeling of people's opinions, personality, and emotions in social media*, pages 36–41.

Bharathi Raja Chakravarthi, Navya Jose, Shardul Suryawanshi, Elizabeth Sherly, and John Philip McCrae. 2020a. A sentiment analysis dataset for code-mixed malayalam-english. In *Proceedings of the 1st Joint Workshop on Spoken Language Technologies for Under-resourced languages (SLTU) and Collaboration and Computing for Under-Resourced Languages (CCURL)*, pages 177–184.

Bharathi Raja Chakravarthi, Vigneshwaran Muralidaran, Ruba Priyadharshini, and John Philip McCrae. 2020b. Corpus creation for sentiment analysis in code-mixed tamil-english text. In *Proceedings of the 1st Joint Workshop on Spoken Language Technologies for Under-resourced languages (SLTU) and Collaboration and Computing for Under-Resourced Languages (CCURL)*, pages 202–210.

Bharathi Raja Chakravarthi, Ruba Priyadharshini, Parameswari Krishnamurthy, Elizabeth Sherly, et al. 2021. Proceedings of the first workshop on speech and language technologies for dravidian languages. In *Proceedings of the First Workshop on Speech and Language Technologies for Dravidian Languages*.

Michele Corazza, Stefano Menini, Elena Cabrio, Sara Tonelli, and Serena Villata. 2020. A multilingual evaluation for online hate speech detection. *ACM Transactions on Internet Technology (TOIT)*, 20(2):1–22.

Jacob Devlin, Ming-Wei Chang, Kenton Lee, and Kristina Toutanova. 2018. Bert: Pre-training of deep bidirectional transformers for language understanding. *arXiv preprint arXiv:1810.04805*.

Suman Dowlagar and Radhika Mamidi. 2021. Offlangone@ dravidianlangtech-eacl2021: Transformers with the class balanced loss for offensive language identification in dravidian code-mixed text. In *Proceedings of the First Workshop on Speech and Language Technologies for Dravidian Languages*, pages 154–159.

Adeep Hande, Ruba Priyadharshini, and Bharathi Raja Chakravarthi. 2020. Kancmd: Kannada codemixed dataset for sentiment analysis and offensive language detection. In *Proceedings of the Third Workshop on Computational Modeling of People's Opinions, Personality, and Emotion's in Social Media*, pages 54–63.

Divyanshu Kakwani, Anoop Kunchukuttan, Satish Golla, NC Gokul, Avik Bhattacharyya, Mitesh M Khapra, and Pratyush Kumar. 2020. Indicnlpsuite: Monolingual corpora, evaluation benchmarks and pre-trained multilingual language models for indian languages. In *Findings of the Association for Computational Linguistics: EMNLP 2020*, pages 4948–4961.

Thomas Mandl, Sandip Modha, Anand Kumar M, and Bharathi Raja Chakravarthi. 2020. Overview of the hasoc track at fire 2020: Hate speech and offensive language identification in tamil, malayalam, hindi, english and german. In *Forum for Information Retrieval Evaluation*, pages 29–32.

Thomas Mandl, Sandip Modha, Prasenjit Majumder, Daksh Patel, Mohana Dave, Chintak Mandlia, and Aditya Patel. 2019. Overview of the hasoc track at fire 2019: Hate speech and offensive content identification in indo-european languages. In *Proceedings of the 11th forum for information retrieval evaluation*, pages 14–17.

Puneet Mathur, Rajiv Shah, Ramit Sawhney, and Debanjan Mahata. 2018. Detecting offensive tweets in hindi-english code-switched language. In *Proceedings of the Sixth International Workshop on Natural Language Processing for Social Media*, pages 18–26.

Shana Poplack and James A Walker. 2003. Pieter muysken, bilingual speech: a typology of code-mixing. cambridge: Cambridge university press, 2000. pp. xvi+ 306. *Journal of Linguistics*, 39(3):678–683.

Ruba Priyadharshini, Bharathi Raja Chakravarthi, Subalalitha Chinnaudayar Navaneethakrishnan, Thenmozhi Durairaj, Malliga Subramanian, Kogilavani Shanmugavadivel, Siddhanth U Hegde, and Prasanna Kumar Kumaresan. 2022. Findings of the shared task on Abusive Comment Detection in Tamil. In *Proceedings of the Second Workshop on Speech and Language Technologies for Dravidian Languages*. Association for Computational Linguistics.

PANDAS@TamilNLP-ACL2022: Emotion Analysis in Tamil Text using Language Agnostic Embeddings

Krithika S
SSN College of Engineering
krithika2010039@ssn.edu.in

Divyasri K
SSN College of Engineering
divyasri2011037@ssn.edu.in

Gayathri G L
SSN College of Engineering
gayathri2010090@ssn.edu.in

Durairaj Thenmozhi
SSN College of Engineering
theni_d@ssn.edu.in

B. Bharathi
SSN College of Engineering
bharathib@ssn.edu.in

B. Senthilkumar
SSN College of Engineering
senthil@ssn.edu.in

Abstract

As the world around us continues to become increasingly digital, it has been acknowledged that there is a growing need for emotion analysis of social media content. The task of identifying the emotion in a given text has many practical applications ranging from screening public health to business and management. In this paper, we propose a language agnostic model that focuses on emotion analysis in Tamil text. Our experiments yielded an F1-score of 0.010.

1 Introduction

Over the past decade, advances in technology have progressed at an extraordinary rate, which in turn has rapidly transformed our methods of communication, expedited by the need for all institutions and establishments to 'go digital'. People have adapted to online modes of communication such as social networking sites and online discussion forums. These platforms have many advantages such as the ability to bring people with similar passions together and enable them to exchange their views, or the capacity to allow people to rally together for a common cause. It would be useful for these platforms to identify people with common interests by filtering through their comments. On the other hand, there are also some disadvantages that arise from the abuse of these tools, which are not limited to, but include, the posting of inappropriate or hurtful comments (O'Keeffe et al., 2011), (Gao et al., 2020). To ensure moderation in content, it is necessary to monitor posts and comments published on various social media (Naslund JA, 2020). Research suggests that monitoring social media can be useful in surveying, understanding and predicting public health (Chancellor and Choudhury, 2020), (Aiello et al., 2020), (Brenda K. Wiederhold, 2020). Social media analytics can also aid in enterprise management (Lee, 2018) and national security (Sykora et al., 2013). A commonly used method to monitor social media is emotion analysis.

Emotions are subjective mental states that are brought about as reactions to our thoughts or memories, or as reactions to external events in our surroundings. Speech and text are both generally associated with an emotion of some kind - joy, sorrow, fear, anger, etc. Classifying a given text into one of the many categories of emotions is a constructive way to analyze and obtain some understanding of the text (Kim and Klinger, 2018). Such textual emotion analysis has many practical applications. For example, Unilever analyzes the emotional expressions of prospective candidates for its entry-level jobs, which helps in saving a significant amount of time during the candidate screening process.

The task of Emotion Analysis in Tamil - DravidianLangTech@ACL 2022[1] (Sampath et al., 2022) aims to classify a set of given comments by predicting the probable emotions associated with each one. A particular trial faced here is that of the dataset being in the Tamil language, for which comparatively less resources are available. In this paper, we have used a Language-Agnostic Sentence Embedder called LaBSE, a popular multilingual BERT embedding model to identify the emotions in Tamil text.

The rest of the paper is organized as follows: section 2 outlines any related works ascertained by a literature survey; section 3 provides a description of the dataset; section 4 details the methodology used for this task; section 5 discusses the results and in section 6, a conclusion is put forward.

2 Related Work

The field of Emotion Analysis allows for a multitude of approaches to be used, some of which have been documented in prominent literature. With the recent research and development in speech to text concepts, various researchers have gone about building and testing fast and accurate models for

[1]https://competitions.codalab.org/competitions/36396

Proceedings of the Second Workshop on Speech and Language Technologies for Dravidian Languages, pages 105 - 111
May 26, 2022 ©2022 Association for Computational Linguistics

Category	Definition	Example	Data points in train	Data points in dev
Neutral	Datapoints which do not express any of the above emotions	இவர் யார்? ஒவ்வொரு வார்த்தையும் முன்னுக்கு பின் முரணாக உள்ளது	4841	1222
Joy	Statements which show happiness	அருமை நண்பா ...தமிழன் என்பதே பெருமை ..	2134	558
Ambiguous	Sentences that express more than one meaning	நண்பா அடுத்து சூரத் போவீங்களா. போறதா இருந்தா உங்களோட நானும் வரலாமா	1689	437
Trust	Expressions that show strong belief that someone is good or honest	உண்மையை உணர வைத்த உத்தமர்!	1254	272
Disgust	Statements that express unpleasantness and non approval	தினமும் ஸ்டாலின் செருப்ப தொடைத்து கொடுக்குற வன் தான் இந்த ராசா	910	210
Anger	Emotions which show antagonization	இதுவும் ஒரு பைத்தியம். என்னடா வாய் இது	834	184
Anticipation	These are comments that show pleasurable expectations	காவல் துறையினரை அனைவரும் கடவுளாக பார்க்க வேண்டும்...	828	213
Sadness	Sentences which express grief	விவேக் ஐயா உங்களை என்னால் மறக்க முடியாது	695	191
Love	Sentences which express deep affection	அம்மா பண்ணாரி அம்மா	675	189
Surprise	Emotions that arise when reacting to an unexpected event	ஏன் உவரும் கோயம்புத்தூர் தான் அக்கா	248	53
Fear	Emotions expressing fright	பாசக்கார அண்ணன் தம்பி	100	23

Table 1: Data distribution

sentiment analysis, especially using inputs from Indian languages. One such work was done by (Uma and Kausika) (V.Uma et al., 2016) by applying the SVM model on an independent corpus of Tamil and English tweets, which were segregated into positive, neutral and negative labels.

Anand Kumar Madasamy, Soman Kotti Padannayil (Seshadri et al., 2016) formulated a tri-layer RNN for the SAIL task of classifying tweets in Indian languages with 1500 lines of Tamil, Hindi and Bengali, which was applied on the Indian textual tweets. This was compared with a Naive Bayes model given by the SAIL task, which gave a significantly lesser accuracy.

Sajeetha Thavareesan and Sinnathamby Mahesan (Thavareesan and Mahesan, 2021) modeled 5 different approaches for sentiment analysis of Tamil texts. They experimented on the UJ_Corpus_Opinions and SAIL-2015 corpus .They extracted the features using TF, BoW , TF-IDF , Word2vec and fastText. They subsequently used Lexicon based and ML based approaches (using SVM , Extreme Gradient Boost EGB, Random Forest RF, Neural Network NN, Linear Regression LR, k nearest Neighbours kNN). They observed that feature extraction using fastText and EGB outperformed the rest. Xiaotian Lin et al (Lin et al., 2021), performed a multilingual text classification - classification into positive, negative ,neutral and mixed emotions using a plain laBSE model, which was comparatively better than the models XLM, XLM RoBERTa and Multilingual BERT. They used the MLM strategy to achieve the desired result. A research work done by Niveditha et al (Nivedhitha et al., 2016) modeled an unsupervised approach on the 2015 SAIL dataset to feature extraction using SentiWordNet and Word2vec embeddings. Kamal et al. (Sarkar, 2015) participated in the SAIL shared task, which included classifying tweets given in the Hindi and Bengali languages. They processed the tweets with the emoticons and used Multinomial Naive Bayes model. For opinion mining in Hindi (into positive, negative, neutral), they used POS tagging in which adjectives were analyzed to perform the task of mining.

Other state of the art models include CNN, RNN, BiLSTM models and ML techniques implemented on these embeddings.

The conclusion from the aforementioned literature is that LaBSE shows encouraging results in feature extraction, and such datasets comprising Tamil and other subcontinental languages are best served by this transformer. Emotional Analysis and classification of emotion is found to be done most effectively by SVM classifier. In summation, a model which incorporates elements of SVM and LaBSE can be expected to be a good approach for this ACL task, and it is also a novel outlook, which has not been examined by the authors listed above.

3 Dataset

The dataset under consideration for the task consists of comments made by YouTube users in the

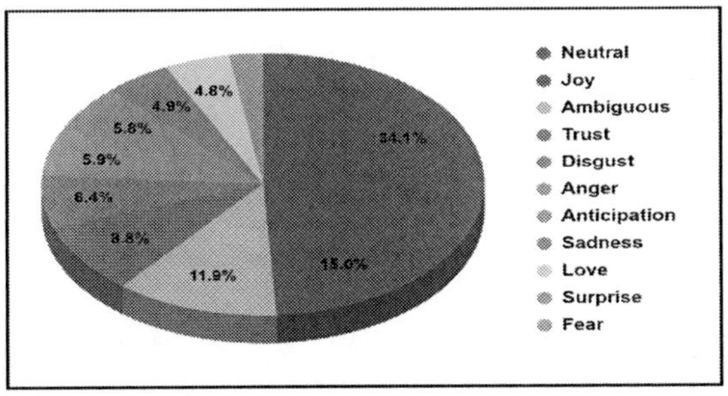

Figure 1: Data distribution of the Training dataset

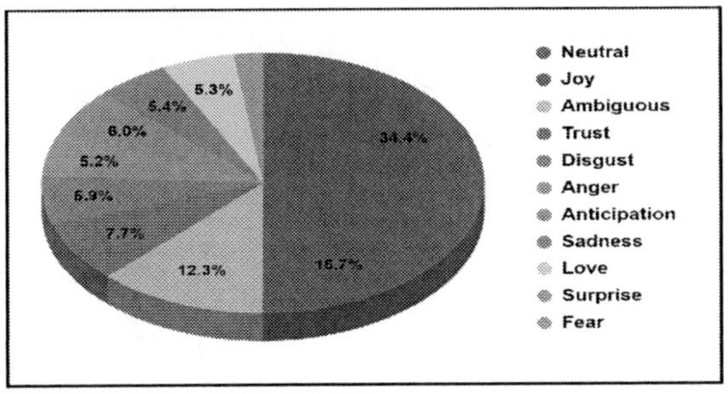

Figure 2: Data distribution of the Development dataset

Tamil language. One of the Dravidian languages and predominantly spoken in Tamil Nadu (India), Tamil has a unique script and an alphabet that is made up of 12 vowels and 18 consonants that when combined in various ways, can give rise to about 216 compound characters.

The comments in this dataset are grouped under 11 different categories based on the emotion that each conveys, as is shown in Table 1. Figure 1 and Figure 2 depict the variance in the training and development datasets. The comments in the training dataset have an average length of 1.18 sentences, with the longest comment having 13 sentences. The average word count per comment is 9.7.

4 Methodology

The proposed methodology for this task includes extracting structural features from the processed data and applying classifier models to them. A schematic diagram illustrating the procedure is given in Figure 3.

4.1 Preprocessing

Any given raw dataset may contain inconsistencies in its data or may contain some unnecessary data known as noise. Before feeding the data to the required algorithm, it is therefore important to clean the dataset. This process of cleaning the data is known as preprocessing and involves a series of steps. The procedure adopted in this task is as follows:

1. Checking for inconsistencies in the dataset: Many models cannot be trained if any inconsistencies, such as empty rows or mismatched values, are present in the dataset. These anomalies were first removed from the dataset.

2. Removal of punctuation and special characters: The model used focuses on identifying words in the text and creating a corpus of the most frequent words in every category of text in the dataset. Punctuation and special characters interfere with this process and hence, they were removed from the text using a list of punctuation marks from the string library and a custom-made list of special characters. In this case, emoticons were also considered to be special characters and have been removed from the text.

3. Transformation of the data: In this step, the text is converted into a form suitable for the mining process. To establish uniformity in the data and thereby reduce misinterpretation, the text was normalized by the conversion of all text to lowercase.

4. Reduction of the data: In any text, there is a considerable amount of fillers or stop words, i.e., words that do not convey any information necessary for the task of analyzing the text. These words may be important for the grammar of the language, but are redundant in the mining process. Such words have been removed from the text using a custom-made list of stop words in Tamil.

5. Balancing of the dataset: As is observed from the dataset, there is an imbalance in the distribution of data in the training dataset. This can lead to huge inaccuracies in the predicted results. To balance out the data, Synthetic Minority Oversampling Technique (or SMOTE)[2] was used. It is a statistical oversampling technique that helps to overcome an imbalance in data by generating synthetic data for the

[2] https://towardsdatascience.com/machine-learning-multiclass-classification-with-imbalanced-data-set-29f6a177c1a

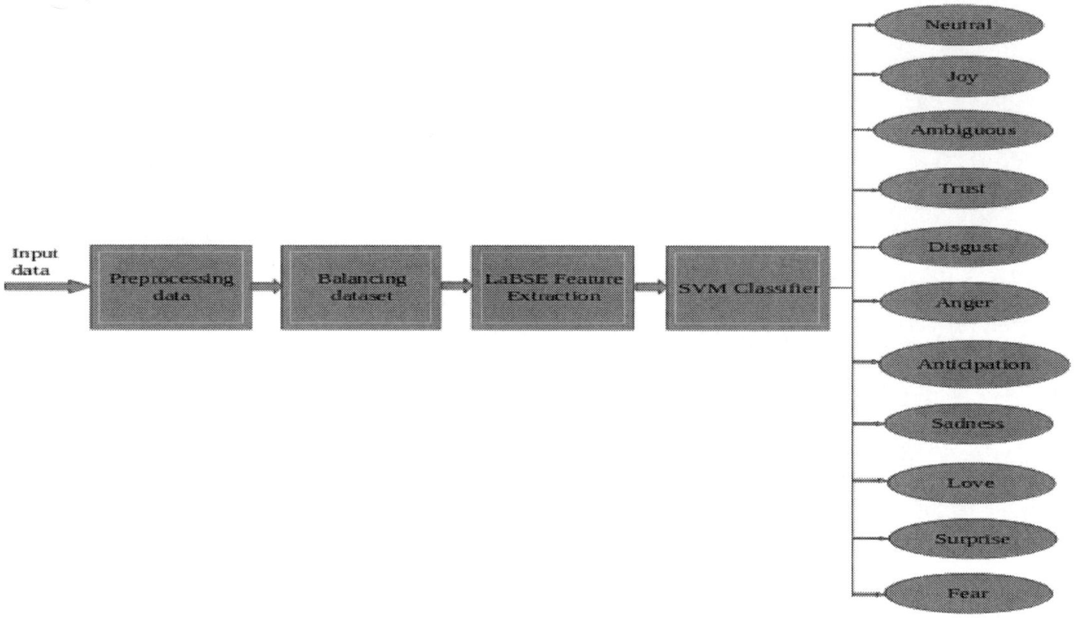

Figure 3: Schematic diagram of the methodology

minority categories in the dataset. It utilizes a k-nearest neighbors algorithm by choosing a minority input vector and adding a new datapoint anywhere between it and one of its nearest neighbors. The process is repeated until the dataset is balanced.

4.2 Embeddings and Feature Extraction

For analyzing text, embedding is used to represent words in the form of real-valued vectors that encode the meaning of the words with the intention that words which are expected to have similar meanings are grouped together.

A feature is a characteristic or property by which a given text can be measured or quantified. Raw data is complex and contains a vast number of features, which makes the process of training a model on the dataset cumbersome. Feature extraction reduces the number of dimensions required to define a large dataset by creating a smaller set of new features and rejecting the larger number of existing ones. In this stage, raw data is transformed into numerical features that can be further processed.

4.2.1 LaBSE feature extraction

Language-Agnostic BERT Sentence Embedding, or LaBSE, is a multilingual language model developed by Google, based on the BERT model. It performs tokenization using Wordpiece, the subword-based tokenization algorithm.

LaBSE is a dual encoder model, with each of its two encoders encoding source and target sentences independently, which are then fed to a scoring function to rank them based on their similarity. This latest technique for sentence embedding encodes sentences into a shared embedding space wherein similar sentences are stored next to each other.

LaBSE is currently a popular model for feature extraction. (Rodríguez et al., 2021) used LaBSE both for feature extraction and as an end to end model for classification and reported that its usage improves the performance for both mono-lingual and cross-lingual sets of data.

For this task, we used LaBSE for embedding the preprocessed data, which was then passed to a Classifier model for classification of the given text based on the emotions associated with them. We used the default parameters for the laBSE model with the learning rate set to 0.001. The model includes 630 dense layers and 1 sigmoid layer.

4.3 Models applied

The models we experimented on for this task include the SVM Classifer and some simple transformers like LaBSE and IndicBERT[3]. After some consideration, we decided on implementing a model that combines LaBSE feature extraction with the SVM Classifier.

[3]https://github.com/AI4Bharat/indic-bert/blob/master

4.3.1 SVM Classifier

Support Vector Machine, or SVM, is a supervised machine learning algorithm that is widely used for classification-based problems (Yang et al., 2015). It works by mapping data to a high-dimensional feature space in which the data points can be easily categorized. Scaling up the dimensionality greatly contributes to the probability of the data being classified accurately, even when linear separation of the data is not possible.

4.4 Experimentation with SMOTE

Since the dataset is highly biased towards 'Neutral' text, we considered the effects of balancing out the data before training the model. The SMOTE technique is used for making a dataset balanced, as discussed above in subsection 4.1. We have tabulated our results for the classification model in Table 2 to compare the case in which SMOTE was used with the case in which it is not used.

Model	Precision	Recall	F1	Accuracy
LaBSE for feature extraction with SVM Classifier without SMOTE preprocessing	0.40	0.23	0.25	0.43
LaBSE for feature extraction with SVM Classifier after SMOTE preprocessing	0.40	0.25	0.27	0.44

Table 2: Training results for the models under consideration

4.4.1 LaBSE embedding with SVM Classifier

The data, stripped of special characters, stop words and inconsistencies, was passed through a LaBSE embedding model for feature extraction. The output was then given to an SVM Classifier and the results were recorded.

4.4.2 LaBSE embedding with SVM Classifier and SMOTE preprocessing

The data, preprocessed with an additional step of balancing out the dataset using an oversampling technique (SMOTE), was allowed to undergo feature extraction using LaBSE, followed by classification of the text using an SVM Classifier.

5 Results and Analysis

It is apparent that the results are slightly better when SMOTE is used along with the classification model, although the dataset seems to be so highly unbalanced that there is very little difference between the two results.

5.1 Performance metrics

This task is evaluated on the macro averages of three performance metrics - Precision, Recall and F1-score[4]. The metrics are computed separately for each class and then the scores are averaged to ensure equal priority for each performance class.

In classification, precision refers to the probability that a classification has been performed accurately. It is the ratio of correctly classified data points to the total number of data points that have been predicted to be of that class.

$$Precision = \frac{TP}{TP + FP}$$

Recall gives some measure of the number of classifications belonging to a particular category that are performed without error. It is the ratio of the correctly classified points of a particular class to the sum of the correctly and incorrectly classified points of the same class.

$$Recall = \frac{TP}{TP + FN}$$

F1-score is the weighted average of precision and recall, and is often used when a balance of both these metrics is needed or when a large class imbalance is encountered.

$$F1 - score = 2 * \frac{Precision * Recall}{Precision + Recall}$$

Team	Precision	Recall	F1	Rank
CUET16	0.220	0.250	0.210	1
GJG_Emotion Analysis_taskA	0.110	0.160	0.050	2
MSDBLSTM _TamilData	0.090	0.080	0.050	2
MSD	0.090	0.100	0.040	2
pandas_tamil	**0.080**	**0.070**	**0.010**	**8**

Table 3: Performance results for the Emotion Analysis task

[4]https://towardsdatascience.com/accuracy-precision-recall-or-f1-331fb37c5cb9

5.2 Results

The development dataset was used for the evaluating the performance of the models after training them. The final performance results on the test dataset for the task are recorded in Table 3.

For the given dataset, LaBSE feature extraction along with the SVM Classifier yielded better results than other models that were experimented with. The accuracy was slightly increased when the data was further preprocessed using the SMOTE technique.

Our submission secured the 8th rank in Task B, i.e., Emotion Analysis on a Tamil dataset. Our model procured an F1-Score of 0.010, a Precision score of 0.080 and a Recall score of 0.070.

6 Conclusion

In this research paper, we have presented a multilingual transformer model for the emotion analysis of Tamil text as required by the DravidianTechLang ACL 2022 shared task. LaBSE, a pre-trained language agnostic BERT model, was found to perform comparatively well on the Tamil dataset. This model yielded an F1-score of 0.010 on the given dataset. We believe that these results can be improved upon highly by using custom embeddings, based on statistical analysis of the language, to process the data before training the model.

References

Allison E. Aiello, Audrey Renson, and Paul N. Zivich. 2020. Social media– and internet-based disease surveillance for public health. *Annual Review of Public Health*, 41(1):101–118. PMID: 31905322.

MBA BCB BCN Brenda K. Wiederhold, PhD. 2020. Cyberpsychology, behavior, and social networking. *International Association of CyberPsychology, Training, and Rehabilitation (iACToR)*, 25.

Stevie Chancellor and Munmun Choudhury. 2020. Methods in predictive techniques for mental health status on social media: a critical review. *npj Digital Medicine*, 3.

Junling Gao, Pinpin Zheng, Yingnan Jia, Hao Chen, Yimeng Mao, Suhong Chen, Yi Wang, Hua Fu, and Junming Dai. 2020. Mental health problems and social media exposure during covid-19 outbreak. *PLOS ONE*, 15(4):1–10.

Evgeny Kim and Roman Klinger. 2018. A survey on sentiment and emotion analysis for computational literary studies. *CoRR*, abs/1808.03137.

In Lee. 2018. Social media analytics for enterprises: Typology, methods, and processes. *Business Horizons*, 61.

Xiaotian Lin, Nankai Lin, Kanoksak Wattanachote, Shengyi Jiang, and Lianxi Wang. 2021. Multilingual text classification for dravidian languages. *CoRR*, abs/2112.01705.

Torous J Aschbrenner KA Naslund JA, Bondre A. 2020. Social Media and Mental Health: Benefits, Risks, and Opportunities for Research and Practice. *J Technol Behav Sci.*, (12):245–257.

E. Nivedhitha, Shinde Pooja Sanjay, M. Anand Kumar, and K. P. Soman. 2016. Unsupervised word embedding based polarity detection for tamil tweets. *Control theory & applications*, 9.

Gwenn Schurgin O'Keeffe, Kathleen Clarke-Pearson, Council on Communications, and Media. 2011. The Impact of Social Media on Children, Adolescents, and Families. *Pediatrics*, 127(4):800–804.

Sebastián E. Rodríguez, Héctor Allende-Cid, and Héctor Allende. 2021. Detecting hate speech in cross-lingual and multi-lingual settings using language agnostic representations. In *Progress in Pattern Recognition, Image Analysis, Computer Vision, and Applications - 25th Iberoamerican Congress, CIARP 2021, Revised Selected Papers*, Lecture Notes in Computer Science (including subseries Lecture Notes in Artificial Intelligence and Lecture Notes in Bioinformatics), pages 77–87. Springer Science and Business Media Deutschland GmbH. Funding Information: Acknowledgment. This work was supported in part by Basal Project AFB 1800082, in part by Project DGIIP-UTFSM PI-LIR-2020-17. Héctor Allende-Cid work is supported by PUCV VRIEA. Publisher Copyright: © 2021, Springer Nature Switzerland AG.; null ; Conference date: 10-05-2021 Through 13-05-2021.

Anbukkarasi Sampath, Thenmozhi Durairaj, Bharathi Raja Chakravarthi, Ruba Priyadharshini, Subalalitha Chinnaudayar Navaneethakrishnan, Kogilavani Shanmugavadivel, Sajeetha Thavareesan, Sathiyaraj Thangasamy, Parameswari Krishnamurthy, Adeep Hande, Sean Benhur, and Santhiya Ponnusamy, Kishor Kumar Pandiyan. 2022. Findings of the shared task on Emotion Analysis in Tamil. In *Proceedings of the Second Workshop on Speech and Language Technologies for Dravidian Languages*. Association for Computational Linguistics.

Kamal Sarkar. 2015. A sentiment analysis system for indian language tweets. volume 9468.

S. Seshadri, M. Kumar, and Soman Kp. 2016. Analyzing sentiment in indian languages micro text using recurrent neural network. 7:313–318.

Martin Sykora, Tom Jackson, Ann O'Brien, and Suzanne Elayan. 2013. National security and social media monitoring: a presentation of the emotive and related systems.

Sajeetha Thavareesan and Sinnathamby Mahesan. 2021. Sentiment analysis in tamil texts using k-means and k-nearest neighbour. In *2021 10th International Conference on Information and Automation for Sustainability (ICIAfS)*, pages 48–53.

Samir E. Abdelrahman V.Uma, N. Kaushikaa, Umar Farooq, and Tej Prasad Dhamala. 2016. Sentiment analysis of english and tamil tweets using path length similarity based word sense disambiguation.

Yujun Yang, Jianping Li, and Yimei Yang. 2015. The research of the fast svm classifier method. *2015 12th International Computer Conference on Wavelet Active Media Technology and Information Processing (ICCWAMTIP)*, pages 121–124.

PANDAS@TamilNLP-ACL2022: Abusive Comment Detection in Tamil Code-Mixed Data Using Custom Embeddings with LaBSE

Gayathri G L
SSN College of Engineering
gayathri2010090@ssn.edu.in

Krithika S
SSN College of Engineering
krithika2010039@ssn.edu.in

Divyasri K
SSN College of Engineering
divyasri2011037@ssn.edu.in

Durairaj Thenmozhi
SSN College of Engineering
theni_d@ssn.edu.in

B. Bharathi
SSN College of Engineering
bharathib@ssn.edu.in

Abstract

Abusive language has lately been prevalent in comments on various social media platforms. The increasing hostility observed on the internet calls for the creation of a system that can identify and flag such acerbic content, to prevent conflict and mental distress. This task becomes more challenging when low-resource languages like Tamil, as well as the often-observed Tamil-English code-mixed text, are involved. The approach used in this paper for the classification model includes different methods of feature extraction and the use of traditional classifiers. We propose a novel method of combining language-agnostic sentence embeddings with the TF-IDF vector representation that uses a curated corpus of words as vocabulary, to create a custom embedding, which is then passed to an SVM classifier. Our experimentation yielded an accuracy of 52% and a macro F1-score of 0.54.

1 Introduction

In recent times, with rapid digitisation, people are increasingly using social media and various other forums available online for interpersonal communication (Riehm et al., 2020). However, these platforms also come with their own share of drawbacks, such as the propagation of fake news (Waszak et al., 2018) and cyberbullying (Whittaker and Kowalski, 2015), to list a few.

Comments that are found to be offensive and often degrading, that may be targeted at an individual or a community as a whole, are categorised as abusive comments. These comments often have negative effects on the mental well-being of people (O'Reilly et al., 2018), with an apparent relation between the time spent on social media and increasing levels of depression (Karim et al., 2020). There is a pressing need for moderation on these websites, which motivates the creation of a system that will be able to classify abusive comments into one of many categories. It could also be useful in identifying and filtering out vitriolic content.

A major challenge faced with this task is that most of the data available contains a mixture of languages (Lin et al., 2021), with people often transliterating from their native language into English, thus posing a hurdle, as most resources available for the task of Abusive language detection are pre-trained on English text.

Tamil is a Dravidian classical language used by the Tamil people of South Asia. Tamil is an official language of Tamil Nadu, Sri Lanka, Singapore, and the Union Territory of Puducherry in India. Tamil is one of the world's longest-surviving classical languages. Malayalam is Tamil's closest significant cousin; the two began splitting during the 9th century AD (Anita and Subalalitha, 2019b,a; Subalalitha and Poovammal, 2018; Subalalitha, 2019; Srinivasan and Subalalitha, 2019; Narasimhan et al., 2018; Sakuntharaj and Mahesan, 2021, 2017, 2016; Thavareesan and Mahesan, 2019, 2020a,b, 2021).

The Task A of Abusive Comment Detection in Tamil-ACL 2022 (Priyadharshini et al.) involves classification of purely Tamil text, whereas task B deals with the classification of code-mixed Tamil English text into 8 categories as listed in Table 1. Our approach for Task B was to create embeddings for each data record and then pass them to the various classifiers. Three types of embeddings were employed - a multilingual BERT that produces language-agnostic embeddings, TF-IDF vectorizer and a combination of both.

The remainder of this paper is organised as follows. Section 2 is dedicated to related works obtained from the literature survey. Section 3 proceeds to describe the dataset used. Section 4 covers the details of the preprocessing steps, outlines the feature extraction process and describes the model employed for this task. Section 5 summarises the results and Section 6 concludes the paper.

Proceedings of the Second Workshop on Speech and Language Technologies for Dravidian Languages, pages 112 - 119
May 26, 2022 ©2022 Association for Computational Linguistics

Category	Definition	Example	Train	Dev
None-of-the-above	Does not belong in any of the other categories	Bala kumar wat ur asking.? 1st olunga kealviya kealunga.	3715	917
Misandry	These are comments indicating contempt against men.	Poda H cha naaye	830	218
Counter-Speech	It is a way of undermining a harsh remark by giving alternate narratives of the story.	Manickam Anbu ammaavai pathi pesurathu sari kidaiyaathu.	348	95
Xenophobia	These are comments that involve hatred towards people of a different culture/ country.	kudisekiram tamilnadu china controll poidum...	297	70
Hope-Speech	These contain sentences that include phrases indicative of hope and other such positive emotions.	DMKJambu Lingaa OK manaviyai mathippom. Malai pola valgaiyil uyarvom.	213	53
Misogyny	These are hateful statements against women.	Gh Wb u pondatti pundaila en Pola Vidava... ungomma punda naaruthu	211	50
Homophobia	Statements with a negative connotation, targeted towards homosexuality.	Nee Naam gay sax pannalam	172	43
Transphobia	Referring to those hateful comments having a prejudice against transgender people.	Pitchakara Moothevinga Train la Ukkara uda maatithunga Parathesinga thuu. Ithungaluku daily azha vendiyatha iruku	157	40

Table 1: Description of the dataset

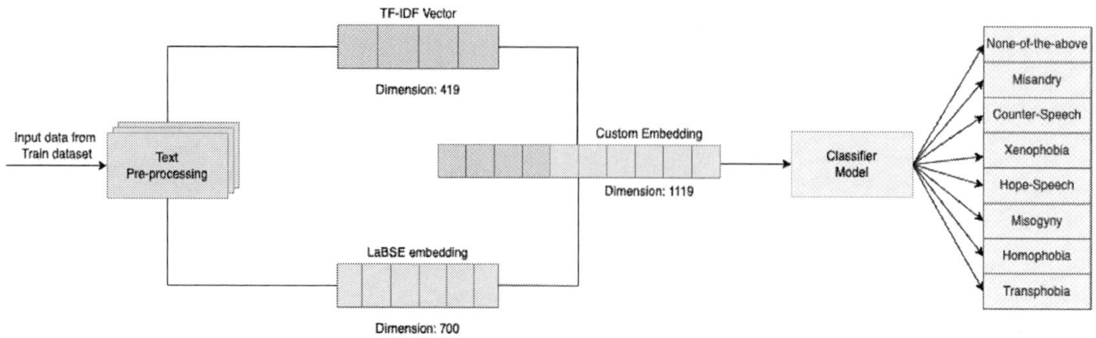

Figure 1: Diagram of the model

2 Related Works

Identification and classification of offensive tasks in a fast and effective manner is very important in the moderation of online platforms (Priyadharshini et al., 2021; Kumaresan et al., 2021; Chakravarthi, 2020; Chakravarthi and Muralidaran, 2021; Sampath et al., 2022; Ravikiran et al., 2022; Chakravarthi et al., 2022; Bharathi et al., 2022). We explored various models to achieve the same.

Ravishankar et al. (Ravishankar and Raghunathan, 2017) proposed three different approaches to classify tamil tweets based on syntactic patterns. These include Tweet weight model, TF-IDF and Domain-Specific Tags (DST), and used Tamil Dictionary (Agarathi).The authors collected tweets from 100 movies which amounted upto 7000 tweets. They proposed three other feature extraction models which include TF-IDF, adjective rules, negation rules, and adjective rules which could be passed into classifiers.

Alison P. Ribeiro et al.(Ribeiro and Silva, 2019) presented their model to identify hate speech against women and immigrants. It consisted of pre-trained word embeddings using FastText and GloVe which they passed through a CNN network.

Younes Samih et al. (Modha et al., 2021) modelled an architecture with Support Vector Machine (SVM) and Deep Neural Networks (DNNs) for task to identify Hate Speech and offensive content. They experimented four different approaches and combined them into an ensemble. They used FastText for the first one, FFNN architecture with four hidden layers for the second one and for the third one they created pretrained word embeddings using Mazajak method which was then passed into a CNN layer and a BiLSTM layer. Their next approach was using BERT. They combined these to create an ensemble which performed well for the given dataset.

Anna Glazkova et al.(Glazkova et al., 2021) for the HASOC 2021 task which focused on detecting offensive, profane and hate content in tweets in six languages . They proposed various models which include pretrained BERT, RoBERTa and LaBSE. Though the performance of the models were similar for the English datasets, LaBSE outperformed the others for Hindi and Marathi datasets.

Shervin et al (Malmasi and Zampieri, 2017) used a corpus of 14.5k English tweets and modelled an approach to classify them as hate speech and non-hate speech. Their model uses character n-grams, word n-grams and word skip-grams for feature extraction which was passed onto a linear SVM classifier.

Burnap et al. in their paper (Burnap and Williams, 2014) wrote about their model - they used unigram , bigram feature extraction techniques and POS (Parts of Speech tagging), they also used the Stanford Lexical Parser, along with a context-free lexical parsing model, to extract typed dependencies within the tweet text. This was further passed to classifiers like Bayesian Logistic Regression, Random Forest Decision Trees and Support Vector Machines.

Aswathi Saravanaraj et al. proposed an approach for the automatic identification of cyberbullying words and rumours. They modelled a Naive Bayes and a Random Forest approach which obtained a greater accuracy then pre-existing models.

From the literature survey performed, it is inferred that an approach involving feature extraction using TF-IDF delivers good results and that transformer models like LaBSE work the best for Indian language datasets, with a particularly high accuracy for the Tamil language. The SVM classifier works well for Hate/Abusive language recognition.

Although various innovative models have been experimented on in the studies discussed above, a model involving TF-IDF feature extraction, LaBSE and SVM, will be a novel approach to this task.

3 Dataset

The dataset used for the study is made up of comments made by subscribers in Tamil language, in relation to a video available on the streaming platform YouTube. The text contents were retrieved and stored following manual annotation. The text statements were organized into 8 different classes: transphobia, counter-speech, misandry, homophobia, hope-speech, xenophobia, misogyny and none-of-the-above, depending on the sentiment reflected through them. The dataset has a highly disproportionate share of expressions being brought under 'none-of-the-above' - 62% from the train dataset and 61% from the development dataset. The data distribution of the train and development datasets is depicted in Table 1. The average number of sentences in a comment is 1.42 with the maximum number being 20 and the minimum number of sentences per data point being 1. The average word count for each row is 12.092.

4 Methodology

The proposed methodology for this task involves extracting lexical and sentence features from the data and applying classifier models, such as SVM, MLP and K neighbours classifier, to them. This is illustrated in Figure 1.

4.1 Preprocessing

Tamil, a Dravidian Language predominantly spoken in the South Asian region, consists of an intricate script consisting of 12 vowels and 18 consonants that can be combined in various ways to give 216 compound characters. The sentences are arranged in the order of Subject Object Verb, and use postpositions. The main difficulty during preprocessing of the code mixed data is the use of different spellings for the same word while typing Tamil sentences in English.

Before mining the text for valuable information, the raw unstructured textual data is stripped of the noise it contains, in the form of punctuations and stop words, to produce meaningful features that might prove instrumental in classifying the samples into the eleven classes available.

1. Text normalisation: Words with different capitalisation may be considered to be different words and, to prevent that from happening, the dataset was standardised by the conversion of the text to lowercase.

2. Removal of punctuations: Since the model involves creating a corpus of the most frequently occurring words in every category, punctuations are removed. The list of punctuations from the string library was used in this process.

3. Removal of extra unwanted characters: The dataset contained a significant number of lines containing noise including emojis and iOS flags which have been filtered out, using RegEx.

4. Removal of stop words: Stop words are words in a language that are used in abundance as a part of the grammatical structure but do not necessarily add to the meaning of the sentence as a whole. These involve propositions, pronouns and articles among others. To achieve this, a curated list of Tamil-English stop words has been created and used. It includes words such as "r" (are), "ur" (your), "nee" (translates to you in Tamil) and "intha" (translates to this in Tamil).

5. Encoding: In the dataset, the data is classified into categories with textual labels. To ensure that the machine learning model is able to understand the data it is being fed, a label encoder is used on the target variable.

4.2 Feature extraction

The training dataset was first preprocessed as described in the above sub-section. Following this, embeddings of the textual data were created as outlined below.

4.2.1 Statistical feature extraction utilising TF-IDF

TF-IDF, standing for term frequency-inverse document frequency, is a method of quantifying a sentence, based on the words it contains. Each row is vectorized using a technique in which every word is essentially given a score that is indicative of its importance in the overall document.

In our implementation, a vocabulary list was first created by extracting the top 100 of the most frequently used words of each category. To ensure

Feature	Classifier	Accuracy	Precision	Recall	F1-score
TF-IDF+LaBSE	SVM	0.74	0.44	0.49	0.70
	MLP	0.67	0.44	0.45	0.49
	Random Forest	0.68	0.34	0.39	0.5
	Gradient Boosting Classifier	0.69	0.55	0.40	0.53
TF-IDF	SVM	0.71	0.28	0.31	0.75
	MLP	0.70	0.41	0.45	0.52
	K Neighbours Classifer	0.66	0.27	0.31	0.44
LaBSE	SVM	0.71	0.32	0.38	0.67
	MLP	0.66	0.38	0.40	0.43

Table 2: Macro-averaged Performance scores of the models deployed

that stop words were not included in the list of most frequent words, they were removed before vectorisation. A TF-IDF vectoriser was then initialised using this custom vocabulary, so that the resultant vector depends upon only the words that are statistically more likely to be found in an abusive comment.

4.2.2 LaBSE feature extraction

Language-Agnostic BERT Sentence Embedding, also known as LaBSE, is the state-of-the-art model in sentence embedding, and works by encoding sentences into a shared embedding space, where similar sentences lie closer to each other (Feng et al., 2020).

LaBSE proves to be a good fit for this task since it is language agnostic and is proven to work better than other previously existing sentence embedders like Doc2Vec and SentenceBERT with regard to languages with low resources (Firmiano and Da Silva, 2021) (Zhu et al., 2021). It is trained on bilingual low-resource sentences as well and works in a way so that it maximises the compatibility between the source sentence and its translation and minimises it with the other samples.

The pre-processed training data is made ready to be classified by encoding it using LaBSE, which creates an embedding with a dimension of 700, for each sentence. The model includes 630 dense layers and 1 sigmoid layer. For this task, the laBSE model was used with the default parameters. The learning rate was set to 0.001.

4.2.3 Custom embeddings

The imbalance of data was first tackled by selecting a number of random data points such that the real life variance is still retained, but the disparity between the number of samples of each type was reduced. In this run, both LaBSE and TF-IDF encodings were used so that the advantages of both these embedding methods could be harnessed in one model.

Individual embeddings of each type were initially created using the methods as described in the above two runs. They were then appended to each other to obtain a custom embedding.

4.3 Classifier Models

Following this, simple ML models such as SVM, MLP, and K Neighbours Classifier were used to classify the embeddings obtained. They are explained as follows;

SVM, also known as Support Vector Machine works by choosing the best hyperplane such that the data classes are segregated better (Mathur and Foody, 2008). RBF kernel has been used in the SVM classifier to optimise the results.

Multilayer Perceptron, abbreviated to MLP, is a feedforward deep learning network consisting of an input layer and output layer that are completely connected to each other by paths. Hidden Layer size of 200 has been used for the optimisation of this particular model, along with rectified linear unit as the activation function.

K neighbours classifier uses the closest K neighbours and identifies the most common class found among them. This label is then assigned to the data point that is to be classified. Here, the classifier uses a value of 3 for the number of neighbours.

Scikit-learn library (Pedregosa et al., 2011) in Python was used to successfully deploy these models and the results are tabulated in Table 2.

5 Results and Analysis

5.1 Performance metrics

This task is evaluated on the Macro averages of Precision, Recall and F1-score, which computes the

Team	Accuracy
abusive-checker	0.650
GJG_TamilEnglish_deBERTa	0.600
UMUteam	0.590
Pandas	**0.520**
Optimize_Prime_Tamil_English_Run2	0.450

Table 3: Results of the shared task

metric individually for each class and then averages the values, so that each class gets equal priority.

In classification, precision refers to the probability that a correct classification has been done. It is the ratio of correctly classified points to the total number of points that have been predicted to be of that class.

$$Precision = \frac{TP}{TP + FP}$$

Recall, on the other hand, gives an idea of the number of classifications of a type that are rightly performed. It is the ratio of the correctly classified points of a particular class to the sum of the correctly and incorrectly classified point of the same class.

$$Recall = \frac{TP}{TP + FN}$$

F1-score is the weighted average of Precision and recall, and is used mostly when a balance of both these metrics is required or when a large class imbalance is encountered.

$$F1 - score = 2 * \frac{Precision * Recall}{Precision + Recall}$$

5.2 Results

The development dataset was used for the unbiased evaluation of the performance of the models that were fit on the training dataset. For this task, the performance metrics used for analysis were accuracy and macro averages, which include precision, recall and F1-score.

For each type of embedding used, SVM was found to be the best classifier and performs better with Radial Basis Function kernel than with Linear kernel, with accuracy scores of 0.70 and 0.71 respectively. From the table, we can also come to the conclusion that an SVM classifier with the custom embedding gives the best performance, with an accuracy of 0.74, outperforming the models employing either LaBSE or TF-IDF, each with an accuracy of only 0.71.

This run secured the 4th rank in Task B which used Tamil English data as is shown in Table 3. The model performed on the test set with a macro F1-Score of 0.34, a precision score of 0.33 and a recall score of 0.37.

6 Conclusion

This paper discusses our approach for the DravidianTechLang ACL 2022 shared task, which aims to identify and classify abusive content in Tamil-English code-mixed text collected from social media. This research contributes to this task by analysing a set of classification models for identifying various types of abusive comments. We have used a combination of embeddings using TF-IDF and LaBSE with the SVM classifier. Our results showed that using this pre-trained multilingual model along with the SVM classifier yielded better results for the code-mixed data.

This model gave us a macro F-1 score of 0.49 and an accuracy of 0.74 on the development dataset, and an accuracy of 0.520 and a weighted F1-score of 0.54 on the test dataset. In the future, we would like to improve our results by using better preprocessing techniques, which may be achieved by acknowledging and utilising the significance of relevant special characters and emoticons in the given text, instead of removing them altogether.

References

R Anita and CN Subalalitha. 2019a. An approach to cluster Tamil literatures using discourse connectives. In *2019 IEEE 1st International Conference on Energy, Systems and Information Processing (ICESIP)*, pages 1–4. IEEE.

R Anita and CN Subalalitha. 2019b. Building discourse parser for Thirukkural. In *Proceedings of the 16th International Conference on Natural Language Processing*, pages 18–25.

B Bharathi, Bharathi Raja Chakravarthi, Subalalitha Chinnaudayar Navaneethakrishnan, N Sripriya, Arunaggiri Pandian, and Swetha Valli. 2022. Findings of the shared task on Speech Recognition for Vulnerable Individuals in Tamil. In *Proceedings of the Second Workshop on Language Technology for Equality, Diversity and Inclusion*. Association for Computational Linguistics.

Peter Burnap and Matthew Leighton Williams. 2014. Hate speech, machine classification and statistical modelling of information flows on twitter: Interpretation and communication for policy decision making.

Bharathi Raja Chakravarthi. 2020. HopeEDI: A multilingual hope speech detection dataset for equality, diversity, and inclusion. In *Proceedings of the Third Workshop on Computational Modeling of People's Opinions, Personality, and Emotion's in Social Media*, pages 41–53, Barcelona, Spain (Online). Association for Computational Linguistics.

Bharathi Raja Chakravarthi and Vigneshwaran Muralidaran. 2021. Findings of the shared task on hope speech detection for equality, diversity, and inclusion. In *Proceedings of the First Workshop on Language Technology for Equality, Diversity and Inclusion*, pages 61–72, Kyiv. Association for Computational Linguistics.

Bharathi Raja Chakravarthi, Ruba Priyadharshini, Thenmozhi Durairaj, John Phillip McCrae, Paul Buitaleer, Prasanna Kumar Kumaresan, and Rahul Ponnusamy. 2022. Findings of the shared task on Homophobia Transphobia Detection in Social Media Comments. In *Proceedings of the Second Workshop on Language Technology for Equality, Diversity and Inclusion*. Association for Computational Linguistics.

Fangxiaoyu Feng, Yinfei Yang, Daniel Cer, Naveen Arivazhagan, and Wei Wang. 2020. Language-agnostic BERT sentence embedding. *CoRR*, abs/2007.01852.

Alan Firmiano and Ticiana L Coelho Da Silva. 2021. Identifying duplicate police reports. In *2021 20th IEEE International Conference on Machine Learning and Applications (ICMLA)*, pages 244–247. IEEE.

Anna Glazkova, Michael Kadantsev, and Maksim Glazkov. 2021. Fine-tuning of pre-trained transformers for hate, offensive, and profane content detection in english and marathi. *arXiv preprint arXiv:2110.12687*.

Fazida Karim, Azeezat A Oyewande, Lamis F Abdalla, Reem Chaudhry Ehsanullah, and Safeera Khan. 2020. Social media use and its connection to mental health: a systematic review. *Cureus*, 12(6).

Prasanna Kumar Kumaresan, Ratnasingam Sakuntharaj, Sajeetha Thavareesan, Subalalitha Navaneethakrishnan, Anand Kumar Madasamy, Bharathi Raja Chakravarthi, and John P McCrae. 2021. Findings of shared task on offensive language identification in Tamil and Malayalam. In *Forum for Information Retrieval Evaluation*, pages 16–18.

Xiaotian Lin, Nankai Lin, Kanoksak Wattanachote, Shengyi Jiang, and Lianxi Wang. 2021. Multilingual text classification for dravidian languages. *arXiv preprint arXiv:2112.01705*.

Shervin Malmasi and Marcos Zampieri. 2017. Detecting hate speech in social media. *arXiv preprint arXiv:1712.06427*.

Ajay Mathur and Giles M Foody. 2008. Multiclass and binary svm classification: Implications for training and classification users. *IEEE Geoscience and remote sensing letters*, 5(2):241–245.

Sandip Modha, Thomas Mandl, Gautam Kishore Shahi, Hiren Madhu, Shrey Satapara, Tharindu Ranasinghe, and Marcos Zampieri. 2021. Overview of the hasoc subtrack at fire 2021: Hate speech and offensive content identification in english and indo-aryan languages and conversational hate speech. In *Forum for Information Retrieval Evaluation*, pages 1–3.

Anitha Narasimhan, Aarthy Anandan, Madhan Karky, and CN Subalalitha. 2018. Porul: Option generation and selection and scoring algorithms for a tamil flash card game. *International Journal of Cognitive and Language Sciences*, 12(2):225–228.

Chikashi Nobata, Joel Tetreault, Achint Thomas, Yashar Mehdad, and Yi Chang. 2016. Abusive language detection in online user content. In *Proceedings of the 25th international conference on world wide web*, pages 145–153.

Michelle O'Reilly, Nisha Dogra, Natasha Whiteman, Jason Hughes, Seyda Eruyar, and Paul Reilly. 2018. Is social media bad for mental health and wellbeing? exploring the perspectives of adolescents. *Clinical child psychology and psychiatry*, 23(4):601–613.

F. Pedregosa, G. Varoquaux, A. Gramfort, V. Michel, B. Thirion, O. Grisel, M. Blondel, P. Prettenhofer, R. Weiss, V. Dubourg, J. Vanderplas, A. Passos, D. Cournapeau, M. Brucher, M. Perrot, and E. Duchesnay. 2011. Scikit-learn: Machine learning in Python. *Journal of Machine Learning Research*, 12:2825–2830.

Ruba Priyadharshini, Bharathi Raja Chakravarthi, Subalalitha Chinnaudayar Navaneethakrishnan, Thenmozhi Durairaj, Malliga Subramanian, Kogilavani Shanmugavadivel, Siddhanth U Hegde, and booktitle = Kumaresan, Prasanna Kumar". Findings of the shared task on Abusive Comment Detection in Tamil.

Ruba Priyadharshini, Bharathi Raja Chakravarthi, Sajeetha Thavareesan, Dhivya Chinnappa, Durairaj Thenmozhi, and Rahul Ponnusamy. 2021. Overview of the DravidianCodeMix 2021 shared task on sentiment detection in Tamil, Malayalam, and Kannada. In *Forum for Information Retrieval Evaluation*, pages 4–6.

Manikandan Ravikiran, Bharathi Raja Chakravarthi, Anand Kumar Madasamy, Sangeetha Sivanesan, Ratnavel Rajalakshmi, Sajeetha Thavareesan, Rahul Ponnusamy, and Shankar Mahadevan. 2022. Findings of the shared task on Offensive Span Identification in code-mixed Tamil-English comments. In *Proceedings of the Second Workshop on Speech and Language Technologies for Dravidian Languages*. Association for Computational Linguistics.

Nadana Ravishankar and Shriram Raghunathan. 2017. Corpus based sentiment classification of tamil movie tweets using syntactic patterns.

Alison Ribeiro and Nádia Silva. 2019. Inf-hateval at semeval-2019 task 5: Convolutional neural networks for hate speech detection against women and immigrants on twitter. In *Proceedings of the 13th International Workshop on Semantic Evaluation*, pages 420–425.

Kira E Riehm, Calliope Holingue, Luther G Kalb, Daniel Bennett, Arie Kapteyn, Qin Jiang, Cindy B Veldhuis, Renee M Johnson, M Daniele Fallin, Frauke Kreuter, et al. 2020. Associations between media exposure and mental distress among us adults at the beginning of the covid-19 pandemic. *American Journal of Preventive Medicine*, 59(5):630–638.

Ratnasingam Sakuntharaj and Sinnathamby Mahesan. 2016. A novel hybrid approach to detect and correct spelling in Tamil text. In *2016 IEEE International Conference on Information and Automation for Sustainability (ICIAfS)*, pages 1–6.

Ratnasingam Sakuntharaj and Sinnathamby Mahesan. 2017. Use of a novel hash-table for speeding-up suggestions for misspelt Tamil words. In *2017 IEEE International Conference on Industrial and Information Systems (ICIIS)*, pages 1–5.

Ratnasingam Sakuntharaj and Sinnathamby Mahesan. 2021. Missing word detection and correction based on context of Tamil sentences using n-grams. In *2021 10th International Conference on Information and Automation for Sustainability (ICIAfS)*, pages 42–47.

Anbukkarasi Sampath, Thenmozhi Durairaj, Bharathi Raja Chakravarthi, Ruba Priyadharshini, Subalalitha Chinnaudayar Navaneethakrishnan, Kogilavani Shanmugavadivel, Sajeetha Thavareesan, Sathiyaraj Thangasamy, Parameswari Krishnamurthy, Adeep Hande, Sean Benhur, Kishor Kumar Ponnusamy, and Santhiya Pandiyan. 2022. Findings of the shared task on Emotion Analysis in Tamil. In *Proceedings of the Second Workshop on Speech and Language Technologies for Dravidian Languages*. Association for Computational Linguistics.

R Srinivasan and CN Subalalitha. 2019. Automated named entity recognition from tamil documents. In *2019 IEEE 1st International Conference on Energy, Systems and Information Processing (ICESIP)*, pages 1–5. IEEE.

C. N. Subalalitha. 2019. Information extraction framework for Kurunthogai. *Sādhanā*, 44(7):156.

CN Subalalitha and E Poovammal. 2018. Automatic bilingual dictionary construction for Tirukural. *Applied Artificial Intelligence*, 32(6):558–567.

Sajeetha Thavareesan and Sinnathamby Mahesan. 2019. Sentiment analysis in Tamil texts: A study on machine learning techniques and feature representation. In *2019 14th Conference on Industrial and Information Systems (ICIIS)*, pages 320–325.

Sajeetha Thavareesan and Sinnathamby Mahesan. 2020a. Sentiment lexicon expansion using Word2vec and fastText for sentiment prediction in Tamil texts. In *2020 Moratuwa Engineering Research Conference (MERCon)*, pages 272–276.

Sajeetha Thavareesan and Sinnathamby Mahesan. 2020b. Word embedding-based part of speech tagging in Tamil texts. In *2020 IEEE 15th International Conference on Industrial and Information Systems (ICIIS)*, pages 478–482.

Sajeetha Thavareesan and Sinnathamby Mahesan. 2021. Sentiment analysis in tamil texts using k-means and k-nearest neighbour. In *2021 10th International Conference on Information and Automation for Sustainability (ICIAfS)*, pages 48–53.

Przemyslaw M Waszak, Wioleta Kasprzycka-Waszak, and Alicja Kubanek. 2018. The spread of medical fake news in social media–the pilot quantitative study. *Health policy and technology*, 7(2):115–118.

Elizabeth Whittaker and Robin M Kowalski. 2015. Cyberbullying via social media. *Journal of school violence*, 14(1):11–29.

Jie Zhu, Braja G Patra, and Ashraf Yaseen. 2021. Recommender system of scholarly papers using public datasets. In *AMIA Annual Symposium Proceedings*, volume 2021, page 672. American Medical Informatics Association.

Translation Techies @DravidianLangTech-ACL2022-Machine Translation in Dravidian Languages

Piyushi Goyal **Musica Supriya** **Dinesh Acharya U** **Ashalatha Nayak**
Department of Computer Science & Engineering
Manipal Institute of Technology
Manipal Academy of Higher Education, Manipal, Karnataka 576104 , India
piyoo.goyal@gmail.com
{musica.supriya, dinesh.acharya, asha.nayak}@manipal.edu

Abstract

This paper discusses the details of submission made by team Translation Techies to the Shared Task on Machine Translation in Dravidian languages- ACL 2022. In connection to the task, five language pairs were provided to test the accuracy of submitted model. A baseline transformer model with Neural Machine Translation(NMT) technique is used which has been taken directly from the OpenNMT framework. On this baseline model, tokenization is applied using the IndicNLP library. Finally, the evaluation is performed using the BLEU scoring mechanism.

1 Introduction

A multilingual country such as India has a diversified population. Several languages are spoken at various parts of the country (Chakravarthi et al., 2019, 2018). Human spoken languages of India are divided into various groups. Indo-Aryan and Dravidian languages are the two primary families. For almost 2600 years, there has been a recorded Tamil literature (Sakuntharaj and Mahesan, 2021, 2017, 2016; Thavareesan and Mahesan, 2019, 2020a,b, 2021). The earliest period of Tamil literature, known as Sangam literature, is said to have lasted from from 600 BC to AD 300. Among Dravidian languages, it possesses the oldest existing literature. The earliest epigraphic documents discovered on rock edicts and 'hero stones' date from the sixth century BC. In Tamil Nadu, the Archaeological Survey of India discovered over 60,000 of the 100,000 odd inscriptions discovered in India (Subalalitha, 2019; Srinivasan and Subalalitha, 2019; Narasimhan et al., 2018). However, the English language dominates the content available on the Internet (Chakravarthi, 2020; Chakravarthi and Muralidaran, 2021). It is a difficult task to have a human translator who can translate texts in across all language pairs. This forms the basic purpose of this shared task. We need constructive and precise computer algorithms that need minimal human intervention to bridge this massive language divide. Machine translation can be used to complete this task effectively.

With various conversational AIs and voice assistants taking the world by storm, translation of native and low-resource languages has become imperative. The Dravidian languages are morphologically rich in nature and are hence, difficult to deal with (Chakravarthi et al., 2020). The scripts are different when compared to the Western scripts and require more attention (Sampath et al., 2022; Ravikiran et al., 2022; Bharathi et al., 2022; Priyadharshini et al., 2022). This task is an attempt to utilise the existing tools for translation of low-resource Dravidian languages. The goal here is to develop a smooth algorithm which will help in knowledge dissemination, and end-to-end speech translation. We have used Neural Machine Translation in our approach towards this problem. The rest of the paper is structured as follows: Section 2 Literature Survey, Section 3 Methodology, Section 4 Results obtained from the shared task and Section 5 Conclusion and Future Scope.

2 Literature Survey

As a result of improved processing capabilities and training data, intensive research on MT began in the early 1950s (Hutchins, 2004), and it has progressed significantly since the 1990s. To accomplish more and more accurate machine translation, a variety of methodologies have been proposed (Hutchins, 2004). Statistical Machine Translation(SMT), a subtype of Corpus-based translation, was the most extensively applied of them because it produced better results previous to the NMT systems.

The statistics-based method to machine translation does not employ traditional language data. It functions on the basis of the probability principle. In this situation, the word in the source language corresponds to the comparable word in the target

Proceedings of the Second Workshop on Speech and Language Technologies for Dravidian Languages, pages 120 - 124
May 26, 2022 ©2022 Association for Computational Linguistics

language. However, a large corpus of trustworthy translations in both the source and target languages is required. This strategy is comparable to that of IBM's research group in the early 1990s, which had some success with speech recognition and machine translation.

NMT approaches are data driven and demands language resources such as a parallel corpora for translation. When it comes to large-scale translation projects like English to German and English to French, (Wu et al., 2016), it outperformed typical MT models. In recent years, several architectures for neural network-based machine translation have been proposed, including a simple encoder-decoder based model, an RNN based model, and an LSTM model that learns problems with long-range temporal dependencies, as well as an Attention mechanism-based model, which is machine translation's most powerful neural model.

The evolution of Machine translation approaches on Indian Languages was surveyed in detail giving an overview from rule based methods used, Statistical machine translation methods implemented on the major Indian languages(J., 2013).

A sequence-to-sequence model based machine translation system for the Hindi language was proposed (Shah et al., 2018) which encouraged the use of NMT architecture on Indian languages.

The neural based approaches in Machine Translation have gained more scope as the accuracy improves based on the quality of the parallel corpora and it may be beneficial to develop an extension of the encoder–decoder paradigm that learns to align and translate together (Bahdanau et al., 2016).

Transformer computes input and output representations using self-attention rather than sequence aligned RNNs or convolution (Vaswani et al., 2017).

This shared task addresses this issue and we have implemented the Transformer model using OpenNMT platform (Klein et al., 2017). The essential principles of n-gram precision are used by BLEU (Papineni et al., 2002) to calculate similarity between the reference and created phrases. Since it employs the average score of all discoveries in the test dataset rather than presenting results for each sentence. Hence, we have used the BLEU metric for the model in this paper.

The base model chosen is Transformer architecture on OpenNMT framework and we have further enhanced this model and applied to given five language pairs. The results are tabulated based on BLEU metric.

3 Methodology

This task explores the transformer approach in OpenNMT framework. With less resources in hand, the OpenNMT framework offers best models to experiment upon. The baseline model was a Transformer architecture directly borrowed from the OpenNMT framework and used on the Dravidian Language pairs. [OpenNMT-py toolkit with commands] The model was used for five language pairs with different sizes of training, validation and testing data as shown in Table 1.

Table 1: The five language pairs and the sizes of their training, validation and testing files (Kumar M et al., 2022).

Source	Target	Dataset size (in lines)		
		Train	Valid	Test
Kannada	Malayalam	90974	2000	2000
Kannada	Sanskrit	9470	1000	1000
Kannada	Tamil	88813	2000	2000
Kannada	Telugu	88503	2000	2000
Kannada	Tulu	8300	1000	1000

The baseline model used the parallel corpora without pre-processing and it was observed that most of the words were tagged as unknown in the output prediction file on the test set. So, the configuration file was altered. In the configuration file, the learning rate is set as 2, training steps as 10,000, valid steps as 500 and checkpoints to save the model was created at every 500 steps. This file was used without any further modification across all given language pairs. It contains the paths to the training source and target files, and the validation files of the same.

On both the encoder and decoder, this configuration will run the default 2-layer LSTM model containing 500 hidden units. The supplied parameters worldsize = 1 and gpu ranks[0], which operates on a single GPU.

The vocab is built using the 'onmt_build_vocab' command present in the OpenNMT-py package installed in the first step. In this, '-n_sample' represents the amount of lines extracted from each corpus, used to create vocabulary.

Without any tokenization or transforms, this is the simplest configuration conceivable. Using this, many unknown tokens and less translated words were obtained. We used the same hyperparameters for all the five language pairs.

In order to get better results, the input datasets were tokenized before training, using the IndicNLP library (Kunchukuttan, 2020). This helped to get way better results for all the language pairs as more translated words, and lesser unknown tokens were produced.

4 Results

The sample text for five language pairs based on training data is shown in Figure 1.

Figure 1: Sample data of all five language pairs from the training set

```
Kannada   : ಭಿನ್ನವಾದದ್ದು ಮಾಡುವ ಬಯಕೆ ಇತ್ತು.
Malayalam : വ്യത്യസ്തമായി എന്തെങ്കിലും ചെയ്യണമെന്ന് ആഗ്രഹിച്ചിരുന്നു.

Kannada   : ಅನುಜನು ವಾಹನವನ್ನು ಚಲಾಯಿಸುತ್ತಿದ್ದಾನೆ
Sanskrit  : अनुजः यानम् चालयति

Kannada   : 40 ಕೋಟಿ ಮಂಜೂರಾಗಿದೆ.
Tamil     : 40 கோடி!

Kannada   : ಆಗುವುದು ಎಲ್ಲಾ ಸಿನಿಮಾ ಇಂಡಸ್ಟ್ರಿಗಳಲ್ಲೂ ಸಹಜ.
Telugu    : సినిమా ఇండస్ట్రీలోనైతే ఆ విషయం నూటికి నూరుపాళ్ళు నిజం.

Kannada   : ದೇವರು ಕೊಡುವಾಗ ಎಲ್ಲವನ್ನೂ ಕೊಡುತ್ತಾರೆ
Tulu      : ದೇವೆರ್ ಕೊರ್ನಗ ಮಾತಲ ಕೊರ್ಪೆರ್
```

After running the model on all the five language pairs of Kannada-Malayalam, Kannada-Sanskrit, Kannada-Tamil, Kannada-Telugu , and Kannada-Tulu; the following BLEU scores in Table 2 were obtained:

Table 2: The BLEU scores calculated for the prediction files of the respective language pairs.

Source	Target	BLEU Score
Kannada	Malayalam	0.0729
Kannada	Sanskrit	0.7482
Kannada	Tamil	0.0798
Kannada	Telugu	0.1242
Kannada	Tulu	0.6149

Despite using the same model and parameters for all the pairs, different BLEU scores were obtained. It can be observed that the model gave best results for Sanskrit and Tulu despite the fact that the dataset was smaller for these two. This is because the test set has similar kind of sentences when compared to train set. There is an overlap of sentences and words used in the source and target sets. As for Telugu, it performed fairly well. The datasets used were small and limited. Hence, our results do not give much insights into the performance of the model. However, the scores can be further improved by enhancing the quality of the dataset and enhancing the model. Better transforms and pre-processing techniques need to be applied on the datasets before training to achieve the same. Some techniques can be byte-pair encoding (Sennrich et al., 2015) and data augmentation (Wei and Zou, 2019) to get more translated words.

5 Conclusion and Future Scope

This paper describes the details of submission made by team Translation Techies to the Shared Task on Machine Translation in Dravidian languages-ACL 2022. The Transformer architecture present in OpenNMT framework along with modifications is implemented in this shared task. The current model can be further improved by providing larger datasets and pre-processing them in detail. We can use data augmentation and byte-pair encoding techniques as well. Subword tokenization is also a good technique to alleviate the problem with such low-resource language pairs (Dhar et al., 2021). The efficient translation of the Dravidian languages is necessary as the need for smart systems are rising rapidly.

References

Dzmitry Bahdanau, Kyunghyun Cho, and Yoshua Bengio. 2016. Neural machine translation by jointly learning to align and translate.

B Bharathi, Bharathi Raja Chakravarthi, Subalalitha Chinnaudayar Navaneethakrishnan, N Sripriya, Arunaggiri Pandian, and Swetha Valli. 2022. Findings of the shared task on Speech Recognition for Vulnerable Individuals in Tamil. In *Proceedings of the Second Workshop on Language Technology for Equality, Diversity and Inclusion*. Association for Computational Linguistics.

Bharathi Raja Chakravarthi. 2020. HopeEDI: A multilingual hope speech detection dataset for equality, diversity, and inclusion. In *Proceedings of the Third Workshop on Computational Modeling of People's Opinions, Personality, and Emotion's in Social Media*, pages 41–53, Barcelona, Spain (Online). Association for Computational Linguistics.

Bharathi Raja Chakravarthi, Mihael Arcan, and John P. McCrae. 2018. Improving wordnets for under-resourced languages using machine translation. In *Proceedings of the 9th Global Wordnet Conference*, pages 77–86, Nanyang Technological University (NTU), Singapore. Global Wordnet Association.

Bharathi Raja Chakravarthi, Mihael Arcan, and John P. McCrae. 2019. WordNet gloss translation for under-resourced languages using multilingual neural machine translation. In *Proceedings of the Second Work-*

shop on Multilingualism at the Intersection of Knowledge Bases and Machine Translation, pages 1–7, Dublin, Ireland. European Association for Machine Translation.

Bharathi Raja Chakravarthi and Vigneshwaran Muralidaran. 2021. Findings of the shared task on hope speech detection for equality, diversity, and inclusion. In *Proceedings of the First Workshop on Language Technology for Equality, Diversity and Inclusion*, pages 61–72, Kyiv. Association for Computational Linguistics.

Bharathi Raja Chakravarthi, Navaneethan Rajasekaran, Mihael Arcan, Kevin McGuinness, Noel E. O'Connor, and John P. McCrae. 2020. Bilingual lexicon induction across orthographically-distinct under-resourced Dravidian languages. In *Proceedings of the 7th Workshop on NLP for Similar Languages, Varieties and Dialects*, pages 57–69, Barcelona, Spain (Online). International Committee on Computational Linguistics (ICCL).

Prajit Dhar, Arianna Bisazza, and Gertjan van Noord. 2021. Optimal word segmentation for neural machine translation into Dravidian languages. In *Proceedings of the 8th Workshop on Asian Translation (WAT2021)*, pages 181–190, Online. Association for Computational Linguistics.

W. John Hutchins. 2004. The georgetown-ibm experiment demonstrated in january 1954. In *Machine Translation: From Real Users to Research*, pages 102–114, Berlin, Heidelberg. Springer Berlin Heidelberg.

Antony P. J. 2013. Machine translation approaches and survey for Indian languages. In *International Journal of Computational Linguistics & Chinese Language Processing, Volume 18, Number 1, March 2013*.

Guillaume Klein, Yoon Kim, Yuntian Deng, Jean Senellart, and Alexander Rush. 2017. OpenNMT: Open-source toolkit for neural machine translation. In *Proceedings of ACL 2017, System Demonstrations*, pages 67–72, Vancouver, Canada. Association for Computational Linguistics.

Anand Kumar M, Asha Hegde, Shubhanker Banerjee, Bharathi Raja Chakravarthi, Ruba Priyadarshini, Shashirekha Hosahalli Lakshmaiah, and John Philip McCrae. 2022. "findings of the shared task on Machine Translation in Dravidian languages". In *Proceedings of the Second Workshop on Speech and Language Technologies for Dravidian Languages*. Association for Computational Linguistics.

Anoop Kunchukuttan. 2020. The Indic-NLP Library. `https://github.com/anoopkunchukuttan/indic_nlp_library/blob/master/docs/indicnlp.pdf`.

Anitha Narasimhan, Aarthy Anandan, Madhan Karky, and CN Subalalitha. 2018. Porul: Option generation and selection and scoring algorithms for a tamil flash card game. *International Journal of Cognitive and Language Sciences*, 12(2):225–228.

Kishore Papineni, Salim Roukos, Todd Ward, and Wei Jing Zhu. 2002. Bleu: a method for automatic evaluation of machine translation.

Ruba Priyadharshini, Bharathi Raja Chakravarthi, Subalalitha Chinnaudayar Navaneethakrishnan, Thenmozhi Durairaj, Malliga Subramanian, Kogilavani Shanmugavadivel, Siddhanth U Hegde, and Prasanna Kumar Kumaresan. 2022. Findings of the shared task on Abusive Comment Detection in Tamil. In *Proceedings of the Second Workshop on Speech and Language Technologies for Dravidian Languages*. Association for Computational Linguistics.

Manikandan Ravikiran, Bharathi Raja Chakravarthi, Anand Kumar Madasamy, Sangeetha Sivanesan, Ratnavel Rajalakshmi, Sajeetha Thavareesan, Rahul Ponnusamy, and Shankar Mahadevan. 2022. Findings of the shared task on Offensive Span Identification in code-mixed Tamil-English comments. In *Proceedings of the Second Workshop on Speech and Language Technologies for Dravidian Languages*. Association for Computational Linguistics.

Ratnasingam Sakuntharaj and Sinnathamby Mahesan. 2016. A novel hybrid approach to detect and correct spelling in Tamil text. In *2016 IEEE International Conference on Information and Automation for Sustainability (ICIAfS)*, pages 1–6.

Ratnasingam Sakuntharaj and Sinnathamby Mahesan. 2017. Use of a novel hash-table for speeding-up suggestions for misspelt Tamil words. In *2017 IEEE International Conference on Industrial and Information Systems (ICIIS)*, pages 1–5.

Ratnasingam Sakuntharaj and Sinnathamby Mahesan. 2021. Missing word detection and correction based on context of Tamil sentences using n-grams. In *2021 10th International Conference on Information and Automation for Sustainability (ICIAfS)*, pages 42–47.

Anbukkarasi Sampath, Thenmozhi Durairaj, Bharathi Raja Chakravarthi, Ruba Priyadharshini, Subalalitha Chinnaudayar Navaneethakrishnan, Kogilavani Shanmugavadivel, Sajeetha Thavareesan, Sathiyaraj Thangasamy, Parameswari Krishnamurthy, Adeep Hande, Sean Benhur, Kishor Kumar Ponnusamy, and Santhiya Pandiyan. 2022. Findings of the shared task on Emotion Analysis in Tamil. In *Proceedings of the Second Workshop on Speech and Language Technologies for Dravidian Languages*. Association for Computational Linguistics.

Rico Sennrich, Barry Haddow, and Alexandra Birch. 2015. Neural machine translation of rare words with subword units. *CoRR*, abs/1508.07909.

Parth Shah, Vishvajit Bakrola, and Supriya Pati. 2018. *Neural Machine Translation System for Indic Languages Using Deep Neural Architecture*, pages 788–795.

R Srinivasan and CN Subalalitha. 2019. Automated named entity recognition from tamil documents. In *2019 IEEE 1st International Conference on Energy, Systems and Information Processing (ICESIP)*, pages 1–5. IEEE.

C. N. Subalalitha. 2019. Information extraction framework for Kurunthogai. *Sādhanā*, 44(7):156.

Sajeetha Thavareesan and Sinnathamby Mahesan. 2019. Sentiment analysis in Tamil texts: A study on machine learning techniques and feature representation. In *2019 14th Conference on Industrial and Information Systems (ICIIS)*, pages 320–325.

Sajeetha Thavareesan and Sinnathamby Mahesan. 2020a. Sentiment lexicon expansion using Word2vec and fastText for sentiment prediction in Tamil texts. In *2020 Moratuwa Engineering Research Conference (MERCon)*, pages 272–276.

Sajeetha Thavareesan and Sinnathamby Mahesan. 2020b. Word embedding-based part of speech tagging in Tamil texts. In *2020 IEEE 15th International Conference on Industrial and Information Systems (ICIIS)*, pages 478–482.

Sajeetha Thavareesan and Sinnathamby Mahesan. 2021. Sentiment analysis in Tamil texts using k-means and k-nearest neighbour. In *2021 10th International Conference on Information and Automation for Sustainability (ICIAfS)*, pages 48–53.

Ashish Vaswani, Noam Shazeer, Niki Parmar, Jakob Uszkoreit, Llion Jones, Aidan N. Gomez, Łukasz Kaiser, and Illia Polosukhin. 2017. Attention is all you need. In *Proceedings of the 31st International Conference on Neural Information Processing Systems*, NIPS'17, page 6000–6010, Red Hook, NY, USA. Curran Associates Inc.

Jason W. Wei and Kai Zou. 2019. EDA: easy data augmentation techniques for boosting performance on text classification tasks. *CoRR*, abs/1901.11196.

Yonghui Wu, Mike Schuster, Zhifeng Chen, Quoc V. Le, Mohammad Norouzi, Wolfgang Macherey, Maxim Krikun, Yuan Cao, Qin Gao, Klaus Macherey, Jeff Klingner, Apurva Shah, Melvin Johnson, Xiaobing Liu, Lukasz Kaiser, Stephan Gouws, Yoshikiyo Kato, Taku Kudo, Hideto Kazawa, Keith Stevens, George Kurian, Nishant Patil, Wei Wang, Cliff Young, Jason Smith, Jason Riesa, Alex Rudnick, Oriol Vinyals, Greg Corrado, Macduff Hughes, and Jeffrey Dean. 2016. Google's neural machine translation system: Bridging the gap between human and machine translation. *CoRR*, abs/1609.08144.

SSNCSE_NLP@TamilNLP-ACL2022: Transformer based approach for Emotion analysis in Tamil language

Josephine Varsha & B. Bharathi
Department of CSE
Sri Siva Subramaniya Nadar College of Engineering
Kalavakkam - 603110
josephine2010350@ssn.edu.in
bharathib@ssn.edu.in

Abstract

Emotion analysis is the process of identifying and analyzing the underlying emotions expressed in textual data. Identifying emotions from a textual conversation is a challenging task due to the absence of gestures, vocal intonation, and facial expressions. Once the chatbots and messengers detect and report the emotions of the user, a comfortable conversation can be carried out with no misunderstandings. Our task is to categorize text into a predefined notion of emotion. In this thesis, it is required to classify text into several emotional labels depending on the task. We have adopted the transformer model approach to identify the emotions present in the text sequence. Our task is to identify whether a given comment contains emotion, and the emotion it stands for. The datasets were provided to us by the LT-EDI organizers Sampath et al. (2022) for two tasks, in the Tamil language. We have evaluated the datasets using the pretrained transformer models and we have obtained the micro-averaged F1 scores as 0.19 and 0.12 for Task1 and Task 2 respectively.

1 Introduction

In today's world, the user has complete liberty to express their opinion on any topic in the form of comments, videos, reels, and reviews. Identifying emotions from a video or a graphic image is simple. By analyzing the body language, facial expressions, and speech modulation we can determine the emotion. However, the identification of emotion from a text is quite challenging due to the absence of discrete evidence. Emotions in the text are not only identified by their cue words such as happy, good, bore, hurt, hate, and fun, but also by the presence of interjections (e.g., "oopsie"), emoticons (e.g., ":)"), idiomatic expressions (e.g., "am on cloud nine"), metaphors (e.g., "sending clouds") and other descriptors mark the existence of emotions in the conversational text (Thenmozhi et al., 2019; Chakravarthi, 2020). With the growth and advancement of text messaging applications, it is possible to detect the emotion during conversation and proceed with the conversation with no miscommunications. In the last years, the recognition of emotions has become a multi-disciplinary research area (Ghanghor et al., 2021a,b; Yasaswini et al., 2021). This plays an important role in HumanMachine interaction (Ram and Ponnusamy, 2014).

There are three main classification levels in Emotion Analysis: document-level, sentence-level, and aspect-level Emotion Analysis. Document-level Emotion analysis aims at classifying an opinion as a positive or a negative opinion or sentiment. Sentence-level emotion analysis strives to classify the emotion expressed in each sentence. The first step is to identify whether the sentence is subjective or objective. If the sentence is subjective, Sentence-level EA will determine whether the sentence expresses positive or negative opinions. The authors Wilson et al. (2005) points out that emotional expressions are not necessarily subjective in nature. The authors Liu (2012) states that there is no fundamental difference between document and sentence level classifications because sentences are just short documents.

Tamil is one of the world's longest-surviving classical languages (Anita and Subalalitha, 2019b,a; Subalalitha and Poovammal, 2018; Subalalitha, 2019). According to A. K. Ramanujan, it is "the only language of modern India that is recognizably continuous with a classical history." Because of the range and quality of ancient Tamil literature, it has been referred to as "one of the world's major classical traditions and literatures." For about 2600 years, there has been a recorded Tamil literature. The earliest period of Tamil literature, known as Sangam literature, is said to have lasted from from 600 BC to AD 300. Among Dravidian languages, it possesses the oldest existing literature. The earliest epigraphic documents discovered on rock edicts and "hero

Proceedings of the Second Workshop on Speech and Language Technologies for Dravidian Languages, pages 125 - 131
May 26, 2022 ©2022 Association for Computational Linguistics

stones" date from the 6th century BC (Sakuntharaj and Mahesan, 2021, 2017,?, 2016; Thavareesan and Mahesan, 2019, 2020a,b, 2021a).

Recently there are many research shared tasks on Tamil and other Dravidian languages conducted by researchers (Priyadharshini et al., 2021; Kumaresan et al., 2021; Chakravarthi and Muralidaran, 2021; Chakravarthi et al., 2020b; Sampath et al., 2022; Ravikiran et al., 2022; Chakravarthi et al., 2022; Bharathi et al., 2022; Priyadharshini et al., 2022). The goal of this task is to determine the emotional state of the user who writes comments. In this paper, we will look into the classification, and analyze the different emotions of the YouTube comments. Our focus lies in the study of emotion analysis in Tamil. The datasets were provided by the LT-EDI organizers in the Tamil language in two forms, namely, Task A and Task B, each consisting of a different number of comments or posts. The language constriction poses several challenges due to the limited resources available for the Tamil language. We have used multilingual models such as BERT, XLNet, and m-BERT transformer models to tackle this issue. In this paper, we investigate the efficacy of different learning models in identifying emotions. We then compare the F1-Score of the different transformer models for both datasets and conclude which is the better model.

The remainder of the paper is organized into 5 sections. Section 2 discusses the related works in the field of Artificial Intelligence, on emotion or sentiment analysis for both Tamil, and other languages. The methodology proposed for the model along with the models implemented are elaborately explained in the 3rd section of this paper. In section 4 the results and the observations are discussed. Section 5 concludes the paper.

2 Related Works

In this section, we will be reviewing the research work reported for emotion analysis from the text. The authors Abdelrahman et al. (2016) had proposed an architectural framework to identify the sentiments of both English and Tamil tweets. Tweets were gathered with the help of Twitter API. They had used the word sense disambiguation technique to determine the correct usage of the word sense and went about classifying the sentiments of tweets using a linear classifier like the Support Vector Machine.

K-means clustering and k-nearest neighbor classifier to predict the sentiments expressed in Tamil texts is used in Thavareesan and Mahesan (2021b). The data points are considered in two different ways for the clustering of the corpus; clustering by considering class-wise information and clustering without considering class-wise information. They extracted features using Tf, BoW, fastText, and word embeddings. The fastText and class-wise clustering method has yielded the best results of accuracy of 89.87

The authors of Jenarthanan et al. (2019) this paper had worked on ACTSEA: Annotated Corpus for Tamil & Sinhala Emotion Analysis, to develop emotion annotated twitter corpus in Sinhala and Tamil Languages. They had adopted the scalable semi-automatic approach and found it an effective process for creating a large-scale emotion corpus with acceptable quality. They've also concluded that it is useful for under-resourced languages.

A research work done by Vas aimed at creating a monolingual corpus for the Tamil language. They advanced the corpus solution and created the TamilEmo, a large dataset for fine-grained emotion detection that has been extensively annotated manually. They've further presented a detailed data analysis that illustrates that the accuracy of the annotations over the whole taxonomy with a high inter-annotator agreement in terms of Krippendorff's alpha

There are many research works on classifying the emotion of document sources into a single type of emotion. In Sharma et al. (2017), provides an insight on how to characterize a person's multiple emotions. The LEXicon Based Emotion AnalyzeR abbreviated as LEXER is employed to analyze the emotion underlying the text. The proposed method contains a dictionary that has different emotional values for words. Emotion values from the vocabulary are allotted to every expression that's being used in the text. A fuzzy set function is used to complement the emotional value of a negated word. This in comparison to polarity reversal is more realistic and reliable. The lexicon assigns an emotional value that is derived from a fuzzy set function. This is an efficient multi-emotion analyzer model which has still not been applied to the best of our understanding.

The authors Chakravarthi et al. (2020a) put forth a model that aimed at creating a gold standard code-mixed dataset for Malayalam-English that ensured providing enough data for research purposes. They

Language	Training	Development	Test
Task A	14208	3552	4440
Task B	30179	4269	4269

Table 1: Dataset description

used Krippendorff's α method among the numerous approaches developed, to measure the degree of agreement between annotators. They used traditional machine learning algorithms such as Logistic regression (LR), Support vector machine (SVM), Decision tree (DT), Random Forest (RF), Multinomial Naive Bayes (MNB), K-nearest neighbors (KNN) on the newly annotated English-Malayalam dataset to show the insights about the dataset.

Seq2Seq deep neural network for detecting the emotions from textual conversations which include a sequence of phrases are adopted in Thenmozhi et al. (2019). The Seq2Seq model is adopted and the sequence of n words is mapped with a target label(n:1 mapping). The sequence was vectorized and sent to the bidirectional LSTM for encoding and decoding.

A study on how sentiment communicates in Dravidian social media language in a code-mixed setting was taken up as a shared task by Chakravarthi et al. (2021). The results of the sentiment analysis shared task on Tamil, Malayalam, and Kannada are presented. The top-performing systems involved the application of attention layers on the contextualized word embeddings.

3 Methodology and Data Pre-processing

In this section, we have illustrated our implementation of the pre-trained machine learning transformer models in detail. Further, we investigate the performance of the various transformer models in the coming sections. The architecture of the proposed model and the steps are given in the Fig.1.

The dataset provided by the LT-EDI organizers Sampath et al. (2022) for the Tamil Tasks A and B, consisted of 22,200 and 38,717 posts/comments respectively. The details are given in Table 1.

In task A we were provided with data annotated for 8-10 emotions for social media comments in Tamil. In task B we were provided with data annotated for fine-grained 30 emotions for social media comments in Tamil Sampath et al. (2022).

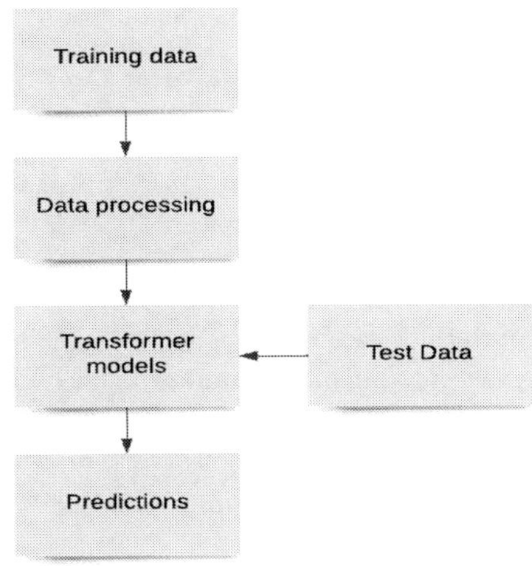

Figure 1: The architecture of the proposed system

3.1 Data-set Analysis

The goal of this task is to identify whether a given comment contains emotions, and which emotion it represents. A comment or post within the corpus may contain more than one sentence but the average sentence length of the corpora is 1. The annotations in the corpus are made at a comment or post level Sampath et al. (2022).

The dataset provided by LT-EDI 2021 organizers, consisted of the training set, development set, and test set of 14208, 3552, and 4440 instances respectively for Task A text, and 30179, 4269, and 4269 instances for the Task B text. The dataset contained text sequences that include user utterances along with the context, followed by the offensive class label. The task is to identify the emotion underlying the text and label them accordingly.

3.2 Data Pre-processing

Data pre-processing is essential for any machine learning problem. The given dataset of YouTube comments shows signs of irregularities in spelling and words. Firstly, the dataset is cleaned and processed before classifying.

- Hashtags, HTML tags, mentions, and URLs are removed
- Annotate emojis, emoticons, and replace them with the text they represent
- Convert uppercase characters to lowercase
- To expand abbreviations

- Remove special characters
- Remove accented characters
- Reduce lengthened words
- Remove extra white spaces

We've implemented data processing with the use of the nltk package, abbreviated as the Natural Language Toolkit, built to work with the NLP (Natural Language Processing). It provides various text processing libraries for classification, tokenization, parsing, semantic reasoning, etc. For our model, we've only used the regular expression (re) module. The re. sub() function was used to clean and scrape the text, remove URLs, remove numbers, and remove tags.

Regexp() module we were able to extract the tokens from the string by using the regular expression with the RegexpTokenizer() method. Tokenizing is a crucial step when it comes to cleaning the text. It is used to split the text into words or sentences, splitting it into smaller pieces that still hold its meaning outside the context of the rest of the text. When it comes to analyzing the text, we need to tokenize by word and tokenize by sentence. This is how unstructured data is turned into structured data, which is easier to analyze.

3.3 Model Description

The dataset text was classified using 3 transformer models, namely BERT, XLNet, and m-BERT

- BERT:
  BERT stands for Bidirectional Encoder Representations from Transformers. BERT is a pre-trained model for the top 104 languages of the world on Wikipedia (2.5B words) with 110 thousand shared word piece vocabulary, using masked language modeling (MLM) objective, which was first introduced in Devlin et al. (2018). BERT uses bi-directional learning to gain context of words from left to right context simultaneously. This is optimized by the Masked Language Modelling. The MLM is different from the traditional recurrent neural networks (RNNs), which generally see the word one after the other. This model randomly masks 15% of the words in the input and predicts the masked words when the entire masked sentence is run through the model.
- XLNet:
  The XLNet transformer model was proposed in 'XLNet: Generalized Autoregressive Pretraining for Language Understanding' Yang et al. (2019). It is pre-trained using an autoregressive model (a model that predicts future behavior based on past behavior) which enables learning bidirectional contexts by maximizing the expected likelihood over all permutations of the factorization order and overcomes the limitations of BERT thanks to its autoregressive formulation Yang et al. (2019). It integrates the Transformer-XL mechanism with a slight improvement in the language modeling approach.
- m-BERT:
  m-BERT is a pre-trained model on a large corpus of multilingual data It is trained on the top 104 languages with the largest Wikipedia using a masked language modeling (MLM) objective. It was first introduced in Devlin et al. (2018)

4 Results and Analysis

The BERT (Bidirectional Encoder Representations from Transformers) models and XLNET were used for the Task A dataset. The BERT model operates on the principle of an attention mechanism to learn contextual relations between words. The transformer encoder used is bidirectional, unlike the other directional methods which read input sequentially. BERT reads the entire sequence of text at once. This bidirectional property of the encoder has made it very useful for classification tasks. The BERT models BERT and m-BERT were trained for 5 epochs. XLNet does not suffer from pre-train fine-tune discrepancy since it does not depend on data corruption. We have trained the XLNet model for 5 epochs. The bert-base-uncased model showed the best F1-Score of 0.19, 0.08 for Task A and Task B respectively.

4.1 Task A

The accuracy obtained by the BERT model was found to be 0.35, XLNet, and m-BERT showed an accuracy of 0.34, and 0.34 respectively. The bert-base-uncased model (BERT) showed the best performance with a weighted F1 score of 0.19. The weighted precision, weighted recall, weighted F1 score, and accuracy are given in the Table 2.

Pre-trained model	Precision	Recall	F1-score	Accuracy
bert-base-uncased	0.18	0.35	0.19	0.35
xlnet-base-cased	0.12	0.34	0.18	0.34
hline bert-base-mulitingual-uncased	0.12	0.34	0.18	0.34
hline				

Table 2: Performance analysis of the proposed system using development data for Task A

Pre-trained model	Precision	Recall	F1-score	Accuracy
bert-base-uncased	0.05	0.19	0.08	0.19
xlnet-base-cased	0.02	0.16	0.04	0.16
hline bert-base-mulitingual-uncased	0.13	0.20	0.12	0.20
hline				

Table 3: Performance analysis of the proposed system using development data for Task B

4.2 Task B

For Task B, the training data was run for the 3 transformer models. The training data with the best F1 score is run with the test data. The bert-base-multilingual-uncased model yielded the best results, with an F1 score of 0.12. The weighted precision, weighted recall, weighted F1 score, and accuracy is given in the Table 3.

4.3 Performance Metrics

In this task we have evaluated the models based on the macro average of Precision, Recall, and F1 Score. They provide us with an evaluation of the performance of the ML algorithm. We've used classification metrics for our research. Classification Metrics evaluate a model's performance and tell you how good or bad the classification is, but each of them evaluates it in a different way.

Precision: Precision is the ratio of true positives and total positives predicted. As the name goes, Precision refers to the accuracy of the classification algorithm.

$$Precision = \frac{TP}{TP + FP}$$

Recall: Recall may be defined as the number of positives returned by our ML model. Recall is the measure of the model correctly identifying the True Positives (TP).

$$Recall = \frac{TP}{TP + FN}$$

F1 Score: The F1-score metric uses a combination of precision and recall. The F1 score is the harmonic mean of the two. Since it takes both, Precision, and Recall into account, it is more useful than accuracy.

$$F1\ Score = 2 * \frac{Precision * Recall}{Precision + Recall}$$

5 Conclusions

In this paper, we have investigated the baseline accuracy of different models as well as their variants on the datasets, and also proposed an approach for identifying emotions from the text. We have achieved F1 scores of 0.19 and 0.12 for Task A and Task B respectively. Due to the time constraint and not promising results, we had not submitted our results to the organizers. Identifying emotions based on text is quite a challenge and the performance of this model can further be enhanced by adopting favorable features.

References

Samir E. Abdelrahman, Umar Farooq, and Tej Prasad Dhamala. 2016. Sentiment analysis of english and tamil tweets using path length similarity based word sense disambiguation.

R Anita and CN Subalalitha. 2019a. An approach to cluster tamil literatures using discourse connectives. In *2019 IEEE 1st International Conference on Energy, Systems and Information Processing (ICESIP)*, pages 1–4. IEEE.

R Anita and CN Subalalitha. 2019b. Building discourse parser for thirukkural. In *Proceedings of the 16th International Conference on Natural Language Processing*, pages 18–25.

B Bharathi, Bharathi Raja Chakravarthi, Subalalitha Chinnaudayar Navaneethakrishnan, N Sripriya,

Arunaggiri Pandian, and Swetha Valli. 2022. Findings of the shared task on Speech Recognition for Vulnerable Individuals in Tamil. In *Proceedings of the Second Workshop on Language Technology for Equality, Diversity and Inclusion*. Association for Computational Linguistics.

Bharathi Raja Chakravarthi. 2020. HopeEDI: A multilingual hope speech detection dataset for equality, diversity, and inclusion. In *Proceedings of the Third Workshop on Computational Modeling of People's Opinions, Personality, and Emotion's in Social Media*, pages 41–53, Barcelona, Spain (Online). Association for Computational Linguistics.

Bharathi Raja Chakravarthi, Navya Jose, Shardul Suryawanshi, Elizabeth Sherly, and John P McCrae. 2020a. A sentiment analysis dataset for code-mixed malayalam-english. *arXiv preprint arXiv:2006.00210*.

Bharathi Raja Chakravarthi and Vigneshwaran Muralidaran. 2021. Findings of the shared task on hope speech detection for equality, diversity, and inclusion. In *Proceedings of the First Workshop on Language Technology for Equality, Diversity and Inclusion*, pages 61–72, Kyiv. Association for Computational Linguistics.

Bharathi Raja Chakravarthi, Ruba Priyadharshini, Thenmozhi Durairaj, John Phillip McCrae, Paul Buitaleer, Prasanna Kumar Kumaresan, and Rahul Ponnusamy. 2022. Findings of the shared task on Homophobia Transphobia Detection in Social Media Comments. In *Proceedings of the Second Workshop on Language Technology for Equality, Diversity and Inclusion*. Association for Computational Linguistics.

Bharathi Raja Chakravarthi, Ruba Priyadharshini, Vigneshwaran Muralidaran, Shardul Suryawanshi, Navya Jose, Elizabeth Sherly, and John P McCrae. 2020b. Overview of the track on sentiment analysis for Dravidian languages in code-mixed text. In *Forum for Information Retrieval Evaluation*, pages 21–24.

Bharathi Raja Chakravarthi, Ruba Priyadharshini, Sajeetha Thavareesan, Dhivya Chinnappa, Durairaj Thenmozhi, Elizabeth Sherly, John P McCrae, Adeep Hande, Rahul Ponnusamy, Shubhanker Banerjee, et al. 2021. Findings of the sentiment analysis of dravidian languages in code-mixed text. *arXiv preprint arXiv:2111.09811*.

Jacob Devlin, Ming-Wei Chang, Kenton Lee, and Kristina Toutanova. 2018. Bert: Pre-training of deep bidirectional transformers for language understanding.

Nikhil Ghanghor, Parameswari Krishnamurthy, Sajeetha Thavareesan, Ruba Priyadharshini, and Bharathi Raja Chakravarthi. 2021a. IIITK@DravidianLangTech-EACL2021: Offensive language identification and meme classification in Tamil, Malayalam and Kannada. In *Proceedings of the First Workshop on Speech and Language Technologies for Dravidian Languages*, pages 222–229, Kyiv. Association for Computational Linguistics.

Nikhil Ghanghor, Rahul Ponnusamy, Prasanna Kumar Kumaresan, Ruba Priyadharshini, Sajeetha Thavareesan, and Bharathi Raja Chakravarthi. 2021b. IIITK@LT-EDI-EACL2021: Hope speech detection for equality, diversity, and inclusion in Tamil , Malayalam and English. In *Proceedings of the First Workshop on Language Technology for Equality, Diversity and Inclusion*, pages 197–203, Kyiv. Association for Computational Linguistics.

Rajenthiran Jenarthanan, Yasas Senarath, and Uthayasanker Thayasivam. 2019. Actsea: annotated corpus for tamil & sinhala emotion analysis. In *2019 Moratuwa Engineering Research Conference (MERCon)*, pages 49–53. IEEE.

Prasanna Kumar Kumaresan, Ratnasingam Sakuntharaj, Sajeetha Thavareesan, Subalalitha Navaneethakrishnan, Anand Kumar Madasamy, Bharathi Raja Chakravarthi, and John P McCrae. 2021. Findings of shared task on offensive language identification in Tamil and Malayalam. In *Forum for Information Retrieval Evaluation*, pages 16–18.

Bing Liu. 2012. Sentiment analysis and opinion mining. *Synthesis lectures on human language technologies*, 5(1):1–167.

Ruba Priyadharshini, Bharathi Raja Chakravarthi, Subalalitha Chinnaudayar Navaneethakrishnan, Thenmozhi Durairaj, Malliga Subramanian, Kogilavani Shanmugavadivel, Siddhanth U Hegde, and Prasanna Kumar Kumaresan. 2022. Findings of the shared task on Abusive Comment Detection in Tamil. In *Proceedings of the Second Workshop on Speech and Language Technologies for Dravidian Languages*. Association for Computational Linguistics.

Ruba Priyadharshini, Bharathi Raja Chakravarthi, Sajeetha Thavareesan, Dhivya Chinnappa, Durairaj Thenmozhi, and Rahul Ponnusamy. 2021. Overview of the DravidianCodeMix 2021 shared task on sentiment detection in Tamil, Malayalam, and Kannada. In *Forum for Information Retrieval Evaluation*, pages 4–6.

C.Sunitha Ram and R. Ponnusamy. 2014. An effective automatic speech emotion recognition for tamil language using support vector machine. In *2014 International Conference on Issues and Challenges in Intelligent Computing Techniques (ICICT)*, pages 19–23.

Manikandan Ravikiran, Bharathi Raja Chakravarthi, Anand Kumar Madasamy, Sangeetha Sivanesan, Ratnavel Rajalakshmi, Sajeetha Thavareesan, Rahul Ponnusamy, and Shankar Mahadevan. 2022. Findings of the shared task on Offensive Span Identification in code-mixed Tamil-English comments. In *Proceedings of the Second Workshop on Speech and*

Language Technologies for Dravidian Languages. Association for Computational Linguistics.

Ratnasingam Sakuntharaj and Sinnathamby Mahesan. 2016. A novel hybrid approach to detect and correct spelling in tamil text. In *2016 IEEE International Conference on Information and Automation for Sustainability (ICIAfS)*, pages 1–6.

Ratnasingam Sakuntharaj and Sinnathamby Mahesan. 2017. Use of a novel hash-table for speeding-up suggestions for misspelt tamil words. In *2017 IEEE International Conference on Industrial and Information Systems (ICIIS)*, pages 1–5.

Ratnasingam Sakuntharaj and Sinnathamby Mahesan. 2021. Missing word detection and correction based on context of tamil sentences using n-grams. In *2021 10th International Conference on Information and Automation for Sustainability (ICIAfS)*, pages 42–47.

Anbukkarasi Sampath, Thenmozhi Durairaj, Bharathi Raja Chakravarthi, Ruba Priyadharshini, Subalalitha Chinnaudayar Navaneethakrishnan, Kogilavani Shanmugavadivel, Sajeetha Thavareesan, Sathiyaraj Thangasamy, Parameswari Krishnamurthy, Adeep Hande, Sean Benhur, and Santhiya Ponnusamy, Kishor Kumar Pandiyan. 2022. Findings of the shared task on Emotion Analysis in Tamil. In *Proceedings of the Second Workshop on Speech and Language Technologies for Dravidian Languages*. Association for Computational Linguistics.

Shikhar Sharma, Piyush Kumar, and Krishan Kumar. 2017. Lexer: Lexicon based emotion analyzer. In *International Conference on Pattern Recognition and Machine Intelligence*, pages 373–379. Springer.

C. N. Subalalitha. 2019. Information extraction framework for kurunthogai. *Sādhanā*, 44(7):156.

CN Subalalitha and E Poovammal. 2018. Automatic bilingual dictionary construction for tirukural. *Applied Artificial Intelligence*, 32(6):558–567.

Sajeetha Thavareesan and Sinnathamby Mahesan. 2019. Sentiment analysis in tamil texts: A study on machine learning techniques and feature representation. In *2019 14th Conference on Industrial and Information Systems (ICIIS)*, pages 320–325.

Sajeetha Thavareesan and Sinnathamby Mahesan. 2020a. Sentiment lexicon expansion using word2vec and fasttext for sentiment prediction in tamil texts. In *2020 Moratuwa Engineering Research Conference (MERCon)*, pages 272–276.

Sajeetha Thavareesan and Sinnathamby Mahesan. 2020b. Word embedding-based part of speech tagging in tamil texts. In *2020 IEEE 15th International Conference on Industrial and Information Systems (ICIIS)*, pages 478–482.

Sajeetha Thavareesan and Sinnathamby Mahesan. 2021a. Sentiment analysis in tamil texts using k-means and k-nearest neighbour. In *2021 10th International Conference on Information and Automation for Sustainability (ICIAfS)*, pages 48–53.

Sajeetha Thavareesan and Sinnathamby Mahesan. 2021b. Sentiment analysis in tamil texts using k-means and k-nearest neighbour. In *2021 10th International Conference on Information and Automation for Sustainability (ICIAfS)*, pages 48–53.

D Thenmozhi, Aravindan Chandrabose, Srinethe Sharavanan, et al. 2019. Ssn_nlp at semeval-2019 task 3: Contextual emotion identification from textual conversation using seq2seq deep neural network. In *Proceedings of the 13th International Workshop on Semantic Evaluation*, pages 318–323.

Theresa Wilson, Janyce Wiebe, and Paul Hoffmann. 2005. Recognizing contextual polarity in phrase-level sentiment analysis. In *Proceedings of human language technology conference and conference on empirical methods in natural language processing*, pages 347–354.

Zhilin Yang, Zihang Dai, Yiming Yang, Jaime G. Carbonell, Ruslan Salakhutdinov, and Quoc V. Le. 2019. Xlnet: Generalized autoregressive pretraining for language understanding. *CoRR*, abs/1906.08237.

Konthala Yasaswini, Karthik Puranik, Adeep Hande, Ruba Priyadharshini, Sajeetha Thavareesan, and Bharathi Raja Chakravarthi. 2021. IIITT@DravidianLangTech-EACL2021: Transfer learning for offensive language detection in Dravidian languages. In *Proceedings of the First Workshop on Speech and Language Technologies for Dravidian Languages*, pages 187–194, Kyiv. Association for Computational Linguistics.

SSN_MLRG1@DravidianLangTech-ACL2022: Troll Meme Classification in Tamil using Transformer Models

Shruthi Hariprasad, Sarika Esackimuthu, Saritha Madhavan
Rajalakshmi Sivanaiah, Angel Deborah Suseelan
Department of Computer Science and Engineering
Sri Sivasubramaniya Nadar College of Engineering
Chennai 603 110, Tamil Nadu, India
{shruthi2010101, sarika2010128, sarithamadhesh}@ssn.edu.in
{rajalakshmis, angeldeborahs}@ssn.edu.in

Abstract

The ACL shared task of DravidianLangTech-2022 for Troll Meme classification is a binary classification task that involves identifying Tamil memes as troll or not-troll. Classification of memes is a challenging task since memes express humour and sarcasm in an implicit way. Team SSN_MLRG1 tested and compared results obtained by using three models namely BERT, ALBERT and XLNet. The XLNet model outperformed the other two models in terms of various performance metrics. The proposed XLNet model obtained the 3rd rank in the shared task with a weighted F1-score of 0.558.

1 Introduction

Memes are interesting ideas that spread the emotions of the people or culture across the internet. Social media plays a pivotal role in facilitating the spread of memes. Memes have become a powerful tool of everyday communication that uses humour to catch the attention of the people and also help in sharing the views (Ghanghor et al., 2021a,b; Yasaswini et al., 2021). And though a good number of them are harmless, there are many memes that are not. Troll memes are such memes whose main goal is to provoke the audience with intent to offend or demean them (Priyadharshini et al., 2021; Kumaresan et al., 2021). Since the internet aids in the widespread propagation of memes it can be utilised in trolling (Sampath et al., 2022; Ravikiran et al., 2022; Chakravarthi et al., 2022; Bharathi et al., 2022; Priyadharshini et al., 2022). Considering the adverse mental effects of troll memes on individuals, the task is to identify and label memes as troll or not in an effort to monitor what is being posted on the internet.

Tamil is one of the world's longest-surviving classical languages. According to A. K. Ramanujan, it is "the only language of modern India that is recognizably continuous with a classical history." Because of the range and quality of ancient Tamil literature, it has been referred to as "one of the world's major classical traditions and literatures." For almost 2000 years, there has been a recorded Tamil literature. The earliest period of Tamil literature, known as Sangam literature, is said to have lasted from from 600 BC to AD 300 (Anita and Subalalitha, 2019b,a; Subalalitha and Poovammal, 2018). Among Dravidian languages, it possesses the oldest existing literature. The earliest epigraphic documents discovered on rock edicts and 'hero stones' date from the third century BC (Subalalitha, 2019; Srinivasan and Subalalitha, 2019; Narasimhan et al., 2018). In Tamil Nadu, the Archaeological Survey of India discovered over 60,000 of the 100,000 odd inscriptions discovered in India. The majority of them are in Tamil, with just around 5% in languages other than Tamil. Inscriptions in Tamil inscribed in Brahmi script have been unearthed in Sri Lanka, as well as on trade products in Thailand and Egypt (Sakuntharaj and Mahesan, 2021, 2017, 2016; Thavareesan and Mahesan, 2019, 2020a,b, 2021).

The task of classifying troll memes is challenging as it needs to discover the intention of the meme. Moreover, memes often use offensive words to express feelings. We used XLNet (Yang et al., 2019), ALBERT (Lan et al., 2019) and BERT (Devlin et al., 2018) models that classify memes as troll and not a troll. The training data set provided contains 2300 memes that have been annotated, out of which 1610 memes were used for training and the rest were used for development of the model. The troll memes are very subjective and the usage of colloquial language, emojis, references, symbols and images without text add more challenges in predicting the trolls.

2 Related Work

Many researchers in the field of Artificial Intelligence and Natural Language Processing have

Proceedings of the Second Workshop on Speech and Language Technologies for Dravidian Languages, pages 132 - 137
May 26, 2022

been working to detect hateful memes (B and A, 2021b,a). In the past couple of years, social media usage has increased drastically and so the data available has also increased (Chakravarthi, 2020; Chakravarthi and Muralidaran, 2021; Chakravarthi et al., 2021).

Shaheen et al. (2020) studied the performance of NLP transformer models BERT, RoBERTa , DistilBERT, XLNet and M-BERT in Large Multi-Label Text Classification (LMTC) and found that RoBERTa and BERT yield best results.

Afridi et al. (2020) presented an inclusive study on meme classification and proposed a generalised framework for visual-linguistic problems. Suryawanshi et al. (2020) created a dataset that has been used for classifying the memes. They have used image classification to address the difficulties in the state-of-the-art methods and concluded that such an image classifier is not feasible for classifying memes.

The findings of previous shared tasks (Suryawanshi and Chakravarthi, 2021), (Suryawanshi et al., 2022) have been shared where submissions show multiple ways to approach the problem. Smitha et al. (2018) stress the importance of visual memes and recommend a framework that could be utilized to categorize the internet memes by certain visual and textual features.

Hegde et al. (2021b) illustrates different textual analysis methods and contrasting multi-modal methods from simple merging to cross attention to using both visual and textual features. Cross-lingual language model XLM was found to perform the best in textual analysis, and the multi-modal transformer performed the best in multi-modal analysis. It was noted that the distribution of the test set does matter and the type of images was different in the test set which could mainly affect the performance of the ImageNet models while fine-tuning.

Du et al. (2020) provided the first large-scale analysis of who shares the image with text (IWT) memes, relative to other forms of expression and provided an analysis of the relationship between the demographics of users and their meme sharing patterns. They also developed an accurate, publicly available classifier to identify IWT memes in other data sets.

Hegde et al. (2021a) have put forth a model using vision transformer for images and Bidirectional Encoder Representations from Transformers (BERT) for captions of memes to achieve an overall F1-score of 0.59 on the test set. They believed that the preprocessing of the images was a huge factor for achieving a great F1-score on the validation set.

In (Sivanaiah et al., 2020), we worked to identify the presence of offensive language in social media posts using BERT. Deep network model with BERT embeddings was found to achieve better F1 score when compared to 1D-CNN model trained with GloVe pretrained embeddings, 2D-CNN and BiLSTM models with Word2Vec embeddings.

ColBERT (Contextualized Late Interaction over BERT), a modification of BERT was used to detect offense and humor in text in (Sivanaiah et al., 2021) which outperformed the machine learning models tested by a large margin.

3 Methodology

The architecture diagram for the offensive text classification is shown in Figure 1.

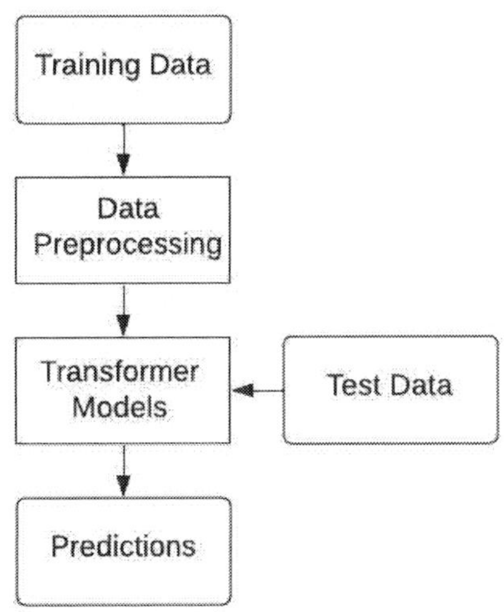

Figure 1: Architecture of the Proposed System

3.1 Dataset

The dataset consists of troll and non-troll images with their captions as text. The training data set provided contained 1018 troll and 1282 not troll memes. And for the test data, 395 of the total memes were annotated with troll and the remaining 272 were not troll. The data distribution of the train and test set is in Table 1.

The data set (Suryawanshi et al., 2020) provided by the organisers was used for the task. It contains image files of the memes as well as transcriptions

Class Label	Train Set	Test Set
Troll	1018	395
Not Troll	1282	272

Table 1: Distribution of Data Set

of the text embedded in the images. Every single one of these memes have been annotated as either troll or not troll and this label is embedded in the file name.

3.2 Data Preprocessing

Data preprocessing is an essential step where the given data set has to be regulated as much as possible in order to have some consistency. The data set was cleaned and processed using methods from NLTK (Loper and Bird, 2002) and spacy (Honnibal and Johnson, 2015) toolkit. In pre-processing, the following changes were made to the data: annotation of emojis and emoticons, conversion of uppercase letters to lowercase, expanding contractions, removal of URLs, reduction of lengthened words, removal of accented characters, removal of stopwords, removal of extra whitespaces, and lemmatization of text.

3.3 Model Description

We classified memes using three models namely BERT (Devlin et al., 2018), ALBERT (Lan et al., 2019) and XLNet (Yang et al., 2019). The first model we used is BERT - Bidirectional Encoder Representations from Transformers. It is a deep learning model based on transformers. The directional models usually read the text input sequentially, but BERT reads the entire sequence of words at once. This characteristic allows the model to learn the context of a word based on all of its surroundings. The BERT model was trained for 4 epochs. The second model that we used is ALBERT, a Lite BERT, shrinks BERT in size while maintaining the performance. This model was trained for 5 epochs.

The next model that we used is XLNet, which is a BERT like pretrained model that has outperformed BERT in some NLP tasks including text classification. It captures bi-directional context using a mechanism called "permutation language modeling". XLNet does not suffer from pre-train fine-tune discrepancy since it does not depend on data corruption. We trained the XLNet model for 4 epochs.

4 Results

The models were tested on the test data with labels provided. The accuracy obtained by the proposed XLNet model is 0.59. BERT and ALBERT showed an accuracy of 0.58 and 0.57 respectively. XLNet was found to have the best performance out of all three models. Weighted F1-score, precision and recall are other performance metrics that have been used to measure the effectiveness of the model. Table 2 shows the results obtained with all three models.

Performance Metrics	BERT	ALBERT	XLNET
Accuracy	0.58	0.57	**0.59**
Weighted Avg. F1-score	0.54	0.54	**0.558**
Weighted Avg. Recall	**0.58**	0.57	0.565
Weighted Avg. Precision	0.55	0.54	**0.555**

Table 2: Performance Metrics of Transformer models

We secured a rank of 3 with the XLNet model in the shared task. The first rank had obtained a weighted average F1 score 0.596 while we obtained 0.558.

4.1 Error Analysis

The confusion matrix for the results obtained with the XLNet model is shown in figure 2. True positive was obtained for 311 memes and true negative was obtained for 69 memes. False positive and false negative was obtained for 203 memes and 84 memes respectively.

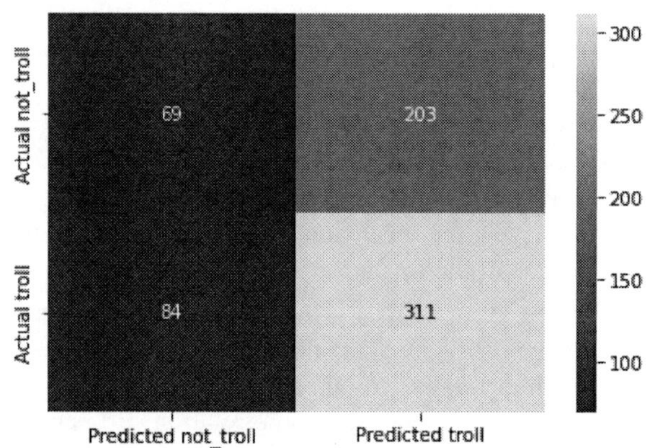

Figure 2: Confusion matrix for results with XLNet

5 Conclusion

We built an XLNet based model for the task Troll Meme Classification in Tamil. The model uses the preprocessed data done using NLTK, which we believe is a key factor for improved accuracy. Classifying a meme based only on the text is a reason for the reduced accuracy. How a meme is perceived is based upon a multitude of factors and cannot be judged using simple conventional models. This is another reason for the reduced precision of classification. The words present in a meme are too intuitive for the models to detect accurately. We intend to further proceed by adding multiple hidden layers and building a complex network structure.

References

Tariq Habib Afridi, Aftab Alam, Muhammad Numan Khan, Jawad Khan, and Young-Koo Lee. 2020. A multimodal memes classification: A survey and open research issues. In *The Proceedings of the Third International Conference on Smart City Applications*, pages 1451–1466. Springer.

R Anita and CN Subalalitha. 2019a. An approach to cluster Tamil literatures using discourse connectives. In *2019 IEEE 1st International Conference on Energy, Systems and Information Processing (ICESIP)*, pages 1–4. IEEE.

R Anita and CN Subalalitha. 2019b. Building discourse parser for Thirukkural. In *Proceedings of the 16th International Conference on Natural Language Processing*, pages 18–25.

Bharathi B and Agnusimmaculate Silvia A. 2021a. SSNCSE_NLP@DravidianLangTech-EACL2021: Meme classification for Tamil using machine learning approach. In *Proceedings of the First Workshop on Speech and Language Technologies for Dravidian Languages*, pages 336–339, Kyiv. Association for Computational Linguistics.

Bharathi B and Agnusimmaculate Silvia A. 2021b. SSNCSE_NLP@DravidianLangTech-EACL2021: Offensive language identification on multilingual code mixing text. In *Proceedings of the First Workshop on Speech and Language Technologies for Dravidian Languages*, pages 313–318, Kyiv. Association for Computational Linguistics.

B Bharathi, Bharathi Raja Chakravarthi, Subalalitha Chinnaudayar Navaneethakrishnan, N Sripriya, Arunaggiri Pandian, and Swetha Valli. 2022. Findings of the shared task on Speech Recognition for Vulnerable Individuals in Tamil. In *Proceedings of the Second Workshop on Language Technology for Equality, Diversity and Inclusion*. Association for Computational Linguistics.

Bharathi Raja Chakravarthi. 2020. HopeEDI: A multilingual hope speech detection dataset for equality, diversity, and inclusion. In *Proceedings of the Third Workshop on Computational Modeling of People's Opinions, Personality, and Emotion's in Social Media*, pages 41–53, Barcelona, Spain (Online). Association for Computational Linguistics.

Bharathi Raja Chakravarthi and Vigneshwaran Muralidaran. 2021. Findings of the shared task on hope speech detection for equality, diversity, and inclusion. In *Proceedings of the First Workshop on Language Technology for Equality, Diversity and Inclusion*, pages 61–72, Kyiv. Association for Computational Linguistics.

Bharathi Raja Chakravarthi, Ruba Priyadharshini, Thenmozhi Durairaj, John Phillip McCrae, Paul Buitaleer, Prasanna Kumar Kumaresan, and Rahul Ponnusamy. 2022. Findings of the shared task on Homophobia Transphobia Detection in Social Media Comments. In *Proceedings of the Second Workshop on Language Technology for Equality, Diversity and Inclusion*. Association for Computational Linguistics.

Bharathi Raja Chakravarthi, Ruba Priyadharshini, Rahul Ponnusamy, Prasanna Kumar Kumaresan, Kayalvizhi Sampath, Durairaj Thenmozhi, Sathiyaraj Thangasamy, Rajendran Nallathambi, and John Phillip McCrae. 2021. Dataset for identification of homophobia and transophobia in multilingual YouTube comments. *arXiv preprint arXiv:2109.00227*.

Jacob Devlin, Ming-Wei Chang, Kenton Lee, and Kristina Toutanova. 2018. Bert: Pre-training of deep bidirectional transformers for language understanding. *arXiv preprint arXiv:1810.04805*.

Yuhao Du, Muhammad Aamir Masood, and Kenneth Joseph. 2020. Understanding visual memes: An empirical analysis of text superimposed on memes shared on twitter. In *Proceedings of the International AAAI Conference on Web and Social Media*, volume 14, pages 153–164.

Nikhil Ghanghor, Parameswari Krishnamurthy, Sajeetha Thavareesan, Ruba Priyadharshini, and Bharathi Raja Chakravarthi. 2021a. IIITK@DravidianLangTech-EACL2021: Offensive language identification and meme classification in Tamil, Malayalam and Kannada. In *Proceedings of the First Workshop on Speech and Language Technologies for Dravidian Languages*, pages 222–229, Kyiv. Association for Computational Linguistics.

Nikhil Ghanghor, Rahul Ponnusamy, Prasanna Kumar Kumaresan, Ruba Priyadharshini, Sajeetha Thavareesan, and Bharathi Raja Chakravarthi. 2021b. IIITK@LT-EDI-EACL2021: Hope speech detection for equality, diversity, and inclusion in Tamil , Malayalam and English. In *Proceedings of the First Workshop on Language Technology for Equality, Diversity and Inclusion*, pages 197–203, Kyiv. Association for Computational Linguistics.

Siddhanth U Hegde, Adeep Hande, Ruba Priyadharshini, Sajeetha Thavareesan, and Bharathi Raja Chakravarthi. 2021a. Uvce-iiitt@ dravidianlangtech-eacl2021: Tamil troll meme classification: You need to pay more attention. *arXiv preprint arXiv:2104.09081*.

Siddhanth U Hegde, Adeep Hande, Ruba Priyadharshini, Sajeetha Thavareesan, Ratnasingam Sakuntharaj, Sathiyaraj Thangasamy, B Bharathi, and Bharathi Raja Chakravarthi. 2021b. Do images really do the talking? analysing the significance of images in tamil troll meme classification. *arXiv preprint arXiv:2108.03886*.

Matthew Honnibal and Mark Johnson. 2015. An improved non-monotonic transition system for dependency parsing. In *Proceedings of the 2015 conference on empirical methods in natural language processing*, pages 1373–1378.

Prasanna Kumar Kumaresan, Ratnasingam Sakuntharaj, Sajeetha Thavareesan, Subalalitha Navaneethakrishnan, Anand Kumar Madasamy, Bharathi Raja Chakravarthi, and John P McCrae. 2021. Findings of shared task on offensive language identification in Tamil and Malayalam. In *Forum for Information Retrieval Evaluation*, pages 16–18.

Zhenzhong Lan, Mingda Chen, Sebastian Goodman, Kevin Gimpel, Piyush Sharma, and Radu Soricut. 2019. Albert: A lite bert for self-supervised learning of language representations. *arXiv preprint arXiv:1909.11942*.

Edward Loper and Steven Bird. 2002. Nltk: The natural language toolkit. *arXiv preprint cs/0205028*.

Anitha Narasimhan, Aarthy Anandan, Madhan Karky, and CN Subalalitha. 2018. Porul: Option generation and selection and scoring algorithms for a tamil flash card game. *International Journal of Cognitive and Language Sciences*, 12(2):225–228.

Ruba Priyadharshini, Bharathi Raja Chakravarthi, Subalalitha Chinnaudayar Navaneethakrishnan, Thenmozhi Durairaj, Malliga Subramanian, Kogilavani Shanmugavadivel, Siddhanth U Hegde, and Prasanna Kumar Kumaresan. 2022. Findings of the shared task on Abusive Comment Detection in Tamil. In *Proceedings of the Second Workshop on Speech and Language Technologies for Dravidian Languages*. Association for Computational Linguistics.

Ruba Priyadharshini, Bharathi Raja Chakravarthi, Sajeetha Thavareesan, Dhivya Chinnappa, Durairaj Thenmozhi, and Rahul Ponnusamy. 2021. Overview of the DravidianCodeMix 2021 shared task on sentiment detection in Tamil, Malayalam, and Kannada. In *Forum for Information Retrieval Evaluation*, pages 4–6.

Manikandan Ravikiran, Bharathi Raja Chakravarthi, Anand Kumar Madasamy, Sangeetha Sivanesan, Ratnavel Rajalakshmi, Sajeetha Thavareesan, Rahul Ponnusamy, and Shankar Mahadevan. 2022. Findings of the shared task on Offensive Span Identification in code-mixed Tamil-English comments. In *Proceedings of the Second Workshop on Speech and Language Technologies for Dravidian Languages*. Association for Computational Linguistics.

Ratnasingam Sakuntharaj and Sinnathamby Mahesan. 2016. A novel hybrid approach to detect and correct spelling in Tamil text. In *2016 IEEE International Conference on Information and Automation for Sustainability (ICIAfS)*, pages 1–6.

Ratnasingam Sakuntharaj and Sinnathamby Mahesan. 2017. Use of a novel hash-table for speeding-up suggestions for misspelt Tamil words. In *2017 IEEE International Conference on Industrial and Information Systems (ICIIS)*, pages 1–5.

Ratnasingam Sakuntharaj and Sinnathamby Mahesan. 2021. Missing word detection and correction based on context of Tamil sentences using n-grams. In *2021 10th International Conference on Information and Automation for Sustainability (ICIAfS)*, pages 42–47.

Anbukkarasi Sampath, Thenmozhi Durairaj, Bharathi Raja Chakravarthi, Ruba Priyadharshini, Subalalitha Chinnaudayar Navaneethakrishnan, Kogilavani Shanmugavadivel, Sajeetha Thavareesan, Sathiyaraj Thangasamy, Parameswari Krishnamurthy, Adeep Hande, Sean Benhur, Kishor Kumar Ponnusamy, and Santhiya Pandiyan. 2022. Findings of the shared task on Emotion Analysis in Tamil. In *Proceedings of the Second Workshop on Speech and Language Technologies for Dravidian Languages*. Association for Computational Linguistics.

Zein Shaheen, Gerhard Wohlgenannt, and Erwin Filtz. 2020. Large scale legal text classification using transformer models. *arXiv preprint arXiv:2010.12871*.

Rajalakshmi Sivanaiah, S Milton Rajendram, Mirnalinee Tt, Abrit Pal Singh, Aviansh Gupta, Ayush Nanda, et al. 2021. Techssn at semeval-2021 task 7: Humor and offense detection and classification using colbert embeddings. In *Proceedings of the 15th International Workshop on Semantic Evaluation (SemEval-2021)*, pages 1185–1189.

Rajalakshmi Sivanaiah, Angel Suseelan, S Milton Rajendram, and Mirnalinee Tt. 2020. Techssn at semeval-2020 task 12: Offensive language detection using bert embeddings. In *Proceedings of the Fourteenth Workshop on Semantic Evaluation*, pages 2190–2196.

ES Smitha, Selvaraju Sendhilkumar, and GS Mahalaksmi. 2018. Meme classification using textual and visual features. In *Computational Vision and Bio Inspired Computing*, pages 1015–1031. Springer.

R Srinivasan and CN Subalalitha. 2019. Automated named entity recognition from tamil documents. In *2019 IEEE 1st International Conference on Energy, Systems and Information Processing (ICESIP)*, pages 1–5. IEEE.

C. N. Subalalitha. 2019. Information extraction framework for Kurunthogai. *Sādhanā*, 44(7):156.

CN Subalalitha and E Poovammal. 2018. Automatic bilingual dictionary construction for Tirukural. *Applied Artificial Intelligence*, 32(6):558–567.

Shardul Suryawanshi and Bharathi Raja Chakravarthi. 2021. Findings of the shared task on Troll Meme Classification in Tamil. In *Proceedings of the First Workshop on Speech and Language Technologies for Dravidian Languages*. Association for Computational Linguistics.

Shardul Suryawanshi, Bharathi Raja Chakravarthi, Mihael Arcan, Susan Levy, Paul Buitaleer, Prasanna Kumar Kumaresan, Rahul Ponnusamy, and Adeep Hande. 2022. Findings of the second shared task on Troll Meme Classification in Tamil. In *Proceedings of the Second Workshop on Speech and Language Technologies for Dravidian Languages*. Association for Computational Linguistics.

Shardul Suryawanshi, Bharathi Raja Chakravarthi, Pranav Verma, Mihael Arcan, John Philip McCrae, and Paul Buitelaar. 2020. A dataset for troll classification of TamilMemes. In *Proceedings of the WILDRE5– 5th Workshop on Indian Language Data: Resources and Evaluation*, pages 7–13, Marseille, France. European Language Resources Association (ELRA).

Sajeetha Thavareesan and Sinnathamby Mahesan. 2019. Sentiment analysis in Tamil texts: A study on machine learning techniques and feature representation. In *2019 14th Conference on Industrial and Information Systems (ICIIS)*, pages 320–325.

Sajeetha Thavareesan and Sinnathamby Mahesan. 2020a. Sentiment lexicon expansion using Word2vec and fastText for sentiment prediction in Tamil texts. In *2020 Moratuwa Engineering Research Conference (MERCon)*, pages 272–276.

Sajeetha Thavareesan and Sinnathamby Mahesan. 2020b. Word embedding-based part of speech tagging in Tamil texts. In *2020 IEEE 15th International Conference on Industrial and Information Systems (ICIIS)*, pages 478–482.

Sajeetha Thavareesan and Sinnathamby Mahesan. 2021. Sentiment analysis in Tamil texts using k-means and k-nearest neighbour. In *2021 10th International Conference on Information and Automation for Sustainability (ICIAfS)*, pages 48–53.

Zhilin Yang, Zihang Dai, Yiming Yang, Jaime Carbonell, Russ R Salakhutdinov, and Quoc V Le. 2019. Xlnet: Generalized autoregressive pretraining for language understanding. *Advances in neural information processing systems*, 32.

Konthala Yasaswini, Karthik Puranik, Adeep Hande, Ruba Priyadharshini, Sajeetha Thavareesan, and Bharathi Raja Chakravarthi. 2021. IIITT@DravidianLangTech-EACL2021: Transfer learning for offensive language detection in Dravidian languages. In *Proceedings of the First Workshop on Speech and Language Technologies for Dravidian Languages*, pages 187–194, Kyiv. Association for Computational Linguistics.

BpHigh@TamilNLP-ACL2022: Effects of Data Augmentation on Indic-Transformer based classifier for Abusive Comments Detection in Tamil

Bhavish Pahwa
Bits Pilani Hyderabad Campus
bhavishpahwa@gmail.com

Abstract

Social Media platforms have grown their reach worldwide. As an effect of this growth, many vernacular social media platforms have also emerged, focusing more on the diverse languages in the specific regions. Tamil has also emerged as a popular language for use on social media platforms due to the increasing penetration of vernacular media like ShareChat and Moj, which focus more on local Indian languages than English and encourage their users to converse in Indic languages. Abusive language remains a significant challenge in the social media framework and more so when we consider languages like Tamil, which are low-resource languages and have poor performance on multilingual models and lack language-specific models. Based on this shared task, "Abusive Comment detection in Tamil@DravidianLangTech-ACL 2022", we present an exploration of different techniques used to tackle and increase the accuracy of our models using data augmentation in NLP. We also show the results of these techniques.

1 Introduction

The growth of social media platforms has been a significant factor in increasing awareness and connecting the world. Social media has changed the conventional way of communication and has introduced certain short forms and slang that are not present in the traditional vocabulary of any language.[1] At the same time, social media platforms have given rise to a new dynamic of cyber harassment utilizing the veil of anonymity that most platforms provide. Abusive language is a broad term often used to describe the posts and comments on social media platforms written to cyberbully, spread toxicity, spread hate, hurt others based on sex, caste, or creed(Pamungkas et al., 2021).

In the recent past, many social media platforms have updated their guidelines and added moderation policies to curb the spread of abusive language on them. Platforms like Facebook, YouTube, and Twitter have added features to report several posts/videos and comments. Many social media platforms also employ content moderators to clamp down on abusive language on their platforms. Still, this strategy is not sustainable for the long term as social media users continue to grow, and this approach cannot scale (Saha et al., 2021). Many content moderators feel the mental and psychological effects of viewing and moderating several extreme contents and are profoundly affected by such content.[2] Hence many platforms have started building automated abusive language detection and classification systems to improve their moderation capabilities.

In India, vernacular media faces more challenging problems dealing with more diverse languages and code-mixed data. For example, dealing with a vernacular language like Tamil is challenging as it is a low-resource language. Hence, it has insufficient datasets and code-mixed data, and data belonging to both Tamil script and transliterated data. Sometimes these challenges can lead to difficulty for the social media platforms to detect and remove the abusive language, leading to skirmishes with the government.[3]

Sharechat and Moj also organized a challenge recently to improve the abusive language detection systems in Indic languages and released their proprietary dataset for further research.[4] A shared task on "Offensive language detection in Dravidian Languages" was also introduced in the "First Workshop on Speech and Language Technologies for Dravidian Languages at EACL 2021". This shared task consisted of a large cor-

[1] https://www.languageservicesdirect.co.uk/social-media-changing-english-language/

[2] https://www.theverge.com/

[3] https://www.npr.org

[4] https://www.kaggle.com

Proceedings of the Second Workshop on Speech and Language Technologies for Dravidian Languages, pages 138 - 144
May 26, 2022

pus of comments/posts in code-mixed languages Tamil-English, Kannada-English, and Malayalam-English(Chakravarthi et al., 2020b,a, 2021; Hande et al., 2020). Further extending this shared task, the organizers of "The Second Workshop on Speech and Language Technologies for Dravidian Languages at ACL 2022" have released a shared task on "Abusive Comment Detection in Tamil" this task focuses specifically on abusive language detection in Tamil. It consists of datasets of both Tamil as well as code-mixed Tamil-English(Priyadharshini et al., 2022; Chakravarthi, 2020; Chakravarthi and Muralidaran, 2021; Hande et al., 2021).

Our paper makes a two-fold contribution to the shared task. First, we experiment with the state-of-the-art transformer models pre-trained on Indian languages. Secondly, we show how data augmentation techniques in NLP perform in this task and how training with word-level augmented sentences affect our model accuracy. We also provide the trained model weights and the implementation code.[5]

2 Related Work

Steimel et al. (2019) investigated multilingual abusive comment detection focusing on English and German languages. They used a publicly available dataset of Twitter hate speech made by Waseem and Hovy (2016) for English and for German they used the 2018 GermEval shared task data set(Wiegand et al., 2018). They experimented with different text classification algorithms and found that there was no single algorithm which gave the best results on both the languages. They got best results on the German dataset by using SVM , 72.01 F-score and best results on English dataset were obtained using XGBoost, 80.49 F-score.

Pamungkas et al. (2021) wrote a summary paper on multilingual and multi domain abusive language detection, in the paper the authors highlighted various different techniques and datasets created and used by different researchers to properly define and solve the multilingual challenges related to abusive language detection. In the papers the author mentions several Transformer architecture based models like Multilingual BERT and XLM RoBERTa which are pre trained on corpus of several languages and can be finetuned for various tasks. They also mention various datasets in Indic languages like Hindi and code mixed hindi-english which are created specifically for the purpose of Hate speech/Abusive language detection, like HASOC, 2019.[6]

Khanuja et al. (2021) published a research paper along with a new transformer language model 'MURIL' based on the BERT architecture which is specifically designed for Indian languages. In the paper the authors also compared performance of both Multilingual BERT and MURIL on various tasks in Indian languages.The model currently has support for 17 Indian languages. In the papers the author shows that MURIL beats Multilingual BERT across all tasks and benchmarks in Indian languages. On the famous XTREME benchmark, Multilingual BERT gives an average performance of 59.1 whereas MURIL gives a 68.6 average performance.

Feng et al. (2021) published a survey paper on data augmentation approaches utilized in NLP. The paper's authors discussed how data augmentation techniques could help fix the class imbalance. They also discussed various data augmentation methods like BACKTRANSLATION (Sennrich et al., 2016) and EASY DATA AUGMENTATION (EDA)(Wei and Zou, 2019).

Kobayashi (2018) presented a novel data augmentation technique called contextual augmentation. In this technique the authors used a bi-directional language model to replace words in the given input with other words according to the context. They further showed how this technique helps improve the accuracy of classifiers based on Recurrent Neural Networks(RNN) and Convolutional Neural Networks(CNN).

3 Dataset Description

The shared task on Abusive comment detection in Tamil-ACL 2022(Priyadharshini et al., 2022) is a comment classification problem that can be further described as a multi-class text classification problem in Tamil native script and Tamil-English code-mixed. The main objective is to build two separate systems that can classify comments, one for Tamil native script and another for code-mixed Tamil-English.

The purpose can also be redefined as developing a common system that can classify comments of both Tamil and Tamil-English languages. This paper treats the objective as building a common

[5]https://github.com/bp-high

[6]https://hasocfire.github.io

system for both languages rather than separate, to have a more standard approach.

The dataset was generated by scraping Youtube comments belonging to Tamil and Tamil-English code-mixed languages and annotated on comment level by linguists/annotators based on the platform's set guidelines and code of conduct. The dataset is split into two datasets based on the language. The labels used for annotation of the dataset are Misogyny, Misandry, Homophobia, Transphobia, Xenophobia, Counter Speech, Hope Speech, and None of the above. The dataset is further split into the training and development sets. The dataset consists of rows that contain the comment text and the label assigned to that comment.

4 Methodology

This section discusses the experiments and approaches undertaken to build a system for abusive comment detection. As explained earlier, we create a common system for both Tamil and Tamil-English languages, and hence for this purpose, we combine the dataset of Tamil and Tamil-English languages to make a combined dataset. Figure 1 shows a flowchart of the different approaches that we explored.

4.1 Transformer Model

Recently Transformer models have become quite widely used in NLP due to their property to capture context and the attention mechanism. In many downstream tasks in NLP, Transformers based models are state of the art, and due to organizations like Hugging Face, their implementation and Fine-tuning have become quite accessible.

We build a classifier using the **MURIL Transformer**(Khanuja et al., 2021) as our embedding layer(all layers frozen) and attach a classifier head by adding subsequent convolution and dense layers. The final output dense layer has softmax activation, which gives us the final predictions. The details of the model structure are present in Figure 2.

We used the MURIL Transformer as our embedding layer as it supports both Tamil and Tamil-English code-mixed as it was trained on both translated and transliterated document pairs.

Also, pre-processing of the comments is done using the MURIL tokenizer, also from Khanuja et al. (2021) we can see that MURIL produces lesser sub-words per word when compared to other multilingual models trained for Indian languages

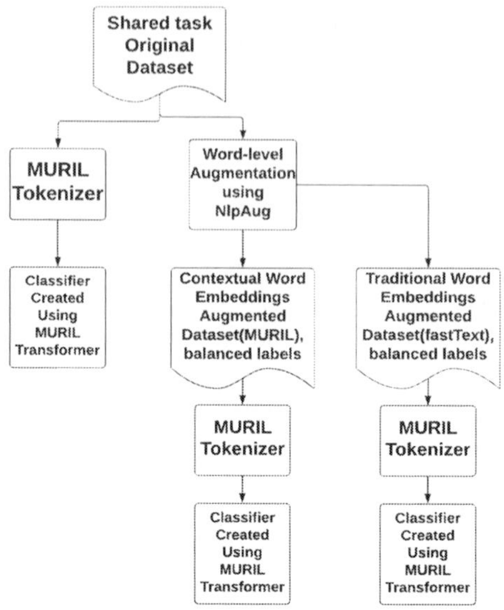

Figure 1: Flowchart of the different approaches

and has higher preservation of semantic meaning for Indian languages.

4.2 Data Augmentation in NLP

The labels in the initial dataset were unbalanced, with an overwhelming number of labels belonging to the "None of the above" class. We use data augmentation techniques in NLP to balance the dataset by performing word-level augmentation on the sentences belonging to the classes with lower representation in the dataset to reach a net balanced representation of all classes. We take the help of the NlpAug library[7](Ma, 2019), which provides the methods to perform word-level augmentation using contextual models as well as non-contextual word embeddings like Word2vec(Mikolov et al., 2013), fastText(Bojanowski et al., 2017), and Glove(Pennington et al., 2014).

$$M(i) = \lfloor (maximum_{j \in L}(N_j)) / N_i \rfloor$$

The above equation shows us the multiplier value M, used while generating the augmented sentences. M refers to the value by which the number of occurrences of a label should change, and N is the number of occurrences of a label, also called the value count of a label. L refers to the set of class labels. In terms of words, the above equation conveys that the multiplier value M(i) for label i is equal to the floor division of the value count for the

[7]https://github.com/makcedward/nlpaug

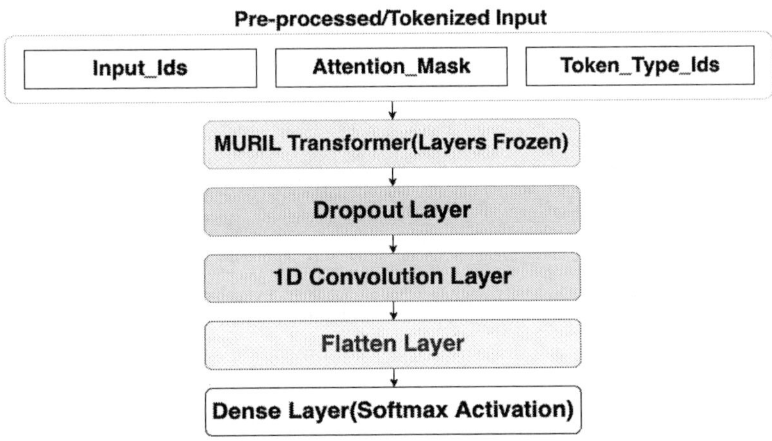

Figure 2: Structure of the classifier based on MURIL Transformer

Approach	Language	Accuracy	Macro-avg F1-score	Weighted-avg F1-score
No Augmentation	Tamil	0.64	0.17	0.56
No Augmentation	Tamil-English	0.67	0.19	0.59
Augmentation(MURIL)	Tamil	0.55	0.16	0.48
Augmentation(MURIL)	Tamil-English	0.59	0.13	0.50
Augmentation(Tamil fastText)	Tamil	0.49	**0.25**	0.52
Augmentation(Tamil fastText)	Tamil-English	0.52	**0.27**	0.56

Table 1: Results of all the approaches on test dataset

label having maximum count and the value count for label i. Using the mentioned equation we apply two word-level augmentation approaches on our train dataset. One using the contextual model and the other using the traditional non-contextual word embedding. Do note that no changes are made to the development/validation dataset.

4.2.1 Data Augmentation using Contextual Model

We use the **MURIL Transformer**(Khanuja et al., 2021) again as a "Contextual Word Embedding Augmenter" to generate word-level augmented sentences(Kumar et al., 2020). Then we train our classifier using this new balanced version of the train dataset.

4.2.2 Data Augmentation using Non-Contextual Word Embedding

We use the IndicNLP tokenizer for Indian languages[8] for pre-processing the input sentences and the **Tamil fastText model** from the IndicNLP suite(Kakwani et al., 2020) as a 'Word Embeddings Augmenter' to generate word-level augmented sentences. Then we train our classifier using this new balanced version of the train dataset.

[8]Indic NLP library

MODEL PARAMETERS	VALUE
Fixed Parameters	
Batch Size	32
Optimizer	Adam
Learning Rate Schedule	Exponential Decay
Max Sequence Length	64
Tuned Parameters	
No Augmentation	
Num Epochs	50
Dropout	0.5
Learning Rate	0.01
Augmentation(MURIL)	
Num Epochs	60
Dropout	0.5
Learning Rate	0.001
Augmentation(Tamil fastText)	
Num Epochs	50
Dropout	0.3
Learning Rate	0.01

Table 2: Hyperparameters optimized for different approaches

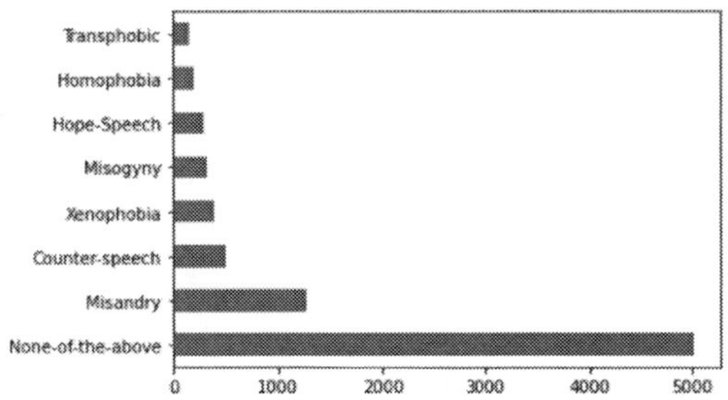

Figure 3: Bar graph of the number of occurrences of each label in the original train dataset

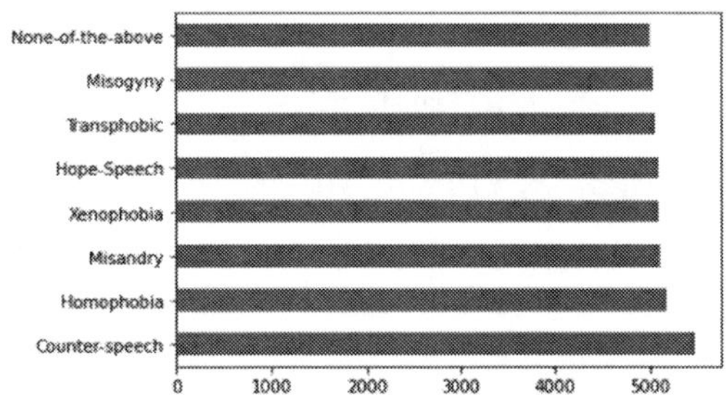

Figure 4: Bar graph of the number of occurrences of each label in the augmented train datasets generated

5 Results

We optimize the hyperparameters of the transformer-based classifier in all of our approaches on the training and development set and then get the predictions on the test set to observe the results of our approaches. The test dataset results on both languages are present in Table-1. In this task the approaches are evaluated with Macro-avg F1-score and the best performing approach for each language has been highlighted. For both the languages Tamil and Tamil-English, we observe that using the original dataset and training it with our transformer-based classifier yields better results than the data augmentation approach using **MURIL** and then training it with the transformer-classifier. However we observe that the results for the data augmentation approach using **Tamil fastText** produced better results for both the languages. See Table-2 for details in our training setup for the transformer-based classifier for all our approaches.

6 Conclusion

We explored the effects of data augmentation techniques on the Indic-Transformer based classifier created using MURIL Transformer on the task of Abusive Comment Detection in Tamil. We observe a negative result in the case of word-level augmentation using Contextual Models(**MURIL**) and an improvement in performance in the case of augmentation using Non-Contextual Word Embeddings(**Tamil fastText**).

As we further try to speculate why our augmentation technique based on Contextual Models failed to yield a better result, we consider the reasons stated in Longpre et al. (2020), which show that data augmentation techniques help improve performance on the task only when the approaches provide a language pattern that is not seen before during pretraining of the Transformer model. As both the Contextual Model for augmentation and the Indic-Transformer used to create the classifier is MURIL transformer, we cannot observe new linguistic patterns.

Also, in Kobayashi (2018), the authors observe that augmentation based on Contextual Models might not be able to remain compatible with the annotated labels of the original input and thus might harm the training process. They suggest using information from both label and context to generate word-level augmentations to control this incompatibility.

References

Piotr Bojanowski, Edouard Grave, Armand Joulin, and Tomas Mikolov. 2017. Enriching word vectors with subword information. *Transactions of the Association for Computational Linguistics*, 5:135–146.

Bharathi Raja Chakravarthi. 2020. HopeEDI: A multilingual hope speech detection dataset for equality, diversity, and inclusion. In *Proceedings of the Third Workshop on Computational Modeling of People's Opinions, Personality, and Emotion's in Social Media*, pages 41–53, Barcelona, Spain (Online). Association for Computational Linguistics.

Bharathi Raja Chakravarthi, Navya Jose, Shardul Suryawanshi, Elizabeth Sherly, and John Philip McCrae. 2020a. A sentiment analysis dataset for code-mixed Malayalam-English. In *Proceedings of the 1st Joint Workshop on Spoken Language Technologies for Under-resourced languages (SLTU) and Collaboration and Computing for Under-Resourced Languages (CCURL)*, pages 177–184, Marseille, France. European Language Resources association.

Bharathi Raja Chakravarthi and Vigneshwaran Muralidaran. 2021. Findings of the shared task on hope speech detection for equality, diversity, and inclusion. In *Proceedings of the First Workshop on Language Technology for Equality, Diversity and Inclu-*

sion, pages 61–72, Kyiv. Association for Computational Linguistics.

Bharathi Raja Chakravarthi, Vigneshwaran Muralidaran, Ruba Priyadharshini, and John Philip McCrae. 2020b. Corpus creation for sentiment analysis in code-mixed Tamil-English text. In *Proceedings of the 1st Joint Workshop on Spoken Language Technologies for Under-resourced languages (SLTU) and Collaboration and Computing for Under-Resourced Languages (CCURL)*, pages 202–210, Marseille, France. European Language Resources association.

Bharathi Raja Chakravarthi, Ruba Priyadharshini, Navya Jose, Anand Kumar M, Thomas Mandl, Prasanna Kumar Kumaresan, Rahul Ponnusamy, Hariharan R L, John P. McCrae, and Elizabeth Sherly. 2021. Findings of the shared task on offensive language identification in Tamil, Malayalam, and Kannada. In *Proceedings of the First Workshop on Speech and Language Technologies for Dravidian Languages*, pages 133–145, Kyiv. Association for Computational Linguistics.

Steven Y. Feng, Varun Gangal, Jason Wei, Sarath Chandar, Soroush Vosoughi, Teruko Mitamura, and Eduard Hovy. 2021. A survey of data augmentation approaches for NLP. In *Findings of the Association for Computational Linguistics: ACL-IJCNLP 2021*, pages 968–988, Online. Association for Computational Linguistics.

Adeep Hande, Ruba Priyadharshini, and Bharathi Raja Chakravarthi. 2020. KanCMD: Kannada CodeMixed dataset for sentiment analysis and offensive language detection. In *Proceedings of the Third Workshop on Computational Modeling of People's Opinions, Personality, and Emotion's in Social Media*, pages 54–63, Barcelona, Spain (Online). Association for Computational Linguistics.

Adeep Hande, Ruba Priyadharshini, Anbukkarasi Sampath, Kingston Pal Thamburaj, Prabakaran Chandran, and Bharathi Raja Chakravarthi. 2021. Hope speech detection in under-resourced kannada language. *arXiv preprint arXiv:2108.04616*.

Divyanshu Kakwani, Anoop Kunchukuttan, Satish Golla, Gokul N.C., Avik Bhattacharyya, Mitesh M. Khapra, and Pratyush Kumar. 2020. IndicNLPSuite: Monolingual corpora, evaluation benchmarks and pre-trained multilingual language models for Indian languages. In *Findings of the Association for Computational Linguistics: EMNLP 2020*, pages 4948–4961, Online. Association for Computational Linguistics.

Simran Khanuja, Diksha Bansal, Sarvesh Mehtani, Savya Khosla, Atreyee Dey, Balaji Gopalan, Dilip Kumar Margam, Pooja Aggarwal, Rajiv Teja Nagipogu, Shachi Dave, Shruti Gupta, Subhash Chandra Bose Gali, Vish Subramanian, and Partha P. Talukdar. 2021. Muril: Multilingual representations for indian languages. *CoRR*, abs/2103.10730.

Sosuke Kobayashi. 2018. Contextual augmentation: Data augmentation by words with paradigmatic relations. In *Proceedings of the 2018 Conference of the North American Chapter of the Association for Computational Linguistics: Human Language Technologies, Volume 2 (Short Papers)*, pages 452–457, New Orleans, Louisiana. Association for Computational Linguistics.

Varun Kumar, Ashutosh Choudhary, and Eunah Cho. 2020. Data augmentation using pre-trained transformer models. In *Proceedings of the 2nd Workshop on Life-long Learning for Spoken Language Systems*, pages 18–26, Suzhou, China. Association for Computational Linguistics.

Shayne Longpre, Yu Wang, and Chris DuBois. 2020. How effective is task-agnostic data augmentation for pretrained transformers? In *Findings of the Association for Computational Linguistics: EMNLP 2020*, pages 4401–4411, Online. Association for Computational Linguistics.

Edward Ma. 2019. Nlp augmentation. https://github.com/makcedward/nlpaug.

Tomas Mikolov, Kai Chen, Greg Corrado, and Jeffrey Dean. 2013. Efficient estimation of word representations in vector space.

Endang Wahyu Pamungkas, Valerio Basile, and Viviana Patti. 2021. Towards multidomain and multilingual abusive language detection: a survey.

Jeffrey Pennington, Richard Socher, and Christopher Manning. 2014. GloVe: Global vectors for word representation. In *Proceedings of the 2014 Conference on Empirical Methods in Natural Language Processing (EMNLP)*, pages 1532–1543, Doha, Qatar. Association for Computational Linguistics.

Ruba Priyadharshini, Bharathi Raja Chakravarthi, Subalalitha Chinnaudayar Navaneethakrishnan, Thenmozhi Durairaj, Malliga Subramanian, Kogilavani Shanmugavadivel, Siddhanth U Hegde, and Prasanna Kumar Kumaresan. 2022. Findings of the shared task on Abusive Comment Detection in Tamil. In *Proceedings of the Second Workshop on Speech and Language Technologies for Dravidian Languages*. Association for Computational Linguistics.

Debjoy Saha, Naman Paharia, Debajit Chakraborty, Punyajoy Saha, and Animesh Mukherjee. 2021. Hate-alert@DravidianLangTech-EACL2021: Ensembling strategies for transformer-based offensive language detection. In *Proceedings of the First Workshop on Speech and Language Technologies for Dravidian Languages*, pages 270–276, Kyiv. Association for Computational Linguistics.

Rico Sennrich, Barry Haddow, and Alexandra Birch. 2016. Improving neural machine translation models with monolingual data. In *Proceedings of the 54th Annual Meeting of the Association for Computational*

Linguistics (Volume 1: Long Papers), pages 86–96, Berlin, Germany. Association for Computational Linguistics.

Kenneth Steimel, Daniel Dakota, Yue Chen, and Sandra Kübler. 2019. Investigating multilingual abusive language detection: A cautionary tale. In *Proceedings of the International Conference on Recent Advances in Natural Language Processing (RANLP 2019)*, pages 1151–1160, Varna, Bulgaria. INCOMA Ltd.

Zeerak Waseem and Dirk Hovy. 2016. Hateful symbols or hateful people? predictive features for hate speech detection on Twitter. In *Proceedings of the NAACL Student Research Workshop*, pages 88–93, San Diego, California. Association for Computational Linguistics.

Jason Wei and Kai Zou. 2019. EDA: Easy data augmentation techniques for boosting performance on text classification tasks. In *Proceedings of the 2019 Conference on Empirical Methods in Natural Language Processing and the 9th International Joint Conference on Natural Language Processing (EMNLP-IJCNLP)*, pages 6382–6388, Hong Kong, China. Association for Computational Linguistics.

Michael Wiegand, Melanie Siegel, and Josef Ruppenhofer. 2018. Overview of the germeval 2018 shared task on the identification of offensive language. In *Overview of the GermEval 2018 Shared Task on the Identification of Offensive Language*.

MUCS@DravidianLangTech@ACL2022: Ensemble of Logistic Regression Penalties to Identify Emotions in Tamil Text

Asha Hegde[1 a], **Sharal Coelho**[1 b], **Hosahalli Lakshmaiah Shashirekha**[1 c]
[1]Department of Computer Science, Mangalore University, Mangalore, India
{[a]hegdekasha,[b]sharalmucs,[c]hlsrekha}@gmail.com

Abstract

Emotion Analysis (EA) is the process of automatically analyzing and categorizing the input text into one of the predefined sets of emotions. In recent years, people have turned to social media to express their emotions, opinions or feelings about news, movies, products, services, and so on. These users' emotions may help the public, governments, business organizations, film producers, and others in devising strategies, making decisions, and so on. The increasing number of social media users and the increasing amount of user generated text containing emotions on social media demands automated tools for the analysis of such data as handling this data manually is labor intensive and error prone. Further, the characteristics of social media data makes the EA challenging. Most of the EA research works have focused on English language leaving several Indian languages including Tamil unexplored for this task. To address the challenges of EA in Tamil texts, in this paper, we - team MUCS, describe the model submitted to the shared task on Emotion Analysis in Tamil at DravidianLangTech@ACL 2022. Out of the two subtasks in this shared task, our team submitted the model only for Task a. The proposed model comprises of an Ensemble of Logistic Regression (LR) classifiers with three penalties, namely: L1, L2, and Elasticnet. This Ensemble model trained with Term Frequency - Inverse Document Frequency (TF-IDF) of character bigrams and trigrams secured 4th rank in Task a with a macro averaged F1-score of 0.04. The code to reproduce the proposed models is available in github[1].

1 Introduction

Emotions are a form of psychological state of human mind and in texts the emotions are commonly represented through content bearing words such as happiness, anger, joy, disgust, boredom, depression, etc. The process of automatically analyzing and categorizing the input text into one of the predefined sets of emotions like happy, sad, angry and so on is called Emotion Analysis (Priyadharshini et al., 2021; Kumaresan et al., 2021). Analyzing the text for emotions helps to improve an existing process, grab new opportunities, capture the real response of audiences for their movies and reality shows, recognize and predict the market trends, and so on (Sampath et al., 2022; Ravikiran et al., 2022; Chakravarthi et al., 2022; Bharathi et al., 2022; Priyadharshini et al., 2022). Today internet and social media have become a popular platform for users to express the emotions, views, sentiments and opinions. The freedom to users to express their emotions about anything and everything on social media is increasing the social media text containing emotions (Chakravarthi, 2020; Chakravarthi and Muralidaran, 2021). Further, the freedom of the use of language on social media makes the analysis of social media text very challenging. The large volume and complexity of social media data makes the analysis of such data very challenging and interesting.

Most the EA works focus on English language leaving the task in several Indian languages including Tamil unexplored for the task (Vasantharajan et al., 2022). Due to the availability of a large volume of user-generated social media data in Tamil containing different emotions, EA in Tamil is gaining popularity (Jenarthanan et al., 2019). In recent years, there has been an increase in the EA of text in classical languages like Tamil The growing number of Tamil users on social media platforms and the increasing number of posts and comments shared by these users are making it nearly impossible to track and control the content manually (Sakuntharaj and Mahesan, 2021, 2017, 2016; Thavareesan and Mahesan, 2019, 2020a,b, 2021). Hence, there is a need for tools or models to analyse the emotions in the social media comments automatically. EA is an open-ended issue because of the creative users' cre-

[1]https://github.com/hegdekasha/Emotion-analysis-in-Tamil

Proceedings of the Second Workshop on Speech and Language Technologies for Dravidian Languages, pages 145 - 150
May 26, 2022 ©2022 Association for Computational Linguistics

ative posts on social media (B and A, 2021b,a). To address the challenges of EA in Tamil, in this paper, we - team MUCS, describe the model submitted to "Emotion Analysis in Tamil"[2] shared task organized by DravidianLangTech@ACL 2022. This task aims to classify the input comment in Tamil into one of eleven emotion categories. The proposed methodology consists of an Ensemble of LR classifiers with different regularizations or penalties, namely: LASSO (L1) regularization, Ridge (L2) regularization and Elasticnet regularization. TF-IDF of character bigrams and trigrams is used to train the LR classifiers and soft voting is used to classify the input comment into one of eleven categories.

The following is a breakdown of the paper's structure. Section 2 contains the literature review and Section 3 explains the proposed methodology. Section 4 describes the experiments conducted to identify and determine type of emotions, as well as the outcomes and the paper concludes in Section 5 with future work.

2 Literature Review

Researchers are trying to develop tools for processing the Tamil language for various applications such as EA, Text Summarization, Sentiment Analysis (SA) and so on (Nandwani and Verma, 2021).

Chiorrini et al. (2021) analyzed the performance of SA and emotion recognition using Bidirectional Encoder Representations from Transformers (BERT) models on real-world Twitter dataset. The experimental results showed that the models scored 0.92 and 0.90 accuracies for SA and emotion recognition, respectively. Vasantharajan et al. (2022) developed the largest manually annotated dataset of over 42k Tamil YouTube comments and categorized them into 31 emotions in order to recognize emotional statements. They established three distinct groups of emotions that are of 3-class, 7-class, and 31-classes. For the 3-class group dataset, they used Multilingual Representations for Indian Languages (MuRIL) pre-trained model trained on English and 16 Indian languages and obtained a macro average F1-score of 0.60. For 7-class and 31-class groups, the Random Forest (RF) model performed well with macro average F1-scores of 0.42 and 0.29, respectively.

To determine the category of emotions, Alotaibi (2019) trained Support Vector Machine (SVM), k-Nearest Neighbors (kNN), and LR classifiers on the International Survey on Emotion Antecedents and Reactions (ISEAR) dataset using TF-IDF features. LR classifier obtained 0.86 and 0.85 as precision and F1-score respectively. Using the benefits of Convolutional Neural Network (CNN) and Bidirectional Long Short Term Memory (BiLSTM), Ahmad et al. (2020) proposed an attention-based C-BiLSTM model to classify emotional states of poetry texts into different emotional states like love, joy, hope, sadness, anger, etc. Experimental results showed an accuracy of 88% for their model.

Even though several techniques have been developed to detect emotions in the text, very few attempts have been made for the Tamil language. This opens up lots of possibilities to conduct experiments on EA of Tamil texts including social media data.

3 Methodology

Inspired by Anusha and Shashirekha (2020) and Balouchzahi and Shashirekha (2020) an Ensemble of LR classifiers is proposed to identify the emotions in Tamil text and classify them into one of the given eleven categories and the framework of the proposed model is shown in Figure 1. The proposed model consists of three modules, namely: Pre-processing, Feature Extraction and Classifier Construction which are described briefly below:

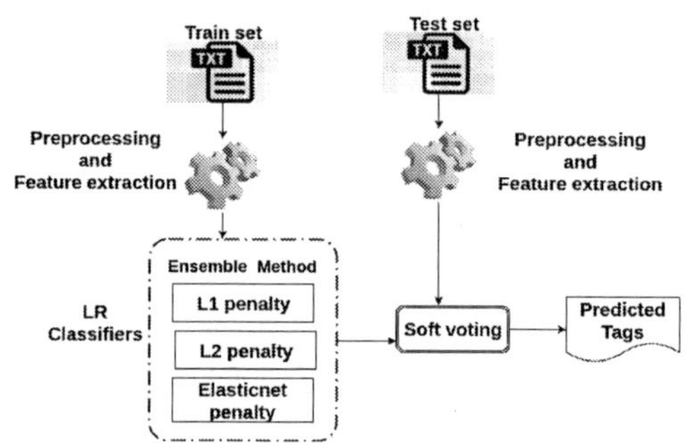

Figure 1: Framework of the proposed model

3.1 Pre-processing

Pre-processing step is essential to clean the text to improve the quality of data. The text is preprocessed by removing punctuation marks, digits, unrelated characters, and stopwords, as these features do not contribute to the task of classification. Tamil stopwords[3] list available in github repository

[2] https://competitions.codalab.org/competitions/36396

[3] https://gist.github.com/arulrajnet/

are used to remove Tamil stopwords from the given corpus as stop words do not contribute to the classification. Further, emojis are also removed as the dataset has enough textual content.

3.2 Feature Extraction

Feature extraction is one of the key steps in classification. TF-IDF expresses the relative importance between a word in the document and the entire corpus and TF-IDF of character n-grams has shown good performance (Kanaris et al., 2007). Hence, all the character bigrams and trigrams are extracted from the dataset and are vectorized using TFidfVectorizer[4]. The number of character bigrams and trigrams extracted from the datasets amounts to 13,808.

3.3 Classifier Construction

Model performance is heavily dependent on the features of the dataset and the classifier employed. No classifier produces good results for every dataset. Due to this, in general, no classifier can be considered as the best. An ensemble of classifiers, where the weakness of one classifier is compensated by the strength of another, produces better results than a single classifier. The proposed Ensemble of LR models with L1, L2 and Elasticnet penalties are trained on character bigrams and trigrams and soft voting is used to classify the input text into one of the emotion categories.

LR algorithm is a Machine Learning (ML) classifier used to predict categorical variables with the use of dependent variables and regularization to reduce overfitting (Indra et al., 2016). The penalties used in the LR models are described below:

- **L1 regularization -** The term LASSO stands for Least Absolute Shrinkage and Selection Operator and is also known as L1 regularization. In L1 regularization, L1 penalty which is equal to the absolute magnitude of coefficients is added to the loss function. L1 penalty uses shrinkage to determine regression coefficients and shrinkage occurs when a data value is shrunk towards zero.

- **L2 regularization -** The Ridge regularization also known as L2 regularization adds a squared magnitude of the coefficient to the loss function as a penalty. If the loss is zero then the regularization leads to an ordinary least square.

- **Elasticnet regularization -** L1 regularization eliminates many features, whereas L2 regularization manifests the loss by adding large weights. Elasticnet regularization is a popular type of regularized LR that combines L1 and L2 penalties. More precisely, elasticnet combines feature elimination from L1 regularization and feature coefficient reduction from L2 regularization to improve the model's predictions.

[4]https://scikit-learn.org/stable/modules/generated /sklearn.feature_extraction.text.TfidfVectorizer.html

Classes	Training set	Dev set
Neutral	4,841	1,222
Joy	2,134	558
Ambiguous	1,689	437
Trust	1,254	272
Disguist	910	210
Anger	834	184
Anticipation	828	213
Sadness	695	191
Love	675	189
Surprise	248	53
Fear	100	23

Table 1: Statistics of Tamil dataset used for Task a

4 Experiments and Results

Statistics of the dataset for Task a in the EA shared task is summarized in Table 1 and the sample Tamil comments with their corresponding labels are shown in Table 2. The observation of the dataset shows the imbalance in the distribution of samples.

Several experiments were conducted with different values of the hyperparameters for the classifiers. The values of the hyperparameters which gave good results on the Development (Dev) set were used to conduct experiments on the Test set and such values of the hyperparameters are given in Table 3. For final evaluation and ranking, the predicted outputs on the Test set were submitted to the organizers of the shared task. A macro-averaged Precision, macro-averaged Recall, and macro-averaged F1-score were used by the organizers to measure the performance of the classifier for EA task and the results of the proposed model are shown in Table 4. The comparison of the performances of the best models of the shared task

Sl. No	Tamil sentences	Label
1.	அண்ணன் கிட்டுக்கு வாழ்த்துக்கள்	Joy
2.	வேல்ராஜ் வேலையா தான் இருக்கும்	Anticipation
3.	ஆமா நானும் இதான் யோசித்தேன்	Trust
4.	இவர் சொன்னது உன் மை	Neutral
5.	எந்த ஊர் சொல்லுறங்க அக்கா	Ambiguous
6.	ஏஒறுவனிடம் தோர்க போகும் பழசு	Sadness
7.	இந்த நிமிடமும் தமிழகத்தின் முதல்வர் எடப்பாடமு	Surprise
8.	பொணம் இன்னி பசங்க அரசாங்கம்	Anger
9.	உங்களை பார்களும் சகோதரா	Love
10.	இதே வேலை யா போச்சு இவனுகளுக்கு	Disguist
11.	நாம் டம்ளர் டெபாசிட் போச்சா	Fear

Table 2: Sample Tamil comments with their labels

Type of regularizations	Hyperparameters
L1	C=1, penalty="l1", tol=0.01, solver="saga"
L2	C=1, penalty="l2", tol=0.01, solver="saga"
Elasticnet	penalty="elasticnet", l1_ratio=0.5

Table 3: Details of hyperparameters used in the proposed model

with that of the proposed model in terms of macro-averaged F1-score is shown in Figure 2.

The proposed model obtained macro-averaged F1-scores of 0.20 and 0.04 for Dev set and Test set respectively. It is clear that the scores for Dev set and Test set were low because of imbalanced nature of the dataset. Class distribution has a significant impact on the predictions and the same is reflected in the results. 'Neutral' class has the maximum distribution of 34.07% of the overall distribution, whereas 'Fear' class has a least distribution of 0.70%. The proposed model exhibited a low F1-score because of the large difference between the number of samples in the classes.

Datasets	Precision	Recall	Macro averaged F1-score
Dev set	0.38	0.19	0.20
Test set	0.11	0.13	0.04

Table 4: Results of the proposed model

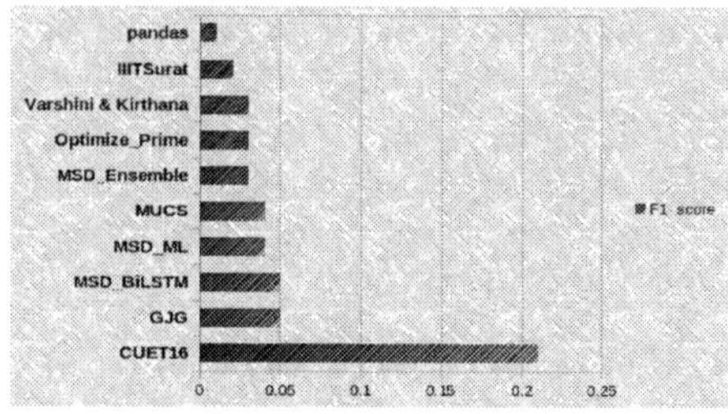

Figure 2: Comparison of the macro-averaged F1-scores of the proposed model with that of the other best models in the shared task

5 Conclusion and Future Work

In this paper, we, team MUCS, have presented the description of the proposed model submitted to a shared task on EA in Tamil at DravidianLangTech@ACL 2022 to identify the different categories of emotions from social media comments in Tamil. The proposed Ensemble of LR classifiers with L1, L2 and Elasticnet penalties obtained macro-averaged F1-score of 0.04 and secured 4th place in the shared task. In future, we intend to investigate sets of features and different re-sampling methods for identifying emotions in Tamil text.

References

Shakeel Ahmad, Muhammad Zubair Asghar, Fahad Mazaed Alotaibi, and Sherafzal Khan. 2020. Classification of Poetry Text into the Emotional States using Deep Learning Technique. volume 8, pages 73865–73878. IEEE.

Fahad Mazaed Alotaibi. 2019. Classifying Text-based Emotions using Logistic Regression.

M. D. Anusha and H. L. Shashirekha. 2020. An Ensemble Model for Hate Speech and Offensive Content Identification in Indo-European Languages. In *FIRE (Working Notes)*, pages 253–259.

Bharathi B and Agnusimmaculate Silvia A. 2021a. SSNCSE_NLP@DravidianLangTech-EACL2021: Meme classification for Tamil using machine learning approach. In *Proceedings of the First Workshop on Speech and Language Technologies for Dravidian Languages*, pages 336–339, Kyiv. Association for Computational Linguistics.

Bharathi B and Agnusimmaculate Silvia A. 2021b. SSNCSE_NLP@DravidianLangTech-EACL2021: Offensive language identification on multilingual code mixing text. In *Proceedings of the First Workshop on Speech and Language Technologies for Dravidian Languages*, pages 313–318, Kyiv. Association for Computational Linguistics.

Fazlourrahman Balouchzahi and H. L. Shashirekha. 2020. LAs for HASOC-Learning Approaches for Hate Speech and Offensive Content Identification. In *FIRE (Working Notes)*, pages 145–151.

B Bharathi, Bharathi Raja Chakravarthi, Subalalitha Chinnaudayar Navaneethakrishnan, N Sripriya, Arunaggiri Pandian, and Swetha Valli. 2022. Findings of the shared task on Speech Recognition for Vulnerable Individuals in Tamil. In *Proceedings of the Second Workshop on Language Technology for Equality, Diversity and Inclusion*. Association for Computational Linguistics.

Bharathi Raja Chakravarthi. 2020. HopeEDI: A multilingual hope speech detection dataset for equality, diversity, and inclusion. In *Proceedings of the Third Workshop on Computational Modeling of People's Opinions, Personality, and Emotion's in Social Media*, pages 41–53, Barcelona, Spain (Online). Association for Computational Linguistics.

Bharathi Raja Chakravarthi and Vigneshwaran Muralidaran. 2021. Findings of the shared task on hope speech detection for equality, diversity, and inclusion. In *Proceedings of the First Workshop on Language Technology for Equality, Diversity and Inclusion*, pages 61–72, Kyiv. Association for Computational Linguistics.

Bharathi Raja Chakravarthi, Ruba Priyadharshini, Thenmozhi Durairaj, John Phillip McCrae, Paul Buitaleer, Prasanna Kumar Kumaresan, and Rahul Ponnusamy. 2022. Findings of the shared task on Homophobia Transphobia Detection in Social Media Comments. In *Proceedings of the Second Workshop on Language Technology for Equality, Diversity and Inclusion*. Association for Computational Linguistics.

Andrea Chiorrini, Claudia Diamantini, Alex Mircoli, and Domenico Potena. 2021. Emotion and Sentiment Analysis of Tweets using BERT. In *EDBT/ICDT Workshops*.

ST Indra, Liza Wikarsa, and Rinaldo Turang. 2016. Using Logistic Regression Method to Classify Tweets into the Selected Topics. In *2016 international conference on advanced computer science and information systems (icacsis)*, pages 385–390. IEEE.

Rajenthiran Jenarthanan, Yasas Senarath, and Uthayasanker Thayasivam. 2019. ACTSEA: Annotated Corpus for Tamil & Sinhala Emotion Analysis. In *2019 Moratuwa Engineering Research Conference (MERCon)*, pages 49–53. IEEE.

Ioannis Kanaris, Konstantinos Kanaris, Ioannis Houvardas, and Efstathios Stamatatos. 2007. Words versus Character N-grams for Anti-spam Filtering. volume 16, pages 1047–1067. World Scientific.

Prasanna Kumar Kumaresan, Ratnasingam Sakuntharaj, Sajeetha Thavareesan, Subalalitha Navaneethakrishnan, Anand Kumar Madasamy, Bharathi Raja Chakravarthi, and John P McCrae. 2021. Findings of shared task on offensive language identification in Tamil and Malayalam. In *Forum for Information Retrieval Evaluation*, pages 16–18.

Pansy Nandwani and Rupali Verma. 2021. A Review on Sentiment Analysis and Emotion Detection from Text. volume 11, pages 1–19. Springer.

Ruba Priyadharshini, Bharathi Raja Chakravarthi, Subalalitha Chinnaudayar Navaneethakrishnan, Thenmozhi Durairaj, Malliga Subramanian, Kogilavani Shanmugavadivel, Siddhanth U Hegde, and Prasanna Kumar Kumaresan. 2022. Findings of the shared task on Abusive Comment Detection in Tamil. In *Proceedings of the Second Workshop on Speech and Language Technologies for Dravidian Languages*. Association for Computational Linguistics.

Ruba Priyadharshini, Bharathi Raja Chakravarthi, Sajeetha Thavareesan, Dhivya Chinnappa, Durairaj Thenmozhi, and Rahul Ponnusamy. 2021. Overview of the DravidianCodeMix 2021 shared task on sentiment detection in Tamil, Malayalam, and Kannada. In *Forum for Information Retrieval Evaluation*, pages 4–6.

Manikandan Ravikiran, Bharathi Raja Chakravarthi, Anand Kumar Madasamy, Sangeetha Sivanesan, Ratnavel Rajalakshmi, Sajeetha Thavareesan, Rahul Ponnusamy, and Shankar Mahadevan. 2022. Findings of the shared task on Offensive Span Identification in code-mixed Tamil-English comments. In *Proceedings of the Second Workshop on Speech and Language Technologies for Dravidian Languages*. Association for Computational Linguistics.

Ratnasingam Sakuntharaj and Sinnathamby Mahesan. 2016. A novel hybrid approach to detect and correct spelling in Tamil text. In *2016 IEEE International Conference on Information and Automation for Sustainability (ICIAfS)*, pages 1–6.

Ratnasingam Sakuntharaj and Sinnathamby Mahesan. 2017. Use of a novel hash-table for speeding-up suggestions for misspelt Tamil words. In *2017 IEEE International Conference on Industrial and Information Systems (ICIIS)*, pages 1–5.

Ratnasingam Sakuntharaj and Sinnathamby Mahesan. 2021. Missing word detection and correction based on context of Tamil sentences using n-grams. In *2021 10th International Conference on Information and Automation for Sustainability (ICIAfS)*, pages 42–47.

Anbukkarasi Sampath, Thenmozhi Durairaj, Bharathi Raja Chakravarthi, Ruba Priyadharshini, Subalalitha Chinnaudayar Navaneethakrishnan, Kogilavani Shanmugavadivel, Sajeetha Thavareesan, Sathiyaraj Thangasamy, Parameswari Krishnamurthy, Adeep Hande, Sean Benhur, Kishor Kumar Ponnusamy, and Santhiya Pandiyan. 2022. Findings of the shared task on Emotion Analysis in Tamil. In *Proceedings of the Second Workshop on Speech and*

Language Technologies for Dravidian Languages. Association for Computational Linguistics.

Sajeetha Thavareesan and Sinnathamby Mahesan. 2019. Sentiment analysis in Tamil texts: A study on machine learning techniques and feature representation. In *2019 14th Conference on Industrial and Information Systems (ICIIS)*, pages 320–325.

Sajeetha Thavareesan and Sinnathamby Mahesan. 2020a. Sentiment lexicon expansion using Word2vec and fastText for sentiment prediction in Tamil texts. In *2020 Moratuwa Engineering Research Conference (MERCon)*, pages 272–276.

Sajeetha Thavareesan and Sinnathamby Mahesan. 2020b. Word embedding-based part of speech tagging in Tamil texts. In *2020 IEEE 15th International Conference on Industrial and Information Systems (ICIIS)*, pages 478–482.

Sajeetha Thavareesan and Sinnathamby Mahesan. 2021. Sentiment analysis in Tamil texts using k-means and k-nearest neighbour. In *2021 10th International Conference on Information and Automation for Sustainability (ICIAfS)*, pages 48–53.

Charangan Vasantharajan, Sean Benhur, Prasanna Kumar Kumarasen, Rahul Ponnusamy, Sathiyaraj Thangasamy, Ruba Priyadharshini, Thenmozhi Durairaj, Kanchana Sivanraju, Anbukkarasi Sampath, Bharathi Raja Chakravarthi, et al. 2022. TamilEmo: Finegrained Emotion Detection Dataset for Tamil.

BPHC@DravidianLangTech-ACL2022-A comparative analysis of classical and pre-trained models for troll meme classification in Tamil

Achyuta Krishna V **Mithun Kumar S R** **Aruna Malapati** **Lov Kumar**
BITS Pilani, Hyderabad Campus
{f20180165,p20190503,arunam,lovkumar}@hyderabad.bits-pilani.ac.in

Abstract

Trolling refers to any user behavior on the internet to intentionally provoke or instigate conflict, predominantly on social media. This paper aims to classify troll meme captions in Tamil-English code-mixed form. Embeddings are obtained for raw code-mixed text, and the translated and transliterated version of the text and their relative performances are compared. Furthermore, this paper compares the performances of 11 different classification algorithms using Accuracy and F1- Score. We conclude that we were able to achieve a weighted F1 score of 0.74 through MuRIL pretrained model.

1 Introduction

Technology is ingrained in every aspect of our lives. We require it to communicate with others and thrive in the modern world. We increasingly rely on text-based mediums to interact with technology every day. Hence there is a need for machines to understand natural human languages. However, it is challenging for computers to understand natural languages because of the inherent ambiguity in both the syntax and the semantics of natural language (Priyadharshini et al., 2021; Kumaresan et al., 2021).

With the ease of accessing the internet and the surge in the number of social media platforms, social media has become an essential and influential aspect of everyone's life (Chakravarthi, 2020; Chakravarthi and Muralidaran, 2021). It has also brought about a change in the way regional languages are expressed. Native script of the regional language is not used for exchanges on social media platforms (Chakravarthi et al., 2021). Instead, native speakers use Roman script combined with English words or phrases through code-mixing to express their ideas. The text generated by users in social media contains a high amount of spelling mistakes, phonetic typing, wordplay characters, and modern internet slang (Sampath et al., 2022; Ravikiran et al., 2022; Chakravarthi et al., 2022; Bharathi et al., 2022; Priyadharshini et al., 2022). This is mainly due to the limitation of the English keyboard and the speed at which the modern world moves. Thus, the study of text expressed in code-mixed form is essential (Priyadharshini et al., 2020).

In this paper, we explain our submission to DravidianLangTech-ACL2022 for the task of Troll-meme classification in Tamil. Tamil is a member of the southern branch of the Dravidian languages, a group of about 26 languages indigenous to the Indian subcontinent (Subalalitha, 2019; Srinivasan and Subalalitha, 2019; Narasimhan et al., 2018). The earliest Old Tamil documents are small inscriptions in Adichanallur dating from 905 BC to 696 BC (Anita and Subalalitha, 2019b,a; Subalalitha and Poovammal, 2018). Tamil, one of the 22 scheduled languages in the Indian Constitution, was the first to be designated as a classical language of India (Sakuntharaj and Mahesan, 2021, 2017, 2016; Thavareesan and Mahesan, 2019, 2020a,b, 2021). We brief on all the embedding techniques like TF-IDF, m-BERT, MuRIL, IndicFT, etc., and various classification algorithms, including Logistic Regression, Decision tree, SVM, etc., that were implemented in the process. The rest of the paper is organized as follows. Section 2 details the related works done in the field, and Section 3 describes the dataset used. Section 4 expands on the methodology and experimental setup, Section 5 discusses the results obtained, and Section 6 elucidates the conclusions.

2 Related work

There has been a rapid rise in the number of interesting studies performed in the domain of Dravidian code-mixed text analysis in the last few years (Chakravarthi et al., 2021, 2020; Ghanghor et al., 2021a,b; Yasaswini et al., 2021).

Sub-word level or morpheme level embedding

Proceedings of the Second Workshop on Speech and Language Technologies for Dravidian Languages, pages 151 - 157
May 26, 2022 ©2022 Association for Computational Linguistics

technique obtained using a 1D convolution layer with ReLU activation was proposed by Joshi et al. (2016). After getting a morpheme-level feature map, a 1-D maximum pooling layer is used to obtain its most prominent features. LSTMs are used to obtain the connections between each of these features due to their ability to process sequences and retain information.

Bharathi et al. (2021) proposed using TF-IDF and m-BERT embeddings coupled with classification models like Random Forest, Naive Bayes, and Multi-Layer Perceptron for the task of classifying English text code-mixed with Dravidian languages as offensive or not-offensive.

Selective translation and transliteration was performed by Sai and Sharma (2021), to convert the whole text to Tamil text in native script. XLM-RoBERTa multilingual model was used to obtain embeddings. Multiple classification algorithms were used to classify code-mixed text as offensive and not-offensive, and logistic regression was found to perform the best.

An ensembling of multiple classification algorithms applied on TF-IDF embedding was experimented in Kumar et al. (2021). It was found to perform well for shorter Dravidian code-mixed sentences like YouTube comments, which can be considered to be similar to meme captions.

We hypothesized translation and transliteration should improve the overall classification accuracy of the text when the troll script is code mixed. In addition, using language-specific embeddings would yield an improvement.

3 Data

3.1 Data description

The dataset used is the official dataset released in DravidianLangTech-ACL2022, which comprises captions from memes, and each caption is labelled as either troll or not troll. The data is represented in the Tamil-English code-mixed form, with the sentences comprising Tamil and English words but written in Roman script. (Suryawanshi et al., 2020)(Suryawanshi and Chakravarthi, 2021)(Suryawanshi et al., 2022)

Examples of the meme captions and its labels in Figure 1

3.2 Data distribution

The training data contains 2300 captions, each labelled as either troll or not troll, with a distribution of 1282 captions labelled as troll and 1018 captions labelled as not troll. The test dataset contains 667 captions, with 395 labelled as troll and 272 labelled as not troll.

Dataset	Troll	Not troll	Total
Train	1282	1018	2300
Test	395	272	667

Table 1: Distribution of the dataset

4 Methodology

4.1 Data pre-processing

The raw dataset was initially pre-processed to convert the text to lower case and remove URLs, special characters, extra spaces, and emoticons. Apostrophe abbreviated words like "they're", "it's", "I'm" etc., were converted to the long-form "they are", "it is", and "I am", respectively. The words were lemmatized and stop words were removed using NLTK[1]. Named entity recognition was performed using the spaCy[2] library.

4.2 Experimental setup

4.2.1 Raw Tamil-English code-mixed text

The first set of techniques obtains embeddings from the dataset in the Tamil-English code-mixed form itself. The techniques under this category include TF-IDF, sub-word LSTM and m-BERT (Devlin et al. (2018)). TF-IDF was implemented using an n-gram range of (1,5), which was proven to perform better for the required use case (Bharathi et al., 2021). The hyperparameters for the sub-word LSTM model were tuned in accordance with the suggestions proposed by Joshi et al. (2016).

4.2.2 Translated and transliterated text

The second set of embedding techniques acts on the translated and transliterated version of the preprocessed dataset. The English words in the dataset were translated to Tamil using the deep translator API[3], and the Tamil words written in Roman script were transliterated to Tamil script using Indic transliteration API[4]. Embeddings for the resulting dataset were obtained using TF-IDF, IndicFT (Kakwani et al. (2020)), MuRIL (Khanuja et al. (2021)), and m-BERT.

[1] https://www.nltk.org/
[2] https://spacy.io/
[3] https://pypi.org/project/deep-translator/
[4] https://pypi.org/project/indic-transliteration/

	imagename	captions
2072	troll_238.jpg	Thangachi pasathula bamalaya minchiruva polaya...
1271	troll_1225.png	BUS'IL SINGLE'AAGA PAYANAM SAIBAVARGALUKKU MAT...
1430	troll_137.png	WHATSAPP GROUP CONVERSATIONS AFTER CREATING TH...
1567	troll_1539.jpg	*Beardless boys : Aiyoo perumale enna PET sir ...
733	Not_troll_742.jpg	idhe velaiya dhaan alaierangala kaalailairundhu..

Figure 1: Troll meme data

4.3 Classifier models

Eleven different classification algorithms, Logistic Regression (LR), MultinomialNaive Bayes (NB), Support Vector Machine - Linear kernel (L-SVM), Support Vector Machine - RBF kernel (R-SVM), Support Vector Machine - Polynomial kernel (P-SVM), Random Forest (RF), k-Nearnest Neighbours classifier (k-NN), Extra-tree classifier (ExT), AdaBoost classifier (AdB), XGBoost classifier (XgB), Multilayer Perceptron (MLP) and a voting ensemble of all the eleven classifiers were applied on the embeddings obtained from each of the above techniques.

Method	A	F1-m	F1-w
LR	0.62	0.53	0.57
NB	0.62	0.53	0.57
L-SVM	0.61	0.55	0.58
R-SVM	0.60	0.52	0.56
P-SVM	0.61	0.55	0.58
RF	0.61	0.57	0.60
k-NN	0.45	0.41	0.38
ExT	0.60	0.55	0.57
AdB	0.60	0.47	0.52
XgB	0.62	0.52	0.56
MLP	0.60	0.53	0.57
Voting	0.61	0.54	0.58

Table 2: TF-IDF - raw text

5 Results and Discussions

Tables 2, 3 and 4 depict the results obtained by performing experiments on raw code-mixed text. Tables 5, 6, 7 and 8 depict the results obtained by performing experiments on translated and transliterated text.

A weighted F1 score of 0.74 was achieved with MuRIL, beating our own previously published competition result of 0.60 obtained by random forest classifier, which held the top position in the rankings. This performs best due to the nature of input text which is code mixed and predominantly in Tamil and written either in Roman script or Tamil

Method	A	F1-m	F1-w
LR	0.57	0.47	0.51
NB	0.57	0.49	0.53
L-SVM	0.57	0.47	0.51
R-SVM	0.56	0.46	0.50
P-SVM	0.56	0.46	0.51
RF	0.57	0.49	0.53
k-NN	0.57	0.49	0.52
ExT	0.58	0.49	0.53
AdB	0.56	0.47	0.51
XgB	0.57	0.47	0.52
MLP	0.56	0.48	0.52
Voting	0.57	0.48	0.52

Table 3: Sub-word LSTM - raw text

Method	A	F1-m	F1-w
m-BERT	0.60	0.49	0.53

Table 4: m-BERT - raw text

Method	A	F1-m	F1-w
LR	0.59	0.51	0.55
NB	0.61	0.52	0.56
L-SVM	0.57	0.51	0.54
R-SVM	0.58	0.51	0.55
P-SVM	0.57	0.51	0.54
RF	0.56	0.51	0.54
k-NN	0.43	0.38	0.35
ExT	0.56	0.51	0.54
AdB	0.54	0.53	0.54
XgB	0.55	0.50	0.53
MLP	0.57	0.52	0.55
Voting	0.58	0.52	0.55

Table 5: TF-IDF - Translated, transliterated text

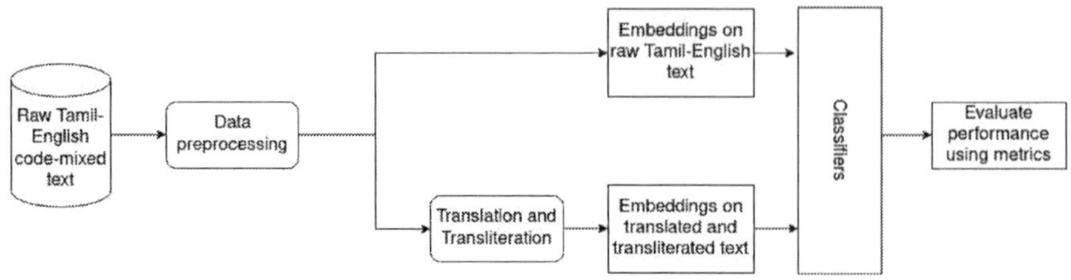

Figure 2: Experimental framework

Method	A	F1-m	F1-w
LR	0.59	0.37	0.74
NB	0.54	0.52	0.54
L-SVM	0.59	0.37	0.74
R-SVM	0.59	0.37	0.74
P-SVM	0.59	0.37	0.74
RF	0.53	0.48	0.55
k-NN	0.52	0.51	0.52
ExT	0.58	0.48	0.52
AdB	0.57	0.49	0.53
XgB	0.56	0.48	0.60
MLP	0.56	0.46	0.61
Voting	0.58	0.46	0.50

Table 6: MuRIL - Translated, transliterated text

Method	A	F1-m	F1-w
LR	0.60	0.49	0.66
NB	0.57	0.51	0.61
L-SVM	0.59	0.48	0.53
R-SVM	0.58	0.41	0.70
P-SVM	0.59	0.46	0.67
RF	0.55	0.50	0.56
k-NN	0.59	0.44	0.68
ExT	0.54	0.45	0.49
AdB	0.56	0.49	0.52
XgB	0.58	0.48	0.52
MLP	0.59	0.48	0.65
Voting	0.58	0.45	0.50

Table 7: IndicFT - Translated, transliterated text

Method	A	F1-m	F1-w
m-BERT	0.58	0.50	0.55

Table 8: m-BERT - Translated, transliterated text

script. With a pre-trained model like MuRIL, which is specifically trained on Tamil, we see a higher accuracy. IndicFT, a fastText model that is also trained on Indian languages, achieves a weighted F1 of 0.70. Another word embedding technique, m-BERT, performed slightly better with translated-transliterated text with an F1 score of 0.55 compared to 0.53 without. Translation and transliteration on TF-IDF, contrary to our hypothesis, performed poorly relative to direct usage of tokens in their raw form on all three metrics; Accuracy, macro F1 and weighted F1 scores. This could be attributed to the lower level of confidence in the translation and transliteration capabilities in code-mixed text.

6 Conclusion and Future Work

We compared the weighted F1 score of the various classifiers between the raw text and translated-transliterated text in Tamil-English code mixed troll memes. Language-specific word embedding techniques significantly improve the classification metrics like accuracy, macro F1 and weighted F1 scores. With a comparison between the various pre-trained models, MuRIL performs best with an F1 score of 0.74 relative to others. We have only considered text captions and not the images. We hypothesize that a unified framework to combine image with text will yield even better results. In the future, we would want to integrate a deep learning model that could take both the caption text and the images together.

References

R Anita and CN Subalalitha. 2019a. An approach to cluster Tamil literatures using discourse connectives.

In *2019 IEEE 1st International Conference on Energy, Systems and Information Processing (ICESIP)*, pages 1–4. IEEE.

R Anita and CN Subalalitha. 2019b. Building discourse parser for Thirukkural. In *Proceedings of the 16th International Conference on Natural Language Processing*, pages 18–25.

B Bharathi, Bharathi Raja Chakravarthi, Subalalitha Chinnaudayar Navaneethakrishnan, N Sripriya, Arunaggiri Pandian, and Swetha Valli. 2022. Findings of the shared task on Speech Recognition for Vulnerable Individuals in Tamil. In *Proceedings of the Second Workshop on Language Technology for Equality, Diversity and Inclusion*. Association for Computational Linguistics.

B Bharathi et al. 2021. Ssncse_nlp@ dravidianlangtech-eacl2021: Offensive language identification on multilingual code mixing text. In *Proceedings of the First Workshop on Speech and Language Technologies for Dravidian Languages*, pages 313–318.

Bharathi Raja Chakravarthi. 2020. HopeEDI: A multilingual hope speech detection dataset for equality, diversity, and inclusion. In *Proceedings of the Third Workshop on Computational Modeling of People's Opinions, Personality, and Emotion's in Social Media*, pages 41–53, Barcelona, Spain (Online). Association for Computational Linguistics.

Bharathi Raja Chakravarthi and Vigneshwaran Muralidaran. 2021. Findings of the shared task on hope speech detection for equality, diversity, and inclusion. In *Proceedings of the First Workshop on Language Technology for Equality, Diversity and Inclusion*, pages 61–72, Kyiv. Association for Computational Linguistics.

Bharathi Raja Chakravarthi, Vigneshwaran Muralidaran, Ruba Priyadharshini, and John Philip McCrae. 2020. Corpus creation for sentiment analysis in code-mixed Tamil-English text. In *Proceedings of the 1st Joint Workshop on Spoken Language Technologies for Under-resourced languages (SLTU) and Collaboration and Computing for Under-Resourced Languages (CCURL)*, pages 202–210, Marseille, France. European Language Resources association.

Bharathi Raja Chakravarthi, Ruba Priyadharshini, Thenmozhi Durairaj, John Phillip McCrae, Paul Buitaleer, Prasanna Kumar Kumaresan, and Rahul Ponnusamy. 2022. Findings of the shared task on Homophobia Transphobia Detection in Social Media Comments. In *Proceedings of the Second Workshop on Language Technology for Equality, Diversity and Inclusion*. Association for Computational Linguistics.

Bharathi Raja Chakravarthi, Ruba Priyadharshini, Rahul Ponnusamy, Prasanna Kumar Kumaresan, Kayalvizhi Sampath, Durairaj Thenmozhi, Sathiyaraj Thangasamy, Rajendran Nallathambi, and John Phillip McCrae. 2021. Dataset for identification of homophobia and transophobia in multilingual YouTube comments. *arXiv preprint arXiv:2109.00227*.

Jacob Devlin, Ming-Wei Chang, Kenton Lee, and Kristina Toutanova. 2018. BERT: pre-training of deep bidirectional transformers for language understanding. *CoRR*, abs/1810.04805.

Nikhil Ghanghor, Parameswari Krishnamurthy, Sajeetha Thavareesan, Ruba Priyadharshini, and Bharathi Raja Chakravarthi. 2021a. IIITK@DravidianLangTech-EACL2021: Offensive language identification and meme classification in Tamil, Malayalam and Kannada. In *Proceedings of the First Workshop on Speech and Language Technologies for Dravidian Languages*, pages 222–229, Kyiv. Association for Computational Linguistics.

Nikhil Ghanghor, Rahul Ponnusamy, Prasanna Kumar Kumaresan, Ruba Priyadharshini, Sajeetha Thavareesan, and Bharathi Raja Chakravarthi. 2021b. IIITK@LT-EDI-EACL2021: Hope speech detection for equality, diversity, and inclusion in Tamil , Malayalam and English. In *Proceedings of the First Workshop on Language Technology for Equality, Diversity and Inclusion*, pages 197–203, Kyiv. Association for Computational Linguistics.

Aditya Joshi, Ameya Prabhu, Manish Shrivastava, and Vasudeva Varma. 2016. Towards sub-word level compositions for sentiment analysis of hindi-english code mixed text. In *Proceedings of COLING 2016, the 26th International Conference on Computational Linguistics: Technical Papers*, pages 2482–2491.

Divyanshu Kakwani, Anoop Kunchukuttan, Satish Golla, NC Gokul, Avik Bhattacharyya, Mitesh M Khapra, and Pratyush Kumar. 2020. Indicnlpsuite: Monolingual corpora, evaluation benchmarks and pre-trained multilingual language models for indian languages. In *Findings of the Association for Computational Linguistics: EMNLP 2020*, pages 4948–4961.

Simran Khanuja, Diksha Bansal, Sarvesh Mehtani, Savya Khosla, Atreyee Dey, Balaji Gopalan, Dilip Kumar Margam, Pooja Aggarwal, Rajiv Teja Nagipogu, Shachi Dave, et al. 2021. Muril: Multilingual representations for indian languages. *arXiv preprint arXiv:2103.10730*.

SR Mithun Kumar, Nihal Reddy, Aruna Malapati, and Lov Kumar. 2021. An ensemble model for sentiment classification on code-mixed data in dravidian languages. Technical report, EasyChair.

Prasanna Kumar Kumaresan, Ratnasingam Sakuntharaj, Sajeetha Thavareesan, Subalalitha Navaneethakrishnan, Anand Kumar Madasamy, Bharathi Raja Chakravarthi, and John P McCrae. 2021. Findings of shared task on offensive language identification in Tamil and Malayalam. In *Forum for Information Retrieval Evaluation*, pages 16–18.

Anitha Narasimhan, Aarthy Anandan, Madhan Karky, and CN Subalalitha. 2018. Porul: Option generation and selection and scoring algorithms for a tamil flash card game. *International Journal of Cognitive and Language Sciences*, 12(2):225–228.

Ruba Priyadharshini, Bharathi Raja Chakravarthi, Subalalitha Chinnaudayar Navaneethakrishnan, Thenmozhi Durairaj, Malliga Subramanian, Kogilavani Shanmugavadivel, Siddhanth U Hegde, and Prasanna Kumar Kumaresan. 2022. Findings of the shared task on Abusive Comment Detection in Tamil. In *Proceedings of the Second Workshop on Speech and Language Technologies for Dravidian Languages*. Association for Computational Linguistics.

Ruba Priyadharshini, Bharathi Raja Chakravarthi, Sajeetha Thavareesan, Dhivya Chinnappa, Durairaj Thenmozhi, and Rahul Ponnusamy. 2021. Overview of the DravidianCodeMix 2021 shared task on sentiment detection in Tamil, Malayalam, and Kannada. In *Forum for Information Retrieval Evaluation*, pages 4–6.

Ruba Priyadharshini, Bharathi Raja Chakravarthi, Mani Vegupatti, and John P McCrae. 2020. Named entity recognition for code-mixed Indian corpus using meta embedding. In *2020 6th international conference on advanced computing and communication systems (ICACCS)*, pages 68–72. IEEE.

Manikandan Ravikiran, Bharathi Raja Chakravarthi, Anand Kumar Madasamy, Sangeetha Sivanesan, Ratnavel Rajalakshmi, Sajeetha Thavareesan, Rahul Ponnusamy, and Shankar Mahadevan. 2022. Findings of the shared task on Offensive Span Identification in code-mixed Tamil-English comments. In *Proceedings of the Second Workshop on Speech and Language Technologies for Dravidian Languages*. Association for Computational Linguistics.

Siva Sai and Yashvardhan Sharma. 2021. Towards offensive language identification for dravidian languages. In *Proceedings of the first workshop on speech and language technologies for Dravidian languages*, pages 18–27.

Ratnasingam Sakuntharaj and Sinnathamby Mahesan. 2016. A novel hybrid approach to detect and correct spelling in Tamil text. In *2016 IEEE International Conference on Information and Automation for Sustainability (ICIAfS)*, pages 1–6.

Ratnasingam Sakuntharaj and Sinnathamby Mahesan. 2017. Use of a novel hash-table for speeding-up suggestions for misspelt Tamil words. In *2017 IEEE International Conference on Industrial and Information Systems (ICIIS)*, pages 1–5.

Ratnasingam Sakuntharaj and Sinnathamby Mahesan. 2021. Missing word detection and correction based on context of Tamil sentences using n-grams. In *2021 10th International Conference on Information and Automation for Sustainability (ICIAfS)*, pages 42–47.

Anbukkarasi Sampath, Thenmozhi Durairaj, Bharathi Raja Chakravarthi, Ruba Priyadharshini, Subalalitha Chinnaudayar Navaneethakrishnan, Kogilavani Shanmugavadivel, Sajeetha Thavareesan, Sathiyaraj Thangasamy, Parameswari Krishnamurthy, Adeep Hande, Sean Benhur, Kishor Kumar Ponnusamy, and Santhiya Pandiyan. 2022. Findings of the shared task on Emotion Analysis in Tamil. In *Proceedings of the Second Workshop on Speech and Language Technologies for Dravidian Languages*. Association for Computational Linguistics.

R Srinivasan and CN Subalalitha. 2019. Automated named entity recognition from tamil documents. In *2019 IEEE 1st International Conference on Energy, Systems and Information Processing (ICESIP)*, pages 1–5. IEEE.

C. N. Subalalitha. 2019. Information extraction framework for Kurunthogai. *Sādhanā*, 44(7):156.

CN Subalalitha and E Poovammal. 2018. Automatic bilingual dictionary construction for Tirukural. *Applied Artificial Intelligence*, 32(6):558–567.

Shardul Suryawanshi and Bharathi Raja Chakravarthi. 2021. Findings of the shared task on Troll Meme Classification in Tamil. In *Proceedings of the First Workshop on Speech and Language Technologies for Dravidian Languages*. Association for Computational Linguistics.

Shardul Suryawanshi, Bharathi Raja Chakravarthi, Mihael Arcan, Susan Levy, Paul Buitaleer, Prasanna Kumar Kumaresan, Rahul Ponnusamy, and Adeep Hande. 2022. Findings of the second shared task on Troll Meme Classification in Tamil. In *Proceedings of the Second Workshop on Speech and Language Technologies for Dravidian Languages*. Association for Computational Linguistics.

Shardul Suryawanshi, Bharathi Raja Chakravarthi, Pranav Verma, Mihael Arcan, John Philip McCrae, and Paul Buitelaar. 2020. A dataset for troll classification of tamilmemes. In *Proceedings of the WILDRE5–5th workshop on indian language data: resources and evaluation*, pages 7–13.

Sajeetha Thavareesan and Sinnathamby Mahesan. 2019. Sentiment analysis in Tamil texts: A study on machine learning techniques and feature representation. In *2019 14th Conference on Industrial and Information Systems (ICIIS)*, pages 320–325.

Sajeetha Thavareesan and Sinnathamby Mahesan. 2020a. Sentiment lexicon expansion using Word2vec and fastText for sentiment prediction in Tamil texts. In *2020 Moratuwa Engineering Research Conference (MERCon)*, pages 272–276.

Sajeetha Thavareesan and Sinnathamby Mahesan. 2020b. Word embedding-based part of speech tagging in Tamil texts. In *2020 IEEE 15th International Conference on Industrial and Information Systems (ICIIS)*, pages 478–482.

Sajeetha Thavareesan and Sinnathamby Mahesan. 2021. Sentiment analysis in Tamil texts using k-means and k-nearest neighbour. In *2021 10th International Conference on Information and Automation for Sustainability (ICIAfS)*, pages 48–53.

Konthala Yasaswini, Karthik Puranik, Adeep Hande, Ruba Priyadharshini, Sajeetha Thavareesan, and Bharathi Raja Chakravarthi. 2021. IIITT@DravidianLangTech-EACL2021: Transfer learning for offensive language detection in Dravidian languages. In *Proceedings of the First Workshop on Speech and Language Technologies for Dravidian Languages*, pages 187–194, Kyiv. Association for Computational Linguistics.

SSNCSE_NLP@TamilNLP-ACL2022: Transformer based approach for detection of abusive comment for Tamil language

Josephine Varsha & B. Bharathi
Department of CSE
Sri Siva Subramaniya Nadar College of Engineering
Kalavakkam - 603110
josephine2010350@ssn.edu.in
bharathib@ssn.edu.in

Abstract

Social media platforms along with many other public forums on the Internet have shown a significant rise in the cases of abusive behavior such as Misogynism, Misandry, Homophobia, and Cyberbullying. To tackle these concerns, technologies are being developed and applied, as it is a tedious and time-consuming task to identify, report and block these offenders. Our task was to automate the process of identifying abusive comments and classify them into appropriate categories. The datasets provided by the DravidianLangTech@ACL2022 organizers were a code-mixed form of Tamil text. We trained the datasets using pre-trained transformer models such as BERT,m-BERT, and XLNET and achieved a weighted average of F1 scores of 0.96 for Tamil-English code mixed text and 0.59 for Tamil text.

1 Introduction

Abusive comment detection is the method of categorizing and detecting the user-generated offensive comments to any type of insult, vulgarity, or profanity that debases the target Schmidt and Wiegand (2017). Over the last decade, there has been an exponential growth of user-generated content on social media. Given this increase in usage of online platforms, technology must be leveraged in the detection of abusive comments, cyber-bullying, hate speech, and trolling. Social media companies have utilized multiple resources to censor comments demeaning others (Chakravarthi et al., 2021a,b, 2020a; Priyadharshini et al., 2020; Chakravarthi, 2020). It's nearly impossible to succeed at perfecting the detector, as a comment's tendency to be abusive depends on the thread of the previous comments (B and A, 2021a). Its subjectivity to the individual and its context-dependent characteristics has been one of the major reasons for its failure. This task aims to train these models to identify abusive language that directly targets an individual or a group without bias.

Our team SSN_CSE_NLP has participated in the shared task of Abusive comment detection. To this effect, we were provided with datasets for code mixed Tamil text comprising comments from YouTube. This poses several challenges due to the low availability of resources for the Tamil language. The task focused on the multilingual offensive language detection, categorization of offensive language, and target identification Kumaresan et al. (2021); Priyadharshini et al. (2022). We have used pre-trained machine learning transformers like BERT,m-BERT, and XLNET. In this paper, we investigate the efficacy of different learning models in detecting abusive languages. We then compare the F1-Score of the different transformer models for both datasets.

Tamil is one of the world's longest-surviving classical languages (Anita and Subalalitha, 2019b,a; Subalalitha and Poovammal, 2018; Subalalitha, 2019). According to A. K. Ramanujan, it is "the only language of modern India that is recognizably continuous with a classical history." Because of the range and quality of ancient Tamil literature, it has been referred to as "one of the world's major classical traditions and literatures." For about 2600 years, there has been a recorded Tamil literature. The earliest period of Tamil literature, known as Sangam literature, is said to have lasted from from 600 BC to AD 300 (Sakuntharaj and Mahesan, 2021, 2017,?, 2016). Among Dravidian languages, it possesses the oldest existing literature. The earliest epigraphic documents discovered on rock edicts and "hero stones" date from the 6th century BC (Thavareesan and Mahesan, 2019, 2020a,b, 2021).

The remainder of the paper is organized into 5 sections. Section 2 discusses the related works in the field of Artificial Intelligence, on abusive com-

Proceedings of the Second Workshop on Speech and Language Technologies for Dravidian Languages, pages 158 - 164
May 26, 2022 ©2022 Association for Computational Linguistics

ment detection, for both Tamil and other languages. The methodology proposed for the model along with the models implemented are elaborately explained in the 3rd section of this paper. In section 4 the results and the observations are discussed. Section 5 concludes the paper.

2 Related works

A lot of research is being done on detecting offensive language from social media platforms in the field of Artificial Intelligence and Natural Language Processing(Priyadharshini et al., 2021; Chakravarthi and Muralidaran, 2021; Chakravarthi et al., 2020b; Sampath et al., 2022; Ravikiran et al., 2022; Chakravarthi et al., 2022; Bharathi et al., 2022; Priyadharshini et al., 2022). In this section, we will be reviewing the research work.

The authors of (Vasantharajan and Thayasivam, 2021) has analyzed various techniques and neural network models to detect offensive language in code-mixed romanized social media text in Tamil. They have implemented selective translation and transliteration for text conversion in romanized and code-mixed settings, and are positive that this can be extended to romanized and code-mixed contexts of other languages.

The authors of B and A (2021b) identified offensive language content of the code-mixed dataset of comments/posts in Dravidian Languages (Tamil-English, Malayalam-English, and Kannada-English) collected from social media. The basic TFIDF and count vectorizer features were found to perform best when compared to sentence embeddings. They detected that machine learning models are giving better performance than deep learning models.

A large transliterated Bengali corpus Sazzed (2021) introduced, consisting of 3000 comments collected from YouTube, which are manually annotated into abusive and non-abusive categories. The comparative performances of various supervised ML and deep learning-based classifiers are given, and BiLSTM, the deep learning-based architecture, obtains a relatively lower F1 score compared to LR and SVM, which could be attributed to the small size (i.e.,3000 comments) of the corpus.

The authors of Hande et al. (2021) emphasized on improving offensive language identification by prioritizing the construction of a bigger dataset and generating pseudo-labels on the transliterated dataset, combining the latter with the former to have extensive amounts of data for training.

Language	Training	Development	Test
Tamil	2240	560	700
Tamil-English	5948	1488	1859

Table 1: Dataset description

A three-level classification system with Naive Bayes classifier in the first level, Multinomial Updatable Naive Bayes in the second level, and a rule-based classifier named DTNB in the third level is used in Pang et al. (2002).

The authors Zampieri et al. (2020) reported the lexical features, static and deep contextualized embedding for the Support Vector Machine classifiers to detect Arabic offensive language and also determined the topics, dialects, and genders which are associated with the offensive tweets.

The addition of the sentiment and contextual features provide significantly improved performance to a basic TFIDF model in Yin et al. (2009).

The authors of Mishra et al. (2019)proposed an approach based on graph convolutional networks to show that author profiles that directly capture the linguistic behavior of authors along with the structural traits of their community significantly advance the current state of the art.

The authors of Pitsilis et al. (2018) shows an approach that outperforms all other models and has achieved better performance in classifying short messages. The approach taken did not rely on pre-trained vectors, which provides a serious advantage when dealing with short messages.

3 Methodology and Data pre-processing

In this section, we have illustrated our implementation of the pre-trained machine learning transformer models in detail. Further, we will investigate the performance of the various transformer models in the coming sections. The architecture of the proposed model and the steps are given below 1.

The dataset provided by the LT-EDI 2021 Priyadharshini et al. (2022) for the Tamil, and code-mixed Tamil text consisted of 3499, and 9293 Youtube comments respectively. The details are given in Table 1.

3.1 Data-set Analysis

The goal of this task is to identify whether a given comment contains an abusive comment. A com-

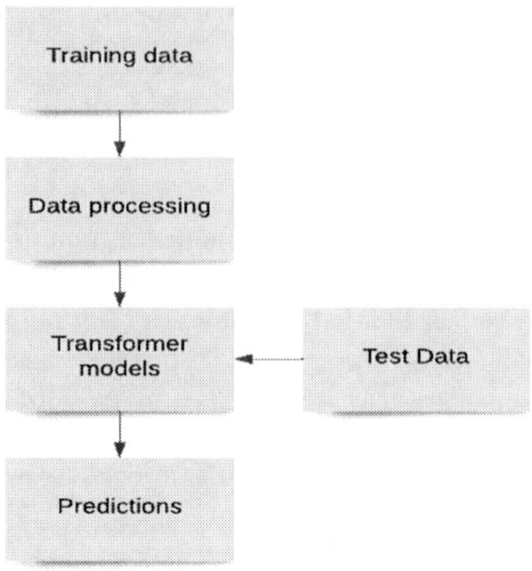

Figure 1: The architecture of the proposed system

ment or post within the corpus may contain more than one sentence but the average sentence length of the corpora is 1. The annotations in the corpus are made at a comment/post level in Priyadharshini et al. (2022)

The dataset provided by LT-EDI 2021 organizers, consisted of the training set, development set, and test set of 2240, 560, and 699 instances respectively for the Tamil text, and 5948, 1488, and 1857 instances for the code-mixed text. It contained text sequences that include user utterances along with the context, followed by the offensive class label. The task was to classify and label them under any of the following: Misogyny, Misandry, Homophobia, Transphobia, Xenophobia, Counter Speech, Hope Speech.

3.2 Data Pre-processing

Data pre-processing is essential for any machine learning problem since the real-world data generally contains noise, and missing values, and may be in an unusable format that cannot be directly used for machine learning models. Data preprocessing is required for cleaning the data and making it suitable for a machine learning model which also increases the accuracy and efficiency of a machine learning model. First, the dataset is cleaned and processed before classifying. During pre-processing :

- Hashtags, HTML tags, mentions and URLs are removed
- Annotate emojis, emoticons, and replace them with the text they represent
- Convert uppercase characters to lowercase
- To expand abbreviations
- Remove special characters
- Remove accented characters
- Reduce lengthened words
- Remove extra white spaces

We've implemented data processing with the use of the nltk package, abbreviated as the Natural Language Toolkit, built to work with the NLP (Natural Language Processing). It provides various text processing libraries for classification, tokenization, parsing, semantic reasoning, etc. For our model, we've only used the regular expression (re) module. The re. sub() function was used to clean and scrape the text, remove URLs, remove numbers, and remove tags.

Using tokenize. regexp() module we were able to extract the tokens from the string by using the regular expression with the RegexpTokenizer() method. Tokenizing is a crucial step when it comes to cleaning the text. It is used to split the text into words or sentences, splitting it into smaller pieces that still hold its meaning outside the context of the rest of the text. When it comes to analyzing the text, we need to tokenize by word and tokenize by sentence. This is how unstructured data is turned into structured data, which is easier to analyze.

3.3 Model Description

The abusive comment text was classified using 3 transformer models, namely BERT, XLNet, and m-BERT

- BERT:
  BERT stands for Bidirectional Encoder Representations from Transformers. BERT is a pre-trained model on the top 104 languages of the world on Wikipedia (2.5B words) with 110 thousand shared word piece vocabulary, using masked language modeling (MLM) objective, which was first introduced in Devlin et al. (2018). BERT uses bi-directional learning to gain context of words from left to right context simultaneously. This is optimized by the Masked Language Modelling. The MLM

is different from the traditional recurrent neural networks (RNNs), which generally see the word one after the other. This model randomly masks 15% of the words in the input and predicts the masked words when the entire masked sentence is run through the model.

- XLNet:
  The XLNet transformer model was proposed in 'XLNet: Generalized Autoregressive Pretraining for Language Understanding' Yang et al. (2019). It is pre-trained using an autoregressive model (a model that predicts future behavior based on past behavior) which enables learning bidirectional contexts by maximizing the expected likelihood over all permutations of the factorization order and overcomes the limitations of BERT thanks to its autoregressive formulation Yang et al. (2019). It integrates the Transformer-XL mechanism with a slight improvement in the language modeling approach.

- m-BERT:
  m-BERT is a pre-trained model on a large corpus of multilingual data It is trained on the top 104 languages with the largest Wikipedia using a masked language modeling (MLM) objective. It was first introduced in Devlin et al. (2018)

4 Results and Analysis

The BERT (Bidirectional Encoder Representations from Transformers) models and XLNET were used for the Task A dataset. The BERT model operates on the principle of an attention mechanism to learn contextual relations between words. The transformer encoder used is bidirectional, unlike the other directional methods which read input sequentially. BERT reads the entire sequence of text at once. This bidirectional property of the encoder has made it very useful for classification tasks. The BERT models BERT and m-BERT were trained for 5 epochs. XLNet does not suffer from pre-train fine-tune discrepancy since it does not depend on data corruption. We have trained the XLNet model for 5 epochs. The bert-base-uncased model showed the best F1-Score of 0.96 and 0.59 for code mixed Tamil text and Tamil dataset respectively.

4.1 Tamil-English Dataset

The accuracy obtained by the BERT model was found to be 0.96, XLNet and m-BERT showed an accuracy of 0.88, and 0.95 respectively. The bert-base-uncased model (BERT) showed the best performance with a weighted F1 score of 0.96. The weighted precision, weighted recall, weighted F1 score, and accuracy are given in the table below 2.

Pre-trained model	Precision	Recall	F1-score	Accuracy
bert-base-uncased	0.96	0.96	0.96	0.96
xlnet-base-cased	0.87	0.88	0.87	0.88
bert-base-mulitingual-uncased	0.96	0.95	0.95	0.96

Table 2: Performance analysis of the proposed system using development data for Tamil-English Dataset

Pre-trained model	Precision	Recall	F1-score	Accuracy
bert-base-uncased	0.56	0.65	0.59	0.65
xlnet-base-cased	0.46	0.61	0.48	0.61
bert-base-mulitingual-uncased	0.56	0.64	0.59	0.64

Table 3: Performance analysis of the proposed system using development data for Tamil Dataset

4.2 Tamil Dataset

The accuracy obtained by the BERT model was found to be 0.65, XLNet and m-BERT showed an accuracy of 0.61, and 0.64 respectively. The bert-base-uncased model (BERT) showed the best performance with a weighted F1 score of 0.59. The weighted precision, weighted recall, weighted F1 score, and accuracy are given in the Table 3.

The development dataset was used for evaluating the performance of the models after training them. The final performance results for the task are recorded in Table 4.

4.3 Error analysis

The adopted model fails to attain a perfect F1 score of 1. To investigate and analyze this, we have plotted the confusion matrix for the code-mixed Tamil dataset, and the Tamil dataset. The Fig.2 shows the confusion matrix of the code-mixed dataset. This is an 8 X 8 matrix that evaluates the performance of the BERT model, where 8 is the number of target classes. The Fig.3 shows the

Results	Tamil-English	Tamil
Accuracy	0.530	0.060
macro average Precision	0.260	0.130
macro average Recall	0.240	0.140
macro average F1score	0.250	0.090
weighted average Precision	0.510	0.040
weighted average Recall	0.530	0.060
weighted average F1score	0.520	0.030

Table 4: Performance analysis of the proposed system using test data for Tamil and Tamil-English Dataset

confusion matrix of the Tamil dataset. This is a 9 X 9 matrix that evaluates the performance of the BERT model, where 8 is the number of target classes. With the confusion matrix, it is possible to compute the performance metrics of the classification model, namely, Precision, Recall, and F1-score

Precision refers to the number of True Positives (TP) to the total number of predictions

$$Precision = \frac{TP}{TP + FP}$$

Recall refers to the number of Positives returned by the model.

$$Recall = \frac{TP}{TP + FN}$$

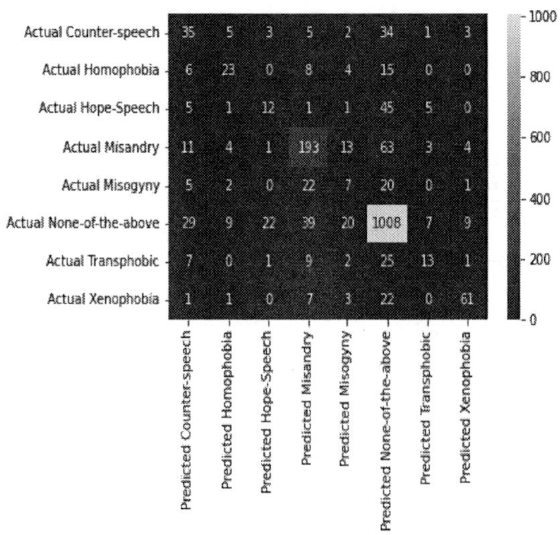

Figure 2: Confusion matrix of tamil-english dataset

5 Conclusions

In this paper, we have investigated the baseline accuracy of different models as well as their variants on the test datasets. There is an increase in demand for abusive language identification on social media, and the goal of this task was to detect whether the comment contains abusive language or not. Our team had secured the 8th rank in the shared Task for the code-mixed Tamil dataset, and the 12th rank for the Tamil dataset. Our models performed the baseline for both the tasks but performance can further be improved by adopting favorable features.

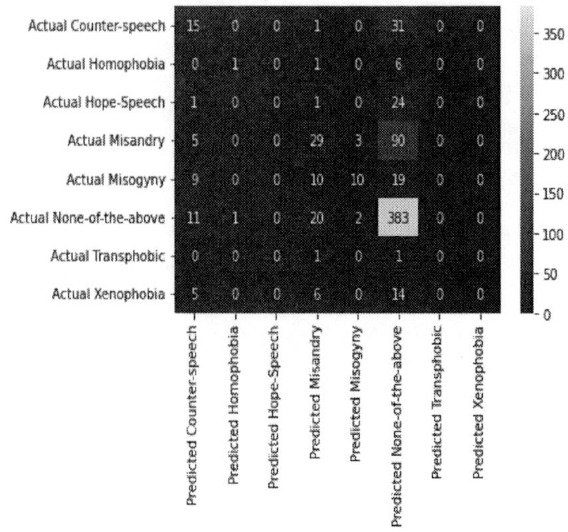

Figure 3: Confusion matrix of tamil dataset

References

R Anita and CN Subalalitha. 2019a. An approach to cluster tamil literatures using discourse connectives. In *2019 IEEE 1st International Conference on Energy, Systems and Information Processing (ICESIP)*, pages 1–4. IEEE.

R Anita and CN Subalalitha. 2019b. Building discourse parser for thirukkural. In *Proceedings of the 16th International Conference on Natural Language Processing*, pages 18–25.

Bharathi B and Agnusimmaculate Silvia A. 2021a. SSNCSE_NLP@DravidianLangTech-EACL2021: Meme classification for Tamil using machine learning approach. In *Proceedings of the First Workshop on Speech and Language Technologies for Dravidian Languages*, pages 336–339, Kyiv. Association for Computational Linguistics.

Bharathi B and Agnusimmaculate Silvia A. 2021b. SSNCSE_NLP@DravidianLangTech-EACL2021: Offensive language identification on multilingual code mixing text. In *Proceedings of the First Workshop on Speech and Language Technologies for Dravidian Languages*, pages 313–318, Kyiv. Association for Computational Linguistics.

B Bharathi, Bharathi Raja Chakravarthi, Subalalitha Chinnaudayar Navaneethakrishnan, N Sripriya, Arunaggiri Pandian, and Swetha Valli. 2022. Findings of the shared task on Speech Recognition for Vulnerable Individuals in Tamil. In *Proceedings of the Second Workshop on Language Technology for Equality, Diversity and Inclusion*. Association for Computational Linguistics.

Bharathi Raja Chakravarthi. 2020. HopeEDI: A multilingual hope speech detection dataset for equality, diversity, and inclusion. In *Proceedings of the Third*

Workshop on Computational Modeling of People's Opinions, Personality, and Emotion's in Social Media, pages 41–53, Barcelona, Spain (Online). Association for Computational Linguistics.

Bharathi Raja Chakravarthi and Vigneshwaran Muralidaran. 2021. Findings of the shared task on hope speech detection for equality, diversity, and inclusion. In *Proceedings of the First Workshop on Language Technology for Equality, Diversity and Inclusion*, pages 61–72, Kyiv. Association for Computational Linguistics.

Bharathi Raja Chakravarthi, Vigneshwaran Muralidaran, Ruba Priyadharshini, and John Philip McCrae. 2020a. Corpus creation for sentiment analysis in code-mixed Tamil-English text. In *Proceedings of the 1st Joint Workshop on Spoken Language Technologies for Under-resourced languages (SLTU) and Collaboration and Computing for Under-Resourced Languages (CCURL)*, pages 202–210, Marseille, France. European Language Resources association.

Bharathi Raja Chakravarthi, Ruba Priyadharshini, Thenmozhi Durairaj, John Phillip McCrae, Paul Buitaleer, Prasanna Kumar Kumaresan, and Rahul Ponnusamy. 2022. Findings of the shared task on Homophobia Transphobia Detection in Social Media Comments. In *Proceedings of the Second Workshop on Language Technology for Equality, Diversity and Inclusion*. Association for Computational Linguistics.

Bharathi Raja Chakravarthi, Ruba Priyadharshini, Vigneshwaran Muralidaran, Shardul Suryawanshi, Navya Jose, Elizabeth Sherly, and John P McCrae. 2020b. Overview of the track on sentiment analysis for Dravidian languages in code-mixed text. In *Forum for Information Retrieval Evaluation*, pages 21–24.

Bharathi Raja Chakravarthi, Ruba Priyadharshini, Rahul Ponnusamy, Prasanna Kumar Kumaresan, Kayalvizhi Sampath, Durairaj Thenmozhi, Sathiyaraj Thangasamy, Rajendran Nallathambi, and John Phillip McCrae. 2021a. Dataset for identification of homophobia and transophobia in multilingual YouTube comments. *arXiv preprint arXiv:2109.00227*.

Bharathi Raja Chakravarthi, Priya Rani, Mihael Arcan, and John P McCrae. 2021b. A survey of orthographic information in machine translation. *SN Computer Science*, 2(4):1–19.

Jacob Devlin, Ming-Wei Chang, Kenton Lee, and Kristina Toutanova. 2018. Bert: Pre-training of deep bidirectional transformers for language understanding.

Adeep Hande, Karthik Puranik, Konthala Yasaswini, Ruba Priyadharshini, Sajeetha Thavareesan, Anbukkarasi Sampath, Kogilavani Shanmugavadivel, Durairaj Thenmozhi, and Bharathi Raja Chakravarthi. 2021. Offensive language identification in low-resourced code-mixed dravidian languages using pseudo-labeling. *arXiv preprint arXiv:2108.12177*.

Prasanna Kumar Kumaresan, Ratnasingam Sakuntharaj, Sajeetha Thavareesan, Subalalitha Navaneethakrishnan, Anand Kumar Madasamy, Bharathi Raja Chakravarthi, and John P McCrae. 2021. Findings of shared task on offensive language identification in Tamil and Malayalam. In *Forum for Information Retrieval Evaluation*, pages 16–18.

Pushkar Mishra, Marco Del Tredici, Helen Yannakoudakis, and Ekaterina Shutova. 2019. Abusive language detection with graph convolutional networks. *arXiv preprint arXiv:1904.04073*.

Bo Pang, Lillian Lee, and Shivakumar Vaithyanathan. 2002. Thumbs up? sentiment classification using machine learning techniques. *arXiv preprint cs/0205070*.

Georgios K Pitsilis, Heri Ramampiaro, and Helge Langseth. 2018. Detecting offensive language in tweets using deep learning. *arXiv preprint arXiv:1801.04433*.

Ruba Priyadharshini, Bharathi Raja Chakravarthi, Subalalitha Chinnaudayar Navaneethakrishnan, Thenmozhi Durairaj, Malliga Subramanian, Kogilavani Shanmugavadivel, Siddhanth U Hegde, and Prasanna Kumar Kumaresan. 2022. Findings of the shared task on Abusive Comment Detection in Tamil. In *Proceedings of the Second Workshop on Speech and Language Technologies for Dravidian Languages*. Association for Computational Linguistics.

Ruba Priyadharshini, Bharathi Raja Chakravarthi, Sajeetha Thavareesan, Dhivya Chinnappa, Durairaj Thenmozhi, and Rahul Ponnusamy. 2021. Overview of the DravidianCodeMix 2021 shared task on sentiment detection in Tamil, Malayalam, and Kannada. In *Forum for Information Retrieval Evaluation*, pages 4–6.

Ruba Priyadharshini, Bharathi Raja Chakravarthi, Mani Vegupatti, and John P McCrae. 2020. Named entity recognition for code-mixed Indian corpus using meta embedding. In *2020 6th international conference on advanced computing and communication systems (ICACCS)*, pages 68–72. IEEE.

Manikandan Ravikiran, Bharathi Raja Chakravarthi, Anand Kumar Madasamy, Sangeetha Sivanesan, Ratnavel Rajalakshmi, Sajeetha Thavareesan, Rahul Ponnusamy, and Shankar Mahadevan. 2022. Findings of the shared task on Offensive Span Identification in code-mixed Tamil-English comments. In *Proceedings of the Second Workshop on Speech and Language Technologies for Dravidian Languages*. Association for Computational Linguistics.

Ratnasingam Sakuntharaj and Sinnathamby Mahesan. 2016. A novel hybrid approach to detect and correct spelling in tamil text. In *2016 IEEE International Conference on Information and Automation for Sustainability (ICIAfS)*, pages 1–6.

Ratnasingam Sakuntharaj and Sinnathamby Mahesan. 2017. Use of a novel hash-table for speeding-up suggestions for misspelt tamil words. In *2017 IEEE International Conference on Industrial and Information Systems (ICIIS)*, pages 1–5.

Ratnasingam Sakuntharaj and Sinnathamby Mahesan. 2021. Missing word detection and correction based on context of tamil sentences using n-grams. In *2021 10th International Conference on Information and Automation for Sustainability (ICIAfS)*, pages 42–47.

Anbukkarasi Sampath, Thenmozhi Durairaj, Bharathi Raja Chakravarthi, Ruba Priyadharshini, Subalalitha Chinnaudayar Navaneethakrishnan, Kogilavani Shanmugavadivel, Sajeetha Thavareesan, Sathiyaraj Thangasamy, Parameswari Krishnamurthy, Adeep Hande, Sean Benhur, and Santhiya Ponnusamy, Kishor Kumar Pandiyan. 2022. Findings of the shared task on Emotion Analysis in Tamil. In *Proceedings of the Second Workshop on Speech and Language Technologies for Dravidian Languages*. Association for Computational Linguistics.

Salim Sazzed. 2021. Abusive content detection in transliterated bengali-english social media corpus. In *CALCS*.

Anna Schmidt and Michael Wiegand. 2017. Proceedings of the fifth international workshop on natural language processing for social media. Association for Computational Linguistics.

C. N. Subalalitha. 2019. Information extraction framework for kurunthogai. *Sādhanā*, 44(7):156.

CN Subalalitha and E Poovammal. 2018. Automatic bilingual dictionary construction for tirukural. *Applied Artificial Intelligence*, 32(6):558–567.

Sajeetha Thavareesan and Sinnathamby Mahesan. 2019. Sentiment analysis in tamil texts: A study on machine learning techniques and feature representation. In *2019 14th Conference on Industrial and Information Systems (ICIIS)*, pages 320–325.

Sajeetha Thavareesan and Sinnathamby Mahesan. 2020a. Sentiment lexicon expansion using word2vec and fasttext for sentiment prediction in tamil texts. In *2020 Moratuwa Engineering Research Conference (MERCon)*, pages 272–276.

Sajeetha Thavareesan and Sinnathamby Mahesan. 2020b. Word embedding-based part of speech tagging in tamil texts. In *2020 IEEE 15th International Conference on Industrial and Information Systems (ICIIS)*, pages 478–482.

Sajeetha Thavareesan and Sinnathamby Mahesan. 2021. Sentiment analysis in tamil texts using k-means and k-nearest neighbour. In *2021 10th International Conference on Information and Automation for Sustainability (ICIAfS)*, pages 48–53.

Charangan Vasantharajan and Uthayasanker Thayasivam. 2021. Towards offensive language identification for tamil code-mixed YouTube comments and posts. *SN Computer Science*, 3(1).

Zhilin Yang, Zihang Dai, Yiming Yang, Jaime G. Carbonell, Ruslan Salakhutdinov, and Quoc V. Le. 2019. Xlnet: Generalized autoregressive pretraining for language understanding. *CoRR*, abs/1906.08237.

Dawei Yin, Zhenzhen Xue, Liangjie Hong, Brian D Davison, April Kontostathis, and Lynne Edwards. 2009. Detection of harassment on web 2.0. *Proceedings of the Content Analysis in the WEB*, 2:1–7.

Marcos Zampieri, Preslav Nakov, Sara Rosenthal, Pepa Atanasova, Georgi Karadzhov, Hamdy Mubarak, Leon Derczynski, Zeses Pitenis, and Çağrı Çöltekin. 2020. Semeval-2020 task 12: Multilingual offensive language identification in social media (offenseval 2020). *arXiv preprint arXiv:2006.07235*.

Varsini_and_Kirthanna@DravidianLangTech-ACL2022-Emotional Analysis in Tamil

Varsini S, Kirthanna Rajan, Angel Deborah S, Rajalakshmi S, R.S.Milton, T.T.Mirnalinee
Department of Computer Science and Engineering
Sri Sivasubramaniya Nadar College of Engineering
Chennai , India
{varsini.sathianantha,kirthanna.rajan}@gmail.com,
{angeldeborahs,rajalakshmis,miltonrs,mirnalineett}@ssn.edu.in

Abstract

In this paper, we present our system for the task of Emotion analysis in Tamil. Over 3.96 million (Gaubys) people use these platforms to send messages formed using texts, images, videos, audio or combinations of these to express their thoughts and feelings. Text communication on social media platforms is quite overwhelming due to its enormous quantity and simplicity. The data must be processed to understand the general feeling felt by the author. We present a lexicon-based approach for the extraction emotion in Tamil texts. We use dictionaries of words labelled with their respective emotions. The process of assigning an emotional label to each text, and then capture the main emotion expressed in it. Finally, the F1-score in the official test set is 0.0300 and our method ranks 5th.

1 Introduction

Emotion Detection is the process of detecting the different human emotions such as anger, disgust, joy, sadness, surprise, love, anticipation, so on and so forth (Cherry). "Emotion Identification", "Emotion Analysis" and "Emotion detection" all mean the same and can be used interchangeably (Munezero et al., 2014). People who are users of social media use these platforms as a way to express their feelings, thoughts and opinions on a wide range of topics. These feelings may be positive or neutral or negative. The book "Emotions In Social Psychology", written by W. Gerrod Parrot, in 2001 (Parrott, 2001). In which he explained that the human emotion system can be formally classified into an emotion hierarchy with six classes at the primary level, namely Surprise, Love, Anger, Fear, Sadness and Joy, while certain other words fall in the secondary and tertiary levels.

Emotion detection is used in various fields such as the business world to analyze how people feel about their new product; in the medical world by identifying the way people respond to a pandemic (Ravikiran et al., 2022; Chakravarthi et al., 2022; Bharathi et al., 2022; Priyadharshini et al., 2022; Chakravarthi et al., 2021; Chakravarthi, 2020; Chakravarthi and Muralidaran, 2021).Emotion identification is also used in monitoring the feelings and emotions of the Users who use social platforms such as Instagram, Facebook, YouTube, Twitter and many more (Rajendram et al., 2017, 2022).

Analyzing the emotions felt by the author using the text is quite challenging while also interesting and essential, as most of the time these text messages not only express the emotion directly by using emotional words and emojis but also the interpretation of the meaning of concepts. Furthermore, new slang or terminologies or short-forms are being created as each day passes, which make emotion detection from text a more interesting as well as a challenging problem for us to tackle (Angel Deborah et al., 2021).

Tamil Language is a Dravidian Language that is natively spoken by the people of Tamil Nadu in South Asia. It is also the official Language of two sovereign nation, Sri Lanka and Singapore as well as the official language of the Union Territory of Puducherry (Sakuntharaj and Mahesan, 2021, 2017, 2016; Thavareesan and Mahesan, 2019, 2020a,b, 2021). Tamil was known as Tamilakam in the time period of the 6th century to the 3rd century CE. Tamil is the first Indian classical language to listed as classical language, and is one of the world's oldest classical languages that is still spoken. There are 12 vowels, 18 consonants, and one special character, the aytam, in the present Tamil script. The vowels and consonants merge to form 216 compound characters, for a total of 247 characters (12 vowels + 18 consonants + 1 aytam + (12 x 18) combinations) (Chakravarthi et al., 2020; Anita and Subalalitha, 2019b,a; Subalalitha and Poovammal, 2018; Subalalitha, 2019; Srinivasan

Proceedings of the Second Workshop on Speech and Language Technologies for Dravidian Languages, pages 165 - 169

and Subalalitha, 2019; Narasimhan et al., 2018).

The paper is organized as follows. Section 2 discusses the related work on emotion analysis. The data set about the shared task is in Section 3.1. Section 4 outlines the features of the proposed system. Section 5 concludes the paper.

2 Related Work

Emotional Analysis from text is considered as an interesting as well as a challenging task in NLP. However due to lack of data set in Tamil language it is difficult to conduct high level research in this area.

The TamilEmo (Vasantharajan et al., 2022)introduced a labelled data set that is manually annotated of more than 42,000 Tamil YouTube comments and is labelled for 31 emotions including neutral. The main aim of the data set is to improve the detection of emotions from Tamil texts. They have also created three different groupings of emotions namely 3-class, 7-class and 31-class.

ACTSEA (Jenarthanan et al., 2019) presented a corpus for emotion analysis that is a scalable semi-automatic approach for creating annotated corpus for Tamil and Sinhala. They gathered data from an online social platform, Twitter, and then manually annotated them after cleaning it. They collected 6,00,280 Tamil Tweets and 3,18,308 Sinhala tweets which now make them have one of the largest data sets for the languages Tamil and Sinhala.

In the year 2007, two people - Strapparava and Mihalcea presented three detailed systems that took part in the SemEval 2007 Affective Text task. The three systems were rule-based, unsupervised and supervised systems. They noted that the rule based system performed the best for 4 emotion classes out of 6, while the supervised system did the best in the remaining two emotion classes. This was done for the language, English.

In the year 2007, Yang et al. proved that sequence labellers can outperform traditional classifier (Support Vector System) on a dataset of blogs, increasing the accuracy to 43.35 from 32.88.

3 Document Body

3.1 Data Description

Competition organizers provided data with text as features (Sampath et al., 2022). The text feature contains the 14,208 total data with emotions being classified as Ambiguous, Anger, Anticipation, Disgust, Fear, Joy, Love, Neutral, Sadness, Surprise, Trust. The detailed contents of the data set are shown in the Table 1.

Table 1. Class Distribution for Emotion Classification in Tamil

Label	Training set
Ambiguous	1689
Anger	834
Anticipation	828
Disgust	910
Fear	100
Joy	2,134
Love	675
Neutral	4,841
Sadness	695
Surprise	248
Trust	1,254

3.2 Emotion Identification using Keyword Spotting

The Emotion Identification is finding the frequency of the emotion word by checking the Emotion Word Knowledge Base (Jenarthanan14) and finding the frequency of the emoji by checking the Emotion Emoji Knowledge Base. This is done by tokenizing the given string (text message) into many substrings (words in the text message) and matching each substring to find a match in the Knowledge Bases. The Knowledge Base consists of emotions namely – anger, sadness, disgust, joy, surprise, fear, love, anticipation and so on and so forth.

This process for identifying emotion contains eight steps as given in Figure 1, here the text message is given as input and the returned value is the emotion felt in the text message. After getting input, we perform tokenization using space " " as the separating delimiter and create a list of substrings, that represent the words as well as the emojis in the text. These substrings are used to analyze the frequency of the emotion. Then the emotion is the output.

3.3 Lexical Affinity Method

The Lexicon-based method is a keyword-based search method that checks for emotion keywords assigned to some Emotional Classes(Abdaoui et al., 2017).

It is based on the idea of detecting emotions based on related keywords such as emotional words and

emojis. This is pretty easy to implement and a straightforward approach. This is more of an extension to the above "Emotion Identification using Keyword Spotting", by assigning a number to the respective emotion. It increments the respective emotion variable's value each time a word or emoji of that emotion is found. For example, if a smiley face is found 3 times in a text, the value of happiness is incremented by 3.
The flowchart is given in Figure 1.

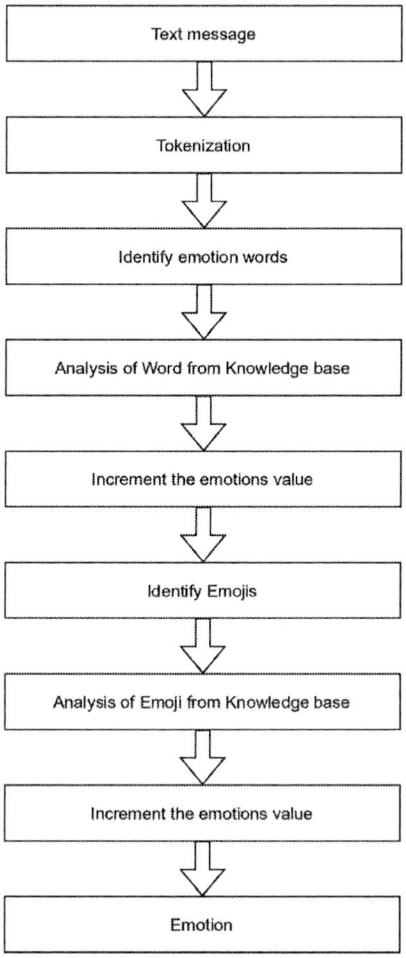

Figure 1: Lexical Affinity Approach Flowchart

4 Our System

Methods described in the previous section, i.e., Section 3 are modified and integrated to extend their capabilities and to improve the performance for which a simple and easy to understand model is designed shown in Figure 2.

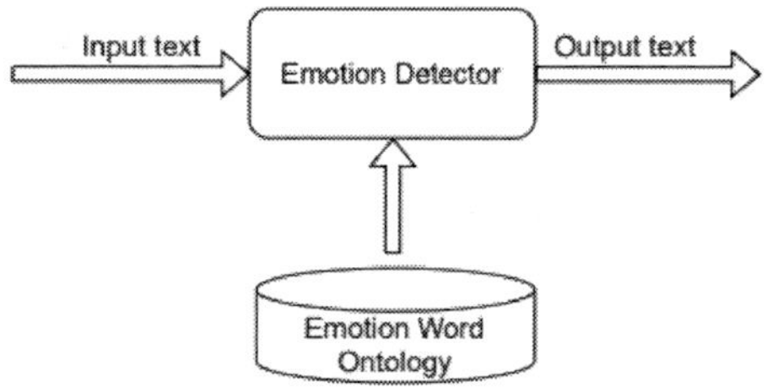

Figure 2: Our system model

4.1 Emotion Word Ontology

The Emotion Word Ontology is a combination of two Knowledge Bases of both words (in Tamil) (Jenarthanan14) and emojis.
The Word Knowledge Base consists of a list of emotional keywords that are matched to their respective emotion class. For example, words that express anger in Tamil are under the class "Anger" and are in all forms (past/present/future as well as singular/plural), while the words that express disgust in Tamil are under the class "Disgust" and are in all forms.
Similarly, there is an Emoji Knowledge Base that consists of emotion icons that are matched to their respective emotions. For example, icons that have a heart are under the class "Love", while the icons with tears are under the class "Sadness".

4.2 Emotion Detector

This is a function that helps in detecting the emotion of the Tamil message that is given as the input. The function assigns a value for each emotion, it also increments the values of the respective emotion variable when it encounters the same word or emoji in the Emotion Word Ontology. The emotion variable that has the greatest value is taken as the detected emotion.

5 Conclusion

In conclusion, the proposed system analyses emotions from text messages that are written in Tamil, using a very simple and straightforward method. Research in the domain of Emotion Analysis has flourished significantly over the past few years, making it a need to take a look back at the big picture that these individual works have led to. There are many methods and models to analyse emotions on text. (Tripathi et al., 2016) The dictionary-based approach is quite straightforward and adaptable to apply to any language.

Acknowledgement

We would like to thank Sri Sivasubramaniya Nadar College of Engineering and its Department of Computer Science and Engineering for providing us with the opportunity to work on this paper. We would also like to take this opportunity to thank The Association of Computational Linguistics (ACL) for inviting us to the DravidianLangTech Workshop and providing us with the opportunity to work on this problem and paper. We also thank Tamil-Sinhala-Emotion-Analysis (Jenarthanan14) (Jenarthanan et al., 2019)for providing us with their Data Set.

References

Amine Abdaoui, Jérôme Azé, Sandra Bringay, and Pascal Poncelet. 2017. Feel: a french expanded emotion lexicon. *Language Resources and Evaluation*, 51(3):833–855.

S Angel Deborah, TT Mirnalinee, and S Milton Rajendram. 2021. Emotion analysis on text using multiple kernel gaussian... *Neural Processing Letters*, 53(2):1187–1203.

R Anita and CN Subalalitha. 2019a. An approach to cluster Tamil literatures using discourse connectives. In *2019 IEEE 1st International Conference on Energy, Systems and Information Processing (ICESIP)*, pages 1–4. IEEE.

R Anita and CN Subalalitha. 2019b. Building discourse parser for Thirukkural. In *Proceedings of the 16th International Conference on Natural Language Processing*, pages 18–25.

B Bharathi, Bharathi Raja Chakravarthi, Subalalitha Chinnaudayar Navaneethakrishnan, N Sripriya, Arunaggiri Pandian, and Swetha Valli. 2022. Findings of the shared task on Speech Recognition for Vulnerable Individuals in Tamil. In *Proceedings of the Second Workshop on Language Technology for Equality, Diversity and Inclusion*. Association for Computational Linguistics.

Bharathi Raja Chakravarthi. 2020. HopeEDI: A multilingual hope speech detection dataset for equality, diversity, and inclusion. In *Proceedings of the Third Workshop on Computational Modeling of People's Opinions, Personality, and Emotion's in Social Media*, pages 41–53, Barcelona, Spain (Online). Association for Computational Linguistics.

Bharathi Raja Chakravarthi and Vigneshwaran Muralidaran. 2021. Findings of the shared task on hope speech detection for equality, diversity, and inclusion. In *Proceedings of the First Workshop on Language Technology for Equality, Diversity and Inclusion*, pages 61–72, Kyiv. Association for Computational Linguistics.

Bharathi Raja Chakravarthi, Ruba Priyadharshini, Thenmozhi Durairaj, John Phillip McCrae, Paul Buitaleer, Prasanna Kumar Kumaresan, and Rahul Ponnusamy. 2022. Findings of the shared task on Homophobia Transphobia Detection in Social Media Comments. In *Proceedings of the Second Workshop on Language Technology for Equality, Diversity and Inclusion*. Association for Computational Linguistics.

Bharathi Raja Chakravarthi, Ruba Priyadharshini, Rahul Ponnusamy, Prasanna Kumar Kumaresan, Kayalvizhi Sampath, Durairaj Thenmozhi, Sathiyaraj Thangasamy, Rajendran Nallathambi, and John Phillip McCrae. 2021. Dataset for identification of homophobia and transophobia in multilingual YouTube comments. *arXiv preprint arXiv:2109.00227*.

Bharathi Raja Chakravarthi, Navaneethan Rajasekaran, Mihael Arcan, Kevin McGuinness, Noel E. O'Connor, and John P. McCrae. 2020. Bilingual lexicon induction across orthographically-distinct under-resourced Dravidian languages. In *Proceedings of the 7th Workshop on NLP for Similar Languages, Varieties and Dialects*, pages 57–69, Barcelona, Spain (Online). International Committee on Computational Linguistics (ICCL).

Kendra Cherry. The 6 types of basic emotions and their effect on human behavior.

Justas Gaubys. How many people use social media in 2022? [updated jan 2022].

Rajenthiran Jenarthanan, Yasas Senarath, and Uthayasanker Thayasivam. 2019. Actsea: Annotated corpus for tamil amp; sinhala emotion analysis. In *2019 Moratuwa Engineering Research Conference (MERCon)*, pages 49–53.

Jenarthanan14. Jenarthanan14/tamil-sinhala-emotion-analysis.

Myriam Munezero, Calkin Suero Montero, Erkki Sutinen, and John Pajunen. 2014. Are they different? affect, feeling, emotion, sentiment, and opinion detection in text. *IEEE Transactions on Affective Computing*, 5(2):101–111.

Anitha Narasimhan, Aarthy Anandan, Madhan Karky, and CN Subalalitha. 2018. Porul: Option generation and selection and scoring algorithms for a tamil flash card game. *International Journal of Cognitive and Language Sciences*, 12(2):225–228.

W Gerrod Parrott. 2001. *Emotions in social psychology: Essential readings*. psychology press.

Ruba Priyadharshini, Bharathi Raja Chakravarthi, Subalalitha Chinnaudayar Navaneethakrishnan, Thenmozhi Durairaj, Malliga Subramanian, Kogilavani Shanmugavadivel, Siddhanth U Hegde, and Prasanna Kumar Kumaresan. 2022. Findings of the shared task on Abusive Comment Detection in Tamil. In *Proceedings of the Second Workshop on Speech and Language Technologies for Dravidian Languages*. Association for Computational Linguistics.

S Milton Rajendram, TT Mirnalinee, et al. 2017. Ssn_mlrg1 at semeval-2017 task 5: fine-grained sentiment analysis using multiple kernel gaussian process regression model. In *Proceedings of the 11th International Workshop on Semantic Evaluation (SemEval-2017)*, pages 823–826.

S Milton Rajendram, Mirnalinee TT, et al. 2022. Contextual emotion detection on text using gaussian process and tree based classifiers. *Intelligent Data Analysis*, 26(1):119–132.

Manikandan Ravikiran, Bharathi Raja Chakravarthi, Anand Kumar Madasamy, Sangeetha Sivanesan, Ratnavel Rajalakshmi, Sajeetha Thavareesan, Rahul Ponnusamy, and Shankar Mahadevan. 2022. Findings of the shared task on Offensive Span Identification in code-mixed Tamil-English comments. In *Proceedings of the Second Workshop on Speech and Language Technologies for Dravidian Languages*. Association for Computational Linguistics.

Ratnasingam Sakuntharaj and Sinnathamby Mahesan. 2016. A novel hybrid approach to detect and correct spelling in Tamil text. In *2016 IEEE International Conference on Information and Automation for Sustainability (ICIAfS)*, pages 1–6.

Ratnasingam Sakuntharaj and Sinnathamby Mahesan. 2017. Use of a novel hash-table for speeding-up suggestions for misspelt Tamil words. In *2017 IEEE International Conference on Industrial and Information Systems (ICIIS)*, pages 1–5.

Ratnasingam Sakuntharaj and Sinnathamby Mahesan. 2021. Missing word detection and correction based on context of Tamil sentences using n-grams. In *2021 10th International Conference on Information and Automation for Sustainability (ICIAfS)*, pages 42–47.

Anbukkarasi Sampath, Thenmozhi Durairaj, Bharathi Raja Chakravarthi, Ruba Priyadharshini, Subalalitha Chinnaudayar Navaneethakrishnan, Kogilavani Shanmugavadivel, Sajeetha Thavareesan, Sathiyaraj Thangasamy, Parameswari Krishnamurthy, Adeep Hande, Sean Benhur, and Santhiya Ponnusamy, Kishor Kumar Pandiyan. 2022. Findings of the shared task on Emotion Analysis in Tamil. In *Proceedings of the Second Workshop on Speech and Language Technologies for Dravidian Languages*. Association for Computational Linguistics.

R Srinivasan and CN Subalalitha. 2019. Automated named entity recognition from tamil documents. In *2019 IEEE 1st International Conference on Energy, Systems and Information Processing (ICESIP)*, pages 1–5. IEEE.

C. N. Subalalitha. 2019. Information extraction framework for Kurunthogai. *Sādhanā*, 44(7):156.

CN Subalalitha and E Poovammal. 2018. Automatic bilingual dictionary construction for Tirukural. *Applied Artificial Intelligence*, 32(6):558–567.

Sajeetha Thavareesan and Sinnathamby Mahesan. 2019. Sentiment analysis in Tamil texts: A study on machine learning techniques and feature representation. In *2019 14th Conference on Industrial and Information Systems (ICIIS)*, pages 320–325.

Sajeetha Thavareesan and Sinnathamby Mahesan. 2020a. Sentiment lexicon expansion using Word2vec and fastText for sentiment prediction in Tamil texts. In *2020 Moratuwa Engineering Research Conference (MERCon)*, pages 272–276.

Sajeetha Thavareesan and Sinnathamby Mahesan. 2020b. Word embedding-based part of speech tagging in Tamil texts. In *2020 IEEE 15th International Conference on Industrial and Information Systems (ICIIS)*, pages 478–482.

Sajeetha Thavareesan and Sinnathamby Mahesan. 2021. Sentiment analysis in Tamil texts using k-means and k-nearest neighbour. In *2021 10th International Conference on Information and Automation for Sustainability (ICIAfS)*, pages 48–53.

Vaibhav Tripathi, Aditya Joshi, and Pushpak Bhattacharyya. 2016. Emotion analysis from text: A survey. *Center for Indian Language Technology Surveys*.

Charangan Vasantharajan, Sean Benhur, Prasanna Kumar Kumarasen, Rahul Ponnusamy, Sathiyaraj Thangasamy, Ruba Priyadharshini, Thenmozhi Durairaj, Kanchana Sivanraju, Anbukkarasi Sampath, Bharathi Raja Chakravarthi, and John Phillip McCrae. 2022. Tamilemo: Finegrained emotion detection dataset for tamil.

CUET-NLP@DravidianLangTech-ACL2022: Investigating Deep Learning Techniques to Detect Multimodal Troll Memes

Md. Maruf Hasan[Ψ], **Nusratul Jannat**[Ψ], **Eftekhar Hossain**[$],
Omar Sharif[Ψ] and **Mohammed Moshiul Hoque**[Ψ]
[Ψ]Department of Computer Science and Engineering
[$]Department of Electronics and Telecommunication Engineering
[$Ψ]Chittagong University of Engineering & Technology, Chattogram-4349, Bangladesh
{u1604089, u1604115}@student.cuet.ac.bd
{eftekhar.hossain, omar.sharif, moshiul_240}@cuet.ac.bd

Abstract

With the substantial rise of internet usage, social media has become a powerful communication medium to convey information, opinions, and feelings on various issues. Recently, memes have become a popular way of sharing information on social media. Usually, memes is visuals with text incorporated into them and quickly disseminate hatred and offensive content. Detecting or classifying memes are challenging due to their region-specific interpretation and multimodal nature. This work presents a meme classification technique in Tamil developed by the CUET NLP team under the shared task (DravidianLangTech-ACL2022). Several computational models have been investigated to perform the classification task. This work also explored visual and textual features using VGG16, ResNet50, VGG19, CNN and CNN+LSTM models. Multimodal features are extracted by combining image (VGG16) and text (CNN, LSTM+CNN) characteristics. Results demonstrate that the textual strategy with CNN+LSTM achieved the highest weighted f_1-score (0.52) and recall (0.57). Moreover, the CNN-Text+VGG16 outperformed the other models concerning the multimodal memes detection by achieving the highest f_1-score of 0.49, but the LSTM+CNN model allowed the team to achieve 4th place in the shared task.

1 Introduction

The **Meme** refers to an element of a culture or system of behaviour conveyed from one individual to another by imitation or other non-genetic actions. Memes appear in various formats, including but not limited to photographs, videos, tweets, and have a growing influence on social media communication (French, 2017; Suryawanshi et al., 2020b). Images with embedded text are the most widely used form of memes. Memes facilitate transmitting ideas or feelings spontaneously. Posting and sharing memes have recently become a popular way of disseminating information on social media since memes can propagate information humorously or sarcastically (Ghanghor et al., 2021a,b; Yasaswini et al., 2021). Propagation of malicious memes and other related activities via memes such as trolling, cyberbullying is rapidly rising (Chakravarthi, 2020; Chakravarthi and Muralidaran, 2021). The implicit meaning of the memes, presence of ambiguous, humorous, sarcastic terms, and usage of attractive, comical, theatrical images have made meme classification even more complicated (Kumari et al., 2021; Chakravarthi et al., 2021). For example, in Figure 1, text and image individually exhibit no means of attack. However, considering both modalities, it insults the persons by directing the age gap in their marriage. To facilitate research in this arena, this work presents our system to classify multimodal troll memes for the Tamil language.

Tamil is a member of the southern branch of the Dravidian languages, a group of about 26 languages indigenous to the Indian subcontinent. It is also classed as a member of the Tamil language family, which contains the languages of around 35 ethno-linguistic groups, including the Irula and Yerukula languages (Sakuntharaj and Mahesan, 2021, 2017, 2016; Thavareesan and Mahesan, 2019, 2020a,b, 2021). Tamil is an official language of Tamil Nadu, Sri Lanka, Singapore, and the Union Territory of Puducherry in India. Significant minority speak Tamil in the four other South Indian states of Kerala, Karnataka, Andhra Pradesh, and Telangana, as well as the Union Territory of the Andaman and Nicobar Islands (Bharathi et al., 2022; Priyadharshini et al., 2022). It is also spoken by the Tamil diaspora, which may be found in Malaysia, Myanmar, South Africa, the United Kingdom, the United States, Canada, Australia, and Mauritius. Tamil is also the native language of Sri Lankan Moors. Tamil, one of the 22 scheduled languages in the Indian Constitution, was the first to be designated as a classical language of India (Anita and Subalalitha, 2019b,a; Subalalitha and Poovam-

Proceedings of the Second Workshop on Speech and Language Technologies for Dravidian Languages, pages 170 - 176
May 26, 2022

mal, 2018; Subalalitha, 2019; Srinivasan and Subalalitha, 2019; Narasimhan et al., 2018).

We experimented with several deep learning models to extract visual and textual features. After investigating the outcomes, an early fusion approach is employed to combine the features from both modalities. The results indicate that the textual models acquired higher f_1-score compared to the visual and multimodal counterparts.

Figure 1: A sample Troll meme

2 Related Work

Over the past few years, trolling, hostility, offensive, and abusive language detection from social media data have been extensively studied by NLP professionals (Kumari et al., 2021; Hossain et al., 2021; Mandl et al., 2020; Sharif et al., 2021a). The majority of these researches were carried out considering only textual information (Li, 2021; Sharif et al., 2021b). However, a meme's existence can be found in an image and text embedded in an image. Few researchers have investigated both textual and visual features of memes to classify trolls, offences and aggression. Sadiq et al. Sadiq et al. (2021) developed and compared several models to identify cyber-trolling tweets. Models include the Multi-Layer Perceptron (MLP) with TF–IDF features, MLP with word embedding, and two deep neural networks: CNN with LSTM and CNN with BiLSTM. Results exhibited that MLP with the TF–IDF features-based model outperformed other models with an accuracy of 0.92. Kumari et al. (2021) proposed a hybrid model in which the image features are retrieved using pre-trained VGG-16, and the textual features are extracted through a layered CNN model. These features are optimized using the binary particle swarm optimization technique (BPSO), contributing to a weighted f_1-score of 0.74. Suryawanshi et al. (2020a) created a multimodal dataset of 743 offensive and not-offensive memes from the 2016 presidential election in the United States. To merge the multimodal characteristics, they used an early fusion method. The combined model received a 0.50 f1-score, but the text-based CNN model outperformed it with a 0.54 f1-score. Most previous studies focused on categorizing memes based on unimodal data: text or image. However, this work considers detecting memes from multimodal data: text and image in Tamil. Pranesh and Shekhar (2020) proposed a multimodal framework (MemSem) consisting of VGG19 for image features and BERT for text features. MemeSem achieved a better result than all unimodal and multimodal baselines with 67.12% accuracy. Gomez et al. (2020) developed a multimodal hate speech dataset containing images and corresponding tweets. The results indicate that the multimodal model (CNN+RNN) was not outperformed the textual model. Bucur et al. (2022) employed a 3-branch network for sentiment analysis. They used EfficientNetV4 and CLIP to extract image features, while a sentence transformer was used to get the text features. The system achieved a weighted f_1-score of 0.5318 with the CORAL loss function.

3 Task and Dataset Descriptions

A troll meme is an image with embedded offensive or sarcastic text which degrade, provoke, or offend a person or group (Suryawanshi et al., 2020b; Gandhi et al., 2019). This work aims to classify troll memes by exploiting the visual and textual information. The task organizers[1] provided a dataset having two types of memes (troll and not troll) in Tamil (Suryawanshi and Chakravarthi, 2021).

Dataset	Train	Test
Troll	1282	395
Not-troll	1018	272
Total	2300	667

Table 1: Meme dataset distribution

Table 1 presents the distribution of the data samples in the train and test set. Dataset is provided in the form of an image with an associated caption. Participants can use the image, caption, or both to perform the classification task. We utilized image,

[1]https://competitions.codalab.org/competitions/36397

text, and multimodal (i.e., image + text) features to address the assigned task.

4 Methodology

The objective of this work is to identify the troll from multimodal memes. Initially, we exploit the visual aspects of the memes and develop several CNN architectures. Subsequently, the textual information is considered, and deep learning-based methods (i.e., LSTM, CNN, LSTM+CNN) are applied for classification. Finally, the visual and textual features are synergistically combined to make more robust meme classification inferences. Figure 2 depicts the abstract process of the troll meme classification system.

4.1 Data preprocessing

In the preprocessing step, unwanted symbols and punctuations are removed from the text automatically using a Python script. The preprocessed text is transformed into a vector of unique numbers. The Keras tokenizer function is utilized to find the mapping of this word to the index. The padding technique is applied to get equal length vectors. Similar to ImageNet's preprocessing method (Deng et al., 2009), all images are transformed into a size of ($224 \times 224 \times 3$) during preprocessing.

4.2 Visual Approach

Several pre-trained CNN architectures including VGG16 (Simonyan and Zisserman, 2014), VGG19, and ResNet50 (He et al., 2016) are employed here. To accomplish the task, this work utilized the transfer learning approach (Tan et al., 2018). At first, the top two layers of the models are frozen and then added a global average pooling layer followed by a sigmoid layer for the classification. The models are trained using the 'binary_crossentropy' loss function and 'adam' optimizer with a learning rate of $1e^{-3}$. Training is performed by passing 32 samples at each iteration. Besides, we use the Keras callback method to save the best intermediate model.

4.3 Textual Approach

In order to extract features from the text modality, various deep learning architectures are used. The investigation employs CNN and RNN architectures, specifically CNN and LSTM with CNN (LSTM+CNN). Firstly, the Keras embedding layer generates the word embeddings for a maximum caption length of 1000. Subsequently, these embeddings are propagated to the models. We construct a CNN model consisting of one convolution layer associated with a filter size of 32 and a ReLU (Rectified Linear Unit) activation function in one architecture. To further downsample the convoluted features, we use a max-pooling layer followed by a classification layer for the prediction. In another architecture, we added a single LSTM layer of 100 neurons at the top of the CNN network and thus created the LSTM + CNN model. Here, the LSTM layer is introduced due to its effectiveness in capturing the long-term dependencies from the long text.

4.4 Multimodal Approach

Visual features are extracted using the pre-trained VGG16 model. Following the VGG16 model, we added a global average pooling layer with fully connected and sigmoid layers. We employed CNN and LSTM models to extract the textual features. Finally, the output layers of the visual and textual models are concatenated to form a single integrated model. The output prediction is produced in all combinations by a final sigmoid layer inserted after the multimodal concatenation layer. All the models are compiled with the 'binary crossentropy' loss function. Aside from that, we utilize the 'adam' optimizer with a learning rate of $1e^{-3}$ and a batch size of 32. Table 2 shows the list of tuned hyperparameters used in the experiment.

Hyperparameters	Values
Dropout rate	0.2
Epoch	15
Optimizer	'adam'
Learning rate	$1e^{-3}$
Batch size	32

Table 2: List of hyperparameters values.

5 Result and Analysis

The task's purpose is to categorize troll memes in Tamil. We experimented with various visual and textual models to deal with each modality. Furthermore, the features from both modalities were merged. The weighted f_1-score determines the models' superiority. Other evaluation criteria, such as precision and recall, are also considered to understand the model's performance better. Table 3 exhibits the evaluation results of the models on the test set. Concerning the multimodal approach, the

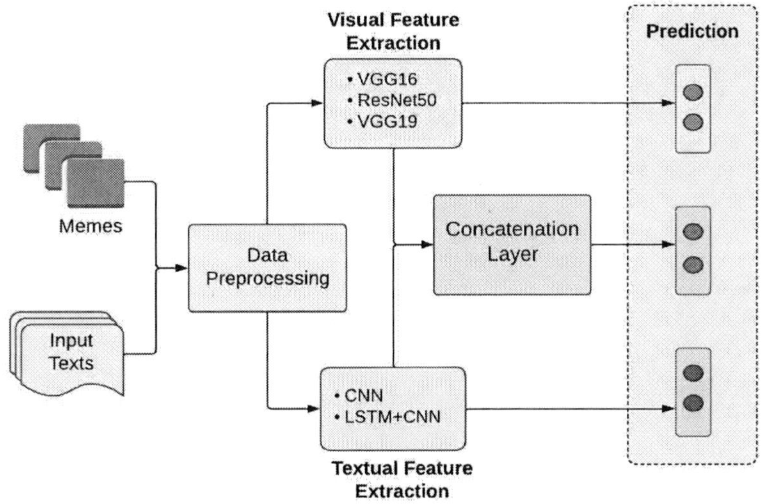

Figure 2: Abstract process of troll meme classification

Approach	Classifier	Accuracy	Precision	Recall	f_1-score
Visual	VGG16	0.58	0.53	0.58	0.50
	ResNet50	0.58	0.50	0.58	0.45
	VGG19	0.55	0.51	0.55	0.50
Textual	CNN	0.55	0.52	0.55	0.52
	LSTM+CNN	0.55	0.54	0.57	0.52
Multimodal	LSTM+VGG16	0.58	0.44	0.58	0.44
	CNN-Text+VGG16	0.59	0.55	0.59	**0.49**
	CNN+LSTM+VGG16	0.59	0.49	0.58	0.46

Table 3: Evaluation results of visual, textual and multimodal models on the test set

CNN_Text+VGG16 model obtained a precision of 0.49 (not-troll class) and 0.60 (troll class) with a weighted average precision of 0.55. The overall performance of the models varies between 44% and 56% weighted f_1-score. The results indicate that VGG16 and VGG19 have the same weighted f_1-score, but VGG16 has superior precision and recall. Although ResNet50 has a lower f_1-score, its precision and recall are similar to VGG16. The performance of the text-based models proved superior to that of the image-based models. In the textual approach, CNN and LSTM + CNN both have the same f_1-score of 0.52.

We also conducted experiments by combining features from both modalities into a single model. In the multimodal approach, the LSTM + VGG16 model had a f_1-score of 0.44, whereas the CNN Text + VGG16 model had a 3% higher f_1-score of 0.49. However, their combination with 0.46 f_1-score could not outperform the textual-based models. According to the results, the multimodal model (CNN-Text +VGG16) outdoes others by acquiring the highest recall of 0.59 but could not perform well in terms of f_1-score. The presence of several images in all of the classes could cause this. The dataset contains many memes with the same visual content but distinct captions. Furthermore, many images do not convey any explicit useful information that can be utilized to determine whether a meme is a troll or not. Table 4 shows the performance comparison between the proposed (CUET89109115) and other models developed by shared task participating teams. With 0.529 f_1-score our team (CUET89109115) placed fourth in the competition. The implementation is available on the Github[2].

[2]https://github.com/Maruf089/DravidianLangTech-2022

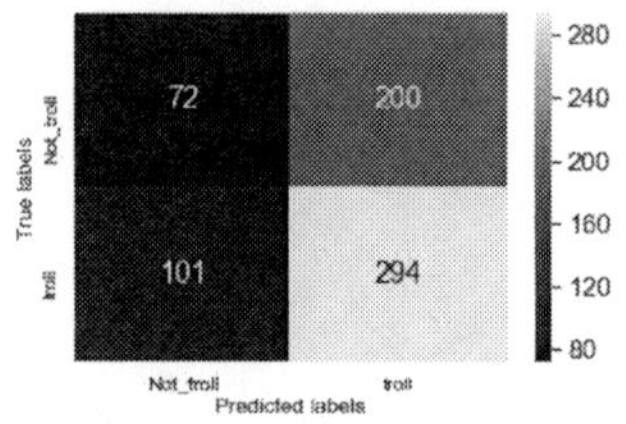

(a) Textual

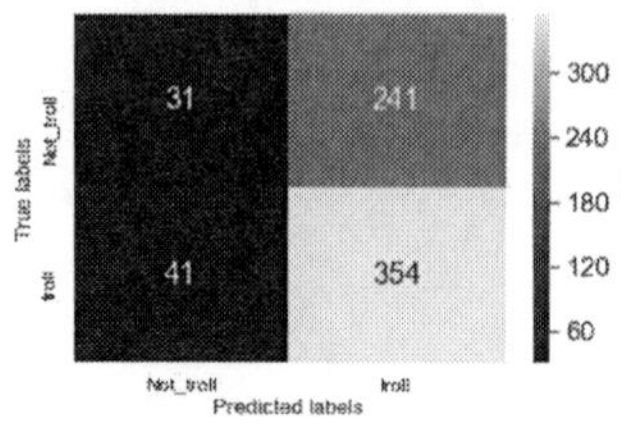

(b) Visual

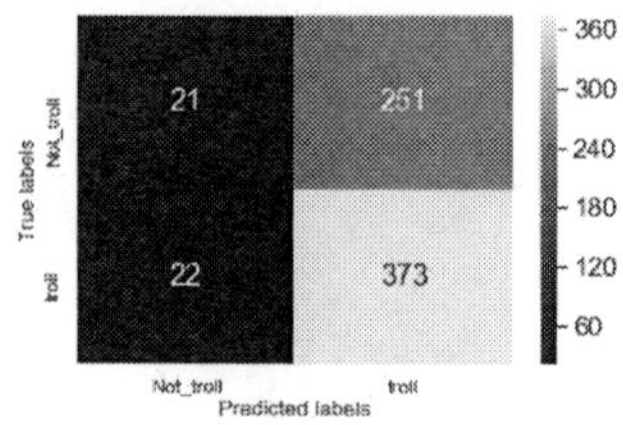

(c) Multimodal

Figure 3: Confusion Matrix of the best model in each approach (based on f_1-score): (a) Textual (b) Visual (c) Multimodal

Team	Precision	Recall	f_1-score
BPHC	0.6	0.613	0.596
hate-alert	0.558	0.567	0.561
SSN_MLRG1	0.555	0.565	0.558
CUET89109115	0.527	0.531	0.529
DLRG_RR	0.529	0.529	0.519
TeamX	0.466	0.544	0.466

Table 4: Summary of performance comparison for all participating teams in the shared task

6 Error Analysis

A detailed error analysis is done on the best model for each modality to gain more insights. Confusion matrices are used to analyze the performance (Figure 3). Figure 3c shows that, out of 395 troll memes, the CNN Text + VGG16 model accurately categorized 373 images while misclassifying 22 as not-troll. However, this model's actual positive rate is lower than its true negative rate since it correctly classified just 21 not-troll memes and incorrectly classified 251 memes. The VGG16 model also performed well in the visual method, successfully detecting 354 troll memes out of 395. However, the model struggled to identify not-troll memes, correctly classifying only 31 of a total of 272 not-troll memes and incorrectly classifying 241 of the exact total. Meanwhile, Figure 3a shows that the CNN text model accurately categorized 294 of 395 troll memes, which is lower than the accuracy of other models. In comparison, the model accurately recognized only 72 non-troll memes out of 272. According to the results of the above investigation, all models are biased toward troll memes and incorrectly label more than 73% of memes as trolls. This improper detection is most likely due to the overlapping nature of memes across all classes. Furthermore, 80 memes in the train set and 34 memes in the test set were missed embedded captions, making it challenging for textual and multimodal models to predict the actual class.

7 Conclusion

This paper presented a deep learning model for detecting troll memes in Tamil. We experimented with visual, textual, and visual-textual fusion techniques. Results revealed that the visual approach obtained the highest weighted f_1-score of 0.50, whereas the textual approach (LSTM+CNN) achieved 0.52 f_1-score. However, after aggregating features from both modalities, we noticed a slight drop in the model performance. The combined CNN-Text+VGG16 model acquired the maximal weighted f_1-score (0.49) with multimodal approach outperformed other models. It will be interesting to catch how the multimodal fusion performs after extracting the visual and textual features with state-of-the-art models. We aim to investigate transformer-based models (e.g., vision transformer, IndicBERT, mBERT, XML-R, Electra, MuRIL) with the extended dataset in the future.

Acknowledgements

This work supported by the ICT Innovation Fund, ICT Division, Ministry of Posts, Telecommunications and Information Technology, Bangladesh.

References

R Anita and CN Subalalitha. 2019a. An approach to cluster Tamil literatures using discourse connectives. In *2019 IEEE 1st International Conference on Energy, Systems and Information Processing (ICESIP)*, pages 1–4. IEEE.

R Anita and CN Subalalitha. 2019b. Building discourse parser for Thirukkural. In *Proceedings of the 16th International Conference on Natural Language Processing*, pages 18–25.

B Bharathi, Bharathi Raja Chakravarthi, Subalalitha Chinnaudayar Navaneethakrishnan, N Sripriya,

Arunaggiri Pandian, and Swetha Valli. 2022. Findings of the shared task on Speech Recognition for Vulnerable Individuals in Tamil. In *Proceedings of the Second Workshop on Language Technology for Equality, Diversity and Inclusion*. Association for Computational Linguistics.

Ana-Maria Bucur, Adrian Cosma, and Ioan-Bogdan Iordache. 2022. Blue at memotion 2.0 2022: You have my image, my text and my transformer.

Bharathi Raja Chakravarthi. 2020. HopeEDI: A multilingual hope speech detection dataset for equality, diversity, and inclusion. In *Proceedings of the Third Workshop on Computational Modeling of People's Opinions, Personality, and Emotion's in Social Media*, pages 41–53, Barcelona, Spain (Online). Association for Computational Linguistics.

Bharathi Raja Chakravarthi and Vigneshwaran Muralidaran. 2021. Findings of the shared task on hope speech detection for equality, diversity, and inclusion. In *Proceedings of the First Workshop on Language Technology for Equality, Diversity and Inclusion*, pages 61–72, Kyiv. Association for Computational Linguistics.

Bharathi Raja Chakravarthi, Ruba Priyadharshini, Rahul Ponnusamy, Prasanna Kumar Kumaresan, Kayalvizhi Sampath, Durairaj Thenmozhi, Sathiyaraj Thangasamy, Rajendran Nallathambi, and John Phillip McCrae. 2021. Dataset for identification of homophobia and transophobia in multilingual YouTube comments. *arXiv preprint arXiv:2109.00227*.

Jia Deng, Wei Dong, Richard Socher, Li-Jia Li, Kai Li, and Li Fei-Fei. 2009. Imagenet: A large-scale hierarchical image database. In *2009 IEEE Conference on Computer Vision and Pattern Recognition*, pages 248–255.

Jean H. French. 2017. Image-based memes as sentiment predictors. In *2017 International Conference on Information Society (i-Society)*, pages 80–85.

Shreyansh Gandhi, Samrat Kokkula, Abon Chaudhuri, Alessandro Magnani, Theban Stanley, Behzad Ahmadi, Venkatesh Kandaswamy, Omer Ovenc, and Shie Mannor. 2019. Image matters: Scalable detection of offensive and non-compliant content / logo in product images.

Nikhil Ghanghor, Parameswari Krishnamurthy, Sajeetha Thavareesan, Ruba Priyadharshini, and Bharathi Raja Chakravarthi. 2021a. IIITK@DravidianLangTech-EACL2021: Offensive language identification and meme classification in Tamil, Malayalam and Kannada. In *Proceedings of the First Workshop on Speech and Language Technologies for Dravidian Languages*, pages 222–229, Kyiv. Association for Computational Linguistics.

Nikhil Ghanghor, Rahul Ponnusamy, Prasanna Kumar Kumaresan, Ruba Priyadharshini, Sajeetha Thavareesan, and Bharathi Raja Chakravarthi. 2021b. IIITK@LT-EDI-EACL2021: Hope speech detection for equality, diversity, and inclusion in Tamil , Malayalam and English. In *Proceedings of the First Workshop on Language Technology for Equality, Diversity and Inclusion*, pages 197–203, Kyiv. Association for Computational Linguistics.

Raul Gomez, Jaume Gibert, Lluis Gomez, and Dimosthenis Karatzas. 2020. Exploring hate speech detection in multimodal publications. In *2020 IEEE Winter Conference on Applications of Computer Vision (WACV)*, pages 1459–1467.

Kaiming He, Xiangyu Zhang, Shaoqing Ren, and Jian Sun. 2016. Deep residual learning for image recognition. In *Proceedings of the IEEE Conference on Computer Vision and Pattern Recognition (CVPR)*.

Eftekhar Hossain, Omar Sharif, and Mohammed Moshiul Hoque. 2021. NLP-CUET@DravidianLangTech-EACL2021: Investigating visual and textual features to identify trolls from multimodal social media memes. In *Proceedings of the First Workshop on Speech and Language Technologies for Dravidian Languages*, pages 300–306, Kyiv. Association for Computational Linguistics.

Kirti Kumari, Jyoti Prakash Singh, Yogesh K. Dwivedi, and Nripendra P. Rana. 2021. Multi-modal aggression identification using convolutional neural network and binary particle swarm optimization. *Future Generation Computer Systems*, 118:187–197.

Zichao Li. 2021. Codewithzichao@DravidianLangTech-EACL2021: Exploring multimodal transformers for meme classification in Tamil language. In *Proceedings of the First Workshop on Speech and Language Technologies for Dravidian Languages*, pages 352–356, Kyiv. Association for Computational Linguistics.

Thomas Mandl, Sandip Modha, Anand Kumar M, and Bharathi Raja Chakravarthi. 2020. Overview of the hasoc track at fire 2020: Hate speech and offensive language identification in Tamil, Malayalam, Hindi, english and german. In *Forum for Information Retrieval Evaluation*, FIRE 2020, page 29–32, New York, NY, USA. Association for Computing Machinery.

Anitha Narasimhan, Aarthy Anandan, Madhan Karky, and CN Subalalitha. 2018. Porul: Option generation and selection and scoring algorithms for a tamil flash card game. *International Journal of Cognitive and Language Sciences*, 12(2):225–228.

Raj Ratn Pranesh and Ambesh Shekhar. 2020. Memesem:a multi-modal framework for sentimental analysis of meme via transfer learning.

Ruba Priyadharshini, Bharathi Raja Chakravarthi, Subalalitha Chinnaudayar Navaneethakrishnan, Thenmozhi Durairaj, Malliga Subramanian, Kogilavani Shanmugavadivel, Siddhanth U Hegde, and

Prasanna Kumar Kumaresan. 2022. Findings of the shared task on Abusive Comment Detection in Tamil. In *Proceedings of the Second Workshop on Speech and Language Technologies for Dravidian Languages*. Association for Computational Linguistics.

Saima Sadiq, Arif Mehmood, Saleem Ullah, Maqsood Ahmad, Gyu Sang Choi, and Byung-Won On. 2021. Aggression detection through deep neural model on twitter. *Future Generation Computer Systems*, 114:120–129.

Ratnasingam Sakuntharaj and Sinnathamby Mahesan. 2016. A novel hybrid approach to detect and correct spelling in Tamil text. In *2016 IEEE International Conference on Information and Automation for Sustainability (ICIAfS)*, pages 1–6.

Ratnasingam Sakuntharaj and Sinnathamby Mahesan. 2017. Use of a novel hash-table for speeding-up suggestions for misspelt Tamil words. In *2017 IEEE International Conference on Industrial and Information Systems (ICIIS)*, pages 1–5.

Ratnasingam Sakuntharaj and Sinnathamby Mahesan. 2021. Missing word detection and correction based on context of Tamil sentences using n-grams. In *2021 10th International Conference on Information and Automation for Sustainability (ICIAfS)*, pages 42–47.

Omar Sharif, Eftekhar Hossain, and Mohammed Moshiul Hoque. 2021a. Combating hostility: Covid-19 fake news and hostile post detection in social media.

Omar Sharif, Eftekhar Hossain, and Mohammed Moshiul Hoque. 2021b. NLP-CUET@DravidianLangTech-EACL2021: Offensive language detection from multilingual code-mixed text using transformers. In *Proceedings of the First Workshop on Speech and Language Technologies for Dravidian Languages*, pages 255–261, Kyiv. Association for Computational Linguistics.

Karen Simonyan and Andrew Zisserman. 2014. Very deep convolutional networks for large-scale image recognition. *arXiv preprint arXiv:1409.1556*.

R Srinivasan and CN Subalalitha. 2019. Automated named entity recognition from tamil documents. In *2019 IEEE 1st International Conference on Energy, Systems and Information Processing (ICESIP)*, pages 1–5. IEEE.

C. N. Subalalitha. 2019. Information extraction framework for Kurunthogai. *Sādhanā*, 44(7):156.

CN Subalalitha and E Poovammal. 2018. Automatic bilingual dictionary construction for Tirukural. *Applied Artificial Intelligence*, 32(6):558–567.

Shardul Suryawanshi and Bharathi Raja Chakravarthi. 2021. Findings of the shared task on Troll Meme Classification in Tamil. In *Proceedings of the First Workshop on Speech and Language Technologies for Dravidian Languages*. Association for Computational Linguistics.

Shardul Suryawanshi, Bharathi Raja Chakravarthi, Mihael Arcan, and Paul Buitelaar. 2020a. Multimodal meme dataset (MultiOFF) for identifying offensive content in image and text. In *Proceedings of the Second Workshop on Trolling, Aggression and Cyberbullying*, pages 32–41, Marseille, France. European Language Resources Association (ELRA).

Shardul Suryawanshi, Bharathi Raja Chakravarthi, Pranav Verma, Mihael Arcan, John Philip McCrae, and Paul Buitelaar. 2020b. A dataset for troll classification of TamilMemes. In *Proceedings of the WILDRE5– 5th Workshop on Indian Language Data: Resources and Evaluation*, pages 7–13, Marseille, France. European Language Resources Association (ELRA).

Chuanqi Tan, Fuchun Sun, Tao Kong, Wenchang Zhang, Chao Yang, and Chunfang Liu. 2018. A survey on deep transfer learning. In *International conference on artificial neural networks*, pages 270–279. Springer.

Sajeetha Thavareesan and Sinnathamby Mahesan. 2019. Sentiment analysis in Tamil texts: A study on machine learning techniques and feature representation. In *2019 14th Conference on Industrial and Information Systems (ICIIS)*, pages 320–325.

Sajeetha Thavareesan and Sinnathamby Mahesan. 2020a. Sentiment lexicon expansion using Word2vec and fastText for sentiment prediction in Tamil texts. In *2020 Moratuwa Engineering Research Conference (MERCon)*, pages 272–276.

Sajeetha Thavareesan and Sinnathamby Mahesan. 2020b. Word embedding-based part of speech tagging in Tamil texts. In *2020 IEEE 15th International Conference on Industrial and Information Systems (ICIIS)*, pages 478–482.

Sajeetha Thavareesan and Sinnathamby Mahesan. 2021. Sentiment analysis in Tamil texts using k-means and k-nearest neighbour. In *2021 10th International Conference on Information and Automation for Sustainability (ICIAfS)*, pages 48–53.

Konthala Yasaswini, Karthik Puranik, Adeep Hande, Ruba Priyadharshini, Sajeetha Thavareesan, and Bharathi Raja Chakravarthi. 2021. IIITT@DravidianLangTech-EACL2021: Transfer learning for offensive language detection in Dravidian languages. In *Proceedings of the First Workshop on Speech and Language Technologies for Dravidian Languages*, pages 187–194, Kyiv. Association for Computational Linguistics.

PICT@DravidianLangTech-ACL2022: Neural Machine Translation On Dravidian Languages

Aditya Vyawahare *
aditya.vyawahare07@gmail.com

Rahul Tangsali *
rahuul2001@gmail.com

Aditya Mandke †
adeetya.m@gmail.com

Onkar Litake †
onkarlitake@ieee.org

Dipali Kadam ‡
ddkadam@pict.edu

Pune Institute of Computer Technology, India

Abstract

This paper presents a summary of the findings that we obtained based on the shared task on machine translation of Dravidian languages. We stood first in three of the five sub-tasks which were assigned to us for the main shared task. We carried out neural machine translation for the following five language pairs: Kannada to Tamil, Kannada to Telugu, Kannada to Malayalam, Kannada to Sanskrit, and Kannada to Tulu. The datasets for each of the five language pairs were used to train various translation models, including Seq2Seq models such as LSTM, bidirectional LSTM, Conv2Seq, and training state-of-the-art as transformers from scratch, and fine-tuning already pre-trained models. For some models involving monolingual corpora, we implemented backtranslation as well. These models' accuracy was later tested with a part of the same dataset using BLEU score as an evaluation metric.

1 Introduction

Often, it becomes a challenge to develop a robust bilingual machine translation system, and that too with limited resources at hand (Dong et al., 2015). Moreover, for low-resource languages, such as the Dravidian family of languages, achieving high accuracy of translations remains a concern (Chakravarthi et al., 2021). This paper presents the development of machine translation systems for Kannada to other Dravidian languages such as Tamil, Telugu, Malayalam, Tulu, and Sanskrit.

Tamil is a Dravidian classical language used by the Tamil people of South Asia. Tamil is an official language of Tamil Nadu, Sri Lanka, Singapore, and the Union Territory of Puducherry in India (Subalalitha, 2019; Srinivasan and Subalalitha, 2019; Narasimhan et al., 2018). Significant minority speak Tamil in the four other South Indian states of Kerala, Karnataka, Andhra Pradesh, and Telangana, as well as the Union Territory of the Andaman and Nicobar Islands. It is also spoken by the Tamil diaspora, which may be found in Malaysia, Myanmar, South Africa, the United Kingdom, the United States, Canada, Australia, and Mauritius. Tamil is also the native language of Sri Lankan Moors (Sakuntharaj and Mahesan, 2021, 2017, 2016; Thavareesan and Mahesan, 2019, 2020a,b, 2021). Tamil, one of the 22 scheduled languages in the Indian Constitution, was the first to be designated as a classical language of India (Anita and Subalalitha, 2019b,a; Subalalitha and Poovammal, 2018). Malayalam is Tamil's closest significant cousin; the two began splitting during the 13th century AD. Although several variations between Tamil and Malayalam indicate a pre-historic break of the western dialect, the process of separating into a different language, Malayalam, did not occur until the 15th or 17th century (Chakravarthi, 2020; Chakravarthi and Muralidaran, 2021).

One of the approaches implemented consisted of training conventional machine translation models which involved sequence to sequence learning (Seq2Seq) (Sutskever et al., 2014). Seq2Seq is an encoder-decoder approach, in which the encoder reads the input sequence, one word at a time to produce a hidden vector. The decoder produces the output sequence from the vector received from the encoder. We used LSTMs (Hochreiter and Schmidhuber, 1997), Bidirectional LSTMs (BiLSTM) (Clark et al., 2018) which learns bidirectional long-term dependencies between time steps of time series or sequence data, and convolutional Seq2Seq learning (Conv2Seq) (Gehring et al., 2017) which uses multiple stacked layers of CNNs to learn long term dependencies with lower time complexity. The second approach involved training the transformer model (Vaswani et al., 2017) from scratch using the Fairseq library (Ott et al., 2019). We also imple-

* equal contribution
† equal contribution
‡ equal contribution

Proceedings of the Second Workshop on Speech and Language Technologies for Dravidian Languages, pages 177 - 183
May 26, 2022 ©2022 Association for Computational Linguistics

Parallel	kn-ml	kn-ta	kn-te	kn-tu	kn-sn
Official	90,974	88,813	88,503	9,470	8,300
Monolingual	**ml**	**ta**	**te**	**te**	**te**
IndicCorp	80,000	80,000	80,000	-	-

Table 1: Statistics of the dataset used for training

mented the approach of fine-tuning the open-source translation model provided by AI4Bharat on multilingual data for Indic languages.

We also fine-tuned their translation models for monolingual data, and then applied back-translation (Edunov et al., 2018; Sennrich et al., 2016a). Back-translation helps avoid the problems caused by the shortage of data for low-resource languages. It is a typical method of data augmentation that can enrich training data with monolingual data. For the ACL 2022 shared task on machine translation in Dravidian languages, we had to submit our results on the five Indic-Indic language pairs: Kannada-Tamil, Kannada-Telugu, Kannada-Malayalam, Kannada-Tulu, and Kannada-Sanskrit. We have experimented and compared the results of the aforementioned models. The datasets were provided by DravidianLangTech. We have used the BLEU (Papineni et al., 2002) evaluation metric for computing accuracy.

2 Dataset Description

The bilingual dataset provided by the organizers (Madasamy et al., 2022) was divided into three sub-corporas of train, dev and test. The statistics of the training data is given in Table 1. The dev and test data provided also had the same trend with 2,000 sentence pairs each for Kannada-Malayalam, Kannada-Tamil and Kannada-Telugu whereas Kannada-Sanskrit and Kannada-Tulu had 1,000 sentence pairs each test and dev.

To further improve the accuracy of the translations we used back-translation. The monolingual data used for back-translation was taken from indicCorp (Kakwani et al., 2020) (a large publicly-available corpora for Indian languages created by AI4Bharat from scraping through news, magazines, and books over the web). Monolingual data used was 80,000 each for Malayalam, Tamil and Telugu. We chose 80,000 sentences according to the memory limitations of our GPU. We didn't perform backtranslation on Tulu and Sanskrit as we couldn't find good monolingual data for those languages.

From the monolingual data taken we generate pseudo-parallel data. Using the official and the pseudo-parallel data we train models to provide translations from Kannada to the given Indic languages.

3 Data Preparation

In data preprocessing, the sentences present in the given dataset contain punctuations, synonyms, misspelled words, numbers, etc., and they have to be cleaned before we pass it to the model.

For the sentences of Kannada, Malayalam, Tamil and Telugu languages, we used the preprocessing given by indicNLP library [1] , which contains preprocessing for various Indian languages. We normalize (helpful in reducing the number of unique tokens present in the text) and then pre-tokenize (for splitting the text object into smaller tokens for better model training) (Harish and Rangan, 2020) the input given followed by transliterating all the indic data written in their own corresponding scripture to Devanagari scripture, along with applying Byte-Pair Encoding (BPE) (Sennrich et al., 2016b). Finally we pass the data to fairseq-preprocess to binarize training data and build vocabularies from the text of that particular language.

For Seq2Seq models such as LSTM and BiLSTM, we took a smaller portion of the dataset, and split it into training data of corpora size 4000, and dev and test datasets of size 1000 for each language pair. For training the Seq2Seq models as well as for training simple transformers from scratch, we used the Sacremoses tokenization [2], where Sacremoses is a pre-installed dependency in the Fairseq toolkit.

4 System Description

4.1 For Kannada to Malayalam, Tamil, Telugu

In the first system, we download the Indic-Indic model for multilingual neural machine translation given by indicTrans [3] which was trained on the

[1] https://github.com/anoopkunchukuttan/indic_nlp_library
[2] https://github.com/alvations/sacremoses
[3] https://indicnlp.ai4bharat.org/indic-trans/

System	kn-ml	kn-ta	kn-te	kn-tu	kn-sn
LSTM	**0.3531**	0.3537	0.4292	0.5535	**0.8085**
BiLSTM	0.3352	0.3636	**0.4477**	0.4200	0.8059
Conv2Seq	0.0233	0.0303	0.0701	0.3975	0.4400
Transformer From Scratch	0.3431	0.3496	0.4272	**0.8123**	0.5551
Pretrained Model	0.3241	**0.3778**	0.4068	NR	NR
Finetuned+Backtranslation	0.2963	0.3536	0.3687	NR	NR

Table 2: The scores mentioned are the BLEU scores on test data passed. NR represents 'Not Recorded' as the pretrained model did not support translations for those languages. Also, for the LSTM, BiLSTM, and transformer models which were trained from scratch, we used a different test dataset, which was other than the one provided by DravidianLangTech. Results in a similar range would be obtained for the test dataset provided by DravidianLangTech. Highest score achieved for each language pair is marked in bold.

Samanantar dataset (Ramesh et al., 2022). We then generate the pseudo-translations for monolingual data using the same pre-trained transformer_4x multilingual model. Finally, we train the official data and the pseudo-parallel data generated using back-translation to give the translation for the given languages.

The second system which we used was a convolutional neural network (CNN) trained using using the 'fconv' architecture provided by the open-source toolkit fairseq.py. Other Seq2Seq architectures for machine translation included LSTM and BiLSTM, wherein LSTM we construct a standard encoder-decoder LSTM architecture, which is provided in the open-source toolkit fairseq.py

Whereas for BiLSTM we use the same 'lstm' architecture provided, with the only change of making the original encoder parameter as bidirectional. We also trained standard transformer models from scratch, again by using the Fairseq library [4]. Fairseq provides a standard transformer architecture which can be further used for training custom transformer models for machine translation.

4.2 For Kannada to Tulu, Sanskrit

In the case of low-resource languages such as Tulu and Sanskrit, there wasn't any support available for multilingual models to be trained on such languages, especially the transformer_4x model, which is a multilingual NMT model by AI4Bharat, trained on the Samanantar dataset (Ramesh et al., 2022). Hence, we were unable to finetune the transformer_4x model and train the multilingual models for these languages as shown in the Table 2 given as Not Recorded (NR). Seq2Seq models (LSTM, BiLSTM, CNN), and transformer models from scratch were trained. The aformentioned models were trained using the Fairseq toolkit.

[4]https://github.com/pytorch/fairseq

5 Experiments

5.1 Training Details

For training the models we used the fairseq, a sequence model toolkit written in Pytorch (Paszke et al., 2019) developed by Facebook Artificial Intelligence Research (FAIR) team.

We used the custom transformer transformer_4x provided by AI4Bharat and finetuned it on the sum of our official data and pseudo parallel corpora generated. This model was trained with a max-tokens parameter of 1568 and a learning rate of 0.00003 with a label smoothing (Szegedy et al., 2016) of 0.1. For evaluation, we take the best checkpoint from all the checkpoints saved. BLEU was used as the best checkpoint metric and then translations generated were recorded.

We also trained transformer models from scratch which had the architecture consisted of 3 layers each of the encoder and decoder, thus having six stacked layers in the transformer model, The layer size taken was 256 and 3 heads in each attention layer, and the feed forward size for both encoder and decoder was taken to be 512. Each of these transformer models was trained for 10 epochs. The batch size specified during training of these transformer models was 128. Dropout (Srivastava et al., 2014) specified during training was 0.1 . Optimizer used was the Adam optimizer (Kingma and Ba, 2014), and a learning rate of 0.0005. The models were trained on 10 epochs each for every language pair. Using fairseq-generate, we were able to get the BLEU score, which was obtained by comparison between the translated sentences by the model from the source language, with the corresponding target language translations.

For encoder-decoder models involving Seq2Seq learning such as LSTM, BiLSTM and Conv2Seq (using CNNs), we again used the Fairseq toolkit for translation. (reference to the documentation [5]). The LSTM and BiLSTM architectures consisted of a dropout (Srivastava et al., 2014) of 0.2, a learning rate of 0.005, and lr-shrink parameter set to 0.5. Maximum number of tokens in a batch were set to 12000. In case of BiLSTM architectures, the encoder-decoder architecture was made bidirectional. The LSTM and BiLSTM were trained for 25 epochs each. In the case of Conv2Seq, we trained the models for 20 epochs each.

All the above mentioned hyperparameters were giving the best possible results, and hence we proceeded with the use of the same. We finetuned the basic configurations specified in the Fairseq documentation. [6]

5.2 Evaluation Metrics

Average sentence BLEU score was used as the evaluation metric. To calculate the BLEU we calculated the score for every sentence and then we averaged the score for the whole corpora of sentences. The BLEU scores were calculated using the sentence_bleu function given by the translate package [7] in NLTK library (Loper and Bird, 2002) with equal weights set to 0.25 for all 4 grams with equal contribution of all 4 grams in the final score. The BLEU scores recorded in Table 2 and Table 4 is scored out of 1. where, closer to 1 means more similarity.

6 Results

Language	Translations
kn	ಶೈಕ್ಷಣಿಕ ಅರ್ಹತೆ
ml	വിദ്യാഭ്യാസ യോഗ്യതകൾ
ta	கல்வித் தகுதி
te	అర్హతలు
tu	ಶೈಕ್ಷಣಿಕ ವಿದ್ಯಾರ್ಹತೆ
sn	टीकाकारः दक्षता
en	educational qualifications

Table 3: Sample translations taken from the test dataset

For the results, please refer to Table 2. The table contains the BLEU scores for the models on which the test data of the language pairs are tested. For the submission of the translations for the language pairs, we used transformer_4x model from AI4Bharat to obtain the translations from Kannada to Tamil, Telugu, and Malayalam. Whereas for the translations from Kannada to Tulu and Sanskrit, transformer models were built from scratch. Results are according to the NLTK BLEU evaluation metric. (After our submission for the workshop task, we explored other models and were getting much better results for the same. You could see those results in the Table 2)

7 Competition Results

kn-ml	kn-ta	kn-te	kn-tu	kn-sn
0.2963	0.3536	0.3687	0.0054	0.035

Table 4: BLEU scores of the translations submitted to the Machine Translation in Dravidian Languages-ACL2022 shared task

We obtained rank 1 for translations from Kannada to Malayalam, Kannada to Telugu and Kannada to Tamil. For translations from Kannada to Sanskrit and for Kannada to Tulu translations we stood 3rd and 4th respectively (We had initially sent the wrong results for kn-sn and kn-tu for the workshop task submission, hence the low scores were obtained for the same). Results of test sets on the shared task is given in Table 4.

8 Related Work

The domain of neural machine translation tasks has been among the interest topics for many researchers. The first machine translation model using deep neural networks was proposed by Kalchbrenner and Blunsom (Kalchbrenner and Blunsom, 2013) . NMT has since been widely studied across the scientific community.

In encoder-decoder mechanisms, the words are converted into word embeddings in the encoder, which are then passed to the decoder which uses an attention mechanism, encoder representations, and previous words to generate the next word in the translation. The encoder and decoder can be deep neural networks such as RNN (Bahdanau et al., 2014), CNN (Gehring et al., 2017), or feed-forward neural networks (Vaswani et al., 2017). Further, there were self-attention models proposed such as

[5]https://fairseq.readthedocs.io/en/latest/

[6]https://fairseq.readthedocs.io/en/latest/index.html

[7]https://www.nltk.org/api/nltk.translate.html

transformers which aided to further research in NMT. A notable research related to the efficiency of the same was presented at the proceedings of the 7th Workshop on Asian Translation in 2020 (Dabre and Chakrabarty, 2020). Other related works include those presented at previous ACL conferences in 2019 (Sennrich and Zhang, 2019) and 2020 (Araabi and Monz, 2020).

Pertaining to research in machine translation in Dravidian languages, Xie (Xie, 2021) was able to achieve BLEU scores of 38.86, 36.66, and 19.84 for English-Telugu, English-Tamil, and English-Malayalam using multilingual translation and back-translation. (Koneru et al., 2021) worked on implementing a translation system for English to Kannada by limited use of supplementary data between English and other Dravidian languages. Other works include CVIT's submissions to WAT-2019 (Philip et al., 2019), a transformer-based multilingual Indic-English NMT system (Sen et al., 2018), comparison of different orthographies for machine translation of under-resourced Dravidian languages (Chakravarthi et al., 2019), etc.

9 Conclusion

Thus, we implemented neural machine translation systems for Dravidian languages. We utilized different architectures for the same, and analyzed their performance. In future, we plan to train our models with large-scale GPUs. We plan to apply other tokenization methods for the language corpora as well for better training. Also, we plan to train our models with expanded corpora for better results.

References

R Anita and CN Subalalitha. 2019a. An approach to cluster Tamil literatures using discourse connectives. In *2019 IEEE 1st International Conference on Energy, Systems and Information Processing (ICESIP)*, pages 1–4. IEEE.

R Anita and CN Subalalitha. 2019b. Building discourse parser for Thirukkural. In *Proceedings of the 16th International Conference on Natural Language Processing*, pages 18–25.

Ali Araabi and Christof Monz. 2020. Optimizing transformer for low-resource neural machine translation. In *Proceedings of the 28th International Conference on Computational Linguistics*, pages 3429–3435, Barcelona, Spain (Online). International Committee on Computational Linguistics.

Dzmitry Bahdanau, Kyunghyun Cho, and Y. Bengio. 2014. Neural machine translation by jointly learning to align and translate. *ArXiv*, 1409.

Bharathi Raja Chakravarthi. 2020. HopeEDI: A multilingual hope speech detection dataset for equality, diversity, and inclusion. In *Proceedings of the Third Workshop on Computational Modeling of People's Opinions, Personality, and Emotion's in Social Media*, pages 41–53, Barcelona, Spain (Online). Association for Computational Linguistics.

Bharathi Raja Chakravarthi, Mihael Arcan, and John P. McCrae. 2019. Comparison of different orthographies for machine translation of under-resourced dravidian languages. In *LDK*.

Bharathi Raja Chakravarthi and Vigneshwaran Muralidaran. 2021. Findings of the shared task on hope speech detection for equality, diversity, and inclusion. In *Proceedings of the First Workshop on Language Technology for Equality, Diversity and Inclusion*, pages 61–72, Kyiv. Association for Computational Linguistics.

Bharathi Raja Chakravarthi, Priya Rani, Mihael Arcan, and John P McCrae. 2021. A survey of orthographic information in machine translation. *SN Computer Science*, 2(4):1–19.

Kevin Clark, Minh-Thang Luong, Christopher D. Manning, and Quoc Le. 2018. Semi-supervised sequence modeling with cross-view training. In *Proceedings of the 2018 Conference on Empirical Methods in Natural Language Processing*, pages 1914–1925, Brussels, Belgium. Association for Computational Linguistics.

Raj Dabre and Abhisek Chakrabarty. 2020. NICT's submission to WAT 2020: How effective are simple many-to-many neural machine translation models? In *Proceedings of the 7th Workshop on Asian Translation*, pages 98–102, Suzhou, China. Association for Computational Linguistics.

Daxiang Dong, Hua Wu, Wei He, Dianhai Yu, and Haifeng Wang. 2015. Multi-task learning for multiple language translation. In *Proceedings of the 53rd Annual Meeting of the Association for Computational Linguistics and the 7th International Joint Conference on Natural Language Processing (Volume 1: Long Papers)*, pages 1723–1732, Beijing, China. Association for Computational Linguistics.

Sergey Edunov, Myle Ott, Michael Auli, and David Grangier. 2018. Understanding back-translation at scale. In *Proceedings of the 2018 Conference on Empirical Methods in Natural Language Processing*, pages 489–500, Brussels, Belgium. Association for Computational Linguistics.

Jonas Gehring, Michael Auli, David Grangier, Denis Yarats, and Yann N. Dauphin. 2017. Convolutional sequence to sequence learning. *CoRR*, abs/1705.03122.

B S Harish and R Kasturi Rangan. 2020. A comprehensive survey on indian regional language processing. *SN Applied Sciences*, 2.

Sepp Hochreiter and Jürgen Schmidhuber. 1997. Long short-term memory. *Neural computation*, 9:1735–80.

Divyanshu Kakwani, Anoop Kunchukuttan, Satish Golla, Gokul N.C., Avik Bhattacharyya, Mitesh M. Khapra, and Pratyush Kumar. 2020. IndicNLPSuite: Monolingual corpora, evaluation benchmarks and pre-trained multilingual language models for Indian languages. In *Findings of the Association for Computational Linguistics: EMNLP 2020*, pages 4948–4961, Online. Association for Computational Linguistics.

Nal Kalchbrenner and Phil Blunsom. 2013. Recurrent continuous translation models. In *Proceedings of the 2013 Conference on Empirical Methods in Natural Language Processing*, pages 1700–1709.

Diederik Kingma and Jimmy Ba. 2014. Adam: A method for stochastic optimization. *International Conference on Learning Representations.*

Sai Koneru, Danni Liu, and Jan Niehues. 2021. Unsupervised machine translation on dravidian languages. In *Proceedings of the First Workshop on Speech and Language Technologies for Dravidian Languages*, pages 55–64. Association for Computational Linguistics. The First Workshop on Speech and Language Technologies for Dravidian Languages, DravidianLangTech-2021 ; Conference date: 20-04-2021 Through 20-04-2021.

Edward Loper and Steven Bird. 2002. Nltk: The natural language toolkit. In *Proceedings of the ACL-02 Workshop on Effective Tools and Methodologies for Teaching Natural Language Processing and Computational Linguistics - Volume 1*, ETMTNLP '02, page 63–70, USA. Association for Computational Linguistics.

Anand Kumar Madasamy, Asha Hegde, Shubhanker Banerjee, Bharathi Raja Chakravarthi, Ruba Priyadarshini, Shashirekha Hosahalli Lakshmaiah, and John Philip McCrae. 2022. Findings of the shared task on Machine Translation in Dravidian languages. In *Proceedings of the Second Workshop on Speech and Language Technologies for Dravidian Languages*. Association for Computational Linguistics.

Anitha Narasimhan, Aarthy Anandan, Madhan Karky, and CN Subalalitha. 2018. Porul: Option generation and selection and scoring algorithms for a tamil flash card game. *International Journal of Cognitive and Language Sciences*, 12(2):225–228.

Myle Ott, Sergey Edunov, Alexei Baevski, Angela Fan, Sam Gross, Nathan Ng, David Grangier, and Michael Auli. 2019. fairseq: A fast, extensible toolkit for sequence modeling. In *Proceedings of the 2019 Conference of the North American Chapter of the Association for Computational Linguistics (Demonstrations)*, pages 48–53, Minneapolis, Minnesota. Association for Computational Linguistics.

Kishore Papineni, Salim Roukos, Todd Ward, and Wei-Jing Zhu. 2002. Bleu: a method for automatic evaluation of machine translation. In *Proceedings of the 40th Annual Meeting of the Association for Computational Linguistics*, pages 311–318, Philadelphia, Pennsylvania, USA. Association for Computational Linguistics.

Adam Paszke, Sam Gross, Francisco Massa, Adam Lerer, James Bradbury, Gregory Chanan, Trevor Killeen, Zeming Lin, Natalia Gimelshein, Luca Antiga, Alban Desmaison, Andreas Kopf, Edward Yang, Zachary DeVito, Martin Raison, Alykhan Tejani, Sasank Chilamkurthy, Benoit Steiner, Lu Fang, Junjie Bai, and Soumith Chintala. 2019. Pytorch: An imperative style, high-performance deep learning library. In H. Wallach, H. Larochelle, A. Beygelzimer, F. d'Alché-Buc, E. Fox, and R. Garnett, editors, *Advances in Neural Information Processing Systems 32*, pages 8024–8035. Curran Associates, Inc.

Jerin Philip, Shashank Siripragada, Upendra Kumar, Vinay Namboodiri, and C V Jawahar. 2019. CVIT's submissions to WAT-2019. In *Proceedings of the 6th Workshop on Asian Translation*, pages 131–136, Hong Kong, China. Association for Computational Linguistics.

Gowtham Ramesh, Sumanth Doddapaneni, Aravinth Bheemaraj, Mayank Jobanputra, Raghavan AK, Ajitesh Sharma, Sujit Sahoo, Harshita Diddee, Mahalakshmi J, Divyanshu Kakwani, Navneet Kumar, Aswin Pradeep, Srihari Nagaraj, Kumar Deepak, Vivek Raghavan, Anoop Kunchukuttan, Pratyush Kumar, and Mitesh Shantadevi Khapra. 2022. Samanantar: The Largest Publicly Available Parallel Corpora Collection for 11 Indic Languages. *Transactions of the Association for Computational Linguistics*, 10:145–162.

Ratnasingam Sakuntharaj and Sinnathamby Mahesan. 2016. A novel hybrid approach to detect and correct spelling in Tamil text. In *2016 IEEE International Conference on Information and Automation for Sustainability (ICIAfS)*, pages 1–6.

Ratnasingam Sakuntharaj and Sinnathamby Mahesan. 2017. Use of a novel hash-table for speeding-up suggestions for misspelt Tamil words. In *2017 IEEE International Conference on Industrial and Information Systems (ICIIS)*, pages 1–5.

Ratnasingam Sakuntharaj and Sinnathamby Mahesan. 2021. Missing word detection and correction based on context of Tamil sentences using n-grams. In *2021 10th International Conference on Information and Automation for Sustainability (ICIAfS)*, pages 42–47.

Sukanta Sen, Kamal Kumar Gupta, Asif Ekbal, and Pushpak Bhattacharyya. 2018. IITP-MT at WAT2018: Transformer-based multilingual indic-English neural machine translation system. In *Proceedings of the 32nd Pacific Asia Conference on Language, Information and Computation: 5th Workshop on Asian Translation: 5th Workshop on Asian Translation*, Hong Kong. Association for Computational Linguistics.

Rico Sennrich, Barry Haddow, and Alexandra Birch. 2016a. Improving neural machine translation models with monolingual data. In *Proceedings of the 54th Annual Meeting of the Association for Computational Linguistics (Volume 1: Long Papers)*, pages 86–96, Berlin, Germany. Association for Computational Linguistics.

Rico Sennrich, Barry Haddow, and Alexandra Birch. 2016b. Neural machine translation of rare words with subword units. In *Proceedings of the 54th Annual Meeting of the Association for Computational Linguistics (Volume 1: Long Papers)*, pages 1715–1725, Berlin, Germany. Association for Computational Linguistics.

Rico Sennrich and Biao Zhang. 2019. Revisiting low-resource neural machine translation: A case study. In *Proceedings of the 57th Annual Meeting of the Association for Computational Linguistics*, pages 211–221, Florence, Italy. Association for Computational Linguistics.

R Srinivasan and CN Subalalitha. 2019. Automated named entity recognition from tamil documents. In *2019 IEEE 1st International Conference on Energy, Systems and Information Processing (ICESIP)*, pages 1–5. IEEE.

Nitish Srivastava, Geoffrey Hinton, Alex Krizhevsky, Ilya Sutskever, and Ruslan Salakhutdinov. 2014. Dropout: A simple way to prevent neural networks from overfitting. *Journal of Machine Learning Research*, 15(56):1929–1958.

C. N. Subalalitha. 2019. Information extraction framework for Kurunthogai. *Sādhanā*, 44(7):156.

CN Subalalitha and E Poovammal. 2018. Automatic bilingual dictionary construction for Tirukural. *Applied Artificial Intelligence*, 32(6):558–567.

Ilya Sutskever, Oriol Vinyals, and Quoc V. Le. 2014. Sequence to sequence learning with neural networks. In *Proceedings of the 27th International Conference on Neural Information Processing Systems - Volume 2*, NIPS'14, page 3104–3112, Cambridge, MA, USA. MIT Press.

Christian Szegedy, Vincent Vanhoucke, Sergey Ioffe, Jon Shlens, and Zbigniew Wojna. 2016. Rethinking the inception architecture for computer vision. In *2016 IEEE Conference on Computer Vision and Pattern Recognition (CVPR)*, pages 2818–2826.

Sajeetha Thavareesan and Sinnathamby Mahesan. 2019. Sentiment analysis in Tamil texts: A study on machine learning techniques and feature representation. In *2019 14th Conference on Industrial and Information Systems (ICIIS)*, pages 320–325.

Sajeetha Thavareesan and Sinnathamby Mahesan. 2020a. Sentiment lexicon expansion using Word2vec and fastText for sentiment prediction in Tamil texts. In *2020 Moratuwa Engineering Research Conference (MERCon)*, pages 272–276.

Sajeetha Thavareesan and Sinnathamby Mahesan. 2020b. Word embedding-based part of speech tagging in Tamil texts. In *2020 IEEE 15th International Conference on Industrial and Information Systems (ICIIS)*, pages 478–482.

Sajeetha Thavareesan and Sinnathamby Mahesan. 2021. Sentiment analysis in Tamil texts using k-means and k-nearest neighbour. In *2021 10th International Conference on Information and Automation for Sustainability (ICIAfS)*, pages 48–53.

Ashish Vaswani, Noam Shazeer, Niki Parmar, Jakob Uszkoreit, Llion Jones, Aidan N Gomez, Ł ukasz Kaiser, and Illia Polosukhin. 2017. Attention is all you need. In *Advances in Neural Information Processing Systems*, volume 30. Curran Associates, Inc.

Wanying Xie. 2021. GX@DravidianLangTech-EACL2021: Multilingual neural machine translation and back-translation. In *Proceedings of the First Workshop on Speech and Language Technologies for Dravidian Languages*, pages 146–153, Kyiv. Association for Computational Linguistics.

Sentiment Analysis on Code-Switched Dravidian Languages with Kernel Based Extreme Learning Machines

Mithun Kumar S R Uber R&D India, Bangalore
Lov Kumar BITS Pilani, Hyderabad
Aruna Malapati BITS Pilani, Hyderabad
mithunkumar.sr@uber.com, (lovkumar, arunam)@hyderabad.bits-pilani.ac.in

Abstract

Code-switching refers to the textual or spoken data containing multiple languages. Application of natural language processing (NLP) tasks like sentiment analysis is a harder problem on code-switched languages due to the irregularities in the sentence structuring and ordering. This paper shows the experiment results of building a Kernel based Extreme Learning Machines(ELM) for sentiment analysis for code-switched Dravidian languages with English. Our results show that ELM performs better than traditional machine learning classifiers on various metrics as well as trains faster than deep learning models. We also show that Polynomial kernels perform better than others in the ELM architecture. We were able to achieve a median AUC of 0.79 with a polynomial kernel.

1 Introduction

Because of the expansion of user-generated material, it is now possible to automatically detect linked attitudes. A "sentiment" is a good or negative opinion, emotion, feeling, or thinking conveyed by a sentiment bearer (user). In general, sentiment analysis attempts to extract certain sentiments from text automatically (Sakuntharaj and Mahesan, 2021, 2017, 2016; Thavareesan and Mahesan, 2019, 2020a,b, 2021). Sentiment analysis seeks to analyse textual patterns in order to find a sentiment at the word, phrase, or document level. Sentiment analysis is widely used in a variety of sectors today, including public-health monitoring, electoral patterns, predicting terrorist actions, and social network analysis (Sampath et al., 2022; Ravikiran et al., 2022).

Dravidian languages, Tamil, Kannada and Malayalam are widely spoken by over 250 million people, but still is a a sparse language for NLP tasks (Chakravarthi et al., 2021, 2022; Bharathi et al., 2022; Priyadharshini et al., 2022). Dravidian languages are a spoken mostly in southern India, north-east Sri Lanka, and south-west Pakistan (Anita and Subalalitha, 2019b,a; Subalalitha and Poovammal, 2018). There have been tiny but important immigrant groups in Mauritius, Myanmar, Singapore, Malaysia, Indonesia, the Philippines, the United Kingdom, Australia, France, Canada, Germany, South Africa, and the United States since the colonial era (Subalalitha, 2019; Srinivasan and Subalalitha, 2019; Narasimhan et al., 2018). Tamil is a member of the southern branch of the Dravidian languages, a group of about 26 languages indigenous to the Indian subcontinent. It is also classed as a member of the Tamil language family, which contains the languages of around 35 ethnolinguistic groups, including the Irula and Yerukula languages.

The influence of English in the regions where these languages are spoken is higher due to the colonial history and the medium of schooling (Priyadharshini et al., 2021; Kumaresan et al., 2021). However the ease of expression of sentiments switches between the words in the Dravidian language and English with most of the bilinguists versatile in both, especially on online social platforms (Chakravarthi, 2020; Chakravarthi and Muralidaran, 2021). The sentiment analysis of text written in code-switched language between the Dravidian languages and English is analysed in this paper through a novel kernel based ELM.

,

2 Related work

Multi-class classification of text sentiment has been approached in both, traditional machine learning models as well as in deep learning models in the past. Chakravarthi et al. has previously shown the performance of traditional classifiers for Dravidian

Proceedings of the Second Workshop on Speech and Language Technologies for Dravidian Languages, pages 184 - 190
May 26, 2022 ©2022 Association for Computational Linguistics

Language	Positive	Negative	Mixed Feelings	Unknown State
Tamil	20,070	4,271	4,020	5,628
Malayalam	6,421	2,105	926	5,279
Kannada	2,823	1,188	574	711

Table 1: Data split between various classes.

languages. Kumar et al. (2021) showed that the performance metrics was the best with ensemble models in Dravidian language code-mixed dataset. Deep learning models like LSTM have been used by Yadav and Chakraborty (2020) for sentiment classification. However most of the pre-trained models like BERT takes as longer as 84 hours to train and there are optimisation efforts on reducing the time as experimented by You et al. (2020). One of the parallel optimisation technique on neural network is to use a single layer hidden layer which is explored in Extreme learning Machines (ELM) by Huang et al. (2004). There has been no work so far in exploring ELM on code-switched languages and hence this paper explores the possibility of using ELM for sentiment analysis. The following research questions (RQ) are explored through our experiments.

- **RQ1:** Will ELM be faster to train than deep-learning models and yield better results for sentiment analysis on code-switched languages?
- **RQ2:** Will sentiment analysis models perform better with dimensionality reduction, word embedding and data balancing techniques, which we hypothesise to be true.

3 Dataset

We conducted our experiments on the labelled data from the YouTube comments using three code-mixed benchmark datasets published for Dravidian languages. Kannada code-switched corpus, published by Hande et al. (2020) was our primary source. Similarly Tamil code-switched corpus, published by Chakravarthi et al. (2020b) was used. For Malayalam code-switched corpus, we used the data published by Chakravarthi et al. (2020a).

The multi-class dataset contains manually labelled sentiments for code-switched data. This dataset is an imbalanced one with a skew towards the labels containing 'Positive' sentiments. The split between various classes is shown in Table 1.

4 Experiment Setup

A multi-staged pipeline was setup for our experiments as depicted in Figure 1.

4.1 Data preprocessing

The raw corpus in code-switched languages were preprocessed with steps such as case conversion, removing stopwords and emoticons, lemmatizing to retain only the root form of the morpheme. Most of the preprocessing was done using NLTK[1]. Labels in the original dataset were 'Positive', 'Negative', 'Mixed Feelings', 'Unknown State' and 'Not in the target language'. Since we were using an explicit language identifier, langdetect[2], and primarily focusing on sentiment classification, we removed the data with the label 'Not in the target language' and retained the rest for our training.

4.2 Word embedding

Our focus during the experiment was to use a language specific word embedding technique. One such pre-trained word embedding model is provided by FastText[3] in multiple languages including Tamil, Kannada and Malayalam. Sentence vectorisation after the language identification was done using the pre-trained FastText word vectors in 300 dimensions on the preprocessed dataset.

4.3 Feature selection

The vectorised sentences along with the labels after the word embedding was either retained as-is, with all the features (All) or was subjected to dimensionality reduction using Principal Component Analysis (PCA). Two different datasets were created for each of the languages, one with All and the other constrained through PCA.

4.4 Data balancing techniques

Since the data is skewed, the vectorised dataset was then subjected to data balancing techniques. We wanted to study the effect of both, imbalanced as

[1]https://www.nltk.org/

[2]https://pypi.org/project/langdetect/

[3]https://fasttext.cc/docs/en/crawl-vectors.html

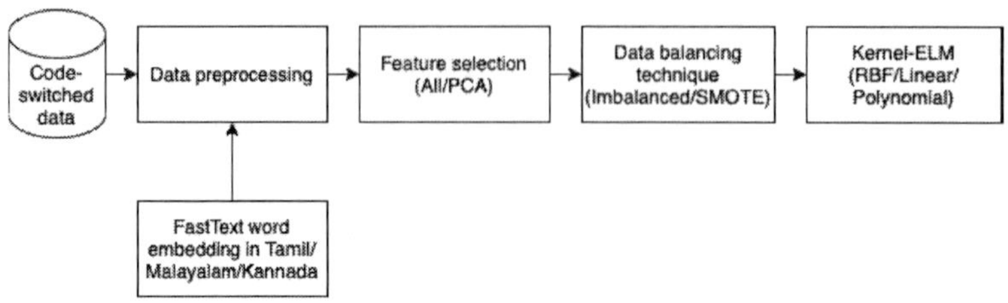

Figure 1: Pipeline of the experimental setup

well as the balanced data. Hence we created two other copies of the data. The first was to retain the data imbalance. The second was to overcome the class imbalance using an oversampling technique, Synthetic Minority Over-sampling TEchnique (SMOTE). This used synthetic minority class samples to build a dataset of equal number of samples in all classes. The dataset was then subjected to a split of training and test data. Data normalisation was done using a 5-fold cross validation on the dataset.

4.5 Kernel-ELMs

We setup a Extreme Learning Machine (ELM) through a single layer feed forward neural network with the same number of hidden layer nodes as the dimension of the sentence vectors in the dataset. The activation layer was through various kernels like Radial Basis Functions (RBF), Linear and Polynomial. Each set of data was trained and evaluated through the Kernel-based ELM. We also ensured that 98% of the variance in the data is present. The training time was around 60 minutes for most of the languages which was faster than deep learning model training time.

5 Observations and Analysis

The combination of features and data-balancing techniques from the pipeline was evaluated separately with each of the ELM kernels. Performance metrics like accuracy as well as the receiver operating characteristic (ROC) curve was determined for each of the dataset. We also measured the Area under the ROC curve (AUC) for each combination of the dataset as observed in Table 2.

5.1 Accuracy analysis

One of the major observations was that all the code-switched languages in combination with the features and data balancing techniques was yielding the best accuracy when all the features were selected instead of dimensionality constraining with techniques like PCA. Balancing techniques like SMOTE was worsening the accuracy instead of bettering it. This pattern is observed with all the language datasets irrespective of the Kernel chosen. Our hypothesis is that this might be due to the over-generalisation with the minority synthetic dataset which might be from the overlapping areas. Since there is larger and less specific decision boundary in SMOTE, there is also a possibility of augmenting noisy regions as also studied by Santos et al. (2018).

5.2 Kernel analysis

One of our research objectives was to analyse the various activation kernels. Linear kernels (LIN) generally perform good for text data. But in our experiments, we subjected the code-switched text data to higher dimension word embedding, where linear kernels did not perform better. This was validated through our experiments where a non-linear kernel like RBF or Polynomial (POLY) of degree 2 was always performing better than linear across the languages. However, between the RBF and Polynomial Kernels, it was a close contest between them, where the values were very similar. For instance, we achieved an accuracy of 0.67 for Malayalam imbalanced data with all features considered, in both RBF and Polynomial Kernels.

5.3 Boxplot analysis

We evaluated the median through the boxplot as in Figure 2 of both accuracy and AUC across the language-feature-data combination. We notice that Polynomial kernel compares better than both, linear as well as RBF kernels in AUC as well as Accuracy evaluation. The median accuracy is 0.63 with a Polynomial kernel compared to 0.55 with Linear and 0.62 with RBF kernels. AUC is also better with Polynomial kernels where it yields 0.79 at the median compared to 0.77 of RBF and 0.74 of linear kernels. Polynomial kernels are known to favor discrete data that has no natural notion of

Code-mixed with English	Features	Data	Acc RBF	Acc LIN	Acc POLY	AUC RBF	AUC LIN	AUC POLY
Tamil	All	Imbalanced	**0.67**	**0.67**	**0.68**	0.72	0.72	0.75
Tamil	PCA	Imbalanced	0.67	0.67	0.67	0.70	0.68	0.71
Tamil	All	SMOTE	0.56	0.51	0.57	**0.79**	**0.76**	**0.80**
Tamil	PCA	SMOTE	0.49	0.46	0.49	0.74	0.72	0.74
Mal	All	Imbalanced	**0.67**	**0.64**	**0.67**	0.76	0.74	0.81
Mal	PCA	Imbalanced	0.61	0.61	0.61	0.70	0.66	0.70
Mal	All	SMOTE	0.63	0.54	0.64	**0.84**	**0.78**	**0.85**
Mal	PCA	SMOTE	0.48	0.43	0.48	0.75	0.70	0.74
Kannada	All	Imbalanced	0.71	**0.59**	**0.70**	0.84	0.77	0.86
Kannada	PCA	Imbalanced	0.60	0.55	0.59	0.78	0.73	0.78
Kannada	All	SMOTE	**0.74**	0.53	0.69	**0.89**	**0.78**	**0.89**
Kannada	PCA	SMOTE	0.57	0.51	0.56	0.81	0.75	0.80

Table 2: Accuracy and AUC values through various kernels and data selection techniques (Best values in bold).

smoothness as studied by Smola et al. (1998).

5.4 Dimensionality reduction analysis

We hypothesised that dimensionality reduction techniques like PCA will better the performance of the model relative to selecting all the features. But across the kernels as well as languages, PCA performed worse by dropping the accuracy margin, than when selecting all the features. Our analysis is that in text embeddings like FastText, the higher the dimensions it better captures the context generally for each word in a 300x1 column vector. The embedding size can be reduced by constraining with techniques like PCA while training in the word vectors but higher dimensions are preferred. Hence, vital spatial information which is important for classification is lost and hence the accuracy degrades.

5.5 Data balancing analysis

While we also hypothesised that data balancing techniques like SMOTE might improve the model's performance, during the experiments we found that the AUC is the best when SMOTE is used along with all the features. This is evident across all the three code-switched languages. For instance, for the Kannada code-switched dataset, selecting all the features yield better results as seen in Figure 3 relative to using SMOTE as shown in Figure 4. We believe that the sentiment classifier achieves good performance on the positive class (high AUC) at the cost of a high false negatives rate (or a low number of true negative).

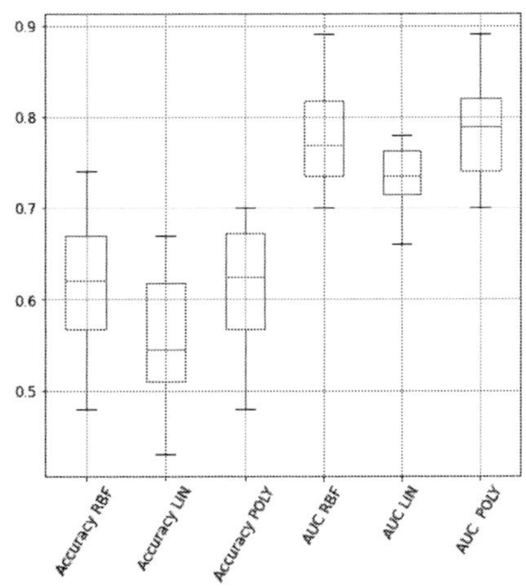

Figure 2: Boxplot of accuracy and AUC with various ELM Kernels

6 Conclusion

In this paper, various Kernel based ELMs like RBF, Linear and Polynomial have been experimented, along with combination of data constraining techniques like PCA and data balancing techniques like SMOTE for accuracy and AUC determination for code-switched languages. Our experimental results show that:

- ELM based techniques are faster to train relative to deep-learning models.
- Polynomial Kernels outperform Linear and RBF Kernels in ELMs across languages.
- SMOTE techniques with all the features favour better AUC in ELM models.

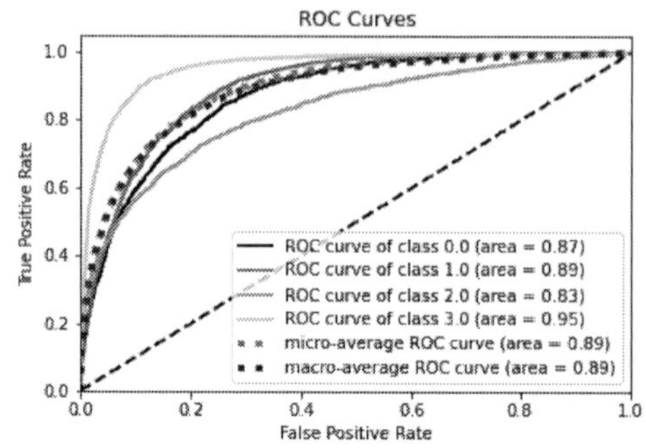

Figure 3: ROC curves of various classes for Kannada dataset with all the features in a Polynomial Kernel

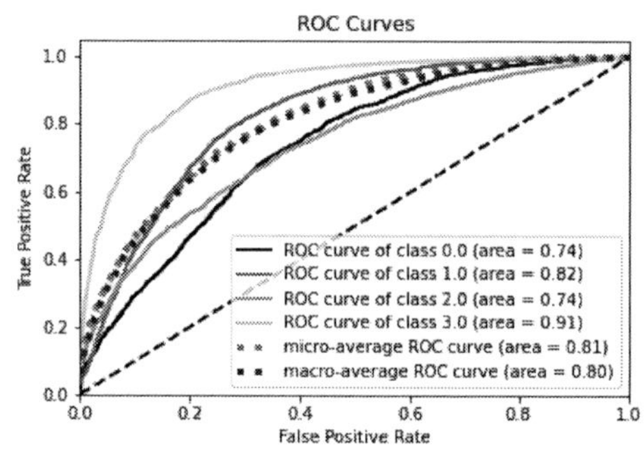

Figure 4: ROC curves of various classes for Kannada dataset constraining with PCA and SMOTE in a Polynomial Kernel

- ELM perform better in the chosen metrics relative to the traditional ensemble classifiers.

The next steps would be to improve on the word embedding and language identification on code-switched data for kernel based ELMs.

References

R Anita and CN Subalalitha. 2019a. An approach to cluster Tamil literatures using discourse connectives. In *2019 IEEE 1st International Conference on Energy, Systems and Information Processing (ICESIP)*, pages 1–4. IEEE.

R Anita and CN Subalalitha. 2019b. Building discourse parser for Thirukkural. In *Proceedings of the 16th International Conference on Natural Language Processing*, pages 18–25.

B Bharathi, Bharathi Raja Chakravarthi, Subalalitha Chinnaudayar Navaneethakrishnan, N Sripriya, Arunaggiri Pandian, and Swetha Valli. 2022. Findings of the shared task on Speech Recognition for Vulnerable Individuals in Tamil. In *Proceedings of the Second Workshop on Language Technology for Equality, Diversity and Inclusion*. Association for Computational Linguistics.

Bharathi Raja Chakravarthi. 2020. HopeEDI: A multilingual hope speech detection dataset for equality, diversity, and inclusion. In *Proceedings of the Third Workshop on Computational Modeling of People's Opinions, Personality, and Emotion's in Social Media*, pages 41–53, Barcelona, Spain (Online). Association for Computational Linguistics.

Bharathi Raja Chakravarthi, Navya Jose, Shardul Suryawanshi, Elizabeth Sherly, and John Philip McCrae. 2020a. A sentiment analysis dataset for code-mixed Malayalam-English. In *Proceedings of the 1st Joint Workshop on Spoken Language Technologies for Under-resourced languages (SLTU) and Collaboration and Computing for Under-Resourced Languages (CCURL)*, pages 177–184, Marseille, France. European Language Resources association.

Bharathi Raja Chakravarthi and Vigneshwaran Muralidaran. 2021. Findings of the shared task on hope speech detection for equality, diversity, and inclusion. In *Proceedings of the First Workshop on Language Technology for Equality, Diversity and Inclusion*, pages 61–72, Kyiv. Association for Computational Linguistics.

Bharathi Raja Chakravarthi, Vigneshwaran Muralidaran, Ruba Priyadharshini, and John Philip McCrae. 2020b. Corpus creation for sentiment analysis in code-mixed Tamil-English text. In *Proceedings of the 1st Joint Workshop on Spoken Language Technologies for Under-resourced languages (SLTU) and Collaboration and Computing for Under-Resourced Languages (CCURL)*, pages 202–210, Marseille, France. European Language Resources association.

Bharathi Raja Chakravarthi, Ruba Priyadharshini, Thenmozhi Durairaj, John Phillip McCrae, Paul Buitaleer, Prasanna Kumar Kumaresan, and Rahul Ponnusamy. 2022. Findings of the shared task on Homophobia Transphobia Detection in Social Media Comments. In *Proceedings of the Second Workshop on Language Technology for Equality, Diversity and Inclusion*. Association for Computational Linguistics.

Bharathi Raja Chakravarthi, Ruba Priyadharshini, Vigneshwaran Muralidaran, Navya Jose, Shardul Suryawanshi, Elizabeth Sherly, and John P McCrae. Dravidiancodemix: Sentiment analysis and offensive language identification dataset for dravidian languages in code-mixed text. *Language Resources and Evaluation*.

Bharathi Raja Chakravarthi, Ruba Priyadharshini, Rahul Ponnusamy, Prasanna Kumar Kumaresan, Kayalvizhi Sampath, Durairaj Thenmozhi, Sathiyaraj Thangasamy, Rajendran Nallathambi, and John Phillip McCrae. 2021. Dataset for identification of homophobia and transophobia in multilingual YouTube comments. *arXiv preprint arXiv:2109.00227*.

Adeep Hande, Ruba Priyadharshini, and Bharathi Raja Chakravarthi. 2020. KanCMD: Kannada CodeMixed dataset for sentiment analysis and offensive language detection. In *Proceedings of the Third Workshop on Computational Modeling of People's Opinions, Personality, and Emotion's in Social Media*, pages 54–63, Barcelona, Spain (Online). Association for Computational Linguistics.

Guang-Bin Huang, Qin-Yu Zhu, and Chee-Kheong Siew. 2004. Extreme learning machine: a new learning scheme of feedforward neural networks. In *2004 IEEE International Joint Conference on Neural Networks (IEEE Cat. No.04CH37541)*, volume 2, pages 985–990 vol.2.

S R Mithun Kumar, Nihal Reddy, Aruna Malapati, and Lov Kumar. 2021. An ensemble model for sentiment classification on code-mixed data in dravidian languages. *Forum for Information Retrieval Evaluation, FIRE 2021*.

Prasanna Kumar Kumaresan, Ratnasingam Sakuntharaj, Sajeetha Thavareesan, Subalalitha Navaneethakrishnan, Anand Kumar Madasamy, Bharathi Raja Chakravarthi, and John P McCrae. 2021. Findings of shared task on offensive language identification in Tamil and Malayalam. In *Forum for Information Retrieval Evaluation*, pages 16–18.

Anitha Narasimhan, Aarthy Anandan, Madhan Karky, and CN Subalalitha. 2018. Porul: Option generation and selection and scoring algorithms for a tamil flash card game. *International Journal of Cognitive and Language Sciences*, 12(2):225–228.

Ruba Priyadharshini, Bharathi Raja Chakravarthi, Subalalitha Chinnaudayar Navaneethakrishnan, Thenmozhi Durairaj, Malliga Subramanian, Kogilavani Shanmugavadivel, Siddhanth U Hegde, and Prasanna Kumar Kumaresan. 2022. Findings of the shared task on Abusive Comment Detection in Tamil. In *Proceedings of the Second Workshop on Speech and Language Technologies for Dravidian Languages*. Association for Computational Linguistics.

Ruba Priyadharshini, Bharathi Raja Chakravarthi, Sajeetha Thavareesan, Dhivya Chinnappa, Durairaj Thenmozhi, and Rahul Ponnusamy. 2021. Overview of the DravidianCodeMix 2021 shared task on sentiment detection in Tamil, Malayalam, and Kannada. In *Forum for Information Retrieval Evaluation*, pages 4–6.

Manikandan Ravikiran, Bharathi Raja Chakravarthi, Anand Kumar Madasamy, Sangeetha Sivanesan, Ratnavel Rajalakshmi, Sajeetha Thavareesan, Rahul Ponnusamy, and Shankar Mahadevan. 2022. Findings of the shared task on Offensive Span Identification in code-mixed Tamil-English comments. In *Proceedings of the Second Workshop on Speech and Language Technologies for Dravidian Languages*. Association for Computational Linguistics.

Ratnasingam Sakuntharaj and Sinnathamby Mahesan. 2016. A novel hybrid approach to detect and correct spelling in Tamil text. In *2016 IEEE International Conference on Information and Automation for Sustainability (ICIAfS)*, pages 1–6.

Ratnasingam Sakuntharaj and Sinnathamby Mahesan. 2017. Use of a novel hash-table for speeding-up suggestions for misspelt Tamil words. In *2017 IEEE International Conference on Industrial and Information Systems (ICIIS)*, pages 1–5.

Ratnasingam Sakuntharaj and Sinnathamby Mahesan. 2021. Missing word detection and correction based on context of Tamil sentences using n-grams. In *2021 10th International Conference on Information and Automation for Sustainability (ICIAfS)*, pages 42–47.

Anbukkarasi Sampath, Thenmozhi Durairaj, Bharathi Raja Chakravarthi, Ruba Priyadharshini, Subalalitha Chinnaudayar Navaneethakrishnan, Kogilavani Shanmugavadivel, Sajeetha Thavareesan, Sathiyaraj Thangasamy, Parameswari Krishnamurthy, Adeep Hande, Sean Benhur, Kishor Kumar Ponnusamy, and Santhiya Pandiyan. 2022. Findings of the shared task on Emotion Analysis in Tamil. In *Proceedings of the Second Workshop on Speech and Language Technologies for Dravidian Languages*. Association for Computational Linguistics.

Miriam Santos, Jastin Soares, Pedro Henriques Abreu, Helder Araujo, and Joao Santos. 2018. Cross-validation for imbalanced datasets: Avoiding overoptimistic and overfitting approaches. *IEEE Computational Intelligence Magazine*, 13:59–76.

Alex J. Smola, Bernhard Schölkopf, and Klaus-Robert Müller. 1998. The connection between regularization operators and support vector kernels. *Neural Netw.*, 11(4):637–649.

R Srinivasan and CN Subalalitha. 2019. Automated named entity recognition from tamil documents. In *2019 IEEE 1st International Conference on Energy, Systems and Information Processing (ICESIP)*, pages 1–5. IEEE.

C. N. Subalalitha. 2019. Information extraction framework for Kurunthogai. *Sādhanā*, 44(7):156.

CN Subalalitha and E Poovammal. 2018. Automatic bilingual dictionary construction for Tirukural. *Applied Artificial Intelligence*, 32(6):558–567.

Sajeetha Thavareesan and Sinnathamby Mahesan. 2019. Sentiment analysis in Tamil texts: A study on machine learning techniques and feature representation. In *2019 14th Conference on Industrial and Information Systems (ICIIS)*, pages 320–325.

Sajeetha Thavareesan and Sinnathamby Mahesan. 2020a. Sentiment lexicon expansion using Word2vec and fastText for sentiment prediction in Tamil texts. In *2020 Moratuwa Engineering Research Conference (MERCon)*, pages 272–276.

Sajeetha Thavareesan and Sinnathamby Mahesan. 2020b. Word embedding-based part of speech tagging in Tamil texts. In *2020 IEEE 15th International Conference on Industrial and Information Systems (ICIIS)*, pages 478–482.

Sajeetha Thavareesan and Sinnathamby Mahesan. 2021. Sentiment analysis in Tamil texts using k-means and k-nearest neighbour. In *2021 10th International Conference on Information and Automation for Sustainability (ICIAfS)*, pages 48–53.

Siddharth Yadav and Tanmoy Chakraborty. 2020. Unsupervised sentiment analysis for code-mixed data.

Yang You, Jing Li, Sashank Reddi, Jonathan Hseu, Sanjiv Kumar, Srinadh Bhojanapalli, Xiaodan Song, James Demmel, Kurt Keutzer, and Cho-Jui Hsieh. 2020. Large batch optimization for deep learning: Training bert in 76 minutes.

CUET-NLP@DravidianLangTech-ACL2022: Exploiting Textual Features to Classify Sentiment of Multimodal Movie Reviews

Nasehatul Mustakim[Ψ], **Nusratul Jannat**[Ψ], **Md. Maruf Hasan**[Ψ], **Eftekhar Hossain**[$], **Omar Sharif**[Ψ] and **Mohammed Moshiul Hoque**[Ψ]

[Ψ]Department of Computer Science and Engineering

[$]Department of Electronics and Telecommunication Engineering

[$Ψ]Chittagong University of Engineering & Technology, Chattogram-4349, Bangladesh

{u1604109, u1604115, u1604089}@student.cuet.ac.bd

{eftekhar.hossain, omar.sharif, moshiul_240}@cuet.ac.bd

Abstract

With the proliferation of internet usage, a massive growth of consumer-generated content on social media has been witnessed in recent years that provide people's opinions on diverse issues. Through social media, users can convey their emotions and thoughts in distinctive forms such as text, image, audio, video, and emoji, which leads to the advancement of the multimodality of the content users on social networking sites. This paper presents a technique for classifying multimodal sentiment using the text modality into five categories: highly positive, positive, neutral, negative, and highly negative. A shared task was organized to develop models that can identify the sentiments expressed by the videos of movie reviewers in both Malayalam and Tamil languages. This work applied several machine learning (LR, DT, MNB, SVM) and deep learning (BiLSTM, CNN+BiLSTM) techniques to accomplish the task. Results demonstrate that the proposed model with the decision tree (DT) outperformed the other methods and won the competition by acquiring the highest macro f_1-score of 0.24.

1 Introduction

Over the years, sentiment analysis has grown to an influential research domain with widespread commercial applications in the enterprise. To date, a significant number of applications have already been used for classifying or analyzing textual sentiment, including customer feedback (Pankaj et al., 2019; Hossain et al., 2021a), recommendation systems (Preethi et al., 2017), medicine analysis (Rajput, 2019), marketing, financial strategies (Jangid et al., 2018) and so on (Sampath et al., 2022; Ravikiran et al., 2022; Chakravarthi et al., 2022; Priyadharshini et al., 2022). Usually, people express their opinions, emotions, and ideas through text over the internet (Chakravarthi, 2020; Chakravarthi and Muralidaran, 2021). However, the mode of communication is gradually shifting from unimodal to multimodal due to the rapid growth of all sorts of media content, including massive collections of videos (e.g., YouTube, Facebook, TikTok), audio clips, and images (Chakravarthi et al., 2020b; Bharathi et al., 2022). Classification of sentiment utilizing multiple modalities is becoming increasingly important and an exciting research topic. Multimodal sentiment analysis can analyze public opinions based on the speaker's language, facial gestures and acoustic behaviours, and voice's intensity (Ghanghor et al., 2021a,b; Yasaswini et al., 2021).

In recent years, a few studies have been performed on unimodal sentiment analysis concerning low-resource languages (e.g., Tamil, Malayalam, Bengali) (Priyadharshini et al., 2020, 2021; Kumaresan et al., 2021; Chakravarthi et al., 2021a, 2020a). The most challenging task in categorizing movie reviews is the interpretation of the words as most of the time, words are anticipated to the elements of a movie, not the opinion of the reviewer (Wöllmer et al., 2013; Mamun et al., 2022). Moreover, most language processing works mainly concentrate on high-resource languages like English, Arabic, and other European languages, where standard datasets are not available for low-resource languages. This work addresses the multimodal sentiment analysis from movie reviews in Tamil.

Tamil is a member of the southern branch of the Dravidian languages, a group of about 26 languages indigenous to the Indian subcontinent. It is also classed as a member of the Tamil language family, which contains the languages of around 35 ethno-linguistic groups, including the Irula and Yerukula languages (Sakuntharaj and Mahesan, 2021, 2017, 2016; Thavareesan and Mahesan, 2019, 2020a,b, 2021). Tamil is an official language of Tamil Nadu, Sri Lanka, Singapore, and the Union Territory of Puducherry in India. Significant minority speak Tamil in the four other South Indian states of Kerala, Karnataka, Andhra Pradesh, and Telangana, as well as the Union Territory of the

Proceedings of the Second Workshop on Speech and Language Technologies for Dravidian Languages, pages 191 - 198
May 26, 2022 ©2022 Association for Computational Linguistics

Andaman and Nicobar Islands. It is also spoken by the Tamil diaspora, which may be found in Malaysia, Myanmar, South Africa, the United Kingdom, the United States, Canada, Australia, and Mauritius (Subalalitha, 2019; Srinivasan and Subalalitha, 2019; Narasimhan et al., 2018). Tamil is also the native language of Sri Lankan Moors. The term "Old Tamil" refers to the time of the Tamil language from the 10th century BC to the 8th century AD. The earliest Old Tamil documents are small inscriptions in Adichanallur dating from 905 BC to 696 BC. These inscriptions are written in Tamil-Brahmi, a variation of the Brahmi script. The Tolkppiyam, an early work on Tamil grammar and poetics, is the first extended book in Old Tamil, with layers dating back to the late 6th century BC (Anita and Subalalitha, 2019b,a; Subalalitha and Poovammal, 2018).

The significant contributions of this work illustrate as follows,

- Developed various machine learning (ML) and deep learning (DL) based techniques to classify the sentiments into five classes (i.e., highly positive, positive, neutral, negative, and highly negative) for the Tamil language.
- Investigated the performance of the developed models with careful experimentation and error analysis.

2 Related Work

With the rapid popularization of social media, people's eagerness to express their views or opinions on these mediums increases sharply. However, sentiment analysis in low-resource languages is still rudimentary due to the scarcity of standard corpora and limited language processing tools. Few ML-based methods such as support vector machine (SVM), logistic regression (LR), naive Bayes (NB) have been used to analyze the textual sentiment in Bengali (Naeem et al., 2020; Sharif et al., 2019). Thavareesan and Mahesan (2019) performed sentiment analysis on five different Tamil text corpora using various ML techniques with BoW and TF-IDF features, which obtained the highest accuracy of 79% with Extreme Gradient Boosting with FastText. Singla et al. (2017) experimented with NB, DT, and SVM with the 10-fold cross-validation achieving 81.75% accuracy with SVM. Phani et al. (2016) used the SAIL corpus to assess the sentiment of tweets. They achieved the best performance in Tamil with NB and Hindi, Bengali with LR. The performance of these models is not very impressive as they were unable to capture semantic and contextual information in the text. The major obstacles are the inherent ambiguity of the language, the computational complexity of exploring large amounts of content, resource-poor language problems, and the contextual understanding of natural language (Zhou et al., 2021; Hossain et al., 2021b).

Different DL models were applied to Malayalam tweets to classify them into positive and negative where Gated Recurrent Unit (GRU) achieved the highest accuracy (Soumya and Pramod, 2019). Several approaches, including lexicon, supervised ML, hybrid, were experimented on Tamil texts (Thavareesan and Mahesan, 2019; Phani et al., 2016; Prasad et al., 2016). Abid et al. (2019) proposed a joint structure that combines CNN and RNN layers along with GloVE embeddings for capturing long-term dependencies of Twitter data. In another similar work, the sentiment lexicon is used to enhance the sentiment features, and then CNN-GRU networks are combined to analyze the sentiment of product reviews (Yang et al., 2020). Pranesh and Shekhar (2020) presented 'MemeSem' where VGG19 is used for visual and BERT for textual modality to analyze the sentiment of memes. MemeSem outperformed all the unimodal and multimodal baseline by 10.69% and 3.41% respectively. Recently, the CNN + Bi-LSTM model (Xuanyuan et al., 2021) has been employed to classify the sentiment of Twitter data and gained the highest accuracy of 90.2% for binary classification (positive and negative).

3 Dataset Description

The dataset we have used for this task is provided by the shared task organizers[1]. It is a collection of videos, audios, and text accumulated from YouTube and manually annotated. The dataset is divided into three sets (i.e., train, validation, and test) and annotated into five classes: highly positive, positive, neutral, negative, and highly negative. The dataset consists of a total of 134 videos, out of which 70 are Malayalam videos and the remaining 64 are Tamil videos (Chakravarthi et al., 2021b; Premjith et al., 2022). The length of the videos is between 1 minute to 3 minutes. Table 1 presents the distribution of the dataset. Table 2 shows the

[1] https://competitions.codalab.org/competitions/36406

number of samples in each category. This work dealt with the Tamil language dataset only.

This work employed textual features to address the assigned task. Participants have the freedom to utilize unimodal data (i.e., video, audio, or text) or multimodal (i.e., a combination of any two or three modalities) features to perform the classification task. Each text is provided in the *.docx file format. Therefore, we extracted all the texts from documents before starting the experimentation and evaluation (Section 4 provides a detailed description).

4 Methodology

The objective of the task is to classify the underlying sentiments from movie reviews using video, audio, and text modalities. However, we have used only textual data to attain this goal. Initially, texts were taken from the *.docx files and preprocessed for further use. Subsequently, feature extraction techniques are applied to get the features. Finally, the extracted features are utilized to develop ML and DL models to perform the classification task. Figure 1 illustrates an abstract view of the sentiment analysis model.

4.1 Feature Extraction

TF-IDF technique has been used to extract the unigram textual features for developing the ML models. On the other hand, Word2vec and FastText (Grave et al., 2018) embeddings are used to train the DL models. This work used pre-trained word vectors which were trained on Common Crawl and Wikipedia texts with a dimension of 300. In case of Word2Vec embeddings, we employed the Keras embedding layer to generate the vectors of length 260.

4.2 Classifiers

Four popular ML models (LR, DT, SVM, and MNB) have been developed to address the task using the 'scikit-learn' library. We devised the LR technique with the regularization parameter (C=5) and 'lbfgs' optimizer. The smoothing parameter (α) settled to 1.0 in the case of MNB. Meanwhile linear kernel with balanced class weight and C = '2' was used for SVM. However, the DT model parameters are: class weight = 'balanced' and criterion = 'gini'.

The task investigates two DL models (CNN and BiLSTM) and their combination (CNN+BiLSTM). For BiLSTM, we utilize the features extracted by the Word2Vec with an embedding dimension of 100. The BiLSTM consists of 128 units, and the dropout rate is set to 0.2 to reduce the overfitting. Finally, features are flattened and passed to the softmax layer for prediction. The model is trained for 30 epochs with a batch size of 32. For the CNN+BiLSTM based approach, we have used pre-trained FastText embedding. The output of Conv1D having 128 filters was fed to the max-pooling layer to downsample the features. These features were propagated to a bidirectional LSTM layer with 128 units. The model was also trained with a batch size of 32 for 30 epochs. For both models, the learning rate settled to 0.001, and 'sparse categorical crossentropy' is used to evaluate the loss. Keras callback function is utilized to save the best model during training used for the final evaluation. Table 3 shows the summary of hyperparameters used in the experiment.

5 Results and Analysis

Table 4 illustrates the performance of the models in terms of precision, recall and $f1$-score measures. The $f1$-score is used to decide the superiority of the model.

The results demonstrate that the DT model outperformed the other ML and DL models. The DT models showed 86.6% of increased performance compared to the ML models and improved by 140% than the best DL model (CNN+BiLSTM). The other ML models, such as LR, SVM, and MNB, were classified all test instances as the positive class. The BiLSTM with Word2Vec features predicts maximum reviews as neutral ones having a macro f_1 score of 0.07. However, after using the pre-trained word embedding with combined CNN and BiLSTM model, the macro f_1-score has grown to 0.10. Thus, the model shows an increase in performance using pre-trained word embedding. However, it cannot beat the DT model developed based on the TF-IDF features.

Table 5 shows the class-wise $f1$-score of the models. The PS class obtained the maximum f_1-score (0.80) in DT model because this class contained the highest number of instances in the dataset. In contrast, the HPS and HNE classes showed the lowest f_1-score (0.0). That means any model cannot predict any sample of HPS and HNE classes due to the minimal number of samples in the dataset. In particular, HPS class contained only

	Tamil			Malayalam			
Dataset	Train	Test	Validation	Train	Test	Validation	Size(MB)
Video	44	10	10	50	10	10	1111.8
Audio	44	10	10	50	10	10	162.2
Text	44	10	10	50	10	10	1.003
Total	132	30	30	150	30	30	1275.003

Table 1: Statistics of dataset

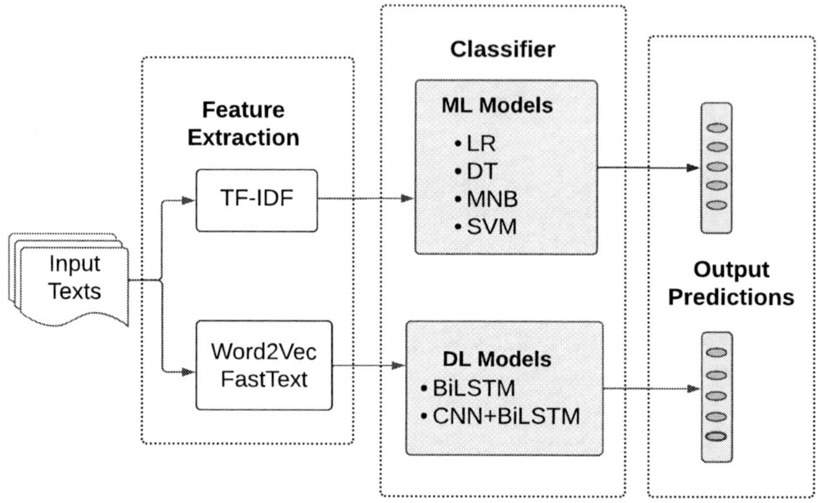

Figure 1: An overview of the sentiment analysis model

Class Label	Tamil	Malayalam
HPS	9	8
PS	39	38
NT	8	8
NE	12	5
HNE	2	5
Total	64	70

Table 2: Class-wise data sample distribution for each language. Here HPS, PS, NT, NE, and HNE indicate highly positive, positive, neutral, negative, and highly negative, respectively

Hyperparameters	Values
Dropout rate	0.2
Optimizer	'adam'
Learning rate	0.001
Epoch	30
Batch size	32

Table 3: Summary of tuned hyperparameters

9 samples whereas, HNE consisting only 2.

5.1 Error Analysis

Table 4 confirmed that the DT model is the best for the assigned task. The model's performance is further investigated using the confusion matrix (Figure 2) with detailed error analysis.

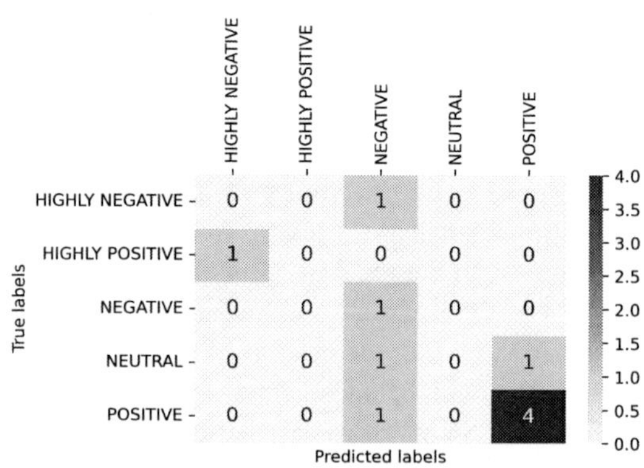

Figure 2: Confusion matrix of the best model (DT)

The model can genuinely predict 4 positive re-

Approach	Classifier	Precision	Recall	$f1$-score
ML models	LR	0.20	0.10	0.13
	DT	**0.21**	**0.36**	**0.24**
	MNB	0.20	0.10	0.13
	SVM	0.20	0.10	0.13
DL models	BiLSTM	0.20	0.04	0.07
	CNN+BiLSTM	0.12	0.09	0.10

Table 4: Performance comparison of various models on the test set

Classifier	HPS	PS	NT	NE	HNE
LR	0.0	0.67	0.0	0.0	0.0
DT	0.0	0.80	0.0	0.40	0.0
MNB	0.0	0.67	0.0	0.0	0.0
SVM	0.0	0.67	0.0	0.0	0.0
BiLSTM	0.0	0.0	0.33	0.0	0.0
CNN+BiLSTM	0.0	0.50	0.0	0.0	0.0

Table 5: Class-wise f_1-score of classifiers

views among 5 reviews. It miss-classifies only one neutral review as the positive class. The model predicted the negative class correctly but miss-classified the highly negative, neutral, and positive class as a negative one. The DT model is failed to predict the highly positive and the neutral classes. The model's low performance can be due to the lack of training data samples. Since this work considered the text modality only, it might miss some essential features associated with video and audio samples. The use of multimodal features might improve the performance of the system.

6 Conclusion

This paper investigated several ML and DL techniques to address the sentiment analysis task on a multimodal dataset in Tamil. Although the provided dataset included text, audio, and video modalities, this work considered the text modality. Results indicate that the DT model outperformed the other ML and DL models obtaining the maximum macro f_1-score (0.24). Surprisingly, DL models showed poor performance compared to their ML counterparts. Since the dataset is too small and crooked, data oversampling techniques or any open source large corpora can be used to create synthetic data to improve performance. The scarcity of training samples might cause lower scores. Moreover, excluding the video and audio features might also hurt the model's performance. We aim to incorporate multimodal features (video, audio, text) and address the task with the recent transformer-based models (i.e., IndicBERT, mBERT, XML-R, MuRIL) in the future.

Acknowledgements

This work supported by the ICT Innovation Fund, ICT Division, Ministry of Posts, Telecommunications and Information Technology, Bangladesh.

References

Fazeel Abid, Muhammad Alam, Muhammad Naveed Yasir, and Chen Li. 2019. Sentiment analysis through recurrent variants latterly on convolutional neural network of twitter. *Future Gener. Comput. Syst.*, 95:292–308.

R Anita and CN Subalalitha. 2019a. An approach to cluster Tamil literatures using discourse connectives. In *2019 IEEE 1st International Conference on Energy, Systems and Information Processing (ICESIP)*, pages 1–4. IEEE.

R Anita and CN Subalalitha. 2019b. Building discourse parser for Thirukkural. In *Proceedings of the 16th International Conference on Natural Language Processing*, pages 18–25.

B Bharathi, Bharathi Raja Chakravarthi, Subalalitha Chinnaudayar Navaneethakrishnan, N Sripriya, Arunaggiri Pandian, and Swetha Valli. 2022. Findings of the shared task on Speech Recognition for Vulnerable Individuals in Tamil. In *Proceedings of the Second Workshop on Language Technology for Equality, Diversity and Inclusion*. Association for Computational Linguistics.

Bharathi Raja Chakravarthi. 2020. HopeEDI: A multilingual hope speech detection dataset for equality, diversity, and inclusion. In *Proceedings of the Third Workshop on Computational Modeling of People's Opinions, Personality, and Emotion's in Social Media*, pages 41–53, Barcelona, Spain (Online). Association for Computational Linguistics.

Bharathi Raja Chakravarthi and Vigneshwaran Muralidaran. 2021. Findings of the shared task on hope speech detection for equality, diversity, and inclusion. In *Proceedings of the First Workshop on Language Technology for Equality, Diversity and Inclusion*, pages 61–72, Kyiv. Association for Computational Linguistics.

Bharathi Raja Chakravarthi, Vigneshwaran Muralidaran, Ruba Priyadharshini, and John Philip McCrae. 2020a. Corpus creation for sentiment analysis in code-mixed Tamil-English text. In *Proceedings of the 1st Joint Workshop on Spoken Language Technologies for Under-resourced languages (SLTU) and Collaboration and Computing for Under-Resourced Languages (CCURL)*, pages 202–210, Marseille, France. European Language Resources association.

Bharathi Raja Chakravarthi, Ruba Priyadharshini, Thenmozhi Durairaj, John Phillip McCrae, Paul Buitaleer, Prasanna Kumar Kumaresan, and Rahul Ponnusamy. 2022. Findings of the shared task on Homophobia Transphobia Detection in Social Media Comments. In *Proceedings of the Second Workshop on Language Technology for Equality, Diversity and Inclusion*. Association for Computational Linguistics.

Bharathi Raja Chakravarthi, Ruba Priyadharshini, Vigneshwaran Muralidaran, Shardul Suryawanshi, Navya Jose, Elizabeth Sherly, and John P McCrae. 2020b. Overview of the track on sentiment analysis for Dravidian languages in code-mixed text. In *Forum for Information Retrieval Evaluation*, pages 21–24.

Bharathi Raja Chakravarthi, Ruba Priyadharshini, Rahul Ponnusamy, Prasanna Kumar Kumaresan, Kayalvizhi Sampath, Durairaj Thenmozhi, Sathiyaraj Thangasamy, Rajendran Nallathambi, and John Phillip McCrae. 2021a. Dataset for identification of homophobia and transophobia in multilingual YouTube comments. *arXiv preprint arXiv:2109.00227*.

Bharathi Raja Chakravarthi, KP Soman, Rahul Ponnusamy, Prasanna Kumar Kumaresan, Kingston Pal Thamburaj, John P McCrae, et al. 2021b. Dravidianmultimodality: A dataset for multi-modal sentiment analysis in Tamil and Malayalam. *arXiv preprint arXiv:2106.04853*.

Nikhil Ghanghor, Parameswari Krishnamurthy, Sajeetha Thavareesan, Ruba Priyadharshini, and Bharathi Raja Chakravarthi. 2021a. IIITK@DravidianLangTech-EACL2021: Offensive language identification and meme classification in Tamil, Malayalam and Kannada. In *Proceedings of the First Workshop on Speech and Language Technologies for Dravidian Languages*, pages 222–229, Kyiv. Association for Computational Linguistics.

Nikhil Ghanghor, Rahul Ponnusamy, Prasanna Kumar Kumaresan, Ruba Priyadharshini, Sajeetha Thavareesan, and Bharathi Raja Chakravarthi. 2021b. IIITK@LT-EDI-EACL2021: Hope speech detection for equality, diversity, and inclusion in Tamil , Malayalam and English. In *Proceedings of the First Workshop on Language Technology for Equality, Diversity and Inclusion*, pages 197–203, Kyiv. Association for Computational Linguistics.

Edouard Grave, Piotr Bojanowski, Prakhar Gupta, Armand Joulin, and Tomas Mikolov. 2018. Learning word vectors for 157 languages. In *Proceedings of the International Conference on Language Resources and Evaluation (LREC 2018)*.

Eftekhar Hossain, Omar Sharif, Mohammed Moshiul Hoque, and Iqbal H. Sarker. 2021a. Sentilstm: A deep learning approach for sentiment analysis of restaurant reviews. In *Hybrid Intelligent Systems*, pages 193–203, Cham. Springer International Publishing.

Eftekhar Hossain, Omar Sharif, and Mohammed Moshiul Hoque. 2021b. Sentiment polarity detection on bengali book reviews using multinomial naïve bayes. In *Progress in Advanced Computing and Intelligent Engineering*, pages 281–292, Singapore. Springer Singapore.

Hitkul Jangid, Shivangi Singhal, Rajiv Ratn Shah, and Roger Zimmermann. 2018. Aspect-based financial sentiment analysis using deep learning. *Companion Proceedings of the The Web Conference 2018*.

Prasanna Kumar Kumaresan, Ratnasingam Sakuntharaj, Sajeetha Thavareesan, Subalalitha Navaneethakrishnan, Anand Kumar Madasamy, Bharathi Raja Chakravarthi, and John P McCrae. 2021. Findings of shared task on offensive language identification in Tamil and Malayalam. In *Forum for Information Retrieval Evaluation*, pages 16–18.

Md Mashiur Rahman Mamun, Omar Sharif, and Mohammed Moshiul Hoque. 2022. Classification of textual sentiment using ensemble technique. *SN Computer Science*, 3(1):1–13.

Saud Naeem, Doina Logofătu, and Fitore Muharemi. 2020. Sentiment analysis by using supervised machine learning and deep learning approaches. pages 481–491.

Anitha Narasimhan, Aarthy Anandan, Madhan Karky, and CN Subalalitha. 2018. Porul: Option generation and selection and scoring algorithms for a tamil flash card game. *International Journal of Cognitive and Language Sciences*, 12(2):225–228.

Pankaj, Prashant Pandey, Muskan, and Nitasha Soni. 2019. Sentiment analysis on customer feedback data: Amazon product reviews. In *2019 International Conference on Machine Learning, Big Data, Cloud and Parallel Computing (COMITCon)*, pages 320–322.

Shanta Phani, Shibamouli Lahiri, and Arindam Biswas. 2016. Sentiment analysis of tweets in three Indian languages. In *Proceedings of the 6th Workshop on South and Southeast Asian Natural Language Processing (WSSANLP2016)*, pages 93–102, Osaka, Japan. The COLING 2016 Organizing Committee.

Raj Ratn Pranesh and Ambesh Shekhar. 2020. Memesem:a multi-modal framework for sentimental analysis of meme via transfer learning.

Sudha Shanker Prasad, Jitendra Kumar, Dinesh Kumar Prabhakar, and Sachin Tripathi. 2016. Sentiment mining: An approach for Bengali and Tamil tweets. pages 1–4.

G. Preethi, P. Venkata Krishna, Mohammad S. Obaidat, V. Saritha, and Sumanth Yenduri. 2017. Application of deep learning to sentiment analysis for recommender system on cloud. In *2017 International Conference on Computer, Information and Telecommunication Systems (CITS)*, pages 93–97.

B Premjith, Bharathi Raja Chakravarthi, B Bharathi, Malliga Subramanian, K.P Soman, Dhanalakshmi Vadivel, K Sreelakshmi, Arunaggiri Pandian, and Prasanna Kumar Kumaresan. 2022. Findings of the shared task on Multimodal Sentiment Analysis in Dravidian languages. In *Proceedings of the Second Workshop on Speech and Language Technologies for Dravidian Languages*. Association for Computational Linguistics.

Ruba Priyadharshini, Bharathi Raja Chakravarthi, Subalalitha Chinnaudayar Navaneethakrishnan, Thenmozhi Durairaj, Malliga Subramanian, Kogilavani Shanmugavadivel, Siddhanth U Hegde, and Prasanna Kumar Kumaresan. 2022. Findings of the shared task on Abusive Comment Detection in Tamil. In *Proceedings of the Second Workshop on Speech and Language Technologies for Dravidian Languages*. Association for Computational Linguistics.

Ruba Priyadharshini, Bharathi Raja Chakravarthi, Sajeetha Thavareesan, Dhivya Chinnappa, Durairaj Thenmozhi, and Rahul Ponnusamy. 2021. Overview of the DravidianCodeMix 2021 shared task on sentiment detection in Tamil, Malayalam, and Kannada. In *Forum for Information Retrieval Evaluation*, pages 4–6.

Ruba Priyadharshini, Bharathi Raja Chakravarthi, Mani Vegupatti, and John P McCrae. 2020. Named entity recognition for code-mixed Indian corpus using meta embedding. In *2020 6th international conference on advanced computing and communication systems (ICACCS)*, pages 68–72. IEEE.

Adil E. Rajput. 2019. Natural language processing, sentiment analysis and clinical analytics. *ArXiv*, abs/1902.00679.

Manikandan Ravikiran, Bharathi Raja Chakravarthi, Anand Kumar Madasamy, Sangeetha Sivanesan, Ratnavel Rajalakshmi, Sajeetha Thavareesan, Rahul Ponnusamy, and Shankar Mahadevan. 2022. Findings of the shared task on Offensive Span Identification in code-mixed Tamil-English comments. In *Proceedings of the Second Workshop on Speech and Language Technologies for Dravidian Languages*. Association for Computational Linguistics.

Ratnasingam Sakuntharaj and Sinnathamby Mahesan. 2016. A novel hybrid approach to detect and correct spelling in Tamil text. In *2016 IEEE International Conference on Information and Automation for Sustainability (ICIAfS)*, pages 1–6.

Ratnasingam Sakuntharaj and Sinnathamby Mahesan. 2017. Use of a novel hash-table for speeding-up suggestions for misspelt Tamil words. In *2017 IEEE International Conference on Industrial and Information Systems (ICIIS)*, pages 1–5.

Ratnasingam Sakuntharaj and Sinnathamby Mahesan. 2021. Missing word detection and correction based on context of Tamil sentences using n-grams. In *2021 10th International Conference on Information and Automation for Sustainability (ICIAfS)*, pages 42–47.

Anbukkarasi Sampath, Thenmozhi Durairaj, Bharathi Raja Chakravarthi, Ruba Priyadharshini, Subalalitha Chinnaudayar Navaneethakrishnan, Kogilavani Shanmugavadivel, Sajeetha Thavareesan, Sathiyaraj Thangasamy, Parameswari Krishnamurthy, Adeep Hande, Sean Benhur, Kishor Kumar Ponnusamy, and Santhiya Pandiyan. 2022. Findings of the shared task on Emotion Analysis in Tamil. In *Proceedings of the Second Workshop on Speech and Language Technologies for Dravidian Languages*. Association for Computational Linguistics.

Omar Sharif, M. Hoque, and E. Hossain. 2019. Sentiment analysis of bengali texts on online restaurant reviews using multinomial naïve bayes. *2019 1st International Conference on Advances in Science, Engineering and Robotics Technology (ICASERT)*, pages 1–6.

Zeenia Singla, Sukhchandan Randhawa, and Sushma Jain. 2017. Sentiment analysis of customer product reviews using machine learning. pages 1–5.

S Soumya and K V Pramod. 2019. Sentiment analysis of Malayalam tweets using different deep neural network models-case study. pages 163–168.

R Srinivasan and CN Subalalitha. 2019. Automated named entity recognition from tamil documents. In *2019 IEEE 1st International Conference on Energy, Systems and Information Processing (ICESIP)*, pages 1–5. IEEE.

C. N. Subalalitha. 2019. Information extraction framework for Kurunthogai. *Sādhanā*, 44(7):156.

CN Subalalitha and E Poovammal. 2018. Automatic bilingual dictionary construction for Tirukural. *Applied Artificial Intelligence*, 32(6):558–567.

Sajeetha Thavareesan and Sinnathamby Mahesan. 2019. Sentiment analysis in Tamil texts: A study on machine learning techniques and feature representation. In *2019 14th Conference on Industrial and Information Systems (ICIIS)*, pages 320–325.

Sajeetha Thavareesan and Sinnathamby Mahesan. 2020a. Sentiment lexicon expansion using Word2vec and fastText for sentiment prediction in Tamil texts. In *2020 Moratuwa Engineering Research Conference (MERCon)*, pages 272–276.

Sajeetha Thavareesan and Sinnathamby Mahesan. 2020b. Word embedding-based part of speech tagging in Tamil texts. In *2020 IEEE 15th International Conference on Industrial and Information Systems (ICIIS)*, pages 478–482.

Sajeetha Thavareesan and Sinnathamby Mahesan. 2021. Sentiment analysis in Tamil texts using k-means and k-nearest neighbour. In *2021 10th International Conference on Information and Automation for Sustainability (ICIAfS)*, pages 48–53.

Martin Wöllmer, Felix Weninger, Tobias Knaup, Björn Schuller, Congkai Sun, Kenji Sagae, and Louis-Philippe Morency. 2013. Youtube movie reviews: Sentiment analysis in an audio-visual context. *IEEE Intelligent Systems*, 28(3):46–53.

Minzheng Xuanyuan, Le Xiao, and Mengshi Duan. 2021. Sentiment classification algorithm based on multi-modal social media text information. *IEEE Access*, 9:33410–33418.

Li Yang, Ying Li, Jin Wang, and R. Simon Sherratt. 2020. Sentiment analysis for e-commerce product reviews in chinese based on sentiment lexicon and deep learning. *IEEE Access*, 8:23522–23530.

Konthala Yasaswini, Karthik Puranik, Adeep Hande, Ruba Priyadharshini, Sajeetha Thavareesan, and Bharathi Raja Chakravarthi. 2021. IIITT@DravidianLangTech-EACL2021: Transfer learning for offensive language detection in Dravidian languages. In *Proceedings of the First Workshop on Speech and Language Technologies for Dravidian Languages*, pages 187–194, Kyiv. Association for Computational Linguistics.

Xuhui Zhou, Maarten Sap, Swabha Swayamdipta, Noah A. Smith, and Yejin Choi. 2021. Challenges in automated debiasing for toxic language detection.

CUET-NLP@TamilNLP-ACL2022: Multi-Class Textual Emotion Detection from Social Media using Transformers

Nasehatul Mustakim[Ψ], **Rabeya Akter Rabu**[Ψ], **Golam Sarwar Md. Mursalin**[Ψ], **Eftekhar Hossain**[$], **Omar Sharif**[Ψ] and **Mohammed Moshiul Hoque**[Ψ]
[Ψ]Department of Computer Science and Engineering
[$]Department of Electronics and Telecommunication Engineering
[$Ψ]Chittagong University of Engineering & Technology, Chattogram-4349, Bangladesh
{u1604109, u1604127, u1604014}@student.cuet.ac.bd
{eftekhar.hossain, omar.sharif, moshiul_240}@cuet.ac.bd

Abstract

Recently, emotion analysis has gained increased attention by NLP researchers due to its various applications in opinion mining, e-commerce, comprehensive search, healthcare, personalized recommendations and online education. Developing an intelligent emotion analysis model is challenging in resource-constrained languages like Tamil. Therefore a shared task is organized to identify the underlying emotion of a given comment expressed in the Tamil language. The paper presents our approach to classifying the textual emotion in Tamil into 11 classes: ambiguous, anger, anticipation, disgust, fear, joy, love, neutral, sadness, surprise and trust. We investigated various machine learning (LR, DT, MNB, SVM), deep learning (CNN, LSTM, BiLSTM) and transformer-based models (Multilingual-BERT, XLM-R). Results reveal that the XLM-R model outdoes all other models by acquiring the highest macro f_1-score (0.33).

1 Introduction

Textual emotion analysis is the automatic process of specifying a text into an emotion class from predefined connotations (Parvin et al., 2022). With the unprecedented growth of the internet, online and social media platforms significantly influence people's lives and interactions. People share opinions, expressions, information, feelings, emotions, ideas and concerns online (Ghanghor et al., 2021a,b; Yasaswini et al., 2021). People seek emotional support from their relatives, friends, or even virtual platforms when they go through challenging or adverse times (Priyadharshini et al., 2021; Kumaresan et al., 2021; Chakravarthi, 2020; Chakravarthi and Muralidaran, 2021). Textual emotion analysis (TEA) has been proven helpful in various applications, for example, consumer feedback on services and products (Hossain et al., 2021b; Mamun et al., 2022). The positive and negative customer experiences help to assess the demand for products and services (Hossain et al., 2021a). However, one cannot fully express his/her attitude only through positive and negative sentiments. For example – *I threw my iPhone in the water, and now it is not working, so I feel awful* (Sadness) vs *What a pain my new iPhone is not working* (Anger). Both texts express negative sentiment, but the first is sadness, and the latter is considered anger. Thus, emotion analysis is very crucial to understand the actual state of mind (Staiano and Guerini, 2014). In recent years, plenty of research has been conducted to analyze textual emotion. However, low-resource languages (i.e. Tamil and Bengali) remained out of focus, and very few research activities have been conducted to date. This deficiency occurs due to the scarcity of resources, limited corpora and unavailability of text processing tools (Sampath et al., 2022; Ravikiran et al., 2022; Chakravarthi et al., 2021, 2022; Bharathi et al., 2022; Priyadharshini et al., 2022). This shared task paper aims to mitigate this gap by presenting computational models for emotion analysis in Tamil.

Tamil is the predominant language of the majority of people living in Tamil Nadu, Puducherry (in India), and the Northern and Eastern regions of Sri Lanka (Sakuntharaj and Mahesan, 2021, 2017, 2016; Thavareesan and Mahesan, 2019, 2020a,b, 2021). The language is spoken by tiny minority communities in various Indian states such as Karnataka, Andhra Pradesh, Kerala, Maharashtra, and in specific places of Sri Lanka such as Colombo and the hill country. Tamil or varieties of it were widely employed as the main language of governance, literature, and general usage in the state of Kerala until the 15th century AD (Subalalitha, 2019; Srinivasan and Subalalitha, 2019; Narasimhan et al., 2018). Tamil was also commonly employed in inscriptions unearthed in the southern Andhra Pradesh regions of Chittoor and Nellore until the 12th century AD. Tamil was employed for inscriptions in southern Karnataka regions such as Kolar, Mysore,

Proceedings of the Second Workshop on Speech and Language Technologies for Dravidian Languages, pages 199 - 206
May 26, 2022 ©2022 Association for Computational Linguistics

Mandya, and Bangalore from the 10th to 14th century (Anita and Subalalitha, 2019b,a; Subalalitha and Poovammal, 2018).

The significant contribution of this work illustrates in the following:

- Developed transformer-based computation models for classifying emotion in Tamil considering 11 predefined emotion categories.
- Investigated the performance of various machine learning (ML), deep learning (DL) and transformer-based techniques to address the task followed by detailed error analysis.

2 Related Work

In the past few years, emotion analysis research has attracted researchers from diverse domains such as computer science, psychology and healthcare. Chaffar and Inkpen (2011) developed a model to recognize six basic emotions from the affective text on ALM's Dataset (1250 texts). They employed several ML techniques where support vector machine (SVM) achieved the highest performance with bag of words (BoW) features. Huang et al. (2019) proposed a contextual model to detect emotion. They combined two LSTM layers hierarchically and formed an ensemble with the BERT model, which achieved 77% accuracy. Vijay et al. (2018) developed a model with SVM and RBF kernel to identify the fear, disgust and surprise emotions from 2866 Hindi-English code-mixed tweets. Wadhawan and Aggarwal (2021) experimented with several DL (CNN, LSTM, BiLSTM) and transformer-based models for recognizing emotions from 149088 Hindi-English code mixed tweets. The transformer-based BERT model outperformed all other techniques and obtained an accuracy of 71.43%. Iqbal et al. (2022) presented a Bengali emotion corpus (BEmoC) containing 7000 texts with six basic emotion categories: *joy, anger, sad, fear, surprise, disgust.* Das et al. (2021) performed an investigation of various ML, DNN, and transformer-based techniques on BEmoD dataset containing 6523 texts. Their results showed that XLM-R outdoes others providing an f_1-score of 69.61%. In a similar work, Parvin et al. (2022) implemented various DL techniques (CNN, GRU, BiLSTM) with different ensemble combinations to recognize six emotions from a corpus containing 9000 Bengali texts. The ensemble of CNN and BiLSTM outperformed other models by achieving f_1-score of 62.46%.

3 Task and Dataset Descriptions

The emotion analysis shared task in Tamil comprises two tasks. We have participated in Task-a, where multi-class categorization of textual emotion is performed. The organizers[1] (Sampath et al., 2022) provided the annotated dataset having 11 types of emotions: Ambiguous, Anger, Anticipation, Disgust, Fear, Joy, Love, Neutral, Sadness, Surprise and Trust. The dataset consists of training, validation and test sets containing 14208, 3552 and 4440 texts. Table 1 shows the number of samples for each set in each class that reveals the dataset's imbalanced nature. Very few samples belong to the fear and surprise classes compared to the neutral class.

Classes	Train	Valid	Test
Neutral	4,841	1,222	1,538
Joy	2,134	558	702
Ambiguous	1,689	437	500
Trust	1,254	272	377
Disgust	910	210	277
Anger	834	184	244
Anticipation	828	213	271
Sadness	695	191	241
Love	675	189	196
Surprise	248	53	61
Fear	100	23	33
Total	14,208	3,552	4,440

Table 1: Class-wise distribution of Tamil emotion dataset

To get better insights, we further analyzed the training set. Table 2 shows the detailed statistics of the training set after removing inconsistencies from the texts. The neutral class retained the highest number of words and unique words, whereas the fear class had the least. On average, all the classes have ≈8-10 words; however, the texts from joy, love and surprise classes tend to be shorter than other classes.

4 Methodology

This work employed four ML, three DL and two transformer-based approaches to identify the underlying emotions of social media comments in

[1] https://competitions.codalab.org/competitions/36396

Classes	Total words	Unique words	Max. length (words)	Avg. words (per text)
Neutral	37,344	17,033	169	7.7
Joy	14,624	6,746	84	6.9
Ambiguous	14,579	8,309	114	8.6
Trust	11,757	6,318	110	9.3
Disgust	8,996	5,651	128	9.9
Anger	7,879	5,149	116	9.4
Anticipation	8,489	5,131	86	10.3
Sadness	6,911	4,485	76	9.9
Love	4,598	2,705	65	6.8
Surprise	1,633	1,362	55	6.9
Fear	1,040	864	108	10.4

Table 2: Detailed statistics of each class in the training set

Tamil. Initially, the unwanted characters (i.e., numbers, extra space, punctuation and URLs) and stop words are removed from the texts. Afterwards, different feature extraction techniques (i.e., TF-IDF, Word2Vec (Mikolov et al., 2013) extract the textual features. Figure 1 depicts the schematic diagram of the emotion classification system.

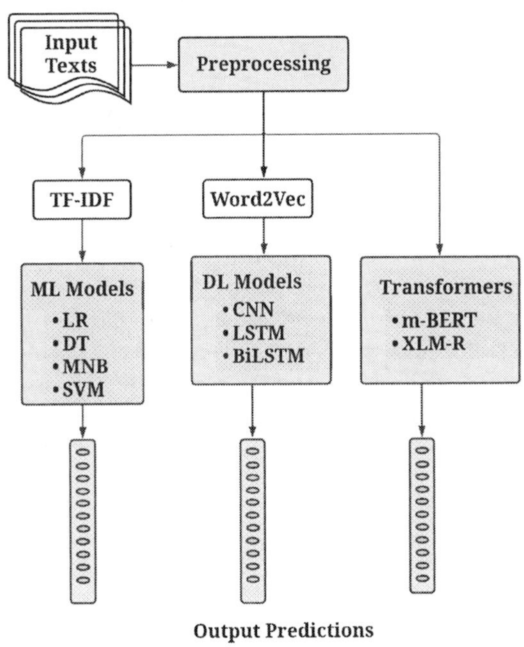

Figure 1: Abstract process of textual emotion classification

4.1 Feature Extraction

To train the ML models, we use the TF-IDF values of the unigram and bigram features, where maximum features are settled to 40000. On the other hand, Word2Vec embedding features are used to develop the DL based methods. The Keras embedding layer is applied to generate the embedding vectors of dimension 100.

4.2 ML-based Methods

Four traditional ML methods such as logistic regression (LR), decision tree (DT), support vector machine (SVM) and multinomial naive Bayes (MNB) have been employed to accomplish the emotion classification task. The models are implemented by using the 'Scikit-learn'[2] library. The LR model is constructed by setting the regularization parameter C at 10, solver to 'lbfgs' along with a balanced class weight. For the DT model, the 'gini' criterion is used for splitting the nodes. Similarly, in the case of MNB, the smoothing parameter α is fine-tuned at 1.50. For SVM, the 'rbf' kernel is used with a regularization value of 7.

4.3 DL-based Methods

This work also employed several DL methods such as CNN, LSTM and BiLSTM to address the task. All the models take word embedding vectors (Word2Vec) as features. We construct a CNN (Kim, 2014) architecture consisting of one convolution layer of 128 filters and a max-pooling layer with a pool size of 2. The flattened output of the pooled layer is then passed to the softmax layer for the classification. Likewise, a layer of LSTM and BiLSTM network of 128 units is developed with a drop-out rate of 0.2 to dissuade the overfitting problem. Finally, the output sentence representation is transferred to the softmax layer for predicting the emotion class. The DL models are implemented by using the Keras library[3] with the TensorFlow (Abadi et al., 2015) backend. 'Adam' (Kingma and Ba, 2014) optimizer with a learning rate of 0.001 is used to compile the models, whereas the 'sparse_categorical_ crossentropy' loss function is used to calculate the errors during the training. We also use the Keras callbacks methods to choose the best intermediate model.

4.3.1 Transformers

Recent advancements in NLP have demonstrated that the transformer-based architecture is superior in solving several classification problems (Puranik et al., 2021; Li et al., 2021; Sharif et al., 2021) irrespective of the language variation. In this work, two

[2]https://scikit-learn.org/stable/
[3]https://keras.io/

Hyperparameters	CNN	LSTM	BiLSTM	m-BERT	XLM-R
Input length	300	300	300	150	150
Embedding dimension	100	100	100	-	-
Filters (layer 1)	128	-	-	-	-
Pooling type	max	-	-	-	-
Kernel size	5	-	-	-	-
LSTM units	-	128	128	-	-
Dropout	-	0.2	0.2		
Optimizer	'adam'	'adam'	'adam'	'adam'	'adam'
Learning rate	$1e^{-3}$	$1e^{-3}$	$1e^{-3}$	$2e^{-5}$	$2e^{-5}$
Epochs	20	3	20	3	5
Batch size	32	32	32	12	12

Table 3: Summary of tuned hyperparameters for DL and Transformer-based models

widely used transformer models such as – m-BERT (Devlin et al., 2018) and XLM-R (Conneau et al., 2019) are employed to address the task. Specifically, we culled the 'bert-base-multilingual-cased' and 'xlm-roberta-base' versions of the models from Huggingface [4] transformers library and fine-tuned them on the dataset. We have trained the models up to five epochs with the help of the Ktrain (Maiya, 2020) package and used the 'adam' optimizer with a learning rate of $2e^{-5}$. Table 3 illustrates the various hyperparameters of the developed models.

5 Results and Analysis

Table 4 reports the performance comparison of the different approaches. The efficacy of the models is determined based on the macro f_1-score. It is observed that amid the ML models, LR achieved the highest f_1-score of 0.23 while MNB performed poorly on the test set. On the other hand, DL based methods did not surpass the performance of the best ML model (f_1-score = 0.23) as both CNN and BiLSTM achieved an identical score of 0.21. However, the transformer model, XLM-R, outperformed all the models by achieving the highest accuracy (0.47), precision (0.36), recall (0.33) and macro f_1-score (0.33).

Table 5 shows the class-wise performance of each model in terms of f_1-score. The XLM-R model achieved the highest f_1-score in seven classes out of eleven as these classes have the most instances in training set. The LR and m-BERT models obtained the highest score in love (0.16) and neutral (0.54) classes, while BiLSTM acquired maximal scores in the remaining classes: fear (0.21) and surprise (0.04).

5.1 Error Analysis

Table 4 illustrates that XLM-R acquired the highest score and outperformed all the other approaches. A quantitative error analysis of the best model has been carried out by using the confusion matrix (Figure 2). It is observed that the model identified 817 instances of the 'neutral' class correctly and incorrectly reckoned 166 and 119 instances as from 'joy' and 'trust' emotion class, respectively. Alternatively, it predicted the 'surprise' class as 'neutral' and 'joy' mostly. Furthermore, we noticed that the model becomes confused among the emotions of 'neutral', 'joy', 'trust' and 'surprise'. The main reason behind this might be the class imbalance problem. There might be plenty of words that are similar for some classes. Apart from this, the number of training texts in the surprise class is only 248, which is inadequate for the model to learn the context effectively. Moreover, the considerable diversity of the Tamil language can also be a potential cause. We have also observed that the most true predictions were made for the neutral and joy class, and an apparent reason for it is that the model saw plenty of texts of that class during the training.

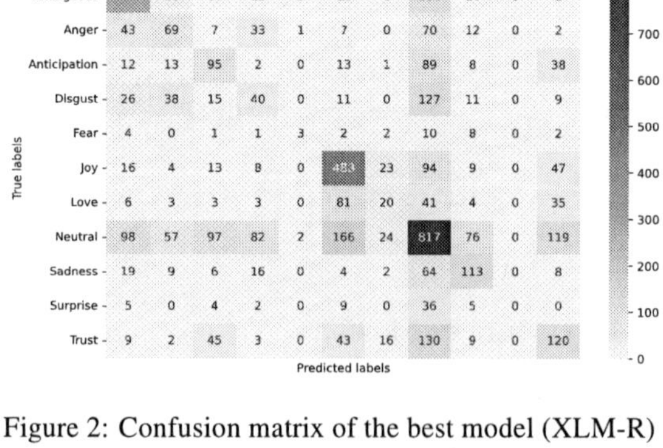

Figure 2: Confusion matrix of the best model (XLM-R)

[4] https://huggingface.co/

Approach	Classifier	Accuracy	Precision	Recall	$f1$-score
ML	LR	0.31	0.23	0.23	0.23
	DT	0.26	0.19	0.19	0.19
	MNB	0.38	0.11	0.16	0.08
	SVM	0.40	0.18	0.35	0.20
DL	CNN	0.29	0.21	0.21	0.21
	LSTM	0.35	0.09	0.03	0.05
	BiLSTM	0.31	0.20	0.23	0.21
Transformers	m-BERT	0.44	0.27	0.23	0.23
	XLM-R	**0.47**	**0.36**	**0.33**	**0.33**

Table 4: Performance comparison of various models on the test set

Classes	LR	DT	SVM	MNB	CNN	LSTM	BiLSTM	m-BERT	XLM-R
Ambiguous	0.31	0.26	0.27	0.00	0.25	0.00	0.21	0.54	**0.58**
Anger	0.18	0.15	0.09	0.00	0.15	0.00	0.16	0.17	**0.30**
Anticipation	0.17	0.14	0.09	0.00	0.17	0.00	0.16	0.30	**0.33**
Disgust	0.12	0.09	0.03	0.00	0.13	0.00	0.14	0.06	**0.17**
Fear	0.20	0.18	0.11	0.00	0.17	0.00	**0.21**	0.00	0.15
Joy	0.52	0.46	0.53	0.35	0.45	0.00	0.47	0.58	**0.63**
Love	**0.16**	0.11	0.11	0.00	0.15	0.00	0.14	0.08	0.14
Neutral	0.38	0.33	0.52	0.52	0.39	0.51	0.44	**0.54**	0.52
Sadness	0.26	0.19	0.19	0.00	0.20	0.00	0.16	0.02	**0.45**
Surprise	0.00	0.00	0.03	0.00	0.02	0.00	**0.04**	0.00	0.00
Trust	0.24	0.18	0.19	0.03	0.21	0.00	0.19	0.21	**0.31**

Table 5: Class-wise performance of models in terms of f_1-score

6 Conclusion

This paper investigated four ML, three DL and two transformer-based models to classify emotion from Tamil texts. Among all models, the XLM-R obtained the highest macro f_1-score of 0.33. Since this work did not use any pre-trained embedding, it might adversely affect the performance of the DL model. Thus, we opt to experiment with pre-trained word embedding in the future. Moreover, we plan to explore other advanced transformer-based models (i.e., Indic-BERT, MuRIL) and ensemble approaches to address the emotion analysis task. Since the dataset is imbalanced, it will be interesting to investigate the impact of resampling on the models in the future.

Acknowledgements

This work was supported by the CUET NLP Lab and Chittagong University of Engineering & Technology, Bangladesh.

References

Martín Abadi, Ashish Agarwal, Paul Barham, Eugene Brevdo, Zhifeng Chen, Craig Citro, Greg S. Corrado, Andy Davis, Jeffrey Dean, Matthieu Devin, Sanjay Ghemawat, Ian Goodfellow, Andrew Harp, Geoffrey Irving, Michael Isard, Yangqing Jia, Rafal Jozefowicz, Lukasz Kaiser, Manjunath Kudlur, Josh Levenberg, Dandelion Mané, Rajat Monga, Sherry Moore, Derek Murray, Chris Olah, Mike Schuster, Jonathon Shlens, Benoit Steiner, Ilya Sutskever, Kunal Talwar, Paul Tucker, Vincent Vanhoucke, Vijay Vasudevan, Fernanda Viégas, Oriol Vinyals, Pete Warden, Martin Wattenberg, Martin Wicke, Yuan Yu, and Xiaoqiang Zheng. 2015. TensorFlow: Large-scale machine learning on heterogeneous systems. Software available from tensorflow.org.

R Anita and CN Subalalitha. 2019a. An approach to cluster Tamil literatures using discourse connectives. In *2019 IEEE 1st International Conference on Energy, Systems and Information Processing (ICESIP)*, pages 1–4. IEEE.

R Anita and CN Subalalitha. 2019b. Building discourse parser for Thirukkural. In *Proceedings of the 16th International Conference on Natural Language Processing*, pages 18–25.

B Bharathi, Bharathi Raja Chakravarthi, Subalalitha Chinnaudayar Navaneethakrishnan, N Sripriya, Arunaggiri Pandian, and Swetha Valli. 2022. Findings of the shared task on Speech Recognition for Vulnerable Individuals in Tamil. In *Proceedings of the Second Workshop on Language Technology for Equality, Diversity and Inclusion*. Association for Computational Linguistics.

Soumaya Chaffar and Diana Inkpen. 2011. Using a heterogeneous dataset for emotion analysis in text. In *Canadian conference on artificial intelligence*, pages 62–67. Springer.

Bharathi Raja Chakravarthi. 2020. HopeEDI: A multilingual hope speech detection dataset for equality, diversity, and inclusion. In *Proceedings of the Third*

Workshop on Computational Modeling of People's Opinions, Personality, and Emotion's in Social Media, pages 41–53, Barcelona, Spain (Online). Association for Computational Linguistics.

Bharathi Raja Chakravarthi and Vigneshwaran Muralidaran. 2021. Findings of the shared task on hope speech detection for equality, diversity, and inclusion. In *Proceedings of the First Workshop on Language Technology for Equality, Diversity and Inclusion*, pages 61–72, Kyiv. Association for Computational Linguistics.

Bharathi Raja Chakravarthi, Ruba Priyadharshini, Thenmozhi Durairaj, John Phillip McCrae, Paul Buitaleer, Prasanna Kumar Kumaresan, and Rahul Ponnusamy. 2022. Findings of the shared task on Homophobia Transphobia Detection in Social Media Comments. In *Proceedings of the Second Workshop on Language Technology for Equality, Diversity and Inclusion*. Association for Computational Linguistics.

Bharathi Raja Chakravarthi, Ruba Priyadharshini, Rahul Ponnusamy, Prasanna Kumar Kumaresan, Kayalvizhi Sampath, Durairaj Thenmozhi, Sathiyaraj Thangasamy, Rajendran Nallathambi, and John Phillip McCrae. 2021. Dataset for identification of homophobia and transophobia in multilingual YouTube comments. *arXiv preprint arXiv:2109.00227*.

Alexis Conneau, Kartikay Khandelwal, Naman Goyal, Vishrav Chaudhary, Guillaume Wenzek, Francisco Guzmán, Edouard Grave, Myle Ott, Luke Zettlemoyer, and Veselin Stoyanov. 2019. Unsupervised cross-lingual representation learning at scale. *arXiv preprint arXiv:1911.02116*.

Avishek Das, Omar Sharif, Mohammed Moshiul Hoque, and Iqbal H. Sarker. 2021. Emotion classification in a resource constrained language using transformer-based approach. pages 150–158.

Jacob Devlin, Ming-Wei Chang, Kenton Lee, and Kristina Toutanova. 2018. Bert: Pre-training of deep bidirectional transformers for language understanding. *arXiv preprint arXiv:1810.04805*.

Nikhil Ghanghor, Parameswari Krishnamurthy, Sajeetha Thavareesan, Ruba Priyadharshini, and Bharathi Raja Chakravarthi. 2021a. IIITK@DravidianLangTech-EACL2021: Offensive language identification and meme classification in Tamil, Malayalam and Kannada. In *Proceedings of the First Workshop on Speech and Language Technologies for Dravidian Languages*, pages 222–229, Kyiv. Association for Computational Linguistics.

Nikhil Ghanghor, Rahul Ponnusamy, Prasanna Kumar Kumaresan, Ruba Priyadharshini, Sajeetha Thavareesan, and Bharathi Raja Chakravarthi. 2021b. IIITK@LT-EDI-EACL2021: Hope speech detection for equality, diversity, and inclusion in Tamil , Malayalam and English. In *Proceedings of the First Workshop on Language Technology for Equality, Diversity and Inclusion*, pages 197–203, Kyiv. Association for Computational Linguistics.

Eftekhar Hossain, Omar Sharif, Mohammed Moshiul Hoque, and Iqbal H. Sarker. 2021a. Sentilstm: A deep learning approach for sentiment analysis of restaurant reviews. In *Hybrid Intelligent Systems*, pages 193–203, Cham. Springer International Publishing.

Eftekhar Hossain, Omar Sharif, and Mohammed Moshiul Hoque. 2021b. Sentiment polarity detection on bengali book reviews using multinomial naïve bayes. In *Progress in Advanced Computing and Intelligent Engineering*, pages 281–292, Singapore. Springer Singapore.

Chenyang Huang, Amine Trabelsi, and Osmar R Zaïane. 2019. Ana at semeval-2019 task 3: Contextual emotion detection in conversations through hierarchical lstms and bert. *arXiv preprint arXiv:1904.00132*.

MD Iqbal, Avishek Das, Omar Sharif, Mohammed Moshiul Hoque, and Iqbal H Sarker. 2022. Bemoc: A corpus for identifying emotion in bengali texts. *SN Computer Science*, 3(2):1–17.

Yoon Kim. 2014. Convolutional neural networks for sentence classification. In *Proceedings of the 2014 Conference on Empirical Methods in Natural Language Processing (EMNLP)*, pages 1746–1751, Doha, Qatar. Association for Computational Linguistics.

Diederik P. Kingma and Jimmy Ba. 2014. Adam: A method for stochastic optimization.

Prasanna Kumar Kumaresan, Ratnasingam Sakuntharaj, Sajeetha Thavareesan, Subalalitha Navaneethakrishnan, Anand Kumar Madasamy, Bharathi Raja Chakravarthi, and John P McCrae. 2021. Findings of shared task on offensive language identification in Tamil and Malayalam. In *Forum for Information Retrieval Evaluation*, pages 16–18.

Xiangyang Li, Yu Xia, Xiang Long, Zheng Li, and Sujian Li. 2021. Exploring text-transformers in aaai 2021 shared task: Covid-19 fake news detection in english. In *International Workshop on Combating On line Ho st ile Posts in Regional Languages dur ing Emerge ncy Si tuation*, pages 106–115. Springer.

Arun S Maiya. 2020. ktrain: A low-code library for augmented machine learning. *arXiv preprint arXiv:2004.10703*.

Md Mashiur Rahaman Mamun, Omar Sharif, and Mohammed Moshiul Hoque. 2022. Classification of textual sentiment using ensemble technique. *SN Computer Science*, 3(1):1–13.

Tomas Mikolov, Ilya Sutskever, Kai Chen, Greg Corrado, and Jeffrey Dean. 2013. Distributed representations of words and phrases and their compositionality.

Anitha Narasimhan, Aarthy Anandan, Madhan Karky, and CN Subalalitha. 2018. Porul: Option generation and selection and scoring algorithms for a tamil flash card game. *International Journal of Cognitive and Language Sciences*, 12(2):225–228.

Tanzia Parvin, Omar Sharif, and Mohammed Moshiul Hoque. 2022. Multi-class textual emotion categorization using ensemble of convolutional and recurrent neural network. *SN Computer Science*, 3(1):1–10.

Ruba Priyadharshini, Bharathi Raja Chakravarthi, Subalalitha Chinnaudayar Navaneethakrishnan, Thenmozhi Durairaj, Malliga Subramanian, Kogilavani Shanmugavadivel, Siddhanth U Hegde, and Prasanna Kumar Kumaresan. 2022. Findings of the shared task on Abusive Comment Detection in Tamil. In *Proceedings of the Second Workshop on Speech and Language Technologies for Dravidian Languages*. Association for Computational Linguistics.

Ruba Priyadharshini, Bharathi Raja Chakravarthi, Sajeetha Thavareesan, Dhivya Chinnappa, Durairaj Thenmozhi, and Rahul Ponnusamy. 2021. Overview of the DravidianCodeMix 2021 shared task on sentiment detection in Tamil, Malayalam, and Kannada. In *Forum for Information Retrieval Evaluation*, pages 4–6.

Karthik Puranik, Adeep Hande, Ruba Priyadharshini, Sajeetha Thavareesan, and Bharathi Raja Chakravarthi. 2021. Iiitt@ lt-edi-eacl2021-hope speech detection: There is always hope in transformers. In *Proceedings of the First Workshop on Language Technology for Equality, Diversity and Inclusion*, pages 98–106.

Manikandan Ravikiran, Bharathi Raja Chakravarthi, Anand Kumar Madasamy, Sangeetha Sivanesan, Ratnavel Rajalakshmi, Sajeetha Thavareesan, Rahul Ponnusamy, and Shankar Mahadevan. 2022. Findings of the shared task on Offensive Span Identification in code-mixed Tamil-English comments. In *Proceedings of the Second Workshop on Speech and Language Technologies for Dravidian Languages*. Association for Computational Linguistics.

Ratnasingam Sakuntharaj and Sinnathamby Mahesan. 2016. A novel hybrid approach to detect and correct spelling in Tamil text. In *2016 IEEE International Conference on Information and Automation for Sustainability (ICIAfS)*, pages 1–6.

Ratnasingam Sakuntharaj and Sinnathamby Mahesan. 2017. Use of a novel hash-table for speeding-up suggestions for misspelt Tamil words. In *2017 IEEE International Conference on Industrial and Information Systems (ICIIS)*, pages 1–5.

Ratnasingam Sakuntharaj and Sinnathamby Mahesan. 2021. Missing word detection and correction based on context of Tamil sentences using n-grams. In *2021 10th International Conference on Information and Automation for Sustainability (ICIAfS)*, pages 42–47.

Anbukkarasi Sampath, Thenmozhi Durairaj, Bharathi Raja Chakravarthi, Ruba Priyadharshini, Subalalitha Chinnaudayar Navaneethakrishnan, Kogilavani Shanmugavadivel, Sajeetha Thavareesan, Sathiyaraj Thangasamy, Parameswari Krishnamurthy, Adeep Hande, Sean Benhur, Kishor Kumar Ponnusamy, and Santhiya Pandiyan. 2022. Findings of the shared task on Emotion Analysis in Tamil. In *Proceedings of the Second Workshop on Speech and Language Technologies for Dravidian Languages*. Association for Computational Linguistics.

Omar Sharif, Eftekhar Hossain, and Mohammed Moshiul Hoque. 2021. NLP-CUET@DravidianLangTech-EACL2021: Offensive language detection from multilingual code-mixed text using transformers. In *Proceedings of the First Workshop on Speech and Language Technologies for Dravidian Languages*, pages 255–261, Kyiv. Association for Computational Linguistics.

R Srinivasan and CN Subalalitha. 2019. Automated named entity recognition from tamil documents. In *2019 IEEE 1st International Conference on Energy, Systems and Information Processing (ICESIP)*, pages 1–5. IEEE.

Jacopo Staiano and Marco Guerini. 2014. Depechemood: a lexicon for emotion analysis from crowd-annotated news. *arXiv preprint arXiv:1405.1605*.

C. N. Subalalitha. 2019. Information extraction framework for Kurunthogai. *Sādhanā*, 44(7):156.

CN Subalalitha and E Poovammal. 2018. Automatic bilingual dictionary construction for Tirukural. *Applied Artificial Intelligence*, 32(6):558–567.

Sajeetha Thavareesan and Sinnathamby Mahesan. 2019. Sentiment analysis in Tamil texts: A study on machine learning techniques and feature representation. In *2019 14th Conference on Industrial and Information Systems (ICIIS)*, pages 320–325.

Sajeetha Thavareesan and Sinnathamby Mahesan. 2020a. Sentiment lexicon expansion using Word2vec and fastText for sentiment prediction in Tamil texts. In *2020 Moratuwa Engineering Research Conference (MERCon)*, pages 272–276.

Sajeetha Thavareesan and Sinnathamby Mahesan. 2020b. Word embedding-based part of speech tagging in Tamil texts. In *2020 IEEE 15th International Conference on Industrial and Information Systems (ICIIS)*, pages 478–482.

Sajeetha Thavareesan and Sinnathamby Mahesan. 2021. Sentiment analysis in Tamil texts using k-means and k-nearest neighbour. In *2021 10th International Conference on Information and Automation for Sustainability (ICIAfS)*, pages 48–53.

Deepanshu Vijay, Aditya Bohra, Vinay Singh, Syed Sarfaraz Akhtar, and Manish Shrivastava. 2018. Corpus creation and emotion prediction for hindi-english code-mixed social media text. In *Proceedings of the 2018 Conference of the North American Chapter of the Association for Computational Linguistics: Student Research Workshop*, pages 128–135.

Anshul Wadhawan and Akshita Aggarwal. 2021. Towards emotion recognition in hindi-english code-mixed data: A transformer based approach. *arXiv preprint arXiv:2102.09943*.

Konthala Yasaswini, Karthik Puranik, Adeep Hande, Ruba Priyadharshini, Sajeetha Thavareesan, and Bharathi Raja Chakravarthi. 2021. IIITT@DravidianLangTech-EACL2021: Transfer learning for offensive language detection in Dravidian languages. In *Proceedings of the First Workshop on Speech and Language Technologies for Dravidian Languages*, pages 187–194, Kyiv. Association for Computational Linguistics.

DLRG@DravidianLangTech-ACL2022: Abusive Comment Detection in Tamil using Multilingual Transformer Models

Ankita Duraphe and **Ratnavel Rajalakshmi***
School of Computer Science and Engineering
Vellore Institute of Technology
Chennai, India
ankitaduraphe@gmail.com
rajalakshmi.r@vit.ac.in

Antonette Shibani
TD School
University of Technology Sydney
Sydney, Australia
antonette.shibani@gmail.com

Abstract

Online Social Network has let people connect and interact with each other. It does, however, also provide a platform for online abusers to propagate abusive content. The majority of these abusive remarks are written in a multilingual style, which allows them to easily slip past internet inspection. This paper presents a system developed for the Shared Task on Abusive Comment Detection (Misogyny, Misandry, Homophobia, Transphobic, Xenophobia, CounterSpeech, Hope Speech) in Tamil DravidianLangTech@ACL 2022 to detect the abusive category of each comment. We approach the task with three methodologies - Machine Learning, Deep Learning and Transformer-based modeling, for two sets of data - Tamil and Tamil+English language dataset. The dataset used in our system can be accessed from the competition on CodaLab. For Machine Learning, eight algorithms were implemented, among which Random Forest gave the best result with Tamil+English dataset, with a weighted average F1-score of 0.78. For Deep Learning, Bi-Directional LSTM gave best result with pre-trained word embeddings. In Transformer-based modeling, we used IndicBERT and mBERT with fine-tuning, among which mBERT gave the best result for Tamil dataset with a weighted average F1-score of 0.7.

1 Introduction

The usage of the Internet and social media has increased exponentially over the previous two decades, allowing people to connect and interact with each other (Priyadharshini et al., 2021; Kumaresan et al., 2021). This has resulted in a number of favourable outcomes such as monitoring pandemic trends, empowering patients and enhancing public communication through social media, amongst others (Cornelius et al., 2020; Househ et al., 2014; Picazo-Vela et al., 2012). At the same time, it has also brought with it hazards and negative consequences, one of which is the use of abusive language on others (Chakravarthi, 2020; Chakravarthi and Muralidaran, 2021).

The rapid spread of abusive content on social networking has become a major source of concern for government organisations. It is very difficult to identify abuse over online social network due to the massive volume of content generated through social media in different online platforms (Sampath et al., 2022; Ravikiran et al., 2022; Chakravarthi et al., 2022; Bharathi et al., 2022). It becomes a bigger problem when most of the communication is in multilingual style (Priyadharshini et al., 2020; Chakravarthi et al., 2021a,b). Hence, there is increasing interest in the use of automated methods for detecting online social abuse (Priyadharshini et al., 2022). It is becoming a major area of research to find solutions with powerful algorithmic systems to curb the growth of abusive content online. One possible way of achieving such a system is by using state-of-the-art Natural Language Processing (NLP) techniques, which can analyse, comprehend and interpret the meaning of the natural language data.

In addition, the detection of abusive language online is harder for some languages like Tamil due to the presence of code-mixed (Barman et al., 2014) and code-switched (Poplack, 2001) data. Code-switching is when in a single discourse, a person switches between two or more languages or language varieties/dialects (B and A, 2021b,a). It refers to using elements from more than one language in a way that is consistent with the syntax, morphology, and phonology of each language or dialect. Code-mixing is the hybridization of two languages (for example, parkear, which uses an English root word and Spanish morphology), which refers to the migration from one language to another. Many such language pairs have a hybrid

*Corresponding Author

Proceedings of the Second Workshop on Speech and Language Technologies for Dravidian Languages, pages 207 - 213
May 26, 2022 ©2022 Association for Computational Linguistics

name.

Tamil is a member of the southern branch of the Dravidian languages, a group of about 26 languages indigenous to the Indian subcontinent. It is also classed as a member of the Tamil language family, which contains the languages of around 35 ethno-linguistic groups, including the Irula and Yerukula languages (Anita and Subalalitha, 2019b,a; Subalalitha and Poovammal, 2018; Subalalitha, 2019). Malayalam is Tamil's closest significant cousin; the two began splitting during the 9th century AD. Although several variations between Tamil and Malayalam indicate a pre-historic break of the western dialect, the process of separating into a different language, Malayalam, did not occur until the 13th or 14th century (Sakuntharaj and Mahesan, 2021, 2017, 2016; Thavareesan and Mahesan, 2019, 2020a,b, 2021). Tanglish is an example which is Tamil+English. In this task, we are given two datasets: One with a Tamil meaning written in English but the content is a combination of Tamil and English. The other is a Tamil+English dataset (Tanglish) which is written in Tamil and English with content in Tamil and English as well. There are also known challenges in the development of computational systems in Tamil because of the lack of linguistic resources (Magueresse et al., 2020). In this paper, we present computational systems for the automated detection of abusive language using the two different data sets containing Tamil and Tamil+English.

2 Related work

In this section, we review the various methodologies and systems previously implemented for similar tasks in under-resourced languages like Tamil. Hope speech is annotated Equality, Diversity and Inclusion (HopeEDI) (Chakravarthi, 2020). They also created several baselines to standard the dataset. (Chakravarthi and Muralidaran, 2021) reports on the shared task of hope speech detection for Tamil, English and Malyalam languages. They presents the dataset used in the shared task and also surveys various competing approaches developed for the shared task and their corresponding results. (Mandalam and Sharma, 2021) presents the methodologies implemented while classifying Dravidian Tamil and Malayalam code-mixed comments according to their polarity and uses LSTM architecture. (Sai and Sharma, 2021; Li, 2021; Que, 2021) use XLM-RoBERTa for offensive language identification. Novel approach of selective translation and transliteration have been used to improve the performance of multilingual transformer networks such as XLMRoBERTa and mBERT by fine-tuning and ensembling. Online messaging has become one of the most popular methods of communication with instances of online/digital bullying. The challenge of detecting objectionable language in YouTube comments from the Dravidian languages of Tamil, Malayalam, and Kannada is viewed as a multi-class classification problem (Andrew, 2021). Several Machine Learning algorithms have been trained for the task at hand after being exposed to language-specific pre-processing.

3 Dataset

The dataset for the current study is taken from the competition [1] which consists of YouTube comments in Tamil and Tamil-English languages annotated for Misogyny, homophobia, transphobic, xenophobia, counter-speech, hope-speech and misandry (and None-of-the-above) (Priyadharshini et al., 2022). Table 1 shows the count of comments for both the datasets under each split. Table 2 gives the class-distribution of each abusive category for both the datasets.

4 Proposed Technique

Raw texts are inaccessible to Machine Learning (ML) and Deep Learning (DL) algorithms. To train the models for classification, feature extraction is necessary. To extract features in ML approaches, the TF-IDF representation is used. For DL models, we use fastText word embeddings feature extraction strategies (Joulin et al., 2016). fastText embedding uses a pre-trained embedding matrix for Tamil language (Grave et al., 2018). To study the results and come up with the best model possible, we follow three approaches - Machine Learning, Deep Learning and Transformer-based.

As it can be clearly seen from Table 1, both the datasets contain class imbalance. Class imbalance is a problem in machine learning when there are great differences in the class-distribution of the dataset. It is seen as a problem when a dataset is biased towards a class in the dataset. If this problem persists, any algorithm trained on the same data will again be biased towards the same class. To resolve

[1] https://competitions.codalab.org/competitions/36403

Class	Tamil+English	Tamil
Train-set	5948	2238
Validation-set	1488	560
Test-set	1857	699

Table 1: Number of comments across both the datasets in each of the three splits.

Class	Tamil+English	Tamil
Misandry	1048	550
Counter-speech	443	185
Xenophobia	367	124
Hope-Speech	266	97
Misogyny	261	149
Homophobia	213	43
Transphobic	197	8
None-of-the-above	4639	1642

Table 2: Class-distribution across both datasets.

the issue of class imbalance, we practice various approaches:

Changing the performance metric: Since accuracy is not always the best metric to use on imbalanced datasets, we use F1-score instead to evaluate the models.

Using a penalized algorithm (cost-sensitive training): This algorithm also handles class imbalance which can be achieved by using 'balanced' as a parameter while computing class weights.

Changing the algorithms: This is why we have used a wide variety of algorithms to get a bigger picture of which models suit the dataset and the classification problem better.

Table 3 provides the details about tuning the hyperparameters in our system both for Tamil+English and Tamil datasets.

To study the results and come up with the best model possible, we follow three approaches - Machine Learning, Deep Learning and Transformer-based, described in the sub-sections below.

4.1 Approach A: Machine Learning/ Non-Neural Network approaches

To start with, we implemented various Machine Learning algorithms which include Logistic Regression (LR), Random Forest (RF), K-nearest neighbors (KNN), Decision Tree, Support Vector Machine (SVM), Gradient Boosting, Adaptive Boosting (AdaBoost), and Ensemble (Husain, 2020). We have used ML algorithms only for Tamil+English dataset due to the poor performance of ML models on Tamil written text (Tamil dataset).

4.2 Approach B: Recurrent Neural Network approaches

To improve the performance of ML models, we dive into deep learning algorithms. Here, we have implemented DL approach for both the datasets. We use two models of Bi-directional LSTM - BiLSTM-M1 and BiLSTM-M2 (Chiu and Nichols, 2015). BiLSTM-M1 is a mix of bidirectional LSTM architecture that uses a convolution and a max-pooling layer to extract a new feature vector from the per-character feature vectors for each word. These vectors are concatenated for each word and sent to the BiLSTM network, which subsequently feeds the output layers. BiLSTM-M2 is an advanced BiLSTM-M1 where we adopted pre-trained word embeddings since BiLSTM and fastText produced better results for classification tasks.

4.3 Approach C: Transformer-based approaches

In natural language processing, the Transformer is a unique design that seeks to solve sequence-to-sequence tasks while also resolving long-range dependencies. It does not use sequence-aligned RNNs or convolution to compute representations of its input and output, instead relying solely on self-attention.

Bidirectional Encoder Representations from Transformers (BERT) (Devlin et al., 2018) is a

Parameters	**Values**
Learning rate	$1x10^{-3}$
Batch Size	32
Epochs	25
Validation Split	0.2

Table 3: Hyperparameters used in our system.

Model name	**P**	**R**	**F1**
RF	**0.91**	**0.71**	**0.78**
Gradient Boosting	0.85	0.71	0.76
SVM	0.78	0.72	0.75
KNN	0.85	0.68	0.75
AdaBoost	0.86	0.69	0.74
LR	0.71	0.71	0.71
Decision Tree	0.72	0.66	0.68
Ensemble	0.71	0.72	0.68
BiLSTM-M1	0.71	0.68	0.7
BiLSTM-M2	0.64	0.61	0.62
IndicBERT	0.55	0.67	0.60

Table 4: Metric evaluation for Tamil+English dataset.

Model name	**P**	**R**	**F1**
BiLSTM-M1	0.63	0.55	0.58
BiLSTM-M2	**0.74**	**0.67**	**0.7**
mBERT	0.64	0.7	0.7

Table 5: Metric evaluation for Tamil dataset.

transformer language model with a variable number of encoder layers and self-attention capabilities.

We again use two BERT models - mBERT (bert-base-multilingual-cased) and IndicBERT

We follow fine-tuning for Transformer models and use pre-trained BERT, bert-base-multilingual-cased (Devlin et al., 2018) and IndicBert classification models (Kakwani et al., 2020) that have been trained on 104 languages and 12 Indian languages respectively, including Tamil, from the largest Wikipedia.

5 Results and Discussion

We ran 8 Machine Learning algorithms, 2 Deep Learning and 1 Transformer model on the Tamil+English dataset. For the Tamil dataset, we used 2 Deep Learning and 1 Transformer model.

For the Tamil+English dataset, the best performance was of Random Forest with macro average F1-score of 0.32 and weighted average F1-score of 0.78. For the Tamil dataset, the best model was BiLSTM-M2 with macro average F1-score of 0.39 and weighted average F1-score of 0.70.

For Tamil, performance improved from switching BiLSTM-M2 to mBERT. And for Tamil+English, the best performer was BiLSTM-M1, followed by BiLSTM-M2 and then IndicBERT and mBERT.

Table 4 and Table 5 show the result of our models across both the datasets. For Tamil language, ML models performed best when DL models were originally expected to perform better. The extensive use of multilingual language in the text could be a reason for the poor performance of DL. Pre-trained word embeddings could not deliver higher performance due to the lack of feature mapping between the words. As a result, DL models might not be able to uncover sufficient relational relationships among the features, and perform poorly.

6 Conclusions and Future Work

In this paper, we presented approaches for the automated detection of abusive comments in Tamil. We used various models to do a comparative study to see which model performed better with the dataset given in the shared task. We found that Deep Learning and Transformer models outperformed Machine Learning models with Tamil data whereas Machine Learning models achieved better results than Deep Learning and Transformer-based for Tamil+English data. We did not apply contextualized embeddings (such as ELMO, FLAIR) which may improve the performance of the system. Implementation of Contextualised embeddings using language modelling with deep learning is the future work to explore.

Acknowledgements

We would like to thank the management of Vellore Institute of Technology, Chennai for their support to carry out this research.

References

Judith Jeyafreeda Andrew. 2021. JudithJeyafreedaAndrew@DravidianLangTech-EACL2021:offensive language detection for Dravidian code-mixed YouTube comments. In *Proceedings of the First Workshop on Speech and Language Technologies for Dravidian Languages*, pages 169–174, Kyiv. Association for Computational Linguistics.

R Anita and CN Subalalitha. 2019a. An approach to cluster Tamil literatures using discourse connectives. In *2019 IEEE 1st International Conference on Energy, Systems and Information Processing (ICESIP)*, pages 1–4. IEEE.

R Anita and CN Subalalitha. 2019b. Building discourse parser for Thirukkural. In *Proceedings of the 16th International Conference on Natural Language Processing*, pages 18–25.

Bharathi B and Agnusimmaculate Silvia A. 2021a. SSNCSE_NLP@DravidianLangTech-EACL2021: Meme classification for Tamil using machine learning approach. In *Proceedings of the First Workshop on Speech and Language Technologies for Dravidian Languages*, pages 336–339, Kyiv. Association for Computational Linguistics.

Bharathi B and Agnusimmaculate Silvia A. 2021b. SSNCSE_NLP@DravidianLangTech-EACL2021: Offensive language identification on multilingual code mixing text. In *Proceedings of the First Workshop on Speech and Language Technologies for Dravidian Languages*, pages 313–318, Kyiv. Association for Computational Linguistics.

Utsab Barman, Amitava Das, Joachim Wagner, and Jennifer Foster. 2014. Code mixing: A challenge for language identification in the language of social media.

B Bharathi, Bharathi Raja Chakravarthi, Subalalitha Chinnaudayar Navaneethakrishnan, N Sripriya, Arunaggiri Pandian, and Swetha Valli. 2022. Findings of the shared task on Speech Recognition for Vulnerable Individuals in Tamil. In *Proceedings of the Second Workshop on Language Technology for Equality, Diversity and Inclusion*. Association for Computational Linguistics.

Bharathi Raja Chakravarthi. 2020. HopeEDI: A multilingual hope speech detection dataset for equality, diversity, and inclusion. In *Proceedings of the Third Workshop on Computational Modeling of People's Opinions, Personality, and Emotion's in Social Media*, pages 41–53, Barcelona, Spain (Online). Association for Computational Linguistics.

Bharathi Raja Chakravarthi and Vigneshwaran Muralidaran. 2021. Findings of the shared task on hope speech detection for equality, diversity, and inclusion. In *Proceedings of the First Workshop on Language Technology for Equality, Diversity and Inclusion*, pages 61–72, Kyiv. Association for Computational Linguistics.

Bharathi Raja Chakravarthi, Ruba Priyadharshini, Thenmozhi Durairaj, John Phillip McCrae, Paul Buitaleer, Prasanna Kumar Kumaresan, and Rahul Ponnusamy. 2022. Findings of the shared task on Homophobia Transphobia Detection in Social Media Comments. In *Proceedings of the Second Workshop on Language Technology for Equality, Diversity and Inclusion*. Association for Computational Linguistics.

Bharathi Raja Chakravarthi, Ruba Priyadharshini, Rahul Ponnusamy, Prasanna Kumar Kumaresan, Kayalvizhi Sampath, Durairaj Thenmozhi, Sathiyaraj Thangasamy, Rajendran Nallathambi, and John Phillip McCrae. 2021a. Dataset for identification of homophobia and transophobia in multilingual YouTube comments. *arXiv preprint arXiv:2109.00227*.

Bharathi Raja Chakravarthi, Priya Rani, Mihael Arcan, and John P McCrae. 2021b. A survey of orthographic information in machine translation. *SN Computer Science*, 2(4):1–19.

Jason P. C. Chiu and Eric Nichols. 2015. Named entity recognition with bidirectional lstm-cnns. *CoRR*, abs/1511.08308.

Joseph Cornelius, Tilia Ellendorff, Lenz Furrer, and Fabio Rinaldi. 2020. COVID-19 Twitter monitor: Aggregating and visualizing COVID-19 related trends in social media. In *Proceedings of the Fifth Social Media Mining for Health Applications Workshop & Shared Task*, pages 1–10, Barcelona, Spain (Online). Association for Computational Linguistics.

Jacob Devlin, Ming-Wei Chang, Kenton Lee, and Kristina Toutanova. 2018. BERT: pre-training of deep bidirectional transformers for language understanding. *CoRR*, abs/1810.04805.

Avishek Garain, Atanu Mandal, and Sudip Kumar Naskar. 2021. JUNLP@DravidianLangTech-EACL2021: Offensive language identification in Dravidian langauges. In *Proceedings of the First Workshop on Speech and Language Technologies for Dravidian Languages*, pages 319–322, Kyiv. Association for Computational Linguistics.

Edouard Grave, Piotr Bojanowski, Prakhar Gupta, Armand Joulin, and Tomas Mikolov. 2018. Learning word vectors for 157 languages. In *Proceedings of the Eleventh International Conference on Language Resources and Evaluation (LREC 2018)*, Miyazaki, Japan. European Language Resources Association (ELRA).

Adeep Hande, Ruba Priyadharshini, Anbukkarasi Sampath, Kingston Pal Thamburaj, Prabakaran Chandran, and Bharathi Raja Chakravarthi. 2021. Hope speech detection in under-resourced kannada language.

Mowafa Househ, Elizabeth Borycki, and Andre Kushniruk. 2014. Empowering patients through social media: the benefits and challenges. *Health Informatics J.*, 20(1):50–58.

Fatemah Husain. 2020. Arabic offensive language detection using machine learning and ensemble machine learning approaches. *CoRR*, abs/2005.08946.

Armand Joulin, Edouard Grave, Piotr Bojanowski, Matthijs Douze, Hérve Jégou, and Tomas Mikolov. 2016. Fasttext.zip: Compressing text classification models. *arXiv preprint arXiv:1612.03651*.

Divyanshu Kakwani, Anoop Kunchukuttan, Satish Golla, Gokul N.C., Avik Bhattacharyya, Mitesh M. Khapra, and Pratyush Kumar. 2020. IndicNLPSuite: Monolingual Corpora, Evaluation Benchmarks and Pre-trained Multilingual Language Models for Indian Languages. In *Findings of EMNLP*.

Prasanna Kumar Kumaresan, Ratnasingam Sakuntharaj, Sajeetha Thavareesan, Subalalitha Navaneethakrishnan, Anand Kumar Madasamy, Bharathi Raja Chakravarthi, and John P McCrae. 2021. Findings of shared task on offensive language identification in Tamil and Malayalam. In *Forum for Information Retrieval Evaluation*, pages 16–18.

Zichao Li. 2021. Codewithzichao@DravidianLangTech-EACL2021: Exploring multilingual transformers for offensive language identification on code mixing text. In *Proceedings of the First Workshop on Speech and Language Technologies for Dravidian Languages*, pages 164–168, Kyiv. Association for Computational Linguistics.

Alexandre Magueresse, Vincent Carles, and Evan Heetderks. 2020. Low-resource languages: A review of past work and future challenges. *CoRR*, abs/2006.07264.

Asrita Venkata Mandalam and Yashvardhan Sharma. 2021. Sentiment analysis of Dravidian code mixed data. In *Proceedings of the First Workshop on Speech and Language Technologies for Dravidian Languages*, pages 46–54, Kyiv. Association for Computational Linguistics.

Sergio Picazo-Vela, Isis Gutiérrez-Martínez, and Luis Felipe Luna-Reyes. 2012. Understanding risks, benefits, and strategic alternatives of social media applications in the public sector. *Gov. Inf. Q.*, 29(4):504–511.

Shana Poplack. 2001. *Code Switching: Linguistic*, pages 2062–2065.

Ruba Priyadharshini, Bharathi Raja Chakravarthi, Subalalitha Chinnaudayar Navaneethakrishnan, Thenmozhi Durairaj, Malliga Subramanian, Kogilavani Shanmugavadivel, Siddhanth U Hegde, and Prasanna Kumar Kumaresan. 2022. Findings of the shared task on Abusive Comment Detection in Tamil. In *Proceedings of the Second Workshop on Speech and Language Technologies for Dravidian Languages*. Association for Computational Linguistics.

Ruba Priyadharshini, Bharathi Raja Chakravarthi, Sajeetha Thavareesan, Dhivya Chinnappa, Durairaj Thenmozhi, and Rahul Ponnusamy. 2021. Overview of the DravidianCodeMix 2021 shared task on sentiment detection in Tamil, Malayalam, and Kannada. In *Forum for Information Retrieval Evaluation*, pages 4–6.

Ruba Priyadharshini, Bharathi Raja Chakravarthi, Mani Vegupatti, and John P McCrae. 2020. Named entity recognition for code-mixed Indian corpus using meta embedding. In *2020 6th international conference on advanced computing and communication systems (ICACCS)*, pages 68–72. IEEE.

Qinyu Que. 2021. Simon @ DravidianLangTech-EACL2021: Detecting offensive content in Kannada language. In *Proceedings of the First Workshop on Speech and Language Technologies for Dravidian Languages*, pages 160–163, Kyiv. Association for Computational Linguistics.

Manikandan Ravikiran, Bharathi Raja Chakravarthi, Anand Kumar Madasamy, Sangeetha Sivanesan, Ratnavel Rajalakshmi, Sajeetha Thavareesan, Rahul Ponnusamy, and Shankar Mahadevan. 2022. Findings of the shared task on Offensive Span Identification in code-mixed Tamil-English comments. In *Proceedings of the Second Workshop on Speech and Language Technologies for Dravidian Languages*. Association for Computational Linguistics.

Siva Sai and Yashvardhan Sharma. 2021. Towards offensive language identification for Dravidian languages. In *Proceedings of the First Workshop on Speech and Language Technologies for Dravidian Languages*, pages 18–27, Kyiv. Association for Computational Linguistics.

Ratnasingam Sakuntharaj and Sinnathamby Mahesan. 2016. A novel hybrid approach to detect and correct spelling in Tamil text. In *2016 IEEE International Conference on Information and Automation for Sustainability (ICIAfS)*, pages 1–6.

Ratnasingam Sakuntharaj and Sinnathamby Mahesan. 2017. Use of a novel hash-table for speeding-up suggestions for misspelt tamil words. In *2017 IEEE International Conference on Industrial and Information Systems (ICIIS)*, pages 1–5.

Ratnasingam Sakuntharaj and Sinnathamby Mahesan. 2021. Missing word detection and correction based on context of Tamil sentences using n-grams. In *2021 10th International Conference on Information and Automation for Sustainability (ICIAfS)*, pages 42–47.

Anbukkarasi Sampath, Thenmozhi Durairaj, Bharathi Raja Chakravarthi, Ruba Priyadharshini, Subalalitha Chinnaudayar Navaneethakrishnan, Kogilavani Shanmugavadivel, Sajeetha Thavareesan, Sathiyaraj Thangasamy, Parameswari Krishnamurthy, Adeep Hande, Sean Benhur, and Santhiya Ponnusamy, Kishor Kumar Pandiyan. 2022. Findings of the shared task on Emotion Analysis in Tamil. In *Proceedings of the Second Workshop on Speech and Language Technologies for Dravidian Languages*. Association for Computational Linguistics.

C. N. Subalalitha. 2019. Information extraction framework for Kurunthogai. *Sādhanā*, 44(7):156.

CN Subalalitha and E Poovammal. 2018. Automatic bilingual dictionary construction for Tirukural. *Applied Artificial Intelligence*, 32(6):558–567.

Sajeetha Thavareesan and Sinnathamby Mahesan. 2019. Sentiment analysis in Tamil texts: A study on machine learning techniques and feature representation. In *2019 14th Conference on Industrial and Information Systems (ICIIS)*, pages 320–325.

Sajeetha Thavareesan and Sinnathamby Mahesan. 2020a. Sentiment lexicon expansion using Word2vec and fastText for sentiment prediction in Tamil texts. In *2020 Moratuwa Engineering Research Conference (MERCon)*, pages 272–276.

Sajeetha Thavareesan and Sinnathamby Mahesan. 2020b. Word embedding-based part of speech tagging in Tamil texts. In *2020 IEEE 15th International Conference on Industrial and Information Systems (ICIIS)*, pages 478–482.

Sajeetha Thavareesan and Sinnathamby Mahesan. 2021. Sentiment analysis in Tamil texts using k-means and k-nearest neighbour. In *2021 10th International Conference on Information and Automation for Sustainability (ICIAfS)*, pages 48–53.

Aanisha@TamilNLP-ACL2022:Abusive Detection in Tamil

Aanisha Bhattacharyya
Institute of Engineering and Management
aanishabhattacharyya@gmail.com

Abstract

In social media, there are instances where people present their opinions in strong language, resorting to abusive/toxic comments.There are instances of communal hatred, hate-speech, toxicity and bullying. And, in this age of social media, it's very important to find means to keep check on these toxic comments, as to preserve the mental peace of people in social media.While there are tools, models to detect and potentially filter these kind of content, developing these kinds of models for the low resource language space is an issue of research.

In this paper, the task of abusive comment identification in Tamil language, is seen upon as a multiclass classification problem.There are different pre-processing as well as modelling approaches discussed in this paper.The different approaches are compared on the basis of weighted average accuracy.

[1]

1 Introduction

With social media being accessible and popular across masses in India, there has been a surge in content in regional languages. People often create content, comment or exchange messages in monolingual or code mixed language (Priyadharshini et al., 2020, 2021; Kumaresan et al., 2021). However,even if there is an abundance of content in Indian language across social media, there is a lack of Indian language datasets (Chakravarthi, 2020; Chakravarthi and Muralidaran, 2021). Hence Indian languages are deemed as low resource language space, due to lack of available datasets, making working in these languages spaces, a challenging research problem (Chakravarthi et al., 2019b, 2018).

Among the messages and comments exchanged on social media there are instances of monolingual comments in regional language as well as transliterated comments. Monolingual comments in transliterated means to write or print (a letter or word) using the closest corresponding letters of a different alphabet or script. Code-Mixing is mixing of two or more language in the same utterance (Sampath et al., 2022; Ravikiran et al., 2022; Chakravarthi et al., 2022a; Bharathi et al., 2022; Priyadharshini et al., 2022).

In this paper, the task is identifying abusive comments in Tamil language. Tamil is a member of the southern branch of the Dravidian languages, a group of about 26 languages indigenous to the Indian subcontinent (Anita and Subalalitha, 2019b,a; Subalalitha and Poovammal, 2018). It is also classed as a member of the Tamil language family, which contains the languages of around 35 ethno-linguistic groups, including the Irula and Yerukula languages (Subalalitha, 2019; Srinivasan and Subalalitha, 2019; Narasimhan et al., 2018). The earliest Old Tamil documents are small inscriptions in Adichanallur dating from 905 BC to 696 BC. This is a multiclass classification problem, with 6 different categories of abusive comments are present. In a multi class classification problem, an instance can belong only to one class. However present Machine Learning or Deep Learning based models cannot be directly applied to Tamil language. Thus several pre-processing techniques have been proposed for Tamil language and models have been fine tuned to suit the task (Sakuntharaj and Mahesan, 2021, 2017, 2016; Thavareesan and Mahesan, 2019, 2020a,b, 2021).

2 Related work

There has been different works done on identifying abusive comments on different languages.

In (Zhao et al., 2021) Performed binary and multiclass classification using a Twitter corpus and studied two approaches: (a)a method which consists in extracting of word embeddings and then using a DNN classifier; (b) fine-tuning the pre-trained

[1]https://github.com/Aanisha/Tamil_Comment_Classification

Proceedings of the Second Workshop on Speech and Language Technologies for Dravidian Languages, pages 214 - 220
May 26, 2022 ©2022 Association for Computational Linguistics

BERT model.However it was only on English language embeddings.

In (Farooqi et al., 2021) Detected hate speech from Hindi-English code mixed conversations on Twitter. The proposed architecture used neural networks, leveraging the transformer's cross-lingual embeddings and further fine tuning them for low-resource hate-speech classification in transliterated Hindi text.

In (Andrew, 2021) as a part of shared task in ACL Dravidian Lang Tech 2021, several Machine learning algorithms were compared and experimented for identifying abusive comment in various Dravidian languages.

3 Dataset

The dataset is provided by (Priyadharshini et al., 2022) as a part of the shared task Abusive comment detection in Tamil.

The dataset has a collection of comments in Tamil language.There are 2240 native Tamil script comments and 5943 transliterated Tamil-English comments in the train data,classified across 7 different categories : 'Hope-Speech', 'Homophobia', 'Misandry', 'Counter-speech', 'Misogyny', 'Xenophobia', Trans-phobic' and 'None-of-the-above'.

The validation data has 560 native Tamil script comments and 1486 transliterated Tamil-English comments.The test data has 699 native Tamil language comments and 1857 transliterated Tamil-English comments.

The most dominant category present across all the datasets is : 'None-of-the-above' and the categories with less no of comments are 'Homophobia' with 207 and 'Trans-phobic' with 163 total comments.

4 Approaches

4.1 Pre-processing

The dataset has a very imbalanced distribution of the categories of comments.

So, for the experiments two separate datasets are generated.

Table 1 shows the distribution of first dataset, is combining both native Tamil script and transliterated Tamil-English comments.

Table 2, shows the distribution of second dataset,which creates a more balanced distribution by a mixed approach of oversampling and under-sampling.

Command	Output
`None-of-the-above`	5011
`Misandry`	1276
`Counter-speech`	497
`Xenophobia`	392
`Misogyny`	336
`Hope-Speech`	299
`Homophobia`	207
`Trans-phobic`	163

Table 1: Distribution of comments in the different categories

Command	Output
`None-of-the-above`	3007
`Misandry`	1276
`Counter-speech`	497
`Xenophobia`	392
`Misogyny`	586
`Hope-Speech`	549
`Homophobia`	457
`Trans-phobic`	413

Table 2: Distribution of comments in the different categories in pre-processed dataset.

The 'None-of-the-above' class comments are downsampled by a percentage of 0.4 in the train data .The lower represented classes 'Misogyny','Hope-speech','Homophobia' and 'Trans-phobic' data samples are over-sampled.

The values are decided on experimental basis.

4.2 Tokenization and feature vectors

For tokenization of the dataset, two different tokenizers have been used.

The MuRil tokenizer is used.MuRIL is a multilingual LMBert specifically built for IN languages.MuRIL is trained on significantly large amounts of IN text corpora only.Can generate embeddings for low resource native script and transliterated Indic languages.(Khanuja et al., 2021).

Another tokenizer used is the the IndicNLP tokenizer. A trivial tokenizer which just tokenizes on the punctuation boundaries. This also includes punctuations for the Indian language scripts (the purna virama and the deergha virama). It returns a list of tokens.(Arora, 2020).

Two kinds of feature vectors are used for the various modelling approaches.MuRil embeddings are generated from pre-trained MuRil model, and used as feature vectors for solving the multiclass classification problem.

Another feature vector used is normalized Tf-Idf vectors from the tokenized text,where

tf(t) = (No. of times term 't' occurs in a document) / (Frequency of most common term in a document)

and,

idf(t) = log e [(1+Total number of documents available) / (1 + Number of documents in which the term t appears)] + 1)

$$tf - idf(t) = tf(t) * idf(t)$$

These feature vectors are generated from the tokenized texts of MuRil and IndicNLP tokenizer respectively.

4.3 Modelling approaches

4.3.1 Logistic Regression

The multiclass logistic regression model is implemented (LR, 2017). The model of logistic regression for a multiclass classification problem forces the output layer to have discrete probability distributions over the possible k classes. This is accomplished by using the softmax function. Given the input vector(z), the softmax function works as follows:

$$\sigma(z_i) = \frac{e^{z_i}}{\sum_{j=1}^{K} e^{z_j}} \quad for\ i = 1, 2, \ldots, K$$

There are n output classes and thus there is a necessity to impose weights connecting each input to each output.

4.3.2 Linear Support Vector Machines

SVMs are very good classification algorithm. The idea is to identify hyper-planes that will separate the various features. The classification decision is thus performed as follows:

$f(x) = sign(W.x + b)$

where x represents the input feature, W represents the model weight and b represents the bias. For the multiclass classification problem, a one-vs-rest (also known as one-vs-all) approach is used.

4.3.3 Gradient Boosting Classifier

Gradient boosting classifiers are a group of machine learning algorithms that combine many weak learning models together to create a strong predictive model. Decision trees are usually used when doing gradient boosting.

Here, this algorithm is used for a multiclass classification.

4.3.4 Transformers

Google introduced the transformer architecture in the paper "Attention is All you need". Transformer uses a self-attention mechanism, which is suitable for language understanding.The transformer has an encoder-decoder architecture. They are composed of modules that contain feed-forward and attention layers.

They have led to advancements in the field of NLP to perform tasks as text classification,machine translation etc.

5 Results

6 Implementation

6.0.1 Logistic Regression

The original training data contains 10227 comments and the test data contains 2555 comments.

The data is first tokenized using the IndicNLP tokenizer and feature vectors are generated by using Tf-Idf with unigrams and bigrams being extracted.

The feature vector are fed to the logistic regression model with a newton-cg solver, to accomodate multiclass classification.

There are two experiments that are run for this model.The model is trained on original dataset and the model is trained on sampled dataset.

6.0.2 Support Vector Machine

The original training data contains 10227 comments and the test data contains 2555 comments.

The data is first tokenized using the IndicNLP tokenizer and feature vectors are generated by using Tf-Idf with unigrams and bigrams being extracted.

The feature vector are fed to the support vector machine with degree=8, to accomodate multiclass classification.The penalty is squared l2.

There are two experiments that are run for this model.The model is trained on original dataset and the model is trained on sampled dataset.

6.0.3 Gradient Boosting Classifier

The original training data contains 10227 comments and the test data contains 2555 comments.

The data is first tokenized using the IndicNLP tokenizer and feature vectors are generated by using Tf-Idf with unigrams and bigrams being extracted.

The feature vector is input to the Gradient Boosting Classifier model, which uses deviance loss function for optimization and a learning rate of 0.1.

Model	Dataset	Acc	Precision	Recall	F1-score
Logistic Regression	Original	0.66	0.62	0.66	0.57
Logistic Regression	Sampled	0.65	0.62	0.65	0.59
Linear SVM	Original	0.59	0.54	0.59	0.47
Linear SVM	Sampled	0.56	0.50	0.56	0.48
Gradient Boost Classifier	Original	0.68	0.67	0.68	0.63
Gradient Boost Classifier	Sampled	0.70	0.67	0.70	0.66
Finetuned MuRIL	Original	0.68	0.60	0.68	0.62
Finetuned MuRIL	Sampled	0.64	0.67	0.64	0.65
Finetuned MuRIL(weighted loss)	Sampled	0.51	0.67	0.51	0.56

Table 3: The results of the experiments conducted.

There are two experiments that are run for this model.The model is trained on original dataset and the model is trained on sampled dataset.

6.0.4 Transformers

The train data contains 8183 comments and the validation data contains 2046 comments.Also the sampled train dataset(details in dataset) is tested on this system.Validation data is same in both the experiments.

The data is tokenised using the Muril tokeniser which has a a vocabulary of 197,285.

The tokenised output from the MuRil tokenizer has 3 elements `Input Id`,`Attention Mask` and `Token Id`.These 3 vectors are fed to the pre-trained MuRil model to generate embeddings.

The model embeddings are input to a 1D convolutional layer which changes the dimension of the embedding from (x,64,768) to (x,64,1).Then it's flattened to have a vector of dimension (x,64).Lastly, there is a fully connected layer with softmax activation to have the output of dim. (x,8).The model output is the probabilities for the sentence to belong to each of the categories.

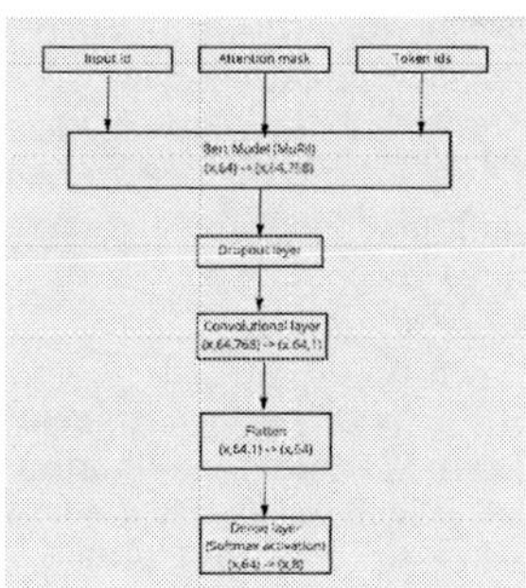

Figure 1: The finetuned MuRil model

For training, the MuRil layers are frozen and pre-trained weights are used.Only trainable layers are the CNN and Dense layers.There is a dropout of 0.2 used.

There are three experiments that are run for this model.The model is trained on original dataset,the model is trained on sampled dataset, and the model is trained on sampled dataset with weighted loss being applied.

The models in each case are trained for 25 epochs.All the transformers are trained on a single GPU and takes around 25-30 mins for one training session.

7 Results

Table 3 contains the results from the different experiments. The best performing model is the Gradient Boost Classifier trained on the sampled dataset. Within the results, the category "None-of-the-above" is more easily detected correctly by most of the models, while the classes "Misogyny" and "counter-speech" are not detected easily. The transformer finetuned on original dataset has the highest accuracy among all the transformer experiments. However it's not able to identify the categories with lower number of datapoints. The transformers trained on sampled dataset is able to perform better in the categories with lower number of datapoints.

8 Future Work

The future work will be primarily to find more efficient sampling techniques for the text data, and compare the performances with further ML models. Also, evaluate performances with other existing transformer models,to check how different suitable models can be fine-tuned to solve this particular task.

9 References

References

BERT and fastText Embeddings for Automatic Detection of Toxic Speech.

Judith Jeyafreeda Andrew. 2021. JudithJeyafreedaAndrew@DravidianLangTech-EACL2021:offensive language detection for Dravidian code-mixed YouTube comments. In *Proceedings of the First Workshop on Speech and Language Technologies for Dravidian Languages*, pages 169–174, Kyiv. Association for Computational Linguistics.

R Anita and CN Subalalitha. 2019a. An approach to cluster Tamil literatures using discourse connectives. In *2019 IEEE 1st International Conference on Energy, Systems and Information Processing (ICESIP)*, pages 1–4. IEEE.

R Anita and CN Subalalitha. 2019b. Building discourse parser for Thirukkural. In *Proceedings of the 16th International Conference on Natural Language Processing*, pages 18–25.

Gaurav Arora. 2020. *iNLTK: Natural Language Toolkit for Indic Languages.*

Bharathi B and Agnusimmaculate Silvia A. 2021a. SSNCSE_NLP@DravidianLangTech-EACL2021: Meme classification for Tamil using machine learning approach. In *Proceedings of the First Workshop on Speech and Language Technologies for Dravidian Languages*, pages 336–339, Kyiv. Association for Computational Linguistics.

Bharathi B and Agnusimmaculate Silvia A. 2021b. SSNCSE_NLP@DravidianLangTech-EACL2021: Offensive language identification on multilingual code mixing text. In *Proceedings of the First Workshop on Speech and Language Technologies for Dravidian Languages*, pages 313–318, Kyiv. Association for Computational Linguistics.

B Bharathi, Bharathi Raja Chakravarthi, Subalalitha Chinnaudayar Navaneethakrishnan, N Sripriya, Arunaggiri Pandian, and Swetha Valli. 2022. Findings of the shared task on Speech Recognition for Vulnerable Individuals in Tamil. In *Proceedings of the Second Workshop on Language Technology for Equality, Diversity and Inclusion*. Association for Computational Linguistics.

Bharathi Raja Chakravarthi. 2020. HopeEDI: A multilingual hope speech detection dataset for equality, diversity, and inclusion. In *Proceedings of the Third Workshop on Computational Modeling of People's Opinions, Personality, and Emotion's in Social Media*, pages 41–53, Barcelona, Spain (Online). Association for Computational Linguistics.

Bharathi Raja Chakravarthi, Mihael Arcan, and John P. McCrae. 2018. Improving wordnets for under-resourced languages using machine translation. In *Proceedings of the 9th Global Wordnet Conference*, pages 77–86, Nanyang Technological University (NTU), Singapore. Global Wordnet Association.

Bharathi Raja Chakravarthi, Mihael Arcan, and John P McCrae. 2019a. Comparison of different orthographies for machine translation of under-resourced Dravidian languages. In *2nd Conference on Language, Data and Knowledge (LDK 2019)*. Schloss Dagstuhl-Leibniz-Zentrum fuer Informatik.

Bharathi Raja Chakravarthi, Mihael Arcan, and John P. McCrae. 2019b. WordNet gloss translation for under-resourced languages using multilingual neural machine translation. In *Proceedings of the Second Workshop on Multilingualism at the Intersection of Knowledge Bases and Machine Translation*, pages 1–7, Dublin, Ireland. European Association for Machine Translation.

Bharathi Raja Chakravarthi and Vigneshwaran Muralidaran. 2021. Findings of the shared task on hope speech detection for equality, diversity, and inclusion. In *Proceedings of the First Workshop on Language Technology for Equality, Diversity and Inclusion*, pages 61–72, Kyiv. Association for Computational Linguistics.

Bharathi Raja Chakravarthi, Vigneshwaran Muralidaran, Ruba Priyadharshini, and John Philip McCrae. 2020a. Corpus creation for sentiment analysis in code-mixed Tamil-English text. In *Proceedings of the 1st Joint Workshop on Spoken Language Technologies for Under-resourced languages (SLTU) and Collaboration and Computing for Under-Resourced Languages (CCURL)*, pages 202–210, Marseille, France. European Language Resources association.

Bharathi Raja Chakravarthi, Ruba Priyadharshini, Thenmozhi Durairaj, John Phillip McCrae, Paul Buitaleer, Prasanna Kumar Kumaresan, and Rahul Ponnusamy. 2022a. Findings of the shared task on Homophobia Transphobia Detection in Social Media Comments. In *Proceedings of the Second Workshop on Language Technology for Equality, Diversity and Inclusion*. Association for Computational Linguistics.

Bharathi Raja Chakravarthi, Ruba Priyadharshini, Vigneshwaran Muralidaran, Navya Jose, Shardul Suryawanshi, Elizabeth Sherly, and John P. McCrae. 2022b. DravidianCodeMix: sentiment analysis and offensive language identification dataset for Dravidian languages in code-mixed text. *Language Resources and Evaluation.*

Bharathi Raja Chakravarthi, Ruba Priyadharshini, Vigneshwaran Muralidaran, Shardul Suryawanshi, Navya Jose, Elizabeth Sherly, and John P McCrae. 2020b. Overview of the track on sentiment analysis for Dravidian languages in code-mixed text. In *Forum for Information Retrieval Evaluation*, pages 21–24.

Bharathi Raja Chakravarthi, Ruba Priyadharshini, Rahul Ponnusamy, Prasanna Kumar Kumaresan,

Kayalvizhi Sampath, Durairaj Thenmozhi, Sathiyaraj Thangasamy, Rajendran Nallathambi, and John Phillip McCrae. 2021a. Dataset for identification of homophobia and transophobia in multilingual YouTube comments. *arXiv preprint arXiv:2109.00227*.

Bharathi Raja Chakravarthi, Ruba Priyadharshini, Bernardo Stearns, Arun Jayapal, Sridevy S, Mihael Arcan, Manel Zarrouk, and John P McCrae. 2019c. Multilingual multimodal machine translation for Dravidian languages utilizing phonetic transcription. In *Proceedings of the 2nd Workshop on Technologies for MT of Low Resource Languages*, pages 56–63, Dublin, Ireland. European Association for Machine Translation.

Bharathi Raja Chakravarthi, Priya Rani, Mihael Arcan, and John P McCrae. 2021b. A survey of orthographic information in machine translation. *SN Computer Science*, 2(4):1–19.

Jacob Devlin, Ming-Wei Chang, Kenton Lee, and Kristina Toutanova. *BERT: Pre-training of Deep Bidirectional Transformers for Language Understanding*.

Zaki Mustafa Farooqi, Sreyan Ghosh, and Rajiv Ratn Shah. 2021. *Leveraging Transformers for Hate Speech Detection in Conversational Code-Mixed Tweets*.

Nikhil Ghanghor, Parameswari Krishnamurthy, Sajeetha Thavareesan, Ruba Priyadharshini, and Bharathi Raja Chakravarthi. 2021a. IIITK@DravidianLangTech-EACL2021: Offensive language identification and meme classification in Tamil, Malayalam and Kannada. In *Proceedings of the First Workshop on Speech and Language Technologies for Dravidian Languages*, pages 222–229, Kyiv. Association for Computational Linguistics.

Nikhil Ghanghor, Rahul Ponnusamy, Prasanna Kumar Kumaresan, Ruba Priyadharshini, Sajeetha Thavareesan, and Bharathi Raja Chakravarthi. 2021b. IIITK@LT-EDI-EACL2021: Hope speech detection for equality, diversity, and inclusion in Tamil , Malayalam and English. In *Proceedings of the First Workshop on Language Technology for Equality, Diversity and Inclusion*, pages 197–203, Kyiv. Association for Computational Linguistics.

Priyanka Gupta, Shriya Gandhi, and Bharathi Raja Chakravarthi. 2021. Leveraging transfer learning techniques-BERT, RoBERTa, ALBERT and DistilBERT for fake review detection. In *Forum for Information Retrieval Evaluation*, pages 75–82.

Simran Khanuja, Diksha Bansal, Sarvesh Mehtani, Savya Khosla, Atreyee Dey, and Pooja Aggarwal Rajiv Teja Nagipogu Shachi Dave Shruti Gupta Subhash Chandra Bose Gali Vish Subramanian Partha Talukdar Balaji Gopalan, Dilip Kumar Margam. 2021. *MuRIL:Multilingual Representations for Indian Languages*.

Prasanna Kumar Kumaresan, Ratnasingam Sakuntharaj, Sajeetha Thavareesan, Subalalitha Navaneethakrishnan, Anand Kumar Madasamy, Bharathi Raja Chakravarthi, and John P McCrae. 2021. Findings of shared task on offensive language identification in Tamil and Malayalam. In *Forum for Information Retrieval Evaluation*, pages 16–18.

Anitha Narasimhan, Aarthy Anandan, Madhan Karky, and CN Subalalitha. 2018. Porul: Option generation and selection and scoring algorithms for a tamil flash card game. *International Journal of Cognitive and Language Sciences*, 12(2):225–228.

Ruba Priyadharshini, Bharathi Raja Chakravarthi, Subalalitha Chinnaudayar Navaneethakrishnan, Thenmozhi Durairaj, Malliga Subramanian, Kogilavani Shanmugavadivel, Siddhanth U Hegde, and Prasanna Kumar Kumaresan. 2022. Findings of the shared task on Abusive Comment Detection in Tamil. In *Proceedings of the Second Workshop on Speech and Language Technologies for Dravidian Languages*. Association for Computational Linguistics.

Ruba Priyadharshini, Bharathi Raja Chakravarthi, Sajeetha Thavareesan, Dhivya Chinnappa, Durairaj Thenmozhi, and Rahul Ponnusamy. 2021. Overview of the DravidianCodeMix 2021 shared task on sentiment detection in Tamil, Malayalam, and Kannada. In *Forum for Information Retrieval Evaluation*, pages 4–6.

Ruba Priyadharshini, Bharathi Raja Chakravarthi, Mani Vegupatti, and John P McCrae. 2020. Named entity recognition for code-mixed Indian corpus using meta embedding. In *2020 6th international conference on advanced computing and communication systems (ICACCS)*, pages 68–72. IEEE.

Manikandan Ravikiran, Bharathi Raja Chakravarthi, Anand Kumar Madasamy, Sangeetha Sivanesan, Ratnavel Rajalakshmi, Sajeetha Thavareesan, Rahul Ponnusamy, and Shankar Mahadevan. 2022. Findings of the shared task on Offensive Span Identification in code-mixed Tamil-English comments. In *Proceedings of the Second Workshop on Speech and Language Technologies for Dravidian Languages*. Association for Computational Linguistics.

Ratnasingam Sakuntharaj and Sinnathamby Mahesan. 2016. A novel hybrid approach to detect and correct spelling in Tamil text. In *2016 IEEE International Conference on Information and Automation for Sustainability (ICIAfS)*, pages 1–6.

Ratnasingam Sakuntharaj and Sinnathamby Mahesan. 2017. Use of a novel hash-table for speeding-up suggestions for misspelt Tamil words. In *2017 IEEE International Conference on Industrial and Information Systems (ICIIS)*, pages 1–5.

Ratnasingam Sakuntharaj and Sinnathamby Mahesan. 2021. Missing word detection and correction based on context of Tamil sentences using n-grams. In

2021 10th International Conference on Information and Automation for Sustainability (ICIAfS), pages 42–47.

Anbukkarasi Sampath, Thenmozhi Durairaj, Bharathi Raja Chakravarthi, Ruba Priyadharshini, Subalalitha Chinnaudayar Navaneethakrishnan, Kogilavani Shanmugavadivel, Sajeetha Thavareesan, Sathiyaraj Thangasamy, Parameswari Krishnamurthy, Adeep Hande, Sean Benhur, Kishor Kumar Ponnusamy, and Santhiya Pandiyan. 2022. Findings of the shared task on Emotion Analysis in Tamil. In *Proceedings of the Second Workshop on Speech and Language Technologies for Dravidian Languages*. Association for Computational Linguistics.

R Srinivasan and CN Subalalitha. 2019. Automated named entity recognition from tamil documents. In *2019 IEEE 1st International Conference on Energy, Systems and Information Processing (ICESIP)*, pages 1–5. IEEE.

C. N. Subalalitha. 2019. Information extraction framework for Kurunthogai. *Sādhanā*, 44(7):156.

CN Subalalitha and E Poovammal. 2018. Automatic bilingual dictionary construction for Tirukural. *Applied Artificial Intelligence*, 32(6):558–567.

Sajeetha Thavareesan and Sinnathamby Mahesan. 2019. Sentiment analysis in Tamil texts: A study on machine learning techniques and feature representation. In *2019 14th Conference on Industrial and Information Systems (ICIIS)*, pages 320–325.

Sajeetha Thavareesan and Sinnathamby Mahesan. 2020a. Sentiment lexicon expansion using Word2vec and fastText for sentiment prediction in Tamil texts. In *2020 Moratuwa Engineering Research Conference (MERCon)*, pages 272–276.

Sajeetha Thavareesan and Sinnathamby Mahesan. 2020b. Word embedding-based part of speech tagging in Tamil texts. In *2020 IEEE 15th International Conference on Industrial and Information Systems (ICIIS)*, pages 478–482.

Sajeetha Thavareesan and Sinnathamby Mahesan. 2021. Sentiment analysis in Tamil texts using k-means and k-nearest neighbour. In *2021 10th International Conference on Information and Automation for Sustainability (ICIAfS)*, pages 48–53.

Konthala Yasaswini, Karthik Puranik, Adeep Hande, Ruba Priyadharshini, Sajeetha Thavareesan, and Bharathi Raja Chakravarthi. 2021. IIITT@DravidianLangTech-EACL2021: Transfer learning for offensive language detection in Dravidian languages. In *Proceedings of the First Workshop on Speech and Language Technologies for Dravidian Languages*, pages 187–194, Kyiv. Association for Computational Linguistics.

Zhixue Zhao, Ziqi Zhang, and Frank Hopfgartner. 2021. *A Comparative Study of Using Pre-trained Language Models for Toxic Comment Classification*.

COMBATANT@TamilNLP-ACL2022: Fine-grained Categorization of Abusive Comments using Logistic Regression

Alamgir Hossain[Ψ], **Mahathir Mohammad Bishal**[Ψ], **Eftekhar Hossain**[$],
Omar Sharif[Ψ] and **Mohammed Moshiul Hoque**[Ψ]
[Ψ]Department of Computer Science and Engineering
[$]Department of Electronics and Telecommunication Engineering
[$Ψ]Chittagong University of Engineering & Technology, Chattogram-4349, Bangladesh
{u1604069, u1604083}@student.cuet.ac.bd
{omar.sharif, eftekhar.hossain, moshiul_240}@cuet.ac.bd

Abstract

With the widespread usage of social media and effortless internet access, millions of posts and comments are generated every minute. Unfortunately, with this substantial rise, the usage of abusive language has increased significantly in these mediums. This proliferation leads to many hazards such as cyber-bullying, vulgarity, online harassment and abuse. Therefore, it becomes a crucial issue to detect and mitigate the usage of abusive language. This work presents our system developed as part of the shared task to detect the abusive language in Tamil. We employed three machine learning (LR, DT, SVM), two deep learning (CNN+BiLSTM, CNN+BiLSTM with FastText) and a transformer-based model (IndicBERT). The experimental results show that Logistic regression (LR) and CNN+BiLSTM models outperformed the others. Both Logistic Regression (LR) and CNN+BiLSTM with FastText achieved the weighted F_1-score of 0.39. However, LR obtained a higher recall value (0.44) than CNN+BiLSTM (0.36). This leads us to stand the 2nd rank in the shared task competition.

1 Introduction

With the rapid growth of user-generated content in social media, the emergence of abusive content also increased dramatically (Priyadharshini et al., 2021; Kumaresan et al., 2021). This insurgence has become a reason of worry for governments, policymakers, social scientists and tech companies since it has detrimental consequences on society (Sharif et al., 2021b; Chakravarthi et al., 2020b). Currently, we are living in an information era where social media plays a vital role in shaping people's minds, and opinions (Perse and Lambe, 2016; Chakravarthi et al., 2021). Therefore mitigating the usage of abusive language has become extremely important (Sharif and Hoque, 2021b). Companies like Facebook, YouTube, Twitter have been trying to achieve this for years (Ghanghor et al., 2021a,b; Yasaswini et al., 2021). It is impossible to monitor and moderate social media content manually because of its large volume and its messy forms (Meyer, 2016). Therefore, it is necessary to develop an intelligent system to tackle this issue. Several studies have been conducted to detect abusive language for English, and other high resource languages (Kumar et al., 2020; Sampath et al., 2022; Ravikiran et al., 2022; Chakravarthi et al., 2022; Bharathi et al., 2022; Priyadharshini et al., 2022). In contrast, a low-resource language like Tamil remained out of focus and has much room for improvement (Priyadharshini et al., 2020; Chakravarthi et al., 2020a).

Tamil is an official language of Tamil Nadu, Sri Lanka, Singapore, and the Union Territory of Puducherry in India (Anita and Subalalitha, 2019b,a; Subalalitha and Poovammal, 2018). Significant minority speak Tamil in the four other South Indian states of Kerala, Karnataka, Andhra Pradesh, and Telangana, as well as the Union Territory of the Andaman and Nicobar Islands (Subalalitha, 2019; Srinivasan and Subalalitha, 2019; Narasimhan et al., 2018). Tamil, as a Dravidian language, descended from Proto-Dravidian, a proto-language, according to Bhadriraju Krishnamurti. Linguistic reconstruction implies that Proto-Dravidian was spoken about the third millennium BC, likely in the peninsular Indian region surrounding the lower Godavari river basin. The material evidence implies that the speakers of Proto-Dravidian belonged to the civilization linked with South India's Neolithic complexes. The earliest Old Tamil documents are small inscriptions in Adichanallur dating from 905 BC to 696 BC. Tamil has the most ancient non-Sanskritic Indian literature (Sakuntharaj and Mahesan, 2021, 2017, 2016; Thavareesan and Mahesan, 2019, 2020a,b, 2021).

This work aims to build a system that can classify abusive language from Tamil text concerning

Proceedings of the Second Workshop on Speech and Language Technologies for Dravidian Languages, pages 221 - 228
May 26, 2022 ©2022 Association for Computational Linguistics

eight different categories: *Hope-Speech, Homophobia, Misandry, Counter-speech, Misogyny, Xenophobia, Transphobia and None-of-the-above*. Various machine learning (ML), deep learning (DL), and transformer-based models have been used to attain this goal. The key contributions of this work are illustrated in the following:

- Developed multiple ML and DL techniques to classify abusive texts in Tamil into eight classes.
- Investigated the performance of the models to find the suitable method for the classification of abusive comments and analyzed in-depth error, providing useful insight into abusive text classification.

2 Related Work

Recently, researchers are trying to develop methods and tools to analyze social media sites like Twitter, Facebook, and Snapchat since these mediums has become integral part of our life (Anand and Eswari, 2019). Studies have already been conducted to detect abusive or offensive comments on social media (Sharif et al., 2021a; Aurpa et al., 2022; Sharif et al., 2020). Few researches has focused on other overlapping domains such as hate speech (Founta et al., 2018; Waseem et al., 2017), cyberbullying (Fosler-Lussier et al., 2012), racism/sexism (Talat et al., 2018), aggression & trolling (Zampieri et al., 2019) and so on. All of these researches primarily conducted for high-resource languages. Very few researches have been carried out to detect abusive language for low-resources languages like Tamil. Eshan and Hasan (2017) evaluated the effectiveness of RF, NB, and SVM classifiers to detect abusive language. Their system achieved the maximum accuracy ($\approx$ 95%) for SVM with linear kernel and tri-gram features. Ishmam and Sharmin (2019) collected roughly 5000 Bengali abusive comments from Facebook and categorized them into six different classes: *hate speech, communal attack, inciteful comments, religious hatred, political hatred etc.* They obtained the highest accuracy of 70.10% utilizing the GRU-based model. Salminen et al. (2020) collected 197,566 comments from Twitter, Wikipedia, Reedit and YouTube, where 20% of the data was hateful. They applied logistic regression, naïve bayes, support vector machines, XGBoost techniques on this dataset and obtained 0.92 F_1-score using XGBoost classifier. Sharif and Hoque (2021a) developed a gold standard dataset on Bengali aggressive comments from social media called 'ATxtC', which contains 7591 annotated data. In the subsequent work they presented a novel Bengali aggressive text dataset (called 'BAD') with two-level of annotation (Sharif and Hoque, 2021b). They proposed a weighted ensemble technique that uses m-BERT, distil-BERT, Bangla-BERT, and XLM-R as base classifiers to identify and categorize aggressive texts in Bengal. The model achieved the highest weighted-score of 93.43% in the identification task and 93.11% in the categorization task.

3 Task and Dataset Description

Task organizers created a gold standard dataset to detect abusive comments from Tamil social networking sites. This task aims to develop a system that can correctly identify abusive texts from a given set of texts in Tamil. We used the corpus provided by the organizers of the workshop[1] (Chakravarthi, 2020; Chakravarthi and Muralidaran, 2021; Hande et al., 2021; Priyadharshini et al., 2022). The shared task required classifying a text into eight predefined classes (i.e., Misogyny, Misandry, Homophobia, Transphobia, Xenophobia, Counter-speech, Hope-speech and None-of-the-above). Table 1 reports the number of samples in the train, validation, and test sets for each class. Dataset is quite imbalanced where Transphobia and Homophobia classes have only 10 and 51 text samples, respectively. Before model development, we preprocessed the dataset to exclude irrelevant characters, numbers, symbols, punctuation marks, and emojis.

Class	Train	Validation	Test
Misogyny	125	24	48
Misandry	447	104	127
Homophobia	35	8	8
Transphobia	6	2	2
Xenophobia	95	29	25
Counter-speech	149	36	47
Hope-speech	87	11	26
None-of-the-above	1296	346	416
Total	2240	560	699

Table 1: Class wise dataset distribution in train, validation and test set

[1]https://competitions.codalab.org/competitions/36403

4 Methodology

The techniques and methods used to detect abusive categories for given YouTube comments are briefly explained in this section. We cleaned the raw data first by stripping away noisy elements and then extracted features (Lewis, 1992) using various feature extraction techniques, including TF-IDF, Word2Vec, and FastText. We used ML and DL based techniques for the baseline evaluation. The schematic process of our approach is depicted in Figure 1.

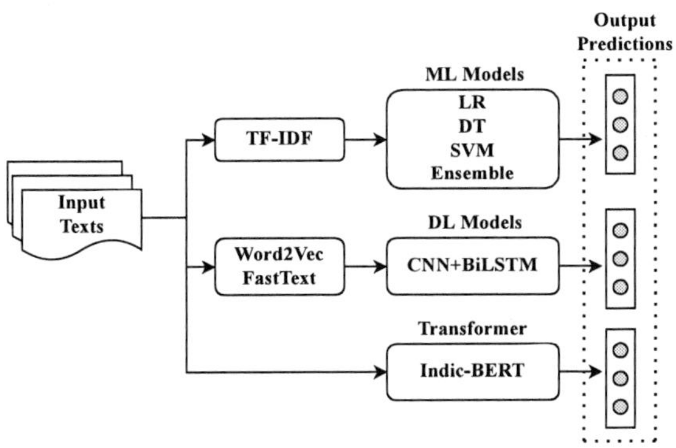

Figure 1: Schematic process of abusive comments classification

4.1 Feature Extraction

Feature extraction is conducted prior to training the models. The TF-IDF (Nayel, 2020) values of the unigram features are calculated and used for training ML models. On the other hand, Word2Vec (Jurgens, 2021) and FastText (Joulin et al., 2017) embeddings are used as feature for the DL models. Keras embedding layer generates the embedding vectors of the dimension of 100. In contrast, a pre-trained embedding matrix is in the case of FastText embedding.

4.2 ML Baselines

In order to design the abusive comment detection system, we developed several ML-based methods such as logistic regression (LR), decision tree (DT), and support vector machine (SVM). After constructing the three models, we also use the majority voting ensemble technique to predict the abusive category of the texts. Furthermore, in search of improved performance, an ensemble approach is applied using the classifiers mentioned earlier. In LR and DT models, the C value is settled at 2, whereas SVM is implemented with a C value of 6.

4.3 DL Baselines

In the case of DL approach (Ruiz et al., 2020), we combined CNN and LSTM (Du et al., 2020) to classify a given comment. A total of seven layers is used to construct the combined model. Initially, a sequence vector of length 260 is fed to the embedding layer. Subsequently, two convolution layers are added with the 'relu' activation function. Features are downsampled through a max-pooling layer before passing to the BiLSTM layer. BiLSTM has 128 units, and the overfitting problem is reduced by setting the dropout rate to 0.2. Finally, a softmax layer is used to get the predictions. We also performed experimentation with pre-trained word vectors (FastText). We use the 'Adam'optimizer with a learning rate of $1e^{-3}$,and a loss function of 'sparse_categorical_crossentropy'. The model has been trained for 25 epochs with a batch size of 32.

4.3.1 Transformers

Considering the recent vogue of transformers, we also employ a transformer-based model. Specifically, we chose Indic-BERT as a pre-trained model is trained on the texts of various Indian languages such as Tamil, Bangla, and Telugu. We chose Indic-BERT because it has far fewer parameters than other multilingual models (i.e., mBERT, XLM-R, etc.) while achieving comparable performance (Kakwani et al., 2020). The maximum length of the input text is settled to 150 and use Ktrain (Maiya, 2020) package to fine-tune the model. The model is compiled using the Ktrain 'fit_onecycle'method along with a learning rate of $2e^{-5}$. Finally, the training is performed for 4 epochs bypassing 12 instances at each iteration. The implementation details of implemented models have been open sourced for reproducibility[2].

5 Results and Analysis

The performance of the various methods on the test set is reported in Table 2. The macro F_1-score measures the supremacy of the models. However, we pay close attention to the other measures such as accuracy (A), precision (P) and recall (R) scores.

It is observed that, among the ML models, the LR model outperformed the DT and SVM models achieving the highest macro F_1-score (0.39). The combination of CNN and BiLSTM (C+B) achieved a very low macro F_1-score (0.16) when trained with

[2]https://github.com/m1n1-coder/ML-and-DL-models-of-Tamil-Abusive-Comment-Detection

Methods	Classifier	P	R	F_1-score	A
ML models	LR	0.38	**0.44**	**0.39**	0.60
	DT	0.31	0.34	0.32	0.57
	SVM	0.54	0.26	0.29	0.66
	Ensemble	0.26	0.44	0.28	0.67
DL models	C+B (Word2Vec)	0.19	0.18	0.16	0.31
	C+B (FastText)	0.52	0.36	0.39	0.63
Transformer	Indic-BERT	0.22	0.20	0.19	0.69

Table 2: Performance of various models on the test set. Here, C+B represents the CNN+BiLSTM model

Word2Vec features. Surprisingly, the performance is improved to 0.39 when we used a pre-trained word embedding (i.e. FastText). Unfortunately, the transformer model, Indic-BERT, could not provide satisfactory performance on the test set. Moreover, we conducted a thorough investigation into all of the employed models. The outcomes of the investigation is presented in Table 3. It is revealed that the LR model predicts 6 of the 8 categories with the highest F_1-score. This demonstrated that the LR model performed admirably and was the best model across all evaluation metrics. However, CNN+BiLSTM with FastText embedding also achieved the same macro F_1-score (0.39). On the other hand, the transformer model performs poorly due to the prevalence of local words across the different abusive classes.

The comparative analysis illustrates that our model (i.e., **COMBATANT**) achieved the 2nd position in the task (Table-4). Although we investigated various ML and DL models on the corpus, the submission included the best three models (LR, SVM, and CNN+BiLSTM (with FastText)). The LR model outperformed the other models by achieving the highest F_1-score.

5.1 Error Analysis

The LR classifier outperformed all models in classifying Tamil abusive comments on the shared task dataset. However, it is necessary to investigate the errors of the model in order to assess how accurately the classifier performed across the different classes. The confusion matrix is used to illustrate the errors (Figure 2). We noticed that, among the classes, **Misandry** and **Counter-Speech** contained a relatively high true positive rate (TPR). Misandry class obtained a TPR of 65.35%, whereas Counter-Speech achieved 53.2%. However, **Transphobia** has a TPR of 0%. With a low TPR, **Homophobia** class also experienced a large number of miss-

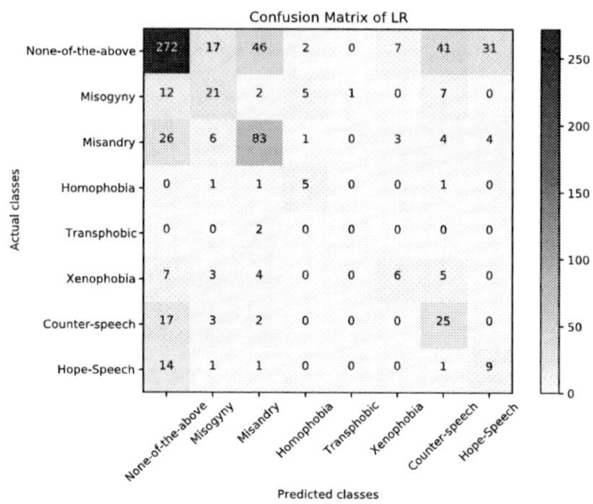

Figure 2: Confusion matrix of the best model (LR).

classification. This lower outcome could be occurred due to inadequacy and class imbalance of data. As a result, many of the test data were incorrectly classified as **None-of-the-above**.

6 Conclusion

This paper presents the various models developed to classify abusive comments in Tamil. This work used three ML, two DL classifiers and one transformer-based model to perform the classification task. The LR model with TF-IDF features outperformed all models by obtaining the highest macro F_1-score (0.39). Although the combined CNN and BiLSTM model (C+B) achieved a similar macro F_1-score (0.39) with FastText features, the LR model obtained a higher recall value (0.44). Surprisingly, Indic-BERT performed poorly compared to the ML and DL models. These inferior results might occur because of the prevalence of local words, which is unknown to the model. It will be interesting to investigate how the model performs if the dataset is used in more advanced transformer models (XML-R, Electra, mBERT, MuRIL).

Classes	LR	DT	SVM	Ensemble	C+B(Word2Vec)	C+B(FastText)	Indic-BERT
Misogyny	**0.42**	0.31	0.21	0.24	0.08	0.14	0.15
Misandry	**0.62**	0.50	0.54	0.55	0.28	0.53	0.42
Homophobia	**0.48**	0.42	0.46	0.43	0.00	0.50	0.15
Transphobic	0.00	0.00	0.00	0.00	0.00	**0.67**	0.03
Xenophobia	**0.29**	0.14	0.07	0.07	0.10	0.10	0.07
Counter-speech	**0.38**	0.28	0.15	0.00	0.21	0.26	0.11
Hope-Speech	**0.26**	0.18	0.14	0.20	0.11	0.14	0.10
None-of-the-above	0.71	0.72	0.78	**0.79**	0.47	0.78	0.49

Table 3: Class-wise performance of models in terms of F_1-score

Team_Names	Precision	Recall	F1-score	Rank
CEN-Tamil	0.380	0.290	0.320	1
COMBATANT	0.290	0.330	0.300	2
DE-ABUSE	0.330	0.290	0.291	3
DLRG	0.340	0.260	0.270	4
TROOPER	0.400	0.230	0.250	5
abusive-checker	0.140	0.140	0.140	6
Optimize_Prime_Tamil_Run1	0.130	0.130	0.130	7
GJG_Tamil	0.130	0.140	0.130	8
umuteam_tamil	0.130	0.130	0.130	9
MUCIC	0.120	0.130	0.120	10
BpHigh_tamil(1)	0.180	0.120	0.060	11
SSNCSE_NLP	0.130	0.140	0.090	12

Table 4: Summary of performance comparison for all participating teams in the shared task

Furthermore, we aim to tackle the data imbalance problem by adding more diverse data to the existing corpus that might improve the model's performance.

Acknowledgements

This work supported by the ICT Innovation Fund, ICT Division, Ministry of Posts, Telecommunications and Information Technology, Bangladesh.

References

Mukul Anand and R Eswari. 2019. Classification of abusive comments in social media using deep learning. In *2019 3rd international conference on computing methodologies and communication (ICCMC)*, pages 974–977. IEEE.

R Anita and CN Subalalitha. 2019a. An approach to cluster Tamil literatures using discourse connectives. In *2019 IEEE 1st International Conference on Energy, Systems and Information Processing (ICESIP)*, pages 1–4. IEEE.

R Anita and CN Subalalitha. 2019b. Building discourse parser for Thirukkural. In *Proceedings of the 16th International Conference on Natural Language Processing*, pages 18–25.

Tanjim Taharat Aurpa, Rifat Sadik, and Md Shoaib Ahmed. 2022. Abusive bangla comments detection on facebook using transformer-based deep learning models. *Social Network Analysis and Mining*, 12(1):1–14.

B Bharathi, Bharathi Raja Chakravarthi, Subalalitha Chinnaudayar Navaneethakrishnan, N Sripriya, Arunaggiri Pandian, and Swetha Valli. 2022. Findings of the shared task on Speech Recognition for Vulnerable Individuals in Tamil. In *Proceedings of the Second Workshop on Language Technology for Equality, Diversity and Inclusion*. Association for Computational Linguistics.

Bharathi Raja Chakravarthi. 2020. Hopeedi: A multilingual hope speech detection dataset for equality, diversity, and inclusion. In *Proceedings of the Third Workshop on Computational Modeling of People's Opinions, Personality, and Emotion's in Social Media*, pages 41–53.

Bharathi Raja Chakravarthi and Vigneshwaran Muralidaran. 2021. Findings of the shared task on hope speech detection for equality, diversity, and inclusion. In *Proceedings of the First Workshop on Language Technology for Equality, Diversity and Inclusion*, pages 61–72, Kyiv. Association for Computational Linguistics.

Bharathi Raja Chakravarthi, Vigneshwaran Muralidaran, Ruba Priyadharshini, and John Philip McCrae. 2020a. Corpus creation for sentiment analysis in code-mixed Tamil-English text. In *Proceedings of the 1st Joint Workshop on Spoken Language Technologies for Under-resourced languages (SLTU) and Collaboration and Computing for Under-Resourced Languages (CCURL)*, pages 202–210, Marseille, France. European Language Resources association.

Bharathi Raja Chakravarthi, Ruba Priyadharshini, Thenmozhi Durairaj, John Phillip McCrae, Paul Buitaleer, Prasanna Kumar Kumaresan, and Rahul Ponnusamy.

2022. Findings of the shared task on Homophobia Transphobia Detection in Social Media Comments. In *Proceedings of the Second Workshop on Language Technology for Equality, Diversity and Inclusion*. Association for Computational Linguistics.

Bharathi Raja Chakravarthi, Ruba Priyadharshini, Vigneshwaran Muralidaran, Shardul Suryawanshi, Navya Jose, Elizabeth Sherly, and John P McCrae. 2020b. Overview of the track on sentiment analysis for Dravidian languages in code-mixed text. In *Forum for Information Retrieval Evaluation*, pages 21–24.

Bharathi Raja Chakravarthi, Ruba Priyadharshini, Rahul Ponnusamy, Prasanna Kumar Kumaresan, Kayalvizhi Sampath, Durairaj Thenmozhi, Sathiyaraj Thangasamy, Rajendran Nallathambi, and John Phillip McCrae. 2021. Dataset for identification of homophobia and transophobia in multilingual YouTube comments. *arXiv preprint arXiv:2109.00227*.

Jinhua Du, Yan Huang, and Karo Moilanen. 2020. Pointing to select: A fast pointer-LSTM for long text classification. In *Proceedings of the 28th International Conference on Computational Linguistics*, pages 6184–6193, Barcelona, Spain (Online). International Committee on Computational Linguistics.

Shahnoor C Eshan and Mohammad S Hasan. 2017. An application of machine learning to detect abusive bengali text. In *2017 20th International Conference of Computer and Information Technology (ICCIT)*, pages 1–6. IEEE.

Eric Fosler-Lussier, Ellen Riloff, and Srinivas Bangalore. 2012. Proceedings of the 2012 conference of the north american chapter of the association for computational linguistics: Human language technologies. In *Proceedings of the 2012 Conference of the North American Chapter of the Association for Computational Linguistics: Human Language Technologies*.

Antigoni Maria Founta, Constantinos Djouvas, Despoina Chatzakou, Ilias Leontiadis, Jeremy Blackburn, Gianluca Stringhini, Athena Vakali, Michael Sirivianos, and Nicolas Kourtellis. 2018. Large scale crowdsourcing and characterization of twitter abusive behavior. In *Twelfth International AAAI Conference on Web and Social Media*.

Nikhil Ghanghor, Parameswari Krishnamurthy, Sajeetha Thavareesan, Ruba Priyadharshini, and Bharathi Raja Chakravarthi. 2021a. IIITK@DravidianLangTech-EACL2021: Offensive language identification and meme classification in Tamil, Malayalam and Kannada. In *Proceedings of the First Workshop on Speech and Language Technologies for Dravidian Languages*, pages 222–229, Kyiv. Association for Computational Linguistics.

Nikhil Ghanghor, Rahul Ponnusamy, Prasanna Kumar Kumaresan, Ruba Priyadharshini, Sajeetha Thavareesan, and Bharathi Raja Chakravarthi. 2021b. IIITK@LT-EDI-EACL2021: Hope speech detection for equality, diversity, and inclusion in Tamil , Malayalam and English. In *Proceedings of the First Workshop on Language Technology for Equality, Diversity and Inclusion*, pages 197–203, Kyiv. Association for Computational Linguistics.

Adeep Hande, Ruba Priyadharshini, Anbukkarasi Sampath, Kingston Pal Thamburaj, Prabakaran Chandran, and Bharathi Raja Chakravarthi. 2021. Hope speech detection in under-resourced kannada language.

Alvi Md Ishmam and Sadia Sharmin. 2019. Hateful speech detection in public facebook pages for the bengali language. In *2019 18th IEEE International Conference On Machine Learning And Applications (ICMLA)*, pages 555–560. IEEE.

Armand Joulin, Edouard Grave, Piotr Bojanowski, and Tomas Mikolov. 2017. Bag of tricks for efficient text classification. In *Proceedings of the 15th Conference of the European Chapter of the Association for Computational Linguistics: Volume 2, Short Papers*, pages 427–431, Valencia, Spain. Association for Computational Linguistics.

David Jurgens. 2021. Learning about word vector representations and deep learning through implementing word2vec. In *Proceedings of the Fifth Workshop on Teaching NLP*, pages 108–111, Online. Association for Computational Linguistics.

Divyanshu Kakwani, Anoop Kunchukuttan, Satish Golla, Gokul N.C., Avik Bhattacharyya, Mitesh M. Khapra, and Pratyush Kumar. 2020. IndicNLPSuite: Monolingual Corpora, Evaluation Benchmarks and Pre-trained Multilingual Language Models for Indian Languages. In *Findings of EMNLP*.

Ritesh Kumar, Atul Kr. Ojha, Bornini Lahiri, Marcos Zampieri, Shervin Malmasi, Vanessa Murdock, and Daniel Kadar, editors. 2020. *Proceedings of the Second Workshop on Trolling, Aggression and Cyberbullying*. European Language Resources Association (ELRA), Marseille, France.

Prasanna Kumar Kumaresan, Ratnasingam Sakuntharaj, Sajeetha Thavareesan, Subalalitha Navaneethakrishnan, Anand Kumar Madasamy, Bharathi Raja Chakravarthi, and John P McCrae. 2021. Findings of shared task on offensive language identification in Tamil and Malayalam. In *Forum for Information Retrieval Evaluation*, pages 16–18.

David D. Lewis. 1992. Feature selection and feature extraction for text categorization. In *Speech and Natural Language: Proceedings of a Workshop Held at Harriman, New York, February 23-26, 1992*.

Arun S Maiya. 2020. ktrain: A low-code library for augmented machine learning. *arXiv preprint arXiv:2004.10703*.

Robinson Meyer. 2016. Twitter's famous racist problem. *The Atlantic*, 7:21.

Anitha Narasimhan, Aarthy Anandan, Madhan Karky, and CN Subalalitha. 2018. Porul: Option generation and selection and scoring algorithms for a tamil flash card game. *International Journal of Cognitive and Language Sciences*, 12(2):225–228.

Hamada Nayel. 2020. NAYEL at SemEval-2020 task 12: TF/IDF-based approach for automatic offensive language detection in Arabic tweets. In *Proceedings of the Fourteenth Workshop on Semantic Evaluation*, pages 2086–2089, Barcelona (online). International Committee for Computational Linguistics.

Elizabeth M Perse and Jennifer Lambe. 2016. *Media effects and society*. Routledge.

Ruba Priyadharshini, Bharathi Raja Chakravarthi, Subalalitha Chinnaudayar Navaneethakrishnan, Thenmozhi Durairaj, Malliga Subramanian, Kogilavani Shanmugavadivel, Siddhanth U Hegde, and Prasanna Kumar Kumaresan. 2022. Findings of the shared task on Abusive Comment Detection in Tamil. In *Proceedings of the Second Workshop on Speech and Language Technologies for Dravidian Languages*. Association for Computational Linguistics.

Ruba Priyadharshini, Bharathi Raja Chakravarthi, Sajeetha Thavareesan, Dhivya Chinnappa, Durairaj Thenmozhi, and Rahul Ponnusamy. 2021. Overview of the DravidianCodeMix 2021 shared task on sentiment detection in Tamil, Malayalam, and Kannada. In *Forum for Information Retrieval Evaluation*, pages 4–6.

Ruba Priyadharshini, Bharathi Raja Chakravarthi, Mani Vegupatti, and John P McCrae. 2020. Named entity recognition for code-mixed Indian corpus using meta embedding. In *2020 6th international conference on advanced computing and communication systems (ICACCS)*, pages 68–72. IEEE.

Manikandan Ravikiran, Bharathi Raja Chakravarthi, Anand Kumar Madasamy, Sangeetha Sivanesan, Ratnavel Rajalakshmi, Sajeetha Thavareesan, Rahul Ponnusamy, and Shankar Mahadevan. 2022. Findings of the shared task on Offensive Span Identification in code-mixed Tamil-English comments. In *Proceedings of the Second Workshop on Speech and Language Technologies for Dravidian Languages*. Association for Computational Linguistics.

Guillermo Ruiz, Eric S. Tellez, Daniela Moctezuma, Sabino Miranda-Jiménez, Tania Ramírez-delReal, and Mario Graff. 2020. Infotec + CentroGEO at SemEval-2020 task 8: Deep learning and text categorization approach for memes classification. In *Proceedings of the Fourteenth Workshop on Semantic Evaluation*, pages 1141–1147, Barcelona (online). International Committee for Computational Linguistics.

Ratnasingam Sakuntharaj and Sinnathamby Mahesan. 2016. A novel hybrid approach to detect and correct spelling in Tamil text. In *2016 IEEE International Conference on Information and Automation for Sustainability (ICIAfS)*, pages 1–6.

Ratnasingam Sakuntharaj and Sinnathamby Mahesan. 2017. Use of a novel hash-table for speeding-up suggestions for misspelt Tamil words. In *2017 IEEE International Conference on Industrial and Information Systems (ICIIS)*, pages 1–5.

Ratnasingam Sakuntharaj and Sinnathamby Mahesan. 2021. Missing word detection and correction based on context of Tamil sentences using n-grams. In *2021 10th International Conference on Information and Automation for Sustainability (ICIAfS)*, pages 42–47.

Joni Salminen, Maximilian Hopf, Shammur A Chowdhury, Soon-gyo Jung, Hind Almerekhi, and Bernard J Jansen. 2020. Developing an online hate classifier for multiple social media platforms. *Human-centric Computing and Information Sciences*, 10(1):1–34.

Anbukkarasi Sampath, Thenmozhi Durairaj, Bharathi Raja Chakravarthi, Ruba Priyadharshini, Subalalitha Chinnaudayar Navaneethakrishnan, Kogilavani Shanmugavadivel, Sajeetha Thavareesan, Sathiyaraj Thangasamy, Parameswari Krishnamurthy, Adeep Hande, Sean Benhur, Kishor Kumar Ponnusamy, and Santhiya Pandiyan. 2022. Findings of the shared task on Emotion Analysis in Tamil. In *Proceedings of the Second Workshop on Speech and Language Technologies for Dravidian Languages*. Association for Computational Linguistics.

Omar Sharif and Mohammed Moshiul Hoque. 2021a. Identification and classification of textual aggression in social media: resource creation and evaluation. In *International Workshop on Combating On line Ho st ile Posts in Regional Languages dur ing Emerge ncy Si tuation*, pages 9–20. Springer.

Omar Sharif and Mohammed Moshiul Hoque. 2021b. Tackling cyber-aggression: Identification and fine-grained categorization of aggressive texts on social media using weighted ensemble of transformers. *Neurocomputing*.

Omar Sharif, Mohammed Moshiul Hoque, A. S. M. Kayes, Raza Nowrozy, and Iqbal H. Sarker. 2020. Detecting suspicious texts using machine learning techniques. *Applied Sciences*, 10(18).

Omar Sharif, Eftekhar Hossain, and Mohammed Moshiul Hoque. 2021a. Combating hostility: Covid-19 fake news and hostile post detection in social media.

Omar Sharif, Eftekhar Hossain, and Mohammed Moshiul Hoque. 2021b. NLP-CUET@DravidianLangTech-EACL2021: Offensive language detection from multilingual code-mixed text using transformers. pages 255–261.

R Srinivasan and CN Subalalitha. 2019. Automated named entity recognition from tamil documents. In *2019 IEEE 1st International Conference on Energy,*

Systems and Information Processing (ICESIP), pages 1–5. IEEE.

C. N. Subalalitha. 2019. Information extraction framework for Kurunthogai. *Sādhanā*, 44(7):156.

CN Subalalitha and E Poovammal. 2018. Automatic bilingual dictionary construction for Tirukural. *Applied Artificial Intelligence*, 32(6):558–567.

Zeerak Talat, James Thorne, and Joachim Bingel. 2018. Bridging the gaps: Multi task learning for domain transfer of hate speech detection. In *Online harassment*, pages 29–55. Springer.

Sajeetha Thavareesan and Sinnathamby Mahesan. 2019. Sentiment analysis in Tamil texts: A study on machine learning techniques and feature representation. In *2019 14th Conference on Industrial and Information Systems (ICIIS)*, pages 320–325.

Sajeetha Thavareesan and Sinnathamby Mahesan. 2020a. Sentiment lexicon expansion using Word2vec and fastText for sentiment prediction in Tamil texts. In *2020 Moratuwa Engineering Research Conference (MERCon)*, pages 272–276.

Sajeetha Thavareesan and Sinnathamby Mahesan. 2020b. Word embedding-based part of speech tagging in Tamil texts. In *2020 IEEE 15th International Conference on Industrial and Information Systems (ICIIS)*, pages 478–482.

Sajeetha Thavareesan and Sinnathamby Mahesan. 2021. Sentiment analysis in Tamil texts using k-means and k-nearest neighbour. In *2021 10th International Conference on Information and Automation for Sustainability (ICIAfS)*, pages 48–53.

Zeerak Waseem, Thomas Davidson, Dana Warmsley, and Ingmar Weber. 2017. Understanding abuse: A typology of abusive language detection subtasks. *arXiv preprint arXiv:1705.09899*.

Konthala Yasaswini, Karthik Puranik, Adeep Hande, Ruba Priyadharshini, Sajeetha Thavareesan, and Bharathi Raja Chakravarthi. 2021. IIITT@DravidianLangTech-EACL2021: Transfer learning for offensive language detection in Dravidian languages. In *Proceedings of the First Workshop on Speech and Language Technologies for Dravidian Languages*, pages 187–194, Kyiv. Association for Computational Linguistics.

Marcos Zampieri, Shervin Malmasi, Preslav Nakov, Sara Rosenthal, Noura Farra, and Ritesh Kumar. 2019. Semeval-2019 task 6: Identifying and categorizing offensive language in social media (offenseval). *arXiv preprint arXiv:1903.08983*.

Optimize_Prime@DravidianLangTech-ACL2022: Emotion Analysis in Tamil

Omkar Gokhale*, **Shantanu Patankar***, **Onkar Litake**†, **Aditya Mandke**†, **Dipali Kadam**
Pune Institute of Computer Technology, Pune, India
omkargokhale2001@gmail.com, shantanupatankar2001@gmail.com, onkarlitake@ieee.org, adeetya.m@gmail.com, ddkadam@pict.edu

Abstract

This paper aims to perform an emotion analysis of social media comments in Tamil. Emotion analysis is the process of identifying the emotional context of the text. In this paper, we present the findings obtained by Team Optimize_Prime in the ACL 2022 shared task "Emotion Analysis in Tamil." The task aimed to classify social media comments into categories of emotion like Joy, Anger, Trust, Disgust, etc. The task was further divided into two subtasks, one with 11 broad categories of emotions and the other with 31 specific categories of emotion. We implemented three different approaches to tackle this problem: transformer-based models, Recurrent Neural Networks (RNNs), and Ensemble models. XLM-RoBERTa performed the best on the first task with a macro-averaged f1 score of 0.27, while MuRIL provided the best results on the second task with a macro-averaged f1 score of 0.13.

1 Introduction

Due to the rise in social media, internet users can voice their opinion on various subjects. Social networking platforms have grown in popularity and are used for a variety of activities such as product promotion, news sharing, and accomplishment sharing, among others (Chakravarthi et al., 2021). Emotion analysis or opinion mining is the study of extracting people's sentiment about a particular topic, person, or organization from textual data. Emotion analysis has many modern-day use-cases in e-commerce, social media monitoring, market research, etc. Tamil is the 18th most spoken language globally (Wikipedia contributors, 2022), with over 75 million speakers. Developing an approach for emotion analysis of Tamil text will benefit many people and businesses.

Emotion Analysis, at its core, is a text classification problem. To date, various approaches have been developed for text classification. Earlier, classification models like logistic regression, linear SVC, etc., were used. RNN based approaches like LSTMs also gained much traction because they produced better results than standard machine learning models. The introduction of transformers (Vaswani et al., 2017) changed the course of text classification due to their consistent performance. Multiple variations of the transformer have been developed like BERT (Devlin et al., 2018), AlBERT (Lan et al., 2019), XLM-RoBERTa (Conneau et al., 2019), MuRIL (Khanuja et al., 2021), etc.

In this paper, we have tried various approaches to detect emotions from social media comments. We have used three distinct ways to get optimal results: Ensemble models, Recurrent Neural Networks (RNNs), and transformer-based approaches. This paper will contribute towards future research in emotion analysis in low-resource Indic languages.

2 Related Work

Emotion Analysis has recently gained popularity, as large volumes of data are added to social networking sites daily. Earlier studies focus more on lexicon-based approaches, and they make use of a pre-prepared sentiment lexicon to classify the text. e.g., in Tkalčič et al. (2016), Wang and Pal (2015) and yan Nie et al. (2015), lexicon-based approaches are used; however, if unrelated words express emotions, this approach fails.

To overcome the limitations of lexical/keyword-based approaches, learning-based approaches were introduced. In this, the model learns from the data and tries to find a relationship between input text and the corresponding emotion. Researchers have tried out both supervised and unsupervised learning approaches. e.g., in Wikarsa and Thahir (2015), tweet classification was performed using naïve Bayes (supervised learning). In Hussien et al. (2016), SVM and multimodal naïve Bayes were used to classify Arabic tweets.

*first author, equal contribution
†second author, equal contribution

Proceedings of the Second Workshop on Speech and Language Technologies for Dravidian Languages, pages 229 - 234
May 26, 2022 ©2022 Association for Computational Linguistics

Emotion	Neutral	Joy	Ambiguous	Trust	Disgust	Anticipation	Anger	Sadness	Love	Surprise	Fear
%	34.24%	15.3%	11.82%	8.6%	6.3%	5.9%	5.7%	5.07%	4.8%	1.63%	0.7%

Table 1: Class-wise distribution of data.

A combination of lexicon-based and learning-based approaches were used to perform classification on a multilingual dataset in Jain et al. (2017). Transfer learning-based approaches work well for low-resource languages. Transfer learning allows us to reuse the existing pre-trained models. For example, Ahmad et al. (2020) used a transfer learning approach to classify text in Hindi.

Lately, transformer-based models have been consistently outperforming other architectures, including RNNs. The development of models like MuRiL (Khanuja et al., 2021), XLM-RoBERTa (Conneau et al., 2019), Indic BERT (Kakwani et al., 2020), and M-BERT (Devlin et al., 2018) has encouraged research in various low resource as well as high resource languages.

3 Dataset Description

The shared task on Emotion Analysis in Tamil-ACL 2022 aims to classify social media comments into categories of emotions. The Emotion Analysis in Tamil Dataset (Sampath et al., 2022) consists of two datasets. The first dataset is for task A and has 11 categories of emotions which are: Neutral, Joy, Ambiguous, Trust, Disgust, Anger, Anticipation, Sadness, Love, Surprise, Fear. While the second is for task B and has 31 more specific categories of emotions. The distribution of data among classes is given in Table 1

3.1 Task A

The train, dev, and test datasets have 14,208, 3,552, and 4,440 data points, respectively. Each data point in the training data has the text in Tamil and its corresponding label in English.

3.2 Task B

The train, dev, and test datasets have 30,180, 4,269, and 4,269 data points, respectively. Each data point in the training data has the text in Tamil and its corresponding label, also in Tamil.
There is a significant class imbalance in the dataset, representing social media comments in real life.

4 Methodology

To classify social media comments into different emotions, we used three different approaches: ensemble models, Recurrent Neural Networks, and transformers. Figure 1. shows the architecture of all the three approaches[1].

4.1 Data Processing

4.1.1 Data cleaning

We removed punctuations, URL patterns, and stop words. For better contextual understanding, we replaced emojis with their textual equivalents. For example, the laughing emoji was replaced by the Tamil equivalent of the word laughter.

Data cleaning boosted the performance of all RNN models and all transformer models except for MuRIL. MuRIL and all ensemble models worked best without data cleaning.

4.1.2 Handling data imbalance

There is a significant class imbalance in the data. To reduce the imbalance, we used the following techniques: over-sampling, over-under sampling, Synthetic Minority Over-sampling (SMOTE) (Chawla et al., 2002), and assigning class weights. In over-under sampling, we under-sample the classes having more instances than expected and over-sample those having lesser instances than expected while keeping the length of the dataset constant. Over-under sampling worked best for all transformer and ensemble models, but it reduced the performance of RNN models. Assigning class weights to the input boosted the performance of the M-BERT - Logistic Regression ensemble model.

4.2 Ensemble model

As shown in the figure, we concatenate different machine learning models with multilingual BERT(M-BERT) (Devlin et al., 2018). Multilingual BERT is a BERT-based transformer trained in 104 languages. It simultaneously encodes knowledge of all these languages. M-BERT generates a sentence embeddings vector of length 768, with

[1] https://github.com/PICT-NLP/Optimize_Prime-DravidianLangTech2022-Emotion_Analysis

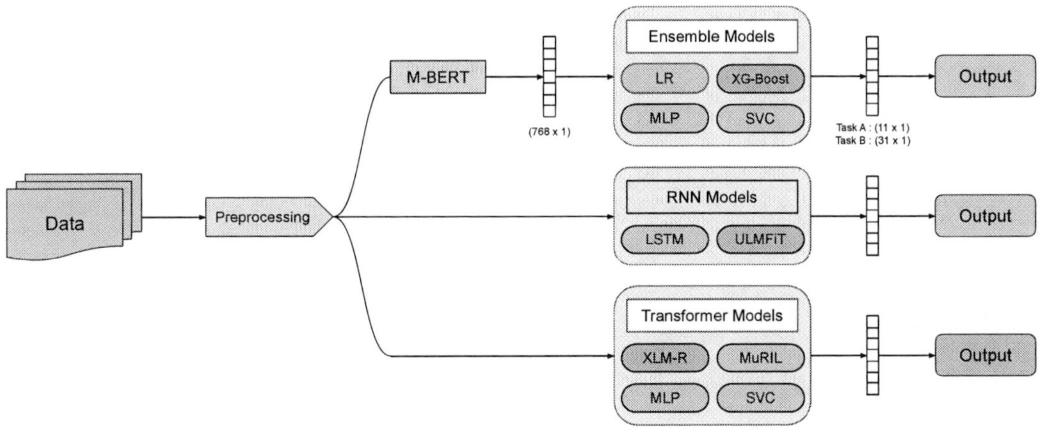

Figure 1: Model architecture (green box represents the classifier with highest f1 score in the group)

context. We then pass these embeddings to different machine learning models like logistic regression, decision trees, and XGBoost. We used grid search with macro-averaged f1 score as the scoring parameter for 3-5 cross-validation folds to fine-tune the hyperparameters.

4.3 RNN Models

We have used two RNN models, Long Short-Term Memory(LSTM) networks and ULM-Fit.

4.3.1 Vanilla LSTM

For setting a baseline for an RNN approach, we built word embeddings from scratch by choosing the top 64,000 most frequently occurring words in the dataset. This is passed through an embedding layer to get 100 dimension word vectors. The rest of the model includes a spatial drop out of 0.2, followed by the classification model consisting of two linear layers followed by a softmax.

4.3.2 ULM-Fit

In transfer learning approaches, models are trained on large corpora, and their word embeddings are fine-tuned for specific tasks. In many state-of-the-art models, this approach is successful (Mikolov et al., 2013). Although Howard and Ruder (2018) argue that we should use a better approach instead of randomly initializing the remaining parameter. They have proposed ULMFiT: Universal Language Model Fine-tuning for Text Classification.

We use team gauravarora's (Arora, 2020) open-sourced models from the shared task at HASOC-Dravidian-CodeMix FIRE-2020. They build corpora for language modeling from a large set of Wikipedia articles. These models are based on the Fastai (Howard and Gugger, 2020) implementation of ULMFiT. We fine-tuned the models on Tamil, codemix datasets individually and on the Tamil-codemix combined dataset.

For tokenization, we used the Senterpiece module. The language model is based on AWD-LSTM (Merity et al., 2018). The model consists of a regular LSTM cell with spatial dropout, followed by the classification model consisting of two linear layers followed by a softmax.

4.4 Transformer Models

Our data sets consist of Tamil and Tamil-English codemixed data; we use four transformers MuRIL, XLM-RoBERTa, M-BERT, and Indic BERT. MuRIL (Khanuja et al., 2021) is a language model built explicitly for Indian languages and trained on large amounts of Indic text corpora. XLM-RoBERTa (Conneau et al., 2019) is a multilingual version of RoBERTa (Liu et al., 2019). Moreover, it is pre-trained on 2.5 TB of filtered CommonCrawl data containing 100 languages. M-BERT (Devlin et al., 2018) or multilingual BERT is pre-trained on 104 languages using masked language modeling (MLM) objective. Indic BERT (Kakwani et al., 2020) is a multilingual ALBERT (Lan et al., 2019) model developed by AI4Bharat, and it is trained on large-scale corpora of major 12 Indian languages, including Tamil. We use HuggingFace (Wolf et al., 2019) for training with SimpleTransformers. The training was stopped early if the f1 score did not improve for three consecutive epochs. A warning was given while training XLM-RoBERTa on the task B dataset using SimpleTransformers, which caused a

Task A			
	Classifier	mf1	wf1
Ensemble Models	LR	0.23	0.32
	SVC	0.18	0.33
	XGBoost	0.16	0.33
	MLP	0.19	0.32
RNN Models	ULMFIT	0.27	**0.41**
	LSTM	0.21	0.33
Transformer Models	MuRIL	0.31	0.37
	XLM-R	**0.32**	0.37
	M-BERT	0.27	0.36
	IndicBERT	0.29	035

Table 2: Results of task A
(mf1: macro avg f1, wf1: weighted avg f1)

Task B			
	Classifier	mf1	wf1
Ensemble Models	LR	0.10	0.17
	SVC	0.09	0.20
	XGBoost	0.07	0.17
	MLP	0.08	0.17
RNN Models	LSTM	0.11	**0.21**
Transformer Models	MuRIL	**0.13**	0.16
	IndicBERT	0.09	0.11

Table 3: Results of Task B
(mf1: macro avg f1, wf1: weighted avg f1)

considerable dip in the score obtained. The solution to this is to make the argument use_multiprocessing equal to False.

5 Results

The results obtained for Task A and Task B are given in Table 2 and Table 3, respectively.

5.1 Ensemble models

In task A, logistic regression achieved the best results with macro-averaged f1 scores of 0.23. MLP achieved a macro averaged f1 score of 0.19. Support Vector Machine also produced decent results with a macro-averaged f1 score of 0.18 and a weighted-average f1 score of 0.33.
For task B, logistic regression got a macro average f1 score of 0.1 and outperformed all the other ensemble models.

5.2 RNNs

For task A, ULMFit performed well with a macro-averaged f1 score of 0.27. For task B, LSTM generated a macro-averaged f1 score of 0.11 and a weighted-average f1 score of 0.21.

5.3 Transformers

For task A, XLM-RoBERTa outperformed all other models with a macro averaged f1 score of 0.32 and a weighted-average score of 0.37. Performance of MuRIL was similar to XLM-Roberta. For task B, MuRIL outperformed all other models with a macro-averaged f1 score of 0.125.

Overall, XLM-RoBERTa performed the best on Task A(11 classes) while MuRIL performed the best on Task B(31 labels)

6 Conclusion

The aim of this paper was to classify social media comments. We used three approaches: Ensemble models, Recurrent Neural Networks (RNNs), and transformers. Out of these models, for task A, XLM-RoBERTa outperformed all other models with a macro-averaged f1 score of 0.27. However, in Task B, MuRIL outperformed all other models with a macro averaged f1 score of 0.125. Overall, it is observed that the models classify emotions like Joy, Sadness, Neutral, and sentences having ambiguity well. However, the models classify more complex emotions like anger, fear, and sadness with much less accuracy. In the future, various techniques like genetic algorithm-based ensembling can be tried to improve the performance of the models.

7 Acknowledgments

We want to thank SCTR's Pune Center for Analytics with Intelligent Learning for Multimedia Data for their continuous support. A special thanks to Neeraja Kirtane and Sahil Khose for their help in drafting the paper.

References

Zishan Ahmad, Raghav Jindal, Asif Ekbal, and Pushpak Bhattachharyya. 2020. Borrow from rich cousin: transfer learning for emotion detection using cross lingual embedding. *Expert Systems with Applications*, 139:112851.

Gaurav Arora. 2020. Gauravarora@ hasoc-dravidian-codemix-fire2020: Pre-training ulmfit on synthetically generated code-mixed data for hate speech detection. *arXiv preprint arXiv:2010.02094*.

Bharathi Raja Chakravarthi, Ruba Priyadharshini, Rahul Ponnusamy, Prasanna Kumar Kumaresan, Kayalvizhi Sampath, Durairaj Thenmozhi, Sathiyaraj Thangasamy, Rajendran Nallathambi, and John Phillip McCrae. 2021. Dataset for identification of homophobia and transophobia in multilingual YouTube comments. *arXiv preprint arXiv:2109.00227*.

Nitesh V Chawla, Kevin W Bowyer, Lawrence O Hall, and W Philip Kegelmeyer. 2002. Smote: synthetic minority over-sampling technique. *Journal of artificial intelligence research*, 16:321–357.

Alexis Conneau, Kartikay Khandelwal, Naman Goyal, Vishrav Chaudhary, Guillaume Wenzek, Francisco Guzmán, Edouard Grave, Myle Ott, Luke Zettlemoyer, and Veselin Stoyanov. 2019. Unsupervised cross-lingual representation learning at scale. *arXiv preprint arXiv:1911.02116*.

Jacob Devlin, Ming-Wei Chang, Kenton Lee, and Kristina Toutanova. 2018. Bert: Pre-training of deep bidirectional transformers for language understanding. *arXiv preprint arXiv:1810.04805*.

Jeremy Howard and Sylvain Gugger. 2020. Fastai: a layered api for deep learning. *Information*, 11(2):108.

Jeremy Howard and Sebastian Ruder. 2018. Universal language model fine-tuning for text classification. *arXiv preprint arXiv:1801.06146*.

Wegdan A Hussien, Yahya M Tashtoush, Mahmoud Al-Ayyoub, and Mohammed N Al-Kabi. 2016. Are emoticons good enough to train emotion classifiers of arabic tweets? In *2016 7th International Conference on Computer Science and Information Technology (CSIT)*, pages 1–6. IEEE.

Vinay Kumar Jain, Shishir Kumar, and Steven Lawrence Fernandes. 2017. Extraction of emotions from multilingual text using intelligent text processing and computational linguistics. *Journal of computational science*, 21:316–326.

Divyanshu Kakwani, Anoop Kunchukuttan, Satish Golla, NC Gokul, Avik Bhattacharyya, Mitesh M Khapra, and Pratyush Kumar. 2020. Indicnlpsuite: Monolingual corpora, evaluation benchmarks and pre-trained multilingual language models for indian languages. In *Findings of the Association for Computational Linguistics: EMNLP 2020*, pages 4948–4961.

Simran Khanuja, Diksha Bansal, Sarvesh Mehtani, Savya Khosla, Atreyee Dey, Balaji Gopalan, Dilip Kumar Margam, Pooja Aggarwal, Rajiv Teja Nagipogu, Shachi Dave, et al. 2021. Muril: Multilingual representations for indian languages. *arXiv preprint arXiv:2103.10730*.

Zhenzhong Lan, Mingda Chen, Sebastian Goodman, Kevin Gimpel, Piyush Sharma, and Radu Soricut. 2019. Albert: A lite bert for self-supervised learning of language representations. *arXiv preprint arXiv:1909.11942*.

Yinhan Liu, Myle Ott, Naman Goyal, Jingfei Du, Mandar Joshi, Danqi Chen, Omer Levy, Mike Lewis, Luke Zettlemoyer, and Veselin Stoyanov. 2019. Roberta: A robustly optimized bert pretraining approach. *arXiv preprint arXiv:1907.11692*.

Stephen Merity, Nitish Shirish Keskar, and Richard Socher. 2018. An analysis of neural language modeling at multiple scales. *arXiv preprint arXiv:1803.08240*.

Tomas Mikolov, Ilya Sutskever, Kai Chen, Greg S Corrado, and Jeff Dean. 2013. Distributed representations of words and phrases and their compositionality. *Advances in neural information processing systems*, 26.

Anbukkarasi Sampath, Thenmozhi Durairaj, Bharathi Raja Chakravarthi, Ruba Priyadharshini, Subalalitha Chinnaudayar Navaneethakrishnan, Kogilavani Shanmugavadivel, Sajeetha Thavareesan, Sathiyaraj Thangasamy, Parameswari Krishnamurthy, Adeep Hande, Sean Benhur, and Santhiya Ponnusamy, Kishor Kumar Pandiyan. 2022. Findings of the shared task on Emotion Analysis in Tamil. In *Proceedings of the Second Workshop on Speech and Language Technologies for Dravidian Languages*. Association for Computational Linguistics.

Marko Tkalčič, Berardina De Carolis, Marco De Gemmis, Ante Odić, and Andrej Košir. 2016. Emotions and personality in personalized services. In *Human-Computer Interaction Series*. Springer.

Ashish Vaswani, Noam Shazeer, Niki Parmar, Jakob Uszkoreit, Llion Jones, Aidan N Gomez, Łukasz Kaiser, and Illia Polosukhin. 2017. Attention is all you need. *Advances in neural information processing systems*, 30.

Yichen Wang and Aditya Pal. 2015. Detecting emotions in social media: A constrained optimization approach. In *Twenty-fourth international joint conference on artificial intelligence*.

Liza Wikarsa and Sherly Novianti Thahir. 2015. A text mining application of emotion classifications of twitter's users using naive bayes method. In *2015 1st International Conference on Wireless and Telematics (ICWT)*, pages 1–6. IEEE.

Wikipedia contributors. 2022. List of languages by number of native speakers — Wikipedia, the free encyclopedia. [Online; accessed 9-April-2022].

Thomas Wolf, Lysandre Debut, Victor Sanh, Julien Chaumond, Clement Delangue, Anthony Moi, Pierric Cistac, Tim Rault, Rémi Louf, Morgan Funtowicz, et al. 2019. Huggingface's transformers: State-of-the-art natural language processing. *arXiv preprint arXiv:1910.03771*.

Chun yan Nie, Ju Wang, Fang He, and Reika Sato. 2015. Application of j48 decision tree classifier in emotion recognition based on chaos characteristics. In *2015 International Conference on Automation, Mechanical Control and Computational Engineering*. Atlantis Press.

Optimize_Prime@DravidianLangTech-ACL2022: Abusive Comment Detection in Tamil

Shantanu Patankar*, **Omkar Gokhale***, **Onkar Litake**†, **Aditya Mandke**†, **Dipali Kadam**
Pune Institute of Computer Technology, Pune, India
shantanupatankar2001@gmail.com, omkargokhale2001@gmail.com,
onkarlitake@ieee.org, adeetya.m@gmail.com, ddkadam@pict.edu

Abstract

This paper tries to address the problem of abusive comment detection in low-resource indic languages. Abusive comments are statements that are offensive to a person or a group of people. These comments are targeted toward individuals belonging to specific ethnicities, genders, caste, race, sexuality, etc. Abusive Comment Detection is a significant problem, especially with the recent rise in social media users. This paper presents the approach used by our team — Optimize_Prime, in the ACL 2022 shared task "Abusive Comment Detection in Tamil." This task detects and classifies YouTube comments in Tamil and Tamil-English Codemixed format into multiple categories. We have used three methods to optimize our results: Ensemble models, Recurrent Neural Networks, and Transformers. In the Tamil data, MuRIL and XLM-RoBERTA were our best performing models with a macro-averaged f1 score of 0.43. Furthermore, for the Code-mixed data, MuRIL and M-BERT provided sublime results, with a macro-averaged f1 score of 0.45.

1 Introduction

The rise in social media platforms like Facebook and Twitter has led to the exchange of massive amounts of information on the internet. With the increase in the number of users and platforms, problems like hate speech and cyberbullying have also increased (Chakravarthi, 2020). Abusive comments are comments that are offensive towards a particular individual or a group of individuals. Online abuse has led to problems like lowered self-esteem, depression, harassment, and even suicide in some severe cases. Hence detecting and dealing with such comments is of utmost importance. Classifying detected comments helps determine the severity of the comment and will also help the authorities take appropriate action against the individual.

Our task is to detect and classify abusive comments written in Tamil. Abusive comment detection is a text classification problem. Text classification is a technique that extracts features from text and assigns a set of predefined categories(classes) to it. Traditionally, text classification was done using linear classifiers on the sentence embeddings of text. This was followed by Recurrent Neural Networks like LSTMs, which gave promising results. After the paper (Vaswani et al., 2017), transformers were introduced in the field of natural language processing. They have an attention layer that provides context to words in the text. The introduction of the transformer architecture has led to the development of many other variations of the transformer like BERT(Devlin et al., 2018), XLM-RoBERTa(Conneau et al., 2019), MuRIL(Khanuja et al., 2021), etc.

In this paper, we use different transformer-based models for abusive comment detection in Tamil. We have also used RNN models like LSTMs, a newer model ULMFit and a type of Ensemble model. We compared the results obtained from all three approaches to determine the optimum model for this task.

2 Related Work

Tamil is a low-resource language, so finding properly annotated data is challenging. In order to encourage research in Tamil, datasets have been created by Chakravarthi et al. (2020). The paper, Pitsilis et al. (2018) tries an RNN based approach for detecting offensive language in tweets. Arora (2020) developed a model for detecting hate speech in Tamil-English codemixed social media comments using a pre-trained version of ULM-FiT. After the introduction of transformers in Vaswani et al. (2017), the use of transformers for NLP tasks increased.

The release of BERT(Devlin et al., 2018) paved

*first author, equal contribution
†second author, equal contribution

Proceedings of the Second Workshop on Speech and Language Technologies for Dravidian Languages, pages 235 - 239
May 26, 2022 ©2022 Association for Computational Linguistics

Dataset	Hope-Speech	Homophobia	Misandry	Counter-Speech	Misogyny	Xenophobia	Transphobic	None-of-these
Tamil	3.51%	1.46%	19.34%	6.62%	5.62%	4.25%	0.2%	59%
Codemix	3.61%	2.91%	14.4%	5.71%	3.42%	4.97%	2.74%	62%

Table 1: Distribution of classes in data

the way for many more variations of transformers. In the paper, Mishra and Mishra (2019) the results for the HASOC in Indo-European languages were showcased where they used MultiLingual BERT and monolingual BERT. Some work has been done by Ziehe et al. (2021) in English, Malayalam, and Tamil, aiming to detect Hope Speech which is also a text classification task. They fine-tuned XLM-RoBERTa (Conneau et al., 2019) for Hope Speech Detection.

The development of models like MuRiL (Khanuja et al., 2021), XLM-RoBERTa (Conneau et al., 2019), Indic BERT (Kakwani et al., 2020), and M-BERT (Devlin et al., 2018) has encouraged research in various low resource as well as high resource languages.

3 Dataset Description

The shared task on Abusive Comment Detection in Tamil-ACL 2022 aims to detect and reduce abusive comments on social media. The main objective of the shared task is to design systems to detect and classify instances of hate speech in Tamil and Tamil-English codemixed YouTube comments. The Abusive Comment Detection Dataset Priyadharshini et al. (2022) consists of Tamil and Tamil-English comments collected from the YouTube comments section. The dataset consists of a comment and its corresponding label belonging to the nine labels in the Dataset: Misandry, Counter-speech, Misogyny , Xenophobia, Hope-Speech, Homophobia, Transphobic, Not-Tamil, and None-of-the-above.

3.1 Tamil Data

The Train, Dev, and Test datasets have 2240, 560 and 700 data points, respectively. Each data point in the training data has the text in Tamil followed by its corresponding label.

3.2 Tamil-English Codemixed

The train, dev, and test datasets have 5948, 1488, and 1859 data points, respectively. Each data point has the actual comment in a codemixed format. Codemixed means text that alternates between two languages. In this case, the two languages are Tamil and English.

There is a significant class imbalance observed in the dataset. The 'Not-Tamil' label has no test or dev data instances, so the classification is done only for eight labels.

4 Methodology

To classify Youtube Comments, we used three different approaches: Ensemble models, Recurrent Neural Networks, and Transformers.[1]

4.1 Data Pre-processing

4.1.1 Data cleaning

We removed punctuations, URL patterns, and stop words from the text. For better contextual understanding, we replaced emojis with their textual equivalents. For example, the laughing emoji was replaced by the Tamil equivalent of laughter.

Data cleaning boosted the performance of all RNN models and all Transformer models except for MuRIL. MuRIL and all Ensemble models worked better without data cleaning.

4.1.2 Handling data imbalance

There is a significant class imbalance in the data. To reduce the class imbalance, we used the following techniques: over-sampling, over-under sampling, Synthetic Minority Over-sampling (SMOTE)(Chawla et al., 2002), and assigning class weights. In over-under sampling, we under-sample the classes having more instances than expected and over-sample those having lesser instances than expected while keeping the length of the dataset constant. Over-under sampling worked best for all transformer and ensemble models, but it reduced the performance of RNN models. Assigning weights boosted the performance of the M-BERT - Logistic Regression ensemble model.

[1]https://github.com/PICT-NLP/Optimize_Prime-DravidianLangTech2022-Abusive_Comment_Detection

4.2 Ensemble model

As shown in figure 1, we concatenate different machine learning models with multilingual BERT(M-BERT)(Devlin et al., 2018). Multilingual BERT is a BERT-based transformer trained in 104 languages. It simultaneously encodes knowledge of all these languages. M-BERT generates a sentence embedding vector of length 768. We then pass these embeddings to different machine learning models, as shown in Table 2. We used grid search with weighted-average f1 score as the scoring parameter for 5 -10 cross-validation folds to fine-tune the hyperparameters.

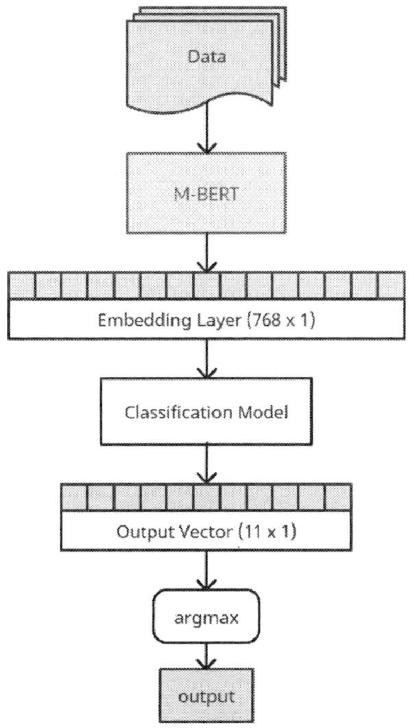

Figure 1: Ensemble model architecture

4.3 RNN Models

We have used two RNN models, Long Short-Term Memory(LSTM) networks and ULM-Fit.

4.3.1 Vanilla LSTM

Long Short-Term Memory (LSTM) (Hochreiter and Schmidhuber, 1997), can capture semantic information and long-term dependencies. We use LSTM to set a baseline score for RNN models. We create word embeddings by choosing the top 64,000 most frequently occurring words in the dataset. The embedding layer then creates 100-dimension vectors. The rest of the model includes a spatial drop out of 0.2, a single LSTM layer, and a final softmax activation function.

4.3.2 ULMFit

In transfer learning approaches, models are trained on large corpora, and their word embeddings are fine-tuned for specific tasks. In many state-of-the-art models, this approach is successful (Mikolov et al., 2013). Although Howard and Ruder (2018) argues that we should use a better approach instead of randomly initializing the remaining parameter. They have proposed ULMFiT: Universal Language Model Fine-tuning for Text Classification.

We use team gauravarora's (Arora, 2020) open-sourced models from the shared task at HASOC-Dravidian-CodeMix FIRE-2020. They build corpora for language modeling from a large set of Wikipedia articles.

These models are based on the Fastai (Howard and Gugger, 2020) implementation of ULMFiT. We tuned the models on Tamil, Codemix data sets individually and on the Tamil - codemix combined dataset.

For tokenization, we used the Senterpiece module. The language model is based on AWD-LSTM (Merity et al., 2018). The model consists of a regular LSTM cell with spatial dropout, followed by the classification model consisting of two linear layers followed by a softmax.

4.4 Transformer models

Our data sets consist of Tamil and Tamil-English codemixed data; we use four transformers MuRIL, XLM-RoBERTa, M-BERT, and Indic BERT. MuRIL (Khanuja et al., 2021) is a language model built explicitly for Indian languages and trained on large amounts of Indic text corpora. XLM-RoBERTa (Conneau et al., 2019) is a multilingual version of RoBERTa (Liu et al., 2019). Moreover, it is pre-trained on 2.5 TB of filtered CommonCrawl data containing 100 languages. M-BERT (Devlin et al., 2018) or multilingual BERT is pre-trained on 104 languages using masked language modeling (MLM) objective. Indic BERT (Kakwani et al., 2020) is a multilingual ALBERT (Lan et al., 2019) model developed by AI4Bharat and, it is trained on large-scale corpora of major 12 Indian languages, including Tamil. We use HuggingFace (Wolf et al., 2019) for training with SimpleTransformers. The training was stopped early if the f1 score did not improve for three consecutive epochs.

Model Type	Classifier	Tamil		Codemix	
		macro f1	weighted f1	macro f1	weighted f1
Ensemble Models	Logistic Regression	0.32	0.60	0.33	0.64
	Decision Trees	0.16	0.50	0.16	0.52
	SVC	**0.33**	**0.61**	0.32	0.64
	Random Forest	0.17	0.53	0.16	0.52
	XG-Boost	0.25	0.59	0.26	0.60
	MLP	**0.33**	0.60	**0.35**	**0.65**
RNN Models	ULMFiT	0.33	**0.63**	**0.40**	**0.68**
	ULMFiT CD*	**0.36**	0.61	0.38	0.62
	Vanilla LSTM	0.21	0.61	0.35	0.66
Transformer Models	MuRIL	**0.43**	**0.68**	**0.45**	0.60
	XLM-R-base	**0.43**	0.66	0.44	**0.62**
	M-BERT	0.40	**0.68**	**0.45**	0.61
	Indic BERT	0.40	0.65	0.35	0.52

Table 2: Results obtained by all the models on the Tamil as well as codemixed data.
*ULMFiT CD is trained by combining Tamil and CodeMix data.

5 Results

The results obtained by all the models can be viewed in Table 2.

5.1 Ensemble Models

In the case of the ensemble models, Support Vector Machine obtained the best result for the Tamil data. A macro-averaged f1 score of 0.33 and weighted-average f1 score of 0.6 was obtained.
In the case of the codemixed data, Multi-Layer Perceptron obtained the best score among the ensemble models. It achieved a macro-averaged f1 score of 0.35 and a weighted-average f1 score of 0.65.
Tree-based algorithms like decision trees, random forest, and XGBoost did not perform well.

5.2 RNNs

Among all the RNN models, ULMFiT fine-tuned on codemix data had the highest macro avg f1 of 0.40 and weighted avg f1 score of 0.68. ULMFit fine-tuned on Tamil data had the highest weighted avg f1 score of 0.63 while ULMFiT finetuned on combined dataset had the highest macro-averaged f1 score of 0.36.

5.3 Transformers

Out of the four transformers, we obtained the best results for MuRIL and XLM-RoBERTa in the case of Tamil. The macro-averaged f1 scores were 0.43 for both models, and the weighted-averaged f1 scores were 0.68 and 0.66 for MuRIL and XLM-RoBERTa, respectively.
MuRIL and M-BERT outperformed all the other models for the Tamil-English codemixed data. The macro-averaged f1 scores of 0.45 and weighted-average f1 scores of 0.61 were obtained by MuRIL and M-BERT.

6 Conclusion

This paper aims to detect and classify abusive comments. We tried three approaches for abusive comment detection in Tamil and Tamil-English Code-Mixed data: Ensemble models, Recurrent Neural Networks, and transformer-based models.
For the Tamil data, MuRIL and XLM-RoBERTa provided the best results with a macro-averaged f1 score of 0.43. Classes like Homophobia and Misandry were predicted with higher accuracy than others like Transphobic and Counter-Speech. Sentences that are not abusive are also classified well.
For the codemixed data, MuRIL and M-BERT outperformed all other models with a macro-averaged f1 score of 0.45. Classes like Xenophobia, Misandry, and Transphobic were predicted with higher accuracy than others for the codemixed data. Sentences that are not abusive are also classified well.
In the future, various techniques can be tried to improve the performance of the models. In order to boost the performance, genetic algorithm-based ensembling methods could be used.

References

Gaurav Arora. 2020. Gauravarora@ hasoc-dravidian-codemix-fire2020: Pre-training ulmfit on synthetically generated code-mixed data for hate speech detection. *arXiv preprint arXiv:2010.02094.*

Bharathi Raja Chakravarthi. 2020. HopeEDI: A multilingual hope speech detection dataset for equality, diversity, and inclusion. In *Proceedings of the Third Workshop on Computational Modeling of People's Opinions, Personality, and Emotion's in Social Media*, pages 41–53, Barcelona, Spain (Online). Association for Computational Linguistics.

Bharathi Raja Chakravarthi, Vigneshwaran Muralidaran, Ruba Priyadharshini, and John P McCrae. 2020. Corpus creation for sentiment analysis in code-mixed tamil-english text. *arXiv preprint arXiv:2006.00206.*

Nitesh V Chawla, Kevin W Bowyer, Lawrence O Hall, and W Philip Kegelmeyer. 2002. Smote: synthetic minority over-sampling technique. *Journal of artificial intelligence research*, 16:321–357.

Alexis Conneau, Kartikay Khandelwal, Naman Goyal, Vishrav Chaudhary, Guillaume Wenzek, Francisco Guzmán, Edouard Grave, Myle Ott, Luke Zettlemoyer, and Veselin Stoyanov. 2019. Unsupervised cross-lingual representation learning at scale. *arXiv preprint arXiv:1911.02116.*

Jacob Devlin, Ming-Wei Chang, Kenton Lee, and Kristina Toutanova. 2018. Bert: Pre-training of deep bidirectional transformers for language understanding. *arXiv preprint arXiv:1810.04805.*

Sepp Hochreiter and Jürgen Schmidhuber. 1997. Long short-term memory. *Neural computation*, 9(8):1735–1780.

Jeremy Howard and Sylvain Gugger. 2020. Fastai: a layered api for deep learning. *Information*, 11(2):108.

Jeremy Howard and Sebastian Ruder. 2018. Universal language model fine-tuning for text classification. *arXiv preprint arXiv:1801.06146.*

Divyanshu Kakwani, Anoop Kunchukuttan, Satish Golla, NC Gokul, Avik Bhattacharyya, Mitesh M Khapra, and Pratyush Kumar. 2020. Indicnlpsuite: Monolingual corpora, evaluation benchmarks and pre-trained multilingual language models for indian languages. In *Findings of the Association for Computational Linguistics: EMNLP 2020*, pages 4948–4961.

Simran Khanuja, Diksha Bansal, Sarvesh Mehtani, Savya Khosla, Atreyee Dey, Balaji Gopalan, Dilip Kumar Margam, Pooja Aggarwal, Rajiv Teja Nagipogu, Shachi Dave, et al. 2021. Muril: Multilingual representations for indian languages. *arXiv preprint arXiv:2103.10730.*

Zhenzhong Lan, Mingda Chen, Sebastian Goodman, Kevin Gimpel, Piyush Sharma, and Radu Soricut. 2019. Albert: A lite bert for self-supervised learning of language representations. *arXiv preprint arXiv:1909.11942.*

Yinhan Liu, Myle Ott, Naman Goyal, Jingfei Du, Mandar Joshi, Danqi Chen, Omer Levy, Mike Lewis, Luke Zettlemoyer, and Veselin Stoyanov. 2019. Roberta: A robustly optimized bert pretraining approach. *arXiv preprint arXiv:1907.11692.*

Stephen Merity, Nitish Shirish Keskar, and Richard Socher. 2018. An analysis of neural language modeling at multiple scales. *arXiv preprint arXiv:1803.08240.*

Tomas Mikolov, Ilya Sutskever, Kai Chen, Greg S Corrado, and Jeff Dean. 2013. Distributed representations of words and phrases and their compositionality. *Advances in neural information processing systems*, 26.

Shubhanshu Mishra and Sudhanshu Mishra. 2019. 3idiots at hasoc 2019: Fine-tuning transformer neural networks for hate speech identification in indo-european languages. In *FIRE (Working Notes)*, pages 208–213.

Georgios K Pitsilis, Heri Ramampiaro, and Helge Langseth. 2018. Detecting offensive language in tweets using deep learning. *arXiv preprint arXiv:1801.04433.*

Ruba Priyadharshini, Bharathi Raja Chakravarthi, Subalalitha Chinnaudayar Navaneethakrishnan, Thenmozhi Durairaj, Malliga Subramanian, Kogilavani Shanmugavadivel, Siddhanth U Hegde, and Prasanna Kumar Kumaresan. 2022. Findings of the shared task on Abusive Comment Detection in Tamil. In *Proceedings of the Second Workshop on Speech and Language Technologies for Dravidian Languages*. Association for Computational Linguistics.

Ashish Vaswani, Noam Shazeer, Niki Parmar, Jakob Uszkoreit, Llion Jones, Aidan N Gomez, Łukasz Kaiser, and Illia Polosukhin. 2017. Attention is all you need. *Advances in neural information processing systems*, 30.

Thomas Wolf, Lysandre Debut, Victor Sanh, Julien Chaumond, Clement Delangue, Anthony Moi, Pierric Cistac, Tim Rault, Rémi Louf, Morgan Funtowicz, et al. 2019. Huggingface's transformers: State-of-the-art natural language processing. *arXiv preprint arXiv:1910.03771.*

Stefan Ziehe, Franziska Pannach, and Aravind Krishnan. 2021. Gcdh@ lt-edi-eacl2021: Xlm-roberta for hope speech detection in english, malayalam, and tamil. In *Proceedings of the First Workshop on Language Technology for Equality, Diversity and Inclusion*, pages 132–135.

Zero-shot Code-Mixed Offensive Span Identification through Rationale Extraction

Manikandan Ravikiran[†*], **Bharathi Raja Chakravarthi**[‡]
[†]Georgia Institute of Technology, Atlanta, Georgia
[‡]Data Science Institute, National University of Ireland Galway
mravikiran3@gatech.edu, bharathi.raja@insight-centre.org

Abstract

This paper investigates the effectiveness of sentence-level transformers for zero-shot offensive span identification on a code-mixed Tamil dataset. More specifically, we evaluate rationale extraction methods of Local Interpretable Model Agnostic Explanations (LIME) (Ribeiro et al., 2016a) and Integrated Gradients (IG) (Sundararajan et al., 2017) for adapting transformer based offensive language classification models for zero-shot offensive span identification. To this end, we find that LIME and IG show baseline F_1 of 26.35% and 44.83%, respectively. Besides, we study the effect of data set size and training process on the overall accuracy of span identification. As a result, we find both LIME and IG to show significant improvement with Masked Data Augmentation and Multilabel Training, with F_1 of 50.23% and 47.38% respectively. *Disclaimer : This paper contains examples that may be considered profane, vulgar, or offensive. The examples do not represent the views of the authors or their employers/graduate schools towards any person(s), group(s), practice(s), or entity/entities. Instead they are used to emphasize only the linguistic research challenges.*

1 Introduction

Offensive language classification and offensive span identification from code-mixed Tamil-English comments portray the same task at different granularities. In the former case, we classify if the code mixed sentence is offensive or not, while the latter concentrates on extracting the offensive parts of the comments. Accordingly, one could do the former using models of the latter and vice versa. Transformer-based architectures such as BERT (Devlin et al., 2019), RoBERTa (Liu et al., 2019) and XLM-RoBERTa (Conneau et al., 2020) have achieved state-of-the-art results on both these tasks (Chakravarthi et al., 2021a). However, often these tasks are treated as independent and model development is often separated.

This paper studies the rationale extraction methods for inferring offensive spans from transformer models trained only on comment-level offensive language classification labels. Such an idea is often vital in the case of code-mixed Tamil-English comments for which span annotations are often costly to obtain, but comment-level labels are readily available. Besides, such an approach will also help in decoding the models' logic behind the prediction of offensiveness.

Accordingly, we evaluate and compare two different methods, namely LIME and IG, for adapting pre-trained transformer models into zero-shot offensive span labelers. Our experiments show that using LIME with pre-trained transformer models struggles to infer correct span level annotations in a zero-shot manner, achieving only 20% F_1 on offensive span identification for code-mixed Tamil-English comments. To this end, we find that a combination of masked data augmentation and multilabel training of sentence transformers helps to better focus on individual necessary tokens and achieve a strong baseline on offensive span identification. Besides, IG consistently surpasses LIME even in cases where there are no data augmentation or multilabel training. Overall the contributions of this paper are as follows.

- We introduce preliminary experiments on offensive language classification transformer models for zero-shot offensive span identification from code-mixed Tamil-English language comments.
- We systematically compare LIME and IG methods for zero-shot offensive span identification.
- We study the impact of data and training process on offensive span identification by

*Corresponding Author

Proceedings of the Second Workshop on Speech and Language Technologies for Dravidian Languages, pages 240 - 247
May 26, 2022

proposing masked data augmentation and multilabel training.

- We further release our code, models, and data to facilitate further research in the field[1].

The rest of the paper is organized as follows. In Section 2, we present LIME and IG methods in brief. Meanwhile section 3 and 4 focus on dataset and experimental setup. In section 5, we present detailed experiments and conclude in section 6 with our findings and possible implications on the future work.

2 Methods

In this section, we present the two rationale extraction methods LIME and IG used to turn sentence-level transformer models into zero-shot offensive span labelers.

2.1 Local Interpretable Model Agnostic Explanation (LIME)

LIME (Ribeiro et al., 2016b) is a model agnostic interpretability approach that generates word-level attribution scores using local surrogate models that are trained on perturbed sentences generated by randomly masking out words in the input sentence. The LIME model has seen considerable traction in the context of rationale extraction for text classification, including work by Thorne et al. (2019), which suggests that LIME outperforms attention-based approaches to explain NLI models. LIME was also used to probe an LSTM based sentence-pair classifier (Lan and Xu, 2018) by removing tokens from the premise and hypothesis sentences separately. The generated scores are used to perform binary classification of tokens, with the threshold based on F_1 performance on the development set. The token-level predictions were evaluated against human explanations of the entailment relation using the e-SNLI dataset (Camburu et al., 2018).

Meanwhile, for offensive span identification in English Ding and Jurgens (2021) coupled LIME with RoBERTa trained on an expanded training set to find expanded training set could help RoBERTa more accurately learn to recognize toxic span. However, though LIME outperforms other methods, it is significantly slower than Integrated Gradients methods, presented in the next section.

[1]The code and data is made available at https://github.com/manikandan-ravikiran/zero-shot-offensive-span

2.2 Integrated Gradients (IG)

Integrated Gradients (Sundararajan et al., 2017) focuses on explaining predictions by integrating the gradient along some trajectory in input space connecting two points. Integrated gradient and its variants are widely used in different fields of deep learning including natural language processing (Sikdar et al., 2021).

Specifically, it is an iterative method, which starts with so-called starting baselines, i.e., a starting point that does not contain any information for the model prediction. In our case involving textual data, this is the set exclusively with the start and end tokens. These tokens mark the beginning and the end of a sentence and do not give any information about whether the evaluation is offensive or not. Following this, it takes a certain number of iterations, where the model moves from the starting baseline to the actual input to the model.

This iterative improvement approach is analogous to the sentence creation process wherein each step, we create the sentence word by word and calculate the offensiveness, which in turn gives us the attribution of the input feature. Across its iterations, whenever IG includes an offensive word, we can expect offensive classification prediction to swing more towards offensive class and vice versa. Such behavior will help calculate the attribution of each word in the identified sentence.

3 Datasets

In this section, we present various datasets used in this study. Details on how they are used across different experiments are presented in Table 3. Finally, the overall dataset statistics are as shown in Table 1.

3.1 Offensive Span Identification Dataset

The Shared task on Offensive Span Identification from Code-Mixed Tamil English Comments (Ravikiran and Annamalai, 2021) focuses on the extraction of offensive spans from Youtube Comments. The dataset contains 4786 and 876 examples across its train and test set respectively. It consists of annotated offensive spans indicating character offsets of parts of the comments that were offensive.

3.2 Masked Augmented Dataset

The data available from both Ravikiran and Annamalai (2021) is minimal, and transformer methods

Dataset	Number of Train Samples	Number of Test Samples	Offensive Language Classification	Offensive Span Identification
Offensive Span Identification Dataset	4786	876	✗	✓
Mask Augmented Dataset	109961	-	✓	✓
Multilabel Dataset	109961	-	✓	✓

Table 1: Dataset statistics of various datasets used in this work.

Steps	Example Output
Offensive Lexicon Creation	[sanghu, thu,thooooo,suthamm,F**k,flop,w*f, p**a,n**y,nakkal]
Data Sourcing	Last scene vera level love u [Last, scene, vera, level, love,u]
Mask Generation	[0,1, 0, 0, 1,1] [1,0, 1, 1, 1,1] [0,0, 0, 0, 1,1]
Offensive Word Augmentation	[Last, sangh, vera, level, thu, n**y] [flop, scene, thooooo, suthamm, F**k, sanghu] [Last, scene, p**a, n**y, love, u]
Position Identification and Multilabel Creation	Last sangh vera level thu n**y [1,0,1] flop scene thooooo suthamm F**k sanghu [1,1,1] Last scene p**a n**y love u [0,1,0]

Table 2: Various steps in Masked Augmented Dataset and Multilabel Dataset creation with sample outputs.

are sensitive to dataset size (Xu et al., 2021). Thus we created an additional dataset using Masked Augmentation. Accordingly, the data is generated by using the following steps.

- **Step 1: Offensive Lexicon Creation**: First, we create an offensive lexicon from the train set of offensive span identification datasets. To do this, we do following
  - Extract the phrases corresponding to annotated offensive spans from the training dataset of Ravikiran and Annamalai (2021).
  - Selecting phrases of size less than 20 characters and word tokenizing them to extract the individual words.
  - Manually, post-processing these words to ignore words that are not offensive. For example, many phrases include conjunctions and pronouns which are not directly offensive.

  Accordingly, an offensive lexicon with 2900 tokens is created.

- **Step 2: Data Sourcing**: In this step, we select the dataset used for creating the Masked Augmented dataset. Specifically, we use the 25425 non-offensive comments from Dravidian Code-Mix dataset (Chakravarthi et al., 2021b).

- **Step 3: Mask Generation**: The mask generation is done as follows
  - Each of 25425 non-offensive comments was tokenized to create respective *maskable token list.*
  - Three random binary masks are generated for each of the tokenized non-offensive comments. These binary masks have same length as that of its maskable token list.

- **Step 4: Offensive Word Augmentation:** Finally, words with a corresponding binary mask of 1 are replaced with words randomly selected from the offensive lexicon from step 1. Additionally, the spans corresponding to the words that were replaced are saved.

Overall, such augmentation resulted in 109961 comments, with 75009 being offensive comments and 34952 non-offensive comments. Table 2 shows an example sentence and masked augmented dataset creation process.

3.3 Multilabel Dataset

All the previously mentioned datasets are restricted to classification only i.e. they contain a binary label indicating if they are offensive or they have annotated offensive spans. Additionally, these sentences does not explicitly encode any position information of the offensive words, which is useful for

Experiment Name	Train dataset	Test dataset
Benchmark	Offensive Span Identification Dataset (Ravikiran and Annamalai, 2021; Ravikiran et al., 2022)	
OS-Baseline	Dravidian CodeMix (Chakravarthi et al., 2021b)	Offensive Span Identification Dataset
OS-Augmentation	Mask Augmented Dataset	
OS-Multilabel	Multilabel Dataset	

Table 3: Relationship between the datasets and experiments.

Name	Value
γ	0.1
max seq length	150
train batch size	64
eval batch size	64
warmup ratio	0.1
learning rate	$3x10^{-5}$
weight decay	0.1
initializer	glorot

Table 4: Model Hyperparameters for Training Transformers.

training. Work of Ke et al. (2021) show encoding relative positional information based attention directly in each head often improves the overall result of corresponding down stream task. Similarly Shaw et al. (2018) also proposed using relative position encoding instead of absolute position encoding and couple them with key and value projections of Transformers to improve overall results. As such, in this work, to encode position we create a multilabel dataset in which the labels indicate the relative position of offensive words. The multilabel dataset is created as follows.

- **Step 1: Dataset Selection:** We first select the 109961 comments from the Masked Augmented Dataset along with their saved spans.

- **Step 2: Position Identification and Multilabel Creation:** From the identified spans, we check if the offensive spans are present in (a) start of the comment (b) end of the comment and (c) middle of the comment. Depending on presence of offensiveness we create three binary labels. For example in Table 2 for sentence `Last scene p**a n**y love u` we can see that the offensive word to be present in the center of the sentence. Accordingly we give it a label [0,1,0]. Meanwhile for comment `Last sangh vera level thu n**y` we can see offensive words to be in center and at the end thus we give label [1,0,1].

4 Experimental Setup

In this section, we present our experimental setup in detail. All of our experiments follow the two steps as explained below.

Transformer Training: We use three different transformer models, namely Multilingual-BERT, RoBERTa, and XLM-RoBERTa, made available by Hugging Face (Wolf et al., 2019), as our transformer architecture due to their widespread usage in the context of code-mixed Tamil-English Offensive Language Identification. In line with the works of Mosbach et al. (2021) all the models were fine-tuned for 20 epochs, and the best performing checkpoint was selected. Each transformer model takes 1 hour to train on a Tesla-V100 GPU with a learning rate of $3x10^{-5}$. Further, all of our experiments were run five times with different random seeds and the results so reported are an average of five runs. The relationship between the datasets used to train the transformers across various experiments is as shown in Table 3. Meanwhile, the model hyperparameters are presented in Table 4.

Span Extraction Testing: After training the transformer models for offensive language identification, we use the test set from the offensive span identification dataset for testing purposes. For LIME, we use individual transformer models' MASK token to mask out individual words and allow LIME to generate 5000 masked samples per sentence. The resulting explanation weights are then used as scores for each word, and tokens below the fixed decision threshold of $\tau = -0.01$ are removed while the spans of the rest of the comments are used for offensive span identification. Meanwhile, for the IG model, for each sentence in the test set, we perform 50 iterations to generate scores for each word and extract the spans in line with LIME.

5 Experiments, Results and Analysis

The consolidated results are presented in Table 5. Each model is trained as an offensive comment classifier and then evaluated for offensive span identification. Though we do not explicitly furnish any

Experiments	Model	$F_1(\%)$	
		LIME	**IG**
Benchmark	BENCHMARK 1	39.834	
	BENCHMARK 2	37.024	
OS-Baseline	BERT	26.35	44.83
	RoBERTa	24.26	37.01
	XLM-RoBERTa	22.86	43.13
OS-Augmentation	BERT	24.97	44.83
	RoBERTa	26.23	44.98
	XLM-RoBERTa	21.93	**50.23**
OS-Multilabel	BERT	47.137	44.83
	RoBERTa	**47.38**	35.83
	XLM-RoBERTa	46.76	42.06

Table 5: Consolidated Results on Offensive Span Identification Dataset. All the values represent character level F_1 measure.

signals regarding which words are offensive, we can see an assortment of behaviors across both the rationale extraction methods when trained differently. For reference comparison, we also include two benchmark baseline models from Ravikiran et al. (2022). `BENCHMARK 1` is a random baseline model which haphazardly labels 50% of characters in comments to belong to be offensive inline. `BENCHMARK 2` is a lexicon-based system, which first extracted all the offensive words from the train samples of offensive span identification dataset (Ravikiran and Annamalai, 2021). These words were scoured in comments from the test set during inference, and corresponding spans were noted. We report the character level F_1 for extracted spans inline with Ravikiran et al. (2022).

5.1 OS-Baseline Experiments

Firstly, both benchmarks exhibit high performance, making the task competitive for LIME and IG methods. To start with, we analyze the results of OS-Baseline experiments. From Table 5, we can see that LIME has moderately low performance compared to IG, which either beats the baseline or produces very close results. Analogizing the LIME and IG, we can see that IG has an average difference of 18% compared to LIME. To understand this, we identify various examples (Table 7) where LIME fails, and IG performs significantly well and vice versa. Firstly, we can see that LIME explicitly focuses on identifying overtly offensive words only. Besides, we can also see LIME focuses primarily on offensive words, while IG accounts for terms such as `"Dei"`, `"understood"`, `"iruku poliye"` etc.

Accordingly, to comprehend their performance on offensive comments of different sizes, we separate results across (a) comments with less than 30 characters (F_1@30), (b) comments with 30-50 characters (F_1@50) (c) comments with more than 50 characters (F_1@>50). The results so obtained are as shown in Table 6. Accordingly, we find interesting outcomes. Firstly we can see that though LIME has lower F_1 overall, it tends to show competitive results against IG for comments with less than 30 characters.

With the increase in the comment length, the performance of LIME tends to lower considerably. We believe such behavior of LIME could be because of two reasons (a) surrogate models may not be strong enough to distinguish different classes and (b) dilution of scores due to LIME's random perturbation procedure. With random perturbations, the instances generated may be quite different from training instances drawn from the underlying distribution. Meanwhile, IG is compatible across all the sizes, and in the case of comments with less than 30 and 50 characters, we can see IG to show the result as high as 50%.

5.2 OS-Augmentation Experiments

Since transformers are very sensitive to dataset size, we focus on estimating the impact of dataset size used to train the transformers for offensive comment classification on the performance of LIME and IG, respectively. To this end, we used the Mask Augmented dataset to finetune the transformers and pose the question *Does adding data make any difference?* The various result so obtained are as shown in Table 5. Firstly, for LIME, we see no such drastic difference in F_1. However, for IG, we can see a significant improvement, especially for RoBERTa and XLM-RoBERTa models. Specifically, we can see the XLM-RoBERTa model to reach an accuracy of 50.23% with an average of 12% higher results compared to benchmark models and 7% compared to OS-Baseline.

Furthermore, analysis of results shows a couple of fascinating characteristics for XLM-RoBERTa. Firstly, we could see many predictions concentrating on words part of the long offensive span annotations. We believe this is because of the ability of the model to learn relations between words in different languages as part of its pretraining, which is not the case with M-BERT and RoBERTa. To verify this again, we separate the results across different comment sizes. From Table 6 we can see that

Experiments	Model	F_1@30 (%)		F_1@50 (%)		F_1@ > 50 (%)	
		LIME	**IG**	**LIME**	**IG**	**LIME**	**IG**
OS-Baseline	**BERT**	47.02	45.79	32.54	50.62	23.27	42.48
	RoBERTa	37.35	36.42	32.75	42.04	20.56	34.95
	XLM-RoBERTa	43.05	51.7	31.54	48.69	18.63	40.49
OS-Augmentation	**BERT**	48.45	45.79	32.62	50.62	21.29	42.48
	RoBERTa	50.21	45.86	32.71	50.71	22.8	42.66
	XLM-RoBERTa	31.19	59.47	27.58	57.01	19.17	47.19
OS-Multilabel	**BERT**	45.7	45.79	57.15	50.62	42.722	42.48
	RoBERTa	58.66	45.86	57.19	50.71	43	42.66
	XLM-RoBERTa	**59.84**	**59.47**	**57.62**	**57.01**	**42.95**	**47.19**

Table 6: Results across different size of comments.

Category	Comment Type	Examples
Correct Prediction	Comments with less than 30 characters	Dei like poda anaithu 9 p***a Semma mokka and as usual a masala movie
	Comments with 30-50 characters	M***u adichutu sagunga da j***i p***********a 81k views 89k likes YouTube be like W*F
	Comments with greater than 50 characters	Old vijayakanth movie parthathu pola irruku..pidikala.... Dei Yappa munjha paarthu Sirichu Sirichu vayiru vazhikuthu
Incorrect Prediction	Comments with less than 30 characters	except last scene its a crap Movie is going to be disaster
	Comments with 30-50 characters	Kandasamy and Mugamoodi mixed nu nenaikre.... Last la psycho ilayaraja nu solitan
	Comments with greater than 50 characters	All I understood from this video was Vikram likes Dosai.. Padam nichiyam oodama poga neriya vaipu iruku poliye ! Oru dislike ah potu vaipom

Table 7: Example of correct and incorrect predictions. Blue highlight shows words attributed by LIME. Green highlight shows words attributed by IG. Pink highlight shows words attributed by both LIME and IG. Yellow highlight shows parts of comments annotated in ground truth but not identified by both LIME and IG.

for longer sized comments, the model tends to outperform M-BERT, RoBERTa when coupled with IG. Meanwhile, LIME has no changes irrespective of used transformers.

5.3 OS-Multilabel Experiments

Finally, we analyze the significance of encoding the position of offensive words as part of the training process. To this end, we ask *Does introducing position information as part of the training process improve zero-shot results?*. As such, we use the multilabel dataset to finetune the transformers to obtain results, as shown in Table 5. Firstly, we can see that introducing multiple labels for training has no impact on the overall results of LG. However, we can see that LIME demonstrates a significant gain in overall results. Specifically, with multilabel training, the baseline results improve by 20% to 47.38%.

Furthermore, we can observe an equivalent trend across the different sizes of comments as seen in Table 6. In fact, for words of less than 30 and 50 characters, LIME outdoes IG models, which aligns with our hypothesis that the position is helpful. Overall from all the results from Table 5-6 we can see XLM-RoBERTa be more suitable for extracting spans, especially with the addition of more data and position information. Meanwhile, IG is consistent in producing explanations irrespective of dataset size or training approach.

6 Conclusion

This work examines rationale extraction methods for inferring offensive spans from the transformer model trained for offensive sentence classification. Experiments revealed that approaches such as LIME do not perform as well when applied to transformers directly, attributing to potential issues with surrogate models and perturbation procedures. Meanwhile, we can see IG as the clear front runner for identifying offensive spans in a zero-shot way. We think this is due to the inherent nature of the method, where it focuses on creating the input at the same time learning the reason for offensiveness.

Besides, we also analyzed LIME and IG under large datasets and incorporated position information in the training process. To this end, we discovered that only augmenting does not improve the performance of LIME. However, when this large data is coupled with labels incorporating position information, both LG and IG improve significantly. Especially LIME prefers this approach with large improvements on F_1, despite IG outperforming LIME.

Additionally, we also found XLM-RoBERTa to be a clear winner among the transformer models owing to its intrinsic learning of relationships which potentially helps with comments that are longer size. However, many details were unexplored, including (i) the effect of random perturbations on overall results (ii) the approach to merge attributions of multilabel predictions, which we plan to explore in the immediate future.

Acknowledgements

We thank our anonymous reviewers for their valuable feedback. Any opinions, findings, and conclusion or recommendations expressed in this material are those of the authors only and does not reflect the view of their employing organization or graduate schools. The work is the part of the final project in CS7643-Deep Learning class at Georgia Tech (Spring 2022). Bharathi Raja Chakravarthi were supported in part by a research grant from Science Foundation Ireland (SFI) under Grant Number SFI/12/RC/2289_P2 (Insight_2), co-funded by the European Regional Development Fund and Irish Research Council grant IRCLA/2017/129 (CARDAMOM-Comparative Deep Models of Language for Minority and Historical Languages).

References

Oana-Maria Camburu, Tim Rocktäschel, Thomas Lukasiewicz, and Phil Blunsom. 2018. e-snli: Natural language inference with natural language explanations. *CoRR*, abs/1812.01193.

Bharathi Raja Chakravarthi, Ruba Priyadharshini, Navya Jose, Anand Kumar M, Thomas Mandl, Prasanna Kumar Kumaresan, Rahul Ponnusamy, Hariharan R L, John P. McCrae, and Elizabeth Sherly. 2021a. Findings of the shared task on offensive language identification in Tamil, Malayalam, and Kannada. In *Proceedings of the First Workshop on Speech and Language Technologies for Dravidian Languages*, pages 133–145, Kyiv. Association for Computational Linguistics.

Bharathi Raja Chakravarthi, Ruba Priyadharshini, Vigneshwaran Muralidaran, Navya Jose, Shardul Suryawanshi, Elizabeth Sherly, and John P. McCrae. 2021b. Dravidiancodemix: Sentiment analysis and offensive language identification dataset for dravidian languages in code-mixed text. *CoRR*, abs/2106.09460.

Alexis Conneau, Kartikay Khandelwal, Naman Goyal, Vishrav Chaudhary, Guillaume Wenzek, Francisco Guzmán, Edouard Grave, Myle Ott, Luke Zettlemoyer, and Veselin Stoyanov. 2020. Unsupervised cross-lingual representation learning at scale. In *Proceedings of the 58th Annual Meeting of the Association for Computational Linguistics, ACL 2020, Online, July 5-10, 2020*, pages 8440–8451. Association for Computational Linguistics.

Jacob Devlin, Ming-Wei Chang, Kenton Lee, and Kristina Toutanova. 2019. BERT: pre-training of deep bidirectional transformers for language understanding. In *Proceedings of the 2019 Conference of the North American Chapter of the Association for Computational Linguistics: Human Language Technologies, NAACL-HLT 2019, Minneapolis, MN, USA, June 2-7, 2019, Volume 1 (Long and Short Papers)*, pages 4171–4186. Association for Computational Linguistics.

Huiyang Ding and David Jurgens. 2021. HamiltonDinggg at SemEval-2021 task 5: Investigating toxic span detection using RoBERTa pre-training. In *Proceedings of the 15th International Workshop on Semantic Evaluation (SemEval-2021)*, pages 263–269, Online. Association for Computational Linguistics.

Guolin Ke, Di He, and Tie-Yan Liu. 2021. Rethinking positional encoding in language pre-training. *ArXiv*, abs/2006.15595.

Wuwei Lan and Wei Xu. 2018. Neural network models for paraphrase identification, semantic textual similarity, natural language inference, and question answering. In *Proceedings of the 27th International Conference on Computational Linguistics*, pages 3890–3902, Santa Fe, New Mexico, USA. Association for Computational Linguistics.

Yinhan Liu, Myle Ott, Naman Goyal, Jingfei Du, Mandar Joshi, Danqi Chen, Omer Levy, Mike Lewis, Luke Zettlemoyer, and Veselin Stoyanov. 2019. Roberta: A robustly optimized BERT pretraining approach. *CoRR*, abs/1907.11692.

Marius Mosbach, Maksym Andriushchenko, and Dietrich Klakow. 2021. On the stability of fine-tuning BERT: misconceptions, explanations, and strong baselines. In *9th International Conference on Learning Representations, ICLR 2021, Virtual Event, Austria, May 3-7, 2021*. OpenReview.net.

Manikandan Ravikiran and Subbiah Annamalai. 2021. DOSA: Dravidian code-mixed offensive span identification dataset. In *Proceedings of the First Workshop on Speech and Language Technologies for Dravidian Languages*, pages 10–17, Kyiv. Association for Computational Linguistics.

Manikandan Ravikiran, Bharathi Raja Chakravarthi, Anand Kumar Madasamy, Sangeetha Sivanesan, Ratnavel Rajalakshmi, Sajeetha Thavareesan, Rahul Ponnusamy, and Shankar Mahadevan. 2022. Findings of the shared task on Offensive Span Identification in code-mixed Tamil-English comments. In *Proceedings of the Second Workshop on Speech and*

Language Technologies for Dravidian Languages. Association for Computational Linguistics.

Marco Túlio Ribeiro, Sameer Singh, and Carlos Guestrin. 2016a. "why should I trust you?": Explaining the predictions of any classifier. In *Proceedings of the 22nd ACM SIGKDD International Conference on Knowledge Discovery and Data Mining, San Francisco, CA, USA, August 13-17, 2016*, pages 1135–1144. ACM.

Marco Túlio Ribeiro, Sameer Singh, and Carlos Guestrin. 2016b. "why should I trust you?": Explaining the predictions of any classifier. In *Proceedings of the Demonstrations Session, NAACL HLT 2016, The 2016 Conference of the North American Chapter of the Association for Computational Linguistics: Human Language Technologies, San Diego California, USA, June 12-17, 2016*, pages 97–101. The Association for Computational Linguistics.

Peter Shaw, Jakob Uszkoreit, and Ashish Vaswani. 2018. Self-attention with relative position representations. In *Proceedings of the 2018 Conference of the North American Chapter of the Association for Computational Linguistics: Human Language Technologies, Volume 2 (Short Papers)*, pages 464–468, New Orleans, Louisiana. Association for Computational Linguistics.

Sandipan Sikdar, Parantapa Bhattacharya, and Kieran Heese. 2021. Integrated directional gradients: Feature interaction attribution for neural NLP models. In *Proceedings of the 59th Annual Meeting of the Association for Computational Linguistics and the 11th International Joint Conference on Natural Language Processing (Volume 1: Long Papers)*, pages 865–878, Online. Association for Computational Linguistics.

Mukund Sundararajan, Ankur Taly, and Qiqi Yan. 2017. Axiomatic attribution for deep networks. In *Proceedings of the 34th International Conference on Machine Learning, ICML 2017, Sydney, NSW, Australia, 6-11 August 2017*, volume 70 of *Proceedings of Machine Learning Research*, pages 3319–3328. PMLR.

James Thorne, Andreas Vlachos, Christos Christodoulopoulos, and Arpit Mittal. 2019. Generating token-level explanations for natural language inference. In *Proceedings of the 2019 Conference of the North American Chapter of the Association for Computational Linguistics: Human Language Technologies, Volume 1 (Long and Short Papers)*, pages 963–969, Minneapolis, Minnesota. Association for Computational Linguistics.

Thomas Wolf, Lysandre Debut, Victor Sanh, Julien Chaumond, Clement Delangue, Anthony Moi, Pierric Cistac, Tim Rault, Rémi Louf, Morgan Funtowicz, and Jamie Brew. 2019. Huggingface's transformers: State-of-the-art natural language processing. *CoRR*, abs/1910.03771.

Peng Xu, Dhruv Kumar, Wei Yang, Wenjie Zi, Keyi Tang, Chenyang Huang, Jackie Chi Kit Cheung, Simon J.D. Prince, and Yanshuai Cao. 2021. Optimizing deeper transformers on small datasets. In *Proceedings of the 59th Annual Meeting of the Association for Computational Linguistics and the 11th International Joint Conference on Natural Language Processing (Volume 1: Long Papers)*, pages 2089–2102, Online. Association for Computational Linguistics.

DLRG@TamilNLP-ACL2022: Offensive Span Identification in Tamil using BiLSTM-CRF approach

Ratnavel Rajalakshmi *, **Mohit Madhukar More, Bhamatipati Naga Shrikriti, Gitansh Saharan, Samyuktha Hanchate, Sayantan Nandy**
Vellore Institute of Technology, Chennai, India
rajalakshmi.r@vit.ac.in, mohitmadhukar.more2019@vitstudent.ac.in, shrikriti4@gmail.com, gitansh18saharan@gmail.com, samyukthahanchate@gmail.com, sayantann11@gmail.com

Abstract

Identifying offensive speech is an exciting and essential area of research, with ample traction in recent times. This paper presents our system submission to the subtask 1, focusing on using supervised approaches for extracting Offensive spans from code-mixed Tamil-English comments. To identify offensive spans, we developed the Bidirectional Long Short-Term Memory (BiLSTM) model with Glove Embedding. With this method, the developed system achieved an overall F1 of 0.1728. Additionally, for comments with less than 30 characters, the developed system shows an F1 of 0.3890, competitive with other submissions.

1 Introduction

Offensive speech, in general, is defined as the speech that causes an individual/group to feel displeased, upset, angry, or annoyed (Pavlopoulos et al., 2019). Often offensive speech is intended to vilify, humiliate, or incite hatred against a group or a class of persons based on race, religion, skin color, sexual identity, gender identity, ethnicity, disability, or national origin (Chakravarthi, 2020; Chakravarthi and Muralidaran, 2021). Predominantly with social media outreach, this is more prevalent. Accordingly, pinpointing such offensive speech is vital to encourage healthy conversation across users. Moreover, such systems are essential in automatic content moderation, with minimal human involvement (Priyadharshini et al., 2021; Kumaresan et al., 2021).

Code-Mixing is yet another social media phenomenon that has crept into daily speech across all languages, including Tamil (B and A, 2021b,a). Often, we see the usage of more than one language like Tamil-English, Kannada-English, etc., which adds a layer of complexity in identifying offensive contents (Ghanghor et al., 2021a,b; Yasaswini et al., 2021). Code-mixing and Code-borrowing have become common among the multi-lingual people (Rajalakshmi and Agrawal, 2017). Even though offensive content classification on Code-mixed language has been studied by few researchers by applying machine learning (Ratnavel Rajalakshmi, 2020) and deep learning algorithms (Rajalakshmi et al., 2021), the span identification of offensive contents are not explored much. Dictionary learning approaches were proposed for short text classification and URL based classification applying machine learning techniques (R. and Aravindan, 2018; Rajalakshmi, 2014) , but the research work in Tamil is limited.

Tamil is a member of the southern branch of the Dravidian languages, a group of about 26 languages indigenous to the Indian subcontinent (Anita and Subalalitha, 2019b,a; Subalalitha and Poovammal, 2018; Subalalitha, 2019). It is also classed as a member of the Tamil language family, which contains the languages of around 35 ethno-linguistic groups, including the Irula and Yerukula languages (Sakuntharaj and Mahesan, 2021, 2017, 2016; Thavareesan and Mahesan, 2019, 2020a,b, 2021). Malayalam is Tamil's closest significant cousin; the two began splitting during the 9th century AD. Although several variations between Tamil and Malayalam indicate a pre-historic break of the western dialect, the process of separating into a different language, Malayalam, did not occur until the 13th or 14th century.

This work, the shared task on offensive span identification handles the code-mixed Tamil-English comments and focuses on identification of character offsets of the offensive parts (?Ravikiran et al., 2022; Chakravarthi et al., 2022; Bharathi et al., 2022; Priyadharshini et al., 2022). There are multiple approaches for extracting spans. In this work, we treat the task of removing offensive span as an approach to token labeling. In this regard, we

*Corresponding Author

Proceedings of the Second Workshop on Speech and Language Technologies for Dravidian Languages, pages 248 - 253
May 26, 2022 ©2022 Association for Computational Linguistics

evaluated Bi-LSTM + CRF-based token labeling system for extracting offensive spans.

The rest of the paper is organized as follows. First, section 2 briefly discusses the literature on offensive span identification-related works. Then, in section 3, our system is described in detail, followed by Section 4, in which the experiments and results are presented. Finally, we conclude with possible implications for future work.

2 Related works

Offensive span can be solved in multiple ways ranging from token labeling to extracting spans using interpretability approaches. Unfortunately, the overall work is still developing for English and code-mixed languages, with very few well-established data sets and methods. (Pavlopoulos et al., 2021; Ravikiran and Annamalai, 2021). Interesting works related to offensive spans include Zhu et al. (2021) that employs token labeling using language models with a mixture of Conditional Random Fields (CRF). Usually, token labeling systems use BIO encoding of the text corresponding to offensive spans. Lexicon-based models (Burtenshaw and Kestemont, 2021) and statistical analysis (Palomino et al., 2021) are also widely explored. Finally, a few strategies utilize custom loss functions tailored explicitly for managing wrong spans. For code-mixed Tamil-English to date, we find there is only by Ravikiran and Annamalai (2021) that again uses token level labeling with language models.

3 Problem and System Description

An example of offensive span identification is shown in Figure 1. Given the input sentence, the task is to extract the range of spans corresponding to offensive content. In the above example, the word `Poramboku` contributes to offensiveness which corresponds to character offset of 47-56. A dataset with offensive span annotations details was released as part of the shared task on Toxic Span identification (Ravikiran et al., 2022). The description of this dataset is presented in Section 3.1.

3.1 Dataset Description

The released shared task dataset consists of two files with span annotations. The training dataset having 4816 samples with offensive spans and testing dataset with 876 samples without annotation. Additionally, the organizers released a stripped down version of train set which consists of span annotations for one or more words, but not the entire sentence. This was used for validation and hyper-parameter tuning.

3.2 Development Pipeline

The overall development pipeline used in this work is depicted in Figure 2. Our pipeline could be broken into three modules namely (a) Pre-processing Module (b) Encoding Module and (c) Bi-LSTM module respectively. Each of which is as described.

3.2.1 Preprocessing Module

In the preprocessing module, we extracted all the offensive parts of the comments from the given dataset and created individual parts it into list of tokens. These tokens are then converted to sequences using Tweet Tokenizer that is available as part of the nltk pipeline. Additionally, all the converted tokens are BIO encoded.

3.2.2 Encoding Module

In the encoding stage we use glove embedding pretrained on twitter data as initializer. We based this approach on the Vector Initialization (VI) alignment method, where after training embedding for one feature space, using it on related domain data will improve existing word embedding catering two new domain of data (code-mixed). We downloaded the Glove embedding which has 400K vocabulary size and each word corresponds to a 100-dimensional embedding vector. To use this embedding, we simply replace the one hot encoding word representation with its corresponding 100-dimensional vector.

3.2.3 Bi-LSTM Module

We follow Bi-LSTM + CRF architecture of Huang et al. (2015). The details of architecture is as shown in Figure 3 and consists of the following components.

- Input layer that accepts the input comments from which the span is to be identified.
- Embedding layer uses Glove embedding to create vectors suitable for training Bi-LSTM.
- The Bi-LSTM layer is more efficient in using the past features (via forward states) and future features (via backward states) for a specific time frame.
- CRF layer, that connects inputs to tags directly in turn identifying the offensive parts of the contents.

Example:
Input Sentence:
2017 Speech Super Star. 1996 endru solavakiran Poramboku Director
Output Spans:
"[47, 48, 49, 50, 51, 52, 53, 54, 55, 56]"

Figure 1: Example of offensive span identification used in the shared task.

Parameter	Value
Dropout	0.1
Recurrent Dropout	0.1
Max Sequence Length	128
Activation	ReLU

Table 1: Hyper-parameters

	F1	F1@30	F1@50	F1@>50
Bi-LSTM + CRF (Ours)	0.1728	0.3890	0.2523	0.1608
Random Baseline (Ravikiran et al., 2022)	0.3975	-	-	-

Table 2: Results obtained by our BiLSTM-CRF method

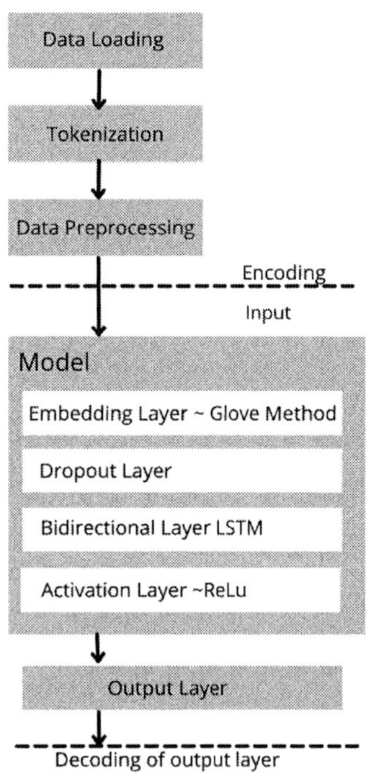

Figure 2: Overall pipeline used in this work

```
Layer (type)                 Output Shape              Param #
===============================================================
input_1 (InputLayer)         (None, 128)               0
_______________________________________________________________
embedding_1 (Embedding)      (None, 128, 100)          119351400
_______________________________________________________________
dropout_1 (Dropout)          (None, 128, 100)          0
_______________________________________________________________
bidirectional_1 (Bidirection (None, 128, 256)          234496
_______________________________________________________________
time_distributed_1 (TimeDist (None, 128, 128)          32896
_______________________________________________________________
crf_1 (CRF)                  (None, 128, 2)            266
===============================================================
Total params: 119,619,058
Trainable params: 119,619,058
Non-trainable params: 0
_______________________________________________________________
```

Figure 3: Overall architecture of Bi-LSTM + CRF used in this work.

Finally the spans corresponding to words mapped as offensive are extracted. The hyper-parameters details are presented in Table 1.

4 Experiments and Results

We have conducted various experiments to study the performance of the model and submitted the best performing version of our model. The results obtained are as shown in Table 2. We can see that our model obtained an F_1 score of 0.1728 which is significantly lower than random baselines used by the organizers. To analyse the performance, we briefly studied the effects of our system on various sizes of text. We found that our model performs well for shorter comments sequences with an F_1 of 0.3890. We believe that, this may be because of lack of LSTM's ability to exploit long range sequences, especially with only one single layer. Accordingly, we plan to revisit this problem with deeper architectures and language models.

5 Conclusion

Offensive Span Identification is still a challenging task with multiple challenges including the need of learning less data and long range contexts. In this work, we studied Bi-LSTM + CRF model to predict offensive spans from code-mixed Tamil-English comments. Accordingly our system obtained the overall F_1 of 0.1728 which is significantly lower. However we found that the developed method is suitable for shorter sequences where we can see higher results. In the future we plan to revisit the architecture in detail with a study on effect of embeddings types, number of layers and advanced architectures.

Acknowledgment

We would like to thank Manikandan Ravikiran and the organizers for all the guidance on the shared tasks. We would also like to thank the management of Vellore Institute of Technology, Chennai, where this research work is carried out.

References

R Anita and CN Subalalitha. 2019a. An approach to cluster Tamil literatures using discourse connectives. In *2019 IEEE 1st International Conference on Energy, Systems and Information Processing (ICESIP)*, pages 1–4. IEEE.

R Anita and CN Subalalitha. 2019b. Building discourse parser for Thirukkural. In *Proceedings of the 16th International Conference on Natural Language Processing*, pages 18–25.

Bharathi B and Agnusimmaculate Silvia A. 2021a. SSNCSE_NLP@DravidianLangTech-EACL2021: Meme classification for Tamil using machine learning approach. In *Proceedings of the First Workshop on Speech and Language Technologies for Dravidian Languages*, pages 336–339, Kyiv. Association for Computational Linguistics.

Bharathi B and Agnusimmaculate Silvia A. 2021b. SSNCSE_NLP@DravidianLangTech-EACL2021: Offensive language identification on multilingual code mixing text. In *Proceedings of the First Workshop on Speech and Language Technologies for Dravidian Languages*, pages 313–318, Kyiv. Association for Computational Linguistics.

B Bharathi, Bharathi Raja Chakravarthi, Subalalitha Chinnaudayar Navaneethakrishnan, N Sripriya, Arunaggiri Pandian, and Swetha Valli. 2022. Findings of the shared task on Speech Recognition for Vulnerable Individuals in Tamil. In *Proceedings of the Second Workshop on Language Technology for Equality, Diversity and Inclusion*. Association for Computational Linguistics.

Ben Burtenshaw and Mike Kestemont. 2021. UAntwerp at SemEval-2021 task 5: Spans are spans, stacking a binary word level approach to toxic span detection. In *Proceedings of the 15th International Workshop on Semantic Evaluation (SemEval-2021)*, pages 898–903, Online. Association for Computational Linguistics.

Bharathi Raja Chakravarthi. 2020. HopeEDI: A multilingual hope speech detection dataset for equality, diversity, and inclusion. In *Proceedings of the Third Workshop on Computational Modeling of People's Opinions, Personality, and Emotion's in Social Media*, pages 41–53, Barcelona, Spain (Online). Association for Computational Linguistics.

Bharathi Raja Chakravarthi and Vigneshwaran Muralidaran. 2021. Findings of the shared task on hope speech detection for equality, diversity, and inclusion. In *Proceedings of the First Workshop on Language Technology for Equality, Diversity and Inclusion*, pages 61–72, Kyiv. Association for Computational Linguistics.

Bharathi Raja Chakravarthi, Ruba Priyadharshini, Thenmozhi Durairaj, John Phillip McCrae, Paul Buitaleer, Prasanna Kumar Kumaresan, and Rahul Ponnusamy. 2022. Findings of the shared task on Homophobia Transphobia Detection in Social Media Comments. In *Proceedings of the Second Workshop on Language Technology for Equality, Diversity and Inclusion*. Association for Computational Linguistics.

Nikhil Ghanghor, Parameswari Krishnamurthy, Sajeetha Thavareesan, Ruba Priyadharshini, and Bharathi Raja Chakravarthi. 2021a. IIITK@DravidianLangTech-EACL2021: Offensive language identification and meme classification in Tamil, Malayalam and Kannada. In *Proceedings of the First Workshop on Speech and Language Technologies for Dravidian Languages*, pages 222–229, Kyiv. Association for Computational Linguistics.

Nikhil Ghanghor, Rahul Ponnusamy, Prasanna Kumar Kumaresan, Ruba Priyadharshini, Sajeetha Thavareesan, and Bharathi Raja Chakravarthi. 2021b. IIITK@LT-EDI-EACL2021: Hope speech detection for equality, diversity, and inclusion in Tamil , Malayalam and English. In *Proceedings of the First Workshop on Language Technology for Equality, Diversity and Inclusion*, pages 197–203, Kyiv. Association for Computational Linguistics.

Zhiheng Huang, Wei Xu, and Kai Yu. 2015. Bidirectional LSTM-CRF models for sequence tagging. *CoRR*, abs/1508.01991.

Prasanna Kumar Kumaresan, Ratnasingam Sakuntharaj, Sajeetha Thavareesan, Subalalitha Navaneethakrishnan, Anand Kumar Madasamy, Bharathi Raja Chakravarthi, and John P McCrae. 2021. Findings of shared task on offensive language identification in Tamil and Malayalam. In *Forum for Information Retrieval Evaluation*, pages 16–18.

Marco Palomino, Dawid Grad, and James Bedwell. 2021. GoldenWind at SemEval-2021 task 5: Orthrus - an ensemble approach to identify toxicity. In *Proceedings of the 15th International Workshop on Semantic Evaluation (SemEval-2021)*, pages 860–864, Online. Association for Computational Linguistics.

John Pavlopoulos, Léo Laugier, Jeffrey Sorensen, and Ion Androutsopoulos. 2021. Semeval-2021 task 5: Toxic spans detection (to appear). In *Proceedings of the 15th International Workshop on Semantic Evaluation*.

John Pavlopoulos, Nithum Thain, Lucas Dixon, and Ion Androutsopoulos. 2019. ConvAI at SemEval-2019 task 6: Offensive language identification and categorization with perspective and BERT. In *Proceedings of the 13th International Workshop on Semantic Evaluation*, pages 571–576, Minneapolis, Minnesota, USA. Association for Computational Linguistics.

Ruba Priyadharshini, Bharathi Raja Chakravarthi, Subalalitha Chinnaudayar Navaneethakrishnan, Thenmozhi Durairaj, Malliga Subramanian, Kogilavani Shanmugavadivel, Siddhanth U Hegde, and Prasanna Kumar Kumaresan. 2022. Findings of the shared task on Abusive Comment Detection in Tamil. In *Proceedings of the Second Workshop on Speech and Language Technologies for Dravidian Languages*. Association for Computational Linguistics.

Ruba Priyadharshini, Bharathi Raja Chakravarthi, Sajeetha Thavareesan, Dhivya Chinnappa, Durairaj Thenmozhi, and Rahul Ponnusamy. 2021. Overview of the DravidianCodeMix 2021 shared task on sentiment detection in Tamil, Malayalam, and Kannada. In *Forum for Information Retrieval Evaluation*, pages 4–6.

Rajalakshmi R. and Chandrabose Aravindan. 2018. An effective and discriminative feature learning for url based web page classification. In *2018 IEEE International Conference on Systems, Man, and Cybernetics (SMC)*, pages 1374–1379.

R. Rajalakshmi and Rohan Agrawal. 2017. Borrowing likeliness ranking based on relevance factor. In *Proceedings of the Fourth ACM IKDD Conferences on Data Sciences*, CODS '17, New York, NY, USA. Association for Computing Machinery.

Ratnavel Rajalakshmi. 2014. Supervised term weighting methods for url classification. *J. Comput. Sci.*, 10:1969–1976.

Ratnavel Rajalakshmi, Yashwant Reddy, and Lokesh Kumar. 2021. DLRG@DravidianLangTech-EACL2021: Transformer based approach for offensive language identification on code-mixed Tamil. In *Proceedings of the First Workshop on Speech and Language Technologies for Dravidian Languages*, pages 357–362, Kyiv. Association for Computational Linguistics.

Yashwanth Reddy B Ratnavel Rajalakshmi. 2020. DLRG@HASOC 2020: A hybrid approach for hate and offensive content identification in multilingual tweets. In *"Proceedings of FIRE '20, Forum for Information Retrieval Evaluation"*, pages 1–7.

Manikandan Ravikiran and Subbiah Annamalai. 2021. DOSA: Dravidian code-mixed offensive span identification dataset. In *Proceedings of the First Workshop on Speech and Language Technologies for Dravidian Languages*, pages 10–17, Kyiv. Association for Computational Linguistics.

Manikandan Ravikiran, Bharathi Raja Chakravarthi, Anand Kumar Madasamy, Sangeetha Sivanesan, Ratnavel Rajalakshmi, Sajeetha Thavareesan, Rahul Ponnusamy, and Shankar Mahadevan. 2022. Findings of the shared task on Offensive Span Identification in code-mixed Tamil-English comments. In *Proceedings of the Second Workshop on Speech and Language Technologies for Dravidian Languages*. Association for Computational Linguistics.

Ratnasingam Sakuntharaj and Sinnathamby Mahesan. 2016. A novel hybrid approach to detect and correct spelling in Tamil text. In *2016 IEEE International Conference on Information and Automation for Sustainability (ICIAfS)*, pages 1–6.

Ratnasingam Sakuntharaj and Sinnathamby Mahesan. 2017. Use of a novel hash-table for speeding-up suggestions for misspelt tamil words. In *2017 IEEE International Conference on Industrial and Information Systems (ICIIS)*, pages 1–5.

Ratnasingam Sakuntharaj and Sinnathamby Mahesan. 2021. Missing word detection and correction based on context of Tamil sentences using n-grams. In *2021 10th International Conference on Information and Automation for Sustainability (ICIAfS)*, pages 42–47.

C. N. Subalalitha. 2019. Information extraction framework for Kurunthogai. *Sādhanā*, 44(7):156.

CN Subalalitha and E Poovammal. 2018. Automatic bilingual dictionary construction for Tirukural. *Applied Artificial Intelligence*, 32(6):558–567.

Sajeetha Thavareesan and Sinnathamby Mahesan. 2019. Sentiment analysis in Tamil texts: A study on machine learning techniques and feature representation. In *2019 14th Conference on Industrial and Information Systems (ICIIS)*, pages 320–325.

Sajeetha Thavareesan and Sinnathamby Mahesan. 2020a. Sentiment lexicon expansion using Word2vec and fastText for sentiment prediction in Tamil texts. In *2020 Moratuwa Engineering Research Conference (MERCon)*, pages 272–276.

Sajeetha Thavareesan and Sinnathamby Mahesan. 2020b. Word embedding-based part of speech tagging in Tamil texts. In *2020 IEEE 15th International Conference on Industrial and Information Systems (ICIIS)*, pages 478–482.

Sajeetha Thavareesan and Sinnathamby Mahesan. 2021. Sentiment analysis in Tamil texts using k-means and k-nearest neighbour. In *2021 10th International Conference on Information and Automation for Sustainability (ICIAfS)*, pages 48–53.

Konthala Yasaswini, Karthik Puranik, Adeep Hande, Ruba Priyadharshini, Sajeetha Thavareesan, and Bharathi Raja Chakravarthi. 2021. IIITT@DravidianLangTech-EACL2021: Transfer learning for offensive language detection in Dravidian languages. In *Proceedings of the First Workshop on Speech and Language Technologies for Dravidian Languages*, pages 187–194, Kyiv. Association for Computational Linguistics.

Qinglin Zhu, Zijie Lin, Yice Zhang, Jingyi Sun, Xiang Li, Qihui Lin, Yixue Dang, and Ruifeng Xu. 2021. HITSZ-HLT at SemEval-2021 task 5: Ensemble sequence labeling and span boundary detection for toxic span detection. In *Proceedings of the 15th International Workshop on Semantic Evaluation (SemEval-2021)*, pages 521–526, Online. Association for Computational Linguistics.

Findings of the Shared Task on Multimodal Sentiment Analysis and Troll Meme Classification in Dravidian Languages

Premjith B[1]**, Bharathi Raja Chakravarthi**[2]**, Malliga Subramanian**[3]**, Bharathi B**[4]**, Soman KP**[1]**, Dhanalakshmi Vadivel**[4]**, Sreelakshmi K**[1]**, Arunaggiri Pandian**[6]**, and Prasanna Kumar Kumaresan**[7]

[1]Center for Computational Engineering and Networking (CEN), Amrita School of Engineering, Coimbatore, Amrita Vishwa Vidyapeetham, India

[2]National University of Ireland Galway, [3]Kongu Engineering College, Tamil Nadu, India

[4]SSN College of Engineering, Tamil Nadu, India, [5]RV Government Arts college , Chengalpattu

[6]Thiagarajar College of Engineerin, Madurai, India

[7]Indian Institute of Information Technology and Management, Kerala

b_premjith@cb.amrita.edu, bharathi.raja@insight-centre.org

Abstract

This paper presents the findings of the shared task on Multimodal Sentiment Analysis and Troll meme classification in Dravidian languages held at ACL 2022. Multimodal sentiment analysis deals with the identification of sentiment from video. In addition to video data, the task requires the analysis of corresponding text and audio features for the classification of movie reviews into five classes. We created a dataset for this task in Malayalam and Tamil. The Troll meme classification task aims to classify multimodal Troll memes into two categories. This task assumes the analysis of both text and image features for making better predictions. The performance of the participating teams was analysed using the F1-score. Only one team submitted their results in the Multimodal Sentiment Analysis task, whereas we received six submissions in the Troll meme classification task. The only team that participated in the Multimodal Sentiment Analysis shared task obtained an F1-score of 0.24. In the Troll meme classification task, the winning team achieved an F1-score of 0.596.

1 Introduction

People use different modes of content, including video, audio and text, to express their opinion or attitude or interact with another person. These types of data are too complex to process because of the ambiguity at various levels. Moreover, such types data are more user-centric and contextual (Schreck and Keim, 2012). The complexity of the computational processing of social media is more for multimodal data, which includes video, audio and text modalities. The machine learning or deep learning model should utilize/extract the features identified from all modalities for better decision making (Chakravarthi, 2020; Kumaresan et al., 2021; Chakravarthi and Muralidaran, 2021; Ravikiran et al., 2022; Chakravarthi et al., 2022; Bharathi et al., 2022; Priyadharshini et al., 2022). This shared task on multimedia social media analysis in Dravidian languages includes two subtasks - Multimodal Sentiment Analysis and Troll meme classification.

Sentiment analysis is a Natural Language Processing (NLP) task to identify the underlying sentiment or opinion about movies, products, government policies etc., expressed by people through various social media platforms (Priyadharshini et al., 2021), (Chakravarthi et al., 2021b). Nowadays, social media users use multiple modalities such as images containing text and videos to express their opinions. It has become common to share review videos about movies and products on YouTube, and Facebook (Castro et al., 2019), (Qiyang and Jung, 2019). Therefore, analysis of multiple modalities has become significant in identifying sentiments from video data. Video data contain modalities such as video frames, speech signals, and text (transcripts). Training a machine learning model requires considering the features of the above three modalities to train a machine learning model.

The shared task on multimodal sentiment analysis aims at inviting researchers for developing machine learning models to draw out the sentiments from movie review videos in Malayalam and Tamil. Malayalam and Tamil are members of the Dravidian language family (Sakuntharaj and Mahesan, 2021, 2017, 2016; Thavareesan and Mahesan, 2019, 2020a,b, 2021). In addition to that, both languages are morphologically rich and agglutinative (Premjith and Soman, 2021), (Premjith et al., 2019). This makes these languages complex for

Proceedings of the Second Workshop on Speech and Language Technologies for Dravidian Languages, pages 254 - 260
May 26, 2022

computational processing (Anita and Subalalitha, 2019b,a; Subalalitha and Poovammal, 2018; Subalalitha, 2019; Srinivasan and Subalalitha, 2019; Narasimhan et al., 2018). Moreover, the complexity increases when we deal with speech and text for learning feature representation from video data. We created the dataset (Chakravarthi et al., 2021a) by downloading movie review videos that have been uploaded on YouTube. The Malayalam dataset consisted of 70 videos, and the Tamil dataset contained 64 videos in it. Videos are classified into five categories: Highly Positive, Positive, Neutral, Negative and Highly Negative by considering the facial expressions of the reviewers and the words used to give a review for the movies.

Memes have become prevalent in social media in recent times. People use memes, which can come in image and video modalities, to express their opinions or attitude on various issues (Suryawanshi and Chakravarthi, 2021a). Some memes are created only for entertainment purposes. However, certain users use memes to inflame individuals or organizations. The computational processing of the meme is challenging because the text that appears in an image or video is difficult to extract (Ghanghor et al., 2021a,b; Yasaswini et al., 2021). In addition to that, the text may appear in different fonts and sizes, increasing the complexity. The objective of the Troll meme classification shared task is to classify a Troll meme into either troll or not-troll categories. We collected Troll memes from social media platforms, namely Facebook, Instagram, Whatsapp, and Pinterest (Suryawanshi et al., 2020a).

This paper presents an overview of the shared task on multimodal sentiment analysis and Troll meme classification in Dravidian languages. We considered data collected from both Malayalam and Tamil for these two tasks. This work also discusses the results of the participating teams. We shared the training and validation data with labels and test data without labels with the participants. The participants submitted the predicted labels for the test data by building machine learning models for the task. In total, 56 teams registered for the multimodal sentiment analysis competition organized by Codalab [1]. However, only one team submitted their results for Tamil test data, whereas six teams participated in the Troll meme classification task.

[1] https://competitions.codalab.org/competitions/36406

The paper is organized into four sections, including the introduction. Section 2 describes the Multimodal Sentiment Analysis shared task and the dataset used in detail. It is followed by Section 3, which summarizes the Troll meme classification task. In Section 4, we discuss the systems and methodologies submitted by participants for both shared tasks and analysis of the results of submitted models. A summary of the tasks and future work are presented in Section 5.

2 Multimodal Sentiment Analysis Task Description

Artificial intelligence models that can recognize emotion and opinions are helpful for a variety of industries to understand user requirements, preferences and reviews. From virtual assistants to content moderation, sentiment analysis has many applications. A great deal of multimodal content has been published in local languages on social media about products making the task of sentiment analysis challenging (Chakravarthi et al., 2021a). The reach of visual information and the traction of smartphones have facilitated people to use videos for sharing their opinions. Hence, our task aims to identify Highly positive, Positive, Neutral, Negative, and Highly Negative videos by taking the video, speech and text modalities.

2.1 Dataset Description

The dataset consists of videos collected from YouTube and annotated manually. The dataset has 70 Malayalam, and 64 Tamil videos split into training, validation and test set. Each video segment includes manual transcription aligned along with sentiment annotation by volunteer annotators. Videos are annotated into five labels.

- **Highly positive state**: Video clip where the reviewer uses overstated words or expressions
- **Positive**: A video clip where reviewer uses positive words with mild facial expressions to give reviews .
- **Neutral**: There is no explicit or implicit indicator of the speaker's emotional state. Examples are asking for like or subscription or questions about the release date or movie dialogue.
- **Negative**: Videos where negative words and

Class Label	Malayalam	Tamil
Highly Positive	9	8
Positive	39	38
Neutral	8	8
Negative	12	5
Highly Negative	2	5
Total	70	64

Table 1: Number of videos in each class, and language.

Dataset	Malayalam	Tamil
Train	50	44
Validation	10	10
Test	10	10

Table 2: Distribution of Multimodal Sentiment Analysis data in Malayalam and Tamil.

sarcastic comments with soft facial expressions are used.

- **Highly Negative**: Videos where exaggerated negative words with a sullen face and taut voice, are used.

Table 1 gives the various classes and statistics of data points in each class, and Table 2 shows the number of data points in train, test and validation datasets used in both languages.

3 Troll meme Classification Task Description

This shared task aims to devise methodologies and models for detecting troll memes in Tamil using textual and visual features. A Troll meme consists of offensive text and non-offensive images and vice versa, intending to degrade, provoke, or offend a person or a group. A dataset with two classes, namely Troll and Not Troll, has been provided for this shared task. The dataset has images associated with captions and comprises memes and transcribed text in Latin, which are annotated and transcribed. The participants used images, captions, or both to do the classification. A sample troll and non-troll meme has been shown in Figure. The task organisers have enhanced the dataset by giving the text as a separate modality for the shared task because the text linked with the meme acts as a context for the image. Both text and image-based classification approach, that is, multimodal classification, was expected from the participants.

Split	Troll	Not-troll	Total
Train	1,282	1,018	2,300
Test	395	272	667
Total	1,677	1,290	2,967

Table 3: Number of images in each class.

Team	Tamil	Rank
cuet_nlp_undergrad	0.24	1
baseline	0.20	2

Table 4: Macro-average F1-score of submitted tasks (for Tamil videos)

3.1 Dataset Description

The dataset consists of images and text associated with a meme in Tamil. The data is labelled into two classes, namely "troll" or "not-troll". The text in the meme is written in Tamil grammar with English lexicon or English grammar with Tamil lexicon. But for consistency the text was transcripted to Latin (Suryawanshi and Chakravarthi, 2021b), (Suryawanshi et al., 2020b).

- **Troll**: The meme has offensive text and non-offensive images, offensive images and non-offensive text, sarcastically offensive text with non-offensive images, or sarcastic images with offensive text to distract, distract, and digressive or off-topic content with the intent to demean or offend particular people, groups or race.

- **Not-Troll**: Images that do not have the above features are Non-Troll memes.

Table 3 gives the various classes and statistics of data points in each class and split up into train and test sets.

4 Methodology

4.1 Multimodal Sentiment Analysis

Multimodal Sentiment Analysis in Dravidian languages is organized for the first time. The task is challenging as the participants have to consider features extracted from three modalities to build a machine learning or deep learning model. Moreover, the size of the dataset in Malayalam and Tamil are 70 and 64, respectively, which is not sufficient to build a machine learning model. Hence, we received only one submission for this task. The rank list for this task is shown in Table 4.

Team	F1-score	Rank
BPHC	0.596	1
hate-alert	0.561	2
SSN_MLRG1	0.558	3
CUET89109115	0.529	4
DLRG_RR	0.519	5
TeamX	0.466	6

Table 5: The Weighted-average F1-score of teams submitted their predictions in Troll meme classification in Tamil

4.2 Troll meme Classification

A meme, also known as a troll, is an image with obscene or satirical text to degrade, provoke, or offend a person or a group. A troll meme can also be an image without any words. This section summarises the shared task for detecting troll memes using images and descriptions submitted by various participants. The main goal of this task is to classify trolling from multimodal memes. While reading the articles, we see that three of the five works submitted employ VGG16, a CNN-based design. Transformer-based models have also been proposed for extracting features from the text modal. One of the submitted tasks has combined the embeddings from text and image-based models. Below, we present a summary of each of the work submitted for this shared task, and the rank list of the task is shown in Table 5.

- TeamX (Rabindra Nath et al., 2022) used TF-IDF for extracting text features and SVM for training and classification of text data. In addition, multilingual BERT has been used for text classification. BERT model has also been trained to extract text from memes using Tesseract (Smith, 2007) and memes in hateful meme dataset (Kiela et al., 2021). Similarly, for image modality, pre-trained models such as EffNet, VGG16, and ResNet have been developed for detecting troll images. For text-only modality, mBERT with code mixed data has the highest accuracy among other models. EffNet has given better accuracy when compared to VGG16 and ResNet for image modality.

- A work by team hate-alert (Mithun et al., 2022) proposed two uni-modal models, one utilizing text features and the other using image-based features. All the texts associated with the meme are sent to a transformer model, MURIL, to get the dimensional feature vectors for each meme and then fed to an output node for the final prediction. For extracting features from images, VGG16 has been used. All the images have been passed to VGG16 and obtained feature vectors. Then, the embeddings from both MURIL and VGG16 models have been concatenated and sent to a classification node for the final prediction. The authors demonstrated that concatenated models give better accuracy than uni-modal models.

- Shruthi et al. (Shruthi et al., 2022) classified memes using three models: BERT, ALBERT, and XLNet. The first model is BERT, which has learned the context of a word based on all of its surroundings. Following this model, two more models, namely ALBERT (a Lite BERT) and XLNet, have also been utilized. The accuracy obtained by the XLNet model is 0.59, which is higher than BERT and ALBERT.

- An attempt by (Achyuta Krishna and Mithun Kumar, 2022) used two techniques to obtain embeddings from raw Tamil-English code-mixed text and another from translated and transliterated version of the dataset. The first approach used TF-IDF, LSTM and mBERT to retrieve embeddings. TF-IDF, IndicFT, MuRIL and mBERT have been used for getting embeddings in the second approach. Then, different machine learning-based classification algorithms, such as Naïve Bayes, Logistic Regression etc., have been used for detecting troll memes. Comparing the various pre-trained models, MuRIL performs best with an F1-score of 0.74 relative to others.

- Team CUET-NLP (Md Maruf et al., 2022) extracted the visual features of memes using CNN architectures such as VGG16, VGG19 and ResNet with transfer learning. Then, to extract the textual features, CNN and CNN with LSTM have been used due to their effectiveness in capturing the long-term dependencies from the long text. Subsequently, the output from the visual and textual models has been concatenated to form a single integrated model. The overall performance of the models is between 44 and 56% weighted F1-score.

From the articles submitted under this shared

task, we find that CNN based VGG models have been the choice of the authors for extracting the visual features from the troll memes and transformer-based models for extracting textual features.

5 Conclusion

We presented two multimodal shared tasks - Multimodal Sentiment Analysis and Troll meme classification in Dravidian languages. Multimodal Sentiment Analysis in Dravidian languages is the first shared task in this area. In addition to the multimodality, the code-mixing nature of the language posed challenges in these two tasks. We created datasets for both tasks to aid the research in the under-researched area. The machine models used by the participants revealed different ways of solving the problems mentioned above. We received one submission in the Multimodal Sentiment Analysis task and six submissions in Troll meme classification.

Acknowledgments

Author Bharathi Raja Chakravarthi was supported in part by a research grant from Science Foundation Ireland (SFI) under Grant Number SFI/12/RC/2289_P2 (Insight_2), co-funded by the European Regional Development Fund and Irish Research Council grant IRCLA/2017/129 (CARDAMOM-Comparative Deep Models of Language for Minority and Historical Languages).

References

V Achyuta Krishna and S R Mithun Kumar. 2022. BPHC@DravidianLangTech-ACL2022: A Comparative Analysis of Classical and Pre-trained Models for Troll Meme Classification in Tamil Code Mixed Captions. In *Proceedings of the Second Workshop on Speech and Language Technologies for Dravidian Languages*. Association for Computational Linguistics.

R Anita and CN Subalalitha. 2019a. An approach to cluster Tamil literatures using discourse connectives. In *2019 IEEE 1st International Conference on Energy, Systems and Information Processing (ICESIP)*, pages 1–4. IEEE.

R Anita and CN Subalalitha. 2019b. Building discourse parser for Thirukkural. In *Proceedings of the 16th International Conference on Natural Language Processing*, pages 18–25.

B Bharathi, Bharathi Raja Chakravarthi, Subalalitha Chinnaudayar Navaneethakrishnan, N Sripriya, Arunaggiri Pandian, and Swetha Valli. 2022. Findings of the shared task on Speech Recognition for Vulnerable Individuals in Tamil. In *Proceedings of the Second Workshop on Language Technology for Equality, Diversity and Inclusion*. Association for Computational Linguistics.

Santiago Castro, Devamanyu Hazarika, Verónica Pérez-Rosas, Roger Zimmermann, Rada Mihalcea, and Soujanya Poria. 2019. Towards multimodal sarcasm detection (an _obviously_ perfect paper). *arXiv preprint arXiv:1906.01815*.

Bharathi Raja Chakravarthi. 2020. HopeEDI: A multilingual hope speech detection dataset for equality, diversity, and inclusion. In *Proceedings of the Third Workshop on Computational Modeling of People's Opinions, Personality, and Emotion's in Social Media*, pages 41–53, Barcelona, Spain (Online). Association for Computational Linguistics.

Bharathi Raja Chakravarthi, P K Jishnu Parameswaran, B Premjith, KP Soman, Rahul Ponnusamy, Prasanna Kumar Kumaresan, Kingston Pal Thamburaj, John P McCrae, et al. 2021a. Dravidian-multimodality: A dataset for multi-modal sentiment analysis in tamil and malayalam. *arXiv preprint arXiv:2106.04853*.

Bharathi Raja Chakravarthi and Vigneshwaran Muralidaran. 2021. Findings of the shared task on hope speech detection for equality, diversity, and inclusion. In *Proceedings of the First Workshop on Language Technology for Equality, Diversity and Inclusion*, pages 61–72, Kyiv. Association for Computational Linguistics.

Bharathi Raja Chakravarthi, Ruba Priyadharshini, Thenmozhi Durairaj, John Phillip McCrae, Paul Buitaleer, Prasanna Kumar Kumaresan, and Rahul Ponnusamy. 2022. Findings of the shared task on Homophobia Transphobia Detection in Social Media Comments. In *Proceedings of the Second Workshop on Language Technology for Equality, Diversity and Inclusion*. Association for Computational Linguistics.

Bharathi Raja Chakravarthi, Ruba Priyadharshini, Sajeetha Thavareesan, Dhivya Chinnappa, Durairaj Thenmozhi, Elizabeth Sherly, John P McCrae, Adeep Hande, Rahul Ponnusamy, Shubhanker Banerjee, et al. 2021b. Findings of the sentiment analysis of dravidian languages in code-mixed text. *arXiv preprint arXiv:2111.09811*.

Nikhil Ghanghor, Parameswari Krishnamurthy, Sajeetha Thavareesan, Ruba Priyadharshini, and Bharathi Raja Chakravarthi. 2021a. IIITK@DravidianLangTech-EACL2021: Offensive language identification and meme classification in Tamil, Malayalam and Kannada. In *Proceedings of the First Workshop on Speech and Language Technologies for Dravidian Languages*, pages 222–229, Kyiv. Association for Computational Linguistics.

Nikhil Ghanghor, Rahul Ponnusamy, Prasanna Kumar Kumaresan, Ruba Priyadharshini, Sajeetha Thavareesan, and Bharathi Raja Chakravarthi. 2021b. IIITK@LT-EDI-EACL2021: Hope speech detection for equality, diversity, and inclusion in Tamil , Malayalam and English. In *Proceedings of the First Workshop on Language Technology for Equality, Diversity and Inclusion*, pages 197–203, Kyiv. Association for Computational Linguistics.

Douwe Kiela, Hamed Firooz, Aravind Mohan, Vedanuj Goswami, Amanpreet Singh, Casey A Fitzpatrick, Peter Bull, Greg Lipstein, Tony Nelli, Ron Zhu, et al. 2021. The hateful memes challenge: competition report. In *NeurIPS 2020 Competition and Demonstration Track*, pages 344–360. PMLR.

Prasanna Kumar Kumaresan, Ratnasingam Sakuntharaj, Sajeetha Thavareesan, Subalalitha Navaneethakrishnan, Anand Kumar Madasamy, Bharathi Raja Chakravarthi, and John P McCrae. 2021. Findings of shared task on offensive language identification in Tamil and Malayalam. In *Forum for Information Retrieval Evaluation*, pages 16–18.

Hasan Md Maruf, Jannat Nusratul, Hossain Eftekhar, Sharif Omar, and Hoque Mohammed Moshiul. 2022. CUET-NLP@DravidianLangTech-ACL2022: Investigating Deep Learning Techniques to Detect Multimodal Troll Memes. In *Proceedings of the Second Workshop on Speech and Language Technologies for Dravidian Languages*. Association for Computational Linguistics.

Das Mithun, Banerjee Somnath, and Mukherjee Animesh. 2022. hate-alert@DravidianLangTech-ACL2022: Ensembling Multi-Modalities for Tamil TrollMeme Classification. In *Proceedings of the Second Workshop on Speech and Language Technologies for Dravidian Languages*. Association for Computational Linguistics.

Anitha Narasimhan, Aarthy Anandan, Madhan Karky, and CN Subalalitha. 2018. Porul: Option generation and selection and scoring algorithms for a tamil flash card game. *International Journal of Cognitive and Language Sciences*, 12(2):225–228.

B Premjith and KP Soman. 2021. Deep learning approach for the morphological synthesis in malayalam and tamil at the character level. *Transactions on Asian and Low-Resource Language Information Processing*, 20(6):1–17.

B Premjith, KP Soman, M Anand Kumar, and D Jyothi Ratnam. 2019. Embedding linguistic features in word embedding for preposition sense disambiguation in english—malayalam machine translation context. In *Recent Advances in Computational Intelligence*, pages 341–370. Springer.

Ruba Priyadharshini, Bharathi Raja Chakravarthi, Subalalitha Chinnaudayar Navaneethakrishnan, Thenmozhi Durairaj, Malliga Subramanian, Kogilavani Shanmugavadivel, Siddhanth U Hegde, and Prasanna Kumar Kumaresan. 2022. Findings of the shared task on Abusive Comment Detection in Tamil. In *Proceedings of the Second Workshop on Speech and Language Technologies for Dravidian Languages*. Association for Computational Linguistics.

Ruba Priyadharshini, Bharathi Raja Chakravarthi, Sajeetha Thavareesan, Dhivya Chinnappa, Durairaj Thenmozhi, and Rahul Ponnusamy. 2021. Overview of the dravidiancodemix 2021 shared task on sentiment detection in tamil, malayalam, and kannada. In *Forum for Information Retrieval Evaluation*, pages 4–6.

Zea Qiyang and Heekyoung Jung. 2019. Learning and sharing creative skills with short videos: A case study of user behavior in tiktok and bilibili. *International association of societies of design research (IASDR), design revolution.*

Nandi Rabindra Nath, Alam Firoj, and Nakov Preslav. 2022. TeamX@DravidianLangTech-ACL2022: A Comparative Analysis for Troll-Based Meme Classification. In *Proceedings of the Second Workshop on Speech and Language Technologies for Dravidian Languages*. Association for Computational Linguistics.

Manikandan Ravikiran, Bharathi Raja Chakravarthi, Anand Kumar Madasamy, Sangeetha Sivanesan, Ratnavel Rajalakshmi, Sajeetha Thavareesan, Rahul Ponnusamy, and Shankar Mahadevan. 2022. Findings of the shared task on Offensive Span Identification in code-mixed Tamil-English comments. In *Proceedings of the Second Workshop on Speech and Language Technologies for Dravidian Languages*. Association for Computational Linguistics.

Ratnasingam Sakuntharaj and Sinnathamby Mahesan. 2016. A novel hybrid approach to detect and correct spelling in Tamil text. In *2016 IEEE International Conference on Information and Automation for Sustainability (ICIAfS)*, pages 1–6.

Ratnasingam Sakuntharaj and Sinnathamby Mahesan. 2017. Use of a novel hash-table for speeding-up suggestions for misspelt Tamil words. In *2017 IEEE International Conference on Industrial and Information Systems (ICIIS)*, pages 1–5.

Ratnasingam Sakuntharaj and Sinnathamby Mahesan. 2021. Missing word detection and correction based on context of Tamil sentences using n-grams. In *2021 10th International Conference on Information and Automation for Sustainability (ICIAfS)*, pages 42–47.

Tobias Schreck and Daniel Keim. 2012. Visual analysis of social media data. *Computer*, 46(5):68–75.

H Shruthi, Esackimuthu Sarika, M Saritha, S Rajalakshmi, and S Angel Deborah. 2022. SSN_MLRG1@DravidianLangTech-ACL2022: Troll Meme Classification in Tamil using Transformer Models. In *Proceedings of the Second*

Workshop on Speech and Language Technologies for Dravidian Languages. Association for Computational Linguistics.

Ray Smith. 2007. An overview of the tesseract ocr engine. In *Ninth international conference on document analysis and recognition (ICDAR 2007)*, volume 2, pages 629–633. IEEE.

R Srinivasan and CN Subalalitha. 2019. Automated named entity recognition from tamil documents. In *2019 IEEE 1st International Conference on Energy, Systems and Information Processing (ICESIP)*, pages 1–5. IEEE.

C. N. Subalalitha. 2019. Information extraction framework for Kurunthogai. *Sādhanā*, 44(7):156.

CN Subalalitha and E Poovammal. 2018. Automatic bilingual dictionary construction for Tirukural. *Applied Artificial Intelligence*, 32(6):558–567.

Shardul Suryawanshi and Bharathi Raja Chakravarthi. 2021a. Findings of the shared task on troll meme classification in tamil. In *Proceedings of the First Workshop on Speech and Language Technologies for Dravidian Languages*, pages 126–132.

Shardul Suryawanshi and Bharathi Raja Chakravarthi. 2021b. Findings of the shared task on troll meme classification in tamil. In *Proceedings of the First Workshop on Speech and Language Technologies for Dravidian Languages*, pages 126–132.

Shardul Suryawanshi, Bharathi Raja Chakravarthi, Pranav Verma, Mihael Arcan, John Philip McCrae, and Paul Buitelaar. 2020a. A dataset for troll classification of tamilmemes. In *Proceedings of the WILDRE5–5th workshop on indian language data: resources and evaluation*, pages 7–13.

Shardul Suryawanshi, Bharathi Raja Chakravarthi, Pranav Verma, Mihael Arcan, John Philip McCrae, and Paul Buitelaar. 2020b. A dataset for troll classification of tamilmemes. In *Proceedings of the WILDRE5–5th workshop on indian language data: resources and evaluation*, pages 7–13.

Sajeetha Thavareesan and Sinnathamby Mahesan. 2019. Sentiment analysis in Tamil texts: A study on machine learning techniques and feature representation. In *2019 14th Conference on Industrial and Information Systems (ICIIS)*, pages 320–325.

Sajeetha Thavareesan and Sinnathamby Mahesan. 2020a. Sentiment lexicon expansion using Word2vec and fastText for sentiment prediction in Tamil texts. In *2020 Moratuwa Engineering Research Conference (MERCon)*, pages 272–276.

Sajeetha Thavareesan and Sinnathamby Mahesan. 2020b. Word embedding-based part of speech tagging in Tamil texts. In *2020 IEEE 15th International Conference on Industrial and Information Systems (ICIIS)*, pages 478–482.

Sajeetha Thavareesan and Sinnathamby Mahesan. 2021. Sentiment analysis in Tamil texts using k-means and k-nearest neighbour. In *2021 10th International Conference on Information and Automation for Sustainability (ICIAfS)*, pages 48–53.

Konthala Yasaswini, Karthik Puranik, Adeep Hande, Ruba Priyadharshini, Sajeetha Thavareesan, and Bharathi Raja Chakravarthi. 2021. IIITT@DravidianLangTech-EACL2021: Transfer learning for offensive language detection in Dravidian languages. In *Proceedings of the First Workshop on Speech and Language Technologies for Dravidian Languages*, pages 187–194, Kyiv. Association for Computational Linguistics.

Findings of the Shared Task on Offensive Span Identification from Code-Mixed Tamil-English Comments

Manikandan Ravikiran[†*], **Bharathi Raja Chakravarthi**[‡], **Anand Kumar Madasamy**[⋆]
Sangeetha Sivanesan [°], **Ratnavel Rajalakshmi** [⊕], **Sajeetha Thavareesan**[◇]
Rahul Ponnusamy [⊖], **Shankar Mahadevan**[⋈]
[†]Georgia Institute of Technology, Atlanta, Georgia
[‡]Data Science Institute, National University of Ireland Galway
[⋆]National Institute of Technology Karnataka Surathkal, India
[°]National Institute of Technology, Trichy, India
[⊕]Vellore Institute of Technology, Chennai, India
[◇]Eastern University, Sri Lanka
[⊖]Indian Institute of Information Technology and Management, Kerala, India
[⋈]Thiagarajar College of Engineering, Madurai, India
mravikiran3@gatech.edu, bharathi.raja@insight-centre.org

Abstract

Offensive content moderation is vital in social media platforms to support healthy online discussions. However, their prevalence in code-mixed Dravidian languages is limited to classifying whole comments without identifying part of it contributing to offensiveness. Such limitation is primarily due to the lack of annotated data for offensive spans. Accordingly, in this shared task, we provide Tamil-English code-mixed social comments with offensive spans. This paper outlines the dataset so released, methods, and results of the submitted systems.

1 Introduction

Combating offensive content is crucial for different entities involved in content moderation, which includes social media companies as well as individuals (Kumaresan et al., 2021; Chakravarthi and Muralidaran, 2021). To this end, moderation is often restrictive with either usage of human content moderators, who are expected to read through the content and flag the offensive mentions (Arsht and Etcovitch, 2018). Alternatively, there are semi-automated and automated tools that employ trivial algorithms and block lists (Jhaver et al., 2018). Though content moderation looks like a one-way street, where either it should be allowed or removed, such decision-making is fairly hard. This is more significant, especially on social media platforms, where the sheer volume of content is overwhelming for human moderators especially. With ever increasing offensive social media contents focusing "racism", "sexism", "hate speech", "aggressiveness" etc. semi-automated and fully automated content moderation is favored (Priyadharshini et al., 2021; Chakravarthi et al., 2020b; Sampath et al., 2022). However, most of the existing works (Zampieri et al., 2020; Chakravarthi et al., 2022a; Bharathi et al., 2022; Priyadharshini et al., 2022) are restricted to English only, with few of them permeating into research that focuses on a more granular understanding of offensiveness.

Tamil is a agglutinative language from the Dravidian language family dating back to the 580 BCE (Sivanantham and Seran, 2019). It is widely spoken in the southern state of Tamil Nadu in India, Sri Lanka, Malaysia, and Singapore. Tamil is an official language of Tamil Nadu, Sri Lanka, Singapore, and the Union Territory of Puducherry in India. Significant minority speak Tamil in the four other South Indian states of Kerala, Karnataka, Andhra Pradesh, and Telangana, as well as the Union Territory of the Andaman and Nicobar Islands (Sakuntharaj and Mahesan, 2021, 2017, 2016; Thavareesan and Mahesan, 2019, 2020a,b, 2021). It is also spoken by the Tamil diaspora, which may be found in Malaysia, Myanmar, South Africa, the United Kingdom, the United States, Canada, Australia, and Mauritius. Tamil is also the native language of Sri Lankan Moors. Tamil, one of the 22 scheduled languages in the Indian Constitution, was the first to be designated as a classical language of India (Subalalitha, 2019; Srinivasan and

*Corresponding Author

Proceedings of the Second Workshop on Speech and Language Technologies for Dravidian Languages, pages 261 - 270
May 26, 2022 ©2022 Association for Computational Linguistics

Subalalitha, 2019; Narasimhan et al., 2018). Tamil is one of the world's longest-surviving classical languages. The earliest epigraphic documents discovered on rock edicts and "hero stones" date from the 6th century BC. Tamil has the oldest ancient non-Sanskritic Indian literature of any Indian language (Anita and Subalalitha, 2019b,a; Subalalitha and Poovammal, 2018). Despite its own script, with the advent of social media, code-switching has permeated into the Tamil language across informal contexts like forums and messaging outlets (Chakravarthi et al., 2019, 2018; Ghanghor et al., 2021a,b; Yasaswini et al., 2021). As a result, code-switched content is part and parcel of offensive conversations in social media.

Despite many recent NLP advancements, handling code-mixed offensive content is still a challenge in Dravidian Languages (Sitaram et al., 2019) including Tamil owing to limitations in data and tools. However, recently the research of offensive code-mixed texts in Dravidian languages has seen traction (Chakravarthi et al., 2021, 2020a; Priyadharshini et al., 2020; Chakravarthi, 2020). Yet, very few of these focus on identifying the spans that make a comment offensive (Ravikiran and Annamalai, 2021). But accentuating such spans can help content moderators and semi-automated tools which prefer attribution instead of just a system-generated unexplained score per comment. Accordingly, in this shared task, we provided code-mixed social media text for the Tamil language with offensive spans inviting participants to develop and submit systems under two different settings. Our CodaLab website[1] will remain open to foster further research in this area.

2 Related Work

2.1 Offensive Span Identification

Much of the literature related to offensive span identification find their roots in SemEval Offensive Span identification shared task focusing on English Language (Pavlopoulos et al., 2021), with development of more than 36 different systems using a variety of approaches. Notable among these include work by Zhu et al. (2021) that uses token labeling using one or more language models with a combination of Conditional Random Fields (CRF). These approaches often rely on BIO encoding of the text corresponding to offensive spans. Alternatively, some systems employ post-processing on these token level labels, including re-ranking and stacked ensembling for predictions (Nguyen et al., 2021). Then, there are exciting works of Rusert (2021); Pluciński and Klimczak (2021) that exploit rationale extraction mechanism with pre-trained classifiers on external offensive classification datasets to produce toxic spans as explanations of the decisions of the classifiers. Lexicon-based baseline models, which uses look-up operations for offensive words (Burtenshaw and Kestemont, 2021) and run statistical analysis (Palomino et al., 2021) are also widely explored. Finally, there are a few approaches that employ custom loss functions tailored explicitly for false spans. For code-mixed Tamil-English to date, there is only preliminary work by Ravikiran and Annamalai (2021) that uses token level labeling.

3 Task Description

Our task of offensive span identification required participants to identify offensive spans i.e, character offsets that were responsible for the offensive of the comments, when identifying such spans was possible. To this end, we created two subtasks each of which are as described. Example of offensive span is shown in Figure 1

3.1 Subtask 1: Supervised Offensive Span Identification

Given comments and annotated offensive spans for training, here the systems were asked to identify the offensive spans in each of the comments in test data. This task could be approached as supervised sequence labeling, training on the provided posts with gold offensive spans. It could also be treated as rationale extraction using classifiers trained on other datasets of posts manually annotated for offensiveness classification, without any span annotations.

3.2 Subtask 2: Semi-supervised Offensive Span Identification

All the participants of subtask 1 were also encouraged to submit a system to subtask 2 using semi-supervised approaches. Here in addition to training data of subtask 1, more unannotated data was provided. Participants were asked to develop systems using both of these datasets together. To this end, the unannotated data was allowed to be used in anyway as necessary to aid in overall model

[1] https://competitions.codalab.org/competitions/36395

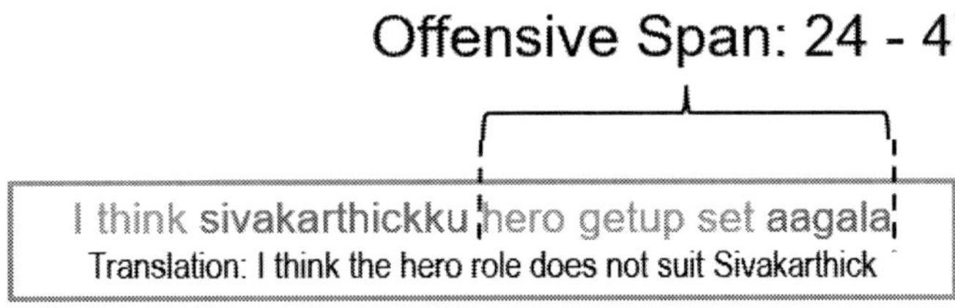

Figure 1: Example Offensive Span Identification from Code-Mixed Tamil-English Text

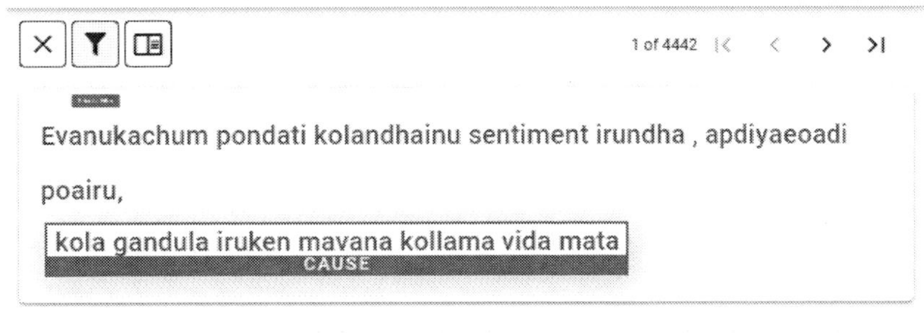

Figure 2: Annotation of offensive spans using Doccano.

development including creating semi-supervised annotations, ranking based on similarity etc.

4 Dataset

For this shared task, we build upon dataset from earlier work of Ravikiran and Annamalai (2021), which originally released 4786 code-mixed Tamil-English comments with 6202 offensive spans. We released this dataset to the participants during training phase for model development. Meanwhile for testing we extended this dataset with new additional annotated comments. To this end, we use dataset of Chakravarthi et al. (2022b) that consist of 10K+ offensive comments. From this we filter out comments that were already part of train set resulting 4442 comments suitable for annotation. Out of this we created (a) 3742 comments were used for creating the test data and (b) 700 comments were used for training phase of subtask 2.

Split	Train	Test
Number of Sentences	4786	876
Number of unique tokens	22096	5362
Number of annotated spans	6202	1025
Average size of spans (# of characters)	21	21
Min size of spans (# of characters)	4	3
Max size of spans (# of characters)	82	85
Number of unique tokens in spans	10737	1006

Table 1: Dataset Statistics used in this shared task

In line with earlier works (Ravikiran and Annamalai, 2021) for the 3742 comments we create span level annotations where at least two annotators annotated every comment. Additionally, we also employ similar guidelines for annotation, anonymity maintenance etc. Besides, no annotator data was collected other than their educational background and their expertise in the Tamil language.

Additionally, all the annotators were informed in prior about the inherent profanity of the content along with an option to withdraw from the annotation process if necessary. For annotation, we use doccano (Nakayama et al., 2018)which was locally hosted by each annotator. Within doccano, all the annotators were explicitly asked to create a single label called **CAUSE** with label id of 1, thus maintaining consistency of annotation labels. (See Figure 2).

To ensure quality each annotation was verified by one or more annotation verifier, prior to merging and creating gold standard test set. The overall dataset statistics is given in the Table 1. Compared to train set, we can see that the test set consists of significantly lesser number of samples, this is because many of the comments were either small or were hard to clearly identify the offensive spans. Overall for the 876 comments we obtained Cohen's Kappa inter-annotator agreement of 0.61 inline with Ravikiran and Annamalai (2021).

5 Competition Phases

5.1 Training Phase

In the training phase, the train split with 4786 comments, and their annotated spans were released for model development. Participants were given training data and offensive spans. No validation set was released; rather, participants were emphasized on cross-validation by creating their splits for preliminary evaluations or hyperparameter tuning. In total, 30 participants registered for the task and downloaded the dataset.

5.2 Testing Phase

Test set comments without any span annotation were released in the testing phase. Each participating team was asked to submit their generated span predictions for evaluation. Predictions are submitted via Google form, which was used to evaluate the systems. Though CodaLab supports evaluation inherently, we used google form due to its simplicity. Finally, we assessed the submitted spans of the test set and were scored using character-based F1 (See section 7.2).

6 System Descriptions

Overall we received only a total of 4 submissions (2 main + 2 additional) from two teams out of 30 registered participants. All these were only for subtask 1. No submissions were made for subtask 2. Each of their respective systems are as described.

6.1 The NITK-IT_NLP Submission

The best performing system from NITK-IT_NLP (Hariharan RamakrishnaIyer LekshmiAmmal, 2022) experimented with rationale extraction by training offensive language classifiers and employing model-agnostic rationale extraction mechanisms to produce toxic spans as explanations of the decisions of the classifier. Specifically NITK-IT_NLP used MuRIL (Khanuja et al., 2021) classifier and coupled with LIME (Ribeiro et al., 2016) and used the explanation scores to select words suitable for offensive spans.

6.2 The DLRG submission

The DLRG team (Mohit et al., 2022) formulated the problem as a combination of token labeling and span extraction. Specifically, the team created word-level BIO tags i.e., words were labelled as B (beginning word of a offensive span), I (inside word of a offensive span), or O (outside of any offensive span). Following which word level embeddings are created using GloVe (Pennington et al., 2014) and BiLSTM-CRF (Panchendrarajan and Amaresan, 2018) model is trained.

6.3 Additional Submission

After testing phase, we also requested each team to submit additional runs if they have variants of approaches. Accordingly we received two additional submissions from NITK-IT_NLP where they replaced MuRIL from their initial submission with (i) Multilingual-BERT (Devlin et al., 2019) and (ii) ELECTRA (Clark et al., 2020) respectively without any other changes. More details in section 7.2.

7 Evaluation

This section focuses on the evaluation framework of the task. First, the official measure that was used to evaluate the participating systems is described. Then, we discuss baseline models that were selected as benchmarks for comparison reasons. Finally, the results are presented.

7.1 Evaluation Measure

In line with work of Pavlopoulos et al. (2021) each system was evaluated F1 score computed on character offset. For each system, we computed the F1 score per comments, between the predicted and the ground truth character offsets. Following this we calculated macro-average score over all the 876 test comments. If in case both ground truth and predicted character offsets were empty we assigned a F1 of 1 other wise 0 and vice versa.

7.2 Benchmark

To establish fair comparison we first created two baseline benchmark systems which are as described.

- `BENCHMARK 1` is a random baseline model which randomly labels 50% of characters in comments to belong to be offensive. To this end, we run this benchmark 10 times and average results are presented in Table 2.
- `BENCHMARK 2` is a lexicon based system, which first extracted all the offensive words from the train set and during inference these words were searched in comments from testset and corresponding spans were extracted.
- `BENCHMARK 3` is RoBERTA (Liu et al., 2019; Ravikiran and Annamalai, 2021) model

trained using token labeling approach with BIO encoded texts corresponding to annotated spans.

Table 2: Official rank and F1 score (%) of the 2 participating teams that submitted systems. The baselines benchmarks are shown in red.

RANK	TEAM	F1 (%)
1	NITK-IT_NLP	44.89
BASELINE	BENCHMARK 1	39.75
BASELINE	BENCHMARK 2	37.84
BASELINE	BENCHMARK 3	38.61
2	DLRG	17.28

Table 2 shows the scores and ranks of two teams that made their submission. NITK-IT_NLP (Section 6.1) was ranked first, followed by DLRG (Section 6.2) that scored 27% lower was ranked second. The median score was 31.08%, which is far below the top ranked team and the benchmark baseline models. Meanwhile the additional submission post testing phase are excluded from ranked table. Instead they are presented separately in Table 3.

BENCHMARK 1 achieves a considerably high score and, hence, is very highly ranked with character F1 of 39.83%. Combination of MuRIL with LIME interpretability by model NITK-IT_NLP is ahead of BENCHMARK 1 by 11%, indicating the language models ability to effectively rationalize and identify the spans. This is inline the results of Rusert (2021) which show higher results than random baseline. Meanwhile BENCHMARK 2 and BENCHMARK 3, also shows F1 of 37.84% and 38.61% which again NITK-IT_NLP model tend to beat significantly. On contrary we could see that DLRG model to show least results of 17.28% lesser than akk the baselines as well as the top performing system. The lexicon-based BENCHMARK 2 and RoBERTA based BENCHMARK 3 too score very high. Especially as it overcomes, the submission of DLRG. This may be attributed to dataset domain itself. Especially, since much of the dataset was collected from Youtube comments section of Movie Trailers, often we see usages of same word or similar words. Such behavior is well established across social media forums including Youtube (Duricic et al., 2021), which begs to ask if indeed the dataset construction needs to be revisited, which forms one potential exploration for immediate future.

8 Analysis and Discussion

Overall we were happy to see the degree of involvement in this shared task with multiple participants registering, requesting access to datasets and potential baseline codes for the shared task. Though only two teams submitted the systems, the resulting diversity of approaches to this problem is fairly encouraging. However we include some of our observations below, from our evaluation and what we have learned from the results.

Table 3: Results of additional runs submitted by NITK-IT_NLP.

Method	F1 (%)
ELECTRA + LIME	37.33
M-BERT + LIME	33.95

8.1 Participation Characteristics

The authors reached out to teams that initially registered but failed to create any systems and the vast majority were undergraduate students who were new into the concept of shared task and were time-limited due to semester exams. The fact that students participated in the task is promising and we plan to consider more ways to introduce Shared tasks on Low-Resource Dravidian Languages in classrooms. To this end, the we used social media and other medium to spread the word around universities.

On the other hand, 60% of the participants did not download dataset after registering and instead chose to participate in other shared tasks, which is problematic and should be addressed. To this end, correspondence with such teams revealed potential favoritism towards classification based problems that are common in undergraduate studies. Moreover we also received multiple queries on the concept of offensive span itself during the training phase, which is a indicates potential need of improving the overall task structure with potential early release of data and task details. Yet, upon extending the number of submissions NITK-IT_NLP submitted additional runs (See Table 3). Additionally both the teams also submitted source codes [2] for their respective models encouraging further development of systems.

[2] https://drive.google.com/drive/folders/1T3kl8mljPt8oXcKVn7OQqaU3d55za2zZ?usp=sharing

Table 4: Results of submitted systems across comments of different lengths.

	F1@30 (%)	F1@50 (%)	F1@>50 (%)
NITK-IT_NLP	42.39	37.05	26.42
DLRG	39.62	23.47	14.05

8.2 General remarks on the approaches

Though neither of teams that made final submissions created any simple baselines, we could see that all the submissions of NITK-IT_NLP use well established approaches in recent NLP focusing on pretrained language models. Meanwhile DLRG used well-grounded Non-Transformer based approach. Yet neither of teams used any ensembles, data augmentation strategies or modifications to loss functions that are seen for the task of span identification in the past across shared tasks.

8.3 Error Analysis

Table 2 shows maximum result of 0.4489 with DLRG failing significantly compared to random baseline. To this end, we wonder if potentially these approaches have any weaknesses or strengths. To understand this, first we study the character F1 results across sentences of different lengths. Specifically we analysis results of (a) comments with less than 30 characters (F1@30) (b) comments with 30-50 characters (F1@50) (c) comments with more than 50 characters (F1@>50). The results so obtained are as shown in Table 4.

Firstly we can see though NITK-IT_NLP shows high results overall for cases of comments with larger lengths the model fails significantly. Specifically, comparing results with ground truth showed that use of LIME often restricts the overall word so selected as the rationale for offensiveness in turn reducing number of character offsets predicted as spans. This is because with larger texts the net score distribution weakens and span extraction is largely off leading to significant drop in results. Meanwhile for DLRG the results are more mixed, especially we can see that for comments with less than 30 characters the model shows improvement in F1. Analysis of results reveal that token labeling is highly accurate, which drops significantly with large size sentences. This may be attributed to non-local interactions between the words that may not be captured by the Bi-LSTM CRF model. Further more much of these sentences often contained only cuss words or clearly abusive words that are easily identifiable and often present in the train set. Also we found few bugs in the training code so used, which was already informed to the authors.

Besides error analysis also showed some implicit challenges in the proposed shared task. First the strong dependency of offensiveness on context makes it particularly difficult to solve as evident from NITK-IT_NLP which used language models. Second, offensiveness often is expressed as sarcasm or even is very subtle. In such cases we often see the offensiveness results to depend only the words bearing the most negative sentiment, meanwhile the ground truth spans annotated are larger thus showing high errors. Finally, many times the nature of offensiveness itself becomes debatable without clear context. Often these are the cases where we find the developed approaches to fail significantly.

9 Conclusion

Overall this shared task on offensive span identification we introduced a new dataset for code-mixed Tamil-English language with total of 5652 social media comments annotated for offensive spans. The task though has large participants, eventually had only two teams that submitted their systems. In this paper we described their approaches and discussed their results. Surprisingly rationale extraction based approach involving combination MuRIL and LIME performed significantly well. Meanwhile Bi-LSTM CRF model was found showing sensitivity towards shorter sentences, though it performed significantly worse than the random baseline. Also extracting offensive spans for long sentences were found to be difficult especially as they are context dependent. To this end, we release the baseline models and datasets to foster further research. Meanwhile in the future we plan to re-do the task of offensive span identification where we could require the participants to identify offensive spans and simultaneously classify different types of offensiveness.

Acknowledgements

We thank our anonymous reviewers for their valuable feedback. Any opinions, findings, and conclusion or recommendations expressed in this material are those of the authors only and does not reflect the view of their employing organization or graduate schools. The shared task was result of series projects done during CS7646-ML4T (Fall 2020), CS6460-Edtech Foundations

(Spring 2020) and CS7643-Deep learning (Spring 2022) at Georgia Institute of Technology (OMSCS Program). Bharathi Raja Chakravarthi were supported in part by a research grant from Science Foundation Ireland (SFI) under Grant Number SFI/12/RC/2289_P2 (Insight_2), co-funded by the European Regional Development Fund and Irish Research Council grant IRCLA/2017/129 (CARDAMOM-Comparative Deep Models of Language for Minority and Historical Languages).

References

R Anita and CN Subalalitha. 2019a. An approach to cluster Tamil literatures using discourse connectives. In *2019 IEEE 1st International Conference on Energy, Systems and Information Processing (ICESIP)*, pages 1–4. IEEE.

R Anita and CN Subalalitha. 2019b. Building discourse parser for Thirukkural. In *Proceedings of the 16th International Conference on Natural Language Processing*, pages 18–25.

Andrew Arsht and Daniel Etcovitch. 2018. The human cost of online content moderation. *Harvard Journal of Law & Technology*.

B Bharathi, Bharathi Raja Chakravarthi, Subalalitha Chinnaudayar Navaneethakrishnan, N Sripriya, Arunaggiri Pandian, and Swetha Valli. 2022. Findings of the shared task on Speech Recognition for Vulnerable Individuals in Tamil. In *Proceedings of the Second Workshop on Language Technology for Equality, Diversity and Inclusion*. Association for Computational Linguistics.

Ben Burtenshaw and Mike Kestemont. 2021. UAntwerp at SemEval-2021 task 5: Spans are spans, stacking a binary word level approach to toxic span detection. In *Proceedings of the 15th International Workshop on Semantic Evaluation (SemEval-2021)*, pages 898–903, Online. Association for Computational Linguistics.

Bharathi Raja Chakravarthi. 2020. HopeEDI: A multilingual hope speech detection dataset for equality, diversity, and inclusion. In *Proceedings of the Third Workshop on Computational Modeling of People's Opinions, Personality, and Emotion's in Social Media*, pages 41–53, Barcelona, Spain (Online). Association for Computational Linguistics.

Bharathi Raja Chakravarthi, Mihael Arcan, and John P. McCrae. 2018. Improving wordnets for under-resourced languages using machine translation. In *Proceedings of the 9th Global Wordnet Conference*, pages 77–86, Nanyang Technological University (NTU), Singapore. Global Wordnet Association.

Bharathi Raja Chakravarthi, Mihael Arcan, and John P. McCrae. 2019. WordNet gloss translation for under-resourced languages using multilingual neural machine translation. In *Proceedings of the Second Workshop on Multilingualism at the Intersection of Knowledge Bases and Machine Translation*, pages 1–7, Dublin, Ireland. European Association for Machine Translation.

Bharathi Raja Chakravarthi and Vigneshwaran Muralidaran. 2021. Findings of the shared task on hope speech detection for equality, diversity, and inclusion. In *Proceedings of the First Workshop on Language Technology for Equality, Diversity and Inclusion*, pages 61–72, Kyiv. Association for Computational Linguistics.

Bharathi Raja Chakravarthi, Vigneshwaran Muralidaran, Ruba Priyadharshini, and John Philip McCrae. 2020a. Corpus creation for sentiment analysis in code-mixed Tamil-English text. In *Proceedings of the 1st Joint Workshop on Spoken Language Technologies for Under-resourced languages (SLTU) and Collaboration and Computing for Under-Resourced Languages (CCURL)*, pages 202–210, Marseille, France. European Language Resources association.

Bharathi Raja Chakravarthi, Ruba Priyadharshini, Thenmozhi Durairaj, John Phillip McCrae, Paul Buitaleer, Prasanna Kumar Kumaresan, and Rahul Ponnusamy. 2022a. Findings of the shared task on Homophobia Transphobia Detection in Social Media Comments. In *Proceedings of the Second Workshop on Language Technology for Equality, Diversity and Inclusion*. Association for Computational Linguistics.

Bharathi Raja Chakravarthi, Ruba Priyadharshini, Vigneshwaran Muralidaran, Navya Jose, Shardul Suryawanshi, Elizabeth Sherly, and John P. McCrae. 2022b. DravidianCodeMix: sentiment analysis and offensive language identification dataset for dravidian languages in code-mixed text. *Language Resources and Evaluation*.

Bharathi Raja Chakravarthi, Ruba Priyadharshini, Vigneshwaran Muralidaran, Shardul Suryawanshi, Navya Jose, Elizabeth Sherly, and John P McCrae. 2020b. Overview of the track on sentiment analysis for Dravidian languages in code-mixed text. In *Forum for Information Retrieval Evaluation*, pages 21–24.

Bharathi Raja Chakravarthi, Ruba Priyadharshini, Rahul Ponnusamy, Prasanna Kumar Kumaresan, Kayalvizhi Sampath, Durairaj Thenmozhi, Sathiyaraj Thangasamy, Rajendran Nallathambi, and John Phillip McCrae. 2021. Dataset for identification of homophobia and transophobia in multilingual YouTube comments. *arXiv preprint arXiv:2109.00227*.

Kevin Clark, Minh-Thang Luong, Quoc V. Le, and Christopher D. Manning. 2020. ELECTRA: pre-training text encoders as discriminators rather than generators. In *8th International Conference on*

Learning Representations, ICLR 2020, Addis Ababa, Ethiopia, April 26-30, 2020. OpenReview.net.

Jacob Devlin, Ming-Wei Chang, Kenton Lee, and Kristina Toutanova. 2019. BERT: pre-training of deep bidirectional transformers for language understanding. In *Proceedings of the 2019 Conference of the North American Chapter of the Association for Computational Linguistics: Human Language Technologies, NAACL-HLT 2019, Minneapolis, MN, USA, June 2-7, 2019, Volume 1 (Long and Short Papers)*, pages 4171–4186. Association for Computational Linguistics.

Tomislav Duricic, Volker Seiser, and Elisabeth Lex. 2021. Cross-platform analysis of user comments in youtube videos linked on reddit conspiracy theory forum. *CoRR*, abs/2109.01127.

Nikhil Ghanghor, Parameswari Krishnamurthy, Sajeetha Thavareesan, Ruba Priyadharshini, and Bharathi Raja Chakravarthi. 2021a. IIITK@DravidianLangTech-EACL2021: Offensive language identification and meme classification in Tamil, Malayalam and Kannada. In *Proceedings of the First Workshop on Speech and Language Technologies for Dravidian Languages*, pages 222–229, Kyiv. Association for Computational Linguistics.

Nikhil Ghanghor, Rahul Ponnusamy, Prasanna Kumar Kumaresan, Ruba Priyadharshini, Sajeetha Thavareesan, and Bharathi Raja Chakravarthi. 2021b. IIITK@LT-EDI-EACL2021: Hope speech detection for equality, diversity, and inclusion in Tamil , Malayalam and English. In *Proceedings of the First Workshop on Language Technology for Equality, Diversity and Inclusion*, pages 197–203, Kyiv. Association for Computational Linguistics.

Manikandan Ravikiran Hariharan RamakrishnaIyer LekshmiAmmal, Anand Kumar Madasamy. 2022. Nitk-it_nlp@tamilnlp-acl2022: Transformer based model for toxic span identification in tamil. In *Proceedings of the Second Workshop on Speech and Language Technologies for Dravidian Languages*. Association for Computational Linguistics.

Shagun Jhaver, Sucheta Ghoshal, Amy S. Bruckman, and Eric Gilbert. 2018. Online harassment and content moderation: The case of blocklists. *ACM Trans. Comput. Hum. Interact.*, 25(2):12:1–12:33.

Simran Khanuja, Diksha Bansal, Sarvesh Mehtani, Savya Khosla, Atreyee Dey, Balaji Gopalan, Dilip Kumar Margam, Pooja Aggarwal, Rajiv Teja Nagipogu, Shachi Dave, Shruti Gupta, Subhash Chandra Bose Gali, Vish Subramanian, and Partha P. Talukdar. 2021. Muril: Multilingual representations for indian languages. *CoRR*, abs/2103.10730.

Prasanna Kumar Kumaresan, Ratnasingam Sakuntharaj, Sajeetha Thavareesan, Subalalitha Navaneethakrishnan, Anand Kumar Madasamy, Bharathi Raja Chakravarthi, and John P McCrae. 2021. Findings of shared task on offensive language identification in Tamil and Malayalam. In *Forum for Information Retrieval Evaluation*, pages 16–18.

Yinhan Liu, Myle Ott, Naman Goyal, Jingfei Du, Mandar Joshi, Danqi Chen, Omer Levy, Mike Lewis, Luke Zettlemoyer, and Veselin Stoyanov. 2019. Roberta: A robustly optimized BERT pretraining approach. *CoRR*, abs/1907.11692.

More Mohit, Naga Shrikriti Bhamatipati, Saharan Gitansh, Hanchate Samyuktha, Nandy Sayantan, and Rajalakshmi Ratnavel. 2022. Dlrg@tamilnlp-acl2022: Offensive span identification in tamil using bilstm-crf approach. In *Proceedings of the Second Workshop on Speech and Language Technologies for Dravidian Languages*. Association for Computational Linguistics.

Hiroki Nakayama, Takahiro Kubo, Junya Kamura, Yasufumi Taniguchi, and Xu Liang. 2018. doccano: Text annotation tool for human. Software available from https://github.com/doccano/doccano.

Anitha Narasimhan, Aarthy Anandan, Madhan Karky, and CN Subalalitha. 2018. Porul: Option generation and selection and scoring algorithms for a tamil flash card game. *International Journal of Cognitive and Language Sciences*, 12(2):225–228.

Viet Anh Nguyen, Tam Minh Nguyen, Huy Quang Dao, and Quang Huu Pham. 2021. S-NLP at SemEval-2021 task 5: An analysis of dual networks for sequence tagging. In *Proceedings of the 15th International Workshop on Semantic Evaluation (SemEval-2021)*, pages 888–897, Online. Association for Computational Linguistics.

Marco Palomino, Dawid Grad, and James Bedwell. 2021. GoldenWind at SemEval-2021 task 5: Orthrus - an ensemble approach to identify toxicity. In *Proceedings of the 15th International Workshop on Semantic Evaluation (SemEval-2021)*, pages 860–864, Online. Association for Computational Linguistics.

Rrubaa Panchendrarajan and Aravindh Amaresan. 2018. Bidirectional LSTM-CRF for named entity recognition. In *Proceedings of the 32nd Pacific Asia Conference on Language, Information and Computation*, Hong Kong. Association for Computational Linguistics.

John Pavlopoulos, Léo Laugier, Jeffrey Sorensen, and Ion Androutsopoulos. 2021. Semeval-2021 task 5: Toxic spans detection (to appear). In *Proceedings of the 15th International Workshop on Semantic Evaluation*.

Jeffrey Pennington, Richard Socher, and Christopher Manning. 2014. GloVe: Global vectors for word representation. In *Proceedings of the 2014 Conference on Empirical Methods in Natural Language Processing (EMNLP)*, pages 1532–1543, Doha, Qatar. Association for Computational Linguistics.

Kamil Pluciński and Hanna Klimczak. 2021. GHOST at SemEval-2021 task 5: Is explanation all you need? In *Proceedings of the 15th International Workshop on Semantic Evaluation (SemEval-2021)*, pages 852–859, Online. Association for Computational Linguistics.

Ruba Priyadharshini, Bharathi Raja Chakravarthi, Subalalitha Chinnaudayar Navaneethakrishnan, Thenmozhi Durairaj, Malliga Subramanian, Kogilavani Shanmugavadivel, Siddhanth U Hegde, and Prasanna Kumar Kumaresan. 2022. Findings of the shared task on Abusive Comment Detection in Tamil. In *Proceedings of the Second Workshop on Speech and Language Technologies for Dravidian Languages*. Association for Computational Linguistics.

Ruba Priyadharshini, Bharathi Raja Chakravarthi, Sajeetha Thavareesan, Dhivya Chinnappa, Durairaj Thenmozhi, and Rahul Ponnusamy. 2021. Overview of the dravidiancodemix 2021 shared task on sentiment detection in Tamil, Malayalam, and Kannada. In *Forum for Information Retrieval Evaluation*, pages 4–6.

Ruba Priyadharshini, Bharathi Raja Chakravarthi, Mani Vegupatti, and John P McCrae. 2020. Named entity recognition for code-mixed Indian corpus using meta embedding. In *2020 6th international conference on advanced computing and communication systems (ICACCS)*, pages 68–72. IEEE.

Manikandan Ravikiran and Subbiah Annamalai. 2021. DOSA: Dravidian code-mixed offensive span identification dataset. In *Proceedings of the First Workshop on Speech and Language Technologies for Dravidian Languages*, pages 10–17, Kyiv. Association for Computational Linguistics.

Marco Túlio Ribeiro, Sameer Singh, and Carlos Guestrin. 2016. "why should I trust you?": Explaining the predictions of any classifier. In *Proceedings of the Demonstrations Session, NAACL HLT 2016, The 2016 Conference of the North American Chapter of the Association for Computational Linguistics: Human Language Technologies, San Diego California, USA, June 12-17, 2016*, pages 97–101. The Association for Computational Linguistics.

Jonathan Rusert. 2021. NLP_UIOWA at Semeval-2021 task 5: Transferring toxic sets to tag toxic spans. In *Proceedings of the 15th International Workshop on Semantic Evaluation (SemEval-2021)*, pages 881–887, Online. Association for Computational Linguistics.

Ratnasingam Sakuntharaj and Sinnathamby Mahesan. 2016. A novel hybrid approach to detect and correct spelling in Tamil text. In *2016 IEEE International Conference on Information and Automation for Sustainability (ICIAfS)*, pages 1–6.

Ratnasingam Sakuntharaj and Sinnathamby Mahesan. 2017. Use of a novel hash-table for speeding-up suggestions for misspelt Tamil words. In *2017 IEEE International Conference on Industrial and Information Systems (ICIIS)*, pages 1–5.

Ratnasingam Sakuntharaj and Sinnathamby Mahesan. 2021. Missing word detection and correction based on context of Tamil sentences using n-grams. In *2021 10th International Conference on Information and Automation for Sustainability (ICIAfS)*, pages 42–47.

Anbukkarasi Sampath, Thenmozhi Durairaj, Bharathi Raja Chakravarthi, Ruba Priyadharshini, Subalalitha Chinnaudayar Navaneethakrishnan, Kogilavani Shanmugavadivel, Sajeetha Thavareesan, Sathiyaraj Thangasamy, Parameswari Krishnamurthy, Adeep Hande, Sean Benhur, and Santhiya Ponnusamy, Kishor Kumar Pandiyan. 2022. Findings of the shared task on Emotion Analysis in Tamil. In *Proceedings of the Second Workshop on Speech and Language Technologies for Dravidian Languages*. Association for Computational Linguistics.

Sunayana Sitaram, Khyathi Raghavi Chandu, Sai Krishna Rallabandi, and A. Black. 2019. A survey of code-switched speech and language processing. *ArXiv*, abs/1904.00784.

R Sivanantham and M Seran. 2019. Keeladi: An urban settlement of sangam age on the banks of river vaigai. *India: Department of Archaeology, Government of Tamil Nadu, Chennai*.

R Srinivasan and CN Subalalitha. 2019. Automated named entity recognition from tamil documents. In *2019 IEEE 1st International Conference on Energy, Systems and Information Processing (ICESIP)*, pages 1–5. IEEE.

C. N. Subalalitha. 2019. Information extraction framework for Kurunthogai. *Sādhanā*, 44(7):156.

CN Subalalitha and E Poovammal. 2018. Automatic bilingual dictionary construction for Tirukural. *Applied Artificial Intelligence*, 32(6):558–567.

Sajeetha Thavareesan and Sinnathamby Mahesan. 2019. Sentiment analysis in Tamil texts: A study on machine learning techniques and feature representation. In *2019 14th Conference on Industrial and Information Systems (ICIIS)*, pages 320–325.

Sajeetha Thavareesan and Sinnathamby Mahesan. 2020a. Sentiment lexicon expansion using Word2vec and fastText for sentiment prediction in Tamil texts. In *2020 Moratuwa Engineering Research Conference (MERCon)*, pages 272–276.

Sajeetha Thavareesan and Sinnathamby Mahesan. 2020b. Word embedding-based part of speech tagging in Tamil texts. In *2020 IEEE 15th International Conference on Industrial and Information Systems (ICIIS)*, pages 478–482.

Sajeetha Thavareesan and Sinnathamby Mahesan. 2021. Sentiment analysis in Tamil texts using k-means and k-nearest neighbour. In *2021 10th International Conference on Information and Automation for Sustainability (ICIAfS)*, pages 48–53.

Konthala Yasaswini, Karthik Puranik, Adeep Hande, Ruba Priyadharshini, Sajeetha Thavareesan, and Bharathi Raja Chakravarthi. 2021. IIITT@DravidianLangTech-EACL2021: Transfer learning for offensive language detection in Dravidian languages. In *Proceedings of the First Workshop on Speech and Language Technologies for Dravidian Languages*, pages 187–194, Kyiv. Association for Computational Linguistics.

Marcos Zampieri, Preslav Nakov, Sara Rosenthal, Pepa Atanasova, Georgi Karadzhov, Hamdy Mubarak, Leon Derczynski, Zeses Pitenis, and Çagri Çöltekin. 2020. Semeval-2020 task 12: Multilingual offensive language identification in social media (offenseval 2020). In *Proceedings of the Fourteenth Workshop on Semantic Evaluation, SemEval@COLING 2020, Barcelona (online), December 12-13, 2020*, pages 1425–1447. International Committee for Computational Linguistics.

Qinglin Zhu, Zijie Lin, Yice Zhang, Jingyi Sun, Xiang Li, Qihui Lin, Yixue Dang, and Ruifeng Xu. 2021. HITSZ-HLT at SemEval-2021 task 5: Ensemble sequence labeling and span boundary detection for toxic span detection. In *Proceedings of the 15th International Workshop on Semantic Evaluation (SemEval-2021)*, pages 521–526, Online. Association for Computational Linguistics.

Overview of the Shared Task on Machine Translation in Dravidian Languages

Anand Kumar Madasamy[1], Asha Hegde[2], Shubhanker Banerjee[3], Bharathi Raja Chakravarthi[3], Ruba Priyadarshini[4], Hosahalli Lakshmaiah Shashirekha[2] and John Philip McCrae[3]

[1]National Institute of Technology Karnataka Surathkal, [2]Mangalore University, [3]National University of Ireland Galway, [4]Madurai Kamaraj University

m_anandkumar@nitk.edu.in

Abstract

This paper presents an outline of the shared task on translation of under-resourced Dravidian languages at DravidianLangTech-2022 workshop to be held jointly with ACL 2022. A description of the datasets used, approach taken for analysis of submissions and the results have been illustrated in this paper. Five sub-tasks organized as a part of the shared task include the following translation pairs: Kannada to Tamil, Kannada to Telugu, Kannada to Sanskrit, Kannada to Malayalam and Kannada to Tulu. Training, development and test datasets were provided to all participants and results were evaluated on the gold standard datasets. A total of 16 research groups participated in the shared task and a total of 12 submission runs were made for evaluation. Bilingual Evaluation Understudy (BLEU) score was used for evaluation of the translations.

1 Introduction

The results of the shared task on Machine Translation (MT) of Dravidian languages held as a part of DravidianLangTech-2022 workshop have been presented in this paper. Five translation sub-tasks featured in this shared task, namely: Kannada to Tamil, Kannada to Telugu, Kannada to Sanskrit, Kannada to Malayalam and Kannada to Tulu. We evaluated the performance of the systems using BLEU scores. Training, development, and test data used in this shared task have been released publicly. MT is one of the fundamental problems in the area of natural language processing. We hope that this shared task and associated datasets can further research and development of translation technology for under-resourced Dravidian languages.

Related works have been described in section 2. A brief description about Dravidian languages and Sanskrit are given in section 3 and section 4 respectively. The task description and the datasets have been discussed in section 5. The description of the systems submitted has been given to section 6. Lastly, the results and the conclusion have been discussed in section 7 and section 8 respectively.

2 Related Works

In the past few years Deep Learning (DL) based architectures have increasingly been applied to tackle the problem of MT (Pan et al., 2021; Du et al., 2021; Chen et al., 2018; Hoang et al., 2018). These architectures require large amounts of data during training and this, in turn, makes them unsuitable for application in development of translation systems for under-resourced languages. Dabre et al. (2019); Aharoni et al. (2019) demonstrate good performance on translation of under-resourced languages using multilingual MT systems. Another noteworthy approach to tackle this problem is the development of universal translation systems (Gu et al., 2018). The key idea driving this line of research is the development of a system that's capable of transferring linguistic attributes across data from different languages. This is aimed at alleviating the need for large bilingual datasets for under-resourced languages.

Data augmentation is another approach that has been explored in building of translation systems of under-resourced languages. Xia et al. (2019) propose a framework for a translation system that uses monolingual target side dataset along with pivots grounded in a third high resource language. Precisely, they propose a two-stage framework based on pivoting to convert data from high-resourced languages to under-resourced languages, thus augmenting the available data for the translation under-resourced languages.

Another avenue of interest that has been popular amongst researchers working in this domain is application of Transfer Learning (TL) based approaches to improve the performance of MT systems for under-resourced languages. Zoph et al. (2016) train a model for under-resourced MT by initializing some parameters of the model with pa-

Proceedings of the Second Workshop on Speech and Language Technologies for Dravidian Languages, pages 271 - 278
May 26, 2022

rameters from a neural model trained on the task of MT for a resource rich language pair. They report an average increase in performance by 5.6 BLEU. Kocmi and Bojar (2018) demonstrate improved performance on translation of under-resourced languages by employing a simple TL based approach wherein they train a parent model for MT of a resource rich language pair followed by fine-tuning on an under-resourced language pair. It is interesting to note that the authors report improved performance even if the languages in the under-resourced setting are altogether different from the languages which are used to train the model. Mahata et al. (2020) study the impact of languages and their relative position in the language family on the performance of TL systems. Furthermore, they try to quantify the impact of shared vocabulary on the performance of such systems.

In the past few years MT of Indian languages has gained increasing traction from the research community. Chakravarthi et al. (2019, 2021) propose a translation system to improve WordNet for Dravidian languages. Chakravarthi et al. (2019) assess the suitability of using orthographically motivated methods to develop translation systems for Dravidian languages. The key idea behind developing these systems is to leverage the orthographic similarity amongst Dravidian languages to build robust systems in under-resourced scenarios. Pathak and Pakray (2019) propose a neural system for MT of Indian languages based on openNMT[1].

3 Dravidian Languages

Dravidian languages, which make up the fifth largest linguistic family in the world, are spoken by around 200 million people in South Asia and diaspora communities around the world. In Dravidian language family, there are 26 languages, including Tamil, Malayalam, Kannada, and Telugu, which are considered as major languages, in addition to 20 non-literary languages (Krishnamurti, 2003). Since the most Dravidian languages have their writing script, they have a separate block in the Unicode computing industry standard (Sarveswaran et al., 2021). All of these languages use left-to-right writing systems and maintain similar features in their word formation and sentence structure. In these languages, sentences are constructed by a sequence of words and words are formed by adding prefixes and/or suffixes to the root word (Priyadharshini et al., 2021; Kumaresan et al., 2021; Chakravarthi and Muralidaran, 2021; Chakravarthi et al., 2020; Sampath et al., 2022; Ravikiran et al., 2022; Chakravarthi et al., 2022; Bharathi et al., 2022; Priyadharshini et al., 2022). Dravidian languages follow an alpha-syllabic writing scheme, with each character being called a syllable. Consonant ligatures are formed when vowels and consonants are tied together with grammar (Thavareesan and Mahesan, 2019a, 2020a).

Tamil was the first language to be listed as a classical language of India and is one of the longest-surviving classical languages of India. Being a scheduled language by the Indian constitution, it is an official language of Tamil Nadu, a state of India and Puducherry, a territory of India. Further, it is also considered as one of the official languages of Sri Lanka and Singapore. Besides Kerala, Karnataka, Andhra Pradesh, Telangana, and the Union Territory of Andaman and Nicobar Islands, Tamil is spoken by significant minorities in four other south Indian states. Tamil script was first recorded in 580 BCE on pottery from Keezhadi, Sivagangai, and Madurai districts of Tamil Nadu, India by the Tamil Nadu State Department of Archaeology and Archaeological Survey of India (Sivanantham and Seran, 2019). The script was known as Tamili or Tamil-Brahmi[2]. The alphabets of Tamil consist of 18 consonants, 12 vowels, and 216 compound letters followed by a special character making total of 247 letters (Hewavitharana and Fernando, 2002). Tamil is an official language of Tamil Nadu, Sri Lanka, Singapore, and the Union Territory of Puducherry in India. Significant minority speak Tamil in the four other South Indian states of Kerala, Karnataka, Andhra Pradesh, and Telangana, as well as the Union Territory of the Andaman and Nicobar Islands (Sakuntharaj and Mahesan, 2021, 2017, 2016; Thavareesan and Mahesan, 2019b, 2020b,c, 2021). It is also spoken by the Tamil diaspora, which may be found in Malaysia, Myanmar, South Africa, the United Kingdom, the United States, Canada, Australia, and Mauritius. Tamil is also the native language of Sri Lankan Moors. Tamil, one of the 22 scheduled languages in the Indian Constitution, was the first to be designated as a classical language of India (Subalalitha, 2019; Srinivasan and Subalalitha, 2019; Narasimhan et al., 2018). Tamil is one of the world's longest-surviving classical languages. The

[1]https://github.com/OpenNMT/OpenNMT-py

[2]Tamil-Brahmi

earliest epigraphic documents discovered on rock edicts and "hero stones" date from the 6th century BC. Tamil has the oldest ancient non-Sanskritic Indian literature of any Indian language (Anita and Subalalitha, 2019b,a; Subalalitha and Poovammal, 2018).

Malayalam belongs to the Dravidian language family and is highly agglutinative. It originated during the last quarter of the 9th Century A.D (Sekhar, 1951). As a result of the steep Western Ghats separating the dialect from the main speech group in the 16th century, it gradually developed into a separate language. The Ramacaritam is the first literary work written in Malayalam, a combined language of Tamil and Sanskrit, utilizing the Tamil Grantha script used in Tamil Nadu for the writing of Sanskrit and foreign words (Andronov, 1996). There are 13 vowels, 36 consonants, 5 chillu, an anuswara, a visarga, and a chandrakkala making total of 57 letters in Malayalam (Kumar and Chandran, 2015). Telugu belongs to the Dravidian language family and is predominantly spoken by the people of Andra Pradesh. It is the official language of Andhra Pradesh and Telangana with more than 2.75 million Telugu speakers[3]. Inscriptions of Telugu date back to 575 CE. There is a total of 52 letters in Telugu with 16 vowels and 36 consonants and the script is called Abugida which belongs to the Brahmi family[4]. Kannada is the second-oldest Dravidian language, spoken primarily by residents of Karnataka. There are around 44 million Kannada speakers worldwide, with over 12.6 million non-Kannada speakers in Karnataka speaking it as a second or third language[5]. It is one of the scheduled languages of the Indian constitution, as well as the official and administrative language of Karnataka, India. It uses the Brahmi script, which comprises 49 letters in total, comprising 13 vowels, 2 diphthongs, and 34 consonants[6]. Kannada has a large number of articles, although they are not all digitized. Tulu is a prominent Dravidian language spoken primarily by the people of Dakshina Kannada and Udupi in Karnataka state, as well as some parts of Kasaragod in Kerala state. Tulu is spoken by around 2.5 million individuals who believe it to be their mother tongue[7]. With its particular sociocultural qualities, religious practices, creative traditions, and dramatic forms, the Tulu-speaking people have made a substantial contribution to Karnataka's cultural history, and via it, to Indian culture and civilization as a whole. It has kept numerous characteristics of the ancient Dravidian languages while also making some advances not seen in other Dravidian languages (Kekunnaya, 1994). Furthermore, Tulu has its own script, Tigalari, which is developed from the Grantha script, which is no longer in use (Antony et al., 2016). There are 52 letters in Tulu with 16 vowels and 36 consonants.

Languages	Train set	Dev set	Test set
Kannada-Tamil	90,974	2,000	2,000
Kannada-Malayalam	88,813	2,000	2,000
Kannada-Telugu	88,503	2,000	2,000

Table 1: Statistics of set I

Languages	Train set	Dev set	Test set
Kannada-Sanskrit	9,470	1,000	1,000
Kannada-Tulu	8,300	1,000	1,000

Table 2: Statistics of set II

4 Sanskrit

The Sanskrit language has been around for hundreds of years, and it uses the Devanagari (Keith, 1993). With its extensive vocabulary, phonology, grammar, and syntax, Sanskrit literature has a long history of use in ancient poetry, drama, science, and philosophy (Macdonell, 1915). It consists of 16 vowels and 36 consonants and belongs to the Indo-European language family. Sanskrit is a highly inflected language divided into eight chapters to make it more structured and understandable (Panini Asthadhyayi) (Kak, 1987). Despite the enormous number of articles, the quantity of digital resources is limited, especially for the parallel corpus.

5 Task Description and Dataset

Codalab was used to host the shared task. Several translation sub-tasks were organized as a part of this task, namely: Kannada to Tamil, Kannada to Malayalam, Kannada to Telugu, Kannada to Sanskrit, and Kannada to Tulu. The participants could choose which sub-tasks they wanted to participate in. For each language pair, participants were provided with training, development, and test datasets.

[3]Telugu language
[4]Teligu-script
[5]Census report 2011
[6]Kannada-script
[7]Tulu language and its script

Objective of the task was to train/develop MT systems for the language pairs that were provided. Participants translated the test data using MT models proposed by them and submitted the results to the workshop organizers. BLEU is selected as the evaluation metric to evaluate the submitted MT models. In order to determine the participants' rank, the submissions were compared with gold-standard data.

5.1 Dataset

Datasets used in this shared task are broadly grouped into two categories: i) Collection of publicly available parallel corpora (set I) (ii) Construction of parallel corpus from scratch (set II). In the set I, parallel corpora were collected from *Samanantar*[8] - a collection of the largest parallel corpora available for Indic languages (Ramesh et al., 2022) and statistics of set I is shown in Table 1. It may be noted that only a small portion is used in this task instead of using whole dataset. For set II, dataset is manually constructed and Table 2 gives the statistics of set II. Since there is no parallel corpus available for the translation of Kannada-Tulu and Kannada-Sanskrit, the construction of parallel corpora will exacerbate entanglement for these under-resourced language pairs. To create these parallel corpora, we collected monolingual Tulu and Sanskrit documents from digitally accessible sources and manually translated the corresponding Kannada sentences.

6 System Description

Out of 16 research groups, 12 run submissions were made by 4 teams. Set II received the maximum number of submissions (4 teams) followed by set I (3 teams). Further, results of the participated systems in terms of BLEU score and system ranks for each language pair are shown in Table 3. Based on the BLEU scores, we evaluated the performance of the submitted systems. The following is a brief description of the participants' systems. For more information, please refer to their papers.

Aditya et al. (2022) have used two distinct models, namely: i) fine-tuned multilingual indicTrans[9] model with pseudo data generated from monolingual data obtained using backtranslation ii) Convolutional Neural Network (CNN), Seq2Seq models like, Long Short Term Memory (LSTM), Bidirectional LSTM (BiLSTM) and transformer models which were trained from scratch using Fairseq[10] library. They report better BLEU scores for transformer (Vaswani et al., 2017) model trained from scratch using Fairseq library for all the language pairs.

Piyushi et al. (2022) have proposed a system based on the openNMT-py implementation of the transformer (Vaswani et al., 2017) for building the baseline model. Furthermore, they also carry out experiments by using the IndicNLP [11] tokenizer to improve upon the baseline and report an improvement in the observed results. They report better BLEU scores for the Kannada - Tulu and Kannada - Sanskrit languages.

7 Results and Discussion

As shown in Table 3 the submissions were evaluated with BLEU scores. The results indicate that Aditya et al. (2022) achieved the best performance across Kannada - Tamil, Kannada - Telugu and Kannada - Malayalam translation tasks. As mentioned in Section 6, they carried out their experiments with multiple models namely LSTM, BiLSTM, ConvS2S, Transformer, pre-trained multilingual transformer using backtranslation. On these translation tasks they report the better performance of the LSTM based architectures as well as the pre-trained transformer model. This indicates that for these 3 language pairs which have comparatively larger datasets available the DL architectures with a large number of parameters perform better than the other models. For the language pairs in Set II (as shown in 2) the models employed by Aditya et al. (2022) didn't achieve the best performance. The primary reason for this is that size of the dataset for these language pairs is not sufficient to either train the LSTM models from scratch or fine-tune the transformer architecture in order to achieve meaningful generalization.

Piyushi et al. (2022) report the best performance across the Kannada - Tulu and Kannada - Sanskrit language pairs. These languages which belong to Set II (as shown in Table 2) have comparatively smaller datasets. The authors have used openNMT system to tackle the problem at hand. The opotimal performance of their approach for the languages

[8] `https://indicnlp.ai4bharat.org/samanantar/`

[9] `https://indicnlp.ai4bharat.org/indic-trans/`

[10] `https://github.com/pytorch/fairseq`

[11] `https://github.com/AI4Bharat/indicnlp_corpus`

Languages	Team	BLEU	Rank
Kannada-Tamil	PICT	0.3536	1
	Anvita	0.1791	2
	Translation_Techies	0.0798	3
Kannada-Telugu	PICT	0.3687	1
	Anvita	0.1959	2
	Translation_Techies	0.1242	3
Kannada-Malayalam	PICT	0.2963	1
	Anvita	0.1301	2
	Translation_Techies	0.0729	3
Kannada-Sanskrit	PICT	0.7482	1
	Anvita	0.6209	2
	PICT	0.035	3
	Unitum	0.0011	4
Kannada-Tulu	Translation_Techies	0.6149	1
	Anvita	0.2788	2
	Unitum	0.007	3
	PICT	0.0054	4

Table 3: Results of the participating systems in BLEU score and ranks

of Set II can particularly be attributed to the hyper-parameter tuning to the openNMT system. Also, it is interesting to note that participants used the indic tokenization scheme provided by IndicNLP and reported improved results. The impact of the tokenization on specific language pairs however cannot be verified using the subtasks presented in this paper and more comprehensive experiments need to be carried out.

8 Conclusion

The shared task on MT in Dravidian Languages opened up a slew of new research opportunities in the field of MT in Dravidian languages. The task also involves Sanskrit, an ancient language, in addition to Dravidian languages. Despite positive reactions and enthusiasm for attending the event, the number of system submissions was not impressive. We collected Kannada-Tamil, Kannada-Malayalam, and Kannada-Telugu from *samanatar*, a collection of parallel corpora. Further, Kannada-Sanskrit and Kannada-Tulu parallel corpora were created manually. The performance and BLEU scores of the participants are not credible, yet they are not discouraging. The main inference from the participants' results is that along with the baseline MT models, efficient dataset preparation methods, namely, backtranslation and subword tokenization also necessary to achieve better performance in the translation of morphologically rich languages. As a final note, we hope to continue conducting this workshop in the coming years to contribute to the advancement of language technology for under-resourced Dravidian languages.

9 Acknowledgement

Author Bharathi Raja Chakravarthi was supported in part by a research grant from Science Foundation Ireland (SFI) under Grant Number SFI/12/RC/2289_P2 (Insight_2), co-funded by the European Regional Development Fund and Irish Research Council grant IRCLA/2017/129 (CARDAMOM-Comparative Deep Models of Language for Minority and Historical Languages).

Author Shubhanker Banerjee was supported by Science Foundation Ireland under Grant Agreement No. 13/RC/2106_P2 at the ADAPT SFI Research Centre at National University Of Ireland Galway. ADAPT, the SFI Research Centre for AI-Driven Digital Content Technology, is funded by Science Foundation Ireland through the SFI Research Centres Programme.

References

Vyawahare Aditya, Tangsali Rahul, Mandke Aditya, Litake Onkar, and Kadam Dipali. 2022. PICT@DravidianLangTech-ACL2022: Neural Machine Translation on Dravidian Languages. In *Proceedings of the Second Workshop on Speech and Language Technologies for Dravidian Languages*.

Roee Aharoni, Melvin Johnson, and Orhan Firat. 2019. Massively Multilingual Neural Machine Translation. In *Proceedings of the 2019 Conference of the North American Chapter of the Association for Computational Linguistics: Human Language Technologies, Volume 1 (Long and Short Papers)*, pages 3874–3884.

Mikhail Sergeevich Andronov. 1996. *A Grammar of the Malayalam Language in Historical Treatment*, volume 1. Otto Harrassowitz Verlag.

R Anita and CN Subalalitha. 2019a. An approach to cluster Tamil literatures using discourse connectives. In *2019 IEEE 1st International Conference on Energy, Systems and Information Processing (ICESIP)*, pages 1–4. IEEE.

R Anita and CN Subalalitha. 2019b. Building discourse parser for Thirukkural. In *Proceedings of the 16th International Conference on Natural Language Processing*, pages 18–25.

PJ Antony, CK Savitha, and UJ Ujwal. 2016. Haar features based handwritten character recognition system for Tulu script. In *2016 IEEE International Conference on Recent Trends in Electronics, Information & Communication Technology (RTEICT)*, pages 65–68. IEEE.

B Bharathi, Bharathi Raja Chakravarthi, Subalalitha Chinnaudayar Navaneethakrishnan, N Sripriya, Arunaggiri Pandian, and Swetha Valli. 2022. Findings of the shared task on Speech Recognition for Vulnerable Individuals in Tamil. In *Proceedings of the Second Workshop on Language Technology for Equality, Diversity and Inclusion*. Association for Computational Linguistics.

Bharathi Raja Chakravarthi, Mihael Arcan, and John P. McCrae. 2019. Comparison of Different Orthographies for Machine Translation of Under-Resourced Dravidian Languages. In *2nd Conference on Language, Data and Knowledge (LDK 2019)*, volume 70 of *OpenAccess Series in Informatics (OASIcs)*, pages 6:1–6:14, Dagstuhl, Germany. Schloss Dagstuhl–Leibniz-Zentrum fuer Informatik.

Bharathi Raja Chakravarthi and Vigneshwaran Muralidaran. 2021. Findings of the shared task on hope speech detection for equality, diversity, and inclusion. In *Proceedings of the First Workshop on Language Technology for Equality, Diversity and Inclusion*, pages 61–72, Kyiv. Association for Computational Linguistics.

Bharathi Raja Chakravarthi, Ruba Priyadharshini, Thenmozhi Durairaj, John Phillip McCrae, Paul Buitaleer, Prasanna Kumar Kumaresan, and Rahul Ponnusamy. 2022. Findings of the shared task on Homophobia Transphobia Detection in Social Media Comments. In *Proceedings of the Second Workshop on Language Technology for Equality, Diversity and Inclusion*. Association for Computational Linguistics.

Bharathi Raja Chakravarthi, Ruba Priyadharshini, Vigneshwaran Muralidaran, Shardul Suryawanshi, Navya Jose, Elizabeth Sherly, and John P McCrae. 2020. Overview of the track on sentiment analysis for Dravidian languages in code-mixed text. In *Forum for Information Retrieval Evaluation*, pages 21–24.

Bharathi Raja Chakravarthi, Priya Rani, Mihael Arcan, and John P McCrae. 2021. A survey of orthographic information in machine translation. *SN Computer Science*, 2(4):1–19.

Mia Xu Chen, Orhan Firat, Ankur Bapna, Melvin Johnson, Wolfgang Macherey, George Foster, Llion Jones, Mike Schuster, Noam Shazeer, Niki Parmar, et al. 2018. The Best of Both Worlds: Combining Recent Advances in Neural Machine Translation. In *Proceedings of the 56th Annual Meeting of the Association for Computational Linguistics (Volume 1: Long Papers)*, pages 76–86.

Raj Dabre, Atsushi Fujita, and Chenhui Chu. 2019. Exploiting multilingualism through multistage finetuning for low-resource neural machine translation. In *Proceedings of the 2019 Conference on Empirical Methods in Natural Language Processing and the 9th International Joint Conference on Natural Language Processing (EMNLP-IJCNLP)*, pages 1410–1416.

Cunxiao Du, Zhaopeng Tu, and Jing Jiang. 2021. Order-agnostic cross entropy for non-autoregressive machine translation. In *International Conference on Machine Learning*, pages 2849–2859. PMLR.

Jiatao Gu, Hany Hassan, Jacob Devlin, and Victor OK Li. 2018. Universal Neural Machine Translation for Extremely Low Resource Languages. In *Proceedings of the 2018 Conference of the North American Chapter of the Association for Computational Linguistics: Human Language Technologies, Volume 1 (Long Papers)*, pages 344–354.

S Hewavitharana and HC Fernando. 2002. A Two Stage Classification approach to Tamil Handwriting Recognition. *Tamil Internet*, 2002:118–124.

Vu Cong Duy Hoang, Philipp Koehn, Gholamreza Haffari, and Trevor Cohn. 2018. Iterative back-translation for neural machine translation. In *Proceedings of the 2nd Workshop on Neural Machine Translation and Generation*, pages 18–24.

Subhash C Kak. 1987. The Paninian Approach to Natural Language Processing. *International Journal of Approximate Reasoning*, 1(1):117–130.

Arthur Berriedale Keith. 1993. *A History of Sanskrit Literature*. Motilal Banarsidass Publishe.

K Padmanabha Kekunnaya. 1994. *A Comparative Study of Tulu Dialects*. Rashtrakavi Govinda Pai Research Centre.

Tom Kocmi and Ondrej Bojar. 2018. Trivial Transfer Learning for Low-Resource Neural Machine Translation. *WMT 2018*, page 244.

Bhadriraju Krishnamurti. 2003. *The Dravidian Languages*. Cambridge University Press.

Manoj Kumar and Sandeep Chandran. 2015. Handwritten Malayalam Word Recognition System using Neural Networks. *Int J Eng Res Technol (IJERT)*, 4(4):90–99.

Prasanna Kumar Kumaresan, Ratnasingam Sakuntharaj, Sajeetha Thavareesan, Subalalitha Navaneethakrishnan, Anand Kumar Madasamy, Bharathi Raja Chakravarthi, and John P McCrae. 2021. Findings of shared task on offensive language identification in Tamil and Malayalam. In *Forum for Information Retrieval Evaluation*, pages 16–18.

Arthur Anthony Macdonell. 1915. *A History of Sanskrit Literature*, volume 3. D. Appleton.

Sainik Kumar Mahata, Subhabrata Dutta, Dipankar Das, and Sivaji Bandyopadhyay. 2020. Performance Gain in Low Resource MT with Transfer Learning: An Analysis Concerning Language Families. In *Forum for Information Retrieval Evaluation*, FIRE 2020, page 58–61, New York, NY, USA. Association for Computing Machinery.

Anitha Narasimhan, Aarthy Anandan, Madhan Karky, and CN Subalalitha. 2018. Porul: Option generation and selection and scoring algorithms for a tamil flash card game. *International Journal of Cognitive and Language Sciences*, 12(2):225–228.

Xiao Pan, Mingxuan Wang, Liwei Wu, and Lei Li. 2021. Contrastive Learning for Many-to-many Multilingual Neural Machine Translation. In *Proceedings of the 59th Annual Meeting of the Association for Computational Linguistics and the 11th International Joint Conference on Natural Language Processing (Volume 1: Long Papers)*, pages 244–258.

Amarnath Pathak and Partha Pakray. 2019. Neural machine translation for Indian languages. *Journal of Intelligent Systems*, 28(3):465–477.

Goyal Piyushi, Supriya Musica, Acharya U Dinesh, and Nayak Ashalatha. 2022. Translation Techies @DravidianLangTech-ACL2022-Machine Translation in Dravidian Languages. In *Proceedings of the Second Workshop on Speech and Language Technologies for Dravidian Languages*.

Ruba Priyadharshini, Bharathi Raja Chakravarthi, Subalalitha Chinnaudayar Navaneethakrishnan, Thenmozhi Durairaj, Malliga Subramanian, Kogilavani Shanmugavadivel, Siddhanth U Hegde, and Prasanna Kumar Kumaresan. 2022. Findings of the shared task on Abusive Comment Detection in Tamil. In *Proceedings of the Second Workshop on Speech and Language Technologies for Dravidian Languages*. Association for Computational Linguistics.

Ruba Priyadharshini, Bharathi Raja Chakravarthi, Sajeetha Thavareesan, Dhivya Chinnappa, Durairaj Thenmozhi, and Rahul Ponnusamy. 2021. Overview of the DravidianCodeMix 2021 shared task on sentiment detection in Tamil, Malayalam, and Kannada. In *Forum for Information Retrieval Evaluation*, pages 4–6.

Gowtham Ramesh, Sumanth Doddapaneni, Aravinth Bheemaraj, Mayank Jobanputra, Raghavan AK, Ajitesh Sharma, Sujit Sahoo, Harshita Diddee, Divyanshu Kakwani, Navneet Kumar, et al. 2022. Samanantar: The Largest Publicly Available Parallel Corpora Collection for 11 Indic Languages. *Transactions of the Association for Computational Linguistics*, 10:145–162.

Manikandan Ravikiran, Bharathi Raja Chakravarthi, Anand Kumar Madasamy, Sangeetha Sivanesan, Ratnavel Rajalakshmi, Sajeetha Thavareesan, Rahul Ponnusamy, and Shankar Mahadevan. 2022. Findings of the shared task on Offensive Span Identification in code-mixed Tamil-English comments. In *Proceedings of the Second Workshop on Speech and Language Technologies for Dravidian Languages*. Association for Computational Linguistics.

Ratnasingam Sakuntharaj and Sinnathamby Mahesan. 2016. A novel hybrid approach to detect and correct spelling in Tamil text. In *2016 IEEE International Conference on Information and Automation for Sustainability (ICIAfS)*, pages 1–6.

Ratnasingam Sakuntharaj and Sinnathamby Mahesan. 2017. Use of a novel hash-table for speeding-up suggestions for misspelt Tamil words. In *2017 IEEE International Conference on Industrial and Information Systems (ICIIS)*, pages 1–5.

Ratnasingam Sakuntharaj and Sinnathamby Mahesan. 2021. Missing word detection and correction based on context of Tamil sentences using n-grams. In *2021 10th International Conference on Information and Automation for Sustainability (ICIAfS)*, pages 42–47.

Anbukkarasi Sampath, Thenmozhi Durairaj, Bharathi Raja Chakravarthi, Ruba Priyadharshini, Subalalitha Chinnaudayar Navaneethakrishnan, Kogilavani Shanmugavadivel, Sajeetha Thavareesan, Sathiyaraj Thangasamy, Parameswari Krishnamurthy, Adeep Hande, Sean Benhur, Kishor Kumar Ponnusamy, and Santhiya Pandiyan. 2022. Findings of the shared task on Emotion Analysis in Tamil. In *Proceedings of the Second Workshop on Speech and Language Technologies for Dravidian Languages*. Association for Computational Linguistics.

Kengatharaiyer Sarveswaran, Gihan Dias, and Miriam Butt. 2021. Thamizhimorph: A Morphological

Parser for the Tamil Language. *Machine Translation*, 35(1):37–70.

A. C. Sekhar. 1951. Evolution of Malayalam. *Bulletin of the Deccan College Research Institute*, 12(1/2):1–216.

R Sivanantham and M Seran. 2019. Keeladi: An Urban Settlement of Sangam Age on the Banks of River Vaigai. *India: Department of Archaeology, Government of Tamil Nadu, Chennai.*

R Srinivasan and CN Subalalitha. 2019. Automated named entity recognition from tamil documents. In *2019 IEEE 1st International Conference on Energy, Systems and Information Processing (ICESIP)*, pages 1–5. IEEE.

C. N. Subalalitha. 2019. Information extraction framework for Kurunthogai. *Sādhanā*, 44(7):156.

CN Subalalitha and E Poovammal. 2018. Automatic bilingual dictionary construction for Tirukural. *Applied Artificial Intelligence*, 32(6):558–567.

Sajeetha Thavareesan and Sinnathamby Mahesan. 2019a. Sentiment analysis in Tamil texts: A Study on Machine Learning Techniques and Feature Representation. In *2019 14th Conference on Industrial and Information Systems (ICIIS)*, pages 320–325. IEEE.

Sajeetha Thavareesan and Sinnathamby Mahesan. 2019b. Sentiment analysis in Tamil texts: A study on machine learning techniques and feature representation. In *2019 14th Conference on Industrial and Information Systems (ICIIS)*, pages 320–325.

Sajeetha Thavareesan and Sinnathamby Mahesan. 2020a. Sentiment Lexicon Expansion using Word2vec and fastText for Sentiment Prediction in Tamil texts. In *2020 Moratuwa Engineering Research Conference (MERCon)*, pages 272–276. IEEE.

Sajeetha Thavareesan and Sinnathamby Mahesan. 2020b. Sentiment lexicon expansion using Word2vec and fastText for sentiment prediction in Tamil texts. In *2020 Moratuwa Engineering Research Conference (MERCon)*, pages 272–276.

Sajeetha Thavareesan and Sinnathamby Mahesan. 2020c. Word embedding-based part of speech tagging in Tamil texts. In *2020 IEEE 15th International Conference on Industrial and Information Systems (ICIIS)*, pages 478–482.

Sajeetha Thavareesan and Sinnathamby Mahesan. 2021. Sentiment analysis in Tamil texts using k-means and k-nearest neighbour. In *2021 10th International Conference on Information and Automation for Sustainability (ICIAfS)*, pages 48–53.

Ashish Vaswani, Noam Shazeer, Niki Parmar, Jakob Uszkoreit, Llion Jones, Aidan N Gomez, Łukasz Kaiser, and Illia Polosukhin. 2017. Attention Is All You Need. *Advances in neural information processing systems*, 30.

Mengzhou Xia, Xiang Kong, Antonios Anastasopoulos, and Graham Neubig. 2019. Generalized Data Augmentation for Low-Resource Translation. In *Proceedings of the 57th Annual Meeting of the Association for Computational Linguistics*, pages 5786–5796.

Barret Zoph, Deniz Yuret, Jonathan May, and Kevin Knight. 2016. Transfer Learning for Low-Resource Neural Machine Translation. In *Proceedings of the 2016 Conference on Empirical Methods in Natural Language Processing*, pages 1568–1575.

Findings of the Shared Task on Emotion Analysis in Tamil

Anbukkarasi Sampath [1], Durairaj Thenmozhi [2], Bharathi Raja Chakravarthi,[3]
Ruba Priyadharshini[4], Subalalitha Chinnaudayar Navaneethakrishnan[5],
Kogilavani Shanmugavadivel[1], Sajeetha Thavareesan[6], Sathiyaraj Thangasamy[7],
Parameswari Krishnamurthy[8], Adeep Hande[9] ,Sean Benhur[10],
Kishore Kumar Ponnusamy[11], Santhiya Pandiyan[1]
[1] Kongu Engineering College, India, [2] SSN College of Engineering, India
[3]Insight SFI Research Centre for Data Analytics,National University of Ireland Galway, Ireland
[4]Madurai Kamaraj University, India, [5]SRM Institute Of Science And Technology, Tamil Nadu,India
[6]Eastern University, Sri Lanka,[7]Sri Krishna Adithya College of Arts and Science, India
[8] University of Hyderabad, India
[9] Indian Institute of Information Technology Tiruchirappalli, India
[10] PSG College of Arts and Science, India, [11] Guru Nanak College, India.
anbu.1318@gmail.com

Abstract

This paper presents the overview of the shared task on emotional analysis in Tamil at DravidianLangTech-ACL 2022. This overview paper presents the dataset used in the shared task, task description, the methodologies used by the participants and the evaluation results of the submissions. Emotion analysis in Tamil shared task consists of two sub tasks. Task A aims to categorize the social media comments in Tamil to 11 emotions and Task B aims to categorize the comments into 31 fine-grained emotions. For conducting experiments, training and development datasets were provided to the participants and results are evaluated for the unseen data. In total, we have received around 24 submissions from 13 teams. For evaluating the models, Precision, Recall, micro average metrics are used.

1 Introduction

Emotional analysis is the process of mining emotions in texts for categorization, which is used in a variety of natural language applications such as e-commerce review analysis, public opinion analysis, comprehensive search, customized suggestion, health-care, and online teaching. Emotions are mental states that are frequently represented through behavior or words. Emotional analysis assists in analyzing the text and extracting the emotions portrayed in the text. There are a variety of monolingual datasets available for Dravidian languages, which may be used for a variety of research purposes (Priyadharshini et al., 2021; Kumaresan et al., 2021; Chakravarthi and Muralidaran, 2021; Chakravarthi et al., 2020b). There have, however, been few attempts to create code-mixed datasets for Tamil, Kannada, and Malayalam (Chakravarthi et al., 2021a,b, 2020a). We will assist Tamil in overcoming this resource barrier by producing this dataset, which will provide Tamil with cost-effective and quick natural language processing support in emotional analysis. We gathered comments on several Tamil movie trailers and teasers from YouTube to develop resources for a Tamil scenario.

Data on social media platforms such as Twitter, Facebook, and YouTube is rapidly changing and may have a significant impact on an individual's or community's perception or reputation (Ravikiran et al., 2022; Chakravarthi et al., 2022; Bharathi et al., 2022; Priyadharshini et al., 2022). This highlights the need of automation in emotional analysis. Because of its numerous content offerings, such as movies, trailers, music, tutorials, product reviews, and so on, YouTube is a popular social media network in the Indian subcontinent (Priyadharshini et al., 2020; Chakravarthi, 2020). YouTube allows users to create content as well as participate and interact with it through activities such as like and commenting. As a result, more user-generated content is available in underdeveloped languages (Chakravarthi et al., 2019, 2018; Yasaswini et al., 2021).

In this paper the results of the shared task on emotional analysis in Tamil are presented and held at DravidianLangTech. This task consists of two

Proceedings of the Second Workshop on Speech and Language Technologies for Dravidian Languages, pages 279 - 285
May 26, 2022 ©2022 Association for Computational Linguistics

sub tasks, namely Task A and Task B. The first task is focused on analysing the emotion in social media Tamil comments with 11 emotions. The second task is focused on analysing 31 fine-grained emotions in social media Tamil comments. The task is focused on analysing emotions on Tamil language which is a low resource language that belongs to Dravidian family. All the data including training data, testing data, development data along with results are made publicly available. We strongly believe that the curated dataset will contribute more in advancing the research in the field of emotional analysis field of Tamil.

2 Related Work

As the availability of text data is more today, there are many good works carried out in the field of Natural Language Processing (NLP). Identifying the emotions in a given text data helps in various applications, including online teaching, recommendation systems, public opinion analysis. Even though many researchers contribute in emotion analysis domain, very few works have been made in Dravidian languages like Tamil. In recent days, deep learning based techniques yield good results in this domain. With social media content, emotion detection from code mixed Hindi and English language (Sasidhar et al., 2020) is performed. They created an emotion annotated corpus using 12000 code-mixed text sentences from different social media sites as the data availability in their field of interest is less. It is reported that the CNN-BiLSTM model provides good accuracy. Xu et al. (2020) performed emotion analysis using the proposed CNN_Text_Word2vec model in Chinese microblog. All the words in the microblog are trained using word2vec neural network model. The trained feature vectors are fed as input feature for attention-based convolution neural network model which classifies the text emotion into positive and negative. Sina Weibo microblog is used for experimental analysis in which 40000 training and 40000 test microblog samples were considered.

A combination of cognitive linguistic and deep learning features are used for performing emotion analysis on Persian text (Sadeghi et al., 2021). These models help to identify emotions including anger, happiness, sadness, surprise and fear. For performance measurement, a self-labeled 23,000 Persian documents are taken. They used Word2Vec embedding technique for vector conversion. The deep learning based architectures (Tocoglu et al., 2019) such as Artificial Neural Network, Convolutional Neural Network, and Long Short-Term Memory based Recurrent Neural Network are examined for Turkish tweets emotional prediction (S.Anbukkarasi and S.Varadhaganapathy, 2020). To curate a dataset, the lexicon-based approach is proposed for automatic annotation of Turkish tweet text and compared the deep learning based architectures that outperformed the traditional machine learning techniques for emotion recognition in Turkish. Hybrid model is proposed to identify the emotions in Arabic text (Alswaidan and Menai, 2020). Human-Engineered feature-based model and deep feature-based model are investigated in which Human-Engineered Feature-based model is used to select the features based on various kinds of the text like lexical, stylistics, and semantic. Deep Feature based model contains stacked neural network that reinserts the embedding layer several times to delay the learning process. From the study, it is clear that there is a research gap in emotional analysis field for Tamil language with advanced techniques.

3 Tamil

Tamil is a classical Dravidian language spoken by Tamil people of South Asia. It is the official language of the Indian state, Tamil Nadu, Singapore and Sri lanka. Tamil is one of the longest surviving classical languages and it was the first to be listed as classical language of India. It is one of the 22 scheduled languages in Indian constitution. The history of Tamil language is categorized into Old Tamil, Middle Tamil and Modern Tamil. Tamil has 247 alphabets including 12 vowels, 18 consonants, 216 compound letters and one special character known as ayudham (S.Anbukkarasi and S.Varadhaganapathy, 2020; Chakravarthi et al., 2018; Ghanghor et al., 2021a,b)

4 Task Description

4.1 Task

Two sub tasks are carried out as part of this shared task: Emotional analysis with 11 emotions annotated data for social media comments in Tamil and Task B were organized with 31 fine-grained emotions annotated data for social media comments in Tamil. The dates followed for releasing the training and testing data is provided in Table 1. Participants are encouraged to participate in any one of the tasks or both the tasks. For this task, training, testing development datasets with the comments and corresponding emotion label is given to all the participants. The task was to classify the given comment with corresponding emotion.

4.2 Dataset

The data has been collected from various comments of Youtube videos. The data for Task A consists of around 22,200 Tamil Youtube comments with 11 emotions and Task B (Vasantharajan et al., 2022) consists of around 46,000 YouTube comments with 31 emotions. The YouTube Comment Scraper tool is used to collect Tamil comments from various domains such as sports, news and movies, and most of the sentences contain the English text, Tamil text and code-mixed Tamil-English text. For identifying the Tamil language, the language detection library known as langdetect [1] is used to find the Tamil comments from the sentences which are written fully in Tamil and discarded the other language comments. For annotation, the guidelines are given in both English and Tamil and each sentence in the dataset is annotated by minimum three annotators. The personal information of the annotators are gathered to understand about them and informed them the reason for collecting the information. Those who accepted to annotate are given with the instructions and data. They were given the freedom of relieving from the task at any point of time. This process was done for annotating data for both Task A and Task B.

4.3 System Description

We received around 16 submissions for Task A and 8 submissions for Task B, with total of 8 teams for Task A and 7 teams for Task B. For the teams that have submitted multiple submissions, we have considered the highest scoring submission. The system descriptions of each teams are given in this section.

1. **MUCS** (Hegde et al., 2022)- This team participated in Task A and used an ensemble of logistic regression models with three penalties, L1, L2 and Elasticnet. The team ranked 4th with macro average F1 score of 0.04.

2. **Judith Jeyafreeda** (Andrew Jayafreeda, 2022) - has used pretrained word embeddings with CNN model for classifying emotions, the system achieved 0.094 Macro F1 for Task A and 0.057 for Task B and achieved 6th place in Task B.

3. **pandas** - This team has participated in Task A and have used LaBSE (Feng et al., 2020) feature extraction method with SVM classifier. To handle class imbalance problem, they have oversampled the dataset with SMOTE.

4. **CUET-NLP** (Mustakim et al., 2022) - The team has participated in Task A, and has experimented with multiple classical Machine Learning models such as logistic regression,naive bayes, decision tree, SVM and Pretrained multilingual transformer models, mBERT(Devlin et al., 2019) and XLM-R (Lample and Conneau, 2019) base model, The XLM-R model achieved the highest Macro F1 score of 0.210 and were ranked 2nd in the Task A.

5. **Varsini And Kirthanna** (S et al., 2022) - Partcipated in Task A and have used a combination of Keyword spotting and Lexical affinity based methods, using emojis and external datasets. The system ranked 5th place with Macro F1 score of 0.030.

6. **GJG** (Prasad et al., 2022) - Used pretrained transformers XLM-R and Deberta. They participated in both of the Tasks A and B, in Task B they achieved the Macro F1 score of 0.45 in Task A and 0.26 in Task B. The participants achieved Rank 1st in Task A.

7. **Optimize_Prime** (Gokhale et al., 2022) - Have experimented with multiple methods, an ensemble of class machine learning models, RNN based models such as LSTM and ULMFIT (Howard and Ruder, 2018), and pretrained transformer models such as XLM-R, Indic-BERT and MuRIL. They have participated in both subtasks, In Task A XLM-R achieved best result of 0.030 Macro F1 ranking 5th place and in Task B, MuRIL achieved best result of 0.125 ranking second place.

8. **UMUTeam** (García-Díaz and Valencia-García, 2022) - Have participated in both Tasks A and B, used a Model that combines both Linguistic Features such as psychological features, POS tags and contextual em-

[1] `https://github.com/Mimino666/langdetect`

Event	Date
Training Set Release	Nov 20, 2021
Test Set Release	Jan 14, 2022
Submission Deadline	Jan 30, 2022
Results Announcement	Feb 10, 2022
Paper Submission	March 10, 2022

Table 1: Emotional Analysis Task Schedule

beddings from pretrained models and Fasttext. They have achived Rank 1st in Task B with the score of 0.151.

9. **IIITSurat** - Have participated in both Task A and B. They have used an ensemble of deep learning models with oversampling the minority classes. They were able to rank 4 with Macro F1 score of 0.090 in Task B and rank 7th with Macro F1 score of 0.020 in Task A.

10. **MSD** - The team has participated in the Task A and have submitted submissions on Support Vector Machines, BiLSTM and an ensembles. Out of the three submissions, BiLSTM provided higher results than other models.

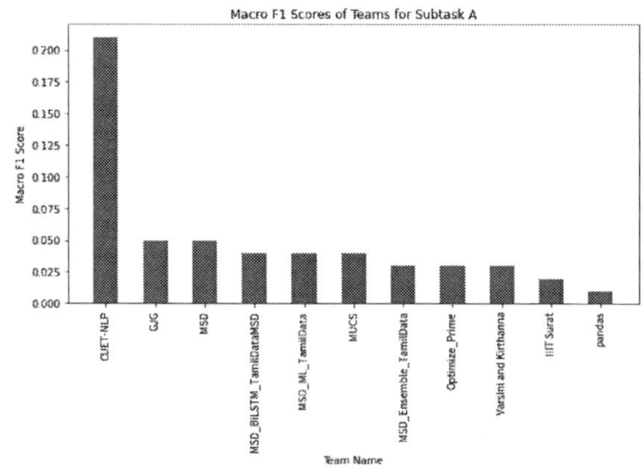

Figure 1: Results for Task A

5 Evaluation

In this section we describe about the evaluation method that were used for the both Tasks A and B. We primarily evaluated the submissions using major classification metrics such as Macro Averaged and Weighted Average Precision, Recall and F1-Score. For ranking the teams, we primarily used Macro Averaged F1 Score as it finds f1 score for each label and find their unweighted mean.

6 Results and Discussion

Fine-grained Emotion Detection is a hard problem, it is even harder for low resource languages such as Tamil, In this shared task teams have submitted results for both Tasks A and B. Figures 1 and 2 depicts the pictorial representation of scores of each team for both Task A and Task B. The results are discussed in Table 2 and Table 3.

In Task A, Team GJG has achieved Rank 1 with Macro F1 Score of 0.310 and UMUTeam has achieved Rank 1 with 0.151 F1-score in Task B. Task A received more number of submissions compared to Task B, we hypothesize that this is due to the fact that Task B is relatively harder than Task A since it contains 31 emotions which are more

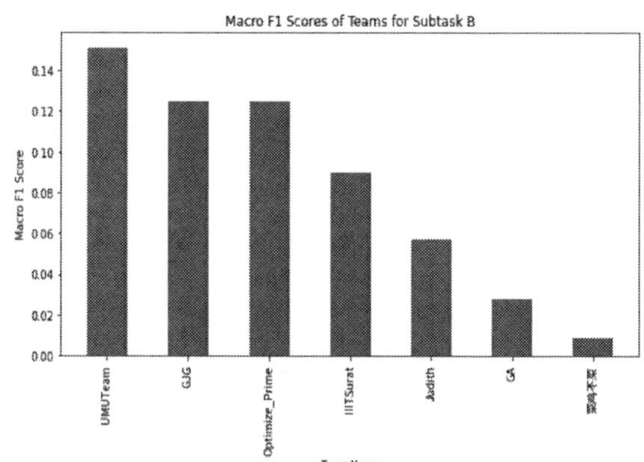

Figure 2: Results for Task B

Team	Precision	Recall	F1-Score	Rank
GJG	0.320	0.310	0.310	1
CUET-NLP	0.220	0.250	0.210	2
MSD	0.090	0.080	0.050	3
MUCS	0.110	0.130	0.040	4
Optimize_Prime	0.090	0.080	0.030	5
Varsini and Kirthanna	0.090	0.110	0.030	5
IIITSurat	0.090	0.090	0.020	7
pandas_tamil	0.080	0.070	0.010	8

Table 2: Results of the Submissions for Task A

Team	Precision	Recall	F1-Score	Rank
UMUTeam	0.150	0.171	0.151	1
GJG	0.142	0.144	0.125	2
Optimize_Prime	0.132	0.140	0.125	2
IIITSurat	0.156	0.099	0.090	4
Judith Jeyafreeda	0.094	0.068	0.057	5
GA	0.033	0.031	0.028	6
菜鸡不菜	0.005	0.032	0.009	7

Table 3: Results of the Submissions for Task B

similar in nature and harder for Machine Learning models to classify.

7 Conclusion and Future Work

Two new datasets with fine-grained emotions for classifying the emotions in Tamil language is created for this shared task. In this paper, various approaches used for analysing emotions from Tamil comments and their results are analyzed. The task has been carried out as two sub tasks. In the Task A, 8 teams have participated and submitted their results. For Task B, 7 teams submitted their results. The XLM-R model produces the highest F1-score for Task A and the combination of techniques including linguistic features, POS tags, contextual embeddings yields remarkable results for Task B. As a future work, we planned to increase the size of the dataset and include more fine grained emotional labels to increase the performance of the system.

Acknowdgements

Author Bharathi Raja Chakravarthi were supported in part by a research grant from Science Foundation Ireland (SFI) under Grant Number SFI/12/RC/2289_P2 (Insight_2), co-funded by the European Regional Development Fund and Irish Research Council grant IRCLA/2017/129 (CARDAMOM-Comparative Deep Models of Language for Minority and Historical Languages).

References

Nourah Alswaidan and Mohamed El Bachir Menai. 2020. Hybrid feature model for emotion recognition in Arabic text. *IEEE Access*, 8:37843–37854.

Judith Andrew Jayafreeda. 2022. JudithJeyafreedaAndrew@TamilNLP-ACL2022:CNN for Emotion Analysis in Tamil. In *Proceedings of the Second Workshop on Speech and Language Technologies for Dravidian Languages*. Association for Computational Linguistics.

B Bharathi, Bharathi Raja Chakravarthi, Subalalitha Chinnaudayar Navaneethakrishnan, N Sripriya, Arunaggiri Pandian, and Swetha Valli. 2022. Findings of the shared task on Speech Recognition for Vulnerable Individuals in Tamil. In *Proceedings of the Second Workshop on Language Technology for Equality, Diversity and Inclusion*. Association for Computational Linguistics.

Bharathi Raja Chakravarthi. 2020. HopeEDI: A multilingual hope speech detection dataset for equality, diversity, and inclusion. In *Proceedings of the Third Workshop on Computational Modeling of People's Opinions, Personality, and Emotion's in Social Media*, pages 41–53, Barcelona, Spain (Online). Association for Computational Linguistics.

Bharathi Raja Chakravarthi, Mihael Arcan, and John P. McCrae. 2018. Improving wordnets for under-resourced languages using machine translation. In *Proceedings of the 9th Global Wordnet Conference*, pages 77–86, Nanyang Technological University (NTU), Singapore. Global Wordnet Association.

Bharathi Raja Chakravarthi, Mihael Arcan, and John P. McCrae. 2019. WordNet gloss translation for under-resourced languages using multilingual neural machine translation. In *Proceedings of the Second Workshop on Multilingualism at the Intersection of Knowledge Bases and Machine Translation*, pages 1–7, Dublin, Ireland. European Association for Machine Translation.

Bharathi Raja Chakravarthi and Vigneshwaran Muralidaran. 2021. Findings of the shared task on hope speech detection for equality, diversity, and inclusion. In *Proceedings of the First Workshop on Language Technology for Equality, Diversity and Inclusion*, pages 61–72, Kyiv. Association for Computational Linguistics.

Bharathi Raja Chakravarthi, Vigneshwaran Muralidaran, Ruba Priyadharshini, and John Philip McCrae. 2020a. Corpus creation for sentiment analysis in code-mixed Tamil-English text. In *Proceedings of the 1st Joint Workshop on Spoken Language Technologies for Under-resourced languages (SLTU) and Collaboration and Computing for Under-Resourced Languages (CCURL)*, pages 202–210, Marseille, France. European Language Resources association.

Bharathi Raja Chakravarthi, Ruba Priyadharshini, Thenmozhi Durairaj, John Phillip McCrae, Paul Buitaleer, Prasanna Kumar Kumaresan, and Rahul Ponnusamy. 2022. Findings of the shared task on Homophobia Transphobia Detection in Social Media Comments. In *Proceedings of the Second Workshop on Language Technology for Equality, Diversity and Inclusion*. Association for Computational Linguistics.

Bharathi Raja Chakravarthi, Ruba Priyadharshini, Vigneshwaran Muralidaran, Shardul Suryawanshi, Navya Jose, Elizabeth Sherly, and John P McCrae. 2020b. Overview of the track on sentiment analysis for Dravidian languages in code-mixed text. In *Forum for Information Retrieval Evaluation*, pages 21–24.

Bharathi Raja Chakravarthi, Ruba Priyadharshini, Rahul Ponnusamy, Prasanna Kumar Kumaresan, Kayalvizhi Sampath, Durairaj Thenmozhi, Sathiyaraj Thangasamy, Rajendran Nallathambi, and John Phillip McCrae. 2021a. Dataset for identification of homophobia and transophobia in multilingual YouTube comments. *arXiv preprint arXiv:2109.00227*.

Bharathi Raja Chakravarthi, Priya Rani, Mihael Arcan, and John P McCrae. 2021b. A survey of orthographic information in machine translation. *SN Computer Science*, 2(4):1–19.

Jacob Devlin, Ming-Wei Chang, Kenton Lee, and Kristina Toutanova. 2019. Bert: Pre-training of deep bidirectional transformers for language understanding. *ArXiv*, abs/1810.04805.

Fangxiaoyu Feng, Yinfei Yang, Daniel Cer, Naveen Arivazhagan, and Wei Wang. 2020. Language-agnostic BERT sentence embedding.

José Antonio García-Díaz and Rafael Valencia-García. 2022. UMUTeam@TamilNLP-ACL2022: Emotional Analysis in Tamil. In *Proceedings of the Second Workshop on Speech and Language Technologies for Dravidian Languages*. Association for Computational Linguistics.

Nikhil Ghanghor, Parameswari Krishnamurthy, Sajeetha Thavareesan, Ruba Priyadharshini, and Bharathi Raja Chakravarthi. 2021a. IIITK@DravidianLangTech-EACL2021: Offensive language identification and meme classification in Tamil, Malayalam and Kannada. In *Proceedings of the First Workshop on Speech and Language Technologies for Dravidian Languages*, pages 222–229, Kyiv. Association for Computational Linguistics.

Nikhil Ghanghor, Rahul Ponnusamy, Prasanna Kumar Kumaresan, Ruba Priyadharshini, Sajeetha Thavareesan, and Bharathi Raja Chakravarthi. 2021b. IIITK@LT-EDI-EACL2021: Hope speech detection for equality, diversity, and inclusion in Tamil , Malayalam and English. In *Proceedings of the First Workshop on Language Technology for Equality, Diversity and Inclusion*, pages 197–203, Kyiv. Association for Computational Linguistics.

Omar Gokhale, Shantanu Patankar, Onkar Litake, Aditya Mandke, and Dipali Kadam. 2022. Optimize_Prime@TamilNLP-ACL2022: Emotion Analysis in Tamil. In *Proceedings of the Second Workshop on Speech and Language Technologies for Dravidian Languages*. Association for Computational Linguistics.

Asha Hegde, Sharat Coelho, and Shashrekha H.L. 2022. MUCS@DravidianLangTech@ACL2022: ensemble of logistic regression penalties to identify Emotions in Tamil Text. In *Proceedings of the Second Workshop on Speech and Language Technologies for Dravidian Languages*. Association for Computational Linguistics.

Jeremy Howard and Sebastian Ruder. 2018. Universal language model fine-tuning for text classification. In *Proceedings of the 56th Annual Meeting of the Association for Computational Linguistics (Volume 1: Long Papers)*, pages 328–339, Melbourne, Australia. Association for Computational Linguistics.

Prasanna Kumar Kumaresan, Ratnasingam Sakuntharaj, Sajeetha Thavareesan, Subalalitha Navaneethakrishnan, Anand Kumar Madasamy, Bharathi Raja Chakravarthi, and John P McCrae. 2021. Findings of shared task on offensive language identification in Tamil and Malayalam. In *Forum for Information Retrieval Evaluation*, pages 16–18.

Guillaume Lample and Alexis Conneau. 2019. Cross-lingual language model pretraining. *Advances in Neural Information Processing Systems (NeurIPS)*.

Nasehatul Mustakim, Rabeya Rabu Aktar, Golam Sarwar Md Mursalin, Eftekhar Hossain, Omar Sheriff, and Mohammed Hoque Moshiui. 2022. CUET-NLP@TamilNLP-ACL2022 multi-class textual emotion detection from social media using transformers. In *Proceedings of the Second Workshop on Speech and Language Technologies for Dravidian Languages*. Association for Computational Linguistics.

Janvi Prasad, Gaurang Prasad, and Gunavathi Chellamuthu. 2022. GJG@TamilNLP-ACL2022: emotion analysis and classification in Tamil using Transformers. In *Proceedings of the Second Workshop on Speech and Language Technologies for Dravidian Languages*. Association for Computational Linguistics.

Ruba Priyadharshini, Bharathi Raja Chakravarthi, Subalalitha Chinnaudayar Navaneethakrishnan, Thenmozhi Durairaj, Malliga Subramanian, Kogilavani Shanmugavadivel, Siddhanth U Hegde, and Prasanna Kumar Kumaresan. 2022. Findings of the shared task on Abusive Comment Detection in Tamil. In *Proceedings of the Second Workshop on Speech and Language Technologies for Dravidian Languages*. Association for Computational Linguistics.

Ruba Priyadharshini, Bharathi Raja Chakravarthi, Sajeetha Thavareesan, Dhivya Chinnappa, Durairaj Thenmozhi, and Rahul Ponnusamy. 2021. Overview of the DravidianCodeMix 2021 shared task on sentiment detection in Tamil, Malayalam, and Kannada. In *Forum for Information Retrieval Evaluation*, pages 4–6.

Ruba Priyadharshini, Bharathi Raja Chakravarthi, Mani Vegupatti, and John P McCrae. 2020. Named entity recognition for code-mixed Indian corpus using meta embedding. In *2020 6th international conference on advanced computing and communication systems (ICACCS)*, pages 68–72. IEEE.

Manikandan Ravikiran, Bharathi Raja Chakravarthi, Anand Kumar Madasamy, Sangeetha Sivanesan, Ratnavel Rajalakshmi, Sajeetha Thavareesan, Rahul Ponnusamy, and Shankar Mahadevan. 2022. Findings of the shared task on Offensive Span Identification in code-mixed Tamil-English comments. In *Proceedings of the Second Workshop on Speech and Language Technologies for Dravidian Languages*. Association for Computational Linguistics.

Varsini S, Kirthana S Ranjan, Angel S Deborah, S Rajalakshmi, R.S Milton, and T.T Mirnalinae. 2022. Varsini_and_Kirthanna@DravidianLangTech-ACL2022-Emotional Analysis in Tamil. In *Proceedings of the Second Workshop on Speech and Language Technologies for Dravidian Languages*. Association for Computational Linguistics.

Seyed Soheil Sadeghi, Hassan Khotanlou, and Mohammad Rasekh Mahand. 2021. Automatic persian text emotion detection using cognitive linguistic and deep learning. *Journal of AI and Data Mining*.

S.Anbukkarasi and S.Varadhaganapathy. 2020. Analyzing sentiment in Tamil tweets using deep neural network. In *2020 Fourth International Conference on Computing Methodologies and Communication*. IEEE.

T Tulasi Sasidhar, Premjith B, and Soman K P. 2020. Emotion detection in Hinglish(Hindi+English) code-mixed social media text. *Procedia Computer Science*, 171:1346–1352. Third International Conference on Computing and Network Communications (CoCoNet'19).

Mansur Alp Tocoglu, Okan Ozturkmenoglu, and Adil Alpkocak. 2019. Emotion analysis from Turkish tweets using deep neural networks. *IEEE Access*, 7:183061–183069.

Charangan Vasantharajan, Sean Benhur, Prasanna Kumar Kumarasen, Rahul Ponnusamy, S. Thangasamy, Ruba Priyadharshini, Thenmozhi Durairaj, Kanchana Sivanraju, Anbukkarasi Sampath, Bharathi Raja Chakravarthi, and John P. McCrae. 2022. TamilEmo: finegrained emotion detection dataset for Tamil. *ArXiv*, abs/2202.04725.

Dongliang Xu, Zhihong Tian, Rufeng Lai, Xiangtao Kong, Zhiyuan Tan, and Wei Shi. 2020. Deep learning based emotion analysis of microblog texts. *Information Fusion*, 64:1–11.

Konthala Yasaswini, Karthik Puranik, Adeep Hande, Ruba Priyadharshini, Sajeetha Thavareesan, and Bharathi Raja Chakravarthi. 2021. IIITT@DravidianLangTech-EACL2021: Transfer learning for offensive language detection in Dravidian languages. In *Proceedings of the First Workshop on Speech and Language Technologies for Dravidian Languages*, pages 187–194, Kyiv. Association for Computational Linguistics.

Findings of the Shared Task on Multi-task Learning in Dravidian Languages

Bharathi Raja Chakravarthi[1], **Ruba Priyadharshini**[2], **CN Subalalitha**[3]
Sangeetha Sivanesan[4], **Malliga Subramanian**[5], **Kogilavani Shanmugavadivel**[5],
Parameswari Krishnamurthy[6], **Adeep Hande**[7], **Siddhanth U Hegde**[8]
Roshan Nayak[9], **Swetha Valli**[10]
[1] National University of Ireland Galway, [2]Madurai Kamaraj University
[3]SRM Institute Of Science And Technology, [4]NIT Tiruchirappalli,[5]Kongu Engineering College
[6]University of Hyderabad, [7]Indian Institute of Information Technology Tiruchirappalli
[8]University Visvesvaraya College of Engineering, [9]BMS College of Engineering
[10]Thiyagarajar college of engineering
bharathi.raja@insight-centre.org

Abstract

We present our findings from the first shared task on Multi-task Learning in Dravidian Languages at the second Workshop on Speech and Language Technologies for Dravidian Languages. In this task, a sentence in any of three Dravidian Languages is required to be classified into two closely related tasks namely *Sentiment Analyis* (**SA**) and *Offensive Language Identification* (**OLI**). The task spans over three Dravidian Languages, namely, Kannada, Malayalam, and Tamil. It is one of the first shared tasks that focuses on Multi-task Learning for closely related tasks, especially for a very low-resourced language family such as the Dravidian language family. In total, 55 people signed up to participate in the task, and due to the intricate nature of the task, especially in its first iteration, 3 submissions have been received.

1 Introduction

The term "Social media" provides a channel through which people engage in interactive communities and networks by creating, sharing, and exchanging thoughts and information. It has received users from almost all generations and all around the world (Chakravarthi et al., 2020a). Users can interact and connect with others and form communities through social media. It allows users to share their ideas, views and information openly on various topics. This gives license to the users to write hateful and offensive comments sometimes. People come from a variety of racial backgrounds and hold a diversity of belief systems. This can often cause conflict of opinions during their interactions on social media platforms (Chakravarthi et al., 2021a,b, 2020b; Priyadharshini et al., 2020; Chakravarthi, 2020). Due to the COVID 19 pandemic, the internet community has become more popular than it has ever been. The amount of false narratives and derogatory remarks shared on online platforms has risen exponentially. A large number of social media users share malicious posts despite understanding that they are infringing on their rights to free expression (Bhardwaj et al., 2020). Sentiment analysis is a text mining task that identifies and extracts personal information from source material, allowing a company/researcher to better understand the social sentiment of its brand, product, or service while monitoring online conversations.

Multi-task learning (MTL) is a practical approach to improving system performance by utilising shared characteristics of tasks (Caruana, 1997). The goal of MTL is to use learning multiple tasks at the same time to improve system performance (Martínez Alonso and Plank, 2017). Because SA and OLI are essentially sequence classification tasks, we were motivated to conduct the shared task, due to the recent developments in large language modeling. Kannada and Malayalam are Dravidian languages that are widely spoken in South India and are also official languages in the states of Karnataka and Kerala (Reddy and Sharoff, 2011; Chakravarthi et al., 2020a, 2019, 2018; Ghanghor et al., 2021a,b). Tamil is an official language in Tamil Nadu, India, as well as Sri Lanka, Singapore, Malaysia, and other parts of the world. Dravidian languages are morphologically rich; with code-mixing, processing these languages becomes even more difficult, and they are under-resourced (Priyadharshini et al., 2021; Kumaresan et al., 2021;

Proceedings of the Second Workshop on Speech and Language Technologies for Dravidian Languages, pages 286 - 291
May 26, 2022

Chakravarthi and Muralidaran, 2021; Chakravarthi et al., 2020c; Sampath et al., 2022; Ravikiran et al., 2022; Chakravarthi et al., 2022a; Bharathi et al., 2022; Priyadharshini et al., 2022). Significant minority speak Tamil in the four other South Indian states of Kerala, Karnataka, Andhra Pradesh, and Telangana, as well as the Union Territory of the Andaman and Nicobar Islands (Sakuntharaj and Mahesan, 2021, 2017, 2016; Thavareesan and Mahesan, 2019, 2020a,b, 2021). It is also spoken by the Tamil diaspora, which may be found in Malaysia, Myanmar, South Africa, the United Kingdom, the United States, Canada, Australia, and Mauritius. Tamil is also the native language of Sri Lankan Moors. Tamil, one of the 22 scheduled languages in the Indian Constitution, was the first to be designated as a classical language of India (Subalalitha, 2019; Srinivasan and Subalalitha, 2019; Narasimhan et al., 2018). Tamil is one of the world's longest-surviving classical languages. The earliest epigraphic documents discovered on rock edicts and "hero stones" date from the 6th century BC. Tamil has the oldest ancient non-Sanskritic Indian literature of any Indian language (Anita and Subalalitha, 2019b,a; Subalalitha and Poovammal, 2018).

The shared task on MTL in Dravidian Languages investigates whether it is beneficial to train models using MTL, as obtaining extensive annotated data for under resourced languages is difficult. Additionally, SA and OLI have discourse properties in common (Chakravarthi et al., 2022b). The lack of large labelled data for user-generated code-mixed datasets motivated the selection of these tasks. Past studies have shown us that the benefits to MTL are two folds, namely, reducing the space/time complexity, and the ability for the model to learn from each other tasks (Hande et al., 2021). Our dataset contains a wide range of code-mixing, from simple script mixing to morphological mixing. The task is to determine the polarity of sentiment and offensiveness in a code-mixed dataset of Tamil-English, Malayalam-English, and Kannada-English comments or posts. This paper presents an overview of the task description, dataset, description of the participating systems, analysis, and provide insights from the shared task.

2 Dataset

The DravidianCodeMix dataset (Chakravarthi et al., 2022b) is the primary resource of the shared task. It comprises of over 60,0000 manually annotated comments scraped from YouTube. Additionally, DravidianCodeMix spans three languages in the Dravidian language family, namely, Kannada, Malayalam, and Tamil. The Kannada code-mixed dataset has 7,273 comments, while the Malayalam and Tamil codemixed datasets have 12,711 and 43,349 comments, respectively. Following the removal of repetitive sentences, Figure 1 shows the class-wise distribution of the datasets which will be split into train, validation, and test sets.

Sentiment Analysis:

- **Positive state:** Comment contains an explicit or implicit clue in the text suggesting that the speaker is in a positive state.
- **Negative state:** Comment contains an explicit or implicit clue in the text suggesting that the speaker is in a negative state.
- **Mixed feelings:** Comment contains an explicit or implicit clue in both positive and negative feeling.
- **Neutral state:** Comment does not contain an explicit or implicit indicator of the speaker's emotional state.
- **Not in intended language:** For Kannada if the sentence does not contain Kannada script or Latin script then it is not Kannada.

Offensive Language Identification :

- **Not Offensive**: Comment does not contain offence or profanity.
- **Offensive Untargeted** : Comment contains offence or profanity without any target. These are comments which contain unacceptable language that does not target anyone.
- **Offensive Targeted Individual**: Comment contains offence or profanity which targets the individual.
- **Offensive Targeted Group**: Comment contains offence or profanity which targets the group.
- **Offensive Targeted Other**: Comment contains offence or profanity which does not belong to any of the previous two categories (e.g., a situation, an issue, an organization or an event).

Kannada				
	Sentiment analysis		Offensive language identification	
Sl. No.	Class	Distribution	Class	Distribution
1	Positive	3,291	Not offensive	4,121
2	Negative	1,481	Offensive untargeted	274
3	Mixed feelings	678	Offensive targeted individual	624
4	Neutral	820	Offensive targeted group	411
5	Other language	1,003	Offensive targeted others	145
6	-	-	Other anguages	1,698
	Total	7,273	Total	7,273
Tamil				
	Sentiment analysis		Offensive language identification	
Sl. No.	Class	Distribution	Class	Distribution
1	Positive	24,501	Not offensive	31,366
2	Negative	5,190	Offensive untargeted	3,594
3	Mixed feelings	4,852	Offensive targeted individual	2,928
4	Neutral	6,748	Offensive targeted group	3,110
5	Other languages	2,058	Offensive targeted others	582
6	-	-	Other languages	1,769
	Total	43,349	Total	43,349
Malayalam				
	Sentiment analysis		Offensive language identification	
Sl. No.	Class	Distribution	Class	Distribution
1	Positive	5,565	Not offensive	11,357
2	Negative	1,394	Offensive untargeted	171
3	Mixed feelings	794	Offensive targeted individual	179
4	Neutral	4,063	Offensive targeted group	113
5	Other languages	955	Other languages	951
	Total	12,771	Total	12,771

Figure 1: Classwise distribution of the datasets for Kannada, Malayalam, and Tamil

- **Not in indented language**: Comment not in the Kannada language.

In general, all languages have similar class types. Kannada and Tamil code-mixed datasets have six classes in OLI, while Malayalam has five classes. The Malayalam dataset lacks the Offensive Language Others (OTO) class.

2.1 Training Phase

In the first phase, data is made available for training and/or development of offensive language detection models. Participants were given training and validation datasets for preliminary evaluations or tuning of hyper-parameters. They were also given the option of performing cross-validation on the training data. In total, 57 people registered for the task and downloaded the data.

2.2 Evaluation Phase

In the second phase, test sets for all three languages are made available for evaluation. Each team that took part submitted their generated prediction for evaluation. Predictions have been submitted to the organising committee via Google form for evaluation. CodaLab is a well-known platform for organising collaborative tasks. However, due to issues with running the evaluation, we decided to evaluate manually. The macro average F1 score is the metric used for evaluation.

3 System Description

MUCIC (Gowda et al., 2022) - The authors submitted their predictions for all three languages. They treated this as a single task and fine-tuned the multilingual DistilBERT language model, and aggregated the outputs.

MUCS (Hegde and Coelho, 2022) - The authors submitted their predictions for all three languages. Similar to the other team, they treated it a single task. They used Dynamic Meta Embedding as a feature in training a DL-based LSTM model to predict test set labels.

4 Evaluation, Results and Discussion

The submissions were primarily evaluated using major classification metrics such as Macro Aver-

Team Name	Kannada		Rank
	Sentiment Analysis	**Offensive Language Identification**	
MUCS	0.201	0.221	1
MUCIC	0.177	0.199	2
Team Name	**Malayalam**		**Rank**
	Sentiment Analysis	**Offensive Language Identification**	
MUCIC	0.192	0.245	1
MUCIC	0.148	0.079	2
Team Name	**Tamil**		**Rank**
	Sentiment Analysis	**Offensive Language Identification**	
MUCS	0.296	0.176	1
MUCIC	0.255	0.171	2

Table 1: Macro Average F1-Score of the systems submitted for the MTL shared Task.

aged and Weighted Average Precision, Recall, and F1-Score. We predominantly used Macro Averaged F1 Score to rank the teams because it identifies the F1 score to every label and calculates their unweighted mean.

MTL in its essence is a very challenging problem, especially when we focus this aspect on low-resourced language family such as Dravidian Languages (Kannada, Malayalam, and Tamil). Table 1 represents the results of the teams **MUCS** (Hegde and Coelho, 2022) and **MUCIC** (Gowda et al., 2022) on the two tasks of the three languages.

5 Conclusion

In its first iteration, the shared task on MTL for Dravidian Languages opened up new avenues for research in low-resource Multi-task Learning. The task involved multiple languages, namely, Kannada, Malayalam, and Tamil. This overview article analyzed the systems that were submitted to the shared task. The main inference from the participants is that MTL is a very challenging problem, especially for morphologically rich languages and all participants performed Single Task Learning and aggregated the outputs.

References

R Anita and CN Subalalitha. 2019a. An approach to cluster Tamil literatures using discourse connectives. In *2019 IEEE 1st International Conference on Energy, Systems and Information Processing (ICESIP)*, pages 1–4. IEEE.

R Anita and CN Subalalitha. 2019b. Building discourse parser for Thirukkural. In *Proceedings of the 16th International Conference on Natural Language Processing*, pages 18–25.

B Bharathi, Bharathi Raja Chakravarthi, Subalalitha Chinnaudayar Navaneethakrishnan, N Sripriya, Arunaggiri Pandian, and Swetha Valli. 2022. Findings of the shared task on Speech Recognition for Vulnerable Individuals in Tamil. In *Proceedings of the Second Workshop on Language Technology for Equality, Diversity and Inclusion*. Association for Computational Linguistics.

Mohit Bhardwaj, Md Shad Akhtar, Asif Ekbal, Amitava Das, and Tanmoy Chakraborty. 2020. Hostility detection dataset in hindi.

Rich Caruana. 1997. Multitask learning. *Machine learning*, 28(1):41–75.

Bharathi Raja Chakravarthi. 2020. HopeEDI: A multilingual hope speech detection dataset for equality, diversity, and inclusion. In *Proceedings of the Third Workshop on Computational Modeling of People's Opinions, Personality, and Emotion's in Social Media*, pages 41–53, Barcelona, Spain (Online). Association for Computational Linguistics.

Bharathi Raja Chakravarthi, Mihael Arcan, and John P. McCrae. 2018. Improving wordnets for under-resourced languages using machine translation. In *Proceedings of the 9th Global Wordnet Conference*, pages 77–86, Nanyang Technological University (NTU), Singapore. Global Wordnet Association.

Bharathi Raja Chakravarthi, Mihael Arcan, and John P. McCrae. 2019. WordNet gloss translation for under-resourced languages using multilingual neural machine translation. In *Proceedings of the Second Workshop on Multilingualism at the Intersection of Knowledge Bases and Machine Translation*, pages 1–7, Dublin, Ireland. European Association for Machine Translation.

Bharathi Raja Chakravarthi, Navya Jose, Shardul Suryawanshi, Elizabeth Sherly, and John Philip McCrae. 2020a. A sentiment analysis dataset for code-mixed Malayalam-English. In *Proceedings of the 1st Joint Workshop on Spoken Language Technologies for Under-resourced languages (SLTU) and Collaboration and Computing for Under-Resourced Languages (CCURL)*, pages 177–184, Marseille, France. European Language Resources association.

Bharathi Raja Chakravarthi and Vigneshwaran Muralidaran. 2021. Findings of the shared task on hope speech detection for equality, diversity, and inclusion. In *Proceedings of the First Workshop on Language Technology for Equality, Diversity and Inclusion*, pages 61–72, Kyiv. Association for Computational Linguistics.

Bharathi Raja Chakravarthi, Vigneshwaran Muralidaran, Ruba Priyadharshini, and John Philip McCrae. 2020b. Corpus creation for sentiment analysis in code-mixed Tamil-English text. In *Proceedings of the 1st Joint Workshop on Spoken Language Technologies for Under-resourced languages (SLTU) and Collaboration and Computing for Under-Resourced Languages (CCURL)*, pages 202–210, Marseille, France. European Language Resources association.

Bharathi Raja Chakravarthi, Ruba Priyadharshini, Thenmozhi Durairaj, John Phillip McCrae, Paul Buitaleer, Prasanna Kumar Kumaresan, and Rahul Ponnusamy. 2022a. Findings of the shared task on Homophobia Transphobia Detection in Social Media Comments. In *Proceedings of the Second Workshop on Language Technology for Equality, Diversity and Inclusion*. Association for Computational Linguistics.

Bharathi Raja Chakravarthi, Ruba Priyadharshini, Vigneshwaran Muralidaran, Navya Jose, Shardul Suryawanshi, Elizabeth Sherly, and John P. McCrae. 2022b. DravidianCodeMix: sentiment analysis and offensive language identification dataset for Dravidian languages in code-mixed text. *Language Resources and Evaluation.*

Bharathi Raja Chakravarthi, Ruba Priyadharshini, Vigneshwaran Muralidaran, Shardul Suryawanshi, Navya Jose, Elizabeth Sherly, and John P McCrae. 2020c. Overview of the track on sentiment analysis for Dravidian languages in code-mixed text. In *Forum for Information Retrieval Evaluation*, pages 21–24.

Bharathi Raja Chakravarthi, Ruba Priyadharshini, Rahul Ponnusamy, Prasanna Kumar Kumaresan, Kayalvizhi Sampath, Durairaj Thenmozhi, Sathiyaraj Thangasamy, Rajendran Nallathambi, and John Phillip McCrae. 2021a. Dataset for identification of homophobia and transophobia in multilingual YouTube comments. *arXiv preprint arXiv:2109.00227.*

Bharathi Raja Chakravarthi, Priya Rani, Mihael Arcan, and John P McCrae. 2021b. A survey of orthographic information in machine translation. *SN Computer Science*, 2(4):1–19.

Nikhil Ghanghor, Parameswari Krishnamurthy, Sajeetha Thavareesan, Ruba Priyadharshini, and Bharathi Raja Chakravarthi. 2021a. IIITK@DravidianLangTech-EACL2021: Offensive language identification and meme classification in Tamil, Malayalam and Kannada. In *Proceedings of the First Workshop on Speech and Language Technologies for Dravidian Languages*, pages 222–229, Kyiv. Association for Computational Linguistics.

Nikhil Ghanghor, Rahul Ponnusamy, Prasanna Kumar Kumaresan, Ruba Priyadharshini, Sajeetha Thavareesan, and Bharathi Raja Chakravarthi. 2021b. IIITK@LT-EDI-EACL2021: Hope speech detection for equality, diversity, and inclusion in Tamil , Malayalam and English. In *Proceedings of the First Workshop on Language Technology for Equality, Diversity and Inclusion*, pages 197–203, Kyiv. Association for Computational Linguistics.

Anusha Gowda, Fazlourrahman Balouchzahi, HL Shashirekha, and G Sidorov. 2022. MUCIC@DravidianLangTech-ACL2022: multi-task learning for dravidian languages. In *Proceedings of the Second Workshop on Speech and Language Technologies for Dravidian Languages*. Association for Computational Linguistics.

Adeep Hande, Siddhanth U. Hegde, Ruba Priyadharshini, Rahul Ponnusamy, Prasanna Kumar Kumaresan, Sajeetha Thavareesan, and Bharathi Raja Chakravarthi. 2021. Benchmarking multi-task learning for sentiment analysis and offensive language identification in under-resourced dravidian languages. *CoRR*, abs/2108.03867.

Asha Hegde and Sharal Coelho. 2022. MUCS@DravidianLangTech@ACL 2022: Multi-task Learning for Sentiment Analysis and Offensive Language Identification in Dravidian Languages using Dynamic Meta Embedding. In *Proceedings of the Second Workshop on Speech and Language Technologies for Dravidian Languages*. Association for Computational Linguistics.

Prasanna Kumar Kumaresan, Ratnasingam Sakuntharaj, Sajeetha Thavareesan, Subalalitha Navaneethakrishnan, Anand Kumar Madasamy, Bharathi Raja Chakravarthi, and John P McCrae. 2021. Findings of shared task on offensive language identification in Tamil and Malayalam. In *Forum for Information Retrieval Evaluation*, pages 16–18.

Héctor Martínez Alonso and Barbara Plank. 2017. When is multitask learning effective? semantic sequence prediction under varying data conditions. In *Proceedings of the 15th Conference of the European Chapter of the Association for Computational Linguistics: Volume 1, Long Papers*, pages 44–53, Valencia, Spain. Association for Computational Linguistics.

Anitha Narasimhan, Aarthy Anandan, Madhan Karky, and CN Subalalitha. 2018. Porul: Option generation and selection and scoring algorithms for a tamil flash card game. *International Journal of Cognitive and Language Sciences*, 12(2):225–228.

Ruba Priyadharshini, Bharathi Raja Chakravarthi, Subalalitha Chinnaudayar Navaneethakrishnan, Thenmozhi Durairaj, Malliga Subramanian, Kogilavani Shanmugavadivel, Siddhanth U Hegde, and Prasanna Kumar Kumaresan. 2022. Findings of the shared task on Abusive Comment Detection in Tamil. In *Proceedings of the Second Workshop on Speech and Language Technologies for Dravidian Languages*. Association for Computational Linguistics.

Ruba Priyadharshini, Bharathi Raja Chakravarthi, Sajeetha Thavareesan, Dhivya Chinnappa, Durairaj Thenmozhi, and Rahul Ponnusamy. 2021. Overview of the dravidiancodemix 2021 shared task on sentiment detection in Tamil, Malayalam, and Kannada. In *Forum for Information Retrieval Evaluation*, pages 4–6.

Ruba Priyadharshini, Bharathi Raja Chakravarthi, Mani Vegupatti, and John P McCrae. 2020. Named entity recognition for code-mixed Indian corpus using meta embedding. In *2020 6th international conference on advanced computing and communication systems (ICACCS)*, pages 68–72. IEEE.

Manikandan Ravikiran, Bharathi Raja Chakravarthi, Anand Kumar Madasamy, Sangeetha Sivanesan, Ratnavel Rajalakshmi, Sajeetha Thavareesan, Rahul Ponnusamy, and Shankar Mahadevan. 2022. Findings of the shared task on Offensive Span Identification in code-mixed Tamil-English comments. In *Proceedings of the Second Workshop on Speech and Language Technologies for Dravidian Languages*. Association for Computational Linguistics.

Siva Reddy and Serge Sharoff. 2011. Cross language POS taggers (and other tools) for Indian languages: An experiment with Kannada using Telugu resources. In *Proceedings of the Fifth International Workshop On Cross Lingual Information Access*, pages 11–19, Chiang Mai, Thailand. Asian Federation of Natural Language Processing.

Ratnasingam Sakuntharaj and Sinnathamby Mahesan. 2016. A novel hybrid approach to detect and correct spelling in Tamil text. In *2016 IEEE International Conference on Information and Automation for Sustainability (ICIAfS)*, pages 1–6.

Ratnasingam Sakuntharaj and Sinnathamby Mahesan. 2017. Use of a novel hash-table for speeding-up suggestions for misspelt Tamil words. In *2017 IEEE International Conference on Industrial and Information Systems (ICIIS)*, pages 1–5.

Ratnasingam Sakuntharaj and Sinnathamby Mahesan. 2021. Missing word detection and correction based on context of Tamil sentences using n-grams. In *2021 10th International Conference on Information and Automation for Sustainability (ICIAfS)*, pages 42–47.

Anbukkarasi Sampath, Thenmozhi Durairaj, Bharathi Raja Chakravarthi, Ruba Priyadharshini, Subalalitha Chinnaudayar Navaneethakrishnan, Kogilavani Shanmugavadivel, Sajeetha Thavareesan, Sathiyaraj Thangasamy, Parameswari Krishnamurthy, Adeep Hande, Sean Benhur, Kishor Kumar Ponnusamy, and Santhiya Pandiyan. 2022. Findings of the shared task on Emotion Analysis in Tamil. In *Proceedings of the Second Workshop on Speech and Language Technologies for Dravidian Languages*. Association for Computational Linguistics.

R Srinivasan and CN Subalalitha. 2019. Automated named entity recognition from tamil documents. In *2019 IEEE 1st International Conference on Energy, Systems and Information Processing (ICESIP)*, pages 1–5. IEEE.

C. N. Subalalitha. 2019. Information extraction framework for Kurunthogai. *Sādhanā*, 44(7):156.

CN Subalalitha and E Poovammal. 2018. Automatic bilingual dictionary construction for Tirukural. *Applied Artificial Intelligence*, 32(6):558–567.

Sajeetha Thavareesan and Sinnathamby Mahesan. 2019. Sentiment analysis in Tamil texts: A study on machine learning techniques and feature representation. In *2019 14th Conference on Industrial and Information Systems (ICIIS)*, pages 320–325.

Sajeetha Thavareesan and Sinnathamby Mahesan. 2020a. Sentiment lexicon expansion using Word2vec and fastText for sentiment prediction in Tamil texts. In *2020 Moratuwa Engineering Research Conference (MERCon)*, pages 272–276.

Sajeetha Thavareesan and Sinnathamby Mahesan. 2020b. Word embedding-based part of speech tagging in Tamil texts. In *2020 IEEE 15th International Conference on Industrial and Information Systems (ICIIS)*, pages 478–482.

Sajeetha Thavareesan and Sinnathamby Mahesan. 2021. Sentiment analysis in Tamil texts using k-means and k-nearest neighbour. In *2021 10th International Conference on Information and Automation for Sustainability (ICIAfS)*, pages 48–53.

Overview of Abusive Comment Detection in Tamil - ACL 2022

Ruba priyadharshini[1], Bharathi Raja Chakravarthi[2], Subalalitha Chinnaudayar Navaneethakrishnan [3], Thenmozhi Durairaj [4], Malliga Subramanian[5] Kogilavani Shanmugavadivel [5], Siddhanth U Hegde [6], Prasanna Kumar Kumaresan [7]

[1]Madurai Kamaraj University,Tamil Nadu, India, [2]National University of Ireland Galway,
[3]SRM Institute Of Science And Technology, Tamil Nadu, India,
[4]SSN College of Engineering, Tamil Nadu, India,
[5]Kongu Engineering College, Tamil Nadu, India,
[7]University Visvesvaraya College of Engineering, Karnataka, India,
[6]Indian Institute of Information Technology and Management, Kerala, India.
bharathi.raja@insight-centre.org

Abstract

The social media is one of the significant digital platforms that create a huge impact in peoples of all levels. The comments posted on social media is powerful enough to even change the political and business scenarios in very few hours. They also tend to attack a particular individual or a group of individuals. This shared task aims at detecting the abusive comments involving, Homophobia, Misandry, Counter-speech, Misogyny, Xenophobia, Transphobic. The hope speech is also identified. A dataset collected from social media tagged with the above said categories in Tamil and Tamil-English code-mixed languages are given to the participants. The participants used different machine learning and deep learning algorithms. This paper presents the overview of this task comprising the dataset details and results of the participants.

1 Introduction

Their distribution of digital information has increased to a greater extent. The importance of the Online Social Networks (OSNs) has grown significantly in recent years, and they have become a go-to source for acquiring news, information, and entertainment (Halevy et al., 2022; Priyadharshini et al., 2021; Kumaresan et al., 2021). However, despite many positive impacts of employing OSNs, a growing body of evidence indicates that there is an ever-increasing number of malevolent actors who are exploiting these networks to spread poison and cause harm to other individuals (Chakravarthi, 2020; Chakravarthi and Muralidaran, 2021). The term "Hate Speech" (HS) refers to any form of communication that is abusive, insulting, intimidating, and/or incites violence or discrimination and that disparages an individual or a vulnerable group on the basis of characteristics such as ethnicity, gender, sexual orientation, or religious affiliation (Whillock and Slayden, 1995; Sampath et al., 2022; Ravikiran et al., 2022; Chakravarthi et al., 2022; Bharathi et al., 2022; Priyadharshini et al., 2022). Because of this diversity in thematic foci, we refer to them as themes. Examples of topics include misogyny, sexism, racism, transphobia, homophobia, and xenophobia (Chakravarthi et al., 2020, 2021; Ghanghor et al., 2021a,b; Yasaswini et al., 2021). The abusive comments targeting people have a huge impact on them psychologically(Wiegand et al., 2021). This task lays a foundation on how these comments can be detected for Dravidian language Tamil. Tamil is a Dravidian classical language used by the Tamil people of South Asia. Tamil is an official language of Tamil Nadu, Sri Lanka, Singapore, and the Union Territory of Puducherry in India. Significant minority speak Tamil in the four other South Indian states of Kerala, Karnataka, Andhra Pradesh, and Telangana, as well as the Union Territory of the Andaman and Nicobar Islands (Subalalitha, 2019; Srinivasan and Subalalitha, 2019; Narasimhan et al., 2018). It is also spoken by the Tamil diaspora, which may be found in Malaysia, Myanmar, South Africa, the United Kingdom, the United States, Canada, Australia, and Mauritius. Tamil is also the native language of Sri Lankan Moors (Sakuntharaj and Mahesan, 2021, 2017, 2016; Thavareesan and Mahesan, 2019, 2020a,b, 2021). Tamil, one of the 22 scheduled languages in the Indian Constitution, was the first to be designated as a classical language of India. Tamil is one of the world's longest-surviving classical languages. The earliest epigraphic documents discovered on rock edicts and "hero stones" date from the 6th century BC. Tamil has the oldest ancient non-Sanskritic Indian literature of any Indian language (Anita and Subalalitha, 2019b,a; Subalalitha and Poovammal, 2018). Since the comments posted online contain mixture of languages that are familiar with the users that are posting the comments, the task also considers detecting

Proceedings of the Second Workshop on Speech and Language Technologies for Dravidian Languages, pages 292 - 298
May 26, 2022

the comments from the Tamil-English code mixed language.

The goal of this task is to identify whether a given comment contains abusive comment. A comment/post within the corpus may contain more than one sentence but the average sentence length of the corpora is 1. The annotations in the corpus are made at a comment/post level. The participants were provided development, training and test dataset in Tamil and Tamil-English languages. The dataset is tagged using various classes namely, Homophobia, Misandry, Counter-speech, Misogyny, Xenophobia, Transphobic and Hope Speech. To the best of our knowledge, this is the first shared task on abusive detection in Tamil at this fine-grained level. 11 teams participated for detecting abusive comments in Tamil language and Tamil-English language tasks.

2 Task Description

The task is primarily a comment/post-level classification task. Given a YouTube comment, the systems submitted by the participants should classify it abusive categories. The participants were provided with development, training and test dataset in Tamil and Tamil-English. The dataset is tagged using various classes namely, Homophobia, Misandry, Counter-speech, Misogyny, Xenophobia, Transphobic and hope speech. 10 teams participated for detecting abusive comment in Tamil language and 11 teams participated for the Tamil-English language.

3 Data Description

The Tamil language training data contains 2240 comments, the validation set contains 560 comments, and the test data set includes 699 comments. The Tamil-English language test data set contains 5943 comments, the validation set contains 1486 comments and the 1857 test comments. The distribution of the seven categories in the whole dataset is shown in Table 1.

4 Participant's methodology

4.1 Pre-processing strategies

The participants have predominantly used "transliteration" as one of the pre-processing strategies. The Tamil-English code-mixed texts necessitate this approach. Apart from transliteration, removal of punctuation, stop words have also been used. Class balancing of the data has also been attempted as the distribution of the class labels in the given training dataset.

4.2 Participant's Systems

Term Frequency- Inverse Document Frequency (TF- IDF) and BERT embeddings have been used to extract and represent the features in the feature extraction phase. The participants have used a wide variety of machine learning algorithms, deep learning models, and transformers. Logistic Regression, Linear Support Vector Machines, Gradient Boost classifier, and K neighbor classifier have been used as machine learning algorithms. Ensemble models attempted composed of a mixture of these machine learning models. Multi-layered perceptron, Recurrent Neural Networks (RNN), Vanilla LSTM (Schuster and Paliwal, 1997) were opted as deep learning models. On the transformers front, mBERT(Devlin et al., 2018), MuRIL BERT (Khanuja et al., 2021), XLM RoBERTa (Liu et al., 2019), and ULMFit (Howard and Ruder, 2018) models have been opted. The MuRIL BERT models have shown the best performance compared to the other models. This is primarily because it is trained exclusively for Indian languages. The ranking of the teams for both of the language tasks is shown in Tables 2 and 3. The ranking is given based on their f1 score and how intense their system is, which counts their pre-processing techniques and the number of models used to prove their performance.

5 Error Analysis of the Systems

The participants have used the standard metrics such as Weighted Precision, Weighted Recall, and Weighted F-score to evaluate the performance of their systems. The equations of these metrics are given below.

$$Precision = \frac{TP}{TP + FP} \tag{1}$$

$$Recall = \frac{TP}{TP + FP} \tag{2}$$

where, TP= Number of True Positives and FP= Number of false Positives

$$F - Score = 2 * \frac{Precision * Recall}{Precision + Recall} \tag{3}$$

Comment category	Count in the datasets
None of the above	5011
Misandry	1276
Counter-speech	497
Xenophobia	392
Misogyny	336
Hope Speech	299
Homophobia	207
Transphobic	163

Table 1: Distribution of Comment Categories in the dataset

TeamName	Precision	Recall	F1-Score	Rank
CEN-Tamil(S N et al., 2022)	0.380	0.290	0.320	1
COMBATANT	0.290	0.330	0.300	2
DE-ABUSE(Palanikrmar et al., 2022)	0.330	0.29	0.290	3
DLRG(Diraphe et al., 2022)	0.340	0.260	0.270	4
TROPER	0.400	0.230	0.250	5
abusive-checker	0.140	0.140	0.140	6
Optimize_Prime(Patankar et al., 2022)	0.130	0.130	0.130	7
GJG	0.130	0.140	0.130	8
umuteam	0.130	0.130	0.130	9
MUCIC	0.120	0.130	0.120	10
BpHigh(Pahwa, 2022)	0.180	0.120	0.060	11
SSNCSE_NLP(Varsha and Bharathi, 2022)	0.130	0.140	0.090	12

Table 2: Rank list based on weighted average F1-score along with other evaluation metrics (Precision and Recall) for Tamil Language

TeamName	Precision	Recall	F1-Score	Rank
abusive-checker	0.460	0.380	0.410	1
GJG	0.370	0.340	0.350	2
umuteam	0.350	0.370	0.350	3
pandas(G L et al., 2022)	0.330	0.370	0.340	4
Optimize_Prime(Patankar et al., 2022)	0.310	0.380	0.320	5
MUCIC	0.400	0.280	0.290	6
CEN-Tamil(S N et al., 2022)	0.300	0.230	0.250	7
SSNCSE_NLP(Varsha and Bharathi, 2022)	0.260	0.240	0.250	8
IIITDWD	0.380	0.170	0.180	9
DLRG(Diraphe et al., 2022)	0.180	0.150	0.140	10
BpHigh(Pahwa, 2022)	0.140	0.160	0.100	11

Table 3: Rank list based on weighted average F1-score along with other evaluation metrics (Precision and Recall) for Tamil-English Language

$$P_{weighted} = \sum_{i=1}^{L}(Precisionofi \times Weightofi) \tag{4}$$

, where i is the test sample size.

$$R_{weighted} = \sum_{i=1}^{L}(Recallofi \times Weighti) \tag{5}$$

$$F\text{-}Score_{weighted} = \sum_{i=1}^{L}(F\text{-}Scoreofi \times Weighti) \tag{6}$$

The participants have also used accuracy, Macro-Precision, Macro-Recall, and Macro-F-scores to evaluate the system. It can be observed that the highest F-score achieved by the systems is 0.41. This is primarily due to the inability of the techniques to handle the errors observed consistently in all the systems during the classification. The various scenarios of errors are explained below.

Scenario 1: The systems fail to classify the sentences whenever the sentences do not contain even a single Tamil word. In other words, the sentences contain only the English transliterated words. For example, the comment, "World health enda ilukara ara kora nayae, " is classified as "Xenophobia" by all the systems while the actual label is "None of the above. The comment is actually against a xenophobic person. On the other comment, "sornam lakshmi mudiyathu mooditu" is classified as "Misandry" by all the systems while the actual class is "Misogyny." The name "sornam lakshhmi " refers to a woman but none of the systems labeled this right.

Scenario 2: The comments contain spelling mistakes and could not be handled during the preprocessing step. For example, This is classified

சாதி வெறி காட்டுமிராண்டி நாய்ங்க எவன்

as "None of the above " by all the systems while it is supposed to be "Misandry." This is due to the spelling mistake in the comment. The word

"எவன்" should have been "இவன்"

Scenario 3: The pre-processing strategies have had a harmful effect on the text and have resulted

"திருட வந்த பயல்களின் மதம் பின்பற்றும் நீ இந்தியனல்ல" is changed to "பயல மதம யனல"

in spelling mistakes. For example, the text, This has lead to the misclassification.

Scenario 4: Certain comments were too short and had references that were not captured by the systems. For example, the comment give below is

"ரெட் shirt நாகரீகம் தெரியாதவன்"

supposed to be classified as "Misandry." It is instead classified as "None of the above." Apart from these scenarios, the systems could never classify incomplete comments and double entendre comments correctly. Specific comments had hyperlinks that had the main content, which was missed by the systems.

6 Conclusion

This shared task aims at detecting the categories of abusive comments that are posted on social media. This kind of analysis would quantify the negativity that is spread in the society, which in turn should be turned into positivity either by enacting laws to enforce restrictions on posting comments on social media. This has been the motivation behind hosting this shared task which has attempted to aggregate the comments from social media in two languages, namely, Tamil and in code mixed language containing Tamil and English scripts. These comments were trained by various machine learning, deep learning, and transfer learning models. 11 teams participated in Tamil and Tamil-English languages tasks. 7 categories of abusive categories were tagged in the collected comments. The ranking of the teams was done based on the performance shown by the systems that were used by the participants and the in-depth analysis done by them. It was observed that the transformer models showed better performance when compared to that of the rest of the systems.

References

R Anita and CN Subalalitha. 2019a. An approach to cluster Tamil literatures using discourse connectives. In *2019 IEEE 1st International Conference on Energy, Systems and Information Processing (ICESIP)*, pages 1–4. IEEE.

R Anita and CN Subalalitha. 2019b. Building discourse parser for Thirukkural. In *Proceedings of the 16th*

International Conference on Natural Language Processing, pages 18–25.

B Bharathi, Bharathi Raja Chakravarthi, Subalalitha Chinnaudayar Navaneethakrishnan, N Sripriya, Arunaggiri Pandian, and Swetha Valli. 2022. Findings of the shared task on Speech Recognition for Vulnerable Individuals in Tamil. In *Proceedings of the Second Workshop on Language Technology for Equality, Diversity and Inclusion*. Association for Computational Linguistics.

Bharathi Raja Chakravarthi. 2020. HopeEDI: A multilingual hope speech detection dataset for equality, diversity, and inclusion. In *Proceedings of the Third Workshop on Computational Modeling of People's Opinions, Personality, and Emotion's in Social Media*, pages 41–53, Barcelona, Spain (Online). Association for Computational Linguistics.

Bharathi Raja Chakravarthi and Vigneshwaran Muralidaran. 2021. Findings of the shared task on hope speech detection for equality, diversity, and inclusion. In *Proceedings of the First Workshop on Language Technology for Equality, Diversity and Inclusion*, pages 61–72, Kyiv. Association for Computational Linguistics.

Bharathi Raja Chakravarthi, Ruba Priyadharshini, Thenmozhi Durairaj, John Phillip McCrae, Paul Buitaleer, Prasanna Kumar Kumaresan, and Rahul Ponnusamy. 2022. Findings of the shared task on Homophobia Transphobia Detection in Social Media Comments. In *Proceedings of the Second Workshop on Language Technology for Equality, Diversity and Inclusion*. Association for Computational Linguistics.

Bharathi Raja Chakravarthi, Ruba Priyadharshini, Vigneshwaran Muralidaran, Shardul Suryawanshi, Navya Jose, Elizabeth Sherly, and John P McCrae. 2020. Overview of the track on sentiment analysis for Dravidian languages in code-mixed text. In *Forum for Information Retrieval Evaluation*, pages 21–24.

Bharathi Raja Chakravarthi, Ruba Priyadharshini, Rahul Ponnusamy, Prasanna Kumar Kumaresan, Kayalvizhi Sampath, Durairaj Thenmozhi, Sathiyaraj Thangasamy, Rajendran Nallathambi, and John Phillip McCrae. 2021. Dataset for identification of homophobia and transophobia in multilingual YouTube comments. *arXiv preprint arXiv:2109.00227*.

Jacob Devlin, Ming-Wei Chang, Kenton Lee, and Kristina Toutanova. 2018. Bert: Pre-training of deep bidirectional transformers for language understanding. *arXiv preprint arXiv:1810.04805*.

Ankita Diraphe, Ratnavel Rajalakshmi, and Antonette Shibani. 2022. Dlrg@dravidianlangtech-acl2022: Abusive comment detection intamil using multilingual transformer models. In *Proceedings of the Second Workshop on Speech and Language Technologies for Dravidian Languages*. Association for Computational Linguistics.

Gayathri G L, Krithika S, Divyasri K, Thenmozhi Durairaj, and B. Bharathi. 2022. Pandas@tamilnlp-acl2022: Abusive comment detection in tamil code-mixed data using custom embeddings with labse. In *Proceedings of the Second Workshop on Speech and Language Technologies for Dravidian Languages*. Association for Computational Linguistics.

Nikhil Ghanghor, Parameswari Krishnamurthy, Sajeetha Thavareesan, Ruba Priyadharshini, and Bharathi Raja Chakravarthi. 2021a. IIITK@DravidianLangTech-EACL2021: Offensive language identification and meme classification in Tamil, Malayalam and Kannada. In *Proceedings of the First Workshop on Speech and Language Technologies for Dravidian Languages*, pages 222–229, Kyiv. Association for Computational Linguistics.

Nikhil Ghanghor, Rahul Ponnusamy, Prasanna Kumar Kumaresan, Ruba Priyadharshini, Sajeetha Thavareesan, and Bharathi Raja Chakravarthi. 2021b. IIITK@LT-EDI-EACL2021: Hope speech detection for equality, diversity, and inclusion in Tamil , Malayalam and English. In *Proceedings of the First Workshop on Language Technology for Equality, Diversity and Inclusion*, pages 197–203, Kyiv. Association for Computational Linguistics.

Alon Halevy, Cristian Canton-Ferrer, Hao Ma, Umut Ozertem, Patrick Pantel, Marzieh Saeidi, Fabrizio Silvestri, and Ves Stoyanov. 2022. Preserving integrity in online social networks. *Communications of the ACM*, 65(2):92–98.

Jeremy Howard and Sebastian Ruder. 2018. Universal language model fine-tuning for text classification. *arXiv preprint arXiv:1801.06146*.

Simran Khanuja, Diksha Bansal, Sarvesh Mehtani, Savya Khosla, Atreyee Dey, Balaji Gopalan, Dilip Kumar Margam, Pooja Aggarwal, Rajiv Teja Nagipogu, Shachi Dave, et al. 2021. Muril: Multilingual representations for indian languages. *arXiv preprint arXiv:2103.10730*.

Prasanna Kumar Kumaresan, Ratnasingam Sakuntharaj, Sajeetha Thavareesan, Subalalitha Navaneethakrishnan, Anand Kumar Madasamy, Bharathi Raja Chakravarthi, and John P McCrae. 2021. Findings of shared task on offensive language identification in tamil and malayalam. In *Forum for Information Retrieval Evaluation*, pages 16–18.

Yinhan Liu, Myle Ott, Naman Goyal, Jingfei Du, Mandar Joshi, Danqi Chen, Omer Levy, Mike Lewis, Luke Zettlemoyer, and Veselin Stoyanov. 2019. Roberta: A robustly optimized bert pretraining approach. *arXiv preprint arXiv:1907.11692*.

Anitha Narasimhan, Aarthy Anandan, Madhan Karky, and CN Subalalitha. 2018. Porul: Option generation and selection and scoring algorithms for a tamil flash card game. *International Journal of Cognitive and Language Sciences*, 12(2):225–228.

Bhavish Pahwa. 2022. Bphigh@tamilnlp-acl2022: Augmentation strategies for indic transformer-based abusive comment detection in tamil. In *Proceedings of the Second Workshop on Speech and Language Technologies for Dravidian Languages*. Association for Computational Linguistics.

Vasanth Palanikrmar, Sean Benhur, Adeep Hande, and Bharathi Raja Chakravarthi. 2022. Deabuse@tamilnlp-acl 2022: Transliteration as data augmentation for abuse detection in tamil. In *Proceedings of the Second Workshop on Speech and Language Technologies for Dravidian Languages*. Association for Computational Linguistics.

Shantanu Patankar, Omkar Gokhale, Onkar Litake, Aditya Mandke, and Dipali Kandam. 2022. Optimize_prime@tamilnlp-acl2022: Abusive comment detection in tamil. In *Proceedings of the Second Workshop on Speech and Language Technologies for Dravidian Languages*. Association for Computational Linguistics.

Ruba Priyadharshini, Bharathi Raja Chakravarthi, Subalalitha Chinnaudayar Navaneethakrishnan, Thenmozhi Durairaj, Malliga Subramanian, Kogilavani Shanmugavadivel, Siddhanth U Hegde, and Prasanna Kumar Kumaresan. 2022. Findings of the shared task on Abusive Comment Detection in Tamil. In *Proceedings of the Second Workshop on Speech and Language Technologies for Dravidian Languages*. Association for Computational Linguistics.

Ruba Priyadharshini, Bharathi Raja Chakravarthi, Sajeetha Thavareesan, Dhivya Chinnappa, Durairaj Thenmozhi, and Rahul Ponnusamy. 2021. Overview of the DravidianCodeMix 2021 shared task on sentiment detection in Tamil, Malayalam, and Kannada. In *Forum for Information Retrieval Evaluation*, pages 4–6.

Manikandan Ravikiran, Bharathi Raja Chakravarthi, Anand Kumar Madasamy, Sangeetha Sivanesan, Ratnavel Rajalakshmi, Sajeetha Thavareesan, Rahul Ponnusamy, and Shankar Mahadevan. 2022. Findings of the shared task on Offensive Span Identification in code-mixed Tamil-English comments. In *Proceedings of the Second Workshop on Speech and Language Technologies for Dravidian Languages*. Association for Computational Linguistics.

Prasanth S N, R Aswin Raj, Adhithan P, Premjith B, and Soman K P. 2022. Cen-tamil@dravidianlangtech-acl2022: Abusive comment detection in tamil using tf-idf and random kitchen sink algorithm. In *Proceedings of the Second Workshop on Speech and Language Technologies for Dravidian Languages*. Association for Computational Linguistics.

Ratnasingam Sakuntharaj and Sinnathamby Mahesan. 2016. A novel hybrid approach to detect and correct spelling in Tamil text. In *2016 IEEE International Conference on Information and Automation for Sustainability (ICIAfS)*, pages 1–6.

Ratnasingam Sakuntharaj and Sinnathamby Mahesan. 2017. Use of a novel hash-table for speeding-up suggestions for misspelt Tamil words. In *2017 IEEE International Conference on Industrial and Information Systems (ICIIS)*, pages 1–5.

Ratnasingam Sakuntharaj and Sinnathamby Mahesan. 2021. Missing word detection and correction based on context of Tamil sentences using n-grams. In *2021 10th International Conference on Information and Automation for Sustainability (ICIAfS)*, pages 42–47.

Anbukkarasi Sampath, Thenmozhi Durairaj, Bharathi Raja Chakravarthi, Ruba Priyadharshini, Subalalitha Chinnaudayar Navaneethakrishnan, Kogilavani Shanmugavadivel, Sajeetha Thavareesan, Sathiyaraj Thangasamy, Parameswari Krishnamurthy, Adeep Hande, Sean Benhur, Kishor Kumar Ponnusamy, and Santhiya Pandiyan. 2022. Findings of the shared task on Emotion Analysis in Tamil. In *Proceedings of the Second Workshop on Speech and Language Technologies for Dravidian Languages*. Association for Computational Linguistics.

Mike Schuster and Kuldip K Paliwal. 1997. Bidirectional recurrent neural networks. *IEEE transactions on Signal Processing*, 45(11):2673–2681.

R Srinivasan and CN Subalalitha. 2019. Automated named entity recognition from tamil documents. In *2019 IEEE 1st International Conference on Energy, Systems and Information Processing (ICESIP)*, pages 1–5. IEEE.

C. N. Subalalitha. 2019. Information extraction framework for Kurunthogai. *Sādhanā*, 44(7):156.

CN Subalalitha and E Poovammal. 2018. Automatic bilingual dictionary construction for Tirukural. *Applied Artificial Intelligence*, 32(6):558–567.

Sajeetha Thavareesan and Sinnathamby Mahesan. 2019. Sentiment analysis in Tamil texts: A study on machine learning techniques and feature representation. In *2019 14th Conference on Industrial and Information Systems (ICIIS)*, pages 320–325.

Sajeetha Thavareesan and Sinnathamby Mahesan. 2020a. Sentiment lexicon expansion using Word2vec and fastText for sentiment prediction in Tamil texts. In *2020 Moratuwa Engineering Research Conference (MERCon)*, pages 272–276.

Sajeetha Thavareesan and Sinnathamby Mahesan. 2020b. Word embedding-based part of speech tagging in Tamil texts. In *2020 IEEE 15th International Conference on Industrial and Information Systems (ICIIS)*, pages 478–482.

Sajeetha Thavareesan and Sinnathamby Mahesan. 2021. Sentiment analysis in Tamil texts using k-means and k-nearest neighbour. In *2021 10th International Conference on Information and Automation for Sustainability (ICIAfS)*, pages 48–53.

Josephine Varsha and B. Bharathi. 2022. Ssncse nlp@tamilnlp-acl2022: Transformer based approach for detection of abusive comment for tamil language. In *Proceedings of the Second Workshop on Speech and Language Technologies for Dravidian Languages*. Association for Computational Linguistics.

Rita Kirk Whillock and David Slayden. 1995. *Hate speech*. ERIC.

Michael Wiegand, Josef Ruppenhofer, and Elisabeth Eder. 2021. Implicitly abusive language–what does it actually look like and why are we not getting there? In *Proceedings of the 2021 Conference of the North American Chapter of the Association for Computational Linguistics: Human Language Technologies*, pages 576–587. Association for Computational Linguistics.

Konthala Yasaswini, Karthik Puranik, Adeep Hande, Ruba Priyadharshini, Sajeetha Thavareesan, and Bharathi Raja Chakravarthi. 2021. IIITT@DravidianLangTech-EACL2021: Transfer learning for offensive language detection in Dravidian languages. In *Proceedings of the First Workshop on Speech and Language Technologies for Dravidian Languages*, pages 187–194, Kyiv. Association for Computational Linguistics.

Author Index

Association for Computational Linguistics
209 N. Eighth Street
Stroudsburg, Pennsylvania 18360

ISBN 978-1-7138-6735-7

CURRAN ASSOCIATES INC.
proceedings.com